"When drunk is very bold"

White Maryland Runaways, 1763-1769

Compiled by

Joseph Lee Boyle

CLEARFIELD

Copyright © 2011 by Joseph Lee Boyle
All Rights Reserved

Printed for
Clearfield Company by
Genealogical Publishing Company
Baltimore, Maryland
2011

ISBN 978-0-8063-5545-0

Made in the United States of America

INTRODUCTION

One of the many neglected episodes of American history is that of the many thousands of white Europeans did not come to the colonies as free men and women. Instead they came as indentured servants, political exiles, or transported convicts. White servitude was a major institution of the social and economic fabric of colonial British America. Bound whites preceded the used of black slaves in every colony. It is estimated that from 350,000 to 500,000 servants were imported through 1775. Though by the start of the eighteenth century the importation of black slaves increased dramatically in the Chesapeake and southern colonies, white bound labor remained significant.

There were thousands of white people who wanted to leave their home countries, but were unable or unwilling to pay the cost of their passage, so they became servants for a period of years to a colonial master who purchased them. Others were convicts or exiles. More than half the whites who came to the colonies south of New England were servants. Those who came voluntarily hoped for a better life. Most indentures were from four to seven years, though this varied.

Some were kidnapped to the colonies, as made famous in Robert Louis Stevenson's *Kidnapped*, but many are likely to have made the claim to escape the terms of their indenture. Others may have runaway from home to leave their families, debt, or other personal problems.

Of course the numbers of both free and indentured immigrants depended on economics. For example, the Irish came in a wave in 1770-1775 due to the collapse of the linen industry. Crop failures, wars, and economic disruptions in general added to the level of immigrants.

Underwriting of transportation was sometimes assumed by the planter, or more often by English merchants specializing in the sale of indentured servants. Recruiting agents called "crimps" hired drummers to recruit, sometimes making extravagant promises about the good life in the colonies. Illiterates were likely the most easily taken advantage of.

Though convicts were sent to the colonies before, the Transportation Act of 1718 opened the floodgates for exiled criminals, those convicted of minor crimes could be sent to the colonies for seven year terms. Capital crimes meant terms of fourteen years. After serving their time, they were eligible for royal mercy, and could return to England, but returning early was a capital offense. Convicts were attractive as they were relatively cheap, their sales prices were about one-third that of African slaves, and female felons sold for only two-thirds the price of males. From 1718 to 1773, some 50,000 convicts from all parts of Europe were sent to America.

Importation of servants into Maryland reached its height in the middle of the eighteenth century, while convicts arrived in ever-increasing numbers. In Maryland there was always a market for "His Majesty's Seven-Years Passengers" despite prejudice against them. The perceived evils of the consignment of convicts to Maryland and Virginia, resulting in those colonies passing laws by 1723. But the Lords Proprietor rejected this. Maryland passed a number of other acts to regulate the convict trade, such as imposing duties on each one imported.

After arrival in America, "soul drivers" sometimes drove coffles of convicts from town to town, selling them as they progressed into the interior of a colony drove coffles of convicts from town to town, selling them as they progressed into the interior of a colony. This was not without risks to the drivers. In 1774 a Baltimore merchant purchased a parcel of convicts, most of which he sold, except four men before he reached Frederick. One complained that he was too tired to go on, and they rested by a tree, the driver then insisted they go on, but they refused, threw him over a tree, dragged him into the woods, and cut his throat from ear to ear. All four were hanged for their crime.

Benjamin Franklin noted convicts that "must be ruled with a Rod of Iron" and considered "emptying their jails into our settlements is an insult and contempt, the cruellest, that ever one people offered to another." While the colonists were incensed about receiving so many convicts, surviving court records do not show that they committed an inordinate number of crimes. Perhaps the lack of large towns, commercial activity, and general lack of opulence did not lend themselves to crimes the way the cities of England did, nor was there an existing criminal subculture.

There were also "redemptioners," initially German, and then British. They promised to pay ship captains on their arrival in America. If they could not pay, or find a relative or countryman to do so, the captain was free to dispose of them for a number of years, (usually two to seven) to defray the cost of their passage. For many this must have been a distress sale, as they could not return to Europe. Coming in family or large groups, they sold their own, or their children's labor for the cost of passage. The redemptioners were often called "free-willers."

These potential immigrants had the opportunity to negotiate the cost before they embarked. The time involved varied, depending on the amount owed. Upon arrival the immigrant usually had up to fourteen days to negotiate a sale of his services. If he could not do so, the shipper recovered his costs by selling the indenture to the highest bidder.

The Chesapeake colonies received the highest number of servants, followed by Pennsylvania. So many Irish Catholics came to Maryland, that the Protestants became alarmed and a duty was imposed on them, while Protestant servants came in free. The Irish were more likely to come than the English as they were not bound to their parishes by the Poor Laws, and provided with a meager sustenance.

There was money to be made at multiple levels. The contractor who arranged the transportation profited, the ship owner and captain profited, and if the transport involved convicts, the county sheriff in England or Ireland had his palm out to facilitate the process. At one time Irish sheriffs received five pounds a head for convicts sentenced to transportation, but paid out only three pounds to the merchant transporters. Subject to supply and demand at the ports, agents would sometimes keep servants on shipboard or in houses until a sale at a good price could be arranged. Once in America, if the servant ran away, local officials were eager to earn rewards for their capture.

There were risks at all levels of the investment. Some absconded before boarding the ship. While ship captains wanted to make as much as possible from transportation the servants, the less they paid for food, the more they made. Though high shipboard mortality was regrettable, some always occurred after six to eight weeks at sea. While convict cargoes were generally chained, there were cases of uprisings with the ship's crew being overpowered.

Ship arrivals in the colonies tended to be seasonal, with the fall preferred, so that ships could take cured tobacco back to Europe, and new arrivals would have cooler weather to adjust to their new environment. The term "seasoning" was applied to newcomers, whose death rate varied, but was rarely less than ten percent, and as high as forty percent. Malaria in particular was a chronic problem in the Chesapeake area.

Masters purchased their labor, not their bodies, but it was a risky investment. Death, injuries, chronic maladies, running away, or a shirking worker could mean loss of income. But cheap labor was more important than quality labor.

While the terms of indentures varied a great deal, the master was usually required to provide his servants with "sufficient meat, Drink, Apparell, Washing and Lodging." Of course what was "sufficient" from the master's view, was often not deemed such by the servant. White servants had the right to go appeal their treatment to the courts. Maryland courts often took masters to task for the denial of rest, sleep, food, drink, and lodging. A third offense by a master was grounds to set a servant free.

On the other hand, colonial courts could impose servitude, usually for larceny or debt, if restitution could not be made, and fines and court costs paid. A 1692 Maryland law provided that a white woman who married a Negro would become a servant for seven years, if the Negro were free, he was to become a servant for the rest of his life. These individuals, as well as apprentices are included in this collection.

If servitude was to be a significant source of reliable labor, runaways could not be permitted to go free with impunity. As might be expected most runaways departed April through October, staying closer to home during winter weather. Non-English speakers might have runway less, whereas the Irish might have runaway more, due to the general anti-Irish feelings of the time. The not infrequent references to iron collars in these ads, show that running away was common. The collars were intended to make an example of the truants and to make identification easier.

Passes were required for those more than a certain distance away from home. Those who appeared to be suspicious characters, or could not give satisfactory accounts of themselves were committed to jail and held temporarily. Even if no master appeared to pay the costs of the man being held, he still might be remanded to servitude.

Unsuccessful flight also added to the time of servitude. In Maryland, a law was passed in 1661 that added ten days service for every day away. This was done partly as punishment, and partly to compensate for the costs of capture, reward and return. On the other hand bad or abusive masters were sometimes punished by the judicial system with the shortening or cancelling of indentures.

All forms of servitude were an important factor in the development of a landed aristocracy in the Chesapeake colonies. They were also vital in the nascent American industrial scene. Many of the runaways left from iron forges or furnaces.

For those fulfilled the terms of their indentures "well and faithfully [in] such employments as the master may assign" for a set period of time, the average man had a better chance of attaining a decent standard of living than he did in Europe. The master had paid for passage to the colonies, and for food, drink, clothing and shelter during the time of the indenture, and depending on the individual transaction, some form of "freedom dues," which could be money, land, tools, livestock, etc.

For the ambitious servant, the term of servitude was a time of preparation. He was used to the climate and ways of the new land. He learned farming or another skill as practiced in the New World. He made contacts in the area he lived, and if an artisan, might have a ready list of customers when on his own. Abbott Emerson Smith estimated that one in ten would take up land and become prosperous, and that one in ten would become an artisan. The other eight died in servitude, returned to England, and or became "poor whites."

The American Revolution stopped the transport of convicts and regular migration. Though regular immigration resumed, and limited indentured servitude resumed after the war, convicts were not permitted. Botany Bay in Australia became the dumping ground for those undesirables beginning in 1786.

The runaway ads provide a first-hand view of history, as well as valuable demographic information with the age, sex, height, place of origin, clothing, occupation, speech, as well as physical imperfections, etc. They often display attitudes of the owners, and personality traits of the runaway, such as a common affection for alcohol. Some ads give extensive vignettes of individuals with their perceived idiosyncrasies. They provide a bonanza of information for the social historian. Those interested in tracking their ancestors will also find a goldmine of details

It is impossible to know how many runaways there really were. Escapees of low value or close to the end of their terms may not have been advertised. Given that so many of the servants appear to be scapegraces, one wonders why their masters spent money to advertise for them, let alone pay a reward for their return. Those who were useful workers with lots of time remaining were likely to be the most sought after. Masters were likely to ignore those who left for a few days of dissipation, particularly planters during the slow season.

Some masters may have not wanted to pay the cost of the ads. Those masters whose servants absconded from the lower Eastern and Western shores of Maryland, and the farther western parts of the colony may not have bothered to advertise in papers printed in distant Annapolis and Baltimore. One wonders why John Moore bothered to advertise for John Harris who had been gone for three years and "drinks hard, and swears much, and used to have a sore leg."

The reader will note that many of those who appear only in Pennsylvania newspapers were from Cecil County, Maryland. Relative proximity to Philadelphia was part of the reason, but the barrier of the Susquehanna river was another. Ferrymen would demand passes, and supplementing their incomes with rewards was always appealing

All of the legible ads for runaways appearing in the *The Maryland Gazette*, the only newspaper then published in that colony. These include fugitives from Delaware, New Jersey, Pennsylvania, Virginia, New York, and even one from St. Vincent in the Caribbean. Maryland, Pennsylvania and New York newspapers are represented. The *Virginia Gazette* was not included in this compilation as it is online. I have retained the original spelling, punctuation, and capitalization of the ads. Illegible words or letters are indicated by brackets.

This compilation lists only white men and women. In the Maryland newspapers ads, wherein whites and blacks are listed together, I list the names of the blacks without any details. For blacks the reader is referred to: Lathan A. Windley, *Runaway Slave Advertisements: A Documentary History from the 1730s to 1790, Volume 2, Maryland* (Westport, Conn.: Greenwood Press, 1983).

Sometimes the ads in different papers are very similar and only the ad which occurs first in time is included, with references to the later ones. Minor differences in the advertisements are considered to be capitalization, spelling such as trousers/trowsers and 7/seven. If the ads are substantially different, each appears at the time it is first run. The three ads John Collins/Thomas Lockier illustrate the differences as well as the use of aliases by runaways. Advertisements that are largely illegible are not included.

It will be noticed that far more men were runaways than women. In part this was due to the imbalance in the ratio of those who were indentured. A 1755 census in Maryland showed that of 1,981 transported convicts that year, almost 80 percent were men.

The reader may wonder was John Gardner really only four feet 5 inches tall? Was John Hall advertising for a servant named John Hall, or was there a misprint? And how did John Chappel, one captain of a man of war, become a servant? There are a numerous variations in the spelling of names such as John Rawlings/Rolings. It also appears that Michael Hayne is probably Michael Hern/Kern/Hewne/Keirn.

For further reading:

Blumenthal, Walter Hart. *Brides From Bridewell: Female Felons Sent to Colonial America* (1962, reprint, Westport, Conn.: Greenwood Press, 1973).

Boyle, Joseph Lee. *"Drinks hard, and swears much": White Maryland Runaways, 1770-1774* (Baltimore: Clearfield Books, 2010).

Coldham, Peter Wilson. *Emigrants in Chains: A Social History of Forced Emigration to the Americas of Felons, Destitute Children, Political and Religious Non-Conformists, Vagabonds, Beggars and Other Undesirables, 1607-1776* (Baltimore: Genealogical Publishing Company, 1992).

Ekirch, A. Roger. *Bound for America: The Transportation of British Convicts to the Colonies, 1775-1778* (Oxford: Clarendon Press, 1987)

Fogleman, Aaron S. "From Slaves, Convicts, and Servants to Free Passengers: The Transformation of Immigration in the Era of the American Revolution," *The Journal of American History* 85 (1998), 43-76.

Galenson, David W. *White Servitude in Colonial America: An Economic Analysis* (Cambridge: Cambridge University Press, 1981)

Kellow, Margaret M. R. "Indentured Servitude in Eighteenth-Century Maryland," *Histoire Sociale — Social History* 17 (November 1984), 229-255.

Lancaster, R. Kent. "Almost Chattel: The Lives of Indentured Servants at Hampton-Northampton, Baltimore County," *Maryland Historical Magazine* 94 (1999), 340-362.

McCormac, E. I. *White Servitude in Maryland, 1634-1820* (Johns Hopkins University Studies in Historical and Political Science, Series XXII, Baltimore, 1904).

Meaders, Daniel. *Dead or Alive: Fugitive Slaves and White Indentured Servants Before 1830* (New York: Garland Publishing, 1993).

Menard, Russell R. "From Servants to Slaves: The Transformation of the Chesapeake Labor System," *Southern Studies*, 16 (1977), 355-388.

Miller, William. "The Effects of the American Revolution on Indentured Servitude." *Pennsylvania History* 7, 3 (July, 1940), 131-41.

Morgan, Kenneth. "Convict Runaways in Maryland, 1745-1775," *Journal of American Studies* 23 (August 1989), 253-68.

Morgan, Kenneth. "The Organization of the Convict Trade to Maryland: Stevenson, Randolph and Cheston, 1768-1775," *The William and Mary Quarterly* third series 42, (April 1985), 201-227.

Prude, Jonathan. "To Look Upon the "Lower Sort": Runaway Ads and the Appearance of Unfree Laborers in America, 1750-1800," *The Journal of American History* 78 1 (June, 1991), 124-159.

Semmes, Raphael. *Crime and Punishment in Early Maryland* (Baltimore: The Johns Hopkins University Press, 1938, reprint 1996.

Sollers, Basil. "Transported Convict Laborers in Maryland During the Colonial Period," *Maryland Historical Magazine* 2 (1907), 17-47.

Smith, Abbot Emerson. *Colonists in Bondage: White Servitude and Convict Labor in America, 1607-1776* (1947; reprint; Gloucester, Mass.: Peter Smith, 1965)

Tomlins, Christopher L. *Reconsidering Indentured Servitude: European Migration and the Early American Labor Force, 1600-1775*. American Bar Foundation Working Paper #9920 American Bar Association, 1999.

NEWSPAPERS CONSULTED

It should be noted that many of these newspapers did not have a complete run for the period. For example, *The Boston Chronicle* did not begin publication until October 22, 1767. Also, there were no newspapers published in Delaware or New Jersey for the entire period, colonies where ads for Maryland runaways might have been numerous, particularly Delaware.

Boston Chronicle
Boston Evening Post
The Boston Gazette, and Country Journal
The Boston News-Letter
Boston Post Boy
Connecticut Courant
Connecticut Gazette
Connecticut Journal
Essex Gazette
The Maryland Gazette
The New-Hampshire Gazette
The New-London Gazette
The New-York Gazette
The New-York Gazette; and the Weekly Mercury
The New-York Journal; or, The General Advertiser
The New-York Mercury
The Pennsylvania Chronicle
The Pennsylvania Gazette
The Providence Gazette; And Country Journal
Der Wöchentliche Pennsylvanische Staatsbote, (Philadelphia),

1763

Baltimore County, Dec. 31, 1762.

RAN away from the Subscriber, on the 29th of this Instant, a Servant Man named *David Wickenden*, an *Englishman*, about 30 Years of Age, about 5 Feet 6 Inches high, dark Skin, thin Visage, black Hair tied behind, and a small Blemish in one of his Eyes: Had on when he went away, a good Felt Hat, and [sic] old Country-Cloth Coat fulled, the Cape lined with Plaid, and a Lead-colour'd Country fulled Jacket with large white Buttons, a small old light-colour'd Coat, old coarse Shirt, old Leather Breeches, mix'd blue and white Yarn Stockings, old Shoes, and round yellow Buckles.

Whoever secures the said Servant so that his Master may have him again, shall receive Forty Shillings Reward if taken in the County; Five Pounds if out of the County; and Seven Pounds Ten Shillings if out of the Province, and reasonable Charges paid if brought home, by
ALEXANDER WELLS.

N. B. He formerly served Seven Years to Mr. *Henry Dorsey* on *Elk-Ridge.*

The Maryland Gazette, January 6, 1763; January 13, 1763; January 20, 1763; January 27, 1763; February 3, 1763; February 10, 1763. See *The Maryland* Gazette, June 16, 1763, and The *Maryland Gazette*, January 5, 1764.

RAN away from the Subscriber, living in *Annapolis*, on the 28th of *Decemb.* last, a Convict Servant Man, named *Richard Stevens*, a *Prussian* Born, and a Taylor by Trade, Speaks broken *English*, and very quick. He is about 5 Feet 8 Inches high, naturally of a pale Complexion, but when he ran away, his Face was much bruised, and had black Eyes, occasioned by Fighting. He carried with him sundry very good Clothes, *viz.* a very good brown Broadcloth Coat and Waistcoat, trimmed with the same Colour, a violet blue Suit of Cloth, with divers other Things too tedious to mention.

Whoever takes up the said Servant, and secures him so that his Master may have him again, shall have TEN POUNDS Reward, paid by
JOHN DUCKER.

The Maryland Gazette, January 6, 1763; January 27, 1763; February 3, 1763; February 10, 1763; February 17, 1763; February 24, 1763; March 3, 1763; March 10, 1763; March 17, 1763; March 24, 1763; March 31, 1763; April 7, 1763; April 14, 1763; April 28, 1763; May 5, 1763; *The Pennsylvania Gazette*, January 27, 1763. Minor differences between the papers.

December 13, 1763.

RAN away from the Subscriber, living on *Kent-Island*, in *Queen Anne's* County, on the 6th Instant, a young Convict Servant Man, named *John Place*, born in *England*, about 5 Feet 8 Inches high, of a fair Complexion, heavy Look, remarkable large white Eyes, dark Hair with drop Curls; he is an artful cunning Fellow, writes a legible Hand, and will probably forge a Pass: His Cloathing is, a light coloured Broad Cloth Coat, with Mohair Buttons, a white Linen Jacket, and Swanskin ditto, Buckskin Breeches, a Pair of grey ribbed Stockings, and a Pair of Block-Tin Shoe Buckles, which has much the Appearance of Silver.

Also one other Servant, named *Samuel Downy*, born in *England*, 5 Feet 5 Inches high, about 35 Years of Age, of a dark Complexion; has had a Bile on one of his Cheeks: His Clothing a light brown Cloth Coat, with white Metal Buttons, a blue Serge Jacket, a grey and brown cut Wig, dark Yarn Stockings, and took several Pair with him, their Colour unknown, Buckskin Breeches, with Jockey Straps, and speaks much in the West-Country Dialect.

Whoever takes up and secures the said Servant, so that their Master may have them again, shall have Fifty Shillings Reward for each, paid by
          JAMES HUTCHINGS.

The Maryland Gazette, January 13, 1763; January 27, 1763.

Baltimore County, Dec. 18, 1762.

RUN away from the Subscribers, the 12th of this Instant, two Servant Men, both Englishmen, and came into this Country as Convicts for seven Years; the one belonging to Jones, aged near 30 Years, about 5 Feet 9 Inches high, of a pale Complexion, by Name William Harding, wears his own Hair hanging about his Ears, which is very straight, and of a brown Colour: He carried with him two dark coloured Cotton Jackets, two Ozenbrigs Shirts, a Pair of old Leather Breeches, a Pair of Cotton Stockings or Legings, a Pair of black Yarn Stockings, two Pair of Shoes, one Pair with Strings, the other with Straps, yellow Metal Buckles, and coarse Felt Hat, not much worn; but it is probable he may change his Name and Apparel, as there is Reason to believe he carried some Cash with him; supposed he likewise carried a Gun with him.—The other is something more than 5 Feet high, by Name Samuel Webb; he carried with him a Country Cloth Jacket, an old Pair of Trowsers, old Felt Hat, and Ozenbrigs Shirts; but expected he has got other Cloathing; his Hair is brown, and curls. Whoever secures the said servants, so that their Masters may have them again, shall have Forty Shillings for each, besides what the Law allows, paid by us,
RICHARD JONES, and WILLIAM SLADE.

The Pennsylvania Gazette, January 13, 1763.

Prince-George's County, *Jan.* 10. 1763.

RAN away about the 8th Instant, from the Subscriber, an indented Servant Man, whose Name, as he says, is *Jonathan Henry*, which he will probably change as soon as he gets over the Bay, as I suppose he is gone that Way. He carried with him a Female Child, in order, as he pretends, to leave with his Wife's Friends: He had on when he went away, a Holland Shirt, Leather Breeches, an old brown Great-Coat, &c.

Whoever secures the said Servant, and brings him to me, or to *William Reynolds* at *Annapolis*, shall have a PISTOLE Reward, besides what the Law allows.   SAMUEL DUVALL BECK.

The Maryland Gazette, January 27, 1763; February 3, 1763; February 10, 1763; February 17, 1763.

TWENTY DOLLARS Reward.

WHEREAS a certain Charles Goldsmith, a handsome young Man, of about 5 Feet 9 Inches high, long light-coloured Hair, commonly plaited; about 28 Years of Age, is remarkable for playing the German Flute, which he took with him; had a Cut across the Ball of his left Thumb, a little Pock-marked, is a Cabinet-maker by Trade: Had on when he went away, a new Coat and Jacket of superfine blue Cloth, a Pair of Buck-skin Breeches, a Pair of Stone Knee-Buckles, a new Beaver Hat, a blue Surtout Coat with a Velvet Collar, a black Cravat, and rode away a small Bay Mare.—He was last heard of, at one Wagstaffe's, in Baltimore, Maryland.

As said Goldsmith has absented himself from his Bail, they are likely to suffer. Any Person that will arrest and take him, so as he may be brought to Justice, may depend on being paid the above Reward of Twenty Dollars, by the Subscriber or Subscribers hereof.—It is likely he will change his Name.—As it is said he is bound for Carolina, all Masters of Vessels are desired not to take him off, at their Peril.
EDMUND MILNE, JAMES BENNETT.

The Pennsylvania Gazette, January 27, 1763. See *The Maryland Gazette*, February 3, 1763.

RAN away from the Subscriber, living at the *Vineyard* near *Annapolis*, on the 23d of *January* last, a Convict Servant Man named *Thomas Smith*, he is a *Welchman*, and speaks but very little *English*. His Apparel was a brown Surtout Coat, a Kersey Vest, and Cotton ditto, Cotton and brown Cloth Breeches, and a Pair of Boots.

Whoever takes up the said Servant, and brings him home, shall receive TEN POUNDS Reward, beside what the Law allows, paid by
NATHAN LANE.

The Maryland Gazette, February 3, 1763; February 10, 1763; February 17, 1763; February 24, 1763; March 3, 1763; March 10, 1763.

RAN away on the 12th of *December* last, from the Subscriber in *Fredericksburg*, a Servant Woman named *Mary Kellock*, born in *England*, about 17 Years of Age, is much mark'd with the Small Pox, has light brown Hair, grey Eyes, and very red Lips: Had on, a light colour'd Camblet Gown, a pink-colour'd Stuff Petticoat, a Check Apron, and a black Sattin Hat. I since heard she went with one *Jarvis* a Drummer in the *Virginia* Regiment, and was dressed in his old blue Cloaths.

Whoever takes up the said Servant, and conveys her to me at *Fredericksburg*, or secures her so that I may have her again, shall receive Forty Shillings Reward, and reasonable Charges, paid by
JANE NEILE.
The Maryland Gazette, February 3, 1763; February 10, 1763.

Philadelphia, January 22, 1763.
TWENTY DOLLARS REWARD.
WHEREAS a certain *Charles Goldsmith*, a handsome young Man of about 5 Feet 9 Inches high, long light-coloured Hair, commonly plaited; about 28 Years of Age; is remarkable for playing the *German Flute*, which he took with him; had a Cut across the Ball of his left Thumb, a little Pock-mark'd, is a Cabinet-maker by Trade: Had on when he went away, a new Coat and Jacket of superfine Cloth, a Pair of Buckskin Breeches, a Pair of Stone Knee-Buckles, a new Beaver Hat, a blue Surtout Coat with a Velvet Collar, a black Cravat, and rode away on a small Bay Mare.—He was last heard of, at one *Wagstaffe's*, in *Baltimore, Maryland*.

N. B. As said *Goldsmith* has absented himself from his Bail, they are likely to suffer. Any Person that will arrest and take him, so as he may be brought to Justice, may depend on being paid the above Reward of *Twenty Dollars*, by the Subscriber or Subscribers hereof.—'Tis likely he will change his Name.—As it's said he is bound for *Carolina*, all Masters of Vessels are desired not to take him off, at their Peril.
EDMUND MILNE,
JAMES BENNETT.
The Maryland Gazette, February 3, 1763; February 10, 1763; February 17, 1763; February 24, 1763. See *The Pennsylvania Gazette*, January 27, 1763.

Salem County, in West-Jersey, January 26, 1763.
WHEREAS a certain Joseph Cartwrite, and Clement Leonard, were advertised by James Baxter, Sheriff of Cecil County, Maryland, and William Murdo; this is to inform the said Sheriff, and Murdo, that the said Joseph Cartwrite, and Clement Leonard, are now in Salem Goal.
The Pennsylvania Gazette, February 10, 1763.

Head of *South-River*, March 9, 1763.
RAN away from the Subscriber on Monday last, an Apprentice Lad, turned of 19 Years of Age, named *Richard Clark*, he about 5 Feet 4 or 5 Inches high, well set, and of a dark Complexion: Had on when he went away, a Pair of old Negro Shoes, grey Worsted Stockings, Serge Breeches, old brown Coat much patched, and old Felt Hat: He has short black Hair, and wears a white Cap.

Whoever brings the said Lad home, or secures him so that his Master may get him again, shall receive Twenty Shillings Reward, paid by
BENJAMIN WILLIAMS.
N. B. All Persons are forewarned from entertaining him, as they will answer it at their Peril.
The Maryland Gazette, March 10, 1763.

March 21, 1763.
TEN POUNDS REWARD.
RAN away last Night from *Kingsbury Furnace*, in *Baltimore* County, two *English* Convict Servants, *viz.*

Thomas Hawkes, aged about 30 Years, wears his own brown Hair, is slow of Speech, thick of Hearing, and has a Mole between his Eyes: Had on a Felt Hat, Osnabrig Shirt, Fearnothing Coat, *Welch* Cotton Jacket and Breeches, Yarn Hose, a Pair of Flats, and several other Things unknown.

Thomas Stringer, aged about 25 Years, 5 Feet 6 Inches high, wears his own short brown Hair, has two Moles on his Face, and speaks pretty fast: Had on and took with him, a new Felt Hat, old *Monmouth* Cap, a Fearnothing Jacket with Metal Buttons, Cotton Jacket and Breeches, Osnabrig Shirt, Yarn Stockings, a Pair of Turn up Shoes, and other Things unknown.

Whoever will take up and secure the said Runaways, so that they may be had again, and give Notice thereof to the Subscriber, shall receive, if 10 Miles from home, Fifteen Shillings; if 20 Miles, Twenty Shillings; if 40 Miles, Forty Shillings; and if out of the Province, Five Pounds for each of them, to be paid by
JOHN ADDISON SMITH.

The Maryland Gazette, March 31, 1763. See *The Maryland Gazette*, March 10, 1768, for Hawkes. See *The Maryland Gazette*, September 8, 1768, and *The Pennsylvania Gazette*, September 15, 1768, for Stringer.

THREE POUNDS Reward.

RUN away from the Subscriber, living between the Branches of Elk, on the First Instant, a Servant Man, named Nathaniel M'Dowell, about 30 Years of Age, born in the North of Ireland, by Trade a Spinning wheel-maker, about five Feet eight Inches high, wears his own black bushy Hair, round Face, and rough Features: Had on when he went away, a blue under jacket, light coloured outside Jacket, with Sleeves and Cuffs, new Cloth Breeches, Thread Stockings, good Shoes, and Check Shirt; is remarkably fond of Smoaking Tobacco, and drinking Spirits. As it is known an Intimacy has subsisted between him and a neighbouring Woman, the Wife of Alexander Logan, who left her Husband about the same Time, and took her Child with her, a promising Boy, six Years old, with white Hair, it is thought they are gone together, and that they will go to Philadelphia. Whoever takes up the said Servant, and secures him in any Goal, so as his Master may have him again, shall have the above Reward, and reasonable Charges, paid by JOHN STRAWBRIDGE.

N. B. All Masters of Vessels are forbid to carry him off.

The Pennsylvania Gazette, May 12, 1763; June 9, 1763.

RUN away from the Subscriber, living in Queen Anne's County, Maryland, an English Convict Servant Man, named Richard Priest, about five Feet six Inches high, thick made, about 20 Years of Age, a little pitted with the Small-pox: Had on when he went away, a Castor Hat, green Broadcloth Coat, about half worn, scarlet Vest, and new Buckskin Breeches. Whoever takes up and secures said Servant, so as his master may have him again, shall have One Guinea Reward, besides what the Law allows, paid by SOLOMON HOLTON.

The Pennsylvania Gazette, May 19, 1763.

May 14, 1763.

FIVE PISTOLES REWARD.

RAN away from the Subscriber, living on *My Lady's Manor* in *Baltimore* County, on Thursday Night last, an *English* Servant Man, named *John Collins*, (but am informed he once went by the Name of *Thomas Lockier*), he is a lusty Fellow, about 26 Years of Age, and about 5 Feet 6 Inches high, of a dark Complexion, pretty much pitted with the Small-Pox, and wears his own Hair tied behind. Had on when he went away, a brown Kersey Coat with flat Brass Buttons, a bluish Cloth Jacket, with round Brass Buttons, and the Skirts cut off, Check and reddish Silk Handkerchiefs, old Leather Breeches, Grey Stockings, Shoes, Buckles, and an old Castor Hat.

Whoever secures the said Fellow, so that his Master may get him again, shall receive, if taken in the County, Five Pounds, and if out of it, Five Pistoles Reward, of
JOSIAS SLADE.

N. B. He is a very saucy Fellow, speaks thick, is acquainted with the Country, and has some Dollars with him. 'Tis supposed a Brindle Dog follows him, and expect he will take a Horse the first Opportunity.

The Maryland Gazette, May 26, 1763; June 9, 1763; June 16, 1763; June 23, 1763. See *The Pennsylvania Gazette*, July 21, 1763, and *The Maryland Gazette*, August 25, 1763.

RAN away the 22d of *May* 1763, from the Subscriber, a Convict Servant Man, named *Richard Lotan*, born in the West of *England*, about 40 Years of Age, 5 Feet 6 Inches high, pretty thick in the Body, has small Legs, much upon the Battle Ham, as he walks with his Knees very close, of a fair and fresh Complexion, short, strait, reddish Hair, and speaks Effeminately; understands Plowing, Sowing, Hedging, and Ditching, and pretends to be a Cobbler. His Apparel, when he went away, was a grey Pea Jacket, Cotton Waist-coat and Breeches, Yarn Stockings, Osnabrigs Shirt, and Negro Shoes; but that he may alter, and may have a Pass.

Whoever takes up the said Servant, and delivers him to me in *Annapolis*, shall have TEN POUNDS Reward, paid in Spanish Dollars at 7/6 each.   NICHOLAS MACCUBIN.

The Maryland Gazette, May 26, 1763.

Baltimore County, *June* 14, 1763.
RAN away from the Subscriber, living near *Soldier's Delight*, on the 9th Instant, a Servant Man, named *David Wickenden*, about 5 Feet 6 Inches high, near 30 Years old, thin Visage, dark Complexion, dark Brown Hair, and has a Blemish in the Sight of his Right Eye: Had on when he went away, an old Felt Hat, old dark coloured Country fulled Great Coat, the Cape lined with Plaid, Osnabrig Shirt, Country Linen Trowsers, old Shoes, and an Iron Collar about his Neck. He is well known in *Baltimore* and *Anne-Arundel* Counties, having served Mr. *Henry Dorsey* on *Elk-Ridge* Seven Years.

Whoever takes up and secures the said Servant, shall have Fifty Shillings Reward; if taken 30 Miles from home, Five Pounds; if out of the

Province, Seven Pounds Ten Shillings; and if brought home, reasonable Charges, paid by ALEXANDER WELLS.

The Maryland Gazette, June 16, 1763; June 30, 1763; July 7, 1763; July 14, 1763; July 28, 1763; August 4, 1763. See *The Maryland Gazette*, January 6, 1763, and The *Maryland Gazette*, January 5, 1764.

BROKE out of *Talbot* County Goal, in *February* last, *Thomas Wales*, a Cooper by Trade, but has for some Years past followed the Bay Trade in a small Shallop, he is a Man of a small Stature, is much given to Drink to Excess; I am inform'd he has past by the Name of *Thomas Spencer*, and has been seen in *Joppa*, in *Baltimore County*, since he made his Escape.

Whoever secures the said *Wales*, in any Goal, so that the Subscriber may get him again, shall be paid THREE POUNDS, by
W. GIBSON, Sheriff of *Talbot* County.

The Maryland Gazette, June 16, 1763; June 30, 1763; July 7, 1763; July 14, 1763.

June 10, 1763.

RAN away from the Subscriber in *London-Town*, a Servant Man named *William Carroll*, alias *Stansley*, an *Irishman*, and speaks very much on the Brogue: he is a short thick Fellow, and has short black Hair: Had on and with him when he went away, a very good white Shirt, double Stitched in the Collar, and work'd in Diamonds between the Stitching; two Check Shirts, two Osnabrigs Ditto, one of which is quite new, two Pair of old white ribb'd Stockings, the Ribs very broad, one Pair of white plain Ditto, long Osnabrigs Trowsers, a blue lappelled Cloth Coat, with Metal Buttons and white Lining, a dark colour'd grey Jacket, a grey Bearskin Great Coat with broad Metal Buttons, and old Fall Shoes newly soled. He talks much about Ditching and Farming.

Whoever takes up the said Runaway, and secures him so as he may be had again, shall have Two Pistoles Reward; and if brought home, reasonable Charges, paid by WILLIAM BROWN.

The Maryland Gazette, June 23, 1763; July 7, 1767; July 21, 1763; August 4, 1763; August 11, 1763.

Anne-Arundel County,

RAN away from the Subscriber, living near *Annapolis*, on the 18th Instant, an Indented Servant Man, named *Ambrose St. Laurance*, about 5 Feet high, near 30 Years old, red Complexion, Sandy colour'd Hair, Battle-hamm'd, and is dis abled in one of his Legs: Had on when he went away, a brown Broad-cloth Coat and Breeches, white Metal Buttons, a white Shirt, *Russia* Drab Jacket, grey Worsted Stockings, black Shoes, and a Cloth colour'd

Great Coat: Rode a remarkable small Dark Bay Mare, with an old Saddle patch'd on the Pummel.

    Whoever takes up the said Servant, and secures him so as he may be had again, shall have Twenty Shillings Reward, beside what the Law allows, paid by   THOMAS RUTLAND.
The Maryland Gazette, June 23, 1763.

RAN away from the Subscriber, living near *Elk-Ridge* Furnace, a Convict Servant Lad, named *Joseph Dickason*, about 18 Years old, 5 Feet high, he was born in *Portugal*, is of a very swarthy Complexion, and some of his Fingers are crippled: Had on and with him, a Bearskin Coat, with large Metal Buttons, a Grey *German* Serge Waistcoat, Osnabrigs Trowsers, white Shirt, one Check Ditto, a Silk Handkerchief, black Stock, Silver Clasps, turn'd Pumps, large Metal Buckles, and an old Felt Hat.

    Whoever takes up and secures the said Servant, so as his Master may have him again, shall receive Twenty Shillings Reward, if 10 Miles from home, if taken at a greater Distance, Thirty Shillings, and reasonable Charges, paid by
July 1, 1763.   THOMAS WELSH, Collier.
The Maryland Gazette, July 7, 1763; July 21, 1763.

                            Annapolis, July 4, 1763.
RAN away last Night from the Subscribers, a Convict Servant Man, named *Henry Talbot*, born in the West of *England*, and speaks much in that Country dialect, of a ruddy Complexion, dark brown Hair, about 5 Feet 10 Inches high, has three or four large Scars on his Head, and is a little disabled in the Wrist of his left Arm, which may be perceived by taking hold of it, as the outside Bone is not knit in the Joint, and is much addicted to Liquor. Had on a dark brown Broad-cloth Coat, a Scarlet Cloth Jacket, a Pair of new Country made Shoes, and a white Shirt.

    Whoever takes up and secures the said Servant, so that the Subscribers may have him again, shall receive FIVE POUNDS Reward.
ISAAC HARRIS,   JONATHAN PINKNEY.
The Maryland Gazette, July 7, 1763. See *The Maryland Gazette*, August 16, 1764.

RAN away from the Subscriber's Plantation at the Head of *Severn (Turkey-Island)* on Monday last, a white Servant Man named *Thomas Watts*, he is a thick well-set Fellow, about 5 Feet 7 Inches high, has a fresh Complexion, a little pitted with the Small-Pox, a large Nose, sharp at the tip End, large staring Eyes, and wears his own black Hair, which he often ties back with a Ribbon: His wearing Apparel is an old light brown *Manchester* Velvet Coat, a blue Halfthick Jacket, Leather Breeches, coarse grey Yarn Stockings, and County made Shoes: He sometimes wears a Fustian Coat, and red Jacket, and he has several Shirts, both Linen and Osnabrigs.

Whoever brings the said Servant to me at *Annapolis*, shall receive THREE POUNDS Reward, beside what the Law allows.

GEO. STEUART.

The Maryland Gazette, July 7, 1763; July 14, 1763; July 21, 1763; August 4, 1763; August 11, 1763.

RAN away from the Subscriber on the 5th of *June* last, from *Yocomico* River, *Northumberland* County, *Virginia*, a Servant Man named *John Payne*, born in *Maryland*, about 5 Feet 7 Inches high, a thin spare Man, of a black Complexion, and about 25 Years of Age. He had on and with him, a Claret or Pompadour coloured Cloth Coat, black Worsted figured Wove Jacket, fine Castor Hat, blue Cloth and Buckskin Breeches, mix'd Yarn and black Worsted Stockings, new Check Trowsers, and a new Check Shirt. It is thought he will made for *North-Carolina* or *Pennsylvania*.

Whoever apprehends the said Servant, and delivers him to his Master, or secures him so that he may be had again, shall have One Pistole Reward, beside what the Law allows, if taken 10 Miles off; Two Pistoles, if 15 Miles; Three Pistoles, if 30 Miles; Five Pistoles, if 50 Miles; or Six Pistoles if out of the Province, paid by   RICHARD BOWES.

The Maryland Gazette, July 7, 1763; July 14, 1763; July 21, 1763; July 28, 1763; August 4, 1767; August 11, 1763. See *The Maryland Gazette*, October 20, 1763.

FIFTEEN POUNDS Reward.

RUN away from Stafford Forge, on Deer Creek, in Baltimore County, Maryland, on the 27th of June, three English Convict Servant Men, viz. William Brooks, about 30 Years of Age, a lusty Man, about 5 Feet 8 Inches high, remarkable large square Shoulders, round Face, much pitted with the Small-Pox, has blue Eyes, and is rough spoken, but speaks very good English: Had on when he went away a Felt Hat, brown Fearnought Jacket, a Pair of Rolls Trowsers, Country made Shoes, Yarn Hose, and Ozenbrigs Shirt. Said Brooks has been used to drive a Coal Waggon.

John Pickron, a middle sized Man, about 40 Years of Age, 5 Feet 5 Inches high, blue Eyes, round red Face, and is a little pitted with the Small Pox: Had on when he went away, a brown Halfthick Coat, with metal

Buttons, a Pair of Leather Breeches, Yarn Hose, Country made Shoes, and Ozenbrigs Shirt.

Richard Poole, 35 Years of Age, about 5 Feet 4 Inches high, well set, long Nose, grey Eyes, of a yellow Complexion, Down-look, and speaks good English. It is likely the above Servants may have changed their Clothes; they were imported into Maryland last Fall. Whoever apprehends said Servants, or either of them, and secures them in any Goal, so that they may be had again, shall have for each of them, if taken Twenty Miles from Home, Forty Shillings; if at a greater Distance Three Pounds, or if out of the Province, Five Pounds Reward, and reasonable Charges, if brought to said Forge by   JEREMIAH SHEREDINE.

The Pennsylvania Gazette, July 7, 1763; August 11, 1763.

Run away on Saturday, the 18th of June last, from the Subscriber, living in George-Town, Kent County, Maryland, A convict Servant Man, named Francis Richard, about 45 Years of Age, a Blacksmith by Trade, and can make Carts and Waggons, he is a very ill down looking Man, about 6 Feet high, and very well made; he talks like a West Countryman: Had on when he went away, A brown Cloth Jacket, with Metal buttons, black Wig, and Felt Hat. He is much given to Liquor. It is supposed he is gone with a Woman named Mary Hoult, alias Mary Brisko, who is likewise very much given to drinking. It is thought they went towards Chester or Philadelphia, as the said Woman lived in Chester and Philadelphia some Time ago. Whoever takes up and secures said Servant, so as his Master may have him again, shall have Three Pounds Reward, paid by Mr. James M'Lacklen, Merchant, or Mrs. Mary M'Cay, in George Town.

The Pennsylvania Gazette, July 7, 1763. See *The Pennsylvania Gazette*, July 21, 1763

Bladensburg, July 12, 1763.
RAN away last Wednesday Morning, an Indented Servant Man, about 19 Years of Age, well-set, about 5 Feet 6 Inches high, fair Complexion, round Visage, his right Arm has been broke, and he can't straiten it. Had on when he went away, a blue Serge Coat, Country Cloth Jacket, and light colour'd German Serge Breeches.

Whoever brings the Servant to the Subscriber in *Bladensburg*, shall receive Five Pounds Reward.
WILLIAM SAUNDERS.

The Maryland Gazette, July 14, 1763.

Baltimore County, Maryland, July 3, 1763.

RUN away, on Saturday, the Second Instant, from Onion's Iron Works, near Joppa, an English Servant Man, named John Collins, about 5 Feet 8 Inches high, about 26 Years of Age, pitted with the Small-Pox, wears his own long black Hair, and speaks very thick: Had on when he went away, a brown Kersey Coat, with Brass Buttons, a Lappel Jacket, old Leather Breeches, Shoes and Stockings, and an old Castor Hat. Since he has been in this Country he has lived at Caleb Dorsey's Iron Works, at Cute's Creek; at Jacob Giles's Works, in Lancaster County; and at the White Horse, in the Great Valley, Pennsylvania, and there went by the Name of Thomas Lockier, but likely he may change his Name, as usual. Whoever secures the said Servant, so as he may be had again, shall receive Five Pistoles, and reasonable Charges, paid by JOSIAH SLADE.

The Pennsylvania Gazette, July 21, 1763. See *The Maryland Gazette*, May 26, 1763, and *The Maryland Gazette*, August 25, 1763.

New Castle, July 13, 1763.

NOW in the Goal of this County, a certain Francis Richard, aged about 45 Years, about six feet high, says he is a Blacksmith by Trade, and that he was a servant to Mrs. Mary M'Cay, in Georgetown, but got his Freedom. His Master or Mistress (if he has any) is hereby desired to come pay Charges, and take him away, otherwise he will be sold out for the same, by ALEXANDER HARVEY, Goaler.

The Pennsylvania Gazette, July 21, 1763. See *The Pennsylvania Gazette*, July 7, 1763.

COMMITTED to *Anne-Arundel* County Goal, on the 15th Instant, as a Runaway, *Thomas Hays*, who says he belongs to *John Gardiner* of *St. Mary's* County, he is about 5 Feet 6 Inches high, of a ruddy Complexion, slim made, and has on a Blue Grey Cloth Jacket, Check Shirt, and Osnabrigs Trowsers.

The said *Hays* appears to be disordered in his Senses.

His Master may have him again on paying Charges.
LANCELOT JACQUES, Sheriff.

The Maryland Gazette, July 28, 1763; August 4, 1763.

RAN away in *June* last, from the Subscriber living in *Dorchester* County, a Servant Man named *Owen Robinson*, an Irishman, a Taylor by Trade, about 40 Years of Age, has had the Small-Pox, but is not much pitted, has a large Scar on his Cheek, near the Corner of his Mouth, torn, as he says, by a

Cow's Horn, in *Ireland*, when a Lad. He had on and with him, an old Cloth Coat Vest, and a Pair of Breeches of Forest Cloth, one white and two check Shirts, a Silk Handkerchief red & spotted, Worsted Stockings, & Thread Ditto, old Shoes, a brown bob Wig, and old Castor Hat. He may have got some other Cloaths, as he was intrusted to work abroad some Time before he went away. Whoever secures the said Servant, so that he may be had again, shall have Three Pounds Reward, paid by
Bartholomew Ennalls.
The Maryland Gazette, August 4, 1763; August 11, 1763; August 18, 1763.

RAN away from the Subscriber, living on the lower Part of *Kent-Island*, on the first of this Instant *August*, Two Convict Servant Men, *viz.*

John Griffitts, of a dark Complexion, has black Hair, is pretty much pitted with the Small-Pox, about 5 Feet 7 Inches high, and is well made. Had on an old Osnabrigs Shirt and Trowsers, an old blue Serge Coat, and a Felt Hat.

John Pritchard, of a fair Complexion, about the same Height with the other, has light colour'd Hair, and has lost the first Joint of each of his great Toes. Had on an old blue Jacket without Sleeves, an old patch'd check Shirt, strip'd Country Cloth Breeches, old Leggings and Shoes, and a Felt Hat.

They went off in a large Canoe, and are supposed to be gone down the Bay.

Whoever takes up the said Servants, and secures them in any Goal, so that the Subscriber may get them again, shall have Forty Shillings Reward for each, paid by   STEPHEN BRYAN.
The Maryland Gazette, August 4, 1763.

Baltimore-Town, August 8, 1763.
RAN away from on board the Ship *Dolphin*, Capt. *Mathew Craymer*, lying in the Ferry Branch of *Patapsco* River, in the Night between the 7th and 8th Instant, five Convict Men, *viz.*

Simon Pugh, a well-set middle sized Man, smooth Face, black Hair, and remarkable fine black Eyes, had with him a blue Surtout, two light coloured Cloth Coats, several Waistcoats, and other Cloaths, and capable of making a genteel Appearance.

Miles Cook, a stout Fellow, in a Jacket and Trowsers, fair Complexion, and one of his Legs thicker than the other.

James Anderson, a little Man, who has lost to Use of one of his Hands by a Shot through the Wrist. The two last are Sailors.

Robert Walker, a tall elderly Man, with his own Hair, much pitted with the Small-Pox. And,

James Donaldson, very much freckled, and black Hair.

They took with them the Ship's Yawl, about 20 Feet long, with one Mast, a Sprit Main-Sail and Jib, turpentined Sides, painted with a Streak of Blue along the Gunwale, and rows five Oars, but had Four only on board.

Whoever takes up the said Runaways, and secures them, so as they may be had again, shall receive Twenty Shilling Reward for each; but if they are brought on board the Ship, Forty Shillings, and the same Sum for the Yawl.   STEWART and LUX.

The Maryland Gazette, August 11, 1763; August 18, 1763; August 25, 1763; September 1, 1763. See *The Pennsylvania Gazette*, August 18, 1763, and *The Pennsylvania Gazette*, December 1, 1763.

Annapolis, August 11, 1763.

RAN away Yesterday Morning, from the Subscriber, an Apprentice Lad named *Thomas Stinsicomb*, about 18 Years of Age, 5 Feet 6 Inches high, has short dark Hair, and grey Eyes. Had on and took with him, a grey Cut Wig, a light colour'd Bearskin Coat, two Waistcoats, one a Country wove black and white, the other Nankeen, with red Glass Buttons, one Castor and a Felt Hat.

He formerly belonged to one *Thomas Pecker*, and inlisted in the *Virginia* Regiment.

Whoever apprehends the said Apprentice, and delivers him to his Master in Annapolis, shall have THREE POUNDS Reward, paid by CHARLES WILSON PEALE.

The Maryland Gazette, August 11, 1763; August 18, 1763.

TWO PISTOLES REWARD.

RAN away from the Subscriber, living in *Kent* County, on the 22d of *July* last, a Servant Man named *Thomas Conner*, an *Irishman*, by Trade a Shoemaker, about 50 Years of Age, 6 Feet high, is very artful, has grey Hair, and a large Scar in one of his Cheeks. Had on when he went away, a brown Cloth Coat with white Metal Buttons, a white Frize Jacket, black Everlasting Breeches, white Thread Stockings, and old Pumps. His other Dress is unknown, as he stole and took with him several other Cloaths, Shoemaker's Tools, Leather, and some ready made Shoes. He has a remarkable Shaking in his Head and Hands when at Work. He takes a great deal of Snuff, and is fond of Liquor, has been a Soldier in *Flanders*, and talks much about it.

Whoever takes up and secures the said Servant in any Goal, so that the Subscriber may get him again, shall have the above Reward; and if brought home, reasonable Charges, paid by
ALEXANDER M'INTOSH.
All Masters of Vessels are forbid to carry him off at their Peril.
The Maryland Gazette, August 18, 1763; August 25, 1763; September 1, 1763.

Philadelphia, August 12, 1763.
RUN away, on the 8th Instant, from on board the Ship Dolphin, Capt. Craymer, from London, lying at Baltimore, in Maryland, the following Convicts, viz.

Simon Pugh, about 5 Feet 6 Inches high, black Hair, tied behind; has with him a blue Surtout Coat, with good Lining, and is 28 Years of Age.

Miles Cook, about 5 Feet 10 Inches high, has one very thick Leg, and is 30 Years of Age.

James Doloson, much freckled, black Hair, in Sailor Dress, 26 Years old, five Feet six Inches high.

James Anderson, who has lost the Use of one Hand, about 5 Feet 5 Inches high, in SailorDress, and 32 Years of Age.

Robert Walker, much Pock marked, about 5 Feet 10 Inches high, 44 Years old, and has a red Jacket.

Whoever apprehends said Servants, shall be paid One Pistole for each, by Mr. M'GLOCHLAN, at the Indian Queen, in Philadelphia.
The Pennsylvania Gazette, August 18, 1763. See *The Maryland Gazette*, August 11, 1763, and *The Pennsylvania Gazette*, December 1, 1763.

FIVE POUNDS REWARD.

RAN away from the Subscriber, living in *Baltimore* County, on the 14th of this Instant *August*, Two *Irish* Servants, a Man and a Woman. The Man named *Patrick Britt*, about 5 Feet high, about 45 Years of Age, and grey headed. Had on and took with him, a Snuff-colour'd Coat, a blue striped Flannel Jacket, a Pair of Osnabrigs Trowsers, old Shoes, a Felt Hat, an old Coat, a white Shirt, Check and Osnabrigs Ditto, with several other Things, The Woman is named *Mary Moran*, about 56 Years of Age, and grey headed. She had on a Check Gown, a Bed Gown striped with red, blue and black, and a Woollen Petticoat striped with black and white, and took with her several other Things.

Whoever will bring the said Servants to the Subscriber, shall receive, if taken in the County, Forty Shillings Pennsylvania Money; and if out of the County, Five Pounds. CHARLES MOTHERBY.

The Maryland Gazette, August 25, 1763; *The Pennsylvania Gazette*, September 15, 1763. Minor differences between the papers.

Baltimore County, *August* 15, 1763.
FIVE POUNDS REWARD.

RAN away last Night, from the Subscriber, an *English* Servant Man named *John Collins*, about 26 Years of Age, and about 5 Feet 6 Inches high, pitted with the Small-Pox, wears his own long black Hair, and speaks thick: Had on when he went away, a lightish brown Cloth Coat, lined with blue, with white Metal Buttons, a brown Cloth Lapel Jacket, a good Pair of Leather Breeches, white ribb'd Worsted Stockings, good Pumps with odd Buckles, a half worn Castor Hat, and a good Check Shirt.

Whoever secures the said Servant, so as his Master may have him again, shall receive, if taken in this County, THREE POUNDS; and if out of the County, FIVE POUNDS Reward, paid by
JOSIAS SLADE.

N. B. He may change his Name, as he once went by the Name of *Thomas Locker*.

The Maryland Gazette, August 25, 1763; September 1, 1763; September 8, 1763; September 15, 1763; September 22, 1763; *The Pennsylvania Gazette*, September 1, 1763. Minor differences between the papers. See *The Maryland Gazette*, May 26, 1763, and *The Pennsylvania Gazette*, July 21, 1763.

August 19, 1763.

RAN away from the *Baltimore* Iron-Works, three Convict Servant Men, lately imported from *Bristol* to *Annapolis*, viz.

John Pinemore, about 22 Years of Age, near 6 Feet high, dark Complexion, speaks in the West-Country Dialect, pretends to be a Farmer and Tinker: Had on when he went away, an Osnabrig Shirt, Crocus Trowsers, Cotton Jacket, new Felt Hat, and Country made Shoes with Brass Buckles.

Mortimore Sales, about 23 Years of Age, fair Complexion, brown curled Hair tied, about 5 Feet 8 Inches high, pretends he is an *Englishman*, but the Brogue on his Tongue discovers him to be an *Irishman*, can write, and says he understands Farming: Had on when he went away, a brown Cloth Jacket with Horn Buttons, Osnabrig Shirt, Crocus Trowsers, a small half-worn Hat, bound with Binding, & a Pair of half-worn turn'd Pumps with a large Pair of carved Silver Buckles.

Thomas Grant, born in *Northamptonshire*, 22 Years of Age, black Hair, about 5 Feet 4 Inches high, can write, and has been a Gentleman's Servant: Had on when he went away, an old Cotton Jacket, Osnabrig Shirt, Crocus Trowsers, half-worn Hat, and old Shoes.

They may all change their Names, and steal other Cloathing. *Pinemore* and *Sales* are Fiddlers.

Whoever apprehends said Servants, so as they may be had again, shall have Thirty Shillings, if taken 10 Miles from home; Forty Shillings, if 20 Miles from home; and if out of the Province, Five Pounds, and reasonable Charges, if brought home.   R. CROXALL.

The Maryland Gazette, August 25, 1763; September 1, 1763.

                       Joppa, Sunday Morning, August 7, 1763.
BRoke out of Baltimore County Goal, the following Prisoners, viz. Gerrard Bewmire (committed for Horse stealing) of a swarthy Complexion, about 6 Feet high: Had on a light coloured Broadcloth Jacket and Breeches, and had with him an old Pair of Velvet Breeches, blue Worsted Stockings, old Pumps, and an old Hat. He came from Monmouth County in East New-Jersey.

John Driver (committed for Debt) had on an old Thickset Coat, black Jacket, Breeches and Stockings, and old Pumps with Steel Buckles; has long black Hair on the back Part of his Head, wears a white Cap, and an old Castor Hat. Whoever takes up the said Prisoners, and brings them to the Subscriber, shall have Three Pounds Reward paid by
         JOHN TAYLOR, GOALER,
N. B. If taken out of the County, Three Pounds Reward will be paid for each.

The Pennsylvania Gazette, August 25, 1763; October 6, 1763.

RAN away, the 21st of *August* last, from the Subscriber living in *Frederick* County, near Mr. *Snowden's* Iron-Works, a Convict Servant Man named *James Allen*, born in *England*, about 5 Feet 7 Inches high, and a Cooper by Trade: Had on, and with him, when he went away, a blue Broadcloth Coat and Jacket, a Pair of Leather Breeches, three old white Shirts, three Pair of Worsted Stockings, a Wig, a Worsted Cap, Felt Hat, and two Pair of *French* Shoes.

Whoever takes up and secures the said Servant, so as his Master may have him again, shall receive FIVE POUNDS Reward, and reasonable Charges if brought home, paid by

THOMAS WATERS.
All Masters of Vessels are forbid to carry him off at their Peril.
The Maryland Gazette, September 1, 1763. See *The Pennsylvania Gazette*, September 8, 1763.

Annapolis, September 3, 1763.
BROKE Goal on the Second of this Instant, at Night: *John Sullivan*, an *Irishman*, a most notorious Rogue, committed for Horse-Stealing: He is 5 Feet 9 Inches high, about 28 Years of Age: Had on a Scarlet Broad Cloth Jacket without Sleeves, striped Breeches, made out of Bed Tick, blue Worsted Stockings, old Pumps, and a white Shirt. The said *Sullivan* is a well-set Fellow, of a fair Complexion, and the Wrist of each Arm is much fretted by the Hand Cuffs.
Also a well-set Mulatto Fellow, with bandy Legs, named *Bob*....
Whoever takes up the said Men, so that they may be had again, shall receive Five Pounds Reward for *Sullivan*, and Three Pounds for *Bob*.
LANCELOT JACQUES, Sheriff.
The Maryland Gazette, September 8, 1763; September 15, 1763; September 22, 1763.

Baltimore-Town, Sept. 5, 1763.
RAN away from the Subscriber on the 27th of last Month, an Apprentice named *Zachariah Riston*, between 19 and 20 Years of Age, he is tall and slim, has a long thin Face, fair Complexion, red Nose, sandy or whitish Eye Brows, a dull simple Look, was born in *Baltimore* County, speaks good high Dutch, a Bricklayer and Stone-mason by Trade, and works Left-handed. Had on and took with him, a blue Cloth Coat lined with white, a white Linen Jacket with black Glass Buttons, an Ash colour'd Cloth Jacket, new Buckskin Breeches, a Pair of Check Linen Trowsers, white and Check Linen Shirts, Worsted Stockings, old Shoes, and a Hat.
There went off in his Company, a Man who goes by the Name of *Absalom Hines* or *Haynes*, who is short and well set, says he has been a Ranger, and among the Indians for some Time past, has a Rifle Gun with him, and says his Mother lives on the Eastern Shore in this Province.
Whoever apprehends the above Apprentice, and secures him in any Goal, so that I may get him again, shall have Three Pounds *Pennsylvania* Currency Reward, if taken in this Province, or FIVE POUNDS if taken elsewhere; if brought home the same Reward, and all reasonable Charges, paid by CONRAD SMITH.

The Maryland Gazette, September 8, 1763; September 15, 1763; September 22, 1763; September 29, 1763. See *The Pennsylvania Gazette,* September 15, 1763, and *The Pennsylvania Gazette,* September 29, 1763.

FIVE POUNDS Reward.

RUN away from the Subscriber, living near Snowdon's Iron-works, in Frederick County, Maryland, a Servant Man, named James Allen, about five Feet seven Inches high, an Englishman, by Trade a Cooper, about 30 Years of Age; Had on when he went away, a blue Broadcloth Coat and Jacket; a Felt Hat, a Wig, and a Worsted Cap, a Pair of Leather Breeches; he also took with him three white Shirts, three Pair Worsted Stockings, and two Pair of French Shoes. Whoever takes up and secures said Servant in any Goal, so that the Subscriber may have him again, shall have the above Reward, and reasonable Charges, if brought Home, paid by
THOMAS WATERS.
All Masters of Vessels are forbid to carry him off at their Peril.
The Pennsylvania Gazette, September 8, 1763. See *The Maryland Gazette,* September 1, 1763.

RUN away from the Subscriber, living in Chester Town, Maryland, two Apprentice Boys, of about 18 Years of Age, the one a lively looking smart Bay; the other has a down Look and a Cast in one Eye; it is supposed they have made for the Jerseys. Whoever will secure said Apprentices, so as the Owner may have them again, shall have Forty Shillings Reward and reasonable Charges, paid by   GEORGE PERKIN.
N. B. The above Lads Names are Francis Lamb, and Michael Flewharty.
The Pennsylvania Gazette, September 8, 1763.

THREE PISTOLES Reward.
RUN away from the Subscriber, living in Bohemia Manor, Cecil County, Maryland, about the Middle of July last, a Servant Man, named John Marren, a Weaver by Trade, about five six Inches [*sic*] high, a well set Fellow, about 22 Years of Age, wears his own blackish Hair: Had on when he went away, a Lead coloured Cloth Coat, with large white Metal Buttons, a home made Tow Linen Shirt and Trowsers, and an old Felt Hat; he is much inclined to singing and swearing, and keeping company, and may probably change his Name and Apparel; he was seen lately in Philadelphia, and is supposed to be gone to his Father Archibald Marren, living in Bucks

County. Whoever takes up said Servant, and secures him in any Goal, so as his Master may have him again, shall have the above Reward, and reasonable Charges, paid by
JOSEPH COCKRAN.
The Pennsylvania Gazette, September 8, 1763.

Frederick County, *Sept.* 7, 1763.
RAN away from the Subscriber, living near *Snowden's* Manor, Two Convict Servant Men, viz.

George Wilkinson, by Trade a Taylor, about 5 Feet high, very slim, and is a thin faced Fellow, pale Complexion, has short yellow Hair, and grey Eyes. Had on a Felt Hat, a Wig, a grey Broadcloth Coat, turned, and trimmed with Mohair Buttons, a Pair of brown Broadcloth Breeches much worn and patch'd, black and white mixed Yarn Stockings, Country made Shoes much worn and has been soaled, odd Buckles, a Check Shirt, and Osnabrigs Ditto.

John Smith, used to Plantation Work, a little short down looking Fellow, has short thick black Hair, dark Eyes, dark Complexion, and has lost two of his fore Teeth. Had on when he went away, a good Castor Hat, red and white striped Handkerchief, a new light colour'd Coat, with a Snuff colour'd Cotton Velvet Cape, flat white Metal Buttons, long Cuffs without Buttons on them, a red Everlasting Jacket, with new Patches on the Corners of the fore Parts, black Stocking Breeches, black Stockings, and a white Shirt much worn.

Whoever apprehends the said Servants, and brings them to their Master, shall have, if taken 20 Miles from home, Three Pounds for each; if upwards of 20 Miles, Five Pounds *Pennsylvania* Currency, paid by
MICHAEL BENCE.
N. B. They took with them a Saddle and Bridle, and are supposed to have stolen a Horse.
The Maryland Gazette, September 15, 1763; September 22, 1763.

Charles County, *August* 29, 1763.
TWO PISTOLES REWARD.
RAN away from the Subscriber, living near *Port-Tobacco*, on the 12th Instant, a Convict Servant Man named *Thomas Brooke*, born in *England*, brought up to the Farmer's Business, about 30 Years of Age, 5 Feet 9 Inches high, has a sly down Look, of a dark Complexion, almost bald on the Top of his Head, born without Toes on his left Foot, and is fond of Drinking. Had on a half worn grey Frize Cloth Coat, trimm'd with Metal Buttons, too small for him, brown Holland Jacket, Check Shirt, Silk

Handkerchief, Osnabrigs Trowsers, blue Worsted Stockings, old Shoes, odd Buckles, and an old Felt Hat.

Whoever brings home, or secures in Goal, the aforesaid Servant, shall receive the above Reward.   DANIEL M'PHERSON.

N. B. All Skippers of Vessels are hereby forewarned carrying him off at their Peril.

The Maryland Gazette, September 15, 1763; September 22, 1763; September 29, 1763; October 13, 1763.

RUN away from the Subscriber, living in Chester Town, on Monday Night, the 22d of August last, one John M'Donnell, about 15 Years of Age, and about 4 Feet 6 Inches high, well set, black hair, and is a talkative Fellow; pretends to have Leave under the Subscriber's Hand to work with who he will: Had on, when he went away, a brown Homespun Coat, with white Lining, a white Linen Jacket, with jet black Buttons, near pair of Buff coloured Breeches, with yellow Metal Buttons, white and blue Stockings, Pumps, with yellow Buckles, three white Shirts, Check Trowsers, Wool Hat, a Taylor by Trade. Whoever takes up said Servant and secures him in any of his Majesty's Goal, shall have Thirty Shillings Reward, and reasonable Charges, paid by   BARNEY DAILY.

The Pennsylvania Gazette, September 15, 1763.

RAN away from the Subscriber, living in Baltimore Town, Maryland, on the 27th of August last, an Apprentice named Zachariah Rigton, between 19 and 20 Years old, by Trade a Bricklayer and Stone Mason, was born in this County, but can speak good high Dutch; he is tall and slim, has a long thin Face, fair Complexion, red Nose, sandy or whitish Eyebrows, and a dull simple Look, at his Trade he works Left-handed: Had on, and took with him, a blue Cloth Coat, lined with white, a Linen Jacket, with black Glass Buttons, an Ash coloured Cloth Jacket, new Buckskin Breeches, a Pair of Check Linen Trowsers, a white Linen and Check Shirts, worsted Stockings, old Shoes, and a Hat. There went off in his Company a Man, who goes by the Name of Absalom Hines or Haynes, who is short and well set, says he has been a Ranger, and among the Indians for some Time past; has a Rifle Gun with him, and says his Mother lives somewhere on the Eastern Shore in this Province. Whoever apprehends the above Apprentice, and secures him in any Goal, so that I may get him again, shall have Three Pounds Pennsylvania Currency Reward, if taken in this Province, or Five Pounds, if taken elsewhere; or if brought home, the same Reward, and all reasonable Charges, paid by   CONRAD SMITH.

The Maryland Gazette, September 8, 1763; September 15, 1763; September 22, 1763; September 29, 1763. See *The Pennsylvania Gazette*, September 15, 1763, and *The Pennsylvania Gazette*, September 29, 1763.

         Kent County, Maryland, September 7, 1763.
BROKE out of the Goal of Kent County, Maryland, on Sunday Night, the 4th Instant, three Prisoners, one named John Andrews, an Englishman, about five Feet six or eight Inches high, by Trade a Blacksmith; he is a little Pock-marked in the Face, black eyed, of a swarthy complexion, a pert Look, and talks much in the West Country Dialect, much inclinable to Drunkenness: Had on when he broke Goal, a brown cut Wig, blue Broadcloth Coat, trimmed with Trimmings of the same Colour, a Plad Jacket, and blue Cloth Breeches: He has lately been a Privateering, and it is supposed he will make towards Philadelphia. Another named Thomas White, an Englishman born, by Trade a Butcher, about 5 Feet 6 or 8 Inches high, red faced, thin visaged, down Look, and crippled in one of his Hands: Had on, when he broke Goal, a brown cut Wig, a white fustian or Russia Drab Coat, much worn, and Breeches of the same; talks fast, and stammers much, and is very fond of Liquor. And the other named Thomas Evans, born in the West of England, about five Feet five or seven Inches high, much Pock-marked, full faced, a down Look, short brown Hair, and has a very great Sore on his Left Leg: Had on, when he broke Goal, a white Cotton Jacket, much worn, an Ozenbrigs Shirt and Trowsers, an old Felt Hat, and an old Pair of Country made Shoes. Whoever takes up and secures the aforesaid John Andrews in any Goal, so that he may be had again, or delivers him to the Sheriff of Kent, shall have Six Pistoles Reward, and for the other two, White and Evans, Two Pistoles Reward for each, to by paid by   THOMAS SMITH, Sheriff.
 The Pennsylvania Gazette, September 15, 1763.

RAN away from on board a Schooner, belonging to the Head of *Elk*, *Thomas Pitcher*, who served his Time to the Sea, a short thick Lad, about 18 Years of Age, born in *England*. Had on a Pair of old wide Petticoat Trowsers, an old Beaver Hat, a coarse spotted double-breasted Flannel Jacket; but no Shoes or Stockings. He is mark'd on the Right Hand T P with Indian Ink. Whoever secures the said *Pitcher*, so that is Master may get him again, shall have Forty Shillings Reward, and reasonable Charges, paid by ROBERT MUIR, at the Head of *Elk*.
N. B. All Masters of Ships, &c. are forewarned not to carry him off.
 The Maryland Gazette, September 22, 1763; October 6, 1763.

Prince-George's County, *Sept.* 19, 1763.
RAN away on Tuesday the 6th Instant, from the Subscriber, living near *Bladensburg*, a Convict Servant Man named *John Graigg*, about 30 Years of Age, born in *Kent* in *England*, about 5 Feet 9 Inches high, full smooth Face, short Black Hair, grey Eyes, square made, slow of Speech, walks with his Toes much in, and has a Sore on his right Leg. Had on when he went away, an old Hat, blue Cloth Vest without Sleeves, with flat white Metal Buttons, Osnabrigs & Check Shirts, Osnabrigs Trowsers, blue Worsted Stockings, and old Shoes.

Whoever takes up the said Runaway, and brings him home, shall receive, if taken in the Province, Two, if out of the Province Three Pounds, more than the Law allows, paid by
JOSHUA BEALL.
N. B. He pretends to be something of a Sailor; all Masters of Vessels are forbid taking him on board.

The Maryland Gazette, September 29, 1763; October 6, 1763; October 13, 1763; October 20, 1763; Ocober 27, 1763; November 3, 1763.

RAN away from the Subscriber, living near *Soldier's Delight*, in *Baltimore* County, on the 20th of this Inst. *September*, a Servant Man named *John Bryan*, an *Irishman*, about 5 Feet high, has black Hair which curls, is a good Scholar, a romancing Fellow, talks very much, and it is imagin'd he has a forged Pass with him. Had on when he went away, an old Castor Hat, an old Cotton Jacket, the Skirts torn off, and the Cuff of the Sleeves mended like a Pea Jacket Sleeve, two old Check Shirts, a Pair of blue Velvet Breeches, Country Cloth Trowsers, blue full'd Stockings, and old Shoes.

Whoever secures the said Servant, and brings him to me, shall have Twenty Shillings Reward, beside what the Law allows, if taken in the Country, and if out of it Forty Shillings, beside what the Law allows, and reasonable Charges, paid by   RICHARD DAVIS.
He pretends to be a Sailor. All Masters of Vessels are forewarned not to carry him off at their Peril.

The Maryland Gazette, September 29, 1763.

RAN away from the Subscriber living in *Frederick-Town*, *Frederick* County, a Servant Man named *John Davis*, by Trade a Carpenter, and pretends to understand Joyner's Work also, he is about 5 Feet 6 or 7 Inches high, wears his own black Hair tied behind, was a Prisoner in this County Jail, from which I reliev'd him last Thursday, says he was born in *England*; this is the same Fellow that was advertised in the *Maryland* Gazette in *October* 1762, as a Deserter from the *Virginia* Regiment: Had on when he went away, a light-coloured blue Coat, blue Jacket, fine whitish colour'd Broadcloth Breeches, a Check Shirt, black Stockings, good Shoes, large Brass Buckles, and an old Castor Hat.

Whoever takes up the said Servant, and brings him to me in *Frederick-Town*, shall receive one Pistole Reward, if taken in this County; and two Pistoles in taken out of it, or secured in any Jail so that he may be had again, paid by
JOHN CARY. *September* 20, 1763.

The Maryland Gazette, September 29, 1763; October 6, 1763; October 13, 1763; October 20, 1763; October 27, 1763; November 3, 1763.

Briton-Ridge, Baltimore County, *Sept.* 21. 1763.
RAN away from the Subscriber on the 14th Instant, a Convict Servant Man named *John Broadbent*, aged 22 Years 5 Feet 2 or 3 Inches high, wears his own Hair, which is short and curls, nearly upon a light sandy Colour, and is a Weaver by Trade: He rode away upon an old dark Bay Horse, branded upon the near Buttock **GH**, and took with him the following Apparel, *viz.* a Castor Hat, two Holland Shirts, one Check Ditto, a Country Cloth Coat of a black and white Colour, a *Russia* Drab Frock, 3 Pair of *Russia* Drab Breeches, 2 Pair of them white, and the other of a darkish Colour, a Pair of Pumps made with the Grain Side outwards, grey Yarn Stockings, and 4 Silk Handkerchiefs, every one of them strip'd.

Whoever takes up the said Servant, and brings him to the Subscriber, shall have Three Pounds Reward, if taken within this Province; and if out of it SIX POUNDS, and reasonable Charges, paid by
GEORGE HAILE, senr.

The Maryland Gazette, September 29, 1763; October 6, 1763.

RUN away, the 18th Inst. from the Ship Elizabeth, Captain Morrison, lying in Patapsco River, Maryland, two Servant Men, viz. one named Henry Talbot, alias Smith, a middle aged Man, an Irish-man, has a very smooth fawning Way of expressing himself, and much addicted, in his Answers, to say, if it please your Honour; can write a very good engrossing Hand, and may probably have forged a Pass from Leghorn, Consul's Name (James Dicks) in the Margin; had on when he went away, a coarse Drab surtout Coat, very dirty, Ozenbrigs Trowsers; and has remarkable grey Eyes.

The other named Dennis Dunnavon, a young lusty Irishman, brought up to the Business of a Taylor, but has been some Time from this Trade, has a round Face, and seemingly a very innocent Look; had on when he went away, a blue Jacket and Russia Drab Breeches.—They took the Ship's Four Oar Yawl, with a white bottom, yellow Streaks, and blue Gunwale, black

bows and Quarters, and a blue Stern. Whoever secures the said Servants, so that they may be sent to the Ship again, shall have Thirty Shillings for each, and Forty Shillings for the Yawl, with reasonable Charges, paid by JAMES FISHWICK.
The Pennsylvania Gazette, September 29, 1763.

Trenton, in Hunterdon County, N. Jersey, Sept. 19, 1763.

TAken up, and committed to the Goal of said County, A certain Zachariah Rigton, who says his Master lives in Baltimore Town, by Trade a Mason, and that his Name is Conrad Smith; his said Master is desired to come and pay Charges, and take him out, otherwise he will be sold out for the same, by Samuel Tucker, Sheriff for said County.
The Pennsylvania Gazette, September 29, 1763. See *The Maryland Gazette,* September 8, 1763, and *The Pennsylvania Gazette,* September 15, 1763.

September 7, 1763.

RUN away Last Night, from Deep-Creek Furnace, near the Head of Nanticoke River, Four Native Irish Men, viz. John Kittle, Martin Kelly, Patrick M'Nealy, and Thomas Clinton; they are all of middle Stature, of fair Complexion, and each of them more or less pitted with the Small-pox; they wore striped Linsey Caps or short Hair; Felt Hats, almost new; check or Ozenbrigs Shirts, and Ozenbrigs Trowsers; about half-worn Shoes: One of them has a Scar above his Eye-brow on his Forehead: Another has a Scar or Blister near his Ear; the same is broke out with several Sores on his Legs, Arms, and some Parts of his Body: One of them had a light-coloured Cloth Jacket, the others striped Lincey Ones. It is thought they will endeavour to pass for Sailors. Whoever takes up and secures the said Servants in any Goal, or brings them to the said Furnace, shall have Thirty Shillings Reward for each, paid by   JONATHAN VAUGHAN.

N. B. These Fellows are expected to make to Philadelphia, or New York, or up that Way.—All Masters of Vessels, and others, are forbid to harbour, or carry them off, at their Peril.
The Pennsylvania Gazette, September 29, 1763.

RAN away from the Subscriber on the Fourth of *October* last, from *Yocomico* River, *Northumberland* County, *Virginia,* a Servant Man named *John Payne,* born in *Maryland,* about 5 Feet 7 Inches high, a thin spare Man, of a black Complexion, and about 25 Years of Age. He had on and with him, a Claret or Pompadour coloured Cloth Coat, black Worsted figured Wove Jacket, fine Castor Hat, blue Cloth and Buckskin Breeches, mix'd Yarn and black Worsted Stockings, new Check Trowsers, and a new Check Shirt. It is thought he will made for *North-Carolina* or *Pennsylvania*.

Whoever apprehends the said Servant, and delivers him to his Master, or secures him so that he may be had again, shall have One Pistole Reward, beside what the Law allows, if taken 10 Miles off; Two Pistoles, if 15 Miles; Three Pistoles, if 30 Miles; Five Pistoles, if 50 Miles; or Six Pistoles if out of the Province, paid by   RICHARD BOWES.

The Maryland Gazette, October 20, 1763; November 3, 1763; November 10, 1763; November 17, 1763; November 24, 1763; December 1, 1763. See *The Maryland Gazette*, July 7, 1763.

RAN away from the Subscriber, on the 17th Instant at Night, a Convict Servant Man named *John Hunter*, about 22 Years of Age, 5 Feet 8 Inches high, fair Complexion, and wears his own Hair, which is short and brown, has had the Small-Pox, was born in *England*, and has been in the Country about 4 Months. Had on when he went away, a cross barr'd double Breasted Waistcoat, and a short blue Cloth one under it, light colour'd Broadcloth Breeches, grey Worsted Stockings, a pair of good Shoes, and white Shirt.

Any Person that will take up said Servant, and bring him to his Mistress in *Baltimore*-Town, shall receive a Reward of Twenty Shillings if 10 Miles from home, if 30 Miles Fifty Shillings, and if further Five Pounds. CAROLINE ORRICK.

The Maryland Gazette, October 20, 1763.

                        Cumberland County, West New-Jersey, Oct. 8, 1763. WAS Committed to the Goal of this Country for want of a Pass, a Man about 26 Years of Age, in poor Habit, and says he was born in Queen Ann's County, Maryland, and that his Name is William Lloyd. If any Person or Persons, has any Demand on said Lloyd, they are desired to come to the Sheriff of said County, and pay the Cost, otherwise he will be discharged in five Weeks from this Date, with paying the Cost.
HOWELL POWELL, Sheriff.

The Pennsylvania Gazette, October 20, 1763.

RAN away the 15th of *October* Inst. from the Subscriber, living near Mr. *John Cooke's* in *Prince-George's* County, a Servant Man named *James Henry*, alias *Molison*, or may change his Name otherways, lately brought from *Scotland*, a Taylor by Trade, but cares not to work, he has a thin Face, with many Pimples in it, middling long black Hair, and on the Crown about two Inches long, speaks fast, and on the *Scots* Tongue, he is about 5 Feet 6 or 7 Inches high, and a great Rogue: Had on when he went away, a grey *German* Serge Coat and Jacket, lined with white Shalloon, and all very dirty, his Jacket had no Flaps, but Binding like a Sailor's, and the Backs of it of another Colour, had blue *German* Serge Breeches not lined, and some Tar on the Seat of them, white Woollen Stockings, old Shoes, two old ragged white Shirts, and a small Felt Hat, with a black Binding. Whoever takes up the said Fellow, and brings him to his Master, or secures him so that he may be had again, shall have Twenty Shillings Reward, beside what the Law allows, paid by   DAVID LOW.

The Maryland Gazette, October 27, 1763. See *The Maryland Gazette*, October 10, 1765.

Talbot County, *October* 25, 1763.

RAN away from his Bail, on the first Instant, a certain *Felix Hall*, about 30 Years of Age, of a small low Stature, fair Complexion, given to Drink, very talkative, and says he was born in *Somerset* County: His Apparel uncertain, but of a lightish Colour. Whoever will take up and secure the said *Felix Hall*, in any Jail in this Province, so as his Bail may have him again, shall have Thirty Shillings Reward, and reasonable Charges, paid by
THOMAS LOVEDAY, living near *Choptank* River.

The Maryland Gazette, November 3, 1763.

Queen-Anne's County, *October* 17, 1763.

RAN away from the Subscribers, living near *Queen's-Town*, Two Convict Servant Men, one named *George Harriss*, a thick, well-set Fellow, about 5 Feet 7 Inches high, wears his own Hair, and has a down Look. The other named *Robert Chant*, a short, thick, well-set Fellow, about 5 Feet 5 Inches high, and very much mark'd with the Small-Pox, and has a bold Look.

They were very meanly Cloathed.

Whoever takes up the said Servants, and secures them so as their Masters may get them again, shall have Forty Shillings Reward, beside what the Law allows, or Twenty Shillings for either, paid by
WILLIAM DARDING,   WILLIAM CORKRILL.

The Maryland Gazette, November 3, 1763.

Kent County, in Maryland.

RUN away from the Subscriber, a Convict Servant Man, named John Williams, born in Bristol, though he says he was born in New England; he was transported and came into Chester River, in Kent County, this Summer; he is a lusty Fellow, about 38 Years of Age, short black curled Hair, blue Coat, green Frize Jacket, Leather Breeches, Shoes and Stockings, one Arm

shorter than the other, a Scar near his Shoulder, on the Short Arm, and another on one of his Legs; he often Acts as a Beggar, and pretends that has no Tongue, makes Signs to People that his Tongue was cut out by the Indians, and other Harms done him by them, which is all false; he has a most excellent Tongue that he draws out of his Throat when provoked, though it is probable he will leave off Begging when he thinks himself safe from his Master. Whoever takes up said Servant, and secures him, so as the Owner may have him again, shall have Forty Shillings Reward, and if brought home, reasonable Charges, paid by
ROBERT ROBERTS.
The Pennsylvania Gazette, November 3, 1763.

Sassafras Neck, November 2, 1763.
RUN away from the Subscriber, on the 29th of October last, at Night, a convict Servant Man, named Henry Carr, born in Cornwall, in England; he is about 6 Feet high, a well set Fellow, speaks broad English: Had on, when he went away, an old blue Plush Coat, Ozenbrigs Trowsers, blue Cloth Waistcoat, without Sleeves, Ozenbrigs Shirt, old black Stockings, a Pair of Shoes, about half-worn, an old grey Wig, and a little old Felt Hat. He came over Schuylkill Ferry, on Monday, to Philadelphia. Whoever takes up said Fellow, and will bring him to Mr. Peter Robeson's, before his Master leaves Town, shall have Three Pounds Reward; or if after he leaves Town, and secures him in any Goal, so that his Master may have him again, shall be paid the abovesaid Reward, by
ROBERT MARCER, living in Caecil County, Maryland.
N. B. All Masters of Vessels are forbid to carry him off at their Peril.
The Pennsylvania Gazette, November 10, 1763.

Run away from the Subscriber, living within 6 Miles of Charles-Town, in Caecil County, Maryland, on the 29th ult. A native Irish Servant Man, named Brian Doran, about 20 Years of Age, 5 Feet 6 or 7 Inches high, well set, has a down look, dark Complexion, and short black Hair: had on when he went away, A short blue Coat, of napped Cloth and Breeches of the same, striped Linsey Jacket, new Shoes, Yarn Stockings, striped Woolen Cap, without a Hat, unless he stole one. Whoever takes up said Servant, and secures him in any Goal, so as his Master may have him again, shall have Forty Shillings Reward, and reasonable Charges, paid by
ISAAC JANNEY.
N. B. All Masters of Vessels are forbid to carry him off at their Peril.
The Pennsylvania Gazette, November 10, 1763. See *The Pennsylvania Gazette*, December 1, 1763.

RAN away from the Subscriber, in the Night of the 23d Instant, a Convict Servant Man named *John Matthews*, (lately imported from *Bristol* by Capt. *Cole*) by Trade a Carpenter and Joiner, he is a middle-siz'd, well-set Person, of a brown Complexion: His Apparel a light brown Fustian Coat, lined with Shalloon, with flat White-Metal Buttons, a striped red and white short Jacket, Leather Breeches, mix'd Yarn Stockings, very dark, black grain'd Shoes, and sometimes wears a brown Wig, at other times, his own dark brown Hair. He is supposed to have gone in Company with a Gardener, belonging to *Charles Carroll*, Esq; Barrister at Law.

Whoever takes up the said Servant, and brings him to the Subscriber in *Annapolis*, or secures him in any Jail so that he may be had again, shall receive FIVE POUNDS in Pieces of Eight at 7/6 each, or *Pennsylvania* Currency, paid by   JOHN BRICE.

The Maryland Gazette, November 24, 1763.

One *John Ferroll*, from *Maryland*, came to my House, on the *Virginia* Side, about 2 Miles from *Rock-Creek* Ferry, about the Middle of *June* last, and worked there about 15 Days, and got acquainted with a Convict Servant Woman of mine, named *Hannah Arthur*, a fresh-looking *English* Woman, from *Dover*, about 22 Years of Age, some Freckles on her Face, and a brown Mark on her right Cheek, that one may cover with their Thumb; and he carried her away on the 13th Day of *August* last, and was seen with her near *Mordecai Broadwater's*, on *Patuxent*, and keeps her secreted about his Father's, *Martin Ferroll's*, who lives near *John Fowler's*, about 2 Miles from Mr. *Snowden's* new Furnace. I have been twice with him, the first Time his Father abused me very much, but he promised to deliver her on my bringing him Five Pounds *Virginia* Money, and I brought the Money last Time, but he would not deliver her. As he is afraid of Officers, and I understand broke out of *Annapolis* Jail, there is no coming at him; but as the Convict Woman will be seen at different Times by People in the Neighbourhood (or perhaps with the Relations of *Martin Ferroll's* Wife, who I understand live near *Annapolis*, and she, the Wife, seems by her Colour to be of the Mulatto breed.

Whoever apprehends the Servant Woman, and gets her committed to any Jail, and advertises it in the *Maryland* Papers, shall have Five Pounds Reward, paid to the Sheriff, before she is taken away, by
HENRY CULLOM.

The Maryland Gazette, November 24, 1763. See *The Maryland Gazette*, February 7, 1765, for John Ferroll.

Baltimore Town, August 8, 1763.
RUN away from on board the Ship Dolphin, Capt. Matthew Craymer, lying on the Ferry Branch of Patapsco River, in the Night between the 7th and 8th Inst. five Convict Men, viz.

Simon Pugh, a well-set middle sized Man, smooth Face, black Hair, and remarkable fine black Eyes; had with him a blue Surtout, two light coloured Cloth Coats, several Waistcoats, and other Cloaths, and capable of making a genteel Appearance.

Miles Cook, a stout Fellow, in a Jacket and Trowsers, fair Complexion, and one of his Legs thicker than the other.

James Anderson, a little Man, who has lost the Use of one of his Hands by a Shot through the Wrist. The two last are Sailors.

Robert Walker, a tall elderly Man, with his own Hair, much pitted with the Small-Pox. And,

James Donaldson, very much freckled, with black Hair.

They took with them the Ship's Yawl, about 20 Feet long, with one Mast, a Sprit Main Sail and Jib, turpentined Sides, painted with a Streak of blue along the Gunwales, and rows five Oars, but had four only on board. Whoever takes up the said Runaways, and secures them, so as they may be had again, shall receive Twenty Shillings Reward for each; but if they are brought on board the Ship, Forty Shillings, and the same Sum for the Yawl.
STEWART and LUX.   Philadelphia, December 1, 1763.

As the first mentioned Convict, Simon Pugh, is now in our Goal, and as we have heard he has since confessed that he, and some others, had agreed to go on the Highway, and swore to be true to one another; there is great Reason to believe the above Convicts are the Persons that have, of late, infested our Roads, and therefore think proper to give this public Notice of them.

The Pennsylvania Gazette, December 1, 1763. See *The Maryland Gazette*, August 11, 1763, and *The Pennsylvania Gazette*, August 18, 1763.

New-Castle, Nov. 21, 1763.
NOW in the Goal of this County, a certain Bryan Doran, taken up as a Runaway Servant; says he came into the Country this Fall, with Capt. Fussell, from Newry; wears a blue Sea Jacket, blue Breeches, and good Shoes.

Also a Negroe Man, calls himself Jack, says he ran from William Corsa, of Queen Anne's County, Wye River, near Queens Town, wears a white Cotton Jacket and Breeches, Ozenbrigs Shirt, and old Felt Hat. Their Masters are hereby desired to pay Fees, and take them away, otherwise they will be sold for the same, by   ALEXANDER HARVEY, Goaler.

The Pennsylvania Gazette, December 1, 1763. See *The Pennsylvania Gazette,* November 10, 1763.

Virginia, Hanover Court House, *Nov.* 29, 1763.
RAN away from the Subscriber, betwixt the 23d and 24th Instant, from Mr. *William Dudley's* in *Caroline* County, brought from on board the *Beverly,* Capt. *Allen,* now lying at *Port-Royal, Rappahannock* River, Two Convict Servant Men; one named *Edward Eagle,* about 6 Feet high, dark Complexion, wearing his own short Hair, very black. Had on when he went away, two red Jackets, a Pair of black Breeches, and grey Stockings. He is a Man of a robust, tho' to Appearance, a slender Body. The other named *William English,* about 5 Feet 6 or 7 Inches high, dark Complexion, wearing a black Wig, brown Coat, red Hair Shag Jacket, Buckskin Breeches, and black Stockings, with either Silver or Plated Buckles in his Shoes. He is a thick strait well-made Fellow, and was formerly Servant to a Recruiting Officer at *Winchester.* Whoever secures the said Runaways in any of the County Goals in *Maryland,* on giving Information, so as they may be had again, to Capt. *Allen* on board the Ship, or to me at *Hanover* Court-House, shall receive Forty Shillings Reward, besides what the Law allows. ROBERT HART.

The Maryland Gazette, December 15, 1763; December 22, 1763; December 29, 1763. The second and third ads state the men were "bought from on board the *Beverly*...."

RAN away from the Subscriber, the 28th of *October* last, a Convict Servant Woman, named *Nancy Partinton,* about 19 Years of Age, a round Face, small black Eyes, light Eye brows, sandy colour'd Hair, of a short Stature, very round shoulder'd, talks very brisk, has a down Look, keeps a Handkerchief tied under her Jaws, and wears a Bonnet set round with Sticks. Had on a red and white checqu'd Holland Bed Gown, a large Woman's new Chintz Gown, with yellowish green Sprigs, a white Cotton Petticoat, black Serge Denim Shoes, old black Stockings, 2 large blue and white spotted Silk Handkerchiefs, a Cotton long Bed Gown, and a red Cloak with a Cap to it. Whoever takes up the said Servant, and delivers her to the Subscriber, living at *Chaptico* in *St. Mary's* County, shall receive Forty Shillings Reward; paid by   RICHARD COOKE.

'Tis supposed she travels under the Name of *Jane M'Gee,* having such a Pass granted her by *Richard Ward Key.*

The Maryland Gazette, December 22, 1763; January 5, 1764; January 12, 1764; January 19, 1764.

1764

RAN away on the 28th of *December* last, from the Subscriber living near *Annapolis*, a Convict Servant Woman, named *Mary Osburn*, about 27 Years of Age, and about 4 [sic] Feet high, her Hair and Eyes are very black, and she is of a brown Complexion. Her Apparel when she went away, was a checquered Stuff Gown, a striped Country Cloth Petticoat, an old patch'd quilted Ditto, Osnabrigs Shift, blue and white ring'd Stockings, flat heel'd Shoes, Linen Handkerchief, Brown Roll Apron, no Cap on, but her Hair tied behind.

Whoever takes up the said Servant, and brings her home, shall receive Forty Shillings Reward, beside what the Law allows, paid by
JOHN LANSDALE.
The Maryland Gazette, January 5, 1764.

TEN POUNDS REWARD.

RAN away from the Subscriber, living near *Soldier's Delight*, in *Baltimore* County, on the 9th of *June* last, a Servant Man, named *David Wickenden*, an *Englishman*, about 5 Feet 6 Inches high, about 30 Years old, thin Visage, dark Complexion, dark brown Hair, has a Speck in the Sight of his Right Eye of a palish blue, stoops a little in his Walk, is fond of Liquor, much given to chewing Tobacco, and is a notorious Rogue. He is well known in *Baltimore* and *Anne-Arundel* Counties, having served Mr. *Henry Dorsey* on *Elk-Ridge* 7 Years. He is fond of Plowing or driving a Team.

Whoever takes up the said Servant, and brings him to the Subscriber, shall have the above Reward, paid by
ALEXANDER WELLS.
The Maryland Gazette, January 5, 1764; January 12, 1764; January 19, 1764; January 26, 1764; February 2, 1764; February 9, 1764. See *The Maryland Gazette*, January 6, 1763, and *The Maryland Gazette*, June 16, 1763.

RUN away from the Subscriber, living in Newtown, Chester River, Maryland, a Convict Servant Man, named Jeremiah Johns, about 40 Years of Age, with one Leg. Had on, when he went away three Jackets, two blue and one white; one Shoe, with a Cap on the Toe; he walks with a Crutch and Stick, is a Shoe-maker by Trade, took with him two Check Shirts, and a Pair of Blue Breeches. Whoever takes up the said Runaway, and secures him in any Goal, so as his Master may have him again, or brings him home, shall have Two Pistoles, and reasonable Charges, paid by me

THOMAS JOHNSON, Cordwainer.
The Pennsylvania Gazette, January 12, 1764.

STOLEN from the Subscriber, living in Kennet Township, Chester County, Pennsylvania, about nine Miles Westward from Wilmington, on the 25th of July last, at Night, a likely brown Mare, 4 Years old Spring coming, about 14 Hands and a Half high, a large Star in her Forehead, Snip on her Nose, the off or near hind Foot white, but which is not certain; she was not fully broke, trotted chiefly, is pretty light, hanging Mane, and switch Tail. It is supposed that one James Stephens, a Taylor by Trade, and pretty well known about his Lordship's Manor, in Ann Arundel County, and in and about Queen Ann Town, in Prince George's County, in Maryland, was the Person that stole here, as he was seen with such a Creature at John Smith's, in Caecil County, and also by several Persons in the above Counties, though by what I am told he, or some other has disfigured her, by trimming her Tail to the Strunt; I am told the said Stephens is about 5 Feet 5 Inches high, of a fair Complexion, wears his own Hair, which is of a sandy Colour, has had his Left Thigh broke, which occasions him to limp, is an Englishman born, pretty talkative, and apt to drink. Whoever secures the said Mare, and delivers her to Gerard Hopkins, or Henry Hall, shall have Twenty Shillings Reward; if the Thief is brought to Justice, and convicted of the Crimes, the Apprehender shall receive Five Pounds.
The Pennsylvania Gazette, January 12, 1764; February 16, 1764.

January 16, 1764.
RAN away on Sunday Night last, from the *Patapsco* Furnace, near *Elk Ridge* Landing, an *English* Convict Servant Woman named *Margaret Tasker*, about 18 Years old, of short Stature, fair Complexion, dark Eyes, brown Hair, and Pock mark'd, was Imported in the Ship *Betsy*, Captain *Nicholas Andrew*, in *November* last. She went off in Company with an Indented Country-born Servant Woman, by Name *Sarah Skinner*, and belongs to *Mordecai Kelley*, who is near the same Stature. Had on an Iron Collar, and has sustained the Loss of one Eye. The said *Margaret Tasker* has on and with her, as her common Dress, a blue Half-thick Waist and Petticoat, an *Irish* Sheeting Linen Shift, a Pair of white ribb'd Yarn Hose, and Lawn Cap; but otherwise took with her, a white ground Country Cotton Gown, strip'd with blue and black, a black Callimanco Quilted Coat, an old red Ditto, a double Cambrick Handkerchief mark'd M. W. a blue and white spotted Silk Romall Ditto, same Mark, two flower'd Bandanoe Ditto, a purple and white Callico Bed Gown, a white figur'd Dimity Ditto, 2 red Cloth Cloaks, a black Sattin Bonnet, an old black Silk Hat, a Pair of

Womens blue Silk Hose, with white Clocks, a Pair of Womens blue Worsted Ditto, two Womens Cambrick Caps, with Lawn Borders, a Pair of Mens turn'd Pumps, with cork'd Heels, lined and bound, and perhaps many other Things not yet discovered. It is probable many of these Articles may be found on the other Woman, as she was meanly clad, and only took a Pair of black Callimanco Shoes, and a Pair of green Worsted Hose, with red Clocks.

    Whoever will take up and secure the said *Margaret Tasker*, so that she may be had again, if with the Goods, Forty Shillings; if without, Twenty Shillings Reward, more than the Law allows, and reasonable Charges if brought home, of Messrs. *Thomas Harrison* and Company, *per*
JOSEPH WATKINS.
The Maryland Gazette, January 19, 1764.

Maryann Furnace, *January* 18, 1764.
TWO PISTOLES REWARD.
RAN away from *Maryann* Furnace, *York* County, in *Pennsylvania*, a Servant Man named *William Young*, of a fair Complexion, about 5 Feet 8 Inches high: Had on when he went away, a blue Broadcloth Coat with Metal Buttons, a red Jacket, lined with green Linen, with white Metal Buttons, old Greasy Buckskin Breeches, and two Shirts, one of them with broad Stripes.

    Whoever takes up the said Servant, and secures him in any Goal, shall have the above Reward, paid by
WILLIAM THOMPSON.
The Maryland Gazette, January 26, 1764; February 2, 1764.

December 21, 1763.
THREE PISTOLES REWARD.
RAN away from *Paradise* Iron-Works, in *York* County, *Pennsylvania*, last Monday Night, an *English* Servant Man named *James Clark*, came from Yorkshire, and speaks that Country Dialect, is about 5 Feet 5 Inches high, and wears his Hair, which is of a light Colour: Had on when he went away, a white Coat, Jacket, and Breeches, made of Half-thicks, new Shoes, and an old Felt Hat. He has a Woman with him, named *Mary*, who (I suppose) will pass for his Wife, she is of a middle Size.

    Whoever takes up the said *James Clark*, and secures him in any Goal, so that the Subscriber may have him again, shall have the above Reward, paid by   JOHN WILKINSON.

    N. B. The said Clark wrought some Time about *Baltimore-Town*, and served four Years with *James Gallion*, in *Bush-River* Neck.

The Maryland Gazette, January 26, 1764; February 2, 1764; February 9, 1764.

SEVEN POUNDS REWARD.
Baltimore County, near Baltimore-Town.

RAN away from the Subscriber, on the 16th Day of *January* 1764, a Country born Servant Man, named *James Hurd*, alias *Barnett*, he is a middle siz'd Fellow, with short light brown Hair, light Eyes, Round shouldered, pitted with the Small-Pox, and a Carpenter by Trade. Had on when he went away, a Felt Hat, Osnabrigs Shirt, a brown Cloth Jacket and Breeches, a red under Jacket, white Yarn Stockings, old Shoes, and an Iron Collar, if not taken off He has been a Soldier in the *Virginia* and *Pennsylvania* Service, is a great Lyar, and very talkative.

Whoever takes up the said Servant, and brings him home, shall have Five Pounds; and if Fifty Miles from home, the above Reward, paid by THOMAS OWINGS.

N. B. He has also Runaway from his Bail, in several Actions.

The Maryland Gazette, February 2, 1764; February 9, 1764; February 16, 1764; February 23, 1764; March 8, 1764; March 15, 1764; March 22, 1764; March 29, 1764; April 5, 1764; April 12, 1764; April 19, 1764. Only the first ad has the line beginning N. B.

Baltimore County, *January* 20, 1764.
THIRTEEN DOLLARS REWARD.

LAST Night the House of the Subscriber was Broke open by a certain *John Dent*, who lived near the Premises; he pretends to be a Carpenter, a slim built Fellow, with black Hair tied behind, a remarkable Scar on his right Cheek, which he says he got by a Stroke from a Cutlass, born in *Charles* County, about 28 or 30 Years old, of a whitish Look, 5 Feet 6 or 8 Inches high, and an uncommon Lyar; a very impudent Fellow to some People, and to others very complaisant and obliging; he may be taken by a Boy of Fifteen Years old, if resolute. His Apparel is an old blue Coat, white Cloth Breeches, a spotted Flannel Waistcoat, blue Worsted Stockings, and a striped Linen Shirt. He stole 2 Coats, 2 Waistcoats, a Pair of Pumps, and a Hat. It is probable he will change his Cloaths. If he should put on those he stole, they are too big for him. He likewise stole a very genteel Saddle, with a Hog-skin Seat, and a neat *English* blue fring'd Housing, and a Pair of old fashion'd Saddle Bags. He also stole out of the Subscriber's Stable, a whitish Grey Mare 8 Years old, about 15 or 16 Hands high, a natural Pacer, very straight hamm'd, her Mane hangs on the right Side, is shod before, her

Brand, (if any) unknown. He likewise took a Half Kirb Bridle, with very long Reins.

Whoever takes up and secures the said *John Dent*, so that he may be brought to Justice, and the Owner may get his Mare, Saddle and Bridle, shall be paid the above Reward, by   EDWARD DAY.

The Maryland Gazette, February 2, 1764; February 9, 1764. See *The Pennsylvania Gazette*, February 16, 1764.

RAN away from the Subscriber, living near the Head of *Maggothy* River in *Anne-Arundel* County, on the 12th of this Instant *February*, an Indented Servant Man named *James Williams*, about 5 Feet 1 Inch high, and has light coloured Hair very short, so that he sometimes wears an old Cut Wig. Had on when he went away, an Osnabrig Shirt, two blue Cloth Jackets, white Cotton Breeches, Country made Yarn Stockings, Country made Shoes, and an old Hat bound round with white Linen. He served his Time with the *Baltimore* Company, and has been in the Country about twelve Years.

Whoever takes up said *Williams*, and secures him so that he may be had again, shall receive Thirty Shillings Reward.
WILLIAM GAMBRILL.

The Maryland Gazette, February 16, 1764. See *The Maryland Gazette*, June 14, 1764.

                Baltimore County, Maryland, January 20, 1764.
                THIRTEEN DOLLARS Reward.
LAST Night the House of the Subscriber was broke open, by a certain JOHN DENT, who lived near the Premises, and has left some Marks of his Villainy behind him; he pretends to be a Carpenter, a slim built Fellow, with black Hair, tied behind, a remarkable Scar on his right Cheek, which he says he got by a Stroke from a Cutlass, born in Charles county, about 28 or 30 Years old, of a whitish Look, 5 Feet 6 or 8 Inches high, a very sorry Fellow as to Manhood, an uncommon Liar; and very daring and impudent to some People, and to others very complaisant and obliging; he may be taken by a Boy of 15 Years old, if resolute; his Apparel an old blue Coat, white Cloth Breeches, spotted Flannel Waistcoat, blue Worsted Stockings, one striped Linen Shirt, but has taken out of the said House two Coats and two Waistcoats, a Pair of Pumps and a Hat, belonging to John Morris, Overseer at the said Place, and it may be thought he may change his Clothes, if he should put on any of Morris's Clothes, it may readily be discovered they are not his, being too big for him. He likewise stole out of said House a very genteel Saddle, with Hogskin Seat, made by Mr. Joseph

Jacobs in Philadelphia, with a neat blue fringed Housing a Pair of Saddle Bags, made to go behind the Saddle, and Buckle to the Girt, old Fashion. And, worse than all, he has stole a remarkable fine Mare out of the Stable close by the House he broke on the same Plantation; the Mare is about 15 or 16 Hands high, 8 Years old, of a whitish grey, her Mane hangs very handsome all to the right Side, is very straight made behind, paces and gallops well. He took a half Kirb Bridle, with very long Reins, made by the foresaid Jacobs.

Whoever takes up the said Thief, and secures him so as to be brought to Justice, and that the Owner may get his Mare, Bridle and Saddle, shall be paid the above Reward by   EDWARD DAY.

N. B. It is thought he has stole many other Things, but at this Time, being in so great a Hurry after him, have not Time to enquire.

The Pennsylvania Gazette, February 16, 1764. See *The Maryland Gazette*, February 2, 1764.

February 28, 1764.

RAN away last Night from the *Baltimore* Iron-Works, on *Patapsco*, in *Maryland, viz.*

John Pinamore, an *Englishman*, near 6 Feet high, very lusty, of a swarthy Complexion, and about 30 Years old, has a down Look, wears short black Hair: Had on and took with him, when he went away, a Cotton Jacket, Buckskin Breeches, Osnabrig Shirt, Country Shoes and Stockings, old Hat, a Pair of ribbed Yarn or Worsted Stockings, and has a Discharge from one *William Banks*.

John Child, a Convict, about 30 Years of age, near 5 Feet 10 Inches high, by Trade a Gardener, marked with the Small Pox, born in *England*, and speaks broad, wears brown curled Hair: Had on when he went away, a new Felt Hat, Cotton Jacket and Breeches, and a Pair of old black Cloth ditto, Country Shoes, grey Yarn Stockings, and Osnabrig Shirt.

Ben, a Country born Mulatto Slave....It is supposed they have stole the following Horses, *viz*. A black Stallion, is a Waggon Horse, about 14½ Hands high, shod round, hanging Mane, and short Tail. A dark brown Gelding, about 14 Hands high, shod round, hanging Mane, and short bob Tail, a Waggon Horse also. A grey Gelding, of the *English* running Breed, near 15 Hands high, gallops and trots well, shod round, hanging Mane, Switch Tail, slender made, and lately trimmed.

Whoever secures said Servants, so that they may be had again, shall have Five Pounds Reward for each, or either of them, and Fifty Shillings for each, or either of the Horses, and reasonable Charges, if brought Home.
R. CROXALL.

N. B. It is thought they have stole a brown Coat with Metal Buttons, two Osnabrig Shirts, and a Pair of ribbed Thread Stockings, and a Pair of new black Shoes.

The Maryland Gazette, March 8, 1764; March 15, 1764; April 5, 1764. See *The Pennsylvania Gazette,* March 8, 1764, *The Maryland Gazette,* May 31, 1764, and August 16, 1764, for Child.

Baltimore, February 24, 1764.
RUN away, last Night, from the Baltimore Iron-works, on Patapsco, in Maryland, two Convict Servant Men, and a Mulatto Slave, viz. John Child, by Trade a Gardiner, born in England, and speaks broad, is about 30 Years of Age, and about 5 Feet 10 Inches high, marked with the Small-Pox, and wears brown curled Hair: Had on, when he went away, a Felt Hat, Ozenbrigs Shirt, Cotton Jacket and Breeches, a Pair of old black Cloth Ditto, Country Shoes, and grey Yarn Stockings. John Penemore, a lusty well-set Fellow, about 6 Feet high, swarthy Complexion, and wears black Hair: Had on and took with him an old Felt Hat, Ozenbrigs Shirt, a blue Coat, and a brown Ditto, trimmed with Metal Buttons, Cotton Jacket, Leather Breeches, Country Shoes and Stockings, and sundry other Things not here described. Ben, a Country-born Mulattoe Slave....It is supposed they have stole the following Horses, viz. a black Stallion, a Waggon Horse, about 14 hands and an Half high, a natural Pacer, shod round, hanging Mane, and short Tail; a dark brown Gelding, about 14 hands high, shod round, paces and trots, hanging Mane, and short bob Tail; a grey Gelding, of the English running breed, near 15 hands high, shod round, trots and gallops, hanging Mane, and switch Tail; he is slender made, and has been lately trimmed. Whoever secures said Servants, so that they may be had again, shall have Five Pounds Reward for each or either of them, and Forty Shillings for each or either of the Horses, and reasonable Charges, if brought home.   JAMES FRANKLIN.

The Pennsylvania Gazette, March 8, 1764; April 19, 1764. See *The Maryland Gazette,* March 8, 1764, *The Maryland Gazette,* May 31, 1764, and August 16, 1764, for Child.

TEN POUNDS Reward.
Run away from the Subscriber, in Baltimore Town, about six Weeks ago, an Irish Convict, named William Dealy, about 5 Feet 7 or 8 Inches High, stout built, has a Mole on one of his Cheeks, wears a Cap or Wig: Had on when he went away, a Snuff coloured Coat, Flannel Jacket, Leather Breeches, and a Pair of Hussar Boots. He carried with him a black Horse, about 14 Hands and a Half high, has a few white Hairs in his Forehead,

used to go in a Curricle, carries himself genteely, can trot and gallop. Whoever brings said Horse and Runaway to Conyngham and Nesbitt, shall have the above Reward; or whoever gives Intelligence, so that the Horse may be had again, shall be thankfully rewarded, and all Charges paid by JOHN STEVENSON.
The Pennsylvania Gazette, March 15, 1764; April 12, 1764; April 19, 1764.

RUN away from the Subscriber, living in North Sasquehannah Hundred, Cecil County, Maryland, on the 15th inst. March, a Servant Man, named Bartholomew Barron, born in the West of Ireland, about 30 Years old, about 5 Feet 9 Inches high, of a fair Complexion, has fair Hair tied behind, very much pock-marked, tender eyed, and has the Brogue on his Tongue; he is a good Scholar, and understand some of the Languages: Had on, when he went away, the following Articles, viz. an old ash-coloured Great Coat, a Strait Coat of the same Kind, black Broadcloth Jacket, old Buckskin Breeches, Check Shirt, light coloured Worsted Stockings, old Shoes, Brass Buckles, but not Fellows, and a halfworn Felt Hat. Whoever takes up the said Servant, and secures him, so that his Master may have him again, shall have Forty Shillings Reward, and reasonable Charges, paid by JOHN ANDERSON.
The Pennsylvania Gazette, March 22, 1764; April 19, 1764.

RUN away from the Subscriber, a Servant Fellow, named George Perepoint, is fresh coloured: Had on, when he went away, a Snuff coloured Coat, with Horn Buttons and White metal Eyes, black Breeches, both Thighs wore cross, and Lining shews white; he has a Mole on his Right Cheek, with some black Hairs in it; it is supposed he has a Pass, and will change his Name; he is a pretty good Scholar, and carried with him a brownish Wig; about 35 Years of Age. Whoever takes up and secures said Servant, so as his Master may have his again, shall have Ten Dollars Reward, besides what the Law allows, paid by SAMUEL COSH, living in Queen Ann's County, near Corseser Creek.
The Pennsylvania Gazette, March 22, 1764; April 12, 1764; April 12, 1764.

Baltimore County, *March* 20, 1764.
RAN away from the from the Subscribers, Two Convict Servant Men, *viz.*
  Elias Hix, about 25 Years of Age, 5 Feet 7 Inches high, of a brown Complexion, very much pitted with the Small-Pox, and has a large Scar over his right Eye: Had on when he went away, an old Castor Hat, a full'd

Country Cloth Great Coat of a light Colour, a yellow Broad-Cloth Jacket, Halfthick Breeches, blue Yarn Stockings, and a Pair of Pumps. He took with him a light colour'd Bay Mare, about 13 Hands high, branded on one of her Buttocks with a Pot-Hook. [*sic*]

Job Grimshaw, about 5 Feet 2 Inches high, of a dark Complexion, a thick set Fellow, near 40 Years of Age: Had on when he went away, a good light colour'd Thickset Coat, an old Felt Hat, old Jacket, old patch'd Breeches, Yarn Stockings, and Country made Shoes, well nail'd. He took with him a white Horse, branded on the near Buttock thus **S O**.

Whoever secures the said Servants, so as their Masters may have them again, shall have Four Pounds Pennsylvania Money Reward, paid by
WILLIAM ISGRIG,   JOHN JONES.

N. B. Grimshaw has a Bag of Tinker's Tools, and it's supposed will pass for a Tinker.

The Maryland Gazette, March 29, 1764; April 5, 1764; April 26, 1764. See *The Pennsylvania Gazette*, April 5, 1764.

Baltimore, March 20, 1764.
RUN away from the Subscriber, two Convict Servant Men, one named Elias Hicks: Had on when he went away, a light coloured Cloth Great Coat, a brown Cloth Jacket double breasted, and a yellow Broad Jacket, Silk Handkerchief, old Castor Hat, Halfthicks Breeches, Yarn Stockings, and a Pair of Pumps; has a large Scar over his Right Eye, which looks like the Blow of a Horse; is of a brown Complexion, about 25 Years of Age, very much pitted with the Small-Pox, is a Shoemaker by Trade, took with him a bright bay Mare, about 13 and an Half Hands high, branded on the Buttock with a Pot-hook, shod before, and trots. The other named Job Grimshaw, about 5 feet 2 Inches high, of a brown Complexion, a thickset Fellow, near 40 Years of Age: Had on, when he went away, an old Felt Hat, a very light coloured Thickset Coat, old Jacket, old patched Breeches, Yarn Stockings, Country made Shoes, well nailed, took with him a white Horse, branded on the Buttock **S O**. Whoever secures the said Servants, so as they may be had again, shall have Five Pounds Pennsylvania Money Reward, and reasonable Charges, paid by
WILLIAM ISGREG, and JOHN JONES.

N. B. Grimshaw has a Bag of Tinkers Tools, and it is expected will pass for a Tinker; the white Horse shod before. All Masters of Vessels are forbid to carry them off at their Peril.

The Pennsylvania Gazette, April 5, 1764; April 19, 1764. See *The Maryland Gazette*, March 29, 1764.

March 26, 1764.

RAN away from the Subscriber, living on *Kent-Island*, the 21st of this Instant, a Convict Servant Man named *John Tongue*, an *Englishman*, he pretends to be a good Scholar, and it is supposed he will write himself a Pass: he is a well set Fellow, about 5 Feet 7 or 8 Inches high, and has a very sly Look; he went off in a small Pettiauger, and it is supposed that he made for *West-River*, as he has often said he had some Relations that lived there. He had on and with him, a lightish colour'd Cloth Jacket, a white Dimity Ditto, one Pair of yellow Fustian Breeches, one Pair of light colour'd Country made Stockings, two Pair of Country made Shoes, one of them he wore with Strings, one Castor Hat, about half worn, and one white knit Cotton Cap.

Whoever takes up the said Servant, and secures him so as his Master may have him again, shall have Twenty Shillings Reward, beside what the Law allows, paid by   JOHN COPPAGE.

The Maryland Gazette, March 29, 1764; April 12, 1764; April 19, 1764.

Anne-Arundel County, *March* 22, 1764.

RAN away last Night, from the Subscriber, a Convict Servant Man, named *Richard Smith*, about 5 Feet 6 Inches high, a well set Fellow, of a swarthy Complexion, and about 20 Years of Age: Had on and took with him, an old Sagathy Coat, lined with yellow Tammy, an old grey Cloth Waistcoat, a Pair of old Buff Breeches, Broad-Cloth Ditto, a Pair of white Thread Stockings, mix'd Yarn Ditto, two Country Cloth Jackets, two Osnabrig Shirts, a Felt Hat, and an Iron Collar.

Whoever takes up the said Servant, and brings him to the Subscriber living on *Elk-Ridge*, shall have TEN DOLLARS Reward, paid by EPHRAIM HOWARD.

The Maryland Gazette, March 29, 1764; April 5, 1764. See *The Pennsylvania Gazette*, August 9, 1764.

March 21, 1764.

RAN away Yesterday, from the Subscriber in *Prince-George's* County, a Convict Servant Man, named *James Corrt*, born in the County of *Kent* in *England*, is about 5 Feet 7 Inches high, of a dark Complexion, and about 24 Years of Age, has an oval Face, his Nose has a cast to one Side, and one of his Feet turns in more than the other, he wears his own Hair, which is short and of a dark Brown: Had on and with him a brown Coat, a red Waistcoat and Breeches, a Check Shirt, and a Pair of grey Yarn Stockings. The said Servant was lately bought from on board the *Neptune*, Capt. *Somervill*, and consequently cannot know much of the Country.

Whoever takes up the said Servant, and brings him home, shall have FIVE POUNDS Reward, and reasonable Charges, paid by
John Frederick Augustus Priggs.

The Maryland Gazette, March 29, 1764; April 5, 1764; April 19, 1764; April 26, 1764; May 3, 1764; May 10, 1764. See *The Maryland Gazette*, June 21, 1764; The *Maryland Gazette*, July 21, 1768, and *The Maryland Gazette*, October 27, 1768.

March 26, 1763. [*sic*]

RAN away from the Subscriber, living on *Kent-Island*, the 21st of this Instant, a Convict Servant Man named *James Tongue*, an *Englishman*, he pretends to be a good Scholar, and it is supposed he will write himself a Pass; he is a well set Fellow, about 5 Feet 7 or 8 Inches high, and has a very sly Look; he went off in a small Pettiauger, and it is supposed that he made for *West-River*, as he has often said he had some Relations that lived there. He had on and with him, a lightish colour'd Cloth Jacket, a white Dimity Ditto, one Pair of yellow Fustian Breeches, one Pair of light colour'd Country made Stockings, two Pair of Country made Shoes, one of them he wore with Strings, one Castor Hat, about half worn, and one white knit Cotton Cap.

Whoever takes up the said Servant, and secures him so as his Master may have him again, shall have Twenty Shillings Reward, beside what the Law allows, paid by   JOHN COPPAGE.

The Maryland Gazette, April 5, 1764.

Kent-Island, April 5, 1764.

RAN away last Week, and made over to the Western Shore in a Canoe, a Convict Servant Man, named *William Richards*, he is about 5 Feet 6 Inches high, wears his Hair which is very black, and is 40 Years of Age: Had on when he went away, an old Hat, a brown Coat, a green Jacket, Osnabrigs Shirt, old Leather Breeches, old Stockings, and an old Pair of half worn Shoes, with plain plaited Buckles in them.

Whoever secures the said Runaway, so as the Subscriber may get him again, shall have Forty Shillings Reward, paid by
AQUILA BROWN.

The Maryland Gazette, April 5, 1764; May 3, 1764.

RAN away from the Subscriber, living in *Talbot* County, *Maryland*, a Convict Servant Man, named *William Colwell*, aged 30 Years, about 5 Feet 10 Inches high, has red Hair, and is much freckled, which appears at first

View like Marks of the Small-Pox, he writes a good Hand, and has been used to keeping School: He had on when he went off, a dark-brown Broadcloth Coat, a Snuff colour'd Vest, a Pair of Sheep-skin Breeches, a grey Bob Wig, and a Felt Hat.
 Whoever secures the said Servant, so that the Owner may get him again, shall have FIVE PISTOLES Reward, paid by
March 27.   JOHN BOZMAN.
 The Maryland Gazette, April 5, 1764; April 12, 1764. See *The Pennsylvania Gazette*, April 26, 1764.

April 2, 1764.
 RAN away this Morning, from the Subscriber's Plantation in *Baltimore* County, near the *Northampton* Iron-Works, a Convict Servant Man, named *Henry* or *John Whiton*, lately imported; he is a lusty Fellow, aged about 24 Years, about 5 Feet 9 Inches high, was born in *Northamptonshire*, and talks much in that Dialect, stoops much in his Shoulders, and wore his Hair, which is black and strait, but it's possible he may cut it off. He had on and took with him, an old greasy brown Surtout Coat, with broad Metal Buttons, *Kendall* Cotton Jacket and Breeches, Yarn Stockings, a Pair of brown Silk and Worsted Ditto, *English* Shoes nail'd all round the Soles, Leather Breeches, two Osnabrig Shirts, a Felt Hat, and a dark colour'd Cloth Jacket, let out in the Back with white Cotton, with Metal Buttons to it.
 Whoever takes up the said Servant, and secures him so as his Master may have him again, shall have if taken above Ten Miles from home, Forty Shillings; if out of the County, Three Pounds; if out of the Province, Five Pounds; and reasonable Charges if brought home, paid by
CHARLES RIDGELY, junr.
 The Maryland Gazette, April 5, 1764; April 12, 1764; April 19, 1764.

RUN away from the Subscriber, living in Queen Ann's County, Maryland, on the 25th of March last, and on the 28th in the Morning, I had a small black Mare missing, branded on the near Buttock **W**, and an old Hunting Saddle, with a Buckskin Seat, which it is likely he might borrow, a Convict Servant Man, named Matthew Humphreys, born in England, 33 Years of Age, a short well set Fellow, fair Complexion and fresh Countenance, pitted with the Small-Pox, and wears his own Hair of a light Colour: had on, when he went away, a Kersey Jacket of white Chain and black Filling, and Breeches of the same, patched on each Knee, a white Kersey Jacket without Sleeves, all homespun, two new Shirts, of Tear Chain and Tow Filling, a Pair of coarse white Stockings, and new Shoes; he is a great Lover of strong

Liquors, and subject to get drunk whenever Opportunity serves. He keeps Company with a Woman that goes by the Name of Jane Heires, and brought up as it is said in the Province of Pennsylvania; it is reported he has a Child by her, which is a Boy, near twelve Months old, and it is likely they may get off together after a small Time. Whoever takes up the said Servant, if in this Province, shall have Forty Shillings Reward, if taken out of this Province, Three Pounds, besides what the Law allows, and reasonable Charges if brought home, paid by WILLIAM WRENCH.

The Pennsylvania Gazette, April 12, 1764; April 19, 1764; April 26, 1764.

St. Mary's County, *April* 9, 1764.

RAN away last Night from the Subscriber, two Indented Servant Men, viz.

Basil Paterson, about 24 Years of Age, about 5 Feet 6 Inches high, a *Scotchman*, pitted with the Small-Pox, fresh Complexion, wears his Hair tied behind, which is of a redish brown Colour, stoops much in his walk, and is round shoulder'd; he is a Schoolmaster, and understands something of the *Latin* Tongue: Had on when he went away, a grey Bearskin Frock Coat, with black Horn Buttons, a Pair of knit black Thread and Cotton Breeches, bound round the Knees with black Sattin, a white Shirt, Shoes and Stockings, and sundry other Things, too tedious to mention.

John Morgan, about 35 Years of Age, about 5 Feet 7 or 8 Inches high, this Country born, has an impudent down Look, of a yellow or dark Complexion, short brown Hair, is much addicted to Drink, something of a Carpenter, and understands keeping a Mill: Had on when he went away, a brown Halfthick Jacket, an old Broadcloth Ditto, old Breeches, new Shoes, old Stockings, and a fine Hat. They took with them a neat stock'd Fowling Piece, a Bed, and several other Things too tedious to mention.

A likely Woman, call'd *Mary Carpenter*, went away with them, who it is imagined will pass for *Paterson's* Wife, and it is probable he will forge a Pass.

Whoever takes up the said Servants, and secures them so as their Master may get them again, shall have Ten Dollars Reward, paid by WILLIAM JORDAN.

The Maryland Gazette, April 12, 1764; April 19, 1764; April 26, 1764.

RAN away from the Subscriber, in *Calvert* County, on the First of this Instant *April*, an *Irish* Servant Man, named *Roger M'Keen*, he was formerly a Soldier in the *Maryland* Service, he is a middle siz'd Fellow, a great Liar, very Talkative, very fond of Drink, and pretends to many Kinds of Business. He had on and took with him, 1 white Shirt, 1 Osnabrig Ditto, 1

Check Ditto, a *German* Serge Vest and Breeches, a new Felt Hat, old Shoes, and two Pair of Stockings. Whoever takes up the said Servant, and brings him home, shall receive Three Pounds Reward.
BENJAMIN MACKALL.
The Maryland Gazette, April 12, 1764; May 3, 1764; May 10, 1764. The second and third ads show he ran away "on the First Day of *April* last...."

RAN away from the Subscribers, living in *Kent* County, Two Convict Servant Men, *viz.*

William Dane, a Blacksmith by Trade, he is a short well-made Fellow, bow legg'd, appears to be about 40 Years old, wears his own Hair which is short and dark, and is very apt to get drunk. Had on a light colour'd *English* Kersey Jacket much worn, Osnabrigs Shirt, red Worsted Plush Breeches, old Stockings, and Shoes plated with Iron.

Rice Price, a short Fellow, of a thin Visage, and a very long Nose, wears his own Hair, which is short and dark, he has a large scar on one of his Legs and is a young Man. Had on a yellow Coat, the Skirts of which are cut off at the Pocket Flaps, an Osnabrigs Shirt, red Breeches, old Stockings, and Pumps with Brass Buckles.

They were both born in the West of *England*, and 'tis supposed will change their Names.

Whoever secures the said Fellows, so that their Masters may get them again, shall have Five Pounds Reward for Dane, and Thirty Shillings for Price, paid by
SIMON WICKES,   ROBERT ROBERTS.
The Maryland Gazette, April 19, 1764. See *The Pennsylvania Gazette*, April 26, 1764.

RAN away from the Subscriber, in *Talbot* County, on the 10th Day of *April* last, a Servant Man named *James Farrow*, an *Irishman*, about 5 Feet 7 Inches high, a lusty well-set Fellow, of a sandy Complexion, with white Eye Brows, a large Scar on his left Arm, which has been out of Joint, and very much disfigured. Had on a Fearnought Jacket, patch'd on the Sides, a blue Jacket without Sleeves, Osnabrig Shirt, Leather Breeches, Osnabrigs Trowsers and good Shoes.

Likewise, A lusty Servant Woman named *Priscilla Laha*, Country-born, about 25 Years of Age. Had on a short chequer'd Gown, a cross barr'd Petticoat, a white Sattin Hat lined with pale red Silk, blue Stockings, good Shoes, and Brass Buckles. They pass for Man and Wife.

Whoever takes up the said Servants, and brings them home, shall have Eight Dollars Reward, and reasonable Charges, paid by
RANDLE JOHNSON.
The Maryland Gazette, April 19, 1764; May 3, 1764.

RAN away from on board the Snow *Prince-William*, on Thursday Night, the Fifth of *April* last, then lying in *South-River*, an *Irish* Indented Servant Man, named *Thomas Burch*, 5 Feet 8 or 8 Inches high, about 26 Years of Age, of a sandy Complexion, much freckled, says he is a Mill-Wright by Trade: Had on when he went away, a blue Cloth Jacket, an old Linen Frock, two old Woollen Vests, black Stocking breeches, black Stockings, and Country made Shoes. He took from *Caleb Burgess*, a light colour'd Sagathy Coat, a Snuff colour'd Broadcloth Jacket, a Pair of Nankeen Breeches, a fine Shirt, a Country made Hat, a grey Cut Wig, and a Gun without a Guard. It is supposed he will try to get over into *Virginia*.

Whoever secures the Said Servant, so that his Master may get him again, shall have Three Pistoles Reward, on giving Notice to JAMES COLE, Commander of the said Snow, at *Wye* River.
The Maryland Gazette, April 19, 1764; May 3, 1764.

FIVE POUNDS Reward.
RUN away from the Subscriber, in Baltimore County, Maryland, near Deer Creek, an Irish Convict Servant Man, named Edward Kennedy, about 5 Feet 2 Inches high, looks red and fresh in the Face: Had on, when he went away, a new Felt Hat, a black cut Wig, a dark coloured fly Coat, old light coloured Cloth Jacket, striped twilled Breeches, with Yarn ribbed Stockings, Ozenbrigs or Check Shirt, good Shoes, with Brass Buckles; it is likely he may change his Name and Apparel. Whoever takes up and secures said Servant in any Goal, shall receive the above Reward, and reasonable Charges, paid by WILLIAM COALE.
The Pennsylvania Gazette, April 19, 1764.

April 20, 1764.
COMMITTED, as Runaways, to the Sheriff of *Frederick* County, about three Weeks ago, a short well-set Fellow, of a black Complexion, wears his own Hair, says he was born in *Virginia*, and that his Name is *Elias Riggs*; his Clothes are, a blue close-bodied Coat and Jacket, lined with red, and Leather Breeches: Is an assuming forward Fellow. He had a young large Bay Horse, and a Gun with him when taken up.

Likewise, a tall slim Mulatto Woman, says her Name is *Hannah Philips*....
The Owners are desired to take them away, and pay Charges.
THOMAS PRATHER, Sheriff.
The Maryland Gazette, April 26, 1764; May 3, 1764.

April 23, 1764.
RAN away last Night from the Subscribers, in *Baltimore-Town*, two Convict Men, *viz*.

John Tummer, an *Englishman*, born in *Norfolk*, a middle-siz'd slim Man, about 22 Years old, of a fair Complexion, black Eyes, wears his own short black Hair, speaks broad, is a Plowman, has an awkward Gait, and a simple Look. Had on an old Felt Hat, thick mix'd Country Cloth Jacket, well full'd, with white Metal Buttons, an old blue Jacket, Osnabrig Shirt, white Country Cloth Breeches, black Yarn Stockings, and strong County made Shoes, tied on: Took with him a light figured Stuff Coat, with a Cape of the same, lined with Shalloon, and had silver'd Buttons, much tarnish'd with Wooden Bottoms; also an old Ash colour'd Sagathy Coat, lined with Dursy of the same Colour, Mohair Buttons, and worn out on one of the Sleeves, near the Shoulder, a new Felt Hat, an old white Shirt, one good Osnabrig Ditto, a Pair of black Worsted Stockings, and a Pair of Boots.

Benjamin Archer, an *Englishman*, born in *St. Ives*, in *Cornwall*, but speaks plain *English*, a Hatter by Trade, a pert looking Fellow, about 5 Feet 9 Inches high, pretty well made, about 22 Years old, of a brown Complexion, and wears his own short dark curled Hair. Had on a Felt Hat, a brown Cloth Coat, lined with Shalloon, and Mohair Buttons, a black Cloth Jacket, Check Shirt, old Leather Breeches, black Yarn Hose, *English* made Shoes, pretty good, and white Metal Buckles: Took with him a white Thickset Coat with Mohair Buttons, two Check Shirts, a black Silk Handkerchief, two Pair of Yarn Hose, and a Gun that screws off in the middle, with Powder, and Shot.

Whoever apprehends the said Servants, and secures them so that their Masters may get them again, shall receive Forty Shillings, if taken within Ten Miles; Three Pounds, if within Twenty Miles; Five Pounds, if within Forty Miles; and Seven Pounds Ten Shillings *Pennsylvania* Currency, if taken out of the Province, for each, with reasonable Charges, if brought Home.   WILLIAM LUX,   ADAM NURSLER.

The Maryland Gazette, April 26, 1764; May 24, 1764; *The Pennsylvania Gazette*, May 3, 1764; May 17, 1764. Minor differences between the papers.

Maryland, Kent County, April [1764]
RAN away from the Subscriber, his special Bail, sometime in *October* last, a certain *George Hayes*, about 30 Years old, a well-set Man, about 5 Feet 10 Inches high, or a brown Complexion, and much Pock-mark'd, is very Talkative, much addicted to Liquor, and is a good Carpenter or Joiner.

Whoever takes up and secures the said *George Hayes*, and puts him in any Goal, and gives Notice to the Subscriber, near *Chester-Town*, so that he may get him to deliver up, shall have FIVE PISTOLES Reward; or if brought and delivered to the Subscriber, shall be also paid the Reward above, and reasonable Charges, by him, or *Thomas* and *William Ringgold*, of *Chester-Town*, Merchants.   JAMES DUNKIN.

The Maryland Gazette, April 26, 1764; May 3, 1764; May 10, 1764.

RAN away from the Subscriber's Quarter, in *Frederick* County, near the Head of *Hawling's* River, on the 11th of this Instant *April*, a Convict Servant Man named *Daniel Boot*, but may change it to *James Watson*, about 5 Feet 7 or 8 Inches high, fair Complexion, short brown Hair, pitted with the Small-Pox. Had on when he went away, an Osnabrig Shirt, full'd Country Cloth Jacket and Breeches, old white Yarn Stockings, Country made Shoes half worn, and an old Felt Hat. He beats the Drum and plays on the Flute.

Whoever takes up the said Servant, and secures him, so as his Master may have him again, shall have a Pistole Reward, beside what the Law allows, paid by   JAMES RIGGS.

The Maryland Gazette, April 26, 1764.

Chester Town, Kent County, Maryland, April 9, 1764.
RUN way from the Subscribers, living in said Town, two Convict Servant Fellows, born in the West of England, one a Blacksmith by Trade, named William Dome, had on when he went away, an old Kersey Jacket, Ozenbrigs Shirt, red Plush Breeches, old Stockings, and Shoes plated with Iron on the Soles, wears his own dark bushey Hair; he is a short well make Fellow, and bow legged. The other named Rice Price, has no Trade that we know of; had on an old yellow Coat, cut off at the Pockets, Ozenbrigs Shirt, red Breeches, old Stockings a Pair of Pumps, with Brass Buckles, and an old Hat; wears his own Hair, and has a very long Nose. Whoever takes up and secures said Servants, so as their Masters may have them again, shall have Eight Dollars Reward, for both, or Thirty Shillings for either, and reasonable Charges if brought home, paid by
ROBERT ROBERTS, and S. WILKES.

The Pennsylvania Gazette, April 26, 1764; May 10, 1764; May 31, 1764. See *The Maryland Gazette*, April 19, 1764.

RUN away from the Subscriber, living in Talbot County, Maryland, on the 21st of March last, a Convict Servant Man, named William Colwell, aged 30 Years, about 5 Feet 10 Inches high, red Hair, and much freckled, which appears at first View like Marks of the Small-Pox; he writes a good Hand, and has been used to keeping School; he had on, when he went away, a dark brown Broadcloth Coat, a Snuff-coloured Vest, and Sheepskin Breeches. Whoever secures the said Servant, so that the Owner may have him again, shall have Four Pistoles Reward, paid by JOHN BOZMAN.

The Pennsylvania Gazette, April 26, 1764; May 24, 1764; June 14, 1764. See *The Maryland Gazette*, April 5, 1764.

RUN away on the Ninth Day of this instant April, from the Subscriber, living on Gunpowder Falls, near Major Thomas Franklin's, in Baltimore County, Maryland, three Servant Men; one named George Smith, about 6 Feet high, of a fair Complexion, thin-visaged, wears a cut Wig, or his own short brown Hair, and has lost the Fore-finger of his Right-hand: Had on a brown Cloth Coat, with Metal Buttons, a light coloured Vest, Leather Breeches, and good Shoes and Stockings. The second named George Woods, about 5 Feet 9 Inches high, of a swarthy Complexion, and has short black Hair: Had on two Vests, one blue, the other a double breasted white Flannel One, old Leather Breeches, good Shoes and Stockings, and an old Felt Hat. The third named Thomas Simpson, is about 5 Feet 8 Inches high, full faced, of a fair Complexion, and has yellow Hair; one of the Fingers of his Left-hand so disabled that he cannot shut it: Had on, when he went away, a brown Vest, old Breeches, the same Cloth of the Vest, a Pair of Trowsers, good Shoes and Stockings, and a Felt Hat, with a narrow Brim, bound round with Cadiz Binding: They are all Englishmen, and it may be they will part. Whoever takes up said Servants, and brings them to their Master, or secures them in any Goal, so as he may have them again, shall have SIX POUNDS Reward, or Forty Shillings for each, paid by JAMES AGER.

The Pennsylvania Gazette, April 26, 1764; May 3, 1764; May 17, 1764; May 31, 1764. See *The Maryland Gazette*, May 3, 1764.

April 27, 1764.
RAN away on the Ninth of this Instant, from the Subscriber, living on *Gunpowder* Falls, near Maj. *Thomas Franklin's*, in *Baltimore* County, *Maryland*, Three Servant Men, *viz.*

George Smith, about 6 Feet high, of a fair Complexion, thin visag'd, wears a cut Wig or his own short brown Hair, has lost the fore Finger of his right Hand: Had on a brown Cloth Coat with Metal Buttons, a light colour'd Vest, Leather Breeches, and good Shoes and Stockings.

George Woods, about 5 Feet 9 Inches high, of a swarthy Complexion, and has short black Hair. Had on two Vests, one blue, and the other a double breasted white Flannel one, old Leather Breeches, good Shoes and Stockings, and an old Felt Hat.

Thomas Simpson, is about 5 Feet 8 Inches high, full faced, of a fair Complexion, and has yellow Hair; one of the Fingers of his left Hand so disabled that he can't shut it: Had on when he went away, a dark brown Coat, a brown Vest, a Pair of Trowsers, good Shoes and Stockings, and Felt Hat, with a narrow Brim, bound round with Cades Binding. They are all *Englishmen*, and it may be they will part.

Whoever takes up the said Servants, and brings them to their Master, or secures them in any Goal, so as he may have them again, shall have SIX POUNDS Reward, or Forty Shillings for either, paid by
JAMES AGER.

The Maryland Gazette, May 3, 1764; May 10, 1764; May 31, 1764.

BROKE out of the *Anne-Arundel* County Goal, on the 30th of *April* last, a Convict Servant Man, belonging to *John Ducker*, committed on Suspicion of Felony; he is a Scotchman, and speaks bad *English*, an assuming forward Fellow, and a good Taylor and Staymaker, about 5 Feet 10 Inches high, squints much, and is of a dark Complexion. His Cloaths are, a double breasted Frize Coat, brown Cloth Breeches, blue Worsted Stockings, a Pair of Pumps, and a brown curled Wig. Likewise, *Richard Parker*, an *Englishman*, and a very slim Fellow. Had on a short Fustian Coat, a spotted Flannel Jacket, a Pair of Trowsers, and ribb'd Worsted Hose.

Whoever takes up and secures the said Runaways, so that the Subscriber may get them again, shall receive a Reward of Two Pistoles and a Half for each.   JOSEPH GALLOWAY, Sheriff.

The Maryland Gazette, May 3, 1764; May 10, 1764.

Annapolis, April 30, 1764.
RAN away from the Subscriber, a Convict Servant Woman, named *Elizabeth Bryan*, is a short spare Woman, about 4 Feet 10 Inches high, and about Thirty Years of Age: Had on when she went away, a Calicoe Bed-Gown, a brown Stuff Petticoat, a Pair of white Yarn Stockings, a Pair of Mens Shoes, and a blue Hat.

She served Part of her Time with Mrs. *Cook* at *Bladensburg,* and is supposed to be gone that Way.

Whoever brings the said Servant to the Subscriber, shall have Twenty Shillings Reward.   JOHN THOMPSON, junior.

The Maryland Gazette, May 10, 1764.

RAN away, on the Sixth of this Instant *May,* from the Subscriber, living near *Snowden's* Manor, in *Frederick* County, a Convict Servant Man, named *John Williams,* 5 Feet 8 or 9 Inches high, pretty well proportion'd, and of a very dark Complexion; he is a Sail Maker or Ship-Rigger by Trade, a very assuming forward Fellow, pretends to be a good Scholar, and may Write himself a Pass. Had on and with him, when he went away, a Claret colour'd close bodied Broadcloth Coat, blue Broadcloth Breeches, a darkish brown Great Coat, a striped Silk and Worsted double-breasted Jacket, an old Castor Hat, new Country made Turn Pumps, [*sic*] 2 or 3 Pair of Worsted Stockings, and 2 white Linen Shirts. Took with him sundry Papers, among which is an Order on Col. *Hunter* of *Virginia* for 16*l.* Sterling, which makes me imagine he will make that Way. He rode off a dark Bay or Brown Horse, about 1[3½] Hands high, paces slow, and gallops well, had a Saddle and Bridle. Whoever apprehends the said Servant, and secures him in any Goal, so that the Subscriber may get him again, shall receive Forty Shillings Reward, besides what the Law allows,
paid by   WILLIAM GARTRELL.

The Maryland Gazette, May 10, 1764; May 17, 1764.

Philadelphia, May 16, 1764.

SINCE the 19th of January last has been committed to the public Goal of this City, the following Persons, who have confessed themselves Runaway Servants, viz. James Hamilton, the Property of William Boon, of Berks County—John Morrow, the Property of William Kelley, of New-Castle—And Benjamin Newport, the Property of John M'Duff, of Caecil County, Maryland. The Masters of the above Servants are desired to take them away within then Days from the Date hereof, otherwise they will be sold to pay Charges, by   JOHN MITCHELL, Goaler.

The Pennsylvania Gazette, May 17, 1764; May 24, 1764.

May 15, 1764.

RAN away on Sunday the 13th past, a Convict Servant Man named *James Hardwick*; he wore a new blue Kersey Coat and Jacket, and he stole some other Cloaths. The Fellow is about 35 Years of Age, his Complexion dark,

his Hair black, short and thick; on his Head are some Scars; he talks smooth, and pronounces some Words very broad; he is fond of strong Drink. Whoever brings the said Servant to the Subscriber, near *King-George* Court House in *Virginia*, shall have Five Pounds Reward if taken in *Virginia*, and Ten Pounds if taken in any other Province.
ALEXANDER ROSE.

The Servant Fellow was very intimate with a noted Rogue belonging to one *Stringfellow*, and it is suspected that they made an Appointment to go off together.

The Maryland Gazette, May 24, 1764; May 31, 1764; June 7, 1764.

RAN away from *Paradise* Iron-Works, in *York* County, on the First of this Instant *May*, an *English* Servant Man, named *Thomas Powny*, about 5 Feet 8 Inches high, and stutters much: Had on when he went away, a short brown Jacket, Osnabrig Shirt, Leather Breeches, Yarn Stockings, old Shoes, and a broad Piece of Leather round each Leg. It is supposed he will change his Name to *John Wells*, as he has past by that Name in several Places.

Whoever takes up said Servant, and secures him in any Goal, shall have Forty Shillings Reward, and reasonable Charges, paid by
JOHN WILKINSON.

The Maryland Gazette, May 24, 1764; May 31, 1764.

May 21, 1764.
RAN away on the first of this Instant from the Subscriber, living at the Head of *Elk*, in *Caecil* County, Two Servant Men, *viz.*

George Scrivener, an *Englishman*, about 5 Feet 7 Inches high, fresh colour'd, has grey Eyes, sandy Hair, and pretty much pitted with the Small-Pox. Had on a brown Cloth Coat, a spotted Flannel Waistcoat, good Buckskin Breeches, a Check Shirt, blue Yarn Stockings, old Shoes, Brass Buckles, and an old Hat.

William Kanare, about 5 Feet 7 Inches high, pretty well-set, fresh colour'd, and of a fair Complexion. Had on a light colour'd Cloth Coat, a black Broad Cloth Waistcoat, Osnabrigs Shirt, Tow Trowsers, a half-worn Castor Hat, old Shoes, with carv'd Silver Buckles.

They probably have other Cloaths with them, and are between 20 and 30 Years old.

Whoever takes up and secures the said Servants in any Gaol, so that their Masters may have them, shall have Three Pounds Rewards for each, and reasonable Charges, paid by ROBERT MUIR.

The Maryland Gazette, May 24, 1764; June 7, 1764.

RUN away the 13th of this inst. May, from the Subscriber, living in Queen Ann's County, Maryland, an Irish Servant Man, named Thomas Fea, about 25 Years of Age, 5 Feet 5 Inches high, middling fair Complexion, very much Pock-marked, slow of Speech: Had on, when he went away, an half-worn Felt Hat, light coloured cut Wig, and his hair about 4 Inches long, of the same Colour, dark grey Coat, long waisted, pretty much worn, a brown Linen Shirt, white long Trowsers, black grey Woollen Stockings, and good Shoes, tied with Strings. His right Arm has been put out of Joint, by reason of which he cannot easily straighten it. Whoever takes up the said Servant, and secures him below Chester county, shall have Three Pounds Reward, and if beyond, Five Pounds, paid by   THOMAS SEGRMES.

N. B. It is supposed he has a Pass, and is gone for New York. All Masters of Vessels are forbid to carry him off.

The Pennsylvania Gazette, May 24, 1764.

RUN away from the Subscriber, at King's-Town, Queen Ann's County, Maryland, on the 22d of this Inst. Two Convict Servant Men, viz. Peter James, born in Cornwell, has the West Country Dialect, about 45 Years of Age: Had on when he went away, a blue Sailor's jacket, and a red under one, Pair of Trowsers, Shoes and Stockings, with a large Pair of Brass Buckles, Felt Hat, black Hair, and has a very sore Leg. The other named Richard Horn, born in Stafford, has the West Country Dialect, about 60 Years of Age, grey bushey Hair, a good fine Hat, no Lining, dark Cloth Coat, with small Cape, Jacket and Breeches of the same, ribbed Stockings, light blue, new soaled Shoes, about 5 Feet 9 Inches high, has a Stoop in his Walk, and has lost his Fore Teeth. Whoever takes them up ,and secures them, so that they may be had again, shall have Four Dollars Reward for each, and reasonable Charges, if brought home, paid by
JOHN BIRSTALL, JOHN KNIGHT.

The Pennsylvania Gazette, May 24, 1764; June 7, 1764.

Lyon's-Creek, *Patuxent* River, *May* 28, 1764.
RAN away from the Snow *Eagle*, whereof the Subscriber is Master, a Servant Man named *Joseph Gillhespy*, of a middle Stature, and a brown Complexion, slender made, pitted with the Small-Pox, and wears dark Hair, is about 5 Feet 4 Inches high, and about 20 Years of Age. He had on a Sailor's Dress.

Whoever takes up the said Servant, and delivers him on board the Ship, or secures him in any Goal, shall have a Reward of Two Pistoles, paid by   WILLIAM MAYNARD.

It is supposed he is gone to *Baltimore*, or to *Choptank*, as he is well acquainted at both those places.
The Maryland Gazette, May 31, 1764; June 7, 1764; June 14, 1764.

FIVE POUNDS REWARD.

RAN away on the 18th of this Inst. *May*, from the *Baltimore* Iron-Works, on *Patapsco*, an *English* Convict Servant Man, named *John Child*, by Trade a Gardener, speaks broad, about 30 Years of Age, has a red Beard, is much mark'd with the Small-Pox, 5 Feet 8 Inches high, and wears brown curl'd Hair: Had on when he went away, a double riveted Steel Collar, Felt Hat, two Osnabrig Shirts, Osnabrig Trowsers, Great Coat of a greyish colour, trimm'd with flat Metal Buttons, blue German Serge Coat, black Cloth Jacket and Breeches, white Cotton Stockings, and a Pair of Pumps almost new.

Whoever secures said Servant so that he may he had again, shall have the above Reward, and reasonable Charges if brought home.
JAMES FRANKLIN.

The Maryland Gazette, May 31, 1764; June 7, 1764; June 21, 1764; June 28, 1764; July 5, 1764. See *The Maryland Gazette*, March 15, 1764, and August 16, 1764.

These are to give Notice, that a certain John Pigman is confined in Lancaster Goal as a Runaway Servant, said to belong to Mr. Joseph Ealgor, of Frederick County, Maryland; he is about 5 Feet 8 or 9 Inches high, wears a blue Coat, a striped Lincey Jacket, a coarse Shirt, of Country Linen, coarse Trowsers, no Stockings, a Pair of Shoes, and Wooll Hat; he is about 18 Years of Age, has a Mark under his Left eye, and is grey eyed. His Master, who is said to be a Mill Carpenter, is desired to come and pay Charges, and take him away, before the First Day of July next.
FELIX DONELLY, Goaler.

The Pennsylvania Gazette, June 7, 1764.

RUN away from the Subscriber, living in Baltimore Town, on the 23d of May last, a Servant Man, named William Fry, about 5 Feet 3 Inches high, well set, of a good clear Complexion, black Hair that curls; he took several old Clothes with him, but it is supposed he will appear in a good Laced Hat, and a good Fustian Coat, with metal Buttons, and a Pair of Buckskin Breeches. The Horse he rode was a roan, branded on the Thigh **C**, and an **I** on the Shoulder; he speaks the West Country Language, and is a very sensible Fellow. Whoever takes up, and brings him to this said Master, shall

have Three Pounds Reward, besides what the Law allows, and reasonable Charges, paid by BRIAN PHILPOT.
The Pennsylvania Gazette, June 7, 1764.

Worcester County, *May* 30, 1764.
TEN PISTOLES REWARD.

RAN away from *Deep-Creek* Iron-Works, near the Head of *Nanticoke* River, a Servant Man named *John Abdell*, about 35 Years of Age, about 5 Feet 6 Inches high, born in this Country, wears his Hair, which is of a brown Colour, thin Visage, and down Look. Had on and took with him, an old brown Jacket without Sleeves, the fore Parts green, Check and Osnabrigs Shirts, Trowsers, old Shoes and Buckles.

Likewise, Ran away from his Bail, *John Severan*, or *Sullivan*, upwards of 40 Years of Age, of middle Stature, Pock mark'd, wore black curled Hair, was born in the West of *England*, and speaks broad, is much given to Drink, and pretends to be well acquainted with driving a Team. Had on and with him, a new Hat, new deep blue Cloth Coat, Check Shirts, Leather Breeches, Check Trowsers, good Shoes, a Callico, or stamped Linen Jacket.

They went off by Water, and 'tis thought intend for *Carolina* or *Virginia*.

Whoever takes up and secures them, so that they may be had again, shall have the above Reward, or Five Pistoles for either, paid by
JONATHAN VAUGHAN,
WILLIAM DOUGLASS.

The Maryland Gazette, June 14, 1764; June 21, 1764; June 28, 1764; July 5, 1764.

RAN away from the Subscriber, on the Fifth of this Instant, *June*, a Servant Man called *James Williams*, about 5 Feet 2 Inches high, wears his own Hair, which is of a light sandy Colour, and he is about 40 Years of Age: Had on when he went away, an Osnabrigs Shirt, old Osnabrigs Trowsers, two old blue Jackets, an old Hat bound round with white Linen, and an Iron Collar round his Neck.

Whoever secures the said Servant in any Goal in the Province, and gives Information thereof to the Subscriber, living near the Head of *Magothy* River, in *Anne-Arundel* County, shall receive a Reward of Twenty Shillings, if taken in the County; and if out of the Province, Three Pounds, paid by   WILLIAM GAMBRILL.

The Maryland Gazette, June 14, 1764. See *The Maryland Gazette*, February 16, 1764.

FOUR PISTOLES REWARD.
RAN away, on the 23d of *May* last, from Mr. *Arnold Livers's*, in *St. Mary's* County, an Indented Servant Man named *Peter Rose*, by Trade a Painter, was born in *Guernsey*, speaks *French*, and very bad *English*, is of middle Stature, and dark Complexion. Had on when he went away, a Suit of blue *German* Serge Clothes almost new. It is supposed he will endeavour to get across the Bay, and make towards *Philadelphia*.
Whoever apprehends the said Servant, and will deliver him to Mr. *Arnold Livers*, in *St. Mary's* County, to Mr. *Henry Bradford*, in *Charles* County, or to the Subscriber, at *Piscataway*, in *Prince-George's* County, shall receive the above Reward.   BENJAMIN DAWSON.
The Maryland Gazette, June 14, 1764; June 21, 1764; July 5, 1764; July 26, 1764; August 2, 1764; *The Pennsylvania Gazette*, August 23, 1764; January 17, 1765; January 31, 1765; February 14, 1765. Minor differences between the papers.

RUN away on Sunday, the 3d of June, from Chester Town, Kent County, Maryland, two Servant Fellows; one an Indentured Servant, named Richard Pearce: Had on, when he went away, a blue Jacket, double-breasted, white Shirt, new Sailor Trowsers, Shoes and Stockings, a Sealskin Cap, and wears his own Hair, which is black and straight. The other is a Convict, was born in the West of England, a Blacksmith by Trade: Had on when he went away, and English Kersey Jacket, Ozenbrigs Shirt, a Pair of red Worsted Plush Breeches, old Yarn Stockings, a Pair of turned Pumps, and Brass Buckles, old Hat, and has dark bushey Hair. Whoever secures said Servants so as their Masters may get them again, shall have Five Pounds Reward for both, or Fifty shillings for either, and reasonable Charges, paid, if brought home, by   ROBERT ROBERTS, and S. WICKES.
The Pennsylvania Gazette, June 14, 1764.

RUN way from the Subscriber, living in Milford Hundred, Caecil County, on the 4th Inst. at Night, A Servant Man, called William Casey, about 5 Feet 3 or 4 Inches high, has brown Hair, is of a brown Complexion, about 19 or 20 Years of Age, pretty well built, speaks English with a Tone: Had on and took with him when he went away, a green regimental Coat, lined with green Serge, the Lappel lined with the same, broke at the Elbows, with small narrow topped Metal buttons, Cloth Scarlet Waistcoat, old blue Broadcloth Breeches, blue Worsted Ribbed Stockings, old Shoes, with Iron buckles, white Linen Shirt, and a coarse Tow ditto, and Felt hat. Came in with Capt. Edward Welsh, from Cork, and arrived in Philadelphia on the 2d

of December last. Whoever takes up said Servant, and brings him to his Master, or secures him, so that he may have him again, shall have Forty Shillings Reward, and reasonable Charges, paid by JOHN MACKY.
The Pennsylvania Gazette, June 14, 1764.

VIRGINIA, *June* 14, 1764.
TEN POUNDS REWARD.

RAN away from the Subscriber, on Sunday the 10th past, an *English* Convict Servant Man, named *John Fricker*, he is about 25 Years of Age, a stout, well made Fellow, about 5 Feet 6 or 7 Inches high, round and full faced, of a ruddy Complexion, and wears his own black Hair tied behind: Had on when he went away, a white Shirt, a Violet colour'd Waistcoat, with yellow gilt Buttons, it has a Flap down the Breast, over the Button Holes, the Skirts of it lined with white Shalloon or Tammy, a brownish colour'd old superfine Broadcloth Coat, lined with Shalloon of the same Colour, with Mohair Buttons partly worn out, a Pair of Buckskin Breeches, white Stockings, and Country made Shoes, lately half soaled. It is suspected he has carried away other Clothes with him. He is a Joiner and House-Carpenter, and pretends to understand the Wheelwright's Business.

Whoever brings the said Servant to me, in Stafford County, shall have the above Reward. WILLIAM BRENT.

The Maryland Gazette, June 21, 1764; June 28, 1764; July 5, 1764; July 12, 1764; July 19, 1764; July 26, 1764. See *The Maryland Gazette*, October 11, 1764.

SIX POUNDS REWARD.

RAN away from the Subscriber, living in *Prince-George's* County, on the 12th of this Instant, *June*, Two Convict Servant Men, and a Convict Servant Woman, *viz*.

William Hyley, about 5 Feet 6 Inches high, born in the West of *England*, and came from *Liverpool*, has been in this Country about 4 Years, is of a dark Complexion, has a remarkable large Wen on the right Side of his Forehead, and is about 40 Years of Age: Had on and with him, a Snuff colour'd Thickset Coat lined with brown Holland, and Breeches of the same as the Coat, a white Shirt, and a new Osnabrig Ditto, 2 Pair of coarse brown Linen Trowsers, Worsted Stockings, Country made Shoes, and a Felt Hat.

James Corrt, alias *Court*, born in the County of *Kent* in *England*, is about 5 Feet 7 Inches high, of a dark Complexion, about 24 Years of Age, has an Oval Face, his Nose has a cast to one Side, and his right Foot turns in more than his Left, and he speaks the *Kentish* Dialect: Had on an Osnabrigs Shirt, coarse brown Linen Trowsers, and an old Hat: He came in this

Country in *February* last, in the *Neptune*, Capt. *Somervill*, ran away soon after, and hired himself as a Freeman to Dr. *Thomas Sprigg Wootton* in *Frederick* County, and was but lately brought home.

The Woman, named *Isabella Watson*, of a fair Complexion, sandy colour'd Hair, has a round Face, much pitted with the Small-Pox, of a middling Stature, but thick, and about 25 Years of Age: Had on and with her, two black Petticoats, one Cotton Ditto, a black Stuff Gown, a coarse brown Linen Apron, and one white Ditto, a black Silk Bonnet, a red Flannel short Gown, blue Worsted Stockings, Country made Womens Pumps, a Necklace of large *French* Beads, 2 brown Sheeting Shifts, 1 white Ditto, Caps, a red flower'd *India* Silk Handkerchief, and sundry other Things in a Check Linen Bag: She came in the same Ship with the above named *James Corrt*. It is supposed they will all keep together, especially the said *Isabella Watson*, and the above described *Wm. Hyley*.

Whoever takes up the said Servants, and brings them to their Master, or secures them in any Goal, and gives Notice thereof, so as he may hear of them soon after their Commitment, shall have Forty Shillings Reward for each, and if brought home, reasonable Charges, paid by
John Frederick Augustus Priggs.

The Maryland Gazette, June 21, 1764; June 28, 1764. See *The Maryland* Gazette, March 29, 1764, for Corrt/Coort, *The Maryland Gazette*, July 21, 1768, for Corrt/Coort and Watson, and *The Maryland Gazette*, October 27, 1768, for Corrt and Watson.

Baltimore County, *Joppa, June* 18.
COMMITTED TO THE Jail of this County, as Runaways, the following, whose Masters are desired to take them away, and pay Charges, *viz.*

John Smith; his Master, who lives on *Kent-Island*, took him out of this Prison, on the 6th of *June*, and he was committed again on the 9th.

William Calle, says he is a Freeman, committed on the 12th. He is about 5 Feet 6 Inches high, says he is a Weaver: Has a light colour'd Coat, coarse Shirt, old Legging and Shoes.

And Three New Negroes. One called himself *James*....Another calls himself *Harry*....The other calls himself *Pompey*....
JOHN TAYLOR, Jailor.

The Maryland Gazette, June 21, 1764; June 28, 1764.

FIVE POUNDS REWARD.
RUN away from the Subscriber, living on Elk Ridge, in Ann-Arundell County, Maryland, a Convict Servant Man, named William Lane, about 25 Years of Age, about 5 Feet 9 Inches high, wears his own brown Hair, brown

Eyes, little pitted with the Small Pox: Had on, when he went away, a new Felt Hat, good Shirt, good brown Cloth Coat, Calicoe Jacket, and Leather Breeches, Worsted Stockings, good Shoes, and sundry other things unknown; he stole a good Saddle, and it is thought he has stole a Horse; it is supposed there is a Convict Servant Man with him, named William Robertson, his Dress unknown; Robertson stole a Broad Sword, which it is thought he carried with him; the said Robertson is very much marked with the Small pox; there is Three Pounds Reward for Robertson, and five Pounds for Lane, if brought home, or secured, so that they may be had again, paid by NATHAN DORSEY.

The Pennsylvania Gazette, June 21, 1764. See *The Maryland Gazette*, August 30, 1764.

Absconded from his Bail, on the 26th Day of May last, John Dixon, an Englishman, by Trade a Wheelwright, about 5 Feet 10 Inches high, of a swarthy Complexion, wears his own Hair, which is black: Had on, when he went away, a new brown Broadcloth Coat, and green Jacket; it is supposed he is gone to Philadelphia. Whoever secures the said Dixon, so that he may be had again, and gives Information thereof to the Subscriber, at the City of Annapolis, in Maryland, shall receive Five Pounds Reward, paid by JONATHAN PINKNEY.

The Pennsylvania Gazette, June 21, 1764.

RUN away from on Board the Schooner Beckey, lying in Patapsco River, near Baltimore Town, An English Convict Servant Man, named Edward Davis, about 5 Feet 9 Inches high: Had on when he went away, a grey Fearnought Sailor's Jacket, a small blue Ditto, with small Metal Buttons, new Felt Hat, Sailor's Trowsers, grey ribbed Stockings, new Country made Shoes, an Ozenbrigs Shirt, and a white Ditto; his Hair lately cut, of a dark swarthy Complexion, much pitted with the Small-pox, and is somewhat bursten; he has been brought up to the Sea from his Childhood. Whoever takes up and secure said Servant, so as his Master may have him again, shall have Three Pounds Reward, and reasonable Charges, paid by
JOHN CALVERT.

N. B. All Masters of Vessels are forbid to carry off said Servant at their Peril.

The Pennsylvania Gazette, June 28, 1764.

RAN away on the 26th of *June* last, from the Subscriber's Quarter in *Baltimore* County, a Convict Servant Man named *William Chandler*, near 6

Feet high, a West Countryman, about 40 or 45 Years of Age, bred a Farmer, two of his upper Fore Teeth stand out pretty much, wears his own brown Hair cut close on the Top of his Head. His Apparel, a brown Surtout Coat, a brown Fearnothing Jacket, Osnabrig Shirt and Trowsers, old Shoes, and old Felt Hat.

 Whoever will take up the said Runaway and bring him to his Master, living near the *Patapsco* Iron Works in *Anne-Arundel* County, or to Mr. *John Hood* on *Elk-Ridge*, shall have Thirty Shillings Reward, and all reasonable Charges, paid by   JOHN WALKER.

 The Maryland Gazette, July 5, 1764; July 12, 1764; July 19, 1764.

      Chester-Town, Kent County, *July* 2, 1764.
Made his Escape from the Subscriber, a certain *Alexander M'Intosh*, who was taken on two *Capias's*, he is an *Irishman*, a Shoemaker by Trade, about 5 Feet 8 Inches high, a thick wellset Fellow, much Pock-mark'd, has a pert Look, very talkative, and pretends to be much of a Man: Had on when he went away, a blue Broad-Cloth Coat, tho' it is probable he may change his Dress, as he has several Suits with him; he wears his own Hair, which is of a brownish Colour, and pretty short; a sharp cock'd Hat, and is a little bald-headed: He took with him a large black Horse, and an Apprentice Boy, and two other Horses, which it is probable he may sell. Whoever takes up and secures the said *Alexander M'Intosh*, so that he may be delivered to the Subscriber, shall receive FIVE PISTOLES Reward.
THOMAS SMYTH, Sheriff.

 The Maryland Gazette, July 5, 1764.

Editor's note: A Capias is writ or process commanding the officer to take the body of the person named in it, that is, to arrest him.

      THREE POUNDS REWARD.
RAN away from the Subscriber, living near *Elk-Ridge*, in *Anne-Arundel* County, on the First of this Inst. *July*, an *English* Convict Servant Man named *James Groves*, a middle sized Fellow, about 40 Years of Age, with short black Hair, dark Eyes, dark Complexion, round shouldered, down Look, speaks bad *English* and quick; was imported into *Maryland, August* last, in the Ship *Albion, John Cole*, Master. Had on when he went away, a new coarse Felt Hat, an old blue Cloth Coat, Check Shirt, old Osnabrig Trowsers, and a pair of strong Country made Shoes.

 He may endeavour to pass for a Freeman, as a Discharge to *Matthew Kelley* is missing, dated *September* 1761, signed by *Cornelius Ragon*.

 Whoever will take up and secure the said Servant, and give Notice thereof, so as he be had again, shall receive, if taken 10 Miles from home,

Twenty Shillings; if 20 Miles, Thirty Shillings; if 30 Miles, Forty Shillings; if out of the Province, the above Reward, and reasonable Charges if brought home, paid by THOMAS FOSTER.

The Maryland Gazette, July 5, 1764; July 26, 1764; August 30, 1764; September 6, 1764; September 13, 1764; September 20, 1764. See *The Pennsylvania Gazette,* August 16, 1764, *The Pennsylvania Gazette,* January 17, 1765.

FIVE POUNDS Reward.

Run away from Onion's Iron-works, in Baltimore County, Maryland, A Convict Servant Man, named Thomas Milliner, a Jeweller by Trade, and lately came into the country, about 20 Years of Age, about 5 Feet 4 Inches high, thin Visage, long Nose, grey Eyes, light brown hair, tied behind, and somewhat pitted with the Small-pox; Had on when he went away, a blue Cloth Jacket, Ozenbrigs Shirt and Trowsers, new Felt hat, old Shoes, and black Stockings. Whoever secures said Servant in any Goal, not exceeding 20 Miles, shall have Thirty Shillings, and if out of the Province the above Reward, with reasonable Charges, paid by
JOHN GRENIFF HOWARD.

The Pennsylvania Gazette, July 5, 1764.

Baltimore-Town, July 2, 1764.
RAN away from the Subscribers, Yesterday Morning, a Convict Servant Man named *Solomon Gabrel,* an *Englishman,* but speaks good Dutch, about 5 Feet 3 Inches high, a thick well-set Fellow, of a down Look, and swarthy Complexion; he wears his own Hair, which is of a light sandy Colour, short, and curls much, and very thin, almost bald on the Top; he is by Trade a Painter, and may pass for a Butcher, as he is a very good one. He took with him when he went away, a white Shirt and a check one, a brown Broad-Cloth Coat, an old blue Waistcoat, with Silver Vellum Button Holes, and touch'd in several Places with Paint of different Colours, a Pair of Leather Breeches, a Pair of black and a Pair of brown Stockings, high quarter'd Shoes, with Yellow Buckles, and a narrow brimm'd Felt Hat.

Whoever brings the said Fellow to the Subscribers, or either of them, shall have, if taken 20 Miles from home, Forty Shillings; and if further, and out of the County, Five Pounds, paid by
THOMAS JONES,
GEORGE WHITE.

The Maryland Gazette, July 12, 1764; July 19, 1764; July 26, 1764. See *The Pennsylvania Gazette,* July 12, 1763, for Gabrel/Gabriel.

COMMITTED to the Custody of the Sheriff of *Calvert* County, as a Runaway, about 4 Weeks ago, *John Gardner*, a *Welchman*, wears brown Hair, is of a light Complexion, about 35 Years old, and 4 Feet [sic] 5 Inches high. Had on an old light colour'd Bearskin Coat, old blue Breeches, and an old Hat.
 His Master may have him, on paying Charges.
TRUEMAN SKINNER.
The Maryland Gazette, July 12, 1774.

 RAN away on the 8th of *July* from *George-Town*, a Servant Man named *Patrick Donerly*, an Irishman, wears his Hair, of a yellowish brown Colour, and a small red Beard, of a middle Size, and of a pale Complexion, large full Eyes, and a remarkable large Hand, cloath'd with an Osnabrigs Shirt and Trowsers, a dark grey colour'd Jacket, Shoes lately mended, a Pair of Brass Buckles, and other Cloathing (I suppose) and is expected to be in Company with Two others; one of them a low well-set Man, named *John Barber*, who pretends to be a Waterman, and wears his Hair tied behind, a light colour'd Cloth Coat and Waistcoat, a Pair of Osnabrigs Trowsers, a Check Shirt with small Stripes, and a Silk Handkerchief with yellow Spots. The other Man, by Trade a Weaver, whose Name is unknown; but wears a coarse dark colour'd Cloth Coat, and a Pair of Leather Breeches dy'd of a Purple Colour, and Strings in his Shoes. Whoever will secure the said *Donerly*, so that his Master may get him again, shall be paid as a Reward Two Pistoles by   SAMUEL BEALL, junior.
 N. B. There is missing a fine Hat, the Lining is sewed in with blue Silk, as also a Pair of Mens new Shoes, which probably they have with them.
The Maryland Gazette, July 12, 1774; July 19, 1764.

TEN POUNDS Reward.

RUN away from the Subscriber, in Baltimore Town, Maryland, on the first of this Instant, two Convict Servant Men, one named Solomon Gabriel, by Trade a Painter, but may pass for a Butcher; he is a middleaged Man, about 5 Feet 3 Inches high, a well set Fellow, has a Down-look, and is of a swarthy Complexion, wears his own short curly hair, and is almost bald on the Top of his Head, is an Englishman, but can talk good Dutch; Had on, and took with him, two Shirts, one white, the other checked; brown Broadcloth Coat, old blue waistcoat, with Silver Vellom Button Holes, and daubed in several Places with Paint of different Colours; Buckskin Breeches, two Pair Stockings, one black, the other brown, high quartered Shoes, with yellow Metal Buckles, and a narrow brimmed Felt Hat.

The other named Richard Rhoads, by Trade a Bricklayer, Mason and Painter, about 5 Feet 6 Inches high, and about 26 Years of Age, a streight square made Fellow, with short black hair, fair Complexion, grey Eyes; Had on, and took with him, a blue Broadcloth Coat, red Cloth Waistcoat, Buckskin Breeches, Thread and Worsted Stockings, double Channel Pumps, some white and Check Shirts, and a Castor hat. They likewise had Trowsers with them. The said Richard has Plenty of Cash, which he took up on his Master's Account. Whoever takes up and secures said Servants, so that their Masters may have them again, shall receive the above Reward, from THOMAS JONES, GEORGE WHITE, or MORDECAI PRICE.

N. B. The said Fellows were seen making toward Philadelphia or New York, and had with them a small black Horse, supposed to be stolen.

The Pennsylvania Gazette, July 12, 1764. See *The Maryland Gazette*, July 12, 1764, for Gabriel/Gabrel.

Oxford, July 13, 1764.
RAN away last Night, from the Ship *Alexander*, *Robert Erskine*, Master, lying at *Oxford*, the following six Sailors, *viz.*

Samuel Gardner, about 5 Feet 8 Inches high, fair Complexion, and pretty lusty.— *James Kennall*, about 5 Feet 7 Inches high, thin Visage, and black Complexion.— *John Summers*, 5 Feet 8 Inches high, of a brown Complexion.— *Francis Dixon*, of a thin Visage, and dark Complexion.— *John Kendall*, about 5 Feet 10 Inches high, of a brown Complexion.— *Augustus Eustus*, 5 Feet 10 Inches high, aged 50 Years, and of a brown Hue.

They went away in a Yawl, 16 Feet Keel, with a white Bottom, and her upper Streak painted blue.

Whoever takes up the said Runaways, and secures them so as they may be had again, shall have Six Pistoles Reward, or One Pistole for each; and One Pistole for the Yawl; and reasonable Charges paid, if brought to Capt. *James Reith's*, at *Annapolis*; *John Glassell's*, at *Oxford*; *Anthony M'Culloch's*, at *Queen's-Town*, or   ROBERT ERSKINE.

The Maryland Gazette, July 19, 1764; August 2, 1764.

NINE POUNDS REWARD.
RAN away from the Subscriber, living on *Elk-Ridge* in *Anne-Arundel* County, Three Servant Men, *viz.*

Henry Lasher, a *Dutchman*, about 5 Feet 6 Inches high, a well made Fellow, has brown Hair tied behind, and a down-cast Look. Had on when he went away, a Check Shirt and Trowsers, green Callimanco Waistcoat, light brown Duffel Coat, new Shoes, Copper Buckles, and a Castor Hat.

The two others are convict Servants, *viz.*

Robert Hooper, about 5 Feet 6 Inches high, a slender made Fellow, has a down-cast Look, much freckled, short curled Hair of a redish Cast. Had on, an Osnabrigs Shirt and Trowsers, blue Sailor's Waistcoat, red Ditto without Sleeves, new Hat, and new Shoes; his Shirt is much stain'd with Bark.

Edward Redkin, about 5 Feet 6 Inches high, a Shoemaker by Trade, a middling well made Fellow, has a down-cast Look, and short black frizzled Hair. Had on, an Osnabrigs Sailor's Trowsers, an Osnabrigs Shirt, a pair of old Pumps, and a new Hat. He has a large Quantity of Shoemaker's Tools with him, a Country made Sheet, a Linsey Blanket, and an old Bearskin Great Coat.

All of them are Bald-headed.

Whoever secures them in any Jail, or brings them to the Subscriber, shall receive the above Reward, or Three Pounds for either of them.
July 15, 1764.   MICHAEL SCOTT.
The Maryland Gazette, July 19, 1774.

Baltimore County, *July* 24, 1764.
BROKE Jail last Night, a certain *Darby Hernly*, a Carpenter by Trade, about 6 Feet high, well made, and a great Lover of RAW RUM, or STRONG GROGG; his Apparel very mean, but may probably be furnish'd with better, by those who are supposed to have help'd him in his Escape, as it is believ'd to have been some Time premeditated. Whoever takes up the said *Darby Hernly*, and delivers him at my Jail at JOPPA, shall receive as a Reward THIRTY POUNDS *Pennsylvania* Money.
AQUILA HALL, Sheriff.
The Maryland Gazette, July 26, 1764; August 2, 1764; August 9, 1764; August 16, 1764; August 23, 1764; August 30, 1764.

RAN away on the 26th of *July* last, from the Subscriber, living on *Soldier's Delight* in *Baltimore* County, an Indented *Irish* Servant Man, named *Dennis Wilson*, about 32 Years of Age, about 5 Feet 6 Inches high, has a large Wart on the left Side of his Neck, black curl'd Hair, fair Complexion, bald headed, and speaks with the Irish Brogue. Had on when he went away, a black Cloth Coat, a striped Lincey Jacket without Sleeves, homespun Shirt and Trowsers, old Felt Hat, and good Shoes with Strings. It is supposed he carried a Sickle with him.

Whoever takes up said Servant, and secures him so that his Master may get him again, shall have Forty Shillings Reward if taken in the Province, and Three Pounds if out of the Province, paid by

JAMES CROSSWELL.
The Maryland Gazette, August 2, 1764; August 9, 1764. See *The Maryland Gazette*, August 23, 1764.

Annapolis, July 13, 1764.
COMMITTED to my Jail this Day, as a Runaway, *Thomas Brookes*, says he belongs to *Daniel M'Pherson* of *Charles* County. Had on, an old Osnabrigs Shirt and Trowsers. Had on, an old Osnabrig Shirt and Trowsers, and an old Country Cloth Jacket.
His Master is desired to take him away, and pay Charges.
JOSEPH GALLOWAY, Sheriff.
The Maryland Gazette, August 2, 1764. See *The Maryland Gazette*, August 7, 1766, for Williams, and *The Maryland Gazette*, October 16, 1766, for Brookes.

RAN away from Fort *Loudon*, in *Pennsylvania*, on the 19th of this Instant *July*, an Indented Servant named *James Casey*, a well-set Fellow, aged 30 Years, 5 Feet 7 Inches high, and has black curl'd Hair. Had on a brown Fustian Frock, and an old Hat bound with black Ferrit; but as he is an artful Fellow, he may probably change his Dress and Name. He has a remarkable maternal Mark on his Shoulder, covered with black Hair. He rode off on a large Sorrel Mare, with a white Face, and had a portmanteau behind him, in which was a Suit of Claret colour'd Cloth, with Gold Buttons, a considerable Sum of Money, a Parcel of fine Holland Shirts, with 2 Suits of *Dresden* Ruffles, and some Silk Stockings; all which Goods, Money, and Mare, he feloniously carried away on the Day abovementioned. 'Tis thought he has made towards the lower Counties of *Pennsylvania* or *Maryland*.
Whoever takes up the said *Casey* and secures him, and the Goods and Money, shall have TEN POUNDS *Pennsylvania* Currency Reward; or FIVE POUNDS for securing the Thief in any of the Jails of *Pennsylvania*, or the neighbouring Provinces.   JOHN ORMSBY.
The Maryland Gazette, August 2, 1764.

TWENTY DOLLARS Reward.
RUN on Sunday, the 3d of June, from the Subscriber, living in Chester Town, Kent County, Maryland, a Convict Servant Man, named William Dane, a Blacksmith by Trade, born in the West of England; he is a short well-made Fellow, bow legged, appears to be about 40 Years of Age, and is a great Lover of strong Liquor: Had on, when he went away, an old light

coloured English Kersey Jacket, red Worsted Plush Breeches, Ozenbrigs Shirt, old Yarn Stockings, Pumps, with Brass Buckles in them, old Castor Hat, and wears his own Hair, which is dark and bushy. He had no Money with him; for which Reason I imagine he has got into Business, in order to get Money to pay his Passage home. Whoever takes up and secures said Servant in any of his Majesty's Goals, so as the Owner may get him again, shall have the above Reward; and if brought home, all reasonable Charges, paid by SIMON WICKES.

The Pennsylvania Gazette, August 2, 1764; August 30, 1764.

Fredericksburg, August 1, 1764.
RAN away from the Subscriber, an *English* Servant Man named *Richard Gouge*, by Trade a Blacksmith; he is a slim made Fellow, about 5 Feet 6 Inches high, about 20 Years of Age, fair Complexion, short brown Hair, which curls much (tho' it is probable he will cut it off); he has remarkable sore Eyes, generally red, occasioned by the Small-Pox, and stammers much in his Speech: Had on and with him, a dark colour'd Bearskin Coat, a light Stuff Jacket, new Thread Stockings, 2 Brown Linen Shirts, 1 fine ditto, 2 Pair of brown long Linen Breeches, new Shoes, new Silver Buckles, and a Felt Hat.

Whoever apprehends the said Runaway, and brings him to the Subscriber in *Fredericksburg*, shall have Four Pounds Reward, paid by WILLIAM HUSTON.

N. B. There are also 4 more Servants run away from the same Place; one belonging to Mr. *Lewis Willis*; another to Capt. *George Widon*, and two belonging to *Nicholas Smith*, who are supposed to be in Company with the above Fellow. They probably may have forged Passes with them, as one of the Company can write a good Hand. Six Pistoles Reward will be paid for apprehending the four last mentioned Servants.

The Maryland Gazette, August 9, 1764; August 16, 1764; August 23, 1764.

FIVE PISTOLES Reward.
Elk-Ridge, in the Province of Maryland, July 22, 1764.
RUN away from the Subscriber, an English Convict Servant Man, named Richard Smith, about 20 Years of Age, near 5 Feet 6 Inches high, has brown Hair, and is of a swarthy Complexion. Had on, and took with him, an old blue German Serge Coat, a blue Shaloon Jacket, a Pair of brown Broadcloth Breeches, an Ozenbrigs Shirt, a Felt Hat, and a Pair of Thread Hose; but he may change his Name and Apparel. He also took with him about Six Pounds in Spanish Dollars, with which he will be able make a more passable Appearance, being a pretty artful Knave, tho' he sometimes

puts on a foolish Face. Whoever apprehends the said Runaway, and brings him to the Subscriber, or secures him, so that his Master may have him again, shall have the above Reward, paid by
EPHRAIM HOWARD.
The Pennsylvania Gazette, August 9, 1764. See *The Maryland Gazette*, March 29, 1764.

August 10, 1764.
FIVE POUNDS REWARD.

RAN away last Night from the *Baltimore* Iron-Works, on *Patapsco*, a Convict Servant Man named *John Child*, by Trade a Gardener, born in *England*, and speaks broad, is about 30 Years of Age, 5 Feet 8 Inches high, wears brown curl'd Hair, and much mark'd with the Small-Pox: Had on and took with him, a fine Hat, new blue *Devonshire* Kersey Surtout Coat, trimm'd with Mohair Buttons, fine Cloth Jacket of a dark grey Colour, new purple Hair Shag Breeches, a pair of *English* Buckskin ditto very dirty, two pair of Country Thread Stockings, a pair of Pumps, two Silk Handkerchiefs, a new Check Shirt, and Osnabrigs Shirt and Trowsers.

Whoever secures said Servant, so that he may be had again, shall have, if taken in the County, Twenty Shillings, and if out of the Province, the above Reward, and reasonable Charges if brought home.
JAMES FRANKLIN.

The Maryland Gazette, August 16, 1764; August 23, 1764; August 30, 1764; *The Pennsylvania Gazette*, August 16, 1764. Minor differences between the papers. See *The Maryland Gazette*, March 15, 1764, and May 31, 1764.

RAN away the 9th Day of *May* last, from on board the Schooner *Becky*, lying in *Patapsco* River, near *Baltimore-Town*, an *English* Convict Servant Man, named *Edward Davis*, who came into the Country last Year in the *Prince William*, Capt. *M'Dougall*. He is the Property of the Hon. *John Tayloe*, Esq: of *Virginia*, is about 5 Feet 9 Inches high, clumsily made, of a very swarthy Complexion, and down Look, had his Hair lately cut off, much pitted with the Small Pox, and has a Rupture which is pretty perceptible. Had on when he went away, a grey Fearnothing Jacket, and a short blue Ditto, full of small Metal Buttons, a new Felt Hat, an Osnabrigs Shirt, one white Linen Ditto, Sailor's Trowsers, grey Worsted ribb'd Stockings, & new Country made Shoes.

As the said Servant was bred up to the Sea, it is more than probable that he would endeavour to get on board of some Ship.

Whoever takes up the said Convict Servant, and secures him so as his Master may have him again, or brings him to *John Calvert*, at Col. *Tayloe's*

Mine Bank in *Baltimore*, or to the Subscriber at Col. *Tayloe's Neabsco* Iron-Works, in *Virginia*, shall receive FIVE POUNDS Reward, and all reasonable Charges, paid by   THOMAS LAWSON.
    N. B. All Masters of Vessels are forbid harbouring on board, or carrying off, the said Servant at their Peril.
    The Maryland Gazette, August 16, 1764.

St. Mary's County, *August* 6, 1764.
RAN away from the Subscriber this Morning, an Indented Servant Man named *Patrick Diggan*, by Birth *Irish*, and by Profession a Taylor. He is about 5 Feet 6 Inches high, of a fair Complexion, and wears his own black Hair tied behind. He had on when he went away, a Frock of *Russia* Drab, a Pair of Cloth Breeches, Check Shirt, an old Castor Hat, brown Thread Stockings, and Shoes pretty much worn, with large Mourning Buckles; but as he carried with him 2 or 3 old Suits, he may probably change his Dress. The Cloaths he carried off, were an old dark colour'd Duroy Coat, and a Coat, Vest and Breeches of light blue Drugget, with a Pair of new Fustian Breeches.
    Any Person who will secure the said Servant, so as his Master may have him again, shall have a Reward of Three Pounds, and reasonable Charges paid, if brought to   EBENEZER FISHER.
    It is conjectured he has carried with him a Black Mare about 14 Hands high, has a small Star in her Forehead, paces, trots and gallops, and is branded with a Square, with 2 Prongs at the Bottom of the upright Stroke. Any Person securing the said Mare, shall have a Reward of Twenty Shillings paid, upon her being delivered to me at Leonard-Town.   E. F.
    The Maryland Gazette, August 16, 1764; August 23, 1764; August 30, 1764; September 6, 1764; September 13, 1764; September 27, 1764.

RAN away on the 11th of this Instant, from the Subscriber, living near *Annapolis*, a Servant Man named *John Ward*, this Country-born, by Trade a Carpenter or Joiner, and pretends to many other Businesses, is between 40 and 50 Years of Age, of middle Stature, is a great Lover of strong Drink, round shouldered, bald on his Forehead, has been a great Traveller, his Hair is black, and wears a Cap. His Apparel mean, but uncertain.
    It is supposed he will make towards *Virginia*, and may have some Joiners Tools with him.
    Whoever takes up and secures the above Servant, so that his Master may have him again, shall receive THREE POUNDS Reward in Dollars at the Current Rate, paid by   THOMAS RUTLAND.
    The Maryland Gazette, August 16, 1764; August 23, 1764.

Annapolis, August 16, 1764.
RAN away from the Subscribers, on the 13th Inst. a Convict Servant Man named *Henry Talbot*, a lusty Fellow, about 5 Feet 10 Inches high, of a ruddy Complexion, born in the West of *England*, and speaks much in that Country Dialect. As he is a quarrelsome Fellow, and much addicted to Liquor, he has a great Number of Scars on his Head. Had on when he went away, a blue Fearnought Jacket, Osnabrigs Shirt and Trowsers, Country made Shoes, and a new Felt Hat. As he has for some Time past been accustomed to work in a Smith's Shop, tho' not a Smith, yet he may pretend to that Business.

Whoever secures the said Servant within the County, so that he may be had again, shall receive Fifty Shillings Reward. If taken and secured in this or any other Province, Five Pounds, paid by
ISAAC HARRIS.   JONATHAN PINKNEY.
The Maryland Gazette, August 16, 1764; August 23, 1764; August 30, 1764; September 6, 1764. See *The Maryland Gazette*, July 7, 1763.

RUN away, on the 9th of July last, from the Subscriber, living in Baltimore County, an Irish Convict Servant Man, named John Hall, born in Dublin; he is of a ruddy Complexion; had on, when he went away, a light coloured Saggathy Coat, lined with brown Shaloon, Whitemetal Buttons, Breeches of the same; he had with him, when he went away, neither Hat nor Wig, a Pair of light coloured grey knit Worsted Hose, and a Pair of Shoes, half worn. Whoever takes up the said Servant, and secures him in any Goal, so that the Owner may have him again, if in the aforesaid County, shall have Forty Shillings Reward, besides what the Law allows, and if out of the County, Five Pounds, paid by   JOHN HALL, of Swan Town.
The Pennsylvania Gazette, August 16, 1764.

Anne-Arundel County, near Elkridge Landing, Maryland,
FIVE POUNDS REWARD.
RUN away from the Subscriber, on the first Day of July, an English Convict Servant Man, named James Groves, a middle sized Fellow, about 40 Years of Age with short black Hair, dark Eyes, and dark Complexion, speaks bad English, and quick, was imported into Maryland last August, in the Ship Albion, John Coal, Master; had on, when he went away, a new coarse Felt Hat, blue Cloth Coat, a Check Shirt, old Ozenbrigs Trowsers, and Country made Shoes; his Beard, when at any Length, is remarkably grey. Whoever takes up and secures said Servant, and gives Notice thereof

to the Subscriber, so that he may be had again, shall receive the above Reward, and reasonable Charges, if brought home, paid by
THOMAS FOSTER.

N. B. The said Servant may attempt to pass for a free Man, as a Discharge is missing to Matthew Kelly, dated September 1761, signed by Cornelius Ragon.

The Pennsylvania Gazette, August 16, 1764; August 30, 1764. See *The Maryland Gazette*, July 5, 1764, and *The Pennsylvania Gazette*, January 17, 1765.

Caecil County, *August* 10, 1764.

MADE his Escape from the Subscriber, on the 7th Inst. a certain *Francis Potter*, by Trade a Taylor, born in *England*, and served his Time in *Virginia*, to which Place it is imagined he is now going. He is about 5 Feet 6 Inches high, well made, and very much marked with the Small Pox: Had on and took with him, a double Allopeen Coat, of a brown Colour, a striped Linen Banyan, white Waistcoat, light coloured Cloth Breeches, blue Worsted Stockings, a Pair of half worn Pumps, with round Brass Buckles, an old brown Wig, and a Linen Cap. He is an impertinent Fellow when in Liquor, which is as often as he can get it.

Whoever takes up the said *Potter*, and will deliver him at *Caecil* County Jail, shall receive Five Pounds *Pennsylvania* Currency Reward, besides reasonable Charges, paid by   RICHARD THOMAS, Sheriff.

The Maryland Gazette, August 23, 1764; August 30, 1764; September 6, 1764; September 13, 1764.

COMMITTED to the Custody of the Sheriff of *Frederick* County, as a Runaway, one *Dennis Wilson*, who says he belongs to one *James Crosswell*, of *Baltimore* County.

His Master is desired to take him away, and pay Charges.
THOMAS PRATHER, Sheriff.

The Maryland Gazette, August 23, 1764. See *The Maryland Gazette*, August 2, 1764.

June 3, 1764.
TWENTY PISTOLES REWARD.

RAN away last Night from the Subscriber, living on *Elk-Ridge*, a Convict Servant Man named *William Lane*, he is about 5 Feet 8 Inches high, well-set, and wears brown Hair. He had on and with him, a good Felt Hat, a good brown Cloth Coat, Callico Jacket, a Fustian Ditto, Leather Breeches, and sundry other Things not particularly known. He is supposed to be in Company with another Convict Servant Man, whose name is *William*

Roberson, and who is much pitted with the Small-Pox. He had on a good Felt Hat, a Cloth Jacket, the hind Parts blue, the fore brown. He also had some other Clothes, and a Broad Sword.

Whoever takes up the said Servants, and brings them home, or secures them, so that their Master may get them again, shall have the above Reward, or Ten Pistoles for either, paid by   NATHAN DORSEY.

The Maryland Gazette, August 30, 1764; September 6, 1764; September 13, 1764; September 20, 1764; September 27, 1764; October 4, 1764; October 11, 1764; October 18, 1764; October 25, 1764; November 1, 1764; November 8, 1764; November 15, 1764; November 22, 1764; November 29, 1764; December 6, 1764. All the ads except the first have the date at the bottom. See *The Pennsylvania Gazette*, June 21, 1764.

BROKE out of *York* Jail, in *York* County, the following five Persons, *viz. Matthew Forsythe*, a thick well-set Fellow, aged about 23 Years, has red Hair, and is much freckled. Had on a white Broad-Cloth Coat, Cotton Velvet Jacket, white Stockings, and old Shoes. He is a very resolute Fellow. *John Maln*, an *Englishman*, 5 Feet 10 Inches high, of a swarthy Complexion, wears a Blanket Coat, short under Jacket, and dark brown Hair. He was confined for Felony, for which he received his Punishment. *William Philips*, a short thick well set Fellow, very remarkable for thick Legs, and is a Shewman. [*sic*] Had on a short strip'd red Jacket, and speaks much on the *Welch* Dialect. *Charles* (a Negro)....*William* (a Mulatto)....

Whoever secures the said *Matthew Forsythe*, shall receive Ten Pounds Reward, and Forty Shillings for any or either of the Rest, or Eight Pounds for the Whole, paid by   ROBERT M'PHERSON, Sheriff.

The Maryland Gazette, September 6, 1764; September 27, 1764.

TEN POUNDS REWARD.

RAN away from *Onion's* Iron-Works, in *Baltimore* County, on Sunday Night the 2d of this Inst. *Sept.* Three Convict Servant Men, *viz.*

John White, an *Irishman*, 5 Feet 9 Inches high, 23 Years of Age, of a fair Complexion, short Hair, talks very pert, and has a remarkable Scar just above his Ancle, on the Inside of his right Leg: Had on when he went away, an old Hat cock'd up two Ways, an old black Jacket, and Osnabrigs Shirt and Trowsers.

Thomas Matthews, an *Irishman*, 23 Years of Age, 5 Feet 9 or 10 Inches high of a swarthy Complexion, wears his own Hair which curls very well, a broad Face, pitted with the Small-Pox, talks very thick, and chews Tobacco: Had on and with him, when he went away, a *Dutch* Cap, blue

Serge Sailor's Jacket with small Buttons on each Side, a Check Shirt, two Frocks, Canvas Trowsers, ribb'd Worsted Stockings, and good Shoes and Buckles. He has been but a short Time in the Country, he is supposed to be a Sailor.

John Jordan, about 20 Years of Age, 5 Feet 4 Inches high, of a modest Look, and yellow Complexion: Had on when he went away, a Wig, brown Coat and Breeches, a flower'd Jacket, good Shoes and Stockings, and sundry other Cloaths in a Bundle.

All Masters of Vessels, and others, are forbid to carry them off at their Peril.

Whoever secures said Servants, and brings them to their Master, shall have, if taken in the County, Three Pounds; if out of the County, Six Pounds; and if out of the Province, the above Reward; and in Proportion for either, with reasonable Charges.   VACHEL WORTHINGTON.

The Maryland Gazette, September 6, 1764

RAN away from the Subscriber, living near *Elk-Ridge* Church, in *Anne-Arundel* County, on the 1st of this Inst. *Sept*. a Convict Servant Man named *William Hall*, an *Englishman*, about 5 Feet 8 Inches high, well made, and is pitted a little with the Small Pox. He had on and with him, a blue Cloth Coat with Metal Buttons, a grey Cloth Jacket, a white Shirt, old Leather Breeches, white ribb'd Worsted Stockings, Crocus Trowsers; two dark brown Cut Wigs, and a Castor Hat bound round the Edges with black Ferrit. As he writes a good Hand, it is probable he has forged a Pass.

Whoever takes up the said Servant, and brings him to the Subscriber, shall have, if taken Ten Miles from Home, Forty Shillings Reward; and if taken out of the County, FIVE POUNDS, paid by
GAITHER SIMPSON.

N. B. It is suspected that he has an Instrument in Writing, setting forth, That he is DUMB, as he had in England, where he was a Begging Impostor.

The Maryland Gazette, September 6, 1764; September 13, 1764. The first ad does not have the sentence beginning N. B.

September 4, 1764.
FIVE POUNDS REWARD.
RAN away last Night from the Subscriber, an Apprentice Lad named *William Young*, about 5 Feet 8 Inches high, very slim made, and round shouldered: Had on when he went away, a blue Coat and Jacket, a Pair of Breeches and blue striped Trowsers, blue Stockings, Check Shirts, two new Handkerchiefs, a Castor Hat, new Shoes, and Brass Buckles. He formerly served his Time in *Pennsylvania* with *William Downing*, Miller, and had

got his Discharge, but afterwards came voluntarily and bound himself Apprentice to me the Subscriber, to learn the Trade of Carpenter. He is supposed to have a Copy of his Discharge with him. Whoever takes up said Apprentice, and brings him to *Baltimore* Town, or secures him in any Jail, so that he may be had again, shall have the above Reward, and reasonable Charges, paid by GEORGE LINDERBERGER.
    The Maryland Gazette, September 13, 1764. See *The Pennsylvania Gazette,* September 20, 1764.

FIVE POUNDS Reward.

RUN away from the Subscriber, on the 3d inst. at Night, an Apprentice Lad, named William Young, about five Feet eight Inches high, very slim made, round shouldered, abut 23 Years of Age; had on and took with him, a blue Coat, with broad Metal Buttons, blue Jacket, with Metal Buttons, blue striped Trowsers, patched before on both Sides, blue Stockings, two Check Shirts, two Pair of old, and one Pair of new Shoes, with Brass Buckles, new Castor Hat, and two Handkerchiefs, which he got out of a Store on my account, old Leather Breeches; he formerly served his Time with Mr. William Downing, Miller, in Pennsylvania, and has got his Discharge; afterwards came and voluntarily bound himself to the Subscriber, to learn the Art of Carpentry; 'tis supposed he will go to the Millers Business again. Whoever takes up said Apprentice, and brings him to Baltimore Town, or secures him in any Goal, so that his master may have him again, shall have Five Pounds Reward, and reasonable Charges, paid by
GEORGE LINDENBERGER.
    The Pennsylvania Gazette, September 20, 1764. See *The Maryland Gazette,* September 13, 1764.

MADE an Escape from *Calvert* County Jail, a Person who assumed the Name of *Richard Richards,* and was Indicted last *June* Court under that Name for passing Counterfeit *New-Jersey* Bills; but has since proved to be a Woman, dress'd in Man's Cloaths. She had on a light colour'd Cloth Suit. Whoever will take her up, and deliver her to the Subscriber, shall receive a Reward of TEN POUNDS, TRUEMAN SKINNER, Sheriff.
    The Maryland Gazette, September 13, 1764; September 20, 1764; September 27, 1764; October 11, 1764.

September 10, 1764.
EIGHT PISTOLES REWARD.

RAN away from the Subscriber living on *Elk-Ridge,* last Night, two Servant Men, *viz.*

John Todd, an *Englishman*, about 35 Years of Age, 5 Feet 7 or eight Inches high, of a sandy Complexion, short yellowish Hair, red Beard, very Clumsy made, and walks chiefly on his Heels. Had on and took with him, an old light colour'd Drab Coat, blue Sagathy Breeches, Osnabrigs Shirt, Crocus Trowsers, old Shoes, and new Felt Hat.

Joseph Neale Bacon, a Baker, an *Englishman*, about 45 Years of Age, 5 Feet 9 or 10 Inches high, a thin Visage, partly owing to having lost several of his Teeth, short black curl'd Hair, walks very straight and upright for a Man of his Age. Had on and took with him a blue Pea Jacket, brown Thickset Breeches, check and white Shirts, Worsted and Yarn Stockings, Shoes lately soal'd, and an old Castor Hat.

It's probable they may cut off their Hair, and change their Dress, and strive to pass for Sailors, as *Bacon* was on board a Man of War for some Time before he came to this Province.

Whoever brings the said Servants to the Subscriber, shall receive as a Reward, Four Pistoles if taken in the Province; and if out of the Province, Eight Pistoles, or half for either, paid by JOHN DORSEY.

The Maryland Gazette, September 13, 1764; September 20, 1764; September 27, 1764; October 4, 1764; October 11, 1764; October 18, 1764.

RAN away from North-East Forge, in *Caecil* County, on the 4th of this Instant *September*, a Convict Servant Man named *William Hatton*, born in *Derbyshire*, and says he is a Stocking Weaver by Trade; he is a down looking Fellow, 25 Years of Age, about 5 Feet 6 Inches high, and well set. Had on when he went away, a Thick-set Coat, a scarlet Cloth Jacket, Leather Breeches, white Shirt, Worsted Stockings, a Pair of Pumps, and a good Castor Hat. He wears his own Hair, which is of a brown Colour. Whoever takes up and secures the said Servant, so that he may be had again, shall receive, if taken within 10 Miles of the said Forge, Twenty Shillings; if above 10 and under 20 Miles, Thirty Shillings; if above 20 and within 40 Miles, Fifty Shillings; and if at a greater Distance than 40 Miles, Five Pounds *Pennsylvania* Currency, and reasonable Charges if brought to the Works, paid by WILLIAM BAXTER.

The Maryland Gazette, September 13, 1764; September 27, 1764; October 4, 1764; October 11, 1764; *The Pennsylvania Gazette*, September 20, 1764. Minor differences between the papers. See *The Maryland Gazette*, October 1, 1767, *The Pennsylvania Gazette*, October 1, 1767, *The Maryland Gazette*, March 10, 1768, *The Maryland Gazette*, September 8, 1768, *The Pennsylvania* Gazette, September 15, 1768, and *The Pennsylvania Gazette*, July 6, 1769.

Baltimore County, September 10, 1764.
COMMITTED to this Jail as Runaways, Negro *Jeffery*....*Samuel Dulany*, a Shoemaker by Trade, about 5 Feet 7 or 8 Inches high, pale faced, black Hair, says he came from *Virginia*, and is thought to be the Man advertised by *George Darrel* of *George-Town*, as a Horse-stealer. *John Robeson*, says he is free, and came from *Nottingham*, has but one Eye; had on a red Jacket, and is very meanly Cloathed. He has a Woman with him, who says she is his Wife.   JOHN TAYLOR, Jailer.
The Maryland Gazette, September 13, 1764.

RUN away from the Ship Albion, Thomas Spencer Master, now lying at Chester Town, Maryland, Thomas Pamer, about 5 Feet 7 Inches high, wearing a Cap or Wig, and had on a green Pea Jacket, and narrow Trowsers. Michael Henley, about 5 Feet 6 Inches high, wears a brown Wig, a dark lappelled Coat, of a swarthy Complexion, and passes for a Native of New England. John Milton, about 5 Feet 5 Inches high, wears a brownish Coat, and his own black Hair. Whoever apprehends the abovesaid Persons, shall have Two Pistoles Reward for each, paid by THOMAS JOHNSTON.
The Pennsylvania Gazette, September 20, 1764.

MADE an Escape from *Calvert* County Jail, a Person who assumed the Name of *Richard Richards*, and was Indicted last *June* Court under that Name for passing Counterfeit *New-Jersey* Bills; but has since proved to be a Woman, dress'd in Man's Cloaths. She had on a light colour'd Cloth Suit. Whoever will take her up, and deliver her to the Subscriber, shall receive a Reward of TEN POUNDS.   TRUEMAN SKINNER, Sheriff.
The Maryland Gazette, September 27, 1764; October 11, 1764.

London-Town, Sept. 24, 1764.
RAN away Yesterday Morning from the Subscriber, Two Servant Men, the one a Convict, named *Daniel Rawson*, an *Irishman*, of a fair Complexion, thin faced, (he has been lately sick) and black Hair, stoops a little in his Shoulders, is about 5 Feet 2 or 3 Inches high: Had on and with him, a mixt Claret coloured Coat with Mohair Buttons, newly turned, a short blue double breasted Jacket, Osnabrig Breeches, and white Worsted Stockings, and is about 28 Years of Age. He is a sly, insinuating Fellow, brags much of having been on board of a Man of War, and as he writes a good Hand, he will probably forge a Pass.
The other an Indented Servant, named *Jacob Verdiman*, this Country born, and served his Time in *Pennsylvania*, is about 5 Feet 10 Inches high,

of a brown Complexion, dark coloured Hair, thin faced, and long Visage, and has a particular Way when speaking to any Person, of shutting his Eyes, especially when he has been drinking, and talks much about the Bricklayer's and Carpenter's Business. He took with him a Bricklayer's Trowil, two Line Pins with the Line, and a Plumb Rule; Had on, an old ragged light coloured Sagathy Coat, Osnabrigs Shirt and Trowsers, but they have other white Shirts with them, old Shoes, and a very good Blanket. *Verdiman* lately lived on *Kent-Island* with *Benjamin Kirby*.

Whoever takes up the said Runaways, and brings them home, shall have Forty Shillings Reward, and reasonable Charges for each, or confines them in any Jail, shall have Thirty Shillings, paid by
WILLIAM BROWN.

The Maryland Gazette, September 27, 1764; October 4, 1764; October 11, 1764.

FIFTEEN POUNDS REWARD.

Elk-Ridge Furnace, *September* 25th, 1764.
RAN away from the Subscriber, Three Convict Servant Men, all late from *England, viz.*

William Driver, about 40 Years of Age, near 6 Feet high, has short thin Hair, a long lean Face, high Forehead, reddish Nose, and round Shoulders; his Legs are long and small, with large Lumps or Knots in the Veins.

Isaac Burritt, a Youth of about 19 Years; he is near 5 Feet 8 Inches high; has many Freckles in his Face, and shews much of the Conjunctiva, or white of his Eyes.

Joseph Clarke, about 25 Years of Age; he is near 5 Feet 8 Inches high, has thin light colour'd Hair, his Complexion is pale, his Eyes black, has lost two of his upper fore Teeth, and when he walks, turns his Toes pretty much in.

They had on, and took with them, as follows, viz. 3 Cotton Jackets, 2 Pair of Breeches, 6 Osnabrigs Shirts, a light colour'd Broad Cloth Coat, with green Lining, light colour'd Fustian Jacket and Breeches, a Pair of Broad Cloth Breeches, a black flower'd Damask Waistcoat without Sleeves, 3 old Hats (one a Castor) a Pair of blue Stockings with white Tops, a Pair of coarse white Yarn Stockings, and coarse Country-made Shoes.

Whoever apprehends the said Runaways, and secures them so that their Master may have them again, shall receive, if taken within 10 Miles of Elk-Ridge Furnace, Three Pounds; and if above 10 Miles and under 20, Five Pounds, and if above 20 Miles, Nine Pounds; and if out of the Province, Fifteen Pounds Reward, (and so in Proportion for one or two) and if brought home, reasonable Charges, paid by   CALEB DORSEY.

The Maryland Gazette, September 27, 1764; October 4, 1764; October 11, 1764; October 18, 1764. See *The Maryland Gazette,* May 16, 1765, for Clarke/Clark.

Stafford County, Virginia, October 1, 1764.
TEN POUNDS REWARD.
RAN away from the Subscriber, Two *English* Servant men, *viz.*

John Buckingham, an Indented Servant, 5 feet 6 or 7 Inches high, remarkably pitted with the Small-Pox, thin visaged, wears his own dark Hair, which is just long enough to tie behind, walks as if he had a Limp in his Gait, he pretends to be a Groom, but is a Coachman. Had on when he went away, a black Velvet Jockey Cap, pretty much worn, a new light grey narrow Broadcloth Coat, lined with Shaloon of the same Colour, with broad white Metal Buttons, a superfine dark brown Broadcloth Waistcoat, with buttons of the same Colour, a Pair of Buckskin Breeches, fine white ribbed Worsted Stockings, and a Pair of channell'd Pumps: He took with him, a white Fustian Frock, the Buttons cover'd with the same, and is unlined; a light colour'd Bearskin Coat, lined with green, trimmed with yellow Metal Buttons, and a Great Coat of the same Colour; a Pink colour'd Jacket, richly trimmed with Livery Lace; and sundry other Cloaths and Linen.

John Fricker, a Convict, by Trade a Joiner and Wheelwright: Had on when he went away, an Osnabrigs Shirt (and sundry white Ones with him) a light blue Jacket without Sleeves, lined with white Tammy or Shaloon, and has yellow Metal Buttons, with a Flap over the Button Holes, a pretty good Felt Hat, and what other Cloaths I can't describe, but has taken many Things with him: It is supposed they have cut up their Blankets, to make Bags or Wallets to carry their Cloaths in. *John Fricker* is a well-made, well-looking, stout young Fellow, about 5 Feet 8 Inches high, and wears his own dark Hair, combed back and tied behind. *Buckingham* has forged a Pass, to which he has put Mr. *Baily Washington's* Name, and mine.
WILLIAM BRENT.

The Maryland Gazette, October 11, 1764; October 18, 1764; October 25, 1764; November 1, 1764; November 8, 1764; November 15, 1764; November 22, 1764. See *The Maryland Gazette,* June 21, 1774, for Fricker.

RAN away from the Subscriber, living *Elk-Ridge* in *Anne-Arundel* County, on the 23d of *Sept.* last, a Servant Man named *Peter Grussely,* about 5 Feet 5 Inches high, of a sandy Complexion: Had on, an Osnabrigs Shirt and Trowsers, an Everlasting Waistcoat, without Sleeves, a Felt Hat, and old Shoes; his left Arm is very remarkable, being near 4 Inches shorter than his

Right. He took with him a Grey Horse, about 13 Hands high, and 4 Years old, no Brand.

Whoever takes up the said Servant and Horse, and secures them so that the Subscriber may get them again, shall have Five Pounds Reward, paid by   ROBERT BROWN.

The Maryland Gazette, October 11, 1764; October 18, 1764.

RAN away from the Subscriber, living at *Broad-Creek*, on *Patowmack* River, in *Prince-George's* County, on Friday the [1]8th of *Sept.* last, a Convict Servant Man, named *Jonathan Darbyshire*, aged about 35 Years, a lusty, well set, strong made Fellow, 6 Feet high, broad over the Shoulders, long black Hair, and dark Complexion: Had on when he went away, an old Drab coloured Cloth Coat, patched on the Shoulders, old Hat, Shoes and Stockings: As he is just come from on Board a Ship, his Cloaths are much Tarr'd. It is supposed he will make towards *Philadelphia*. He is a Miller by Trade, and says he understands Weaving. Whoever will bring the said Servant to his Master, shall, if taken in this Province, receive a Reward of Three Pounds, and if out of the Province, Five Pounds, paid by
ENOCH MAGRUDER.

The Maryland Gazette, October 11, 1764. See *The Maryland Gazette*, October 18, 1764.

RAN away from the Subscriber, living on *Elk-Ridge*, on the 12th of this Instant *October*, a Convict Servant named *John Hubberd*, a likely, fresh colour'd Man, about 25 Years of Age, about 5 Feet 8 Inches high, wears his own brown Hair, has a Scar on his right Cheek, and is marked on his left Hand with Gunpowder I H. His Apparel, a new white Cotton Jacket, old brown Great Coat with one Button, blue Cloth Breeches, old Leather Ditto, Osnabrig Shirt, old Trowsers, old Worsted Stockings, old Shoes, and old Hat. He was a Sailor on board a Man of War, has been in *Philadelphia*, and 'tis probable he will make that Way. All Masters of Vessels, and others, are forbid to carry him off at their Peril.

Whoever takes up the said Servant, and brings him to the Subscriber, shall have, if taken 10 Miles from home, Thirty Shillings beside what the Law allows; if 20 Miles from home, Fifty Shillings; and if out of the Province, Five Pounds, paid by   JAMES WOOD.

The Maryland Gazette, October 18, 1764; October 25, 1764. See *The Pennsylvania Gazette*, December 6, 1764.

RAN away from the Subscriber, living at *Broad-Creek* in *Prince-George's* County, on Sunday Night, the 14th of this Instant *October*, Two Convict Servant Men, *viz.*

Jonathan Darbyshire, a lusty young Fellow, about 6 Feet high, of a dark Complexion, and long black Hair: Had on when he went away, an old Drab Cloth Coat much worn, greased and tarred as he lately came from on board a Ship, an old Jacket and Breeches, Shoes and Stockings, and an old Hat.

Edward Bishen, a lusty well-set young Fellow, about 20 Years of Age, about 5 Feet 10 Inches high, of a fair Complexion, grey Eyes, and by Trade a Shoe-maker: Had on when he went away, an old light colour'd Pea Jacket, black Serge-Denim Breeches, black Worsted Stockings, and Country made Shoes. It is probable he may change his Apparel, as he took with him a Snuff colour'd Cloth Coat, and Cotton Jacket; he also took with him, a Set of Shoe-maker's Tools, and some Soal and Upper Leather.

Whoever will secure the said Servants, and bring them to the Subscriber, shall receive a Reward of Three Pounds, if taken in the Province; and if taken out of the Province, FIVE POUND, and reasonable Charges, paid by   ENOCH MAGRUDER.

The Maryland Gazette, October 18, 1764; October 25, 1764. See *The Maryland Gazette*, October 11, 1764, for Darbyshire.

October 12, 1764.
FIVE POUNDS Reward.

RUN away last Sunday, from the Subscriber, living in Cecil County, Maryland, near Susquehanna, an Irish Servant Man, named Michael Connel, about 25 or 30 Years of Age, of middle Stature, by Trade a Taylor; has black Hair, tied behind, dark brown Eyes, sandy coloured Beard; had on, when he went away, a dark Frize Coat, turned, with Horn Buttons, a light blue Jacket, without Sleeves, lined with different Colours, old Leather Breeches, old Felt Hat, new turned Pumps, with large Pewter Buckles. He was born in Munster, and has much of the Brogue. Whoever takes up said Servant, and secures him, so that his Master may have him again, shall have the above Reward, and, if brought home, reasonable Charges, paid by JAMES BUCHANAN.

The Pennsylvania Gazette, October 18, 1764.

RAN away from the Subscriber, living in *Calvert* County, one *John Rice*, an *Irishman*, who is Indebted to the Subscriber; he has a large Blemish in one of his Eyes, with a pretty full Face, wears his Hair, which is of a brown or sandy Colour, and will pretend to be a Blacksmith, tho' he has worked at the Carpenter's Business; he took with him, a Broad Axe, and some other Carpenter's Tools. He had on a blue Sailor's Waistcoat, a thin red strip'd Ditto, Osnabrigs Shirt, and wide Sailor's Trowsers: He stole from the Landing a large Poplar Canoe, upwards of 25 Feet in Length, with a round Head and Stern, her Stern seat made of Pine Plank, and her Head of Oak Ditto, and has an Iron Chain 8 Feet long.

Whoever will take up and secure him, and the Canoe, so that they may be had again, shall have a Reward of Forty Shillings, or Twenty for either.
SAMUEL CHEW, of Wells.

The Maryland Gazette, October 25, 1764; November 1, 1764.

ALEXANDRIA, *October* 30, 1764.
RAN away the 23d of this Inst. from *Thomas Willcoxen's*, in *Prince-George's* County, in *Maryland*, a Convict Servant called *Jan Jonas Van de Huville*, born in *Rotterdam*, and speaks bad *English*; he is a well made, fresh looking, hearty Fellow, about 40 Years of Age, 5 Feet 10 Inches high, wears black Hair, cued or tied, and has a remarkable Blemish in one of his Eyes, I think the right Eye. Had on when he went away, a blue Broadcloth Coat and Jacket, a Pair of white Cloth Breeches, a Castor Hat, and good Shoes and Stockings: He took with him a Case of Surgeon's Needles, a Silver Probe and Lancets. As he practiced Physic some Time at the said *Willcoxen's*, and received Money of several of my Patients, he may appear like a Gentleman.

Whoever apprehends and secures the said *De Huville*, so that I may have him again, shall have Two Pistoles Reward, beside what the Law allows.   JAMES LAURIE.

The Maryland Gazette, November 1, 1764; November 8, 1764; November 22, 1764; November 29, 1764.

RUN away from the Subscriber, on the 4th of October instant, living in the Fork of Gunpowder, near Major Thomas Franklin's, Baltimore County, Maryland, an indented Irish Servant Lad, named Owen Pharley, about 20 years of Age, 5 Feet 6 Inches high, round Face, fresh Colour, wears his Hair, a Weaver by Trade; Had on, and took with him a new Castor Hat, a whitish coloured German Serge Coat, Buttons bluish, an old Jacket of Irish Cloth, much worn, a Pair of Buckskin Breeches, almost new, a Pair of new Shoes, and Thread Stockings, and 3 Country Linen Shirts; took also an English Saddle, and Snaffle Bridle, half worn, with a whitish Saddle cloth, trimmed with blue Binding, and a sorrel roan Mare, long Blaze down her Face, between 13 and 14 Hands high, bob Tail. whoever secures the said Servant, so that the Owner may get him again, shall receive (if in the

County) Thirty Shillings, Pennsylvania Currency, Reward, besides what the Law allows, and if our of the County Five Pounds, and reasonable Charges, paid by   GEORGE SMITH.
The Pennsylvania Gazette, November 1, 1764; November 29, 1764.

RAN away from the Subscriber on the 1st of *October* last, a Convict Servant Woman named *Margaret Cane*, a tall slim Woman, dark brown Hair, dark Complexion, and is pitted with the Small-Pox, her little Finger and the next to it lies in the Palm of her Left Hand, and was occasioned by a Burn when a Child: Her Dress when she went away, was a blue plain Petticoat, a Linen ditto, a stampt Cotton Jacket, a Linen ditto, Check Apron, a Womans old Hat, and Osnabrigs Shift.

Whoever secures the said Servant in any Jail, shall have SIX DOLLARS Reward; and if brought to the Subscriber, in *Port-Tobacco* Town, in *Charles* County, the above Reward, and reasonable Charges, paid by   BENJAMIN PHILPOTT.

N. B. She is fond of Drink, likes Sailors Company much, and all Masters of Vessels are forewarned carrying her off at their Peril.

The Maryland Gazette, November 8, 1764; November 15, 1764; November 22, 1764; November 29, 1764; December 6, 1764. See *The Maryland Gazette*, December 13, 1764.

Baltimore County, *November* 11, 1764.

RAN away last Night from *Northampton* Iron-Works, an Irish Convict Servant Man, named *Cornelius Trimble*, a Coach Harness-maker by Trade, about 5 Feet 6 Inches high, of a sandy Complexion: Had on & took with him, a light colour'd close-bodied Coat, red Jacket and Breeches, new white Kersey Breeches, old grey Worsted Stockings, new Negro Shoes, with Straps lately sewed to them, Osnabrigs Shirt, half worn Castor Hat, and brown cut Wig. He has a large Scar over his Forehead, occasioned by his Scull being fractured, which is therefore very soft. It is supposed he has a forged Pass.

Whoever secures the said Servant, so as his Masters get him again, shall have, if taken Ten Miles from home, 30 Shillings; if out of the County, 3 Pounds; if out of the Province Four Pounds; and reasonable Charges if brought home; paid by   CHARLES RIDGELY, & Co.

The Maryland Gazette, November 15, 1764; November 22, 1764; November 29, 1764; December 6, 1764; December 13, 1764; December 20, 1764. See *The Maryland Gazette*, January 31, 1765.

RAN away from the Subscribers, in the City of *Annapolis*, on Sunday the 21st Day of *October* last, a Convict Servant Man named *John Clark*, a Blacksmith by Trade, born in the West of *England*, much pitted with the Small-Pox, and has a large Sore on his Right Leg, which occasions him to be lame, and his Leg much swell'd; he is about 5 Feet 9 Inches high, round shoulder'd and stoops in his Walk, is a lusty Fellow, and wears his own Hair, which is black and curls, full faced, and black Eyes; he is about 27 Years of Age. Had on when he went away, a new Felt Hat, white Shirt, blue Fearnought Jacket, and light colour'd Cloth Under-Jacket, a Pair of new Buckskin Breeches, black Worsted Stockings, and a Pair of grey Yarn ditto, and Country made shoes; but as he is an artful Villain, he may have procured other Cloathing. It is supposed he went away in Company with a free Woman, who served her Time with Dr. *John Stevenson* in *Baltimore-Town*, and perhaps they may pass for Man & Wife.

Whoever secures the said Servant, so that he may be had again, shall receive FIVE POUNDS Reward, paid by
ISAAC HARRIS,   JONATHAN PINKNEY.

The Maryland Gazette, November 15, 1764; November 22, 1764; November 29, 1764; December 6, 1764; January 10, 1765; January 17, 1765; January 24, 1765; January 31, 1765; February 7, 1765; February 14, 1765; *The Pennsylvania Gazette*, November 15, 1764; December 13, 1764; January 31, 1765. Minor differences between the papers.

RAN away from the Subscriber, living near *Snowden's* Iron-Works, on Sunday the 6th Day of *October* last, a Convict Servant Woman, named *Mary Brady*, about 5 Feet high, round Face, fresh Colour, black Hair, black Eyes, broad Nose, a remarkable Mole on her left Cheek, thick set: Had on when she went away, a stampt Cotton Gown, full of black Spots, one white Dimity Ditto, a black Quilted Petticoat, one strip'd Country Cloth Ditto, a red Cardinal, one coarse Shift, *English* Shoes, Thread Stockings, and sundry other Things.

Whoever takes up and brings home the said Servant, shall receive Forty Shillings Reward, beside what the Law allows, paid by
ALICE DAVIS.

The Maryland Gazette, November 15, 1764; November 22, 1764.

Calvert County, *Nov*, 14, 1764.
RAN away from the Subscriber, an Indented Servant Man named *William Connant*, a stout Fellow, about 25 Years of Age, and much given to Drinking: His Apparel uncertain, but chiefly such as used by Seamen: He

has some Relation about *Pig-Point*, and has been sometime past in that Neighbourhood, and may still be lurking about there.

Whoever takes up the said Servant, and secures him in any Jail, shall have a Reward of Twenty Shillings, and reasonable Charges if brought home, paid by BETTEY WILKINSON.

The Maryland Gazette, November 22, 1764; November 29, 1774.

November 27, 1764.

RAN away last Night, from the Subscriber at *Patapsco* Ferry in *Anne-Arundel* County, Two *English* Servant Men, *viz.*

John Parker, an Indented Servant, about 5 Feet 6 Inches high, a fresh well looking Fellow, wears his own Hair, which is black, and tied behind with a black Ribbon. Had on a red double breasted Soldiers Jacket, bound round with white and yellow Binding, with Metal Buttons, a Pair of Leather Breeches, with long Trowsers over them, grey Stockings, coarse Negro Shoes, and a good Hat. He appears to be about 25 Years old, has been a Soldier, and perhaps may have a Discharge from the Army. He carried away with him a light colour'd Surtout Coat, white and Check Shirts, and other Things.

The other is a Convict named *John Wilkins*, about 5 Feet 5 Inches high, pitted with the Small-Pox, has a down Look, wears his own dark Hair, which is short. Had on a half worn Felt Hat, a coarse blue Coat, with Metal Buttons, a Pair of Cotton Breeches, with long Trowsers over them, Yarn Stockings, and coarse Negro Shoes. He has lost the first Joint of one of his Fingers.

They are both very well-set Fellows.

Whoever takes up the said Servants, and secures them in any Jail, so that they may be had again, shall have Forty Shillings Reward for each, if taken 40 Miles from home; if out of the Province, Five Pounds Reward for each, and reasonable Charges if brought home, paid by
FLORA DORSEY.

The Maryland Gazette, November 29, 1764. See *The Maryland Gazette*, April 11, 1765, and *The Pennsylvania Gazette*, April 18, 1765, for Wilkins.

RUN away from the Subscriber, living on Elk Ridge, Maryland, an English Convict Servant Man, named John Hubbard, a likely fresh coloured Man, about 25 Years of Age, 5 Feet 8 Inches high, has brown Hair, and a Scar on his Right cheek, and is marked on the Left hand I H, pricked in with Gunpowder, his Apparel a new white Cotton Jacket, blue Cloth Breeches, old Leather Ditto, Ozenbrigs Shirt, new Yarn Stockings, and new Country made Shoes nailed, an old Hat, and had on an Iron Collar. He has been a Sailor on board a Man of War, and has been in Philadelphia, it is probable will make that Way. Whoever takes up the said Servant, and brings him to the Subscriber, shall have, if taken ten Miles from home, Twenty Shillings, and if twenty Miles from home, Forty Shillings, and if out of the Province, Three Pounds, paid by JAMES HOOD.

N. B. All Masters of Vessels, and others, are forbid to carry him off at their Peril.

The Pennsylvania Gazette, December 6, 1764; January 31, 1765. See *The Maryland Gazette*, October 18, 1764

COMMITTED to *Anne-Arundel* County Jail, as Runaways,

John Scham, he is thick and well made, about 5 Feet 10 Inches high, wears his own Hair, had on a red Drugget Coat and Waistcoat, Buckskin Breeches, Osnabrigs Shirt, Yarn Hose, and Country made shoes.

Margaret Cane, a tall slim Woman, much pitted with the Small-Pox, and says she belongs to *Benjamin Philpott*, in *Port-Tobacco*. Their Masters are desired to pay Charges, and take them away.

ROBERT HENWARD, Jailer.

The Maryland Gazette, December 13, 1764; December 20, 1764; December 27, 1764. See *The Maryland Gazette*, November 8, 1764, for Cane.

RUN away from the Subscribers, living in Cecil County, Maryland, the 28th of November last, a Servant Man, named William Hannah, about 39 Years of Age, about 5 Feet 8 Inches high, of a dark Complexion, black Hair mixed with grey, much pitted with the Small-Pox, talks well, much inclined to Drink, a Sadler by Trade; had on, when he went away, a light coloured Coat and Jacket, with Hair Buttons, a Pair of Buckskin Breeches, blue Yarn Stockings, a light coloured Great Coat, a good Beaver Hat. Whoever takes up said Servant, and secures him, so that the Owners may have him again, shall have Three Pounds Reward, and reasonable Charges, paid by THOMAS COOK, and HUGH GLASFORD.

The Pennsylvania Gazette, December 13, 1764.

COMMITTED to Custody of the Sheriff of *Anne-Arundel* County, on Suspicion of being a Runaway, and belonging to Col. *Philip Lee*, in *Virginia*, a Man about 5 Feet 6 Inches high, of a dark Complexion, and had on a light Cloth Great Coat, brown Cloth under Coat, and black Waistcoat,

Buckskin Breeches, and a black bob Wig; and says his name is *William Ferguson*.
His Master is desired to take him away, and pay Charges.
ROBERT HENWARD, Jailer.
The Maryland Gazette, December 20, 1764; December 27, 1764; January 3, 1764.

RAN away about the First of *November* last, from the Subscriber, living near *Bladensburg*, in *Prince-George's* County, *Maryland*, a Convict Servant Man named *Patrick Carroll*, born in *Ireland*, by Trade a Butcher; he is a lusty well-made Fellow, about 5 Feet 8 inches high; he has lost the Fourth Finger of his Left Hand, has remarkable black Hair, which he wears short, and is pitted with the Small-Pox, is very talkative, and excessive fond of strong Liquor. He had on when he went away, a dark Cloth Coat, Check Shirt, and a Pair of Boots: The rest of his Apparel can't be described. He carried with him a dark Chesnut Sorrel Horse, about 13 Hands high. He obtained a Pass from a Magistrate of this County, by making him believe he was a Freeman.
Whoever takes up the said Servant, and secures him in any Jail, so that his Master may get him again, shall receive Two Pistoles Reward, from NATHANIEL POPE.
The Maryland Gazette, December 27, 1764; January 3, 1765; January 10, 1765; *The Pennsylvania Gazette*, January 17, 1765; January 31, 1765. Minor differences between the papers.

1765

Anne-Arundel County, near Elkridge Landing, Maryland.
FIVE POUNDS REWARD.
RUN away from the Subscriber, on the first Day of July, an English Convict Servant Man, named James Groves, a middle-sized Fellow, about 40 Years of Age, with short black Hair, dark Eyes, and dark Complexion, speaks bad English, and quick, was imported into Maryland last August, in the Ship Albion, John Coal, Master; had on, when he went away, a new coarse Felt Hat, blue Cloth Coat, a Check Shirt, old Ozenbrigs Trowsers, and Country made Shoes; his Beard, when at any Length, is remarkably grey. Whoever takes up and secures said servant, and gives Notice thereof to the Subscriber, so that he may be had again, shall receive the above Reward, and reasonable Charges, if brought home, paid by
THOMAS FOSTER.

N. B. The said Servant may attempt to pass for a free Man, as a Discharge is missing to Matthew Kelly, dated September 1762, signed by Cornelius Ragon.
The Pennsylvania Gazette, January 17, 1765; January 31, 1765; February 14, 1765. See *The Pennsylvania Gazette*, August 16, 1764, and *The Maryland Gazette*, July 5, 1764.

RAN away from the Subscriber living near *Annapolis*, on the 19th of this Inst. *January*, a *Welch* Convict Servant Woman, named *Anne Griffin*, of a middle Stature, about 32 Years of Age, fresh colour'd, and of a dark Complexion: Had on and took with her, a Partridge colour'd Gown, an old white Cotton Petticoat, an old quilted Ditto, Osnabrigs Shifts with white Sleeves, old Country made Shoes with high Leather Heels, 1 Blanket, 1 Sheet, 1 Check Apron, 1 Check and 2 Silk Handkerchiefs, a white Country Cloth Petticoat, a Scarlet Cloak, 1 pair of blue Worsted Stockings, a pair of white Cotton Ditto, and 2 pair of Yarn Ditto, a pair of small Stays, and a Man's black Hat.

Whoever takes up the said Servant, and secures her so as the Subscriber may get her again, shall receive Twenty Shillings Reward, paid by   EDWARD OSMOND.
The Maryland Gazette, January 24, 1765.

THERE is in my Custody, committed as a Runaway, a Man about 5 Feet 6 Inches high, clad in a blue Coat, red Jacket, and Breeches, a Scar in his Forehead, is a very simple Fellow, pretends to be a Schoolmaster, and is supposed to be the Man advertised by Mr. *Charles Ridgely*, the 10th of *November* last.

His Master is desired to take him away, and pay Charges.
JEREMIAH JORDAN, Sheriff of *St. Mary's* County.
The Maryland Gazette, January 31, 1765; February 7, 1765; February 14, 1765. See *The Maryland Gazette*, November 15, 1764.

TWENTY POUNDS REWARD.

BROKE out of *Anne-Arundel* County Jail, the Two following Persons, who were committed for Horse-stealing.

John Ferroll, about 5 Feet high, wears his own Hair, and is about 22 Years old.

Dennis Ferroll, about 20 Years of Age, has black Hair, and is about 22 Years old.

Whoever takes up and secures the said Fellows, so that the Subscriber may have them again, shall receive the above Reward, or Ten Pounds for either; and if brought to *Annapolis*, reasonable Charges will be allowed.
JOSEPH GALLOWAY, Sheriff.

The Maryland Gazette, February 7, 1765; February 21, 1765; February 28, 1765; March 21, 1765; March 28, 1765; April 4, 1765. See *The Maryland Gazette*, June 27, 1765, for Dennis Ferroll. See *The Maryland Gazette*, November 24, 1763, for John Ferroll.

FIVE POUNDS REWARD.

RAN away from *Deer-Creek*, in the upper Part of *Baltimore* Country, *Abraham Everhatt*, Taylor, a *German*, speaks broken English very quick, something like the Neutral *French*, about 5 Feet 8 Inches high, of a dark Complexion, and black Hair. Had on when he went away, a blue Surtout Coat; his other Cloaths not known, as he had several Suits with him belonging to Gentlemen who had given him Cloth to make up, and carried away with him a Quantity of blue Broadcloth, and Trimmings, the Number of Yards not known. He rode a remarkable small, pretty, black Horse.

Whoever takes up and secures the said *Everhatt*, so that he may be had again, and gives Information to the Subscriber near *Deer-Creek*, shall receive the above Reward, and reasonable Charges.
NATHANIEL JOHN GILES.

The Maryland Gazette, February 14, 1765; February 21, 1765; February 28, 1765; March 7, 1765; March 21, 1765; March 28, 1765; April 4, 1765.

Virginia, Falmouth, Feb. 15, 1765.

RAN away from the Subscriber, on Wednesday the 13th of this Instant *February*, the Four following Servants, lately Imported into *Rappahannock* River, in the *New Success*, Capt. *Hay*, from *London, viz.*

James Reed, a Sailer, about 5 Feet 8 or 9 Inches high, has a Stoop in his Shoulders, wears his own black Hair, dark Complexion. Had on a blue Sailor's Jacket, black Waistcoat, and Trowsers.

Joshua Cooper, about 5 Feet 7 Inches high, well-set, wears a letter'd Woollen Cap. Had on a Sailor's Jacket, and long wide Trowsers.

Benjamin Hobbs, a very thin made Man, about 5 Feet 8 Inches high, lame in his right Wrist. Had on a blue Waistcoat, and wears his own light brown Hair.

Thomas Watkins, a stout well-made Man, about 5 Feet 6 Inches high, wants a Finger on his right Hand, and wears a Wig. Had on a light Drab Thickset Coat, dark brown Waistcoat, and a Pair of Jockey Boots.

Ran away also from Mr. *Crop's*, at *Deep-Run*, on the 15th Instant, *Robert Roads*, Imported in the same Ship, born in *Staffordshire*, between 30 and 40 Years of Age, about 5 Feet 7 or 8 Inches high, of a pale Complexion, wears straight black Hair, a light Cloth Surtout Coat, black Waistcoat, Buckskin Breeches, blue grey Yarn Hose. On his left Hand he wants a Joint of his two fore Fingers.

Whoever will apprehend the said Servants, and bring them to the Subscriber, shall receive for each Thirty Shillings Reward.
JOHN BRIGGS.
The Maryland Gazette, February 21, 1765; February 28, 1765.

SIX POUNDS Reward.
STOLEN from the Subscriber, near Deer Creek, in Baltimore County, Maryland, a small Mouse coloured Horse, his Mane close trimmed, bob tail, with Saddle and Bridle, by Abraham Stephens, a Dutchman (but says he is an Englishman) about 5 Feet 8 Inches high, by Trade a Taylor, thin faced, swarthy Complexion, short black hair, speaks but indifferent English, much given to drinking and singing; had on, when he went away, a Suit of blue Broadcloth, trimmed with Mohair Buttons, and a blue Surtout, with Metal Buttons; also took with him a small Piece of brown Cotton Velvet, a Piece of double milled Drab, with many other Pieces of Cloth; he said he served some Time in Amboy, and is supposed to have gone that Way. Whoever takes up and secures said Stephens and Horse, shall have the above Reward, paid by ROBERT DUNN.

N. B. Whoever takes up either Stephens or Horse, or both, are desired to write to the Subscriber, either by Post, or otherwise.
The Pennsylvania Gazette, February 21, 1765. See *The New-York Gazette*, February 25, 1765.

Maryland, February 14, 1765.
SIX POUNDS REWARD,
STOLEN from the Subscriber, near Deer Creek, Baltimore County, Maryland, a small mouse-coloured Horse, his Mane close trimmed, bob-tail, with Saddle and Bridle, by one Abraham Stephens, a Dutchman (but says he is an Englishman) about five Feet eight Inches high, by Trade a Taylor, thin faced, short black hair, speaks but indifferent English, much given to Drunkenness, and singing. Had on when he went away, a Suit of blue Broad Cloth trimmed with Mohair Buttons, a blue Surtout with metal buttons. Also took with him a small Piece of brown cotton Velvit, a Piece of double mill'd Drab, with many other Pieces of Cloth. He said, he served some Time in Amboy: It is supposed he is gone that Way. Whoever takes

up and secures said Stephens, and Horse, shall have the above Reward paid by   ROBERT DUNN.
   N. B. Whoever takes up said Stephens, or Horse, or both, are desired to write to the Subscriber by Post, or otherwise.
   The New-York Gazette, February 25, 1765; March 4, 1765; March 18, 1765. See *The Pennsylvania Gazette*, February 21, 1765.

WHEREAS a certain John Patton, that came to these parts of the Country some Time last June from New York, and as we are informed ran away from thence considerably in Debt, and did pretend to follow the FullerBusiness at a Fulling mill belonging to Mr. George Lawson, in Cecil County, Maryland, where he run greatly in Debt, and absconded from the said Place without discharging the same; those that will take up and secure the said Patton in any Goal on the Continent, shall be rewarded with Fifteen Pounds, on giving Notice to the Subscribers. Said Patton is a Scotch man, and has been on board a Man of War, is about 5 Feet 10 Inches high, a well looking Man, wears black Hair; had on, when he went away, a half worn Fur Hat, blue Coat, light coloured Velvet Jacket, black Leather Breeches, blue Stockings, good Shoes, and rode a bay Horse, about 9 Years old, with good Saddle and Bridle; he is pretty talkative, and given to extol himself by the Way of Lying, and pretends to be a Seaman; it is supposed, he will endeavour to get on board some Vessel. Whoever secures the said John Patton, shall be entitled to the above Reward, paid by
THOMAS COOK, JOHN STRAWBRIDGE, JOHN LOCHRIDGE, and ROBERT CORRY.
   The Pennsylvania Gazette, February 28, 1765.

RAN away, the 13th of *January* last, from the Subscriber, living near *Upper-Marlborough* in *Prince-George's* County, a Country-born Servant Man, named *William Thackfeild*, about 5 Feet 8 Inches high, a pert, fresh looking, young Fellow, about 21 or 22 Years of Age, wears his own Hair, tied behind, which is very black, and has a bad Impediment in his Speech. Had on when he went away, a Bearskin Coat, with a Velvet Cape, a blue Cloth Jacket, old Leather Breeches, new Shoes, and mill'd Worsted Stockings. He was an Orphan Boy brought up by one Mr. *Davis* on Elk Ridge, and from thence removed near *Bladensburg,* where he was under the Necessity of becoming a Servant.
   Whoever takes up the said Servant, and brings him home, or secures him in any Jail, so as his Master may have him again, shall have Forty Shillings Reward, paid by   HENRY BROOKES.

The Maryland Gazette, March 7, 1765; March 14, 1765; March 21, 1765; March 28, 1765.

Virginia, February 27, 1765.

RAN away from the Subscriber, on *Rappahannock* River, on Friday Night the 15th Instant, Three Servant Men, imported last Summer in the *Molly*, from *London, viz*.

John Morris, a Groom and Farmer, about 35 Years old, and 5 Feet 10 Inches high, stoops as he walks, of a fair Complexion, thin faced, very slow in his Speech. Had on when he went away, a Bearskin Jacket and Breeches lined with white Plading, trimm'd with black Horn Buttons, old Velvet Cap, and a Worsted one, notwithstanding his own Hair, which is not very long; and has a Wig with him, Plad Stockings, and Country-made Shoes.

James Plato, by Trade a Gardener, about 30 Years old, 5 Feet 8 Inches high, of a fair Complexion, well made, and very talkative. Had on when he went away, a Bearskin Jacket and Breeches lined with white Plading, trimm'd with black Horn Buttons, old brown Cut Wig, Felt Hat, brown Linen Shirt, Plad Stockings, and Country-made Shoes.

John Wood, a Sailor, about 40 or 40 odd Years old, of a dark Complexion, 5 Feet 8 Inches high. Had on when he went away, a Felt Hat, old grey Cut Wig, blue Fearnought Jacket, with black Horn Buttons, Cotton Drawers, old brown Linen Trowsers, brown Linen Shirt, Plad Stockings, and Country-made shoes.

The above Men stole a Boat cieled [*sic*] in the Inside. She was built for a Ferry Boat, and will carry 4 Horses in smooth Water. She is now pretty old, has had several Pieces of Plank put in her Bottom, built low, and very broad. They also stole and carried in her, a new Cast Chimney Back, 3 or 4 new Pails, Abundance of Rugs and Blankets, some of which I have room to think they will make use of for a Sail, and by what I can learn from my Servants, they used frequently to be talking of *Philadelphia*, where, I am told, *Wood* has been; therefore am inclined to think they will endeavour getting there, either by crossing the Bay to the Eastern Shore, or going along the Western Side under the Shore.

Whoever takes up the above Servants, and delivers them to me on *Rappahannock* River, shall have Five Pounds Reward, if taken in this Colony: If out of it, Five Pounds for each, and so in Proportion for as many as are taken.

The Boat would also be worth a Premium the delivering her to
ARCHIBALD RITCHIE.

The Maryland Gazette, March 7, 1765; March 14, 1765; March 21, 1765.

RAN away on the 25th of *February* last, one *George Gibbins*, son of *George*, an Indented Servant belonging to the Subscriber, living near the Eastern Branch of *Patowmack*; he is a thick, well-set Fellow, about 28 Years of Age, wears his own Hair, his fore Finger of one of his Hands is considerably larger than any other of his Fingers, is an idle drunken Fellow, by Trade a House Carpenter and Joiner, understands the Cooper's Trade and Shoemaking, and is a good Hand in a Ship Yard, and about 5 Feet 7 Inches high. He had on a light Frize Coat, with Brass Buttons, an old Check Shirt, a Pair of blue flower'd Everlasting Breeches, Country made Shoes and Stockings, and a Leather Apron. He took with him a Ship Carpenter's Broad Ax. His Father lives in Prince-George's County, about 2 Miles from the Brick Church.

Whoever apprehends the said Servant, and delivers him to the Subscriber, or confines him in any County Jail, so that his Master may have him again, shall have Three Pounds Reward, paid by
WILLIAM HOWARD.
The Maryland Gazette, March 7, 1765.

York Furnace, *Maryland, February* 4, 1765.
RAN away from the Subscriber, an *English* Servant Man, named *William Hulet*, speaks the *West* Country Dialect, has been about 8 Years in the Country, of low Stature, short black Hair: Had on when he went away, a blue Broadcloth Coat, with white Metal Buttons, an Osnabrigs Shirt, Trowsers made of Ravens Duck, old Hat and Stockings, and a new Pair of Shoes.

Whoever takes up the said Servant, so that his Master may have him again, shall have Twenty Shillings Reward, if taken within 20 Miles of the said Furnace; if above that Distance Thirty Shillings, and reasonable Charges, paid by   BENJAMIN SWOPE.

N. B. It is expected the abovemention'd Servant may stop at the Head of Severn, as it is said he has a Brother-in-Law lives near that Place, by Trade a Sail-maker.

The Maryland Gazette, March 7, 1765; March 14, 1765; March 21, 1765; March 28, 1765.

RUN away from the subscriber, living in Kent county, Maryland, a servant man, named James Hawkins, by trade a butcher, an Englishman, came into the country last January, he is a convict, about 5 feet 10 inches high, well made, his eyes remarkably small and black; his apparel is a blue coat and jacket, buckskin breeches very dirty, with stockings for sleeves to his

jacket. Whoever secures said servant, so as his master may have him again, shall receive Two Pistoles reward, paid by   EDWARD COSTOLOW.
The Pennsylvania Gazette, March 28, 1765.

Patuxent Iron-Works, *April* 3, 1765.
RAN away from the Subscriber, the 31st of last Month, an *Irish* Servant Man, named *John Watkins*, he is a thick well made Man, about 5 Feet 8 Inches high, full faced, has a Scar near one Corner of his Mouth, and dark brown Hair. Had on and took with him, a light colour'd Thickset Coat, with Mohair Buttons, a red Cloth Jacket, double breasted, a blue Pea Jacket, white Kersey Breeches, striped Cotton Trowsers, grey ribb'd Stockings, County made Shoes, two Shirts, one brown Sheeting, the other Osnabrigs. It is likely he will pass for a Joiner, or a Sailor, as he has been employed at both.
   Whoever will apprehend the said Servant, and bring him home, shall have Three Pounds Current Money, paid by   SAMUEL SNOWDEN.
The Maryland Gazette, April 4, 1765; April 11, 1765; April 25, 1765.

RAN away from the Subscriber, in *Northumberland* County, *Virginia*, a Convict Servant Man named *James Irwing*, imported last *May* from *London* into *Patowmack*, by the *Trial*, Capt. *M'Gachin*. He is a stout swarthy looking old Fellow, pretends to have been many Years Boatswain of a Ship, and seems to understand the Business very well. Had on a close Pea jacket and Breeches of coarse blue Cloth, with black Horn Buttons and lapelled Breasts (tho' he has probably other Cloaths with him) looks almost as dark as an Indian, and wears his own black curly Hair, a good deal mix'd with grey. He and another Sailor from the *Virginian*, in *Wicomoco* River, stole a Canoe, and were since seen on the *Tangier Islands*, on their Way up the Bay. It is imagined they will push for *Philadelphia*; tho' *Irwing* pretended he was born in *Maryland*, and had a Right to some Land and Negroes in *Somerset* County. The other Sailor is a tight well looking little Man, and pretended also to be a Boatswain. Whoever apprehends the said *Irwing*, and so secures him so that he may be had again, shall have Three Pistoles Reward; and if brought home, or on board the said Ship, Five Pistoles, paid by   DAVID GALLOWAY.
N. B. They will probably endeavour to get on board some Vessel outward bound: All Masters are forewarned from taking Irwing at their Peril.
   The Maryland Gazette, April 4, 1765; April 11, 1765; April 25, 1765; May 2, 1765; May 9, 1765.

RAN away from *Patapsco* Ferry on Sunday the 7th of *April* Instant, two Servant Men, *viz.*

John Wilkins, aged about 25 Years, about 5 Feet 7 Inches high, full faced, pitted with the Small-Pox, down Look, speaks low, his little Finger on the left Hand is off to the first Joint. Had on when he went away, a Felt Hat flapp'd, short black Hair, an old blue Coat with Metal Buttons, red under Jacket, Osnabrigs Shirt, white Cotton Breeches, grey Yarn Stockings, and Country-made Shoes, with Strings.

James Moulton, aged about 22 Years, 5 Feet 6 Inches high, thin Face, pitted with the Small-Pox, bold, and speaks pert. Had on when he went away, a round *Dutch* Cap, short brown Hair, white Cotton Jacket, blue under Jacket, Osnabrigs Shirt, white Cotton Breeches, old blue Yarn Stockings, and Country-made Shoes, with Strings.

Whoever takes up the said Servants, and brings them to the Subscriber, at *Patapsco* Ferry, or secures them so as their Owner may have them again, shall have Forty Shillings Reward; and if out of the County, Three Pounds, besides what the Law allows, paid by
FLORA DORSEY.

The Maryland Gazette, April 11, 1765. See *The Maryland Gazette*, November 29, 1764, and *The Pennsylvania Gazette*, April 18, 1765, for Wilkins, and *The Pennsylvania Gazette*, April 18, 1765, for Moulton/Moalton.

Frederick County, *January* 22d, 1765.
TWENTY-ONE POUNDS REWARD.

WHEREAS *Simon Dixon*, of *Orange* County, *North Carolina*, had a Horse and Mare stole from him in *October* last, and the said Creatures were found in Possession of *Fleetwood Benson*, of *Frederick* County, and *Neal Clark*, junior, of *Anne-Arundel* County: The said *Benson* was taken into Custody, in order to be carried to a Justice, on Suspicion of stealing one or both the said Creatures, when he attempted to murder, and dangerously wounded, the Subscriber, and made his Escape. Upon which the neighbouring Inhabitants have raised the Sum of Sixteen Pounds, and lodged the Subscription Paper with the Subscriber, together with an Advertisement signed *Simon Dixon*, offering Five Pounds Reward for the said Thief, which amounts to the above Reward.

Fleetwood Benson is a middling sized Man, about 22 Years of Age, tolerable fresh and fair Complexion, pitted with the Small-Pox, a brazen Look, narrow Visage, and thoroughly versed in the Art of Dissimulation, wore his own Hair cued behind, a Claret colour'd fine Broad Cloth Coat and Breeches, a black Velvet Waistcoat, &c. &c.

Whoever apprehends the aforesaid *Fleetwood Benson*, so as he may be brought to Justice, shall be intitled to the aforesaid Reward, lodged with the

Subscriber, living near *Richard Brookes's* Store, lower Part of *Frederick* County.   AQUILA DUVALL, Constable.
N. B. The Subscription Paper will be further handed about to make the Reward larger.
The Maryland Gazette, April 11, 1765.

April 12, 1765.

RAN away from the Subscriber, near *Annapolis*, a Convict Servant Woman, named *Anne Griffith*, born in *Wales*, and speaks in that Dialect, she is lusty, of a fresh Complexion, and has dark Hair. Had on and with her, a Partridge colour'd Gown, patch'd in the Body with lighter colour'd Stuff, low heel'd Shoes, black or light colour'd Yarn Hose, a black Woollen Hat with a Ribbon round the Crown, a white Cloth Petticoat, one old quilted Ditto, one Check Handkerchief, and one Silk Ditto.

Whoever secures the said Servant, so as her Master may have her again, shall receive Twenty Shillings Reward.
EDWARD OSMOND.
The Maryland Gazette, April 18, 1765. See *The Maryland Gazette*, July 16, 1767.

April 9, 1765.

RAN away from the Subscribers, living near *Baltimore-Town, Maryland*, Three Convict Servant Men, *viz.*

William Hayward, a Shoemaker by Trade, an *Englishman*, about 25 Years of Age, 5 Feet 8 or 9 Inches high, smooth faced, of a pale Complexion, and has a small Speck near the Sight of one of his Eyes. Had on when he went away, a Check Shirt, Linsey Woolsey mill'd Coat and Breeches, with small Stripes of red and black, Thread Stockings, Turn'd Pumps, and a Felt Hat.

Thomas Simmons, an *Englishman*, about 27 Years of Age, 5 Feet 8 or 9 Inches high, of a pale Complexion, and has a large Scar on one of his Ancles. Had on a light colour'd Cloth Waistcoat and Breeches, Osnabrigs Shirt, Felt Hat, coarse Shoes, and Stockings.

Joseph Andrews, an *Italian*, but speaks good *English*, and some *French*, wears his own Hair, which is black, and tied behind, about 27 Years of Age, about 5 Feet 8 or 9 Inches high, of a brown Complexion, and has lost some of his fore Teeth. Had on a light colour'd Waistcoat, a purple colour'd Ditto, brown Cloth Breeches, a white or check Shirt, Felt Hat, white Yarn Stockings, good Shoes, or Pumps.

It is imagined they will change their Cloaths and Names. They have got Cash with them; and perhaps forged Passes, as two of them are artful Fellows.

They took with them three Horses, viz. A middle siz'd Dark Roan, branded on the near Buttock **S O**. A small Bay, with a Star in his Forehead; the Brand, if any, unknown. A middling large Black Horse; his Brand, if any, is also unknown. They have likewise with them a black Dog, with some white on his Breast and Feet, a neat Brass Pistol, and other Things.

Whoever takes up the said Servants, and secures them in any Jail in this Province, so that their Masters may get them again, shall have a Reward of Fifteen Pounds Currency; and if brought Home, Twenty Pounds. If taken and secured in any Jail out of the Province, Twenty Pounds; and if brought Home, Thirty Pounds; or in Proportion for either of them. A reasonable Reward will likewise be given for bringing Home the Horses.

DAVID GORSUCH.   JOHN ENSOR, junr.

N. B. As they may possibly part, Half the Reward will be given for the Shoe-maker, if taken alone, paid by   DAVID GORSUCH.

The Maryland Gazette, April 18, 1765; *The Pennsylvania Gazette,* April 25, 1765; May 16, 1765. Minor differences between the papers.

Baltimore-Town, *April* 15, 1765.

RAN away from Mr. *Charles Grahame's,* in *Lower Marlborough,* in *Calvert* County, *Maryland,* on Tuesday the 9th of this Instant, an Indented Servant Man named *Robert Milme,* a *Scotchman,* about 5 Feet 8 or 9 Inches high, of a pale Complexion, black straight Hair, tied behind, has a Wig, and may probably cut his Hair off. Had on and carried with him when he went away, a Parson's black grey Coat, a little out at the Elbows, Waistcoat and Breeches of the same, a Drab colour'd Horseman's Coat, several Pair of Stockings and Single Channell'd Pumps. One of his Legs is perceptibly smaller than the other.

Whoever will secure the said Runaway so that the Subscriber may have him again, if taken in this Province, shall have Four Dollars; and if taken out of the Province, Six Dollars Reward, paid by
BENJAMIN ROGERS.

The Maryland Gazette, April 18, 1765.

RUN away on Sunday, the 7th inst. from Patapsco Ferry, two Servant Men, one named John Wilkins, about 25 years of Age, full faced, pitted with the Small-pox, has a down Look, speaks low and wears short black Hair; Had on when he went away, a Felt hat, flapped, blue Coat much worn, with Metal Buttons, short red Jacket, Ozenbrigs Shirt, and white Cotton Breeches, Yarn Stockings, country made Shoes, with Strings in them; he has lost the first Joint of the little Finger on the Left-hand; the other named James Moalton, about 5 Feet 7 Inches high, thin faced, pitted with the

Small-Pox; he is bold, and speaks pert, and has dark brown short Hair; had on, when he went away, a round Dutch Cap, and white Cotton Jacket, a blue under Ditto, Ozenbrigs Shirt, white Cotton Breeches, much-worn, blue Stockings, and Country made Shoes, with Strings in them. Whoever apprehends the said Servants, and brings them to the Subscriber at Patapsco Ferry, or secures them, so as they may be had again, shall have Forty Shillings Reward; if out of the Province, Three Pounds, and what the Law allows, paid by   FLORA DORSEY.

The Pennsylvania Gazette, April 18, 1765. See *The Maryland Gazette*, November 29, 1764, for Wilkins, and *The Maryland Gazette*, April 11, 1765, for Wilkins and Moulton/Moalton.

TEN DOLLARS REWARD.

BROKE out of *Anne-Arundel* County Jail, *Richard Smith*, about 5 Feet 4 Inches high, and wears his Hair; had on nothing more than an old Osnabrigs Shirt, and Cloth Breeches: He belongs to Mr. *Macclesish* on *Elk-Ridge*, where he is supposed to be.

Whoever takes up the said Runaway, and delivers him to the Subscriber, in *Annapolis*, shall receive the above Reward.
JOSEPH GALLOWAY, Sheriff.

The Maryland Gazette, April 25, 1765; May 2, 1765.

April 1, 1765.

COMMITTED to *Anne-Arundel* County Jail, on Suspicion of being a Runaway, *John Stone*, about 5 Feet 10 Inches high, well made; had on a light Drugget Coat and Waistcoat, Buckskin Breeches, a dark Bob Wig, and coarse Castor Hat.

His Master is desired to pay Charges, and take him away.
JOSEPH GALLOWAY, Sheriff.

The Maryland Gazette, April 25, 1765; May 2, 1765; May 9, 1765; May 16, 1765.

NINE POUNDS Reward.

RUN away from the Subscriber, on the Ninth of this instant April, two Servant Men, viz. George Evans, an Irishman, about 5 Feet 10 Inches high, fair Complexion, wears his Hair, which is short, and of a yellowish Colour: Had on, and took with him, one Cotton Waistcoat, two Cloth Ditto, of a dark Colour, two Ozenbrigs Shirts, a Pair of Cotton Breeches, Yarn Hose, and Country made Shoes. Andrew Socket, about 39 Years of Age, near the same Heighth, much pitted with the Small-pox: Had on, when he went

away, a blue Jacket, Ozenbrigs Shirt, Cotton Breeches, Yarn Hose, and Country made Shoes. Negroe Jack....Whoever apprehends the said Servants, and brings them to the Subscriber, living on Elk Ridge, in Ann Arundel County; or to Mr. Benjamin Bell in Annapolis, shall have Forty Shillings Reward for each of them, besides what the law allows, if taken after the Eleventh of April, paid by me,
JAMES RIGGS.
The Pennsylvania Gazette, April 25, 1765.

April 27, 1765.
RAN away from the *Baltimore* Iron-Works on *Patapsco*, in *Maryland*, last Night, Two *English* Convict Servant Men, belonging to *Charles Carroll*, Esq; and Company, viz.

Thomas Plevy, a Bricklayer by Trade, he is of a middle Stature, and about 30 Years of Age, full faced, of a ruddy Complexion, has black Eyes, as is his Hair and Beard, which are turning grey. Had on an old Castor Hat, Osnabrigs Shirt, an old blue Broad-Cloth Coat without Lining, a blue strip'd Flannel Jacket, an old Pair of Leather Breeches, and Country Shoes and Stockings.

John Dabs, he pretends to be a Collier, is of a middle Stature, and about 23 Years of Age, and of a swarthy Complexion, has blue Eyes, and light colour'd Hair. Had on an old Felt Hat, Osnabrigs Shirt, a brown Cloth Coat about half worn, a blue Cloth Jacket, a Pair of old Leather Breeches, and Country Shoes and Stockings.

It is likely they may change their Cloaths in Part, as they stole some Things out of the House they left, *viz.* two brown Wigs, one a Que, the other a bob, one Pair of Thread Stockings, one Pair of mix'd Worsted Ditto, and a Pair turn'd Pumps.

It is expected they will make for *Philadelphia*, as they have both been Soldiers, and have with them their Discharges from the Army.

Plevy was a Soldier at Philadelphia this Time two Years.

Whoever secures the said Servants, so that they may be had again, shall have Six Pounds Reward, or Three Pounds for either of them; and reasonable Charges if brought Home.   R. CROXALL.
The Maryland Gazette, May 2, 1765; May 9, 1765; May 23, 1765; May 30, 1765; June 6, 1765.

WILLIAMSBURG, *April* 23, 1765.
RAN away from the Printing-Office, on Saturday Night, a Servant Man named *George Fisher*, by Trade a Book-Binder, between 25 and 26 Years of Age, about 5 Feet 5 Inches high, very thick, stoops much, and has a

down Look; he is a little Pock-pitted, has a Scar on one of his Temples, in much addicted to Liquor, very talkative when drunk, and remarkably stupid. He had on, and carried away with him, several good white Linen Shirts, a Snuff colour'd Cloth Coat, and a Suit of Light colour'd Sagathy, other good Wearing Apparel, a new Half-cut black Bob Wig, and a Set of Silver Buckles.

Whoever apprehends the said Servant, and conveys him to the Printing-Office, in *Virginia*, shall have Five Pounds Reward, and if taken out of the Colony TEN POUNDS, beside what the Law allows.
JOSEPH ROYLE.

The Maryland Gazette, May 2, 1765.

RAN away from the Subscriber, living in the lower Part of *Frederick* County, near Mr. *John Dorsey's* Mill, on Friday Night last, Two Convict Servant Men, *viz.*

John Shovel, about 5 Feet 4 Inches high, pitted with the Small-Pox. Had on and took with him, two light colour'd Jackets, old Shoes and Stockings, and blue Breeches. He has an Assignment, and a Discharge thereon, from *George Cole*; but is since Indented. He has a scald Head.

Thomas Best, an old Man, about 5 Feet 8 Inches high. Had on an old Great Coat, almost black, a blue Fearnought Jacket, old Shoes and Stockings. He has lost one of his Toes.

Whoever takes up the said Servants, and secures them so that their Master may get them again, shall receive Four Pounds Current Money, besides what the Law allows, paid by
JOHN MUSGROVE.

The Maryland Gazette, May 9, 1765.

RAN away on Sunday the 28th ult. from the Subscriber, at *Mount-Pleasant* Township, in *York* County, *Pennsylvania*, an *Irish* Servant Man named *Charles Nail*, aged about 25 Years, about 5 Feet 5 Inches high, of a reddish Complexion, was brought up to the Sea, and imported into Annapolis last Summer. Had on when he went away, a short blue Jacket, with a red one underneath, a brown Cut Wig, a Felt Hat, and a white Frock, with sundry other Things. He is an artful Fellow, and talks a great deal.

Whoever secures the said Servant in any Jail, so that his Master may get him again, shall have Three Pounds Reward, paid by
PATRICK M'ENERRY.
All Masters of Vessels are forbid to carry him off at their Peril.

The Maryland Gazette, May 9, 1765.

Queen Ann's County, near Queen Ann's Town, April 23, 1765. RUN away from the Subscriber, about two Weeks ago, a Convict Servant Man, named Richard Cox, about 40 Years of Age, of a pale Complexion, round faced, and a little pitted with the Small Pox, about 5 feet 5 Inches high; had on, when he went away, a new Felt Hat, midling short grey Hair, a white twilled Linen Frock, a white Cloth Jacket, Buckskin Breeches, blue and white Stockings, a Pair of Shoes, with large Nails in the Heels, plated Buckles, a fine white Shirt, and a ribbed Stock, and Stock Buckle. Whoever takes up said Servant, and brings him to his Master, shall have Five Pounds Reward, and reasonable Charges, paid by
WILLIAM MODESLEY.
The Pennsylvania Gazette, May 9, 1765; June 6, 1765; June 13, 1765.

RUN away from the Subscriber, in Patapsco Neck, Baltimore County, a Servant Man, named John Cain, alias Farrell, about 6 Feet high, short black Hair, fair Complexion; had on, when he went away, an old Thickset Coat, black Cloth Jacket, black Serge Denim Breeches, black Worsted Stockings (one looks rusty, they not being fellows) old Shoes with Nails in the Soals; he took with him a black grey Horse, branded on the near Shoulder with an H, and an S within it, a Silver Watch with a China Face, Brass Key, a Steel Seal, with a man's Head on one Side, and a Snake, a Bird, a Lion ,and a Sheaff of Wheat on the other; it is supposed he has a short yellow complexioned Woman in Company with him, her Name Mary Leech. Whoever takes up and secures said Servant, so that his Master may have him again, shall receive Three Pounds Reward for the Man and Horse, if taken in the County, of Five Pounds if out of the County, and reasonable Charges if brought home, by   EDMUND TALBOTT.
The Pennsylvania Gazette, May 9, 1765.

RAN away the 14th Instant, from the *Elk-Ridge* Furnace, a Convict Servant Man, named *Joseph Clark*, about 30 Years of Age, near 5 Feet 10 Inches high, is pretty lusty, of a fair Complexion, has black Eyes, and something of a down Look when spoken to; his Hair is of a brown Colour, and curl'd; he has been in the Country about 12 Months, and speaks pretty much in the *English* Country Dialect; he has taken with him a Discharge belonging to one *Benjamin Legate*, which is dated 1764, I think in *July*, which it is probable he will make use of, by changing his Name; he also carried with him a Suit of *Legate's* Cloaths, viz. Coat, Jacket, and Breeches, of a dirty or dark Cloth Colour; the Coat has a slash Sleeve, and the whole trimm'd with yellow Metal Buttons; he also took with him several other Things, as a Castor Hat, Check Shirt, Yarn Stockings, a Pair of Pumps, striped Holland

Trowsers, a Pair of Osnabrigs Sailor's Ditto, and two Silk Handkerchiefs. Whoever takes up and brings the said Runaway to the Subscriber, at the *Elk-Ridge* Furnace, shall have, if taken within 10 Miles of the said Furnace, Thirty Shillings; if 20 Miles from thence, Three Pounds; if 40 Miles, Five Pounds; and if out of the Province, Ten Pounds Reward;
CALEB DORSEY.

The Maryland Gazette, May 16, 1765; May 23, 1765; May 30, 1765; June 6, 1765; June 20, 1765. See *The Maryland Gazette,* September 27, 1764, for Clarke/Clark.

Cecil County, Maryland.
RUN away from his Bail, on Sunday, the 5th of this instant May, one William M'Davett; had on, when he went away, a blue Surtout, with a lappelled Jacket, and flat Buttons; he is a Blacksmith by Trade, and is very apt to get drunk. Whoever takes up said Runaway, and brings him to ELISHA HUGHES, at the Brick Meeting, shall have forty Shillings Reward, and reasonable Charges, paid by
JAMES CORBET.

The Pennsylvania Gazette, May 16, 1765.

FIVE POUNDS REWARD.
VIRGINIA, *Dumfries, May* 13, 1765.
RAN away last Night, or early this Morning, *James Scott,* native of *Ireland,* a Convict Servant, about 5 Feet 7 Inches high, and pitted with the Small-Pox: Took with him a Sailor's blue Jacket, a Pair of coarse Sacking long Breeches, and a full suit of old black Cloaths. He ran away from me in 1757, and was never taken up till this Spring, so that he must be pretty well acquainted with the Country, and will probably impose himself on the Public for a Freeman.

Whoever takes up the said Runaway, and conveys him to me here, shall have Five Pounds Reward.   RICHARD GRAHAM.

The Maryland Gazette, May 23, 1765; June 6, 1765; June 13, 1765; June 20, 1765; June 27, 1765.

RAN away from Subscriber, living near *Lower-Cedar-Point,* in *Charles* County, the 17th of May last, Three Convict Servants, imported in the *Tryal,* Capt. *Errington,* from *London,* viz.

John Thomas, a stout swarthy Man, about 32 Years of Age, upwards of 6 Feet high, has black Eyes, and dark brown Hair. Had on an old Jacket lined with Country Cotton, a red Cloth Cap, an old Check Shirt, old black Worsted knit Breeches, and 3 Pair of Yarn Hose.

James Maund, alias *Philpott,* about 21 Years of age 5½ Feet high, has dark brown Hair, grey Eyes, and Lisps in his Speech. Had on a Snuff colour'd Cloath and blue Breeches, ribb'd Worsted Hose, a Check Shirt, and old Shoes.

James West, about 5 Feet high, 15 or 16 Years of Age, has dark brown curl'd Hair, and grey Eyes. Had on and took with him, a *Scotch* Bonnet, a white Linen Shirt, two Coats, on a dark Cloth, the other a light colour'd Surtout, a Pair of Leather Breeches, ribb'd Worsted Stockings, and a Pair of Pumps.

They took with them two new Osnabrigs Shirts, one Pair of Pumps, one Pair of Shoes, and one Pair of old Shoe Boots.

Whoever takes up and secures the said Servants, so that their Master may have them again, shall have Three Pounds Reward; or Five Pounds if brought home, beside what the Law allows, and in Proportion for either.
THOMAS JAMES.

N. B. All Masters of Vessels are forewarn'd not to carry them off at their Peril.

The Maryland Gazette, June 6, 1765; June 13, 1765; June 20, 1765; June 27, 1765; July 4, 1765; July 11, 1765; July 18, 1765; July 25, 1765; August 1, 1765.

RUN away from the Subscriber, living in Queen Ann's County, Maryland, a Convict servant Man, named Evan Roberts, an Englishman, about 5 Feet high, a well set Fellow, with a down Look, and yellow Complexion; had on, when he went away, an old Felt Hat, whitish coloured Cloth Coat, full trimmed, with a small Cape, Plad Waistcoat, Country Linen Shirt and Trowsers, blue and white mixt Yarn Hose, new Shoes, and what is most remarkable, he has lost the Use of Part of his Left-hand, having the Use of his Thumb and Forefinger only. Whoever takes up and secures said Servant, so that the Owner may have him again, shall have Thirty Shillings Reward, and reasonable Charges, paid by   JOSEPH CHAVIES.

N. B. It is supposed he has a Companion with him, but I cannot give any Description, more than he is an Englishman born.

The Pennsylvania Gazette, June 6, 1765. See *The Pennsylvania Gazette,* March 20, 1766.

COMMITTED to *Anne-Arundel* County Jail, on Suspicion of being a Runaway, an *Irishman,* about 28 Years old, 5 Feet 2 or 3 Inches high. Has on an old black Crape Coat and Waistcoat, and Drab Breeches. He says his name is *Patrick Kelkelly,* and that he belongs to Mr. *Makall,* Merchant at

Hobbs-Hole, in *Virginia*. His Master is desired to pay Charges, and take him away. JOSEPH GALLOWAY, Sheriff.
The Maryland Gazette, June 13, 1765; June 20, 1765.

Philadelphia, June 6, 1765.
WHEREAS a certain *James Millar*, on or about the 2d of May, 1764, Indented himself at *Gravesend*, to Mr. *Sydenham*, Merchant, of *London*, and sailed immediately in the Brig *Brothers*, *James Morrison* Master, bound to *Patapsco* in *Maryland*, and was consigned to Mr. *Fishwick* there. The said *Millar* is of a dark Complexion, about 20 Years of Age, and about 5 Feet 6 or 7 Inches high, and a Carpenter and Joiner by Trade, born at *Stratham* in *Surry*. Whoever will give Information of the said *James Millar* (Alive or Dead) by directing a few Lines to Mr. *Charles Allen*, to be left at Mr. *Joseph Yeates's*, at the *Three Tuns* in *Chesnut-Street, Philadelphia*, the Favour will be most gratefully acknowledged by
CHARLES ALLEN.
The Maryland Gazette, June 13, 1765.

RAN away from the Subscriber, living on *Elk-Ridge* in *Anne-Arundel* County, the 26th of *May* last, a Convict Servant Man named *Samuel Beach*, he is a lusty, well made Fellow, about 5 Feet 8 or 9 Inches high, of a fresh Complexion, wears his own short yellowish Hair, his right Thumb remarkably crooked, and is very apt to get in Liquor. Had on when he went away, an old Felt Hat, Country Cloth fulled Jacket, coarse Country made Linen Shirt and Trowsers, and a Pair of strong Country made Shoes, with a large Nail in the Toe of each.

Whoever takes up the said Servant, and brings him to his Master, or secures him so that he may be had again, shall have Twenty Shillings Reward, if taken 20 Miles from home; Forty Shillings, if out of the County; and Three Pounds *Pennsylvania* Currency, if out of the Province, beside what the Law allows, paid by   BENJAMIN LAWRENCE.
The Maryland Gazette, June 13, 1765; June 20, 1765; July 4, 1765.

June 13, 1765.
WENT away last Night from the Brigantine *Trotman*, (*Richard Hayton*, Commander) at Anchor in *Chesapeak* Bay, off *Annapolis*, Two Men and One Woman, who took a Long-Boat, about 20 Feet Keel, Clinch built, with a Studding Sail and Brass Compass; one of the Men in Country born, named *John Nickles*, about 5 Feet 4 Inches high. The other a Sailor, named *John Ogesen*, a *Dane* born, speaks broken *English*, and is about 5 Feet 7

Inches high. The Woman is about 5 Feet 4 Inches high, named *Lucy Chapell*, and had on a white Linen Hat, and a brown Worsted Gown.

It is imagined they went up the Bay.

Whoever brings or secures the said People, so that the Subscriber gets them again, shall have Four Pounds Reward for the Sailor, and for the other two Forty Shillings each, paid by
RICHARD HAYTON.

The Maryland Gazette, June 13, 1765; June 20, 1765; June 27, 1765.

FIVE POUNDS Reward.

RUN away, the 26th of May last, from Stafford Forge, on Deer Creek, in Baltimore County, Maryland, an English Convict Servant Man, named John Painter, has been used to Farming, about 30 Years of Age, 5 Feet 8 or 10 Inches high, well set, fair Complexion, and grey Eyes; had on, when he went away, an old light coloured Jacket, Felt Hat, Ozenbrigs Shirt, Crocus Trowsers, and Country made Shoes, the Heels and Soals nailed with Hob Nails; he was imported into Maryland last summer. Whoever apprehends the said Servant, and secures him in any Goal, so that he may be had again, shall receive, if taken 10 miles from home, Forty Shillings, if 20 Miles from home, Three Pounds, if out of the Province, Five Pounds, and reasonable Charges, paid when brought home.
JEREMIAH SHEREDINE.

The Pennsylvania Gazette, June 13, 1765.

June 3, 1765.

FIVE POUNDS Reward.

RUN away last Night, from the Subscriber, living in Cecil County, Maryland, a Servant Man, named Charles Farran, about 20 Years of Age, 5 Feet 5 or 6 Inches high, full faced, has a down Look, wears black hair, which is cut on the Top of his Head; had on, and took with him a Felt Hat, dark coloured Frize Coat, with black Lining, Waistcoat and Breeches of the same, one Waistcoat striped with red and white, two Country Linen Shirts, two Pair of Tow Trowsers, blue Yarn Stocks, half worn Shoes, and Brass Buckles. It is thought he took with him some other Clothes, not yet missed. Whoever secures said Servant in any Goal, so that his Master may have him again, shall have the above Reward, and reasonable Charges, if brought home, paid by   HENRY HOLLINGSWORTH.

N. B. All Masters of Vessels are forbid to take him off at their Peril.

The Pennsylvania Gazette, June 13, 1765. See *The Pennsylvania Gazette*, April 10, 1766, *The Pennsylvania Gazette*, June 12, 1766, and *The Pennsylvania Gazette*, August 7, 1766.

Patuxent Iron-Works, *June* 25, 1765.
RAN away last Night from the Subscriber, a Servant Man (just Imported in the Brig *Trotman*, Capt. *Richard Hayton*,) named *Jacob Mathews*, a lusty Fellow, near 6 Feet high, of a dark Complexion, light grey Eyes, black curl'd Hair, and is a Carpenter and Joiner by Trade. He had on, two blue Jackets, double breasted, trimm'd with Metal Buttons, and the Seams bound with Cord, coarse blue Breeches, blue-grey Worsted Stockings, old Check Shirt, Sailor's wove Cap, with a Metal Button.

Whoever secures the said Servant, so that his Master may get him again, shall be paid Forty Shillings, if 20 Miles from home; if out of the Province, Five Pounds; and reasonable Charges if brought home, by
SAMUEL SNOWDEN.

The Maryland Gazette, June 27, 1765; July 25, 1765; August 15, 1765; August 29, 1765.

TEN POUNDS REWARD.
BROKE out of *Anne-Arundel* County Jail, *Dennis Ferroll*, who was committed on Suspicion of Horse-stealing: He had on an old Check Shirt, white Cloth Waistcoat, Drugget Breeches, and a Pair of old Shoes and Stockings. He is about 24 Years old, 5 Feet 8 Inches high, and very brown complexion'd, being of the *Indian* Breed. Whoever secures him, so that the Subscriber may get him again, shall receive the above Reward; and if brought to *Annapolis*, reasonable Charges will be paid, by
JOSEPH GALLOWAY, Sheriff.

The Maryland Gazette, June 27, 1765; July 11, 1765; July 18, 1765; July 25, 1765; August 1, 1765. See *The Maryland Gazette*, February 7, 1765.

Back Creek, June 24, 1765.
RUN away from the Subscriber, living in Cecil County, Maryland, an English Servant Man, calls himself Samuel Downing, dark Complexion, about five Feet eight Inches high, well set, speaks the West of England Dialect: Had on when he went away, a good Pair of Buckskin Breeches, Thread Stockings, good Shoes and Buckles, two fine white Linen Shirts, a blue Jacket, without Sleeves, and a light coloured Coat, supposed to have taken a sorrel Horse, with a Blaze in his Face, along with him. Whoever secures said Servant, in any Goal, so as his Master may have him again, shall have Forty Shillings Reward, and reasonable Charges, paid by
WILLIAM CLARK, Miller.

The Pennsylvania Gazette, June 27, 1765.

RUN away from the Subscriber, living on Patapsco Falls, near the Soldier's Delight, in Baltimore County, a Country born indentured Servant Man, named Christopher Slyder, professes to be a Carpenter, about 35 Years of Age, about 5 Feet 6 Inches high, of a pale Complexion, very down Look, a little Pock-marked, and has long black Hair, tied behind: Had on, when he went away, a brown coloured Great Coat, with Mohair Buttons, half worn, an old Cloth Jacket, without Button, half worn Felt Hat, a new Country Linen Shirt and Trowsers, both coarse. Whoever takes up the said Servant, if 20 Miles from home, shall have Forty Shillings Reward, and reasonable Charges for bringing him home; but if taken out of the County, Four Pounds Reward, and reasonable Charges for bringing him home, paid by SOLOMON STOCKSDALE.
The Pennsylvania Gazette, June 27, 1765.

June 25, 1765.
RAN away on Saturday Night the 22d Instant, from the Subscriber, an *Irish* Servant Boy named *Hugh M'Donald*, about 17 Years of Age, about 5 Feet 3 or 4 Inches high, wears his own Hair, which is of a yellowish Colour, round shoulder'd, one of his Eyes a little sore, Parrot-toed, and had a small Iron Collar on, but it is supposed that he will get it off. He took with him 2 Tow Linen Shirts, and 2 Pair of Trowsers of the same, a half worn black Crape Jacket, without Sleeves, lined with white, two Pair of Worsted Stockings, one Pair ribb'd, a Pair of half worn Shoes, yellow Metal Buckles, an old Wool Hat, and a large Linsey Blanket. He took with him a *Guiney* Negro Boy, about 14 Years of Age, named *Sancho*....They stole a Battoe, and went off by Water, from the Head of *North-East*.
Whoever takes up the said Servant and Negro, and secures them so as their Master may have them again, shall have Twenty Shillings Reward for each, beside what the Law allows, paid by the Subscriber, living near the *North-East* Forge, in *Caecil* County.   JOHN READ.
The Maryland Gazette, July 4, 1765; July 11, 1765; July 18, 1765.

Queen-Anne's County, *July* 1, 1765.
RAN away last Night, from the Subscriber, a *West* Country Convict Servant Man, named *William Cullamore*, about 34 or 35 Years of Age, well set, 5 Feet 2 or 3 Inches high, of a brown Complexion, with blue Eyes, and black Hair: Had on and took with him, a Pair of old patch'd Shoes, a Pair of old dark colour'd Stockings, and a Pair of mix'd black and white Ditto, old red Cloth Breeches, new Osnabrigs Trowsers, two Osnabrigs Shirts, one old greenish colour'd Jacket, one blue Ditto, the back Parts black, a brown

Cloth Coat, with Metal Catgut Buttons, and an old Felt Hat. Whoever takes up the said Servant, and secures him so that his Master gets him again, shall have Thirty Shillings Reward if taken in this County, if taken in any other County in this Province Three Pounds, and if taken out of the Province Four Pounds, paid by   THOMAS ELLIOTT HUTCHINGS.
The Maryland Gazette, July 11, 1765; July 18, 1765.

BALTIMORE-TOWN, *July* 8, 1765.
THREE POUNDS REWARD.

RAN away the 2d of this Instant, from the Subscriber, living at *Marsh Creek*, in *York* County, an *Irish* Convict Servant Man, named *Matthias M'Guier*, about 5 Feet 10 Inches high, of a dark Complexion, with black Hair and black Beard: Had on when he went away, an old Check Shirt, and old red Jacket made Sailor's Fashion, with a large Patch on one Sleeve, an old Felt Hat, an old blue Pair of Breeches, old grey Yarn Stockings, and an old Pair of Shoes. He passes himself for a Soldier who came from Fort *Pitt*, and says he is lame of one Arm, he wants to get where there is Shipping to go to Sea.

Whoever takes up and secures the said Servant, so that his Master may have him again, shall have the above Reward, and reasonable Charges if brought home, paid by   WILLIAM M'CLELLAN.
N. B. All Masters of Vessels are forbid taking him away at their Peril.
The Maryland Gazette, July 11, 1765.

RUN away from the Subscribers, living in Baltimore County, the 23d of June last, two Convict Men, named William Stanton, and William Clark; Stanton wears dark brown Hair, Felt Hat, white Cotton Jacket, Ozenbrigs and Trowsers; Clark also wears his Hair, which is sandy, and neatly curled; he has red Spots in his Face, occasioned by a breaking out; had on, when he went away, an old Castor Hat, Cotton Jacket, Ozenbrigs Shirt and Trowsers, and is a Sow Gelder by Trade. As they stole other Goods, they may have changed their Apparel. They stole two Guns, and two Bridles, and it is supposed will steal Horses the first Opportunity. Whoever takes up the said Servants, and secures them, so that the Owners may have them again, shall have Five Pounds Reward, and reasonable Charges, if brought home, or Fifty Shillings for either, paid by
WILLIAM HARVEY, and RENOLDO MONK.
The Pennsylvania Gazette, July 11, 1765.

Baltimore County, *July* 8, 1765.

RAN away last night from the Subscriber, living on the Little Falls of *Gunpowder*, an *English* Servant Man, who went by the Name of *John Shepherd*, he is a lusty Man, much pitted with the Small-Pox, with black curl'd Hair. He had on and took with him, a light Drab colour'd Coat, with blue Lining, much patch'd, two blue Jackets, and one Country Cloth Ditto, all trimmed with Metal Buttons, two Pair of Trowsers, two Check Shirts, a Felt Hat, a Pair of Shoes, a blue Cloth Jacket, a Common Prayer Book, with five old Almanacks and one new One.

Whoever secures the said Servant, so that the Subscriber may get him again, shall have Thirty Shillings Reward, paid by
THOMAS ELLIOTT.

The Maryland Gazette, July 18, 1765; July 25, 1765; August 1, 1765; August 8, 1765.

THIRTY PISTOLES REWARD.

July 10, 1765.

BROKE out of *Frederick* County Jail, about Two o'clock this Morning, the Six following Persons, *viz*.

John Lewis Davis, about 5 Feet 9 Inches high, wears his own Hair.

Jeremiah Veach, about 6 Feet high, wears his own Hair. Had on when he went away, a full trimmed dark Broad-Cloth Coat, Tow Linen Shirt, a Felt Hat, Linen Breeches, Country made Shoes and Stockings; the Stockings have been burnt, and a Piece knit it. He is bow legg'd.

George Hall, about 5 Feet 6 Inches high; his Legs are remarkably crooked. Had on when he went away, a Thickset Coat, Osnabrigs Shirt and Trowsers, old Hat, grey Stockings, and Country Shoes.

Samuel Jacobs, about 5 Feet 9 Inches high, sandy Complexion, pitted with the Small-Pox, and bald headed. Had on a blue double breasted Camblet Jacket, Country Linen Shirt and Trowsers, old Hat and Shoes.

Michael Burkitt, a well made Man, about 5 Feet 8 Inches high. Had on a light colour'd Cloth Jacket without Sleeves, Check Shirt, red knit Breeches, the Garters of which are white, blue ribb'd Stockings, a Wool Hat, and a Pair of Shoes or Pumps.

Thomas Mullan, about 5 Feet 5 Inches high. Had on a blue Cloth Jacket, Country Linen Shirt and Trowsers, a Pair of Shoes, with Brass Buckles, and a Castor Hat.

Whoever takes up all or either of the said Men, and delivers them to the Subscriber in *Frederick-Town*, shall receive for each a Reward of FIVE PISTOLES.   GEORGE MURDOCK, Sheriff.

The Maryland Gazette, July 18, 1765; July 25, 1765; August 1, 1765.

RAN away on Sunday the 14th of this Instant, from the Subscriber living on *Magothy* River, an *Irish* Servant Man named *Timothy Hearly*, his Hair and Beard are brown, is about 20 Years of Age, about 5 Feet 7 or 8 Inches high, much mark'd with the Small-Pox, by Trade a Sawyer, but has followed the Seas some Years. Had on when he went away, an old Check Shirt, a Pair of patch'd Osnabrigs Trowsers, an old Felt Hat, an old Swanskin Waistcoat with Country Cloth Sleeves, but no Shoes nor Stockings. He took with him a small Country Bed Blanket, and went off in a small Pettiaugre.

Whoever takes up and secures the said Servant, so as his Master may get him again, shall receive Forty Shillings Reward if taken in this Province, Three Pounds if taken in any other Province, and all reasonable Charges if brought home, paid by   WALTER LITTLE.

The Maryland Gazette, July 25, 1765.

Maryland, Patuxent Iron-Works, July 8, 1765.
RUN away from the Subscriber, the 25th of last Month, a Servant Man (just imported in the Brig Trotman, Captain Richard Hayton) named Jacob Matthews, about 28 Years of Age, a lusty Fellow, near 6 Feet high, of a dark Complexion, light grey Eyes, dark brown Hair, and a Carpenter and Joiner by Trade, tho' I imagine that he will endeavour to pass for a Sailor; had on two blue Jackets double breasted, trimmed with small Metal Buttons, and the Seams bound with Cord, coarse blue Breeches, blue grey Worsted Stockings, a Check Shirt, a Sailor's wove Cap, with a Metal Button; it is supposed that he will make towards Philadelphia, as he was born in or near that Place. Whoever secures the said Servant, so that his Master may get him again, shall have Five Pounds Reward, and if out of the Province Ten Pounds, and reasonable Charges, if brought home, from SAMUEL SNOWDEN.

The Pennsylvania Gazette, July 25, 1765. See *The Maryland Gazette,* June 27, 1765.

Rousby-Hall, July 29, 1765.
RAN away from the Subscriber, on Saturday last, a Servant Man, named JOSEPH DENT, about 23 Years of Age; had on, when he went away, a brown Thickset or Fustian Coat and Breeches, a short blue Jacket, and a red Cloth Waistcoat over it; a brown Wig, Yarn Stockings, and common Shoes; and probably has taken more Clothes with him.

He is about 5 Feet 9 Inches high, well made, and active, is full faced, rather of a pale Complexion, marked with the Small-Pox, and hesitates a little in speaking, says he was born in *France,* but went to *England* young. He speaks *French* well, and *English* so well, that no Person would take him for a Foreigner. I purchased him for a Gardener, of which Business he is very ignorant, though he speaks well on the Subject, as he does on many others, being artful, and very smart. He pretends also to understand the Shoemaker's Trade, and some Branches of Husbandry. He has been in the Army a great Part of his Life, and a considerable Time in the *French* Service.

A few Days before he eloped, he applied to one *M'Donald*, a Man who had a Pass from *George Steuart*, Esq: of *Annapolis*, desiring a Copy, so that it is probable he has forged a Pass either in Dr. *Steuart's*, or my Name, as he writes a pretty good Hand.

Whoever apprehends the said Servant, and will deliver him here, shall receive Ten Pounds Reward. WILLIAM FITZHUGH.

The Maryland Gazette, August 1, 1765; August 8, 1765; August 15, 1765' August 22, 1765; August 29, 1765; September 12, 1765. See *The Maryland Gazette*, June 19, 1766, for Dent.

COMMITTED to *Dorchester* County Jail, as a Runaway, *John Harrison*, who says he belongs to *William Jackson*, of *St. Mary's* County, who hired him to Col. *Fitzhugh*, from whose Vessel he ran; he has little or no Cloaths with him, and was taken up the 14th of *July* last, as he cross'd the Bay.

His Master is desired to pay Charges, and take him away.
JOHN DICKINSON, Sheriff.
The Maryland Gazette, August 1, 1765.

July 22, 1765.
FIVE PISTOLES REWARD
RAN away, last Night, from the Subscriber, living on *Elk-Ridge*, in Anne-Arundel County, a Convict Servant Man, named NATHANIEL STAFFORD, about 27 Years of Age, about 5 Feet 2 or 3 Inches, of a dark Complexion, grey Eyes, grim Look, and black Hair; had on, and took with him, a light-coloured Bearskin Coat, a Swanskin Waistcoat, with blue Mohair Buttons, a Linen Ditto, with black Glass Buttons, Claret coloured Cloth Breeches, Old white Shirt, and Osnabrig Ditto, and Trowsers, a Pair of Thread Stockings, Country-made Shoes, Two Red and White Silk Handkerchiefs, and a new Felt Hat.

Whoever takes up, and brings said Servant to the Subscriber, shall have, if taken in the Province, Two Pistoles; and if out of the same, Five Pistoles, and reasonable Charges, from
THO. GASSAWAY, Son of NICHOLAS.
The Maryland Gazette, August 1, 1765; August 8, 1765.

July 29, 1765.
RAN away from the Subscribers, last Night, the following Servants, *viz.*

JOSEPH RODEN, born in *Lincolnshire*, in *England*, imported this Summer in the Brig *Trotman*, is a lusty well-looking young Man, about 19 Years of Age, wears his own Hair, which is dark colour'd, and short.

JOHN SOMERWELL, is a well-looking, likely Lad, imported in said Brig, about 17 Years of Age, wears his own dark Hair, which is long and straight.

RICHARD LOVEWELL, an *East-India* Indian, and very black, tho' he says he was born in *England*, near 50 Years of Age, just imported in the Ship *Ann*, is a sly surly looking Fellow, and a Sailor, very bold and pert spoken, his Hair very black.

They may all pass for Sailors, as they have taken various Kinds of Cloaths, some of which they carry in Bundles or Bags, therefore can't describe them.

Whoever takes up said Servants, and delivers them to their Masters, or to Mr. *Joshua Griffith*, at *Elk-Ridge* Landing, in *Anne-Arundel* County, shall receive Twenty Dollars Reward, or in Proportion for either, paid by
HENRY and ORLANDO GRIFFITH.
If taken out of the Province, Ten Pounds.
The Maryland Gazette, August 1, 1765.

COMMITTED to the Custody of the Sheriff of *Calvert* County, the Three following Persons, as Runaways, *viz. Christopher Clenn, John Thomas*, and *Robert King*. They appear to be Sailors, and say they belong to the Ship *Friendship*, Capt. *Francis Richardson*, who is desired to take them away, and pay Charges.   TRUEMAN SKINNER, Sheriff.
The Maryland Gazette, August 1, 1765. See *The Maryland Gazette*, August 8, 1765.

FIFTY POUNDS REWARD.
MADE their Escape out of Baltimore County Goal, on the 13th of July last, the following Persons, viz.

Hugh Stewart, born in Pennsylvania, about twenty-seven Years old, five Feet eight Inches high, square and well-set, wears short curled yellow Hair, fair Complexion, is freckled, and by Trade a Blacksmith.

Joseph Cooper, an Englishman, about thirty five Years of Age, five Feet eight Inches high, stoops in his Walk, which makes him appear round shouldered, pitted with the Small-Pox, has a sharp Nose, and light brown Hair, and has a Scar near his short Ribs, by a Musket-Ball, but on which Side is uncertain, speaks very broad and fast, and brags much of his Abilities and Skill in every Thing, even that he knows nothing about.

Joseph Barham, an Englishman, seventy [sic] Years old, five Feet six Inches high, a fresh Complexion, wears his own grey Hair, stoops a little, talks loud, and has a bold Look.

James Alexander, an Englishman, forty Years old, five Feet eleven Inches high, by Trade a Butcher, wears short black Hair, and is much pitted with the Small Pox.

Thomas West, a Carpenter, or Mill-wright, Country born, about thirty-five Years old, five Feet four Inches high, wears light coloured short Hair, fair Complexion, speaks fast, but with an effeminate Voice, and it is supposed he will make over Sasquehannah into Cecil, where he has a Wife and Family.

George Collins, a Country born Mulatto, pretends to be a Blacksmith.

John Lemon, an Irishman, by Trade a Weaver, middle-sized and well-set, wears his own brown short Hair, and a good Complexion.

Joseph Lowman, Country born, tall and well-made, about forty-five Years of Age, wears his own Hair, has a fresh Countenance, is very talkative and loves strong Liquor; he lived a few Years ago in Cecil County.

James Hughes, an Englishman, twenty- eight Years of Age, five Feet seven Inches high, was whipt and pillored last June Court for Felony, which may be seen by the Marks on his Back.

Alexander Russel, a Scotchman, he lived in Baltimore-Town, about thirty-two Years of Age, has a dark Complexion, down Look, black short curled Hair, well-set, about 5 Feet 8 or 9 Inches high, by Trade a Joiner and House Carpenter, pretends to understand something of Stone Masonry, speaks a little upon the Scotch Dialect, and very fond of strong Drink.

Whoever takes up, and delivers the above described Persons to the Goaler at Joppa, shall receive the above Reward, or FIVE POUNDS for each, if taken in the Province, and an Addition of FORTY SHILLINGS more for every one taken out of it, paid by
ROBERT ADAIR, Sheriff.

The Pennsylvania Gazette, August 1, 1765; August 8, 1765.

FOUR DOLLARS REWARD.

RAN away from the Subscriber, living in *Annapolis*, on the 6th of this Instant August, a Convict Servant Man named *William Jennings*, an *Englishman*, about 5 Feet 6 or 7 Inches high, his left Thigh has been broke, which occasions him to limp much, one of his Legs is much scarified, wears his own short dark colour'd Hair, and has a very simple Look. Had on and took with him, a light colour'd Cotton Velvet Jacket, lined with green, two Shirts, the one Check, the other Osnabrigs, Buckskin Breeches, Osnabrigs Trowsers, old Shoes, white Stockings, and an old flapp'd Hat.

Whoever takes up the said Servant, and delivers him to his Master, shall have the above Reward, paid by.
WILLIAM FARIS.
N. B. All Masters of Vessels are forbid to carry him off at their Peril.
The Maryland Gazette, August 8, 1765; August 15, 1765; August 22, 1765; August 29, 1765; September 19, 1765.

BROKE out of *Calvert* County Jail, on the 25th of *July* last, the Four following Sailors, Three of whom were committed as Runaways from the Ship *Friendship*, Capt. *Joseph Richardson*, and the other on Suspicion of Felony, named *Christopher Clenn, John Thomas, Robert King,* and *John Commins*. Whoever will apprehend and deliver them to the Subscriber, in *Calvert* County, shall receive a Pistole Reward for each, and reasonable Charges, paid by   TRUEMAN TURNER, Sheriff.
The Maryland Gazette, August 8, 1765; August 29, 1765. See *The Maryland Gazette*, August 1, 1765.

BALTIMORE-TOWN, *July* 31, 1765.
RAN away, last Night, from the *Northampton* Iron-Works, in *Baltimore* County, *Maryland*, Two Convict Servant Men, *viz.*
Godfrey Stone, a *Dutchman*, a lusty Fellow, about 6 Feet high, wears his own short brown Hair, about 35 Years of Age: Had on when he went away, an Osnabrig Shirt, brown Roll Trowsers, half-worn Shoes, and an old Felt Hat.
Thomas Watson, an *Englishman*, a slim Fellow, about 25 Years of Age, about 5 Feet 8 Inches high, has large black Eyes: Had on, when he went away, an Osnabrig Shirt, brown Roll Trowsers, half-worn Shoes, a Bearskin Jacket with Metal Buttons, and a new Felt Hat.
Whoever takes up the said Servants, and delivers them to the said Iron-Works, shall have, if taken above Ten Miles from home, Forty Shillings Reward for each: If taken out of the County and brought home, Four Pounds for each; and if taken out of the Province, and brought home, Five Pounds for each, paid by
CHARLES RIDGELY, senr. & Company.
The Maryland Gazette, August 8, 1765; *The Pennsylvania Gazette*, September 26, 1765. Minor differences between the papers.

RUN away, the 17th of July last, a Convict Servant Man, named Michael Carr, but sometimes called himself Michael Curry, or Michael Davis; he is of a swarthy Complexion, black Hair, much pitted with the Small-pox, thin

visaged, about 5 Feet 7 or 8 Inches high, middle aged; had on a Country Linen Shirt, long Trowsers of the same, old patched Shoes, a blue Pea Jacket, and a small blue Jacket under it, and a patched old Hat, he took with him two Yards and a Half of new Country Linen. Whoever apprehends the said Runaway, and secures him, so that his Master may get him again, shall receive Forty Shillings Reward, and reasonable Charges, for bringing him home, paid by RICHARD FOWLER, living in Baltimore County, near Lancashire Furnace, Maryland.
N. B. It is supposed he is gone towards New York.
The Pennsylvania Gazette, August 8, 1765.

Anne-Arundel County, August 8, 1765.
Ran away, last Night, from the Subscriber, an *English* Servant Man, (Imported in the Ship *Anne,* Capt. *Reid,*) named Edward *Fullerallcary*, about 26 Years of Age, a well-set Fellow, about 5 Feet 6 or 7 Inches high, very much pitted with the Small-Pox, and has a pert bold Countenance: Had on and took with him, an old Castor Hat, brown Cut Wig, a brown Cloth Coat with a Cape to it, 2 Check Shirts, old Leather Breeches, a pair of Flannel Ditto, brown ribb'd Worsted Stockings, and a pair of old Shoes cut near the Toe with an Ax.
Whoever brings the said Servant to the Subscriber, or secures him so as his Master may get him again, shall have Three Pounds Ten Shillings Reward, paid by   JOHN WAYMAN.
The Maryland Gazette, August 15, 1765; August 29, 1765.

FIVE POUNDS REWARD.
RAN away from the Subscriber, at *Vienna*, in *Dorchester* County, on the 30th of *July* last, a Servant Man, named *James Dixon*, a Barber by Trade, was born in *Cumberland*, in *England*, is about 5 Feet 6 Inches high, wears his own Hair, which is near Black, and commonly tied: Had on when he went away, a white Fustian Coat, brown Cloth Jacket, lined with green Shalloon, white Shag Breeches, Check Shirt, and a Beaver Hat. He stole a Canoe from *Hooper's-Island*, the 3d of this Instant *August*, and it is thought he is gone to *St. Mary's*, or *Calvert* County.
Any Person delivering him to the Subscriber, shall receive the above Reward of Five Pounds; or, if secured so as he may be had again, a Reward of Forty Shillings, besides what the Law allows, paid by
REGINALD GRAHAM.
The Maryland Gazette, August 22, 1765; August 29, 1765.

FIVE PISTOLES REWARD.

RAN away from the Ship *Four Friends, William Hamilton* Commander, on the 10th of this Instant, the Five following Seamen, *viz.*
Robert Nesbet, of tall Stature, and wears a Wig.
John Conawa, of middle Stature, and wears a Wig.
Thomas Lewis, middle siz'd, and wears his Hair.
Patrick Colens, of a middle Size, and wears his Hair.
Roger Mere Waters, of middle Stature, and wears a Wig.
Whoever will take up the said Seamen, and deliver them on board the Ship, lying in *Chester* River, shall have a Pistole Reward for each, paid by WILLIAM HAMILTON.
The Maryland Gazette, August 22, 1765; August 29, 1765; September 12, 1765. See *The Pennsylvania Gazette*, September 12, 1765.

TEN POUNDS Reward.

RUN away from Onion's Iron-Works, in Baltimore County, Maryland, the 5th Instant, two Convict Servant Men, viz. Edmund Collins, a Shoemaker by Trade, about 25 Years of Age, 5 Feet 8 Inches high, of a black Complexion, is almost blind of his Left Eye, has a small Scar under his lower Lip, and wears a Wig: Had on, when he went away, an old white Fustian Coat, a white Shirt, half-worn Broadcloth Breeches, new Pumps and Buckles, old ribbed Cotton Stockings, and an old Beaver Hat. William Jordan, alias Edwards, about 32 Years of Age, 5 Feet 5 Inches high, of a dark Complexion, and has short brown Hair: Had on, when he went away, a new Ozenbrigs Shirt and Trowsers, old Castor Hat, a new Coat, of a purple Colour, new Shoes, and sundry other Clothes. Whoever secures the said Servants, and brings them to their Master, shall have, if taken in the County, Four Pounds, if out of the County, Six Pounds, and if out of the Province, the above mentioned Reward, and so in Proportion for either of them, paid by   JOHN GRENIS HOWARD, or BENJAMIN INGRAM.
The Pennsylvania Gazette, August 22, 1765.

August 28, 1765.

RAN away from the Subscriber, last Night, a Convict Servant Man, named *William Lewis*, about 5 Feet 7 Inches high, had his Hair on, but, as he took with him a Grizzle Wig, 'tis supposed he will cut it off. He had with him the Discharge of *Thomas Gray*, by which Name he may probably Pass; also some Papers relating to Work done by *Gray*. He had on, and took with him, a new blue Broad-Cloth Coat, with yellow Buttons, an old grey Cloth Coat, old Leather Breeches, Osnabrig Shirt, old Stockings and Pumps, and Hempen-Roll Trowsers.

Two Negroes are supposed to be gone with him: One named *Sam*....The other named *Bewdly*....

Lewis cannot Read: I think he has a large Scar on one of his Shoulders, occasioned by a Broad Sword. He talks inwardly, has a down Look, and 'tis probable he will soon quit the Negroes.

Whoever will deliver the said *Lewis* to Me, living near *Annapolis*, shall have Three Pistoles Reward; and Four Dollars for each of the Negroes. *N. B.* All Masters of Vessels are forewarn'd from carrying them off, as they will answer the contrary at their Peril.
JOHN WILMOT.

The Maryland Gazette, August 29, 1765; September 5, 1765; September 12, 1765; September 19, 1765.

EIGHT POUNDS Reward.

RUN away, in the Night of the 21st of August, from the Subscriber, living in Cecil County, Maryland, two Convict Servant Men, one named William Callahan, born in Ireland, by Trade a Plaisterer, about 30 years of Age, about 5 Feet 6 Inches high, wear an old grey cut Wig, a light coloured short Kersey Coat, with Metal Buttons, Ozenbrigs Shirt and Trowsers, old Shoes, and Yarn Stockings; he is of a swarthy Complexion, has grey Eyes, pitted with the Small Pox, very talkative, much given to Drink, has served some Time on board a Man of War, and came in the Country about 12 Months ago. The other named Edward Thompson, a Convict, lately imported, an Englishman, a very lusty well looking Man, with black Beard and Eyes: He had on a light coloured Jockey Coat, blue Serve Vest, with Leather Buttons, Shoes and Stockings, an old fine Hat, with a black Crape Band round it; he also took with him a light coloured Bearskin Great-Coat, a Snuff coloured Thickset Coat, and sundry other Things, likewise a small old sorrel Horse, with a Star in his Forehead, paces slow, and very stiff; he is a stout resolute Fellow, is apt to drink, and then very insolent; they are both well acquainted with the Water, and may probably pass for Sailors. Whoever takes up and secures the said Servants in any Goal, so that their Masters may have them again, shall have Five Pounds Reward for Thompson, and Three Pounds for Callahan, if taken out of this Province, paid by
ANDREW PEARCE, HENRY W. PEARCE and JOHN WARD.

The Pennsylvania Gazette, August 29, 1765; October 3, 1765. See *The Pennsylvania Gazette*, September 4, 1766, for Callahan. See *The Pennsylvania Gazette*, April 17, 1766, and *The Maryland Gazette*, April 17, 1766, for Thompson.

Calvert County, *Sept.* 2d, 1765.

RAN away from the Subscriber, on the 25th Day of *August* last, an Indented Servant Man, named *John Chambers*, a Carpenter by Trade, was born in this County, is about 5 Feet 10 Inches high, with a very black Complexion, and a Downish Look. Had on when he went away, a dark coloured Bearskin Coat, a strip'd Country made Waistcoat, Osnabrigs Trowsers and Shirt. Whoever takes up the said Servant, and delivers him at my Plantation, at *Upper Bennett*, shall have Two Pistols, paid by
SAMUEL CHEW, of *Wells.*

The Maryland Gazette, September 5, 1765; September 12, 1765.

BALTIMORE-TOWN, *August* 19, 1765.
TEN POUNDS REWARD.

RAN away last Night from the *Patapsco* Furnace, near *Elk Ridge* in *Anne-Arundel* County, Two *English* Convict Servant Men, *viz.*

William Bostock, about 30 Years of Age, about 5 Feet 4 Inches high, well made, of a fair Complexion, dark Eyes, black curl'd Hair, cut on the Top; he is a very bold talkative pert Fellow, a Weaver by Trade: Had on and took with him, a Felt Hat, 2 Osnabrigs Shirts, a Pair of Osnabrigs Sailor's Trowsers, a Pair of long check Ditto, a Pair of Rolls Ditto, one Osnabrigs Frock, the Body lined with white Flannel, with large Metal Buttons, one Pair of Thread Stockings, and one Pair of Country made Shoes, with carv'd Buckles, plated with Silver: He was Imported in the Ship *Albion*, Capt. *Thomas Spencer*, in *August* 1764.

Richard Purchase, about 30 Years of Age, about 5 Feet 5 Inches high, of a brown Complexion, dark Eyes, brown Hair, has a down surly Look: Had on and took with him, a Felt Hat, a grey Cloth Jacket, with black Horn Buttons, an old brown Holland Ditto, 2 Osnabrigs Shirts, 2 Pair of long Osnabrigs Trowsers, a Pair of white Drawers, with yellow Buttons, a Pair of black and white mix'd ribb'd Yarn Hose, a Pair of grey Ditto, 2 Pair of Shoes, and one Pair of channell'd Pumps, with Copper Buckles. He was imported in the *Betsey*, Capt. *Nicholas Andrew*, in *November* 1763.

It is very probable they will change their Names and Apparel, and pass for Sailors, or may be in Company with a Mulatto Woman named *Amey*, and one *Thomas Key*, about 50 Years of Age, very round shoulder'd, a lusty Fellow.

Whoever will take up and secure the said Servants, so that they may be had again, shall receive, if taken 20 Miles from Home, Thirty Shillings; if 30 Miles, Forty Shillings; if 40 Miles, Fifty Shillings; and if out of the Province, Five Pounds Reward for each, more than the Law allows, and reasonable Charges if brought Home to
Messrs. THOMAS HARRISON, and Company,

JAMES WALKER.
All Masters of Vessels are forewarned carrying them off at their Peril. As there are two Saddles missing, it is supposed they will steal Horses.

The Maryland Gazette, September 5, 1765; September 12, 1765; September 26, 1765; October 3, 1765; October 10, 1765; October 17, 1765; *The Pennsylvania Gazette*, September 12, 1765; October 10, 1765; October 31, 1765. Minor differences between the papers. See *The Maryland Gazette*, October 24, 1765. Bostock and Purchase may be Burgoine and Sheffield.

FIVE POUNDS REWARD.

RAN away, early this Morning, from the Subscriber's Boat, *Thomas Dorney*, Skipper, between *Hill Point* and *Grazin* Creek, *Chester* River.

JOHN TAYLOR, a Taylor by Trade, but has lately used the Water, he is of low Stature, well set, has a boyish Look, had one of his Legs broke, on which is a Scar, and his Hair has been lately cut off. Had on, a light colour'd Sagathy Coat, Nankeen Jacket, and an old white Shirt of his own. He took with him, a new Pair of Check Trowsers, a ruffled Shirt, a *Philadelphia* made hat, half worn, with Silver Loops, and a Silver lace round the Crown, with a large Stone Buckle, and a Pair of Cotton Stockings, of *Thomas Gresham's*.

He likewise stole the Canoe from the Boat, she is almost a new One, made of Chesnut: He also stole out of the Boat, Nineteen Pounds in Dollars.

Whoever takes up the said Runaway, and secures him so that he may be brought to Justice, shall receive the above Reward, paid by
September 1, 1765.   R. GRESHAM.

The Maryland Gazette, September 5, 1765; September 26, 1765. See *The Pennsylvania Gazette*, September 26, 1765.

FIVE POUNDS REWARD.

RAN away from the Subscriber, living in *Queen-Anne's* County, near Col. *Hopper's* Mill, on the 11th of *August* last, a Convict Servant Man named *John Morris*, about 33 Years of Age, of a dark Complexion, short straight black Hair, a small Scar under one of his Eyes; he was born in Wales, and talks much in that Country Dialect. Had on when he went away, an old Castor Hat, a light coloured Cloth Coat, which has been turned and much worn, white Cloth Jacket, Tow Linen Shirt and Trowsers, light blue Worsted Stockings, and old Shoes. He went away in Company with a Woman belonging to *Thomas Spry Morgan*, of a low Stature, a fat well looking Person, with a Cast with one of her Eyes. Her Apparel not known.

Whoever takes up and brings home the Said Servant shall have the above Reward; and Thirty Shillings for the Woman.
RICHARD CLEMENT.

The Maryland Gazette, September 5, 1765; September 12, 1765; September 19, 1765; September 26, 1765.

Prince-George's County, *Sept.* 2, 1765.
RAN away last Night from the Subscriber, a Servant Man named *Philip Cooke*, about 5 Feet 5 Inches high, and 22 Years of Age, born in *London*, by Trade a Taylor, has been but a little while in the Country, and consequently knows little of it; he is of a fair Complexion, has light Eyes, and a wide Mouth, a smiling Countenance, and is pretty well made. He took with him two brown Wigs, one almost new, the other half worn, a good Castor Hat, blue Cloth Coat with Metal Buttons, blue Sattin Waistcoat, white and check Shirts, Silk and Thread Stockings, a red Banian, a Coat and Waistcoat with Vellum Button Holes, a plain Snuff colour'd Cloth Coat and Waistcoat, two white Waistcoats flower'd with Silk.

It is supposed he went away in Company with *George More*, a Schoolmaster, and Servant to Mr. *Basil Waring*. He is about the Size of Taylor, very well made, has black Eyes, Hair, and Beard. Had on a dark Cloth Coat with Hair Twist round the Flaps and Cuffs. He has been in the Army, and 'tis probable will change his Dress.

Whoever secures the said Cooke in any Jail, or brings him to his Master, shall have Two Pistoles, paid by
THOMAS GANTT.

The Maryland Gazette, September 5, 1765. See *The Maryland Gazette*, September 12, 1765.

Talbot County, *August* 28, 1765.
WENT away from his Bail, a certain *James Wilkins*; he is of a fair Complexion, freckled, and pitted with the Small-Pox, and red or sandy Hair, which he wears tied behind, speaks good *English*, and is a Native of *Ireland*, has served 9 Years in the Army in this Country, and has his Discharge with him, which will serve as a Pass. Had on and with him, a dark brown Coat, and Waistcoat of the same, a red Jacket, Osnabrig Trowsers, old Pumps and Hat. Whoever takes up the said *Wilkins*, and secures him in any Jail within this Province, shall have Thirty Shillings Reward, and if out of the Province, Three Pounds, paid by
FREDERICK LEITH,   JAMES CHAPMAN.

N. B. IT is supposed that he went from *Wye* Town, in a Vessel from *Baltimore*. All Masters of Vessels are forbid to take him at their Peril.

The Maryland Gazette, September 5, 1765. See *The Maryland Gazette,* November 27, 1766.

TEN POUNDS Reward.

RUN away, on the 18th of August last, from Stafford Forge, on Deer Creek, in Baltimore County, Maryland, an English Convict Man, named John Williams, of a small Stature, 5 Feet high, well set, ruddy Complexion, about 30 Years of Age, wears short brown Hair, and speaks good English, has been in the Country about 3 Years; had on, and took with him, blue Yarn Stockings, Check Shirt, Felt Hat, country made Pumps, with Buckles in them, and sundry other wearing apparel not known. Whoever apprehends the said Servant and secures him in any Goal, so that he may be had again, shall have, if taken 10 Miles from home, Fifty Shillings, if 20 Miles Five Pounds, or if at a greater distance, and out of this Province, the above Reward, and reasonable Charges, is brought to the said Forge, paid by
JEREMIAH SHEREDINE.

The Pennsylvania Gazette, September 5, 1765.

September 11, 1765.
TEN POUNDS REWARD.

RAN away from his Bail, from *Baltimore* County, JOHN ROWIN, who is a brown dark skinned Person, about 40 Years of Age: He went away in an old Sloop, which went into the Mouth of *Choptank* River, with some Persons who it is said intend for *Carolina.*

Whoever will secure the said *Rowin* in any Jail, so that he may be had again shall have the above Reward, paid by
ISAAC WARNER.

The Maryland Gazette, September 12, 1765; September 26, 1765; October 3, 1765.

RAN away from the Subscriber, living in *Queen-Anne's* County, on the 28th Day of *August* last past, a Convict Servant Man, named *Joseph Jeffcock,* aged about 26 Years, about 5 Feet 6 Inches high, a straight limb'd well proportion'd Fellow, has brown Hair, and a fair Complexion. Had on, a dark Snuff colour'd Coat, with a broad Collar faced with Plush, a blue Cloth Vest without Sleeves, a Pair of Buckskin Breeches, all about half worn, a very thick Wool Hat, a coarse Linen Shirt, and old Shoes and Stockings.

Whoever takes up the said Servant, and secures him in any Jail, and gives Notice to the Subscriber, shall have FIVE POUNDS Reward, paid by

WILLIAM RICHARDSON.
The Maryland Gazette, September 12, 1765; September 26, 1765.

RAN away on the First of this Instant, from the Subscriber, living near *Shrewsbury* Church, in *Kent* County, a Servant Man named *George Burrough*, an *Englishman*, about 5 Feet 10 Inches high, of a fair Complexion, wears his own Hair tied behind, has been a Drummer in the Army at *Minorca*, and very probably may boast of it, has had a Hurt in his left Hand by a Shot, which, he says, makes it stand somewhat inward: Had on and took with him, a whitish Broad-Cloth lapell'd Coat, a Scarlet Jacket without Sleeves, two white Shirts, two Country Linen Ditto, a Pair of blue Broad-Cloth Breeches too short for him, a Pair of Leather Ditto, 2 Pair of Worsted Stockings, one pale blue, the other grey ribb'd, old Shoes with large Brass Buckles in them, and a Country made Castor Hat above half worn.

Whoever takes up and secures the said Servant, so as his Master may get him again, shall have Fifty Shillings Reward, and reasonable Charges if brought Home, paid by   WILLIAM MERRETT.

The Maryland Gazette, September 12, 1765. See *The Pennsylvania Gazette*, September 12, 1765.

Kent County, *Sept.* 1. 1765.

RAN away from the Subscriber, an *Irish* Servant Man named *Garret Fagin*, a lusty well set Fellow, about 6 Feet 2 Inches high, wears his own Hair, of a dark Colour, tied, but it naturally inclines to curl. He had on a dark grey Jacket, Buckskin Breeches, brown Thread Stockings, and a Castor Hat half worn. He went in Company with another Servant Man.

Whoever takes up and secures the said *Fagin*, so that his Master may have him again, shall have a Reward of FORTY SHILLINGS.

THOMAS DERRICK.

The Maryland Gazette, September 12, 1765.

Prince-George's County, *Sept.* 2, 1765.

FIVE POUNDS REWARD.

RAN away last Night, an Indented Servant Man named *Philip Cooke*, a Taylor by Trade, about 22 Years of Age, brought up in *London*, about 5 Feet 5 or 6 Inches high, of a fair Complexion, has a smiling Countenance and Lisps. He took with him, a blue Cloth Coat with Metal Buttons, 1 ditto Pompadour Colour, 1 Suit of Cloth trimm'd with Vellum, 1 blue Sattin Jacket with Vellum Button Holes, 2 white Linen ditto, work'd with Silk, a red Worsted Damask Banian, some Check Linen Shirts, and some white ditto ruffled, Thread and Silk Stockings, 2 brown Bob Wigs, one half worn, the other almost new, and many other Things. He went away in Company with *George Moore*, a Schoolmaster, and Servant to Mr. *Basil Waring*; the said *Moore* is a well set, genteel Person, has black Hair, Eyes and Beard: It is probable he will put on some of the Taylor's best Apparel, and pass for an Officer, as he pretends to have been in the Army; he is a Person of good Address, understands the *Latin* and *French* Tongues, has travel'd much, and gives a good Account of those Places he has seen.

Whoever secures the said Taylor in any Jail, shall have a Reward of Three Pounds, and Five Pounds if brought Home.

THOMAS GANTT.

The Maryland Gazette, September 12, 1765; September 26, 1765; October 3, 1765; October 10, 1765; October 17, 1765; October 24, 1765. See *The Maryland Gazette*, September 5, 1765.

Baltimore-Town, September 2, 1765.

RUN away last Night, being the first of September instant, from the Subscriber, living in Baltimore County, at the Falls of Patapsco, a Convict Servant Man, named Francis Edwin, but very likely he will change his Name; he is about 5 Feet 5 Inches high, with short brown Hair, has a brown beard: He had on when he went away, an old Cotton Jacket, a new Felt Hat, a Country Linen Shirt, and Country Linen Trowsers, a Pair of old Country made Shoes, one of them is fresh mended, and the other is not.

There is also another Servant Man, belonging to William Bennett, supposed to be gone with him: The said Servant Man has taken with him a large grey Horse, belonging to his said Master, the said Horse is branded with a single **R**, he has likewise stole some Pewter, and it is very probable he will pass for a Tinker: He had on a blue Coat, with a double Cape, an old Cotton Jacket, an old Pair of Leather Breeches, an old Hat, with a Metal Button, two Pair of Country Linen Trowsers, a Check Shirt, and a Country Shirt, black Worsted Stockings, an old Pair of Shoes and Buckles, strait black Hair, and a black Beard; he is about 5 Feet 7 Inches high.

Whoever takes up and secures the said Servants, so that their Masters may have them again, shall have Twenty shillings Reward for each, if in the County, and if out of the County, Five Pounds, besides what the Law allows, paid by us, ROBERT TEVIS, and WILLIAM BENNETT.

The Pennsylvania Gazette, September 12, 1765. See *The Pennsylvania Gazette*, November 6, 1766.

FIVE PISTOLES Reward.

RUN away from the Ship Four Friends, now lying at Chester Town, in Chester River, Maryland, on the 11th of August last, the five following Seaman, *viz.* Robert Nisbet, about 6 Feet high, aged 25 Years, born in the North of England, speaks broad, and wears his own Hair or a Wig. John Connoway, about 26 Years of Age, 5 Feet 6 Inches high, fresh Complexion, wears a Wig. Thomas Lewis, about 24 Years of Age, 5 Feet 6 Inches high, pitted with the Small Pox, and wears his Hair. Patrick Collings, about the same Size with Lewis, and wears his Hair. Roger Merryweather, about the same Size, pretty much freckled, and wears a Wig or Cap. Whoever secures said Seamen, and delivers them on board said Ship, at Chester Town, shall receive Five Pistoles Reward, or One Pistole for each.
WILLIAM HAMILTON.

The Pennsylvania Gazette, September 12, 1765. See *The Maryland Gazette*, August 22, 1765.

September 3, 1765.
FIVE POUNDS Reward.

RUN away on Sunday, the 1st instant, from the Subscribers, living in Kent County, Maryland, two Convict Servant Men, one named Garret Fagon, about 30 Years of Age, about 6 Feet high, pitted with the Small-pox, well built, he is a native Irishman, speaks good English, has brown shirt hair, cut on the Top of his Head, and has several Scars on it: Had on, when he went away, an old Castor Hat, a coarse dark grey Broad Cloth Jacket, lined with black Shaloon, a Silk Handkerchief, one Ozenbrigs Shirt, a Pair of good Buckskin Breeches, and Country-knit Thread Stockings, old Shoes and Buckles. The other named George Burrough, a West Countryman born, about 5 Feet 10 Inches high, light coloured Hair, cut in order for buckling: Had on, and took with him, an old Castor Hat, a light coloured lappel Coat, and red Jacket, Sheepskin Breeches, two white Shirts, and two Country Linnen Ditto, one Pair of Trowsers, Worsted Stockings, old Shoes, and brass Buckles. Whoever takes up and secures said Servants, so as their Masters may have them again, shall have the above Reward for both, or Fifty Shillings for either, and reasonable Charges, paid by
THOMAS DARRACH, or WILLIAM MERRITT.

N. B. The said Garret Fagon generally wears his Hair tied. It is supposed they will travel together.

The Pennsylvania Gazette, September 12, 1765; October 10, 1765. See *The Maryland Gazette*, September 12, 1765, for Burrough.

RAN away from the Subscriber, living at *Severn* Ferry, in *Anne-Arundel* County, a Convict Servant Man, named *John Davis*, about 24 or 25 Years of Age, near 6 Feet high; has a down Look and pale Complexion; had on and took with him, one Osnabrig Shirt, one White Ditto, one Pair of Leather Breeches, one blue Jacket, one dark colour'd Pea Ditto, made of full'd Country Cloth, one lightish colour'd Great Coat, with Metal Buttons.

Whoever takes up the said Servant, and secures him, so that he may be had again, shall receive Twenty Shillings Reward, besides what the Law allows, paid by   GEORGE PAGE.

The Maryland Gazette, September 19, 1765.

Sept. 12, 1765.

RAN away from the Subscribers, on Tuesday the 10th of this Instant, *September*, Two Convict Servant Men, *viz. George Tucker*, a Blacksmith by Trade, about Five Feet Eight Inches high, of a thin Visage, a Scar on his Forehead; had on, or carried with him, a brown Surtout Coat, more than half worn, a lapelled Bearskin Waistcoat, Osnabrigs Trowsers and Shirts, also 2 or 3 white Shirts ruffled at the Bosom and Slits of the Sleeves, a Pair of Turn'd Pumps, and a Felt Hat. He is a bold impudent Fellow, and very fond of strong Liquor.

Alexander Connell, a well-set Fellow, about 5 Feet high, wears his own Hair, which is short and black. He took with him 2 Osnabrigs Shirts, 2 Pair of Osnabrigs Trowsers, a Suit of brown Cloth with a Livery lace. He understands the Business of a Farrier, is much addicted to strong Liquor, and will be drunk if he can come at it.

Whoever takes up the said Servants, and secures them in any Jail in this Province, shall receive Three Pounds Currency Reward for each. If brought to *Piscataway*, in *Prince-George's* County, shall receive the same Reward, and all reasonable Charges paid. If taken out of the Province, Five Pounds Reward, and reasonable Charges paid.

FRANCIS KING,   HENRY HARDEY.

N. B. They are supposed to be gone off with two Sailors lately discharged from Capt. *Benjamin Dawson*, at the Mouth of *Piscataway* Creek, and may pass as Sailors with the others. It is also supposed they took with them an Eastern Shore built Pine Canoe, sharp at both Ends, with Iron Hoops fix'd at the Ends, to prevent splitting, with an Iron Chain and a new Pad Lock.

The Maryland Gazette, September 19, 1765.

RAN away from the Subscriber's Quarter, near *Snowden's* Iron-Works, on the 17th of this Inst. *September*, Three Convict Servant Men, *viz.*

John Gardner, a short thick well-set Fellow: Had on when he went away, as is supposed, an Osnabrigs Shirt, coarse Linen Breeches or

Trowsers, an old Cotton Jacket, a Fearnought Pea ditto, a new Felt Hat, and new Shoes. He came from the West of *England*, and speaks pretty broad.

William Waring, a short thick well-set Fellow also: His Apparel much the same with the other.

William Garret, somewhat shorter than the other Two, and wears his own Hair, which is of a light brown Colour: His Dress much the same; though the Whole is uncertain.

Whoever takes up and secures the said Servants in any Jail, so as they may be had again, shall receive Forty Shillings Reward for each: If taken out of the Province, Three Pounds for each, and reasonable Charges, if brought home, paid by　　　　THOMAS RUTLAND.

The Maryland Gazette, September 19, 1765; September 26, 1765.

RAN away, the 16th of this Instant *September*, from the Subscriber, living in *St. Thomas's* Parish, *Baltimore* County, *Maryland*, Two Convict Servant Men, *viz*.

John Finn, an *Irishman*, imported from *Dublin* about 2 Months ago, about 20 Years of Age, of a fair Complexion, is a well-set Fellow, about 5 Feet 6 or 7 Inches high, and a Hatter by Trade: Had on when he went away, a striped Flannel Jacket, a brown Pea Ditto with Horn Buttons, a coarse *Irish* Linen Shirt, a good black and yellow Silk Handkerchief, a Castor Hat, short Brown-Roll Trowsers, Yarn Stockings, and a strong Pair of Shoes with carved Copper Buckles.

John Thomas, an *Englishman*, about 20 Years of Age, of a pale Complexion, has black Hair and grey Eyes, is a well-set Fellow, about 5 Feet 6 or 7 Inches high, and has been in the Country better than 2 Years: Had on when he went away, a redish brown Country Cloth Coat, much too long for him, an old Felt Hat, an old Check Shirt, a black Cloth Jacket, a black Crape Handkerchief, Osnabrigs Trowsers, old Thread Stockings, and half-worn Shoes much too big for him. All these Cloaths he hath stolen, and 'tis probable they will change Apparel with each other.

Whoever takes up and secures the said Servant, [*sic*] so that their Master may get them again, shall have Twenty Shillings Reward for each; if out of the County, Forty Shillings; and if out of the Province, Three Pounds, besides what the Law allows, paid by
MORDECAI HAMMOND.

N. B. The said *John Thomas* has been bred up to the Sea: Therefore, all Masters of Vessels are forbid carrying them off at their Peril.

The Maryland Gazette, September 26, 1765; October 3, 1765.

FOUR POUNDS REWARD.

RUN away from the Subscribers, living in Kent County, Maryland, on the 21st of August past, two Convict Servant Men, the one named Robert Quick, about 40 Years of Age, about 5 Feet 6 or 7 Inches high, well-built, talks on the West Country Dialect, has short black curled Hair, cut on the Top of his Head, and a large black Beard: Had on, when he went away, an old Felt Hat, a darkish coloured Cloth Jacket, lined with dark Coloured Shaloon, a Country linen Shirt, coarse Country Linen Trowsers, old Boots, supposed to have been changed for Shoes and old Yarn Stockings. The other named James Obrian, an Irishman, about 30 Years of Age, about 5 Feet 10 Inches high, of a swarthy Complexion: Had on, when he went off, an old Castor Hat, patched on the Crown, a short blue Coat, with yellow Metal Buttons, and red Lining, a coarse red Waistcoat, a fine Shirt, ruffled at the Bosom, coarse Tow Trowsers, old Shoes, and yellow Buckles. Whoever takes up said Servants and secures them so that their Masters may have them again, shall have the above Reward, or Forty Shillings for either, paid by   THOMAS BOYER and JOHN WALLACE.
N. B. All Masters of Vessels are forbid to carry them off, at their Peril.
The Pennsylvania Gazette, September 26, 1765.

Baltimore Town, Maryland, Sept, 14.
FIVE POUNDS Reward.

RUN away last Night from the Subscriber, a Convict Servant Man, named Charles Aires, a lusty well set Fellow, supposed to be about 35 Years of Age, about 5 Feet 8 Inches high, is very talkative, and has brown Hair: Had on and took with him a Castor Hat, a Russia Drab Coat, with Metal Buttons, a light coloured Surtout Coat, a brown Jacket, greasy Buckskin Breeches, one Pair of brown and a pair of blue Worsted Stockings, Pumps, a Pair of English Falls, both pretty good, two Pair of Ozenbrigs Trowsers, several white Dowlas Shirts, two Ozenbrigs Ditto, and sundry other things unknown. The said Fellow writes a pretty good Hand and probably may forge a Pass; he is known by the Name of my Lord among his Ship mates, and has been in the Country before. Whoever takes up and secures the said Servant, so that his Master may have him again, shall have a Reward of Fifteen Shillings if 15 Miles from Home, if 20 Miles, Twenty Shillings, if 40 Miles, Forty Shillings, and if out of the Province the above Reward, and reasonable Charges, if brought to the Subscriber, living at Kingsbury Furnace, in Baltimore Country, paid by
JAMES SMITH.

The Pennsylvania Gazette, September 26, 1765. See *The Maryland Gazette*, October 31, 1765.

RUN away from the Subscriber, living near George Town, in Kent County, Maryland, a Convict Servant Man, named John Malone, about five Feet seven Inches, about 20 Years of Age, born in Ireland, but speaks good English, has a flat crooked Nose, is much pitted with the Small-pox, knock-kneed, was in the Transport Service last War, pretends to be a Seaman, and it is thought will endeavour to get on board some Vessel in Philadelphia, as he was near being taken at Chester and Schuylkill, on the 23d and 3d Instant, but escaped; the Little Finger on his Left hand grown fast to the next, as far as the Middle Joint. He stole and took with him, a new blue homespun Frock Coat, lined with coarse Sheeting, with long Cuffs to the Elbow, and white Horn Buttons, a white Shirt, and a Check Ditto, Tow Linen Trowsers, Worsted Stockings, old Shoes, and a Felt Hat, also a Kersey Great Coat, and a Hanger or Cutlas, with a Snakeskin over the Scabbard. Whoever secures said Servant, in any Goal, so as his Master may have him again, shall have Three Pistoles Reward, paid by
JOHN SEWELL.
All Masters of Vessels are forbid to carry him off.
The Pennsylvania Gazette, September 26, 1765.

Kent County, Maryland, Sept. 14.
FIVE POUNDS REWARD.
RUN away, the first Instant, from the Subscriber's Boat, Thomas Dorney Skipper, between Hell Point and Grayfin Creek, Chester River, one John Taylor (the Son of Bray Taylor of Kent County, formerly of Baltimore County) a Taylor by Trade, but has lately used the Water; he is of a very low Stature, well set, of a boyish Look has had one of his Legs broke, on which is a Scar, and his Hair has been lately cut off: Had on a light coloured Saggathy Coat, Nankeen Jacket, an old white Shirt, a half worn Philadelphia made hat, with Silver Loops, a Silver Lace round the Brown, with a large Stone Buckle, Check Trowsers, a ruffled Shirt, and a Pair of Cotton Stockings of Thomas Gresham. He likewise stole the Canoe from the Boat, which is almost new, made of Chesnut; he also stole out of the Boat between Eighteen and Nineteen Pounds, in Dollars. Whoever takes up the said Runaway, and secures him, so that he may be brought to Justice, shall receive the above Reward, paid by   R. GRESHAM.
The Pennsylvania Gazette, September 26, 1765. See *The Maryland Gazette*, September 5, 1765.

Piscataway, October 1, 1765.
MADE their Escape from the Subscriber, on Sunday Night last, the following Convict Servant Men, who will probably pass for Sailors:

John Earley, about 45 Years of Age, about 5 Feet 4 or 5 Inches high, with a large Scar on the right Side of his Chin, and has lost Part of his left Hand little Finger: His Apparel was, an old blue Pea Jacket, Check Shirt, Osnabrigs Trowsers, black Worsted Stockings, old Shoes and Hat.

William Mecklenburg, about the same Height, wears his own black Hair, a blue Surtout Coat, red Jacket, Check Shirt, Osnabrigs Trowsers, and old Shoes, and Stockings.

Whoever takes up the said Runaways, and secures them so that they may be had again, shall have a Reward of Thirty Shillings, paid by
FRANCIS KING,   HENRY HARDY, junr.
The Maryland Gazette, October 3, 1765.

COMMITTED to *Anne-Arundel* County Jail, on Suspicion of being a Runaway, *John Goodan*, about 5 Feet 4 Inches high. He has on a Fearnought Jacket, and an Osnabrigs Shirt and Trowsers.

His Master is desired to take him away, and pay Charges.
WILLIAM PRUE, Jailer.
The Maryland Gazette, October 3, 1765.

RAN away from the Subscriber, living in *Dorchester* County, the 21st of *September* last, a Servant Man named *John Gorman*, a lusty well-set Fellow, about 6 Feet high, wears his own Hair, of a light Colour, tied behind, and is a Carpenter and Sawyer by Trade. He has been a Soldier in Fort *Frederick*, and is very much inclined to Liquor. He had on a Shirt and Trowsers, and a Felt Hat.

Whoever takes up and secures the said *Gorman*, so that his Master may have him again, shall have a Reward of FORTY SHILLINGS, paid by
JOHN WOOLFORD.
The Maryland Gazette, October 3, 1765.

September 30, 1765.
NINE PISTOLES REWARD.
RAN away from the Subscribers, living on *Elk-Ridge*, in *Anne-Arundel* County, Three Convict Servant Men, *viz*.

Richard Ryan, an *Irishman*, imported from *Dublin* about 6 Weeks ago, about 18 Years of Age, about 5 Feet 6 or 7 Inches high, of a fair Complexion. He had on and took with him, a blue Broad-Cloth Coat, a red and white double breasted Jacket, a figur'd Ditto, a Pair of red Broad-Cloth Breeches, a brown Wig, a new Castor Hat, two Pair of coarse Yarn Stockings, a Pair of strong Shoes, with Copper Buckles.

Patrick Norton, an *Irishman*, a well-set Fellow, about 24 Years of Age, about 5 Feet 6 or 7 Inches high, and meanly dress'd.

Richard Welsh, an *Englishman*, about 27 Years of Age; he is a slim made Fellow, and also meanly dress'd.

Whoever takes up the said Servants, and brings them to the Subscribers, shall have, if taken in the County, One Pistole for each; if out of the County, Two Pistoles for each; and if out of the Province, Three Pistoles for each. BENJAMIN DORSEY, WILLIAM CHEW BROWN, VALENTINE BROWN, junr.

The Maryland Gazette, October 10, 1765; October 17, 1765; October 24, 1765.

RAN away from the Subscriber, living near *Upper-Marlborough*, the 18th of August last, a Servant Man named *James Henry Aliscram*, tho' probably may assume the Name of *Mollison*, he is a Taylor by Trade, about 24 Years of Age, and about 5 Feet 7 Inches high, has long black Hair, much pitted with the Small-Pox, and many Pimples in his Face: Had on, a grey *German* Serge Pea Jacket, and an Osnabrigs Shirt and Trowsers. It is likely he may change his Dress, as he took other Cloaths with him.

Whoever delivers the said Servant to his Master, shall have, if taken in the County, Twenty Shillings Reward, and reasonable Charges; if out of the County Forty Shillings, and if out of the Province Three Pounds, paid by DAVID LOWE.

N. B. All Masters of Vessels are forewarn'd not to carry him off at their Peril.

The Maryland Gazette, October 10, 1765; October 17, 1765. See *The Maryland Gazette*, October 27, 1763.

Annapolis, October 7, 1765.
TEN POUNDS REWARD.

RAN away, this Morning, from the Subscriber's Plantation, at *Mount-Clare*, near *Baltimore-Town*, a Convict Servant Man named *Joseph Fry*, about 21 or 22 Years of Age: He is about 5 Feet 8 Inches high, a little pitted with the Small-Pox, a short Forehead, and small grey Eyes, a small Nose, flat round Face, short Hair, has a down Look, talks pretty broad, and has a slouch Walk. He carried with him a blue Surtout Coat, a pale grey Broad-Cloth Ditto, a new Felt Hat, brown Cut Wig, a Scarlet and Drab Waistcoat, Buckskin Breeches, a Holland shirt, red Silk Handkerchief, grey Worsted Stockings, Country-made Shoes, with Straps roughly put on, new Copper Buckles, a Cotton Waistcoat, and an Osnabrigs Shirt and Trowsers.

He took with him a Bright Bay Gelding, Half Blood, Four Years old, Fifteen Hands high, with a large Star in his Forehead, hanging Mane, his Ears and Head newly trimmed, has one white Foot behind, a Switch Tail, paces, trots and gallops, and shod all round. Whoever secures the said Horse and Servant, so that the Subscriber may get them again, shall have the above Reward of Ten Pounds, or Five Pounds for either, from   CHARLES CARROLL.

The Maryland Gazette, October 10, 1765; October 17, 1765; October 24, 1765.

New-Castle Goal, October 2, 1765.

IN Custody of the Subscriber, the two following Persons, viz. John Bambridge, committed as a Runaway Servant, is about 5 Feet 5 Inches high; has on a white Coat, blue Jacket, white Shirt, white thread Stockings, Leather Breeches, &c. Also Elizabeth Gold, says that she is a Servant to Thomas Spry Morgan, near Chester Church, Maryland. Their Masters, if any, are desired to pay Charges, and take them away in 6 Weeks from this Date, otherwise they will be sold for the same by
ALEXANDER HARVEY, Goaler.

The Pennsylvania Gazette, October 10, 1765.

RUN away from their Masters, in Somerset County, Maryland, the 12th of September last, two Irish indented Servants, viz. Daniel Freeman, about 5 Feet 4 Inches high, full faced, about 5 Feet 4 Inches high, full-faced, of a pale Complexion, wears his Hair, and by Trade a Taylor: Had on, when he went away, an old Hat, a brown Flannel Waistcoat, a new Check Shirt, narrow Ozenbrigs Breeches, and a Pair of old Shoes. The other called William Murray, about 5 Feet 6 Inches high, thin visaged, wears his Hair, which is very long, and black: Had on, when he went away, an old Hat, bound with Ferrit, a brown Flannel Waistcoat, white Shirt, and a Pair of narrow Ozenbrigs Breeches. The latter, it is said, has a Brother in or near New-Castle, and it is supposed, as they went together, that they are both gone that Way. Whoever secures them in any Goal, upon giving Notice thereof to the Subscribers, in Philadelphia, shall have a Gratuity of Eight Pounds for both of them, or Four Pounds for either, paid by
RICHARD and PETER FOOTMAN.

The Pennsylvania Gazette, October 10, 1765; October 24, 1765; October 31, 1765.

RUN away from the Subscriber, living on My Lady's Manor, Baltimore County, Maryland, a Convict Servant Man, named John Shepard, has gone

by the Name of Jonathan Darbyshire; he is about 30 Years of Age, about 5 Feet 10 Inches high; had on, when he went away, a Felt Hat, a light coloured Coat, with blue Lining; had with him three Jackets, two of which Cloth, the other mixed, two pair of Shoes, Yarn Stockings, Ozenbrigs Shirt, with two new Metal Buttons in the Collar, and a Country Linen Ditto, patched, with new Wristbands; pretends to a Profession of all Trades, a Weaver, a Sawyer, and says he was a Weaver of Cotton Velvet, at Manchester, in Old England; has been in Joppa Goal, till the Irons have worn his Legs almost to the Bone, through his Stockings; is of a brown Complexion, and has black Hair. Whoever takes up said Servant, and secures him, so that the Owner may have him again, shall have Twenty Shillings Reward, and all reasonable Charges, paid by
THOMAS ELLIOT.
The Pennsylvania Gazette, October 17, 1765; October 31, 1765.

September 21, 1765.
RUN away, last Night, from the Bush River Iron works, James Burns, an Irish Servant Fellow, about 35 Years of Age, of a dark Complexion, about 6 Feet high, has lost two of his fore-Teeth, wears his own Hair; had on a blue double-breasted Jacket, and a brown one under it, a Check Shirt, and Ozenbrigs Trowsers, a small Hat, bound with Ferrit, and makes the Appearance of a Sailor. Whoever takes up and secures the said Servant so that his Master may get him again, shall receive (if taken 10 Miles from home) Fifty Shillings, and if upwards of 20 Miles, Four Pounds, paid by
JAMES WEBSTER.
The Pennsylvania Gazette, October 17, 1765; October 31, 1765.

October 16, 1765.
COMMITTED to *Prince-George's* County Jail, as Runaways, the two following Persons, *viz.* One who calls himself *John Burgoine*, about 30 Years of Age, 5 Feet 4 or 5 Inches high, dark Complexion, with black curl'd Hair cut on the Top, and has dark Eyes. Has on a red Duffil great Coat, a Fearnought Jacket, blue and white strip'd Linsey Breeches, an old Beaver Hat, old Shoes and Stockings, and Osnabrig Shirt.

The Other calls himself *John Sheffield*, about 27 Years of Age, 5 Feet 3 or 4 Inches high, dark Complexion, with a down surly Look, much pitted with the Small-Pox, his Hair cut off, and seems to have a scald Head. Has on an old light colour'd Cloth Jacket, lined with white Linen, and large Metal Buttons on it, also an old Kersey Jacket, Osnabrig Shirt and Trowsers, old Stockings, Pumps and Felt Hat.
GEORGE SCOTT, Sheriff.

N. B. They are suppos'd to be the two Servants advertis'd by Mr. *Harrison, Baltimore.*
 The Maryland Gazette, October 24, 1765. See *The Maryland Gazette,* September 5, 1765. Burgoine and Sheffield may be Bostock and Purchase.

SEVEN POUNDS Reward.

RUN away last Sunday Night from the Subscriber, living in Baltimore County, within 20 Miles of Baltimore Town, two Convict Servant Men, one named Charles Lee, about 30 Years of Age, about 5 Feet 10 Inches high, of a black Complexion, has short black Hair, and a Scar down one Side of his Nose: Had on an old Castor Hat, a blue Jockey Coat, with a Velvet Cape to it, a blue Jacket, a Pair of Nankeen Breeches, and old Trowsers. The other named John Burk, about 25 Years of Age, about 5 Feet 4 Inches high, of a fair Complexion, has short black Hair, and two Teeth out before: Had on a good Castor Hat, a curled Wig, a blue Broadcloath Coat, and blue Jacket, a Pair of black Shag Breeches, old Yarn Stockings, old Shoes, and square Copper Buckles. Said Servants took a Woman with them, who is pretty much pitted with the Small-Pox. Whoever takes up said Servants, and secures them in any Goal, so as their Master may have them again, shall have the above Reward, paid by
JOSEPH OSBORN.
 N. B. Said Servants having Money, it is thought they will change their Clothes: Lee is a Watch maker by Trade, and has wrought in Philadelphia and New York.
 The Pennsylvania Gazette, October 24, 1765; October 31, 1765.

*Baltimore-*Town, *September* 14, 1765.
FIVE POUNDS REWARD.

RAN away last Night, from the Subscriber, a Convict Servant Man, named *Charles Aires,* a lusty, well-set Fellow, supposed to be about 35 Years of Age, and about 5 Feet 8 Inches high, is very Talkative, and wears his own brown Hair: Had on and took with, a Castor Hat, *Russia* Drab Coat with Metal Buttons, a light colour'd Surtout Coat, a brown Jacket, and a Pair of greasy Buckskin Breeches, a Pair of brown and a Pair of blue Worsted Stockings, a Pair of Pumps and a Pair of English Falls, both pretty good, 2 Pair of Osnabrig Trowsers, several white Dowlas Shirts, 2 Osnabrigs Ditto, and sundry other Things unknown: The said Fellow writes a pretty good Hand, and probably may forge a Pass.
 Whoever takes up and secures the said Servant, so as his Master may have him again, shall receive a Reward of Fifteen Shillings, if 15 Miles

from home; if 20 Miles, Twenty Shillings; if 40 Miles, Forty Shillings; and if out of the Province, the above Reward; and reasonable Charges if brought to the Subscriber, living at the *Kingsbury* Furnace, in *Baltimore* County, paid by   JAMES SMITH.

N. B. He is known by the Name of *My Lord*, amongst his Ship-Mates, and hath been in the Country before.

The Maryland Gazette, October 31, 1765. See *The Pennsylvania Gazette*, September 26, 1765.

RUN away, on the 12th of October last, from Kent-Island Narrows, in Maryland, a Convict Servant Man, named William Cullimoor, but has changed his Name to William Williams, an Englishman, and speaks in the West Country Dialect, a well set Fellow, about five Feet four Inches high, dark Complexion, with short black Hair, and pretends to be a great Mower and Ditcher: Had on when he went away, a light Cloth Coat, coarse Cotton Waistcoat, white Broadcloth Breeches, grey Cotton Stockings, and a Pair of English Pumps. Whoever takes up and secures the said Servant, so that his Master (now living at Dover) may have him again, shall have seven Dollars Reward, paid by JOHN WINTERTON, Goaler.

The Pennsylvania Gazette, December 12, 1765.

1766

RUN away from the Subscriber, living in Talbot County, Maryland, a Servant Man, named John Reid, aged 22 Years, a little pitted with the Small-Pox, and about 5 Feet 6 Inches high; had on and with him, when he went away, a white Country Kersey Jacket and Breeches, but no Shoes or Stockings: He came over in February 1763, in the Ship Lion, Capt. Taylor. Likewise run away from Hugh Poulk, of Queen Ann's County, a Servant Woman, named Sarah Rogers, of a low Stature, and her Apparel not known. Whoever takes up the said Runaways so that their Master may have them again, shall have Forty Shillings Reward for each, paid by
CORNELIUS DUELY, and HUGH POULK.

The Pennsylvania Gazette, January 2, 1766; January 9, 1766; January 16, 1766; January 23, 1766. See *The Pennsylvania Gazette*, April 3, 1766, and *The Pennsylvania Gazette*, May 22, 1766.

Queen Ann's County, Maryland.
RUN away from the Subscriber, on the 23d of December last, an Apprentice Lad, named Jesse Box, about 18 Years of Age, this Country

born, of low Stature, thick set, a smooth full broad Face, black Eyes, with a Blemish in one of them, short Fingers, and thick Hand: Had on when he went away, a grey Cloth Coat, coarse Shirt, and Trowsers, a Pair of Channel Pumps of his own making, and it is probably he may change his Name and Clothes. Whoever takes up said Apprentice, and brings him Home to his Master, shall have Forty Shillings Reward, and reasonable Charges, if taken out of this Province; or if secured in any Goal, what the Law allows, paid by   THOMAS DOCKERY.
All Masters of Vessels, and others, are forewarned from entertaining him.
The Pennsylvania Gazette, January 2, 1766; January 9, 1766; January 16, 1766; January 23, 1766.

RUN away from the Subscriber, living in Chester Town, Maryland, a Servant Man, named Charles Hysley, about 25 Years of Age, well set, about 5 Feet 6 Inches high, wears a light coloured Saggathy Coat, with green Lining, black Plush Breeches; he is very talkative, particularly about Horse riding and Racing, and at the Time he went off stole a sorrel Mare, that is nearly blind. Whoever takes up and secures the said Servant, so that his Master may have him again, shall have Forty Shillings Reward, paid by RICHARD GRAVES.
The Pennsylvania Gazette, January 23, 1766; January 30, 1766; February 6, 1766.

RUN away, on the 30th of last Month, from the Subscriber, in Frederick-Town, Cecil County, Maryland, an English Convict Servant Man, named Edward Davis, about 30 Years of Age, about 5 Feet 4 Inches high, has lately been sick, which gives his Complexion a yellow Cast, by Trade a Peruke-maker and Barber, and speaks French: Had on, when he went away, a half-worn Felt Hat, old dark cut Wig, mixed Cloth-coloured Surtout Coat, old light-coloured close Coat, scarlet Serge Vest, black Serge Denim Breeches, old striped Holland Trowsers, patched at the Knees, which he wears to hide his bandy Legs. He took with him a white spotted Flannel under Jacket, two or three Cases of Razors, and other Things belonging to the Business. Whoever takes up said Servant, and brings him home, or secures him in any Goal, and gives Notice thereof to his Master, so that he may have him again, shall receive (if taken in the Province) Forty Shillings, and if taken out of the Province, Four Pounds Reward, and reasonable Charges, paid by   JOSEPH EARLE.
N. B. 'Tis supposed he is gone towards Philadelphia. All Masters of Vessels and others are forbid to harbour or carry him off, at their Peril. If he

should offer any of the above mentioned Things for Sale, 'tis requested they may be stopped.
The Pennsylvania Gazette, February 6, 1766; February 20, 1766; February 27, 1766; March 6, 1766; March 13, 1766; March 20, 1766.

RUN away from the Subscriber, at Elk Forge, Maryland, near the Head of Elk, a Servant Man, named John Hoskins, about 5 Feet 9 Inches high, very well built, a Pearl on one Eye, has a very bad Countenance; had on, when he went away, two new Jackets, both of a light colour, home-made Cloth, a new Pair of Buckskin Breeches, Germantown Stockings, a new Felt Hat, an Englishman born, and was last bought out of Chester Goal. Whoever secures said Runaway, so that his Master may have him again, shall have Forty Shillings Reward, and reasonable Charges, paid by
JESSE HOLLINGSWORTH.
The Pennsylvania Gazette, February 6, 1766; February 13, 1766; February 20, 1766; March 13, 1766.

Baltimore Town, Maryland, Feb. 26, 1766.
RUN away from the Subscribers, living in Baltimore-Town, on Monday Night, being the 24th of this Instant, two Irish Servant Men, named John Heron, and James Red; said Heron is about 5 Feet 9 Inches high, of a dark brown Complexion, about 26 Years of Age; and has a natural Mark above his Right Eye, much of the Size and colour of a red Cherry; but rather long than round: Had on when he went away, an old brown Coat, old Scarlet Waistcoat, Deer-Skin Breeches, brown Thread Stockings, a Pair of half worn Shoes, Pinchbeck Buckles, a Shirt of Country made Linen, and a new Wool Hat half worn. He is by Trade a Mason, Bricklayer and Plaisterer.

James Red, about 5 Feet 10 Inches high, of a fair Complexion, and of a slender upright Shape, about 22 Years of Age: Had on, when he went away, a light coloured Cloth Coat, a brown Waistcoat, a Pair of half-worn black Everlasting Breeches, grey Yarn Stockings, new turned Pumps, Pinchbeck Buckles, and half worn Felt Hat, a white or check Shirt, by Trade a Shoemaker. They may very likely change their Apparel.

If taken up in any Place out of this County, and brought to the Subscribers, or secured in any Goal, so that their Owners may have them again, shall have FIVE POUNDS, Reward for both, or for each of them FIFTY SHILLINGS, and reasonable Charges, paid by us
CONRAD SMITH, JOHN CANNON.
The Pennsylvania Gazette, March 13, 1766; April 3, 1766; May 8, 1766. See *The Pennsylvania Gazette*, June 12, 1766.

Petapsco River, Maryland, March 7, 1766.
RUN away from the Baltimore Iron-works, a Convict Servant Man, named John Christopher Cloauss, a Prussian born, speaks pretty good English and lisps a little; was brought up to Physic, which he practised here a Year; he is a genteel Person in Behaviour, having a good Address he is a small Man, dark Complexion, black Eyes, and wears his own (not very long) black Hair; Had on, and took with him, an old Castor Hat, two Check Shirts, an old lapelled blue Cloth Coat, with a bluish Velvet Collar, an old dark coloured Russia Drab Coat and Jacket, coarse Cloth Breeches, all which have Brass Buttons; two Pair Worsted Stockings, Country made Shoes, and Brass Buckles, and an old light coloured great Coat. He also took with him a white Mare, near 14 Hands high, and an old Saddle. He has been to the Northward and Southward of these Colonies, in Men of War, and Letter of Marque Ships, having been in the English Sea Service near nine Years. Whoever secures the said Servant, (with or without the Mare) so as the Subscriber may have him again, shall receive the above Reward, from
JOHN WELSH.
N. B. He has a Case of Surgeons Instruments with him.
The Pennsylvania Gazette, March 20, 1766.

Baltimore-Town, March 14, 1766.
RAN away from the Subscriber's Plantation near *Bush-River*, on the 11th Instant, two Convict Servants, *viz.*

Thomas Dobson, about 5 Feet 7 or Inches high, pitted with the Small-Pox, and has streight black Hair: Had on when he went away, an old blue double-breasted Coat with Metal Buttons, red Shag Breeches, white Yarn Stockings, new coarse Shoes, Brass Buckles, and has not been above two Months in the Country.

Jacob Crawley, an artful Rogue, has been better than two Years in the Country, about 20 Years old, swarthy Complexion, and about 5 Feet 4 Inches high: Had on, an old Felt Hat, brown Coat and Jacket, with Metal Buttons, Cotton Breeches, black and white Yarn Stockings, new coarse Shoes and Brass Buckles.

Perhaps they may change their Dress.

Whoever takes up said Servants, and brings them to the Subscriber in *Baltimore-Town*, or to his Plantation, or secures them in any Jail, shall have Twenty Shillings Reward for each, beside what the Law allows.
HENRY STEVENSON.
The Maryland Gazette, March 27, 1766.

March 19, 1766.
RUN away last Sunday, from the Subscriber, living in Queen Ann's County, Maryland, two Convict Servants, viz. one named Evan Roberts, an

Englishman, about 34 Years of Age, of a dark Complexion, wears black Hair, of middling Stature; had on, when he went away, a new Felt Hat, coarse Ozenbrigs Shirt, a whitish full trimmed Cloth Coat, with a small Cape, white coloured Cloth Waistcoat, dark coloured Fearnought Breeches, new Shoes and Stockings. The other, who goes by the name of Charles, an Englishman, a Weaver by Trade, about 35 Years of Age, limps as he walks, of a Sandy Complexion, a short well-set Fellow, had on, and took with him, when he went away, an old Hat, a yellow cut Wig, a light brown Surtout Coat, a blue Broadcloth right bodied ditto, with white Metal Buttons, a Pair of old Leather Breeches, a Pair of Nankeen Ditto, a Pair of blue and white ribbed Stockings, and good Shoes. Whoever takes up said Runaways and secures them so that the Owner may have them again, shall have four Pounds for them both, or Forty Shillings for either, paid by
JOSEPH CHAIRES.

N. B. What is most remarkable in the above Servants, is their being decriped [sic] each in the left Hand. All Masters of Vessels are forbid to conceal or carry them off at their Peril.

The Pennsylvania Gazette, March 27, 1766; April 24, 1766. See *The Pennsylvania Gazette*, June 6, 1765.

Patuxent Iron-Works, *March* 17, 1766.
FIVE POUNDS REWARD.

RUN away from the Subscribers, on the 26th of *February* last, a Convict Servant Man, named *Henry Glover*, and by Trade a Blacksmith; he is a well-set Fellow, about 5 Feet 7 or 8 Inches high, of a pale Complexion, light grey Eyes, and pitted with the Small-Pox, wears his own dark brown Hair. He had on and took with him, an old light colour'd Cloth Coat, a Cloth Jacket, and a Cotton ditto, brown Cloth Breeches, one white Shirt and one Osnabrigs ditto, Country made Shoes and Stockings, and a Felt Hat about half worn; but it is likely he may change his Dress, as it is conjectured that he has some Money with him. It is supposed that he is gone up towards *Fort Frederick*, as he passed through *Frederick-Town*, and afterwards was seen going up the Road which leads to the Fort. He has with him an old Indenture with a Discharge on the Back of it, Signed by *Christopher Lowndes*, in the Year 1752, and has passed by the Name of the Person mentioned in the same Indenture, (tho' what Name it is we can't find out) by which Means he has deceived many who have questioned him.

Whoever will secure the said Servant, so that the Subscribers may get him again, shall have the above Reward of FIVE POUNDS, and if brought Home, reasonable Charges, paid by
THOMAS, SAMUEL, and JOHN SNOWDEN.

The Maryland Gazette, April 3, 1766; April 17, 1766; April 24, 1766; May 1, 1766; May 8, 1766; May 22, 1766.

RUN away, last June, from Talbot Courthouse, in Maryland, a Servant Man, named John Reid, about five Feet eight Inches high, with broad Shoulders, and pitted with the Small pox; had on when he went away, a Country made Kersey Jacket, without Cuffs, and Breeches of the same. He was bought in February, 1764, from on board the ship Lion, Capt. Taylor, then lying at Choptank. He went to Mother-kill Landing, and from thence to Philadelphia in a Boat, and is thought to be the Person described as in Burlington Goal.

Also run away last June was twelve Months, from Hugh Polk, Merchant, in Queen Ann's, an English Convict Servant Woman, named Sarah Rodgers, she is either in Pennsylvania, or the Jerseys. Whoever takes up and secures said Servants, shall have Five Pounds Reward for both, or Fifty Shillings for either, paid by
CORNELIUS DAILY, and HUGH POLK.

The Pennsylvania Gazette, April 3, 1766; May 8, 1766. See *The Pennsylvania Gazette*, January 2, 1766, and *The Pennsylvania Gazette*, May 22, 1766.

RUN away from the Subscriber, living in George-Town, Kent County, in Maryland, a Convict Servant Man, named James Roe; had on when he went away, a light coloured Surtout Coat, of Whitney, with a Cape, a black Waistcoat, that has been turned, and a Pair of lightish coloured Plush Breeches, much pieced. He is remarkably bald on the Head, about 35 Years of Age, a Taylor by Trade.

He is supposed to be gone away in Company with another Convict Servant, named Johnston, who had on when he went away, a blue Jacket, lined with red, is a very artful Fellow, and knows the Country well. Whoever secures the above Fellows, in any of his Majesty's Goals, so that the Subscriber may have him again, shall have Five Pounds Reward for both, or Fifty Shillings for either, and reasonable Charges, paid by
COLLIN FERGUSON.

N. B. They are thought to be gone towards York, or Sasquehannah.
The Pennsylvania Gazette, April 3, 1766; April 17, 1766.

Stafford County, Virginia, April 4, 1766.
RAN away last Night, from the Subscriber, a Convict Servant Man, named ROBIN CLARKE, lately imported; he is a Groom and Gardener, is about

30 Years of Age, 5 Feet 6 or 7 Inches high, a thick well-set Fellow, sandy Complexion, round Faced, a little mark'd with the Small-Pox, with short curling Hair, a soft smooth Way of Speaking, is a very great Villain, but is an extreme handy Fellow, and can turn his Hand to almost any Business: He was dressed in a Bearskin Jacket and Breeches, but what other Clothes he has with him is not known, except that he has taken with him an old Red Jacket and a Brown Jacket. Also took with him, a small grey blooded Horse, branded **TM**.

Whoever secures the said servant, and brings him Home to the Subscriber, shall receive FIVE DOLLARS Reward.
THOMSON MASON.

The Maryland Gazette, April 10, 1766; April 17, 1766; April 24, 1766; May 1, 1766; May 8, 1766; May 22, 1766.

RAN away from the Subscriber, living in *Dorchester* County, on the 29th of *March* last, an Indentured *English* Servant Man, named *William Payne*; he is about 5 Feet 8 Inches high, rather stout Bodied, his Legs small, his Complexion rather ruddy; is fond of strong Liquor, and is generally Talkative when in Drink: He Indentured as a Sawyer, but as he has formerly been several Years at Sea, it is probable he will attempt to pass as a Sailor. Had on and with him when he went away, a dark grey or brown Cloth Coat, and a blue Cloth Vest, with Metal Buttons to each, one Nankeen Vest, one Pair of brown Cloth Breeches, two Pair of Country Linen Trowsers, two Pair of fine white Country Yarn Hose, two Osnabrigs Shirts, two fine white Linen Shirts, one grey Cut Wig, a Hat bound round the Rim with black Binding, and a Pair of Country Shoes.

Whoever apprehends the said Servant, and secures him in any Jail, shall have FIVE POUNDS *Pennsylvania* Currency REWARD, and if he is brought home, reasonable Charges attending it shall be likewise paid, by WILLIAM ENNALLS.

The Maryland Gazette, April 10, 1766; April 17, 1766; April 24, 1766. See *The Pennsylvania Gazette*, May 15, 1766.

RUN away from the Subscriber, at the Head of Elk, an Irish Servant Man, named Charles Farran, about 20 Years of Age, 5 Feet 7 Inches high, wears black curled Hair, has a down Look, a well set Fellow; had on, when he went away, on old Felt hat, light coloured Country Cloth lappelled Jacket, lined with Tow Linen, with small flat white Metal Buttons, a dark Frize Waistcoat, old Buckskin Breeches, blue grey Yarn Stockings, old Shoes, and Copper Buckles. Whoever takes up and secures said Servant, so that his

Master may have him again, shall have Three Pounds Reward, and reasonable Charges, if brought home, paid by
HENRY HOLLINGSWORTH.
N. B. All Masters of Vessels are forbid to carry him off at their Peril.
The Pennsylvania Gazette, April 10, 1766; May 8, 1766; May 15, 1766; June 5, 1766. See *The Pennsylvania Gazette*, June 13, 1765; *The Pennsylvania Gazette*, June 12, 1766, and *The Pennsylvania Gazette*, August 7, 1766.

FIFTEEN POUNDS REWARD.

RAN away from the Subscribers, in *Sassafrass* Neck, *Caecil* County, on the 9th of this Inst. *April*, Three *English* Convict Servant Men, *viz.*

John Sandals, born *Shropshire*, about 28 or 30 Years of Age, a very stout, likely Fellow, of a sallow Complexion, with short brown Hair, and several large Cuts in his Head: He wears a very light coloured Country Cloth Coat, with Metal Buttons, striped Swanskin Vest, with Lapells, much worn, old Buckskin Breeches, Country Linen Shirt, Castor Hat little worn, Yarn Stockings, and Country Shoes, with large cast Brass Buckles.

John Hockaday, born in *Devonshire*, about 40 Years of Age, a low squat Fellow, fair Complexion'd, with short sandy Hair, and is almost Bald: He wears an old Snuff coloured fine Cloth Coat, bound round the Edges and Button Holes with Worsted Binding of a lighter Colour, and old cut and raised Velvet Vest, a light coloured Country Cloth Pea Jacket, old Leather Breeches, Country Linen Shirt, old ribb'd Worsted Hose, Country Shoes, with large plain Silver Buckles, and a good Felt Hat. He has with him an old green *Rider's* Almanack, an old Twine Purse, and a Silver Stock-Buckle.

Edward Thompson, (belonging to *Henry Ward Pearce*) born in *Shropshire*, about 30 Years of Age, upwards of 6 Feet high, short black Hair, some Scars in his Head, and stoops a little in his Shoulders: He had on a Country Cloth short brown Coat and Breeches, with Metal Buttons, spotted Flannel Jacket, old Whitney Surtout Coat, brown Yarn Stockings, half-worn Shoes, square Brass Buckles, Osnabrig Shirt, and an old fine Hat.

They have taken some Money with them, and have also taken a Servants blue close-bodied Coat, of fine Cloth, some fine Shirts, a Silk and Linen Handkerchief, Stockings, and other Things, so that it's probable they may vary their Dress.—They all ran away last Year, but not altogether, were brought home at considerable Expence, and were forgiven on Promises of Amendment.—As they have now gone off without the least Cause of Complaint, have lived extremely well, and have behaved with the greatest ingratitude, it is hoped every Person will, as far it lies in their Power, hinder their getting off.

Whoever secures them in any Jail, so that they are had again, shall receive a Reward of FIVE POUNDS *Pennsylvania* Currency for each, and if brought home reasonable Charges, paid by
MICHAEL EARLE,   HENRY W. PEARCE.
The Maryland Gazette, April 17, 1766; May 1, 1766; May 8, 1766; May 22, 1766. See *The Pennsylvania Gazette*, April 17, 1766. See *The Pennsylvania Gazette*, August 29, 1765, and *The Maryland Gazette*, April 17, 1766, for Thompson.

April 10, 1766.
FIFTEEN POUNDS Reward.

RUN away, last Night, from the Subscribers, living in Sassafras Neck, Cecil County, Maryland, three English Convict Servant Men, one named John Sandels, born in Shropshire, about 28 Years of Age, a very stout lusty Fellow, of a sallow Complexion, with short brown Hair, has several large Scars on his Head; had on, when he went away, a good Castor Hat a light coloured Country Cloth Coat, with metal Buttons, striped Swanskin lapelled Vest much wore, an old Shirt, old Buckskin Breeches, Yarn Stockings, Country Shoes, with large Brass Buckles.—Another, named John Hawkerday, born in Devonshire, about 40 Years of Age, a low squat Fellow, fair Complexion, with short sandy Hair, and is bald; he wears an old brown Cloth Coat, trimmed round the Edges and Button holes with a lighter coloured Worsted Binding, light coloured Country Cloth Pea Jacket, an old cut and raised Velvet Vest, old Buckskin Breeches, Country Linen Shirt, old ribbed Worsted Stockings, and Country Shoes, with large plain Silver Buckles, and has with him an old Rider's Almanack, with a green Cover, fine Twine Purse, and a large Silver Stockbuckle.—The Third is named Edward Thompson, about 30 Years of Age, upwards of 6 Feet high, short black Hair, some Scars on his Head, and stoops a little in his Shoulders; had on a short brown Country Cloth Coat and Breeches, with Metal Buttons, spotted Flannel Jacket, old Whitney Surtout Coat, brown Yarn Stockings, half-worn, Shoes, square Brass Buckles, an old fine Hat, and Ozenbrigs Shirt. They have also taken a Servant's blue close bodied Coat, of fine Cloth, some Shirts, Silk and Linen Handkerchiefs, Stockings, and other Things, so that they may change their Dress. Whoever secures them in any Goal, so as their Masters may have them again, shall have a Reward of Five Pounds Pennsylvania Currency, for each, and reasonable Charges, if brought home, paid by
MICHAEL EARLE, and HENRY WARD PEARCE.

N. B. Said Servants ran away last Fall, at different Times, were brought home at a considerable Expence, and forgiven, on Promise of Amendment. As they have now gone off, without any Cause or Complaint,

have lived extremely well, and behaved with Ingratitude, it is hoped every Person will so far as it is in their Power hinder their getting off.
The Pennsylvania Gazette, April 17, 1766; June 12, 1766. See *The Maryland Gazette*, April 17, 1766. See *The Pennsylvania Gazette*, August 29, 1765, for Thompson.

Baltimore County, Maryland, April 8, 1766.
TEN POUNDS Reward.

RUN away from his Bale, [sic] on the 6th Instant, James Smith, an Irishman, who calls himself a Tanner by Trade, has lived at different Places in Pennsylvania, and the Jerseys; he is a short well set Fellow, somewhat battle kneed, down Look, and black Hair; has a Knot on one of his Wrists, near the Size of a Nutmeg; had on, when he went away, a short skirted light coloured Jacket, and spotted Flannel one under, old Castor Hat, Leather Breeches, and Yarn Stockings. Whoever takes up and secures the said Fellow, so as he may be delivered to the Subscriber, shall be intitled to the above Reward, paid by JOHN LEE WEBSTER.
The Pennsylvania Gazette, April 17, 1766; April 24, 1766; May 15, 1767; May 22, 1766.

FIVE PISTOLES REWARD.

RAN away last Night, from the Subscriber's Plantation in the Barrens of *Baltimore* County, an Indented Servant Man, named *James Sertain*, born in the West of *England*, and talks much in that Dialect, near or quite 6 Feet high, slim made, has a down roguish sulky Look, about 50 Years of Age, wears his own Hair which is of a dark brown, some grey Hairs in his Beard, and Bald on the Top of his Head: Had on and took with him, an old brown Cloth Coat, brown Kersey Breeches, white Cotton Jacket, Osnabrig Shirts, coarse white Yarn Stockings, old Castor Hat, and old Shoes. He had on an Iron Collar when he went off, but as he is a grand Villain, imagine he soon got rid of it, and will probably change his Apparel. He served 7 Years with *Charles Carroll*, Esq; at the End of which Time, supposed he got a Discharge, by which he will endeavour to pass.

Whoever takes up the said Servant, and delivers him to the Subscriber, living on *Elk-Ridge* in *Anne-Arundel* County, or to *Alexander Todd* at the said Plantation, shall receive as a Reward, if taken 20 Miles from home, Twenty Shillings; if 30 Miles, Forty Shillings; if 40 Miles, Fifty Shillings; if 50 Miles, Three Pounds; and if out of the Province, Five Pistoles, paid by *April* 17, 1766.   JOHN DORSEY.
The Maryland Gazette, April 24, 1766; May 1, 1766; May 8, 1766; May 22, 1766.

Annapolis, *April* 14, 1766.
WHEREAS it has been represented to his Excellency the Governor, that on Sunday Evening the 30th of *March* last, the Store of *Thomas Ewing*, in *Baltimore-Town*, was open'd by a false Key, and stolen out of it, Pieces of Eight and *Pennsylvania* Paper Money, to the amount of about £.70 Currency, by Persons unknown: His Excellency, for the better Discovery and bringing to Justice the Persons who Committed the said Robbery, doth Promise his Lordship's Pardon to any one of them (the Principal only excepted) who shall discover his or her Accomplice or Accomplices in the said Fact, so that he, she or them, may be Apprehended and Convicted thereof.
Signed by *Order*,
UPTON SCOTT, Cl. Con.
AND as a further Encouragement, the Subscriber doth Promise a Reward of Thirty Pounds, to any one who shall made a Discovery of any Person or Persons concerned in the above-mention'd Robbery, so that he, she, or they, be brought to Justice and Convicted thereof.
THOMAS EWING.

 There is one JOHN CHEW, by Trade a Barber, who lived in *Baltimore-Town*, that absconded the Morning after the Robbery, who is supposed to be concerned in the said Robbery: He is a Man of about 35 Years of Age, 5 Feet 8 or 9 Inches high, wears a Grey Surtout Coat, Blue Coat, Black Jacket and Blue Breeches, and a Black Cut Wig; I am told he has formerly been known by the Name of *John Engle*; he is supposed to have two Wives now living, he went towards *George-Town*, in *Caecil* County.
 The Maryland Gazette, April 24, 1766; May 1, 1766; May 8, 1766; May 22, 1766.

RAN away from the Subscriber, in *Northumberland* County, *Virginia*, a Servant named *Samuel Holmes*, by Trade a Taylor, 5 Feet 5 Inches high, has a remarkable yellow Spot on the Outside of one of his Knees, 'tis said by the other Servants to be on the left Knee, and on the Instep of the other Leg there is a very large Scar, he Stammers in his Speech, is Bow legged, and Rolls much in his Walk: Had on a dark Cloth Coat, with white Lining, and Metal Buttons. I expect he will change his Name and Dress; but the above Description of his Person, &c. will always discover him. He ran away once before, and was taken up at *Chester*, in *Pennsylvania*; he then had a forged Pass, and went by the Name of *John Harriss*, but his Knee discovered him. It is supposed he has got a forged Pass. He has told the other Servants he would get on board some Vessel going to Sea, it is therefore begged of all Captains of Vessels not to carry the Rogue away, but to send him on Shore to Justice. He has been long in this Country, and, by his cunning Enquiry, knows most Places, and the Names of the Counties, and the most noted Persons in *Pennsylvania, Maryland,* and *Virginia.*

Whoever secures said Servant, so as he may be had again, shall receive Five Pounds Reward, from

March 12, 1766. WILLIAM TAITE.

The Maryland Gazette, April 24, 1766; May 1, 1766; May 8, 1766; May 15, 1766; May 22, 1766. See *The Pennsylvania Gazette,* May 15, 1766, and *The Maryland Gazette,* July 31, 1766. Holmes/Homes.

RAN away from the Subscriber, living in *Chester-Town, Kent* County, on the 17th of this Inst. *April,* a *Welch* Servant Man, named *John Williams,* about 25 Years of Age, about 5 Feet 8 Inches high, wears his own short dark Hair tied behind, and cut short before, has a great many Pimples in his Face, speaks pretty much in the *Welch* Dialect, one of his Legs is shorter than the other, he walks with his Toes inward, and is a thick set Fellow: Had on, and with him when he went away, an old whited [sic] brown Coat with short Skirts, an old blue Jacket without Sleeves, Leather Breeches, several Pair of Worsted Stockings, and a Beaver Hat almost worn out; several Shirts not made up, of good white Linen, with some Check Shirts half worn out, and a Pair of half worn Shoes.

ALSO, Ran away from the Subscriber, living in *Kingston, Queen-Anne's* County, a *Welch* Servant Man, named *John Lewis,* about 5 Feet 9 Inches high, upwards of 20 Years of Age, wears his own yellowish Hair untied, has a light colour'd Great Coat, the Rest of his Cloaths unknown: They are both gone together, and are suspected to be gone in a Shallop to *Virginia,* as they stole a Canoe from *Queen-Anne's,* in Order to go to the Shallop, which was lying by for them, and was seen talking with the Master of said Shallop. Therefore,

Whoever secures said Servant, so as their Master may have them again, shall receive TEN POUNDS if taken in the Province, and TWENTY POUNDS if taken out of the Province, one Half to be paid by *John Bolton,* if the former is took up, and the other Half to be paid by *John Bennet,* if the later is took up, and all reasonable Charges paid by the Subscribers.

JOHN BOLTON, Mercht. and, JOHN BENNET, *Queen-Anne's.*

The Maryland Gazette, April 24, 1766; May 1, 1766. See *The Pennsylvania Gazette,* May 8, 1766.

RAN away from *Port-Tobacco* in *Charles* County, on Wednesday the 26th of *March* last, an *English* Servant Lad, named *Joseph Smith,* about 19 Years of Age, wears his Hair which is white, and Talks somewhat like a Negro: Had on when he went away, a grey Bearskin Coat, and a brown superfine Cloth Jacket, both pretty much worn, a Pair of Forrest Cloth Breeches, Stockings, and Shoes with black Buckles.

He crossed *South-River* Ferry the Day following with another little Boy, and is supposed to have gone towards *Baltimore*.

Whoever secures the said Servant in any Jail in this Province, shall have Forty Shillings Reward, and if brought home to the Subscriber FIVE POUNDS *Pennsylvania* Currency, paid by
JOHN SEMPLE.

The Maryland Gazette, April 24, 1766; May 1, 1766.

Anti-Eatem Forge, Frederick County, April 27.

RAN away from the above Forge on the 20th Instant, a Servant Man, named THOMAS MECLENE, or ONAN, an *Irishman*, (tho' he says he is a Highlandman) a low squat Fellow, of a very swarthy Complexion, with short black Hair, he had on when he went away a blue Cloth Coat, a double-breasted Jacket of an Ash coloured Bearskin Cloth, trimmed with flat white Metal Buttons, a Pair of Buckskin Breeches, old Shoes, and a Pair of grey mill'd, or worsted Stockings. He commonly wears his Garters under his Knees, is a very talkative Fellow, and pretends to be a Conjuror, and brags much of his Land and Negroes in *Caecil*, or *Kent* County. Whoever brings him, or secures the said Fellow, so as I may have him again, shall receive THREE POUNDS *Pennsylvania* Currency from
SAMUEL BEALL, *jun.* for Self, and Co.

The Maryland Gazette, May 1, 1766; May 8, 1766; May 15, 1766; May 22, 1766; May 29, 1766; June 5, 1766. See *The Pennsylvania Gazette*, July 3, 1766, and August 28, 1766.

RUN away from the Subscriber, living in Dorset County, Maryland, on the 29th of March last, an English Servant Man, named .William Payne; he was imported in the year 1764, in the Ship Dove, from London, by Captain .Jeremiah Banning, of whom the Subscriber bought him, he is about 5 Feet 8 Inches high, rather stout bodied, his Legs small, his Complexion rather ruddy; he is fond of strong Liquor, and is generally talkative when in drink. He indentured as a Sawyer, but as he has formerly been several Years at Sea, it is probably he may attempt to pass as a Sailor; had on and took with him, when he went off, a dark or grey or brown Cloth Coat, a blue Cloth Vest, with Metal Buttons to each, one Nankeen Vest, one Pair brown Cloth Breeches, two Pair Country Linen Trowsers, two Pair fine white Country Yarn Hose, two Ozenbrigs Shirts, two fine white Linen ditto, a grey cut

Wig, a Hat bound round the Rim with black Binding, and a Pair of Country Shoes. Whoever apprehends said Servant, and secures him in any Goal, shall have Five Pounds Pennsylvania Currency Reward, and if brought home, reasonable Charges, paid by   WILLIAM ENNALLS.
The Pennsylvania Gazette, May 1, 1766; May 15, 1767; May 29, 1766; June 12, 1766; July 17, 1766; July 24, 1766. See *The Maryland Gazette*, April 10, 1766.

April 22, 1766.
TEN POUNDS REWARD.

RAN away from the Subscriber's Quarter, on the back of *Elk-Ridge*, near *Poplar Spring* Chapel, on Sunday the 13th of *April*, a Country indented Servant Man named *William Billington*, about 5 Feet 6 Inches high, and pretty well proportioned thereto, fair Complexion, and wears his own short black Hair, under a Cap, has a remarkable down Look when spoke to, and is also a remarkable Liar and Flatterer in Conversation. Had on and with him when he went away, a short green lapell'd Coat, trimm'd with Metal Buttons, one old blue Jacket, Oznabrig Shirt, Cotton Breeches, white Yarn Stockings, and an old Pair of Shoes. He formerly served a Term of Years with Mr. *Joseph Hobbs*, in this County, and has since made a very extensive Acquaintance, some of whom may possibly supply him with Money, and other Cloathing, and its likely he may change his Name.

Whoever takes up the said Servant, and delivers him to the Overseer at the aforesaid Plantation, or to the Subscriber on *Elk-Ridge*, in *Anne-Arundel* County, shall have the above Reward, paid by
H. RIDGELY.
The Maryland Gazette, May 8, 1766; May 22, 1766; June 5, 1766; June 12, 1766; June 26, 1766.

April 14, 1766.

RAN away from the Subscriber, living in *Cockaway* Neck, in *Kent* County, *Maryland*, an *English* Convict Servant Man, named *William Anderson*, about 36 Years of Age, 5 ½ Feet high, with short black Hair, his right Eye-Brow is white, and the other brown. Had on, and took away, a good Felt Hat, a brownish Fly Coat, and double-breasted Jacket, striped with several Colours, and lined with Cross-barr'd Kersey, old Leather Breeches patch'd with Cloth, a new Tow Linen Shirt, an Osnabrigs Ditto pieced a-cross the Back, old blue Stockings, and new Shoes, with white carved Metal Buckles in them.

Whoever takes up and secures the said Servant, so as his Master may get him again, or brings him to Thomas Ringgold, Merchant, in Chester-

Town, shall have FIFTY SHILLINGS Reward, and reasonable Charges, paid by GEORGE CLARK.
The Maryland Gazette, May 8, 1766; May 15, 1766; May 22, 1766.

TWENTY POUNDS Reward.

RUN away, on the 17th of April last, from John Bolton, in Chester-Town, Kent County, Maryland, Merchant, a Welsh Servant Man, named John Williams, about 25 Years of Age, about 5 Feet 8 Inches high, wears his own dark Hair, tied behind, and cut short before; has a good many Pimples in his Face, and speaks a little in the Welsh Dialect: He having had an Imposthume in his Thigh, has contracted it so that one Leg appears a little shorter than the other, walks pretty much with his Toes in and is a thick set Fellow: Had on when he went away, an old light brown Drugget Coat, with short Skirts; old blue Jacket without Sleeves, with two Sorts of Metal Buttons, 3 or 4 of them neatly gilt; a pair Buckskin Breeches, took several Pair of Worsted Stockings, a Castor Hat, much worn; he had also several Shirt Patterns of very good Linen not made up, some Check Shirts, and a Pair of half-worn Shoes. He also stole a Sett of Bills of Exchange for Thirty Pounds, drawn in Favour of John Bolton, besides Cash.

Also, Run-away from John Bennett, in Queen-Ann's County, a Welsh Servant Man, named John Lewes, about 5 Feet 9 Inches high, upwards of 20 Years of Age, wears his own yellowish Hair, not tied behind, has a light-coloured Cloth Great Coat, the rest of his Clothes unknown. Whoever secures the said Servants, so that their Masters may have them again, shall have Five Pounds Reward for John Williams from John Bolton, if taken in the Province, and Ten Pounds if taken out of the Province; and also the same Price for the latter, from John Bennett, and reasonable Charges, paid by JOHN BOLTON, and JOHN BENNETT.

The Pennsylvania Gazette, May 8, 1766; May 22, 1766; June 12, 1766. See *The Maryland Gazette*, April 24, 1766.

Queen-Anne's County, *April* 29, 1766.
TEN POUNDS REWARD.

RAN away the 11th Instant, a Servant Man named WILLIAM KEAN, about 30 Years of Age, about 5 Feet 10 or 11 Inches high, well made, and of a ruddy Complexion; he is a Native of *Ireland*, and retains something of that Dialect, and has a great Impediment in his Speech; wore his Hair (dark colour'd) which was just got to Tie behind. Had on when he went away, an old Hat, light colour'd Cloth Coat and Jacket, blue knit Worsted Breeches, Worsted Stockings, and *English* Shoes.

The said *William Kean* was admitted into the Free-School of this County as Master, in *November* 1764, but by his Ill-Conduct was obliged in *May* 1765 to come under Indenture to Mr. *Anthony M'Culloch* (Merchant at *Queen's-Town*) and Myself, and was settled on *Kent-Island* to teach a private School near Mr. *James Hutchings's*; he was also under Arrest for Debt, for which I am Security to the Sheriff. The said *Kean* is allowed to be an exceeding good classical Scholar, but knows little of Figures, and writes a poor Hand. He has been in several Parts of the World, that when he is sober, is a very agreeable Man, and then has much the Appearance of a distressed Gentleman; that it is very probable he may impose of Gentlemen, tho' he is subject to drink too much, and at that Time to pawn his Cloaths.

Whoever secures the said *William Kean*, that the Subscriber may get him, shall have the above Ten Pounds Reward, and if brought home, reasonable Charges, paid by
NATHAN SAMUEL TURBUTT WRIGHT.
The Maryland Gazette, May 15, 1766; May 22, 1766; May 29, 1766.

COMMITTED to *Frederick* County Jail, as a Runaway, *Margaret Young*, says she belongs to *Henry M'Intyre*, in *Buck's* County, *Pennsylvania*, had on, when committed, a Callicoe Bed-Gown, Linsey-Wolsey Petticoat, Check Apron, Silk Handkerchief, and a Black Hair Hat. She says she was born in *Wales*, and brought up in *Ireland*. She is pitted with the Small-Pox, and has a remarkable Scar on her Throat and each Side of her Neck. The Owner is desired to take her, and pay Fees.
GEO. SCOTT, Sheriff.
The Maryland Gazette, May 15, 1766; May 22, 1766.

RUN away from the Subscriber, in Northumberland County, Virginia, a Servant named Samuel Holmes, by Trade a Taylor, 5 Feet 5 Inches high, has a remarkable yellow Spot on the out side of one of his Knees; it is said by the other Servants it is on the Left Knee, and on the Instep of the other Leg there is a very large Scar; he stammers in his Speech, is bow legged, and roles much in his walk; had on a dark Cloth Coat, with white Lining, and Metal Buttons; I expect he will change his Name and Dress; but the above Description of his Person, &c. will always discover him; he run away once before, and was taken up in Chester Town, Pennsylvania, then had a forged Pass, went by the Name of John Harris, but his Knee discovered him; it is supposed he has got a forged Pass; he has told the other Servants he would get on board some Vessel going to Sea; it is therefore begged of all Captains not to carry any such Rogue, but to send him on Shore to Justice; he has been long in this Country, and, by his cunning Inquiry

knows most Places, and the Names of the Countries, [sic] and the most noted Persons in Pennsylvania, Maryland, and Virginia. Whoever secures him, so as he I may get him again, shall receive Five Pounds Reward, paid by WILLIAM TAITE.
N. B. He was with me in September, on Patuxent River, at Benedict and Lower Marlborough, where no doubt he informed himself of the Names of the most noted Person and Places.

The Pennsylvania Gazette, May 15, 1766; May 29, 1766; July 17, 1767. See *The Maryland Gazette*, April 24, 1766, and *The Maryland Gazette*, July 31, 1766, Holmes/Homes.

RAN away from the Subscriber, in the City of *Annapolis*, on the 19th Instant, an *English* Convict Servant Man named *William Harriss*, by Trade a Shipwright and Caulker, a tall fresh colour'd Fellow, short brown curl'd Hair, talks quick, and is remarkably Impudent: Had on when he went away, a Check Shirt, a Pair of Check Trowsers, and a light colour'd Pea Jacket; he is a very deceiving Fellow, and a most notorious Liar.

Whoever takes up and secures the said Servant, so that his Master may have him again, shall receive THREE POUNDS Reward, besides what the Law allows, paid by WILLIAM ROBERTS.

The Maryland Gazette, May 22, 1766.

RUN away, in June last, from Cornelius Dailey, of Queen-Ann's County, Maryland, a Servant Man, named John Reid. He came from Cork, in the Ship Lion, and was bought of .Murray and Taylor: Had on when he went away, a Country made Jacket, and Breeches of the same two Ozenbrigs Shirts, no Shoes nor Stockings; was landed in Philadelphia by one Taylor from Motherkill, and supposed to go on board a Man of War; is a little pitted with the Small-pox, and has the Brogue on his Tongue; and if not on board a Man of War, it is thought he is in Pennsylvania, or the Jersies; and it is said there is such a Man in Burlington Goal.

Also Run away from Hugh Polk, a Convict English Servant Woman, named Sarah Rogers, she is a little Woman, has a fair Complexion, and says she is a Glover and Breeches Maker. Whoever takes up and secures said Servants, shall have FOUR POUNDS Reward for both or FORTY SHILLINGS for each, paid by CORNELIUS DAILEY, and HUGH POLK.

The Pennsylvania Gazette, May 22, 1766; July 10, 1766. See *The Pennsylvania Gazette*, January 2, 1766, and *The Pennsylvania Gazette*, April 3, 1766.

THREE POUNDS Reward.

RUN away from the Subscriber, living near Fort Frederick, in Frederick County, Maryland, on the Sixth Day of February last, an English Servant Man, named John Hunt, by Trade a Wheelwright, about Twenty Years of Age, 5 Feet 8 or 9 Inches high, has grey Eyes, dark curled Hair, is pale faced, and pitted with the Small-Pox; had on, when he went away, an old brown Frize Coat, Leather Breeches, old Shoes and Stockings, and a long Leather Apron. Whoever takes up said Servant and secures him, so that his Master may have him again, shall have the above Reward, and if brought home, Twenty Shillings more, besides reasonable Charges, paid by
JAMES JOHNSON.

The Pennsylvania Gazette, May 22, 1766; June 12, 1766; July 17, 1766.

Fifth Month, 20, 1766.

RUN away, last Night, from the Subscriber, living at Deer Creek, Baltimore County, Maryland, a Servant Man, named Tobias Tutes, a native Irishman, about 5 Feet 7 Inches high, 24 years of Age, fair Complexion, short brown Hair, and sometimes wears a brown Wig over it, has a Scar on his Head by a Cutlas, and has been trepanned with a Piece of Plate; had on and took with him, a blue Cloth Coat, Fustian Waistcoat, old Velvet Breeches, patched, a Pair of white worsted Stockings, ribbed, coarse Shoes, an Ozenbrigs Shirt, a Check Ditto, and other things; he pretends to be a Carpenter and Joyner; has the Brogue on his Tongue, and is a drunken talkative Fellow. Whoever takes up and secures said Servant, so as his Master may have him again, shall receive Forty Shillings Reward, if taken in this Province, and three Pounds if taken out of the Province, and reasonable Charges, paid by
WILLIAM COX.

The Pennsylvania Gazette, May 29, 1766; June 19, 1766. See *The Pennsylvania Gazette*, July 10, 1766, for Tutes/Tuite

St. Mary's County, May 10, 1766.

RAN away last Night from the Subscriber, a Convict Servant Boy, named *Samuel Mattex*, about 16 Years of Age, sandy Complexion, a down Look, short light colour'd Hair, has been a Drummer in the Army, and is a very great Villain: Had on when he went away, a blue *Kilmarnack* Cap, short Copper colour'd Kersey Jacket, Cotton Breeches, Osnabrig wide Trowsers, and Shoes and Stockings, with large Brass Buckles: Likewise took with him, a Pair of Blankets, and a large Woollen Rugg.

Whoever secures the said Servant, so that the Owner may be him again, shall receive FORTY SHILLINGS Reward.
VERNON HEBB.
The Maryland Gazette, June 5, 1766; June 12, 1766; June 19, 1766; June 26, 1766; July 3, 1766.

COMMITTED to *Anne-Arundel* County Jail, *William Crouch* and *Jos. Landray*, on Suspicion of being Runaways, they confess themselves such, and say they belong to Messrs. *Mudd* and *Murphy*, near *New-Port*.
Their Masters are requested to take them away, and pay Charges.
WILLIAM PRUE, Jailer.
The Maryland Gazette, June 5, 1766; June 12, 1766.

June 3, 1766.
THREE POUNDS REWARD.
RAN away from *Bush-Town*, the 28th of May, *George Williamson*, an *Englishman*, (a Country Indentured Servant,) a Blacksmith by Trade, a broad faced, well-set Fellow, and apt to drink: Had on when he went away, a light colour'd over Jacket, and red under Ditto, Osnabrigs Shirt and Trowsers, Country made Shoes, Felt Hat, and brown Wig. It's likely he may be lurking about some Iron Works, or to and from such Places.
Whoever secures said Servant, so as he may be had again, shall receive the above Reward from
JOHN LEE WEBSTER.
The Maryland Gazette, June 12, 1766.

Reading, in Berks County, June 7, 1766.
NOW in the Goal of this County, a certain Charles Ferran, who says he belongs to one Henry Hollingsworth, at the Head of Elk; these are to desire said Hollingsworth to come in four Weeks from the Date hereof, and page Charges, or he will be sold to pay Costs, by
ISAAC WICKERSAAM, Goaler.
The Pennsylvania Gazette, June 12, 1766; July 17, 1766. See *The Pennsylvania Gazette*, June 13, 1765; *The Pennsylvania Gazette*, April 10, 1766, and *The Pennsylvania Gazette*, August 7, 1766, for Ferran/Farran

FORTY SHILLINGS Reward.
RUN away, in the night of the 8th inst. June, from Mr. Isaac Janvier's, at Christiana Bridge, a certain John Heran, a bricklayer by trade, about 5 feet

9 inches high; had on a white country made jacket, leather breeches, has a very remarkable red spot above his right brow; he has been inlisted with the Royal Americans, and deserted, and was taken up by them again, and put into Philadelphia goal, and taken out of the same by the subscriber, his master of Baltimore, and come with him his said master as far as Christiana Bridge homewards, but went off with a pair of iron hand-cuffs. Whoever takes up the said servant, and puts him in any of his Majesty's goals, or brings him to Mr. Isaac Janvier, or to his said master, shall have the above reward, and reasonable charges, paid by CONRAD SMITH.

The Pennsylvania Gazette, June 12, 1766; June 26, 1766; July 3, 1766.

See *The Pennsylvania Gazette*, March 13, 1766.

TWENTY POUNDS REWARD.

RAN away from *Alexandria* the 20th of last *May*, Four Convict Servant Men, who took with them a small painted Yawl with a white painted Bottom, and are supposed to have made down the River *Patowmack*, and 'tis probable may attempt going down or crossing the Bay.

Francis Wingle, an Englishman, and by Trade a Shoemaker, about 25 Years of Age, 5 Feet 10 or 11 Inches high, a stout, well-made Fellow, smooth Face and brown Complexion, has an impudent Look and speaks very fast, and wears his own Hair, which is short and curley. Had on when he went off, a grey Coat and lappelled Jacket, a Pair of black Plush Breeches, white Shirt and Stockings, and has been in the Country about 12 Months.

Stephen Devorse, an *Englishman*, and by Trade a Baker, about 20 Years of Age, 5 Feet 8 or 9 Inches high, short Hair, a dark brown Complexion, a red Face, and is pretty much pitted with the Small-Pox, and has a dull stupid Look. Had on, a green lappelled Jacket lined with white Flannel, Osnabrigs Shirt and Trowsers, light colour'd Yarn ribb'd Stockings, and strong Shoes: Has been in the Country about two Years.

James Trump, an *Englishman*, about 23 or 24 Years of Age, also a Baker by Trade, and has been sometime at Sea on board of a Man of War, and may perhaps pass for a Seaman, is about 5 Feet 5 Inches high, smooth Face and pale Complexion, speaks pretty fast, and partly has a Cast with one Eye, is remarkable for having a very scabbed Head, which he has had for some Years, and wears a Worsted Cap under his Hat. Had on a grey Jacket, and has been in the Country three Years.

John Hands, also an *Englishman*, about 25 Years of Age, by Trade a Sawyer, and has some Part of his Time kept an *English* School, and may forge himself and the others some kind of Pass, wears his own Hair which has lately been cut short, a brown Complexion, a smooth Face, and has a good Countenance, about 5 Feet 6 or 7 Inches high, one of his Legs considerably shorter than the other, and walks very lame. Had on, a blue Surtout Coat lined with red Shalloon, and had with him Check and Osnabrigs Shirts and Trowsers, blue Broadcloth Breeches, and wears a striped Cotton Cap under his Hat. He has not been long in the Country. It's imagined they will endeavour to be on board some Vessel; therefore, all Masters are at their Peril forbid to take them away.

Whoever takes up and secures the said Servants in any Jail, so as the Owners get them again, shall receive the above Reward of Twenty Pounds, or FIVE POUNDS for each; and if brought and delivered here, reasonable Charges will be allowed: Also ONE PISTOLE for the Yawl, if delivered here, paid by   ROBERT ADAM, and PETER WISE.
ALEXANDRIA, June 7th, 1766.

The Maryland Gazette, June 19, 1766; June 26, 1766; July 20, 1766.

BALTIMORE-TOWN, *June* 7, 1766.
RAN away from the Ship *Essex, John Curling*, Commander, Two Sailors, *viz*.

Joseph Mallett, a stout, sturdy Fellow, of a swarthy Complexion, long Visage, and a sharp Hook Nose. And *John Kelsey*, about 5 Feet 2 Inches high, and of a black swarthy Complexion.

They took with them the Yawl, clean scraped, with a white Bottom, her Stern painted blue, and Quarters flourish'd with white, had a new Spritsail and Foresail, a Mizzen mast, and Oars painted red.

Whoever takes up the said Sailors, and brings them to the said Ship, lying in *Patapsco* River, shall receive a Reward of FIVE POUNDS for the Men and Yawl, and reasonable Charges, paid by
JOHN CURLING.

The Maryland Gazette, June 19, 1766; June 26, 1766.

RAN away from the Subscriber, the 9th of this Instant, *June*, Five Indented Servant Men, *viz*.

William Firth, by Trade a Gardener, and employed in that Capacity by the Subscriber, about 5 Feet 10 Inches high, thin visaged, wore his own light brown Hair, which was shaved as far back as the Crown of his Head, but has a Wig which he wears occasionally over his Hair. Had on when he went off, a striped Flannel Jacket with a black *Manchester* Velvet one over it, a bad blue Coat with yellow Buttons: He is a Man of Education, but remarkably talkative, has been in *America* before in Quality of a School-Master, and may perhaps call himself such now, he is about 45 Years of Age.

John Leary, by Trade a Caulker, a lusty Man, about 5 Feet 8 Inches high, of a ruddy Complexion, wore his own dark brown Hair, which is shaved quite back to the Crown of his Head, lisps very much in his Speech, has a large Mouth and thick Lips. Had on, a blue Jacket very much soiled, long Osnabrigs Trowsers, a small coarse Felt Hat, which he commonly wore flapped before, a Check or Osnabrigs Shirt, having both with him.

James Russell, a Baker, a little Fellow, about 5 Feet high, much pitted with the Small-Pox, has very thin Lips, a remarkable catching in his Speech, and lisps in pronouncing many Words, he has been on board a Man of War, and may perhaps pass for a Sailor. Had on, a blue Sailor's Jacket, with perhaps a striped Flannel one under it as he had both, a Check or Osnabrigs Shirt, long Osnabrigs Trowsers, and wore on his Head commonly, a blue Cloth Cap, but may perhaps have changed it with one of the Men that went with him, for a Leather Cap lined with Leopard's Skin, which turned up round the Cape, this is very probable, as he wore this Cap the Day before they went off.

John Rolings, a Butcher, about 5 Feet 6 Inches high, has a remarkable Stupidity in his Countenance, and is very deaf, has a pretty deep Voice, and speaks very deliberate, tho' seldom. Had on, a blue Jacket, with a striped Flannel one under it, an Osnabrigs Shirt, long Trowsers of the same, a small Felt Hat, or perhaps a Leather Cap lined with Leopard's Skin, or a Cloth Cap, as it was with this Man that the Baker exchanged Caps.

Joseph Dent, a Labourer, this Fellow was purchased by the Subscriber sometime last Summer, as a Gardener, from whom he soon after ran away, but was taken again and thrown into *Calvert* County Jail; he was very particularly described in a former Advertisement, to which the Public is referred for an Account of him.

The above mentioned Servants went off in a small Boat, with a Pitch Bottom, and naked Gunwale. *William Firth*, the Gardener, was formerly a Servant in the *Jerseys*, and will probably endeavour to get there by Way of *Philadelphia*, and as he writes a good Hand, and is an artful, insinuating Villain, it is likely he may forge Passes for the others.

Whoever secures the said Servants, so that they may be had again, shall have FIVE POUNDS Reward, beside what the Law allows, and if brought home be paid reasonable Charges, by
WILLIAM FITZHUGH,   ROUSBY-HALL, *Patuxent* River.

The Maryland Gazette, June 19, 1766; June 26, 1766. See *The Pennsylvania Gazette*, July 24, 1766. See *The Pennsylvania Gazette*, July 31, 1766, for Firth, and *The Maryland Gazette*, August 1, 1765, for Dent.

June 9, 1766.
RUN away last Night, from the Subscriber, living in Kent County, Maryland, a Welch Servant Man, named William Thompson, about 19 Years of Age, wears short dark Hair, about 5 Feet high, very smooth Face, fair Complexion; had on, when he went away, a Fearnothing Jacket, lined with white Kersey, wide Trowsers, no Stockings, and a Pair of half-worn Pumps. Whoever secures said Servant in any Goal, so as his Master may have him again, shall receive Twenty Shillings Reward, and reasonable Charges, paid by   JOHN EUNUCH.
The Pennsylvania Gazette, June 19, 1766; June 26, 1766; July 3, 1766.

RAN away from the Subscriber, about a Fortnight ago, a Convict Servant Man, named *John Morgan*, by Trade a Shoemaker, and pretends to be a Gardener, about 30 Years of Age, 5 Feet 10 Inches high, of a fresh Complexion, short Hair, and one of his Eyes has been lately Hurt by a piece of Mortar falling into it: Had on when he went away, a grey Cloth Coat, and Plush Breeches: He has been seen on *Elk Ridge.*
Whoever secures the said Servant, so that the Subscriber may have him again, shall have Twenty Shillings Reward.
WILLIAM PACA.
The Maryland Gazette, June 26, 1766; July 3, 1766; July 10, 1766; July 17, 1766; July 24, 1766; July 31, 1766; August 7, 1766; August 14, 1766; August 21, 1766; August 28, 1766; September 4, 1766; September 11, 1766; September 18, 1766; September 25, 1766; October 2, 1766; October 9, 1766. The last ten ads have "*Annapolis, June 26, 1766.*" at the top.

RAN away on the 12th Instant, from the *Polly*, Capt. *John Kilty*, lying at *Selby's* Landing, in *Patuxent, James Couley*, 5 Feet 8 Inches high, about 25 Years of Age, of a pale Complexion, and a large Scar or Burn under his Right Eye: Had on when he went away, a blue Jacket, light colour'd Breeches or Trowsers, and white Stockings.
Whoever takes up the said *James Couley*, and lodges him in any Goal, shall have a Reward of TWO PISTOLES, paid by
JOHN KILTY.
The Maryland Gazette, June 26, 1766; July 3, 1766; July 10, 1766.

THREE POUNDS REWARD.
RAN away from the Subscriber, living *in Frederick* County, 7 Miles above *Bladensburg*, on the Fifth of *June* last, a likely well-made *English* Convict Servant Man, named *William Abbutt*, 22 Years of Age, about 5 Feet 8

Inches high, and wears his own brown Hair, tied behind. Had on, and took with him, an old Castor Hat, Part of the Rim tore and sowed on again, a dark brown Coat with a Cape, red Worsted Jacket without Sleeves, Leather Breeches very much soiled, a white Shirt ruffled at the Bosom, one Osnabrigs Ditto, a Muslin Neck-Cloth, grey ribb'd Stockings, a Pair of Country made Ditto, Country Made Shoes, and Steel Buckles.

Whoever takes up the said Servant, and brings him home, or secures him so that his Master may get him again, shall receive the above Reward, paid by   JOHN ADAMSON.

N. B. Perhaps he has changed his Name, and got a false Pass.

The *Maryland Gazette*, June 26, 1766; July 3, 1766. See *The Maryland Gazette*, May 12, 1768.

BROKE out of *Anne-Arundel* County Jail, on the First of this Instant *July*, at Night, the following Persons, viz.

John Kent, a young Fellow, Country Born, his Dress is uncertain, as he has different Suits.

Thomas Woods, an *Irishman*, wears his own Hair; had on a brown Cloth Coat with yellow Metal Buttons; he is Lame in one Leg, it being lately cut, and much swell'd, a Cabinet-maker by Trade. It is supposed he will make to *Philadelphia*.

Thomas Malvill, and *Thomas Winwood*, the one a Weaver and the other a Gardener, both lately imported in the Country.—As they can all Write, its probable they may Forge Passes.

Whoever delivers them to the Subscriber in *Annapolis*, shall receive a Reward of THREE POUNDS for each, and reasonable Charges, paid by JOSEPH GALLOWAY, Sheriff.

The *Maryland Gazette*, July 3, 1766; July 10, 1766; July 17, 1766; July 24, 1766; July 31, 1766; August 7, 1766; August 14, 1766; August 21, 1766; August 28, 1766; September 4, 1766.

COMMITTED as Runaways to the Jail of *Alexandria*, in *Fairfax* County, *Virginia*, the 22d June, Two Men. One is a middle aged white Man, who says his Name is *John Hughes*, and that he has followed the Seas for many Years past, but was incapacitated from going to Sea longer, by a Fall which he got that dislocated one of his Collar Bones (it is still out of Place) and broke Three of his Ribs, &c. He is about 5 Feet 6 Inches high, of a swarthy Complexion, and a very talkative sensible Fellow.

The other is a likely young Mulatto Fellow...calls himself Will Hen[nobie]....

June 29. Wm. TRIPPLETT.

The Maryland Gazette, July 3, 1766.

June 22, 1766.

RAN away from the Subscriber, living in *York-Town, Pennsylvania*, a Servant Man named *John Mackey*, of a small Size, tho' well-set, wears his own black Hair tied behind, and professes to be something of a Doctor: Had on, a red Broadcloth Waistcoat, the Back Part of it is red twilled Worsted, and is ript in the Back, a Blanket Coat, 1 Check Shirt, 1 old pair of Leather Breeches patch'd in the Seat, old Shoes with Pinchbeck Buckles, and a pair of blue Worsted Hose. Took with him, a Black Stone-Horse [sic] shod all round with old Shoes, paces naturally, and then goes a smart Travel, paces very long and clumsey, is about 15 Hands high, thin in Flesh, has a small white Snip on his Nose, and 4 Years old. He also took about Seven Pounds in Silver, and Two *French* Crowns.

Whoever takes up and secures said Servant, so that his Master may have him again, shall receive Three Pounds, or if Man and Horse the above Reward; or for the Horse only Three Pounds Reward; and reasonable Charges, paid by LEVI STEPHENS.

The Maryland Gazette, July 3, 1766; July 10, 1766; July 17, 1766. See *The Maryland Gazette*, September 18, 1766.

COMMITTED to *Kent* County Jail, *Samuel Walker*, as a Runaway, he says his Master's Name is *Nathaniel Nicols*, and lives at *Baltimore*, in *Gunpowder* Neck; said *Walker* has short light colour'd Hair, and says he has been in the Army.

His Master is desired to take him away, and pay Charges.
J. NICHOLSON, Sheriff.
The Maryland Gazette, July 3, 1766.

RUN away, on the 19th of June, from the subscriber, living at Annapolis, an English servant man, named John Haley, about 5 feet 4 or 5 inches high, 24 years of age, thin visage, dark complexion, and black hair, is slow of speech: Had on, when he went away, a bearskin coat, with large side-pockets, two striped linsey jackets, check shirt, and buckskin breeches; but as he has a quantity of cash, it is probable he may change his apparel. He is a baker by trade, but has lately been employed as post-rider from Annapolis to Philadelphia. Whoever takes up and secures said servant in any gaol, so as his master may him again, [sic] shall have FIVE POUNDS Reward, and reasonable charges, paid by WILLIAM NIVEN.
N. B. All masters of vessels are forbid to carry him off at their peril.

The Pennsylvania Gazette, July 3, 1766; July 17, 1766; July 24, 1766.

Anti-Etam Forge, Frederick County, April 27.

RUN away from the above forge on the 20th instant, a servant man, named Thomas Meclene, or Onan, an Irishman, (tho' he says he is a Highlandman) a low squat fellow, of a very swarthy complexion, with short black hair; he had on, when he went away, a blue cloth coat, a double-breasted jacket, of an ash-coloured bearskin cloth, trimmed with flat white metal buttons, a pair of buckskin breeches, old shoes, and a pair of grey milled, or worsted stockings. He commonly wears his garters under his knees, is a very talkative fellow, and pretends to be a conjurer, and brags much of his land and Negroes in Cecil, or Kent county. Whoever brings, or secures the said fellow, so as I may have him again, shall receive THREE POUNDS Pennsylvania Currency from
SAMUEL BEALL, jun. for Self, and Co.

N. B. He served some of his time about Darby, in Chester county, I believe, with one of the Smiths; and he has another man's wife with him.

The Pennsylvania Gazette, July 3, 1766; July 24, 1766; August 28, 1766. See *The Maryland Gazette*, May 1, 1766, and *The Pennsylvania Gazette*, August 28, 1766.

RAN away from the Subscriber, living near the *Northampton* Iron-Works in *Baltimore* County, *Maryland*, a Convict Servant Man, named *John Sanders*, about 25 Years of Age, 5 Feet 6 or 7 Inches high, sandy Complexion, red Eyes, very much pitted with the Small-Pox: Had on when he went away an Osnabrigs Shirt, Country Linen Trowsers, old Felt Hat and old Shoes; had no Coat nor Jacket on when he went away, as we know of.

Whoever takes up the said Servant, and brings him Home to his Master, shall have, if taken in the County Twenty Shillings, if out of the County Forty Shillings, and if out of the Province Three Pounds Reward, and reasonable Charges, paid by
CHARLES RIDGELY, senr.

N. B. He is supposed to have taken a Thick-set Coat much worn, and a light colour'd Jacket without Sleeves.

The Maryland Gazette, July 10, 1766; July 17, 1766; July 24, 1766.

Frederick County, *July* 2, 1766.

RAN away last Night, from the Subscriber's **Plantation** on *Seneca* Creek, a Convict Servant Man named *Evan Morris*, a middle sized Fellow, about 21 Years of Age, fair Complexion, pitted favourably with the Small-Pox, his

Nose rising in the Middle, wore his own brown Hair, talks broad and stammers. Had on, and took with him, a thickset Coat with short Skirts, a white Jacket with green Stone Buttons, 1 yellow Ditto, 1 Pair of Buckskin Breeches, 1 Pair of Trowsers, 1 Pair of Pumps, 1 Pair of Thread Stockings, 3 Holland Shirts, 1 Osnabrigs Ditto, and a new Castor Hat.

Whoever takes up and secures the said Servant, so as he may be had again, shall have Twenty Shillings Reward, and if brought home reasonable Charges, and generous Reward in Proportion to the Distance he is brought, paid by   EDWARD GAITHER, Son of *Benjamin.*

The Maryland Gazette, July 10, 1766.

June 23, 1766.
THREE POUNDS Reward.

RUN away from Bush River Furnace, last night, a native Irish servant man, named Tobias Tuite, 24 years of age, about 5 feet 6 or 7 inches high, fair complexion, light brown hair, and lately wore a wig over it, has a scar on his head, from a cut by a cutlas, and the scull has been trepanned, with a piece of plate; processes to be a carpenter, joiner, and cart wheel-wright; has the brouge on his tongue, and is a drunken talkative Fellow; Had on, and took with him, an old black Coat, full trimmed, a fustian waistcoat, old patched velvet breeches, a pair of new white ribbed worsted stockings, an ozenbrig shirt, and check ditto, old shoes and hat. Whoever takes up and secures said servant, so that his master may get him again, shall have the above reward, paid by me   JAMES WEBSTER.

The Pennsylvania Gazette, July 10, 1766; July 24, 1766; August 28, 1766. See *The Pennsylvania Gazette,* May 29, 1766. Tutes/Tuite

July 7, 1766.

COMMITTED to *Prince-George's* County Jail, as a Runaway, *George Morriss,* a Convict, who says he belongs to Mr. *Edward Gaither.* . .

His Master is desired to take him away, and pay Charges.

Wm. T. WOOTTON, Sheriff.

The Maryland Gazette, July 17, 1766.

Rousby-Hall, Patuxent River, Maryland, June 9, 1766.

RUN away from the Subscriber, five indentured Servant Men, viz. *William Firth,* a Gardiner, an Englishman, about 45 Years of Age, about five Feet ten Inches high, thin visaged, wore his own light brown Hair, which was shaved as far back as the Crown of his Head, but wears a Wig occasionally over his hair. Had on, when he went away, a blue Cloth Coat, pretty much worn, with yellow Buttons, a striped Flannel Jacket, with a black

Manchester Velvet One over it. He stole, and took with him, sundry trifling Things; the most remarkable was, a half-worn Razor, made by Price, and the Maker's Name upon the Shank of it, which is not common. He is a Man of Education, and a most artful Villain, tho' remarkably talkative, and fond of spirituous Liquors; he is a tolerable good Cook, and understands the Management of a Garden, and will probably offer his Service in one or other of these Capacities, or perhaps as a Clerk or Schoolmaster; he has been formerly in the Jerseys, and say, he resided with one Mr. Vanhorn in that Province, if it is likely that he may have forged Passes for himself and the others, and perhaps changed their Names.

John Leary, a Caulker, born in England, a lusty Man, about five Feet eight Inches high, of a ruddy Complexion, wore his own dark brown Hair, shaved back to the Crown of his Head, has thick Lips, a large Mouth, and lisps much in his Speech, had on, when he went away, a blue Jacket, much tarred, a Pair of long Ozenbrigs Trowsers, a small Felt hat, a Check or Ozenbrigs shirt, having both with him.

James Russell, an Englishman, calls himself a Baker, but knows little or nothing of the Business, a short well set Fellow, about five Feet high, pitted with the Small-pox, has thin Lips, a remarkable Catching in his Speech, and lisps in pronouncing many Words; he say he has been in the Navy, and may probably pass for a Sailor; had on, when he went away, a Sailor's blue Jacket, with a striped Flannel One under it, a Check or Ozenbrigs Shirt, long Ozenbrigs Trowsers; he frequently wore on his Head a brown Cloth Cap, but sometimes a leather One lined with a Leopard's Skin, turned up quite round the Cap.

John Rawlings, a Butcher, an Englishman, about five Feet six Inches high, thin visaged, has a remarkable Stupidity in his Countenance, is a little deaf, and speaks slow, and seldom; had on, when he went away, a blue Jacket, and a striped Flannel One under it, an Ozenbrigs Shirt, long Ozenbrigs Trowsers, a Felt Hat, or Leather Cap, lined with a Leopard's Skin.

Joseph Dent, a Shoemaker, calls himself a Gardiner, but is ignorant of the Business, says he is a Frenchman, and speaks French, but appears like an Englishman, and speaks exceeding good English. He is a complicated Villain, and an artful down looking Fellow; he is well made, rather round shouldered, and about five Feet eight Inches high, wears his own dark flaxen Hair, shaved back to the Crown, is much pitted with the Small-pox, has a remarkable Effeminacy in his Voice, and hesitates in speaking. This Man is a good Ploughman, and understands the Business of Farming; had on, when he went away, a blue Half-thick Jacket, with large flat Metal Buttons, Ozenbrigs Shirt, and a Pair of long Ozenbrigs Trowsers.

The said Servants were seen the 14th Day of June, in Sussex, in Pennsylvania, on their Way to the Northward. Whoever takes up the said

Servants, and secures them, so that they may be returned to me, shall receive, as a Reward for *William Firth*, TEN POUNDS, and FIFTY SHILLINGS for each of the others, besides what the law allows, if taken in any Government to the Northward of this Province, after the Publication hereof. Dated the Thirtieth Day of June, in the year of our Lord, 1766.
WILLIAM FITZHUGH.

The Pennsylvania Gazette, July 24, 1766; July 31, 1766; August 28, 1766. See *The Maryland Gazette*, June 19, 1766. See *The Pennsylvania Gazette*, July 31, 1766, and *The Maryland Gazette*, August 1, 1765, for Dent.

July 17, 1766.

RAN away from the Subscriber, living in *Northumberland* County, *Virginia*, a Servant Man, named *Samuel Homes*, by Trade a Taylor. Had on when he went away, a dark colour'd Coat lined, with white Metal Buttons, a Pair of black Stocking Breeches, coarse Shoes, dark mill'd Stockings, much mended, an old Hat bound round with black Ferret; his Hair tied behind, rocks much in his Walk, is Bow legged, has a Scar on his right Cheek, and a small Mole close by it, has a large Flesh Mark on the Outside of his left Knee, resembling the Skin of raw Pork, also a large Scar on the Instep of his right Foot, by a great Sore. Whoever takes up said Runaway, shall receive Twenty Shillings Reward, besides what the Law allows, paid by WILLIAM TAITE.

N. B. If he is taken up in *Maryland*, I will give Five Pounds Reward; it is supposed he will go into *St. Mary's* and *Calvert* Counties, as he was in both a few Days ago, from W. T.

The Maryland Gazette, July 31, 1766; August 7, 1766; August 14, 1766; August 21, 1766; August 28, 1766; September 4, 1766. See *The Maryland Gazette*, April 24, 1766, and *The Pennsylvania Gazette*, May 15, 1766, for Holmes/Homes.

July 21, 1766.

RAN away from the Subscriber, living in *Kent* County, *Maryland*, a Convict Servant Man, named *William Worberton*, a middle sized Man, has a Down Look, is muck [sic] Pock Mark'd, by Trade a Wheelwright, but pretends to understand Joiner's and House-Carpenter's Work. Had on, a dark, nay almost black Broadcloth Jacket and Breeches, black Stockings, new Shoes with large Pewter Buckles, old Castor Hat, Osnabrigs Shirt, and took with him a good Check Shirt. He is a cunning Fellow, and may charge his Apparel and alter his Name, as it is supposed he has Money with him.

Whoever secures the said Servant, shall have Four Pounds Reward, if taken in the Province, and brought home without any further Expence; if out of the Province Five Pounds and all reasonable Charges, paid by

RICHARD GRESHAM.
N. B. If secured in any Prison, Three Pounds, paid by   R. G.
The Maryland Gazette, July 31, 1766. See *The Pennsylvania Gazette*, July 31, 1766.

RUN away from the Subscriber, living in Kent County, Maryland, a Convict Servant Man, named William Warburton; he is of a middle Size, born in England, stoops in his Shoulders, walks with his Toes much out, has short brown Hair, his Beard of sandy Colour, has a Down look, a smooth Tongue, and much pitted with the Small-pox, and often makes use of the Words, Yes sure, Ay sure, and, No sure. He is Wheelwright by Trade, but pretends to understand Joyners and House carpenters Work. Had on, when he went away, a dark, or almost black, Broadcloth Jacket and Breeches, much worn, and has with him black and white Stockings, Check and white Shirts, a Pair of new Shoes, black grain, with large Pewter Buckles, and an old Castor Hat; but as he is a cunning artful Fellow, may change his Name and Apparel, as it is supposed he has Money. Whoever secures the said Servant and brings him home, shall have Four Pounds Currency Reward; and if taken out of the Province Five Pounds; or if secures in any Prison out of the Province, and immediate Notice given, Three Pounds, and all Charges allowed and paid by RICHARD GRESHAM.
N. B. It is probable he may have a forged Pass. All masters of Vessels are forbid to carry him off at their Peril.
The Pennsylvania Gazette, July 31, 1766; August 7, 1766; August 28, 1766; October 9, 1766; October 30, 1766. See *The Maryland Gazette*, July 31, 1766.

WAS committed to Gloucester County Goal, a runaway Servant, named William Firth, belonging to Colonel William Fitzhugh, of Rousby-Hall, on Patuxent River, Maryland, agreeable to his Advertisement, bearing Date June 30, 1766.
The Pennsylvania Gazette, July 31, 1766; August 28, 1766; September 11, 1766; September 18, 1766. See *The Maryland Gazette*, June 19, 1766; and *The Pennsylvania Gazette*, July 24, 1766.

RAN away from the Subscriber, living near *Patapsco* Ferry, on the 3d of this Instant, two Convict Servant Men, *viz.*
Edward Jenkins, a short well-set Fellow, about 5 Feet 4 Inches high, wears his own short brown Hair, and has a remarkable wide Mouth: Had on and took with him, a good Hat, with a white Metal Button to it, two Check

Shirts much wore, one Osnabrig ditto, a striped Flannel lappel'd Jacket, lined with white, Leather Breeches, Crocus Trowsers, Osnabrig Petticoat ditto, three Pair of Yarn or Worsted Hose, some of them ribb'd, and Country made Pumps. As he has been in the Country before, it's probable he will give a good Account of himself, and pass as a Sailor, as he may dress in a Sailors' Habit.

Richard Harbett, a young Fellow, about 20 or 21 Years of Age, smooth Face, and wears his own Hair: Had on and took with him, an old Felt Hat, red Kersey Jacket, old white Shirt, two Osnabrig ditto, short *Russia* Drab Breeches, Crocus Trowsers, and no shoes that are known of.

Whoever takes up the said Servants so that their Master may get them again, shall have a Reward of Four Pounds for *Jenkins*, if taken Twenty Miles from Home, and if taken from on board of any Vessel, outward Bound, Six Pounds, and reasonable Charges if brought Home: And for the other Forty Shillings, paid by
JOSEPH JACOBS.

The Maryland Gazette, August 7, 1766; August 14, 1766; August 21, 1766; August 28, 1766; September 4, 1766; September 11, 1766.

BALTIMORE COUNTY, *July* 24, 1766.
RAN away last Night, from Col. *Charles Ridgely's*, near the *Northampton* Iron Works, an *Irish* Servant Man, named *John Garraughty*, about 25 Years of Age, 5 Feet 2 Inches high, of a swarthy Complexion, black Eyes, looks very bold and fierce, and wears his own straight black Hair, and has much of the *Irish* Brogue in his talk: Had on and took with him when he went away, an old light colour'd Bearskin Coat, lin'd with green Tammy, has a Pocket in the left Inside, full trimm'd, with Lappels and yellow gilt Buttons, two Osnabrig Shirts, old Thickset Breeches, Country Linen Trowsers, old brown Cut Wig, and an old Castor Hat, has neither Shoes nor Stockings with him as we know of: It's very probable he may endeavour to make for *New-Castle*, in *Pennsylvania*, as he was imported there about a Year ago, and from thence Sold in *Baltimore-Town*.

Whoever takes up the said Servant, and secures him in any Goal and give Notice thereof, so that his Masters may get him again, shall have, if taken in the County Forty Shillings, if out of the County Three Pounds, and if out of the Province Five Pounds Reward, and reasonable Charges if brought Home, paid by
WILLIAM GOODWIN,   JOHN HOLLIDAY.
N. B. All Masters of Vessels are forwarned Harbouring him at their Peril.

The Maryland Gazette, August 7, 1766; August 14, 1766; August 21, 1766. See *The Maryland Gazette*, September 25, 1766.

RAN away from the Subscriber, in *Frederick* County, about a Month ago, a Servant Lad named *Francis Dial*, about 5 Feet high, of a pale Complexion, short black Hair, and had a very sore Leg: Had on, an old Castor Hat, Kersey wove Waistcoat, of a yellow Colour, old coarse Shirt and Trowsers, and carried with him an old white Shirt.

    Whoever takes up and secures the said Servant, so as the Subscriber gets him again, shall have a Reward of Three Pounds, if taken out of the Province; if taken in the Province Forty Shillings, paid by
SARAH NELSON.
    The Maryland Gazette, August 7, 1766. See *The Maryland Gazette*, October 30, 1766.

August 4, 1766.

COMMITTED to *Prince-George's* County Jail, as a Runaway, by the Name of *Thomas Williams*, who says he is the Servant of *William Pursley*, of *St. Mary's* County.

    His Master is desired to take him away, and pay Charges.
Wm. T. Wootton, Sheriff.
    The Maryland Gazette, August 7, 1766; August 14, 1766; August 21, 1766. See the *The Maryland Gazette*, August 2, 1764.

July 28, 1766.

RAN away from *Dorsey's* Forge, on the main Falls of *Patapsco* River, a Convict Servant Man, named *John Smith*, about 5 Feet 4 Inches high, 25 Years of Age, short black Hair, a Hazle Eye, a small Scar in his Forehead, and another on the Outside of his left Leg, he is mark'd in both Arms with India-Ink, in one W C 1756, and in the other I C 1759, which last Letters he says are the two first Letters of his real Name *John Cox*. Had on an Osnabrig Shirt and Crocus Trowsers, and it's supposed he will steal Cloaths, as he is an artful Rogue, and must be well secured.

    Whoever takes up the said Servant, and brings him home, or secures him in any Jail, so as his Master may have him again, shall have, if under 10 Miles, Twenty Shillings; if above 20 Miles, Thirty Shillings; if at a greater Distance, Forty Shillings; if at a greater Distance, Forty Shillings; and reasonable Charges, if brought home, paid by
CALEB DORSEY.
    The Maryland Gazette, August 7, 1766; August 14, 1766; August 21, 1766.

Head of Elk, Cecil County, Maryland, July 24, 1766.

MADE his Escape last Night from Way's Tavern, at the Sign of the Waggon, on the Road leading from Philadelphia to Lancaster, an Irish

Servant Man, named Charles Farran, a thick well-set Fellow, about 20 Years of Age, 5 Feet 6 Inches high, has a Down-look, a little Knock-kneed, wears his own black Hair, cut on the Top of his Head, a great Snuffer, and very quarrelsome: Had on, when he made his Escape, an old Felt Hat, a light coloured Country Cloth lappelled Jacket, much worn, lined with Tow Linen, and small flat white Metal Buttons, a Country Linen Shirt, Tow Trowsers, old Calf-skin Shoes, with Copper Buckles. He was ironed with Handcuffs, which it is probably he may get off, as it is thought he has Confederates. He was lately taken out of Reading Goal, and it is thought he will make towards to Back-Country. Whoever takes up and secures said Servant in any Goal, shall have Forty Shillings, and if brought home Four Pounds Reward, paid by   HENRY HOLLINGSWORTH.
The Pennsylvania Gazette, August 7, 1766; September 4, 1766; October 9, 1766. See *The Pennsylvania Gazette*, June 13, 1765; *The Pennsylvania Gazette*, April 10, 1766, and *The Pennsylvania Gazette*, June 12, 1766.

Baltimore County, Maryland, July 21, 1766.
RUN from the Subscribers, last Night, two Convict Servant Men, named William Oak, and George Hails; Oak is about 5 Feet 7 Inches high, of a fair Complexion, short brown Hair, a likely well behaved Fellow, and has good Learning; had on, when he went away, a blue Coat and Breeches, with a Ozenbrig Trowsers over them, Worsted Stockings, and a Pair of good Shoes, a white Shirt and Neckcloth, and a good Hat; his Voice is very effeminate. Hails is about 5 Feet 8 or 9 Inches high, well set, and of a very dark Complexion, short black Hair, talks broad, and is a Brickmaker by Trade, but has lately worked a little at the Blacksmith's Business; had on, when he went away, a light coloured Thickset Coat and Jacket, Country Linen Shirt, Ozenbrigs Trowsers, a good Pair of Shoes, black Stockings, and a good Hat. They came lately in the Country, and have both sore Legs; they have some Cash with them, and are each about 22 or 23 Years of Age. Whoever takes up and secures said Servant, so that their Masters may have them again, shall have Three Pounds Reward, if taken in the County, Five Pounds, if taken out of the County, and Twenty Dollars, if taken out of the Province, paid by THOMAS TALBOTT, and TOBIAS RUDISELY.
The Pennsylvania Gazette, August 7, 1766; August 28, 1766; September 18, 1766;October 9, 1766; October 30, 1766; November 6, 1766; November 20, 1766; December 4, 1766. See *The Maryland Gazette*, July 28, 1768.

Philadelphia, August 13, 1766.
RUN away from the Subscriber, living near the Head of Elk, Caecil County, Maryland, on the 10th of this Instant, an indented Scotch Servant Man,

named John Gordon, about five Feet six Inches high, a well set Man, has a small Lisp in his Speech, freckled in the Face, short sandy Hair, well countenanced, about 18 Years old: Had on, when he went away, a Sailor's blue Jacket, and a Flannel white under Jacket, Ticking Breeches, white Yarn Stockings, and Pumps, a Wool Hat, and a Check Shirt. Whoever takes up and secures said Servant in any of his Majesty's Goals, so that the Subscriber may have him again, shall receive THREE POUNDS Reward, and reasonable Charges, paid by me SAMUEL SHARP.

N. B. It is supposed that he will endeavour to get off by Water, therefore all Masters of Vessels are forbid, at their Peril, taking him away.

The Pennsylvania Gazette, August 14, 1766; August 28, 1766; September 11, 1766. See *The New-York Mercury*, August 25, 1766, and *The Pennsylvania Gazette*, September 11, 1766.

York-Town, August 2, 1766.

NOTICE is hereby given,
THAT I have in my Custody the two following Servants, viz. Patrick Rorck, who says he belongs to William Cox, living near Deer Creek, in Baltimore County, Maryland. John Hughes; who says he belongs to Captain Richards, in Philadelphia. Also James Willis, taken up on suspicion of being a Runaway, a young Lad, about 17 Years of Age, of short Stature, and thin Visage; had on, when committed, a new Felt Hat, and old white Cotton Jacket, coarse Shirt and Trowsers, Thread Stockings, and half worn Shoes. He says he came from Seneca Creek, in Frederick County, Maryland. The Masters of the two above mentioned Servants are desired to come and fetch them away, otherwise they will be sold out for their Costs, in 4 Weeks from this Date; as also the last mentioned Lad, except his Master, if any, or some other, come for him.
JACOB GRAYBELL, Goaler

The Pennsylvania Gazette, August 14, 1766; August 28, 1766; September 11, 1766.

August 9, 1766.

RAN away last Night, from the *Patapsco* Furnace, near *Elk-Ridge* Landing, two *English* Convict Servant Men, viz.

William Lewis, aged about 27 Years, 5 Feet 7 Inches high, spare made, of a fair Complexion, thin Visage, light brown Hair, and grey Eyes: he has been under a Doctor for some Time, with a sore Leg, which causes him to go Lame. Had with him, an old Felt Hat, Osnabrigs Shirt, Matchcoat Jacket, Rolls Trowsers, and Country made Shoes.

John Wright, aged about 25 Years, about 5 Feet 5 Inches high, a bluff faced Fellow, of a fair Complexion, light brown Hair, grey Eyes, and is much Pock-mark'd, has a swelling in his right Knee, which causes him to go Lame. Had with him, a new Felt Hat, Osnabrigs Shirt, a grey Fearnought Jacket, and a blue Cloth under Ditto, Rolls Trowsers, and Country made Shoes.

Whoever takes up and secures the said Servants, so as they may be had again, shall receive for each, if taken 10 Miles from home, Twenty Shillings; if 20 Miles, Thirty Shillings; and if out of the Province, Three Pounds, and reasonable Charges if brought home to the Furnace, of *Thomas Harrison*, and Company.   *per* James Walker.

The Maryland Gazette, August 21, 1766; August 28, 1766; September 4, 1766; September 11, 1766; September 18, 1766.

Baltimore County, Aug. 11, 1766.

RUN away last night from the subscribers, living in Patapsco Neck, in Baltimore county, Maryland, a convict servant man, named John Clark, about 50 Years of age, about 5 feet 9 inches high, dark complexion; he had on, and took with him, when he went away, a striped holland shirt, two ozenbrigs ditto, two Pair ozenbrigs trowsers, a fulled country cloth jacket, lined with white flannel, and large metal buttons, a small red ditto, two pair shoes, and buckles; he has a down-look and remarkable large hump on his back.

From James Wood, an English convict servant man, named James Craytan, about 27 or 28 years of age, about 5 feet 8 or 9 inches high, of a fair red complexion, wears his own brown short curled hair, has a large scar upon his right-leg, a little below his knee; had on, and took with him, a new ozenbrigs shirt, two pair ozenbrigs trowsers, half worn shoes, with a patch upon one of them, and an old beaver hat, without bowlings.

And from Thomas Colegate, an English convict servant man, named John Ancell, about 5 feet 6 or 7 inches high, a well set fellow, about 30 years of age, or upwards, of a dark complexion, wears his own black strait hair, has a large black beard, and black eyes; had on, and took with him when he went away, a lightish coloured fulled cloth country jacket, with small pewter buttons, a coarse brown country linen shirt, and ozenbrigs ditto, new ozenbrigs trowers, with several patches of new ozenbrigs in the seat, coarse half worn shoes, and old coarse felt hat.

Whoever takes up and secures the said servants in any goal, so that their masters may have them again, shall receive for each, if taken in the county, Thirty Shillings reward, if taken out of the county, Forty Shillings, and if taken out of the province, Three Pounds, with reasonable charges, paid by JOSIAS BOWEN, JAMES WOOD, THOMAS COLEGATE.

N. B. It is supposed they are gone by water, there being a small pettiauger missing; they took with them a large black spaniel dog, with some white under his throat.

The Pennsylvania Gazette, August 21, 1766; October 30, 1766.

RUN away from the Subscriber, living near the Head of Elk, Caecil County, Maryland, on the 10th of August, an inded [sic] Scotch Servant Man, named John Gordon, about 5 feet 6 inches high, a well set man, has a small lisp in his speech, freckled in the face, short sandy hair, well countenanced, about 18 years old: Had on, when he went away, a sailor's blue jacket, ticking breeches, white yarn stockings, and pumps, a wool hat, and a check shirt. Whoever takes up and secures said servant in any of his Majesty's goals, so that the subscriber may have him again, shall receive THREE POUNDS reward, and reasonable Charges, paid by me
SAMUEL SHARP.

The New-York Mercury, August 25, 1766; September 1, 1766. See *The Pennsylvania Gazette*, August 14, 1766, and *The Pennsylvania Gazette*, September 11, 1766.

August 11, 1766.
COMMITTED to *Frederick* County Jail, on the 8th Instant, an *Irish* Man, who says he belongs to Mr. *Henry Hollingsworth*, Tavern Keeper, at the Head of *Elk* River, *Caecil* County, and confesses his Name to be *John Armstrong*.

His Master is desired to take him away, and pay Charges.
GEORGE SCOTT, Sheriff.

The Maryland Gazette, August 28, 1766; September 4, 1766.

FOUR DOLLARS reward, if taken in the county, and
EIGHT DOLLARS, if taken out of the county.

RUN away from the subscriber, living in Baltimore county, on Tuesday, the 5th of August, a convict Irish servant lad, named Patrick Brenon, about 18 years of age, 5 feet 2 or 3 inches high, down look, brown hair, cut on top of his head; had on, when he went away, a shirt and trowsers of brown roles, [sic] and felt hat, about half worn. Whoever takes up the said servant and brings him to the subscriber, shall receive the above reward from
JOSEPH BOSLEY, Jun.

The Pennslvania Gazette, August 28, 1766; September 11, 1766; September 18, 1766.

New-Castle Goal, August 22, 1766.
In Custody of the Subscriber, a certain Thomas Meclene, committed on Suspicion of being a Servant to Samuel Beal, of Anti-Etam Forge, Frederick County. His Master (if he has any) is desired to come, pay Charges, and take him away, otherwise he will be sold for the same, by ALEXANDER HARVEY, Goaler.

The Pennsylvania Gazette, August 28, 1766; September 11, 1766. See *The Maryland Gazette*, May 1, 1766, and *The Pennsylvania Gazette*, July 3, 1766.

RUN away from the Subscriber, an Irish Servant Man, named George Pinshen, of a low Stature, round Face, pitted with the Small-pox, came from Cork, and pretends to be a Cooper, calls himself Brown; he was taken on board at the new Wharff, in Kent, on Delaware, by one Liverton, a Shallopman, and landed at Philadelphia, and said he was going to one White; he wore a Country made Kersey Jacket, Ozenbrigs Shirt and Trowsers, and an old Hat, with Holes in the Crown. Whoever takes up the said Servant, and secures him in any of his Majesty's Goals so that his Master may have him again, shall have Forty Shillings Reward, and reasonable Charges, if brought home, paid by
CORNELIUS DAILY, at Talbot Courthouse, in Maryland.

The Pennsylvania Gazette, August 28, 1766; September 4, 1766; September 18, 1766.

RAN away from the Subscriber, near *Annapolis*, a Convict Servant Man, named JOHN STILLING, a slim made Fellow, about Five Feet Six or Seven Inches high; he is of a fair Complexion, short brown Hair, is pitted with the Small-Pox; his apparel is very remarkable, a Fearnought Jacket, Two Quarters grey, and Two blue, with Leather Buttons, Osnabrig Shirt, and Crocus Trowsers; has neither Hat, Shoes, or Stockings. Whoever takes up and secures the said Servant, so that his Master shall get him again, shall have a Reward of Twenty Shillings, and reasonable Charges, paid by
THOMAS RUTLAND.

The Maryland Gazette, September 4, 1766; September 11, 1766; September 18, 1766; September 25, 1766; October 2, 1766; October 9, 1766; October 16, 1766; October 23, 1766.

RAN away from the Subscribers, of *Prince-George's* County, on the 2d Instant, a Convict Servant Man, named *John Evans* (Alias *Harris*), by Trade a Taylor, about 5 Feet 7 Inches high, well made, has an Impediment in his Speech, a round smooth Face, down Look, short black Hair, and a thin black Beard. Had on, and carried with him, an old light coloured Sagathy Coat, white Linen Waistcoat without Sleeves, a Pair of light Cloth Breeches, and a Pair of Linen Ditto, two old white Shirts, a Pair of brown Thread Stockings, a Pair of Cotton Ditto, and a Pair of Shoes.

Whoever secures the said Servant, so that the Subscribers may get him again, shall receive Forty Shillings Reward, beside what the Law allows, and reasonable Charges if brought home, paid by
BASIL WARING, JOHN WARING.

The Maryland Gazette, September 4, 1766; September 11, 1766; September 18, 1766; September 25, 1766; October 2, 1766. See *The Maryland Gazette*, January 7, 1768.

Bohemia, Cecil County, August 18, 1766.
RUN away from the Subscriber, on the 17th Day of this Instant, a Servant Man, named William Callahan, an Irishman, about 32 or 33 Years or Age, and about 5 Feet 6 or 7 Inches high, of a sandy Complexion, wears short light brown Hair, cut close on the Top of his Head; had on, an old Ozenbrigs Shirt and Trowsers, the Trowsers patched between the Legs with a Piece of new tow Linen, an old Hat, and old short Coat, of mixed grey Cloth; he had neither Shoes nor Stockings, nor any other Cloaths with him; is a Plaisterer by Trade, but as he has been some Time on board a Man of War, it is like he may pretend to be a Sailor, and endeavour to get on board some Vessel. Whoever secures said Servant in any Goal, so that this Master may have him again, shall receive Five Dollars Reward from
ANDREW PEARCE.

The Pennsylvania Gazette, September 4, 1766; October 30, 1766. See *The Pennsylvania Gazette*, August 29, 1765.

Chester county, August 30, 1766.
NOW in the subscriber's custody, the four following described persons, committed as runaway servants, viz. John Norris, alias Patrick Norris, who says he is a servant to Mr. Charles Vallaly, at Pottsgrove. William Matthewson, who declares himself to be a servant to Mr. Derrick Pennybacker, in Berks county. John Arens, a Dutch man, about 5 feet 5 inches high, of a very dark complexion, short black hair, says he came from Maryland, and follows the sea. Benjamin Taylor, a lad about 15 years old, fair complexion, and much freckled, short yellow hair, says he came from Bristol, in Old England, in the ship Bristol Packet, captain Veasy, commander. The masters of said fellows (if any) are desired to come, pay charges, and take them away, in six weeks from this date, otherwise they will be sold for the same, by

JOSEPH THOMAS, goaler.
The Pennsylvania Gazette, September 4, 1766; September 25, 1766.

VIRGINIA, *August* 13, 1766.
RAN away from the *Neabsco* Furnace, on or about the 25th of July last, a Convict Servant, named *Arundale Carnes*, the Property of the Hon. *John Tayloe*, Esq; and was imported into this Country, last *April*, in the *Tryall*, from *London*. He is a Lad about 17 Years of Age, 5 Feet, 6 Inches high, very slim made, smooth faced, wears his own brown Hair, tied behind, and very short on the Forehead, has grey Eyes, and very large dark Eye-brows; had on, or with him, when he went away, a new blue Fearnought Pea-Jacket, an Osnabrig, and strip'd Cotton Shirt, Osnabrig Sailor's Trousers, a large half worn Castor Hat, a Pair of Country-made Shoes, large yellow Buckles, and, if drest, would make a genteel enough Appearance. Though he pretends to be somewhat of a Doctor, besides knowing how to wait on a Gentleman, yet it is more than presumable he will endeavour to pass as a Sailor, and get on board some Ship or Vessel, which all Masters of such are hereby forewarned, at their Peril, from indulging him in. He went from hence in a large Canoe, and would probably make for the *Maryland* Shore. Whoever apprehends the said Servant, and brings him to the *Neabsco* Furnace, shall receive, if taken in this Colony, Forty Shillings, if in any other Province, Four Pistoles Reward, besides what the Law allows.
THOMAS LAWSON.
The Maryland Gazette, September 11, 1766; September 18, 1766; September 25, 1766; October 2, 1766.

Baltimore-Town, Sept. 1, 1766.
RAN away from the Ship *Baltimore*, in *Patapsco* River, *William Hamilton* Master, the Three following Sailors, *viz.*

Alexander Taylor, born in *Scotland*, but says he served his Apprenticeship in *Norfolk, Virginia*; about 30 Years of Age, Five Feet Five Inches high, much Pitted with the Small Pox; has very sore Eyes, and much given to Swearing and Drinking, of a swarthy Complexion, and a diminutive Appearance.

Andrew Burt, a *Scotsman*, about 5 Feet 7 Inches high, about 24 Years of Age, a likely fresh complexion'd young Fellow.

Thomas Snell, a North-Country *Englishman*, and speaks in that Dialect, as if his Mouth was full, of a brown Complexion, and about 22 Years of Age.

Whoever secures the said Seaman, and sends them on board the said Ship, in *Patapsco* River, shall receive One Pistole Reward for *Taylor*, and Two Pistoles for each of the other Two, from
WILLIAM HAMILTON.
N. B. It is suppos'd they were decoyed away, and went with a Ship that lately sailed from this River to complete her Loading in *Patuxent*.— They all Three wore either Caps or Wigs.
The Maryland Gazette, September 11, 1766; September 18, 1766; September 25, 1766; October 2, 1766.

COMMITTED, the 4th of *Sept.* last, to *Calvert* County Jail, as a Runaway, one *John Crawford*, born in *Ireland*, says he is a Shoemaker, and belongs to *Henry Osburn* of *Philadelphia*.
His Master is desired to take him away, and pay Charges.
JOSEPH VANSWARINGGEN, Jailer.
The Maryland Gazette, September 11, 1766; September 25, 1766; October 2, 1766; October 9, 1766; October 16, 1766.

Burlington, September 2, 1766.
WAS committed to this goal, a certain John Gordon, about 5 feet 6 inches high, about 18 years of age, says he belongs to one Samuel Sharp, in Cecil county, Maryland; this is to inform said Sharp, or any other person it may concern, that except they come, pay charges, and take him away, he will be sold out in a little time for the same, by me
EPHRAIM PHILLIPS, goaler.
The Pennsylvania Gazette, September 11, 1766; September 18, 1766; October 2, 1766. See *The Pennsylvania Gazette*, August 14, 1766, and *The New-York Mercury*, August 25, 1766.

Carlisle goal, in Cumberland county, August 27, 1766.
WAS committed to the said goal, the 23d of this instant, on suspicion of being a runaway, Thomas Christopher, about 25 years of age, 5 feet 8 inches high, red complexion, very thin fleshed; wears a wig, and ragged cloathing; says he is acquainted in Baltimore Town, and neighbourhood. Also Edward Kelly, who confesses he belongs to, and run away from, John Starland, of Derry township, Lancaster county. Also a young Negroe fellow, called Cato, or Philip....Their Masters (if any there by) are hereby desired to come forthwith, pay charges, and take them away; otherwise they will be sold for the same, 4 weeks after the date hereof, by
HENRY CUNNINGHAM, goaler.
The Pennsylvania Gazette, September 11, 1766; October 9, 1766.

September 16, 1766.
FIVE POUNDS REWARD.

RAN away from the Subscriber's Plantation, at *Mount-Clare*, near *Baltimore-Town*, a Convict Servant Man, called *Richard Green*, a lusty swarthy Fellow, about 50 Years of Age: Had on and with him, a grey Fearnought Jacket, a light colour'd Cloth Coat, a black Cloth Waistcoat, a Pair of Crocus Trowsers, brown Worsted Stockings, and old Country-made Shoes; but it is probably he will get other Cloathes, and has a Forged Discharge.

Whoever secures him, and brings him to the Subscriber, or gives Notice, so that he may get him again, shall have the above Reward.
   CHARLES CARROLL.
The Maryland Gazette, September 18, 1766.

COMMITTED to *Talbot* County Jail, the 15th of *July* last, as a Runaway, a Man who says his Name is *John Mackey*, and that he belongs to *Levi Stephen*, Surveyor of Land in *York Town*, in *Pennsylvania*. His Master is desired to take him away, and pay Charges.
   JOHN BOZMAN, Sheriff.
The Maryland Gazette, September 18, 1766; September 25, 1766; October 2, 1766. See *The Maryland Gazette*, July 3, 1766.

COMMITTED to *Charles* County Jail as a Runaway, a Servant Lad about 17 or 18 Years of Age, of a middle Size, who says his Name is *William Newman*, and belongs to *John Burgess*, at *Elk-Ridge*.

His Master is desired to take him away, and pay Charges.
   CHARLES S. SMITH, Sheriff.
The Maryland Gazette, September 18, 1766; September 25, 1766; October 2, 1766.

RUN away, the 22d of August, from the subscriber, living in Queen Anne's county, Maryland, an indebted servant man, named Thomas Dance, about 30 years of age, 5 feet 4 or 5 inches high, born in the west of England, has brown short hair; had on a half worn felt hat, new check shirt, and new ozenbrig trowers, a pair of old pumps, and white worsted stockings. Whoever brings the said servant to his master, or secures him, so that he may be had again, shall have Twenty Shillings more than the law allows, paid by SWEATNAM BURN.
The Pennsylvania Gazette, September 18, 1766; October 9, 1766; November 20, 1766. See *The Pennsylvania Gazette*, October 30, 1766.

York County, September 1, 1766.
WAS committed to my custody, on the 25th day of August last, a certain Joseph Williams, being convicted on the oath of Joseph Witmore, that he was a runaway servant, belonging to Daniel Delany, in the province of Maryland, 6 years ago. His master is desired, if any he has, to come and pay charges, and take him away in 4 weeks time from the date hereof, otherwise he will be sold out for his fees, by
   JACOB GRAYBILL, goaler.
The Pennsylvania Gazette, September 18, 1766.

Baltimore County, *September* 15, 1766.
RAN away last Night from the Subscriber's Plantation, near the *Northampton* Furnace, in *Baltimore* County, *Maryland*, two Convict Servant Men, *viz.*

Stephen Pane, an *Englishman*, a Shoemaker by Trade, about 5 Feet 8 or 9 Inches high, about 24 Years of Age, swarthy Complexion, much pitted with the Small-Pox, short strait black Hair, has grey Eyes and looks very bold, much Knock-Knee'd, one of his Great Toes has lately been cut with an Ax, and is now sore: Had on and took with him, an old Cotton Jacket, two Osnabrig Shirts, Country Linen Trowsers, Felt Hat, old Shoes, with a Piece cut out against the sore Toe, a red Calf-Skin Knapsack, with the Hair on the outside, and so Shoemaker's Tools in it.

John Garraughty, an *Irishman*, and has much of the Brogue, about 5 Feet 2 Inches high, 24 Years of Age, swarthy Complexion, short strait black Hair, black Eyes, looks very Fierce, and has a large Scar across his Throat where he has attempted to cut it: Had on and took with him, an old Bearskin Coat, full trimm'd, with yellow Gilt Buttons, lined with green Tammy, and has Lappels to it, with a Pocket in the left Inside, Osnabrig Shirt, Country Linen Trowsers, an old Castor Hat, and old single Channel Pumps.

Whosoever takes up the said Servants, and secures them in any Goal, so that their Masters may get them again, shall have Forty Shillings Reward if taken Ten Miles from Home, Four Pounds if Twenty Miles, and Six Pounds if out of the County, and Ten Pounds if out of the Province, or Half as much for either, and reasonable Charges if brought Home, paid by
CHARLES RIDGELY, senior.

N. B. The above Fellows had Iron Collars on when they went away: All Masters of Vessels are forewarn'd harbouring them at their peril.
The Maryland Gazette, September 25, 1766. See *The Maryland Gazette*, August 7, 1766, for Garraughty.

RAN away on the 9th of *September* last, from the Subscriber, living on LADY'S MANOR, near *Gunpowder-Falls*, in *Baltimore* County, an *English* Convict Servant Man, named WILLIAM DENNIT, about 27 Years of Age, 5 Feet 7 or 8 Inches high, has black curled Hair, dark Eyes and Eyebrows, is pitted with the Small-Pox, and has a pleasant Countenance: Had on and took with him when he went away, an old blue Surtout Coat, a Great Coat of a dark grey Colour, made of this Country Cloth, a Pair of old Leather Breeches, a Pair of old Trowsers, Two Tow Linen Shirts, and a Pair of old Shoes; likewise a bay Mare, near 14 Hands high, about 12 Years old, with a Star in her Forehead, and branded on the Near Buttock **AB**.

Whoever takes up the said Servant and Mare, and secures them so that the Subscriber may get them again, shall, if taken in the County receive SEVEN POUNDS, and if taken out of the County TEN POUNDS Reward, paid by   WALTER WYLE.

The Maryland Gazette, October 2, 1766; October 9, 1765; October 16, 1766; October 23, 1766.

September 24, 1766.

RAN away from the Subscriber's Ship, lying at the Mouth of *Piscataway* Creek in *Patowmack* River, Two Indented Servants, *viz*. *Thomas Holmes*, an *Englishman*, about 5 Feet, 8 Inches high, Thirty Years of Age, and a Gardiner by Trade, wears his own Hair, tied behind, and had on when he went away a striped red and white Flannel Jacket.—The other, named *William George*, by Trade a Farmer, was born in *Cornwal*, [sic] is about 5 Feet 6 or 7 Inches high, of a light Complexion, wears his own Hair, and had on when he went away, a white Cloth Coat, a white Flannel Jacket, and a Pair of Trowsers; but, as it is supposed they took sundry other Clothes with them, 'tis probable they may change their Apparel, and pass for Seamen.

Whoever apprehends the said Runaways, and delivers them on board said Ship, or secures them in any Goal, so as they may be had again, shall receive a Reward of One Pistole for each, from
          DAVID LEWIS.

The Maryland Gazette, October 2, 1766; October 9, 1766; October 16, 1766; October 23, 1766.

September 27, 1766.

RAN away last Night from the Subscriber, living near *Snowden's* Iron-Works, in *Anne-Arundel* County, a Convict Servant Man, named *John Hill*, a stout well made Fellow, about 5 Feet 10 Inches high, has short yellow Hair, much pitted with the Small Pox, and has a leering Roguish Look. Had on and took with him when he went away, a Bearskin Jacket, one strip'd Flannel ditto, one white Lappel'd ditto, one Osnabrig Shirt, a Pair of

Osnabrig Trowsers, a Pair of striped Flannel short Breeches, old Shoes, and a good Felt Hat.

Whoever takes up and secures the said Fellow, so that his Master may get him again, shall receive FORTY SHILLINGS Reward, besides what the Law allows, paid by.   JAMES ELDER.

The Maryland Gazette, October 2, 1766; October 9, 1766; October 16, 1766.

September 29, 1766.

RAN away last Night from the Subscriber, near *Snowden's* Manor, in *Frederick* County, Two Convict Servant Men, *viz*.

John Wright, about 25 Years of Age, 5 Feet 6 or 7 Inches high, a brisk active Fellow, a Brick-maker by Trade, dark Complexion, short Visag'd, grey Eyes, and short brown Hair: Had on and took with him, an old light colour'd Cloth Coat, old Castor Hat, One white Shirt, and two Osnabrig ditto, strip'd Flannel Waistcoat and Breeches, Two Pair of light colour'd ribb'd Worsted Hose, and old Shoes.

William White, about the same Age, 5 Feet 7 or 8 Inches high, a lusty clumsy Fellow, yellow Complexion, grey Eyes, short brown Hair, and a large Scar on one of his Legs: Had on and took with him, an Osnabrig Shirt, blue Pea Jacket, and light colour'd ditto, without Sleeves, a Pair of greasy Leather Breeches eaten in the Seat by Rats, Two Pair of grey Worsted Hose, old Shoes and Hat; it is supposed they have stolen Horses, chang'd their Dress, and may endeavour to get a Passage Home.

Whoever secures the said Servants, so that their Masters may get them again, shall receive FIVE POUNDS Reward, or Half that Sum for either, and reasonable Charges if brought home, paid by
RICHARD BROOK,   EDWARD OWEN, junr.

The Maryland Gazette, October 2, 1766; October 9, 1766; October 16, 1766.

Dorchester County, Maryland, Sept. 21, 1766.
FIVE POUNDS REWARD.

RUN away from his Bail, on or about the 20th of June last, a certain Thomas Cross, who came to Philadelphia on Pretence of heiring a Part of the Estate of the Rev. Robert Cross, deceased; he is a Man of a sandy Complexion, slender made, wears green Broadcloth Clothes, is about 5 Feet 10 Inches high, and it is supposed he may go to School-keeping. Whoever takes up the said Runaway, so that his Bail may have him brought to Justice, shall receive the above Reward, and reasonable Charges, from
     JOSEPH HICKS.

The Pennsylvania Gazette, October 2, 1766; October 9, 1766; October 23, 1766.

Carlisle goal, in Cumberland county, October 1, 1766.
BROKE out of the garret window of said goal, in the night of the 30th of last month, the eight following described fellows, viz. Patrick M'Mullan.... John Lefavour....Philip Connally.....William Sheppard....William Ellis....William Guiddine, a short, pock marked, ill looking rascal; says he is servant to Mr. Harrison, of Baltimore. And James Biggar....Whoever takes up any, or all of the above fellows, and brings them to Carlisle goal, shall have Forty Shillings reward for each of the two first named fellows, and Four dollars for each of the others, paid by
JOHN HOLMES, sheriff, or HENRY CUNNINGHAM, goaler.

The Pennsylvania Gazette, October 9, 1766; October 16, 1766. *The Maryland Gazette*, December 1, 1768. See *The Maryland Gazette*, March 17, 1768, and *The Maryland Gazette*, December 1, 1768, for Biggar.

Prince-George's County, *Octob.* 13, 1766.
A FELLOW who was advertised as committed to my Custody on the 4th Day of *August* last, by the Name of *Thomas Williams*, and belonging to *William Pursley*, of *St. Mary's* County, now confesses that his Name is *Thomas Brookes*, and belongs to Mr. *Daniel M'Pherson*, of *Charles* County, the said Fellow has no Toes on his left Foot. His Master is desired to take him away, and pay Charges.
Wm. T. WOOTTON, Sheriff.

The Maryland Gazette, October 16, 1766. See *The Maryland Gazette*, August 2, 1764, for Brookes, and *The Maryland Gazette*, August 7, 1766, for Williams.

FIVE POUNDS Reward.
RUN away from the subscriber, about the middle of August last, living on Potomack river, near Frederick town, in Maryland, a convict servant man, named John Bath, a Scotchman, about 5 feet 6 inches high, well set, has had a leg broke, which is set crooked, and is commonly sore, especially after a drunken touch, which he is much given to, a Weaver, by trade, an excellent workman; he had on, and took with him, an old greyish coat and jacket, and a blue jacket, brown linen shirts and trowsers, &c. Whoever secures the said servant and gives notice to the owner, is intitled to the above reward and reasonable charges, if brought home.   JOSIAS CLAPHAM.

The Pennsylvania Gazette, October 16, 1766; November 6, 1766; November 20, 1766.

RAN away from the Subscriber, near *Joppa*, in *Baltimore* County, the 28th of *Sept.* last, a Convict Servant Man, named *Riely Johnson*, by Trade a Shoemaker, about 5 Feet 9 Inches high, about 50 Years of Age: He had on, a brown double-breasted short Jacket, Thickset Breeches, white Shirt and Stockings, good Shoes, and Brass Buckles: He is a homely Fellow, walks fast, and when in Liquor, which he is fond of, talks much of his Performance as a Doctor, he can Bleed, and Draw Teeth, having both those Instruments with him. He may probably write himself a Pass, as he did once before, and gave himself the Name of *Thomas Scot*. All Masters of Vessels are forbid to take him on Board.

Whoever secures the said Servant in any Jail, so that his Master gets him again, shall have Three Pounds Reward, and if brought home the same beside what the Law allows.   Wm. YOUNG.

The Maryland Gazette, October 23, 1766; October 30, 1766; November 6, 1766.

RAN away from the Subscriber, living in *Fogg's* Manor, *Chester* County, *Pennsylvania*, on the 12th Instant, an *Irish* Servant Man, named *Thomas O'Driskill*, about 35 Years of Age, 5 Feet 7 or 8 Inches high, a broad well-set Fellow, of a dark Complexion, and has short black Hair: Had on and took with him when he went away, and old blue Beaver Hat, a light colour'd Great Coat, a blue strait Body'd ditto, a white Flannel Jacket, a striped Linen ditto, 2 white Linen Shirts, blue Plush Breeches, Buckskin Ditto, Yarn Stockings, and a Pair of good Shoes with Copper Buckles in them.

Whoever takes up the said Servant, and secures him in any Jail, so that his Master may get him again, shall receive Forty Shillings Reward, and reasonable Charges, paid by   JOHN BLAIR.

N. B. He was seen the 16th Instant, within 5 Miles of *Baltimore-Town*; As he is a pretty good Scholar, its probable he may forge himself a Pass: All Masters of Vessels are forewarn'd Harbouring him on Board at their Peril.   J. B.

The Maryland Gazette, October 23, 1766; October 30, 1766.

RUN away, the 27th of September last, from Benjamin Vansant, near Georgetown, in Kent County, Maryland, two Taylor Apprentices; the one named Joshua Burgon, about 20 Years old, about 5 Feet 2 Inches high, brown Hair, of a pale Complexion, long visage, has an Impediment in his Speech; had on, when he went away, a blue broad cloth Coat, claret coloured Waistcoat, blue Breeches, blue Stockings and old beaver Hat. The

other named Cuthbert Cole, about 20 Years old, about 5 Feet 8 Inches high, of a brown Complexion, straight built, wears his own dark brown Hair, commonly tyed, has a mark on his right Cheek, of a whiter colour than the rest of his Skin; had on, when he went away, a brown broadcloth Coat, almost new, with gilt metal Buttons, a turned brown Waistcoat, blue saggathy Breeches, blue and white thread, and Yarn Stockings, a pair of turned Pumps, with Silver plated Buckles, and an old beaver Hat. Any Person that apprehends the said Apprentices, shall have Forty Shillings Reward for each, and all reasonable Charges, paid by the Subscriber,
    BENJAMIN VANSANT.
The Pennsylvania Gazette, October 23, 1766; November 6, 1766; November 27, 1766.

October 29, 1766.
RAN away from the Subscriber, living in *Frederick* County, about the middle of last *July*, a Servant Lad named *Francis Dial*, about 5 Feet high, of a pale Complexion, short black Hair, and had a very sore Leg: Had on, an old Castor Hat, Kersey wove Waistcoat, of a yellow Colour, old coarse Shirt and Trowsers, and carried with him an old white Shirt.

Whoever takes up and secures the said Servant, so as the Subscriber gets him again, shall have a Reward of Three Pounds, if taken out of the Province; if taken in the Province Forty Shillings, paid by
    SARAH NELSON.
The Maryland Gazette, October 30, 1766; November 6, 1766. See *The Maryland Gazette*, August 7, 1766.

RUN away, the 22d of August, from the subscriber, living in Queen Anne's county, Maryland, an indebted servant man, named Thomas Dance, about 30 years of age, 5 feet 4 or 5 inches high, born in the west of England, has brown short hair; had on a half worn felt hat, new check shirt, a green jacket, with white metal buttons, has no lining, but is much worn at the elbows, also a new stuff jacket, of a red and white colour check, lined with brown holland, new ozenbrigs trowers, white worsted stockings, and a pair of half-worn pumps, with large pinchbeck buckles. I have reson to believe he has crossed the bay, and got into Baltimore county. Whoever brings the said servant to his master, or secures him, so that he may be had again, shall have Forty Shillings more than the law allows, paid by
    SWEATNAM BURN.
The Pennsylvania Gazette, October 30, 1766; November 6, 1766; November 20, 1766. See *The Pennsylvania Gazette*, September 18, 1766.

October 29, 1766.

RAN away from the Subscriber, in *Queen-Anne's* County, *Kent-Island*, on the 12th of this Instant, a Convict Servant Man, named *Thomas Evans*, born in *Wales*, about 40 Years of Age, 5 Feet 4 or 5 Inches high, of a fresh Complexion, and light colour'd Hair: Had on and took with him, a Surtout Cloth colour'd Coat, a brown double breasted Broad-Cloth Jacket, Osnabrig Shirt, Country Linen Trowsers, black Yarn Stockings, Thread ditto, good Shoes, and a Hat bound round with black Worsted Binding.

Whoever takes up the said Man, and secures him in any Goal, so that his Master may get him again, shall receive Twenty Shillings Current Money Reward, and reasonable Charges if brought home, paid by
WILLIAM HORN.

The Maryland Gazette, November 6, 1766; November 13, 1766; November 20, 1766; November 27, 1766; December 4, 1766.

TWENTY DOLLARS REWARD.

RUN away from the Subscriber, living in Baltimore County, Maryland, the two following Convict Servant Men, viz. Francis Edwin, a short thick well set Fellow, about 5 Feet 5 Inches high, round full Face, hazle Eyes, of a yellowish Complexion, and has a thick sandy red Beard; had on and with him, a light coloured Fearnought jacket, an old Felt Hat, a Country Linen Shirt and Trowsers, a Pair of old Leather Breeches, white Yarn Stockings, old Shoes, and a Pair of Dog-skin Pumps, with yellow Metal Buttons in them. John Evans, by Trade a Shoemaker, aged about 21 Years, about 5 Feet 8 or 9 Inches high, of a dark Complexion, black Eyes, short black Hair, and thin black Beard: Had on and with him, a yellow Cotton, and a black Cloth Jacket, with a Cape and Horn Buttons, an Ozenbrigs and a Check Shirt, old Felt Hat, old Leather Breeches, Yarn Stockings, and a Pair of Dog-Skin Pumps, with Strings in them. Whoever takes up said Servants, and secures them in any Goal, so as they may be had again, shall have the above Reward of TWENTY DOLLARS, or TEN for either, and reasonable Charges if brought home, paid by
ROBERT TEVES.

The Pennsylvania Gazette, November 6, 1766; December 4, 1766; December 18, 1766; December 25, 1766; January 1, 1767; February 5, 1767; February 26, 1767. See *The Pennsylvania Gazette*, September 12, 1765, for Edwin.

ST. VINCENT, *August* 29, 1766.
EIGHTY POUNDS REWARD.

RAN away from the Sloop *Betsey, Estes Howe*, Master, lying in *Cumberland Bay*, on the Night between the 26th and 27th Instant,

George Brown, Mate, born in the North of *England*, about 5 Feet 7 Inches high, short black Hair, fresh coloured, aged about 27 Years, he was formerly in the Employ of Mr. *Robson* of *Carewacow*, and ran away with his Shallop about a Year ago.

Charles Haney, born in the North of *Ireland*, about 5 Feet 9 Inches high, short black Hair, freckled and mark'd with the Small-pox, wellset, and about 28 Years of Age.

Henry Haney, born in *Ireland*, about 5 Feet 10 Inches high, has long Flaxen Hair, much mark'd with the Small-Pox, a very high *Roman* Nose, aged about 20 Years.

William Haslup, from the North of *England*, about 5 Feet high, wellset, has short light Hair, smooth Face, and 22 Years of Age; he formerly sailed with Capt. *Taylor* of this Island.

They carried off with them a Moses built BOAT almost new, pay'd inside and out with *Spanish* Brown and Tar, and 4 Oars, with a Barrel of Beef, and a Barrel of Bread; they broke open a large Trunk, and a small One that was in it, took out the Papers and carried away the small Trunk and Two Hundred and Thirty-eight Pounds Fifteen Shillings, mostly Johannes's, one Stone Gold Ring, one Pair of Money Scales and Weights.

Whoever will apprehend the above Runaways, or any of them, and bring them to Lieut. Governor *Scott*, of *Dominica*; *John Simpson*, Naval Officer, at *St. Vincent*; Mr. *David Purviance*, at the *Grenado*; Mr. *John Hyligar*, in *Montserrat*; Mr. *John Linsey*, at *Antigua*; Messrs. *Smith* and *Bailey*, at *St. Christophers*; *William Moore*, in *Barbados*; Mr. *Joseph Fitch*, in *Jamaica*; Capt. *Philip Lewis*, in *St. Eustatia*; Mr. *Thomas Forsey*, at *St. Croix*; or, to Mr. *John Philips*, at *St. Thomas*; shall receive as follows, for *George Brown* Fifty Pounds Currency, and for the other Three Thirty Pounds, or Ten Pounds for each; the like Sum to have them secured in any Jail or Fort, and Advice given to any of the above Gentlemen, so that they may be brought to Justice.

If the Boat or Money is found about any of them, it is hoped it will be secured. Whoever secures any of the above Thieves, as above, shall be paid the said Sum or Sums, by   ESTES HOWE.

The Maryland Gazette, November 13, 1766; November 20, 1766.

October 28, 1766.
FORTY SHILLINGS Reward.

RUN away from the Subscriber, living in Kent county, Maryland, a Dutch servant man, named John Dowsman, a baker by trade; he is about 5 feet 8 or 9 inches high, speaks bad English, of a pale complexion, grey eyes, has long black hair, tied behind, about 20 years of age, took with him a suit of blue cloaths, with flat brass buttons, also a brown fine fustian coat, white breeches and waistcoat, white cotton stockings, good shoes, with large silver buckles; took with him two felt hats, and a wallet, with three silk handkerchiefs, sundry white shirts, and other wearing apparel, and an old gun, half stocked; he had five or six pounds in dollars, and has silver sleeve buttons; he is an artful fellow, and has been in the country about two years, which time he lived at Annapolis. Both his legs are sore, have been very much hurt, and look blackish. Whoever takes up said servant and brings him to his master, or secures him in any of his Majesty's goals, shall have the above reward, paid by   CORNELIUS VANSTAVOREN.

The Pennsylvania Gazette, November 13, 1766; December 4, 1766; December 11, 1766; December 18, 1766; December 25, 1766.

Talbot County, Nov. 8, 1766.
FIVE POUNDS REWARD.

RAN away from his Bail, in *August* 1765, a certain *James Wilkins*, about 5 Feet 6 or 7 Inches high, a Native *Irishman*, speaks good *English*, but with his Country's Tone, has been lately here with his Wife, and a Child of 2 Years old, of a fair Complexion, much pitted with the Small-Pox, wears his own Hair, of a reddish or Sandy Colour, commonly tied with an Eel's Skin. He served his Time here, saws well with the Whip-Saw, is a good Hand by Water, and has been seen at *Baltimore*, or on a Plantation belonging to Mr. *Stephen West*. Whoever apprehends the above Person, so as the Subscribers may him again, [*sic*] shall receive the above Reward, from
FREDERICK LEITH, and JAMES CHAPMAN.

The Maryland Gazette, November 20, 1766; November 27, 1766; December 4, 1766; December 11, 1766; December 18, 1766; January 1, 1767. See *The Maryland Gazette*, September 5, 1765

RUN away, on the 12th of this inst. November, from Stafford Forge, on Deer Creek, in Baltimore County, Maryland, an English Convict Servant Man, named Levy Barnett, has been used to the Sea, and has light coloured short Hair, curls behind, cut short on the Top of his Head; had on, an old Felt Hat, grey Fearnought Jacket, blue Cloth under Ditto, double breasted, with Leather buttons, Ozenbrigs Shirt, Petticoat Trowsers, made of Country Linen, a Pair of brown Yarn Hose, a Pair of light coloured English knit ribbed Ditto, and Country made Shoes; has been in the Country about 12 Months. Whoever will apprehend the said Servant, and secure him in any Goal, so that he may be had again, shall have, if taken ten Miles from home,

Forty Shillings, if 20 Miles, Three Pounds, if out of this Province, Five Pounds Reward, and reasonable Charges, if brought to said Forge, paid by JEREMIAH SHEREDINE.

The Pennsylvania Gazette, November 20, 1766; December 4, 1766; December 11, 1766; December 25, 1766.

Nov. 20, 1766.

RAN away, last Night, from the Subscriber, in *Bladensburg*, a *Dutch* Servant Man, named *Matthias Strictfoot*, a Taylor by Trade, born in *Germany*, about 40 Years of Age, 5 Feet 5 or 6 Inches high: has been in the Country near 15 Years, and can speak *English* pretty well, a strong well-made Fellow, of a dark Complexion, short black curl'd Hair, mixed with grey, very full faced, has much the Appearance of a Sailor; had on and took with him, a Double-breasted Half-thick Jacket, with a small Pocket on each Side; Check Shirt, old white Linen, ditto; new blue Serge Breeches, light coloured Yarn-Stockings, good Shoes, and an old Castor Hat.

Whoever takes up the said Man, and secures him, so that his Master may get him again, shall receive a Reward of Forty Shillings, paid by MICHAEL PENCE.

The Maryland Gazette, November 27, 1766; December 4, 1766; December 11, 1766.

Prince-George's County, *Nov. 25, 1766.*
EIGHT POUNDS REWARD.

BROKE Jail last Night, and made their Escape, the Three following Persons, *viz.*

James Thomas, who was committed for stealing Mr. *Samuel Marlow's* Great Coat, a bold impertinent well made Fellow, about Five Feet Seven Inches high.

William White, a Convict, who was committed for stabbing *Benedict Wood*, who is since dead, a well made young Fellow, has on a light coloured Waistcoat and Breeches, a very old Shirt, no Shoes, a Pair of strong Hand-Cuffs, and an Iron Collar about his Neck.

Mulatto *Jack*....

Whoever takes up the said *William White*, and delivers him at the Jail aforesaid, shall be paid Five Pounds, and for the other Two Thirty Shillings each. Wm. T. WOOTTON, Sheriff.

The Maryland Gazette, November 27, 1766; December 4, 1766.

SEVEN POUNDS REWARD.

RAN away from the Subscriber, in *Frederick* County, *Maryland*, Three Convict Servants, on the 30th of *November* past, *viz.*

THOMAS RAVEN, an *Englishman*, a Blacksmith by Trade, about 5 Feet 6 Inches high, about 27 Years of Age, has sore Eyes; had on and took with him, a brown Cut Wig, brown Coat full big and long with a large Cape, black Velvet Jacket and Breeches, with black Horn Buttons, Coarse white Yarn Stockings, a Pair of Ribb'd Worsted Ditto; and has a loud forward Way of Speaking.

WILLIAM BARTLEY, an *Irishman*, about 26 Years of Age, about 5 Feet 9 Inches high, has a remarkable large Head, thick Neck, and red Hair about Three Inches long; had on a Worsted Cap, brown Coat and Breeches, strip'd Linsey Jacket, and coarse white Yarn Stockings.

JAMES REED, an *Englishman*, about 29 Years of Age, the End of his Nose flat, was formerly a Sailor, and has been several Times in the Country before, is slender made, about 5 Feet 8 Inches high, and has black Hair; he had on a Castor Hat bound round with Ferrett, blue double-breasted Sailor's Jacket lined with red, the Button-holes not Worked, brown Cloth Under-Jacket lined with Flannel, brown Breeches not lined, and a Check Shirt.

Whoever takes up the said Servants, or secures them, so as the Subscriber may get them again, shall receive, for *Thomas Raven*, Three Pounds, and Forty Shillings for each of the other Two, with reasonable Charges, paid by   WALTER BEALL.

N. B. All Masters of Vessels are forewarn'd to carry them off, at their peril.

The Maryland Gazette, December 11, 1766; December 18, 1766; January 1, 1767.

ABsconded from the Schooner *Tryall*, lying in the River *Severn*, on Saturday the 6th Instant, an *Irish* Creole, who calls himself *George O'Brien*, and pretends to be the Son of one *O'Brien*, a Wealthy Planter in *Montserrat*, he is about 5 Feet 6 Inches high, wears his own dark Hair, tied behind, and a little pitted with the Small Pox; had on and took with him a blue Broad-Cloth Coat, with Gold Lace, entirely worn out, a red Waistcoat and Breeches, a light coloured bound Great Coat with a double Cape, 2 white Shirts, 1 Check Ditto, 2 Pair of Worsted Hose, Turn'd Pumps, and Brass Buckles, and a half worn Castor Hat: The above Person plays extremely well on the Violin, and values himself much on being a Free-Mason. Whoever apprehends him, so as he may be brought to Justice, and the Things taken away recovered, shall receive Forty Shillings Reward, and reasonable Charges, by applying on board the said Schooner, to
ABRAHAM VAN BEBBE.

The Maryland Gazette, December 11, 1766.

York Goal, December 3, 1766.

ABOUT the Beginning of October last was taken up, at Hammond's Tavern, seven Miles from York, leading from York to Peach-bottom Ferry, a Runaway Servant Boy, about twelve Years of Age, who calls himself Andrew M'Collins, and says his Master lives near Deer-Creek, in Baltimore County, Maryland, who is called Andrew Cunningham. The Owner of said Servant is desired to come directly, pay Charges, and take him away, otherwise he will be sold, by Order of Court, for his Charges, by ALEXANDER RAMSAY, Goaler.

The Pennsylvania Gazette, December 11, 1766; December 18, 1766; January 1, 1767.

New Castle County, Dec. 5, 1766.

NOW in the custody of the subscriber, the three following persons, viz. Samuel Galloway....

Also a certain William Muheaw, about 20 years of age, about 5 feet 4 inches high, light brown hair, by trade a tinker; had on, when committed, a brown broadcloth coat and waistcoat, with mohair buttons, striped Holland trowsers, white worsted stockings, and half boots, committed 21st of October last as a runaway; says his master's name is Thomas Beech, and lives in Arundel County, in the province of Maryland.

Also a negroe lad...Cato....Their masters (if any they have) are desired to come, pay charges, and take them away in six weeks, or they will be sold out for the same by   THOMAS PUSEY, Goaler.

The Pennsylvania Gazette, December 11, 1766; January 1, 1767; January 15, 1767; February 26, 1767.

SIX PISTOLES Reward.

RUN away from New Town, on Chester River, Kent County, Maryland, on the 29th Day of November last, the three following Men, viz. Simon Trayner, an Irishman, about 5 Feet 8 Inches high, smooth faced, fresh coloured, knock kneed, about 26 Years of Age; had on, and took with him, a new Beaver Hat, blue Broadcloth Coat, spotted Flannel Jacket, old Buckskin Breeches, with a Hole on the Right Thigh near the Pocket, and has been lately mended, good Worsted Stockings, and Shoes, with carved Whitemetal Buckles. Michael M'Kenney, an Irishman, about 26 years of Age, 5 Feet 5 Inches high, a little knock kneed; had on, and took with him, an old Beaver Hat, a brown Broadcloth Coat, lined with white Shalloon, a spotted Flannel Jacket, a red Cloth Ditto, light coloured Plush Breeches, new Yarn Stockings, new Shoes, and Brass Buckles; snuffles as he speaks, occasioned by having his Nose broke. Michael Mooney, an Irishman, about 28 Years of Age, about 6 Feet high, pale Complexion, long Hair, tied

behind, had on, an old Castor Hat, old blue Cloth Coat, Leather Breeches, old Pumps, but may have got new ones; they are all acquainted in New-Castle County, the Jerseys, and Bucks County, as they have worked in those Parts some Time ago, and were seen travelling up that Way. They stole and took with them, a brown Broadcloth Coat, lined white Shalloon, which M'Kinney wears, a new Beaver Hat, which Trayner wears, a new Pair of Shoes, an old Beaver Hat, and several Things, too tedious to mention; they likewise had with them, a Piece of Check Linen, and a Piece of Irish Ditto. Whoever secures the said Fellows, and brings them to the Subscriber, shall receive the above Reward, and reasonable Charges, if brought home; otherwise if secured in any Goal so as the Subscriber may have them again, shall have One Pistole for each, paid by
ALEXANDER M'INTOSH.

The Pennsylvania Gazette, December 18, 1766; January 1, 1767.

RUN away from the Subscriber, living in Chester Town, Kent County, Maryland, a Convict Servant Man, named Joseph Sprout, aged 22 Years, or thereabouts, 5 Feet 9 Inches high, thin pale Face, and stoops in his Shoulders when he walks; he had on, when he went away, a thick white Cotton Cap, an old Felt Hat, a blue Surtout, with a Manchester Velvet Cape to it, a red Plush close bodied Coat, an old thin Pair of black Silk knit Breeches, and a Pair of clouded Worsted Stockings. Whoever secures the said Servant in any Goal, so that his Master may have him again, and gives Notice thereof, shall receive Forty Shillings Reward, from
JOSEPH NICHOLSON, jun.

The Pennsylvania Gazette, December 18, 1766; December 25, 1766; January 8, 1767; February 19, 1767; March 19, 1767.

1767

Baltimore-Town, *December* 29, 1766.
RAN away from *Kingsbury* Furnace, in *Baltimore* County, last Night, Three Convict Servant Men, *viz.*

JOHN FRYER, by Trade a Wheel-wright, about 30 Years of Age, about 5 Feet 7 Inches high, dark brown curled Hair, fresh Complexion, had on and took with him the following Things, one Castor and one Felt Hat, a blue grey broad Cloth Coat, red Jacket, blue Duffil Breeches, one Pair of light coloured Plush ditto, blue grey Stockings, one Pair *English* Falls, one Pair Country made Pumps, one white Shirt of *English* Linen, several Oznabrig Shirts, one or two silk Handkerchiefs, and several other Things unknown.

SAMUEL SEARSON, a lusty well made Fellow, fresh Complexion, down-look, about 28 or 30 Years of Age, about 5 Feet 9 Inches high, wears his own dark brown Hair, had on and took with him a pretty good *English* Castor, and one Felt Hat, one of them bound round with black Binding, several pretty good white Linen Shirts, one Pair of Buckskin Breeches, one light coloured Kersey or Drab surtout Coat, double breasted, and Hair Buttons, one Pair of good black ribbed Stockings, and one Pair dark plain ditto, one Pair *English* Pumps, and two Pair *English* Falls, nailed in the Soles, one Pair square Steel, and one Pair Brass figured Buckles, 2 Oznabrig Shirts, Cotton Jacket and Breeches, and several other Things unknown.

THOMAS NORTH, a tall stout Fellow, thin Visaged, pale Complexion, short brown Hair, sour down-look, about 5 Feet 9 or 10 Inches high, about 28 or 30 Years of Age; had on and took with him, one Pair of old Leather Breeches, one Pair of old Cloth ditto, one Pair of Cotton ditto, one Cotton Jacket, one Spotted old Swanskin ditto, one Dowlas Shirt, 2 Oznabrigs ditto, 2 Pair of dark coloured Stockings, one Pair of them ribbed, *English* Falls, one pretty good Felt Hat, and several other Things unknown.

It is supposed the above Servants are gone by Water, and have all got forged Passes.—Whoever apprehends them, so that they may be had again, shall receive, if within 10 Miles of Home, 20 *s.* If 20 Miles from Home, 40 *s.* and if out of the County, £. 3 for each, and if out of the Province, £. 5 each for *North* and *Searson*, and £. 10 for *John Fryer*, with reasonable Charges if brought to the said Furnace, to be paid by
FRANCIS PHILLIPS.

The Maryland Gazette, January 1, 1767; January 8, 1767; January 15, 1767. See *The Pennsylvania Gazette*, January 8, 1767.

NOW in the Goal of Cecil County, Maryland, a white Servant Man, named Daniel M'Clane, supposed to belong to William Denny, of Uwchland Township, as he advertised such a Person some Time since: This is therefore to give Notice to whomsoever he does belong, that unless they come in six Weeks from the Date hereof, and pay his Goal Fees, and other Costs, he will be sold out for the same, according to an Act of the Province of Maryland, by   DANIEL TURNER, Goaler and Under Sheriff.
N. B. There is likewise in said Goal, a new Negroe Man, named Sam.... December 21, 1766.

The Pennsylvania Gazette, January 1, 1767; February 5, 1767.

December 28, 1766.
RUN away, last Night, from Kingsbury Furnace, in Baltimore County, three Convict Servant Men, viz.

John Fryer, by Trade a Wheelwright, aged about 30 Years, and about 5 Feet 7 Inches high, brown curled Hair, and fresh Complexion; had on, and took with him, the following Things, viz. one Castor, and one Felt Hat, blue grey Broadcloth Coat, red Jacket, blue duffil Breeches, and a Pair of light coloured Ditto, blue grey Stockings, one Pair English Falls, and one Pair Country made Pumps, two white English Linen Shirts, one or two Silk Handkerchiefs, and several other Things unknown. The said Fryer writes a pretty good Hand.

Samuel Searson, a lusty well made Fellow, fresh Complexion, down Look, aged about 28 or 30 Years, has short brown Hair, and about 5 Feet 9 Inches high; had on, and took with him, one light coloured Kersey or Drab Surtout Coat, double breasted, with hair Buttons, one Cotton Jacket and Breeches, one light coloured Cloth Jacket, one Pair Buckskin Breeches, one Castor and one Felt Hat, one of them bound round with black binding, some white Dowlas Shirts, and two Ozenbrig Ditto, two Pair Ozenbrigs Trowsers, one Pair black ribbed Stockings, and one Pair drab coloured Yarn Ditto, one Pair English Pumps, and one Pair English Falls, nailed in the Bottoms, one Pair square Steel, and one Pair Brass figured Buckles, and several other Things unknown.

Thomas North, a tall stout Fellow, of thin Visage, pale Complexion, marked with the Small-pox, and has short brown Hair, has a sour down Look, aged about 30 Years, and about 5 Feet 9 or 10 Inches high; had on, and took with him, one Cotton Jacket and Breeches, one old Swanskin Jacket, one Pair of Leather Breeches, one Felt Hat, one Dowlas, and two ozenbrigs Shirts, and two Pair Ozenbrigs Trowsers, two Pair dark coloured Stockings, one Pair of them ribbed, one Pair English Falls, and several other Things unknown. It is supposed the above Servants will all have forged passes. Whoever apprehends the said Servants, so that they may be had again, shall have the following Reward,. viz. if taken within 10 Miles from home, Twenty Shillings; if 20 Miles from home, Forty Shillings; if out of the County, Three Pounds for each of them; and if out of the Province, Five Pounds each for North and Searson, and Ten pounds for Fryer, with reasonable Charges, if brought to the said Furnace, paid by
FRANCIS PHILLIPS.

The Pennsylvania Gazette, January 8, 1767; March 19, 1767. See *The Maryland Gazette*, January 1, 1767.

January 15, 1767.

WAS taken up and committed to the Work house of Philadelphia, the 4th of this Instant, one Bridget M'Cormick; says she belongs to one James Morris, over Sasquehannah, in Maryland; this is to inform said Morris, or any Person she belongs to, that if they don't come or send for her in three

Weeks from this Date, and pay her Charges, she will be sold out for the same, by the Keeper of the said Work-house.
The Pennsylvania Gazette, January 15, 1767.

Baltimore-Town, January 23, 1767.
FIVE POUNDS REWARD.

RAN away last Night, from the Subscriber, a Convict Servant Man, named *William Graham*, alias *Scholar*, about 5 Feet 6 Inches high, a likely, artful young Fellow, has black Hair, commonly curled: Had on a Claret coloured Coat and Jacket, with Metal Buttons, Buckskin Breeches, Boots, and a blue Surtout; carried with him, a likely old Bay Horse, marked **WN**, joined together, on his near Buttock, and a very good Hogskin Saddle, the Horse is well known on the Road.

Whoever brings said Fellow, with the Horse and Saddle to me, in *Baltimore-Town*, shall have the above Reward; or, for the Horse and Saddle alone, Fifty Shillings.   ROBERT CHRISTIE, junr.

The Maryland Gazette, January 29, 1767; February 5, 1767; February 12, 1767; February 19, 1767. See *The Pennsylvania Gazette*, February 26, 1767.

RUN away from the subscriber, the sixth of this instant January, a servant man, named John Glanding, country born, 25 years of age, about 5 feet 7 inches high, well set, fresh coloured, and has light hair, pretends to be a shoemaker; had on, when he went away, a new castor hat, a light coloured broadcloth coat and breeches, the coat lined with green, and a saggathy waistcoat, of another colour, lined with green, white worsted ribbed stockings, old shoes, and plated buckles, a white shirt, and check one, and sundry other clothes with him. Whoever takes up the said Glanding, and brings him to the subscriber, living in Queen Ann's county, Maryland, shall have Forty Shillings reward, and reasonable charges paid, or if secured in any goal, Forty Shillings, paid by   HENRY WRENCH.

The Pennsylvania Gazette, January 29, 1767; February 19, 1767; April 9, 1767; May 7, 1767; May 14, 1767.

Annapolis, January 28, 1767.
COMMITTED to *Anne-Arundel* County Jail, as Runaways, *viz.*

   Samuel Brown, who says he was born in *New-England*, and denies that he is a Servant.
   Negro *Frank*....
   His Master [*sic*] is desired to take him away, and pay Charges.

WILLIAM STEUART, Sheriff.
The Maryland Gazette, February 5, 1767.

January 22, 1767.

RAN away from the Subscriber, living at *Port-Royal*, in *Virginia*, on the 14th Instant, a likely Convict Servant Lad, named *John Bevan*, and, as he says, a Plaisterer by Trade, about 17 Years of Age, of a small slender Make, fair Complexion, has dark Eyes, short black Hair, a delicate smooth Skin, and a very innocent Aspect: Had on and carried with him, an old light coloured Cloath Coat and Waistcoat, a light coloured Welton Cloth Coat, almost new, a Pair of black knit Worsted, and a Pair of dirty Leather Breeches, all rather too large for him; Two fine Shirts, an old Beaver Hat, without Lining, and a Pair of yellow Metal Shoe Buckles. He went off with a Man who confessed he came from *North Carolina*, about Five Feet and an Half high, has a Down Look, is well set, though round-shoulder'd, of a dark Complexion, has short brown Hair, and was dressed in a Brown or Snuff coloured Coat and Waistcoat, green knit Worsted Breeches, and sometimes a Pair of dirty Leather ones, had a Pair of Half-Boots, and Leather Saddle-Bags, and pretended to be a Watchmaker, travelling Northward, and enquired the way to *Hoe's* Ferry, and *Boyd's-Hole*. He answers, in every Respect, the Description of a Person, advertiz'd in the *Virginia* Gazette, for Horse-Stealing, by *Daniel Earle*, for which a Reward of 40s. was offered. They stole, while here, a middle-siz'd grey Horse, with a Switch Tail, and hanging Mane, and a Cut in one of his Ears, and a Crack down the Middle of each Fore-Hoof, shod only behind, and the Shoe of the Near-Foot is a Plate of Iron, covering most Part of the Sole and Frog.

Whoever apprends [sic] the said *Bevan*, so that he may be legally prosecutted, or delivered to me, shall receive THREE POUNDS *Virginia* Currency, and the same Sum for the Horse, if not disabled.
JOHN TENNENT.
N. B. The above Persons are Englishmen.
The Maryland Gazette, February 5, 1767.

COMMITTED to *Prince-George's* County Jail, as a Runaway, by the Name of *Michael M'Cowan*, an *Irishman*, wears his own black Hair, has on an old Thickset Coat, Fustian Breeches, Yarn Stockings, and a Pair of Turned Pumps. He says he is a Freeman, a Taylor by Trade, and lately lived on *Rock-Creek*, in *Frederick* County.

His Master (if any) is desired to take him away, and pay Charges.
WILLIAM T. WOOTTON, Sheriff.
The Maryland Gazette, February 12, 1767.

ANNAPOLIS, *February* 14, 1767.
RAN away on the second Instant, from a Plantation at the upper End of *Anne-Arundel* County, near Mr. *Samuel Mansell's*, Two Servant Men, viz.

JAMES M'DANIEL, an *Irishman*, lately imported, about 5 Feet 8 Inches high, with dark brown Hair: Had on when he went away, a Felt Hat, old Bearskin Coat, striped double-breasted Flannel Waistcoat, a Pair of Buckskin Breeches, white Yarn Stockings, Country-made Shoes, and a white Holland and Osnabrig Shirt.

JOHN NORMAN, an *Englishman*, about 5 Feet high, with dark brown Hair, fresh Complexion, and when spoke to, has a down cast Look: Had on and took with him when he went away, a new Felt Hat, yellow double-breasted Cotton Jacket, two black and white striped Ditto, Leather Breeches, black Yarn Stockings, Country made Shoes, and a white Holland and Osnabrig Shirt, with several other Things they have taken from other Servants. There are missing two Bay Horses, about 13 Hands high, one branded **NH** joined together, about 15 Years old; the other with a Brand unknown, about 9 Years old, which it is supposed they have taken.

Whoever takes up the said Servants, or either of them, and secures them in any Jail, or brings them to *Thomas King*, Overseer at the aforesaid Plantation, or to the Subscribers, if taken in the Province, shall have THREE POUNDS Reward for each; it out, FIVE POUNDS each, and reasonable Charges, paid by
SAMUEL CHASE,   PHILIP HAMMOND,
              Annapolis.
It is supposed they have wrote themselves passes.

The Maryland Gazette, February 19, 1767; February 26, 1767; March 5, 1767.

FIVE POUNDS Reward.
RUN away, the 22d Inst. from the Subscriber, a Convict Servant Man, named William Graham, alias Scholar, about 5 Feet 6 or 7 Inches high, a likely artful young Fellow, has black Hair, commonly cued; had on a Claret coloured Broadcloth Coat and Jacket, with gilt Buttons, Buckskin Breeches, Boots, and a blue Surtout; carried with him a likely old bay Horse, marked **WM** on the near Buttock, and a very good Hogskin Saddle, the Horse is well known on the Road. Whoever brings said Fellow, with the Horse and Saddle to me, in Baltimore, shall have the above Reward; or for the Horse and Saddle alone, Fifty Shillings.
JAMES CHRISTIE, jun.

The Pennsylvania Gazette, February 26, 1767. See *The Maryland Gazette*, January 29, 1767.

March 3, 1767.
RAN away Yesterday, from the Subscriber's Plantation, in the Fork of *Gunpowder*, in *Baltimore* County, *Maryland*, the Two following Servants, viz.

JOHN WHITTON, an *English* Convict, has been in the Country about 3 Years, is about 35 Years of Age, 5 Feet 8 Inches high, dark Complexion, has short dark brown, or black Hair; he can Read and Write; had on and took with him, two Country Fulled Jackets, with Leather Buttons, white Kersey Breeches, coarse Yarn Stockings, and Country made Shoes, nail'd in the Soles and Heels, a Felt Hat, and two Osnabrigs Shirts.

PATRICK FACHY, an Indented *Irish* Lad, has been in the Country about 4 Months, is about 5 Feet 7 Inches high, has brown Hair, and grey Eyes, fair Complexion, and a fresh Colour, has a Scar below his under Lip, speaks very pert and lively, and can Read and Write, and says he understands Navigation; had on and took with him, a dark-grey Cloth Coat, faced with Serge, a brown Cloth Jacket, with Mohair Buttons, a new Country Fulled Jacket, with Leather Buttons, a Pair of old Leather, and a Pair of white Kersey Breeches, two Pair of Yarn Stockings, one Pair blue, a Pair of old Pumps, and a Pair of strong Shoes nail'd in the Heels, two Osnabrigs, and two old Check Shirts, and a new Felt Hat.

Whoever takes up the said Servants, or either of them, and secures them in any Jail, so that their Master gets them again, shall have Twenty Shillings for each, if taken 10 miles from home; if out of the County, Forty Shillings for each; if out of the Province, Three Pounds Reward for each, and reasonable Charges, if brought home, paid by
CHARLES RIDGELY, junr.

The Maryland Gazette, March 5, 1767. See *The Maryland Gazette*, April 30, 1767, and *The Pennsylvania Gazette*, May 14, 1767; for Fachy.

RUN away from Bushtown, on the 20th of February, a servant man, named Thomas Bowman, a tall slim fellow, wears his hair, has a kind of blink or cast in one eye, sharp-fac'd, one of his legs battle-hamm'd much more than the other, is an Englishman born, and pretends to be something of a gardiner: Had on, when he went away, a new frize jacket, a felt hat, oxenbrigs shirt, and what other clothes is uncertain. It is supposed he travelled towards Philadelphia or New-York. Whoever takes up and secures the said fellow, so that he may be returned to his master, shall receive Five Pounds reward, paid by   JOHN LEE WEBSTER.

The Pennsylvania Gazette, March 5, 1767; March 19, 1767.

Annapolis, March 16, 1767.
RAN away last Night, from the Subscriber, living near *Annapolis*, Two Convict Servants, *viz.*

William Newcomb, alias *John Dodson*, a Butcher by Trade, has a Steel, with his own Name on the Blade, of a ruddy Complexion, 5 Feet 5 Inches high, much pitted with the Small-Pox, and wears his own short sandy colour'd Hair, is a Native of *Gloucester*, and speaks in that Dialect. Had on and took with him, an old blue Coat, white Frock, plaid Jacket, a blue grey Broadcloth ditto, a light colour'd Drab Great Coat, Leather Breeches, a Pair of Boots and Silver Spurs, and a Pair of Silver Buckles. 'Tis thought he will make for *New-York*, as he says he has an Uncle there.

Sarah Plint, alias *Powell*, alias *Merchant*, a very likely Woman, of a middle Size, has black Eyes and Hair, a little mixed with grey, and has lost one of her fore Teeth. Had on and took with her, a white Cloak and Hat, a black Bonnet and Cardinal, a strip'd yellow and brown Silk Gown; but 'tis probable she may change her Dress, as she has got different Suits: She is very artful, and 'tis thought they will pass for Man and Wife. They took with them a small Bay Horse, shod before, has a Star in his Forehead, Hog Mane, Bob Tail, and is a natural Pacer; and also a Bay Mare, with a short Tail, if branded, the Marks uncertain: They likewise took with them Two Saddles, one a Man's common Saddle, the other a Woman's, with a deep blue Housing, and a Fringe and Lace round it.

Whoever takes up the said Servants and Horses, and brings them home, shall receive, if taken in this County, THREE POUNDS Reward; if out of the same, FIVE POUNDS; and, if out of the Province, TEN POUNDS, paid by   JOHN MACDONALL.

The Maryland Gazette, March 19, 1767; March 26, 1767.

Elk-Ridge Furnace, *March* 15, 1767.
RAN away from the Subscriber, Three Convict Servant Men, *viz.*

Samuel Newcomb, about 23 Years of Age, 5 Feet 5 or 6 Inches high, has short brown Hair, and went off in his working Cloaths.

Dennis Igo, a stout able-bodied Fellow, about 6 Feet high, and about 27 Years of Age, he has dark brown Hair, and went off in his working Cloaths.

William Snow, a low well-set Fellow, has long black Hair, and a very hooked Nose.

Whoever takes up the said Runaways, and brings them home, shall receive for each, if taken within 10 Miles, Twenty Shillings; if above 10 Miles, and under 20, Thirty Shillings, if above 20 Miles, and within the

Province, Forty Shillings; and, if out of the Province, THREE POUNDS Reward, and reasonable Charges, including what the Law allows, paid by CALEB DORSEY.

The Maryland Gazette, March 19, 1767. See *The Maryland Gazette*, May 11, 1769, for Snow.

Baltimore Town, Feb. 26, 1767.

FIVE POUNDS Reward.

RUN away from the Subscriber, living in Baltimore Town, an English Servant Man, named William Thompson, a Joyner by Trade, about 30 Years of Age, has very little Beard, wears his own Hair, of a black Colour, tied behind, about 5 Feet 4 Inches high; had on, when he went away, a blue Broadcloth Coat, without Lining, with yellow Metal Buttons, a white Cotton Jacket, and brown Broadcloth Breeches; he is very apt to get drunk, and brags much of his Trade when he is drunk; it is supposed that he wrote himself a Pass, as being free from me the Subscriber. Whoever takes up the said Servant, and commits him to any Goal, so that his Master may have him again, shall receive the above Reward, and if brought Home reasonable Charges paid by me   WILLIAM HOFFMAN.

The Pennsylvania Gazette, March 19, 1767; April 2, 1767; April 9, 1767.

TEN POUNDS Reward.

Run away from the Subscribers, living on Deer Creek, in Baltimore County, Maryland, on the Fifteenth of March, three Servant Men, viz.

PARTRICK CARRAVAN, an Irishman, a Blacksmith by Trade, a lusty well-set Fellow, of a pale Complexion, much pitted with the Small-Pox, and speaks good English: Had on and took with him, a brown Bearskin upper Jacket, white Cotton under Ditto, Cotton Breeches, blue milled Stockings, Felt Hat; and Country-made Shoes, Ozenbrigs Shirt, is much given to strong Drink.

NICHOLAS KELLY, an Irishman, of a middle Stature and ruddy Complexion, has dark brown Hair, curled behind, speaks good English: Had on and took with him, a light brown Surtout Coat, brown under Jacket, Leather Breeches, Ozenbrigs Shirt, brown Yarn Stockings, Country-made Shoes, and Felt Hat.

EDWARD PERRY, born in the West of England, of a middle Stature, and wears his own dark brown Hair: Had on and took with him, a grey Country-made upper Jacket, with broad Metal Buttons, spotted double breasted under Jacket, old light coloured Broadcloth Breeches, both Holland and Ozenbrigs Shirts, new English Shoes, and new Felt Hat, and will frequently in his Discourse make use of the Words "behappen so," or

"behappen not." Whoever apprehends the said Servants, and secures them in any Goal, so that they may be had again; shall have for each, if taken twenty Miles from Home, Thirty Shillings; and if Thirty Miles, Forty-Five Shillings; and if out of the Province, Three Pounds Six and Eight Pence, and reasonable Charges if brought Home, paid by
JERREMIAH SHERRIDIN,   NATHANIEL GILES,
March 16, 1767.   JOHN WILSON.

The Pennsylvania Chronicle, and Universal Advertiser, From Monday, March 16, to Monday, March 23, 1767; From Monday, March 23, to Monday, March 30, 1767. In the second ad, the first name of the first runaway is Patrick, and the first name of the first advertiser is Jeremiah. *The Pennsylvania Gazette*, March 26, 1767. Minor differences between the papers. The *Gazette* does not have the date at the bottom, and spells the name of the first man as Patrick

RAN away the 15th of *March* last, from the Subscribers, living in *Frederick* County, *Maryland*, Two *Irish* Convict Servant Men, viz.

William Dunn, about 5 Feet 7 Inches high, and about 30 Years of Age; he appears well dress'd: Had on when he went away, a blue Surtout Coat, and a coarse Cloth ditto, between a Claret and a brown Colour, Breeches of the same, and a blue Jacket.

Patrick Connerly, about 5 Feet 9 Inches high, and about 22 Years Age: Had on, a new Felt Hat, a Coat the same Colour of *Dunn's*, a Linsey Jacket with blue Stripes, brown Cloth Breeches with a large Patch on the fore Part of each Thigh.

Whoever takes up the said Servants, and brings them home, shall receive a Reward of THREE POUNDS Currency, and all reasonable Charges, paid by us.
JOHN TRUNDLE,   WALTER BEALL.

The Maryland Gazette, March 26, 1767; April 2, 1767; April 9, 1767.

ANNAPOLIS, *March* 17, 1767.

RAN away from on board a small Schooner, lying in *Pocomoke* River, a white Convict Servant, belonging to the Subscriber, goes by the Name of *Charles Bener*, is of a dark Complexion, wears his own Hair, a little pitted with the Small-Pox, a short well set Fellow, has lost one of the Fingers of his right Hand, is between 30 and 40 Years of Age; had on when he went away, a white Fearnought Jacket, a Red ditto, a blue great Coat, a Pair of thick Yarn Stockings, Country Made Shoes, but no Buckles.

Whoever takes up said Servant, and secures him, so as the Owner may have him again, shall have FIFTEEN SHILLINGS Reward, and all reasonable Charges paid by NATHANIEL ADAMS.

The Maryland Gazette, April 9, 1767; April 16, 1767; April 23, 1767; April 30, 1767; May 7, 1767; May 14, 1767.

Piscataway, April 7, 1767.

RAN away from the Subscriber, on Sunday Night last, an *Irish* Servant Woman, named *Catherine Lacey,* alias *Dunn,* and supposed to have taken with her sundry wearing Apparel, *viz.* A Stripped Cotton Holland Gown, a new Velvet Queen's fashioned Bonnet, a black Velvet Hood, a Country Cloth stripped Petticoat, a Pair of Woman's Leather Pumps, a Pair of Silver Buckles, cut in imitation of Bristol Stone, a brown Drugget Gown, Two blue Linen Aprons, and several other Things, such as Shifts, Stockings, Caps, Handkerchiefs, &c. too tedious to mention, she is a tall Woman, red Complexion, talks her own Country Dialect.

Whoever takes up the said Servant, and will bring her to Mrs. *Mary Dent,* at *Mattawoman,* or to *Alexander Burrell,* in *Piscataway,* shall receive TWENTY SHILLINGS Reward, if taken in the County, and FORTY SHILLINGS, if out of the County. THOMAS DAVY.

The Maryland Gazette, April 16, 1767.

RUN away, on the 3d inst. April from the Subscriber, living in Cecil County, Maryland, near the Head of Elk, a native Irish Servant Man, named Charles Cosgrove, about 20 Years of Age, about 5 Feet 6 Inches high, stoop shouldered, lightish brown Hair, about 3 Inches long, light grey Eyes, and has no Beard; had on, when he went away, a brown Country Cloth Jacket, without Lining, a red under Ditto, without Sleeves, old Buckskin Breeches, very black and greasey, grey Yarn Stockings, a Pair of old Shoes, newly half soaled, with Strings to them, a Calfskin Apron, a half-worn Tow Shirt, and Felt Hat; had an Iron Collar about his Neck when he went away, without Horns. Whoever takes up and secures said Servant, so as his Master may have him again, shall have Forty Shillings Reward, and reasonable Charges, paid by NOBLE BIDDLE.

The Pennsylvania Gazette, April 16, 1767; April 30, 1767; May 7, 1767; May 14, 1767.

FIVE POUNDS REWARD.

RAN away from the Subscriber the 16th of last Month, a Convict Servant Man, named *Joseph Green,* alias *Joseph Gale,* but as he can write (and has got Pen, Ink, and Paper with him) it is not unlikely that he will forge a Pass, and go by some other Name, he was imported last *November* into *Rappahannock* River, in the *Justitia*, Capt. *Colin Somerwell*; he is a lusty well set Man, and seems to be about 35 Yeas of Age, and is about 5 Feet 9 Inches high, of a fresh Complexion, marked with the Small-Pox, has very black Hair which he has lately cut short, and is very hairy on the Breast, his Eye-lids were red and inflamed with a Cold, when he went away.

He is a Farmer, and says that he was born in *Wiltshire*, and speaks (somewhat) in the West Country Dialect; he has *English* Money with him, also Paper Money; as he broke open a House about a Week before he ran away, where he got some.

He stole a Horse of a dark brown Colour, with mealy Hams, and a bobb'd Tail, and roach'd Mane; on whose Breast and Forehead Tar had lately been applied, which was not quite worn off; and a *Virginia* made Portmanteau Saddle, with Iron Rings behind, and Brass Buttons before, to put Straps through, and an old Snaffle Bridle.

He had on, and with him, the following Cloaths, *viz.* a blue napped Cotton Pea Jacket, with Cuffs to the Sleeves, and black Gimp Buttons on it, and open Pockets without Flaps. An old red Jacket without Sleeves, an old New-market blue Cloth Coat, a Pair of old greasy Leather Breeches, which seemed to be too small for him, and a Pair of brown Sagathy Breeches, a Pair of very coarse Shoes (made by himself) on the back Seam of one of which, a bit of brown Leather hath been since sewed; and a Pair of old *English* Shoes, one of which has a cut across the Insole, near to the Toe, a Pair of large white Metal or Pewter Buckles, one old fine check Shirt, and two Shirts made of brown Scotch Linen, a Pair of very coarse grey *(English)* Yarn Stockings, a Pair of old dark colour'd *Virginia* Stockings and a Pair of old black Silk ribbed Stockings, an old Hat worn very smooth, and greasy or tarred on the Crown, and a Hole burnt in the Brim of it, and a black String either Worsted or Silk for an Hatband; and he commonly wears a blue and white spotted Handkerchief or Hatband Crape over the Hatband to keep his Hat on, and sometimes the Crape or Handkerchief round his Neck.

Three Pounds Reward, if he is taken up in *Virginia*, or Five Pounds Reward if he is taken up in any other Colony, shall be paid to any Person, who will apprehend and secure him, so that he shall be delivered to NICHOLAS FLOOD.

All Masters of Vessels are cautioned not to receive him on board.
Virginia, April 2, 1767.

The Maryland Gazette, April 23, 1767; May 7, 1767; May 14, 1767.

April 27, 1767.

RAN away last Night from the *Northampton* Furnace, in *Baltimore* County, *Maryland*, the Three following Convict Servants, *viz.*

Edmund Grimshaw, born in *Lancashire*, in *England*, about 5 Feet 9 Inches high, has short red Hair, fair Complexion, much pitted with the Small-Pox, has a large Pit or small Scar about an Inch from the left Corner of his Mouth, his right Eye-Tooth doubles over his other Teeth, aged about 21 Years, is a Weaver and Taylor by Trade, and has been in the Country 8 or 9 Months: Had on when he went away, a dark Fearnought Pea Jacket, a white Cotton ditto, Hempen Roll Trowsers, new Osnabrigs Shirt, Felt Hat, and new Shoes nailed in the Heels.

John Hardy, born in *Lancashire*, a well-set Fellow, about 5 Feet 9 Inches high, much pitted with the Small-Pox, the Bridge of his Nose broken, about 38 Years old, has black Eyes, and short black Hair: Had on when he went away, an old brown Cloth Coat, old brown Fustian Jacket, new Osnabrigs Shirt, Hempen Roll Trowsers, Felt Hat, new Shoes nailed in the Heels, and has been in the Country about 4 Months.

Thomas Mahoney, an *Irishman*, a well set Fellow, about 5 Feet 7 Inches high, has short brown Hair, about 20 Years old: Had on when he went away, a Claret colour'd Penniston Coat, white Cotton Jacket, new Osnabrigs Shirt, Hempen Roll Trowsers, Felt Hat, new Shoes nailed in the Heels, and has been in the Country about 3 Months: They have all work'd this Spring with the Colliers, and their Cloaths are very black. They have stolen and took with them the following Horses, *viz.*

A large old sorrel Horse, has a bob Tail, a small Blaze in his Face, is low in Flesh, and Paces fast.

A light bay Mare, about 13½ Hands high, 6 Years old, has a small Star in her Forehead, no Brand that we know of, she paces, trots, and gallops, is in good Order, has been close trimmed about the Head and Feet, and shod before.

A large black Horse 15 Hands high, had a bob Tail, has drawn in a Chaise, is galled on the near Shoulder by the Shaft, is shod all round, and is remarkable for trotting. They have also taken 3 blind Bridles, with Rope Reins, and 3 Blankets.

Whoever takes up the said Servants and Horses, and secures them so that their Masters get them again, shall have Forty Shillings for each Man and Horse, if taken above 20 Miles from home, Three Pounds if out of the County, Five Pounds if out of the Province, and reasonable Charges if brought home; for each Horse, if taken without the Servants, Fifteen Shillings, if above 20 Miles, Twenty Shillings, and if further, Forty Shillings, paid by   CHARLES RIDGELY, senr. & Co.

The Maryland Gazette, April 30, 1767. See The Maryland Gazette, June 18, 1767, and The Pennsylvania Gazette, August 13, 1767, for Grimshaw and Hardy.

April 29, 1767.

RAN away last Night from the Subscriber's Plantation, in the Fork of Gunpowder, in Baltimore County, Maryland, viz.

Charles Campbell, a Convict, born in the West of England, and speaks in that Dialect, about 5 Feet 8 Inches high, has sandy Hair, grey Eyes, a well set Fellow, has a very simple Look, and stutters: Had on when he went away, a light fulled Country Cloth Jacket, blue lappell'd under ditto, without Sleeves, old white Cotton Breeches much patched, Osnabrigs Shirt, new Felt Hat, grey Yarn Stockings, and old Shoes.

Patrick Fachy, an indented Irish Lad, about 5 Feet 8 Inches high, very spare, has long brown Hair, grey Eyes, fair Complexion, and speaks very pert: Had on when he went away, a light fulled Country Cloth Jacket, a Snuff colour'd under ditto, old white Cotton Breeches much patched, Osnabrigs Shirt, Felt Hat, white Yarn Stockings, and old Shoes with large broad headed Nails in the Heels. They had on Iron Collars, and have taken with them an old grey Cloth Coat, fac'd or lin'd with Shalloon, a striped Jacket patched, two Check, and one Osnabrigs Shirt.

Whoever takes up the said Servants, and secures them so that their Master gets them again, shall have Twenty Shillings Reward for each, if taken out of the County Forty Shillings for each, if out of the Province, Three Pounds for each, and reasonable Charges if brought home, paid by
CHARLES RIDGELY, junr.

N. B. They have been in the Country about Six Months.

The Maryland Gazette, April 30, 1767; May 7, 1767; May 14, 1767. See The Maryland Gazette, March 5, 1767, for Fachy. See The Pennsylvania Gazette, May 14, 1767.

Ran away the 17th of April last, from the Subscriber's Plantation in Gunpowder Forest, Baltimore County, a Convict Servant Lad, named Edward Tylor, about 17 Years of Age: Had on a white Kersey Jacket, Osnabrigs Shirt, Cotton Breeches, old blue Stockings, NegroShoes, nailed in the Soles, and Felt Hat; was born in the West of England, and speaks in that Dialect.

Whoever takes up and brings home the said Servant, if out of the County, shall have Three Pounds Reward, paid by
GEORGE RISTEAU.

The Maryland Gazette, May 7, 1767; April 14, 1767.

RAN away from the Subscriber, on the 30th of *April* last, a Prisoner, for Debt, whose Name is *John Elwood*, is a short, thick, well-set Fellow, of a red Complexion, smooth Face, about 5 Feet 5 or 6 Inches high, and very dark Hair, which he generally wears tied behind: Had on when he went away, an old flap'd Hat, old brown Forest-Cloth Coat, good Buckskin Breeches, with Strings at the Knees, an old Osnabrigs Shirt, blue Worsted Hose, and old Shoes, with Brass Buckles.

He has been a Prisoner for two or three Years past, in which Time this is his second Elopement, the first Time he got as far as *Deer-Creek* in *Baltimore County*, where he has a Sister living, who is Wife to one *William Williams*, and it's likely he will make that Way again.

Whoever takes up the said *John Elwood*, and brings him to the Subscriber, shall receive Three Pounds Reward; or, Forty Shillings if secured in any Jail.

JOHN WEEMS, junr. Sheriff of *Calvert* County.

The Maryland Gazette, May 14, 1767; May 21, 1767; May 28, 1767; June 4, 1767; June 11, 1767; June 25, 1767; July 9, 1767; July 16, 1767; July 23, 1767.

RUN away from the subscriber, in Cecil county, Maryland, 10 miles from Christiana bridge, on Saturday night, the 2d of this instant May, two indented servant men, one named Patrick M'Kogh, a native Irishman, about 20 years of age, came in last fall from Ireland, talks much on the brogue, and is by trade a cooper; had on, when he went away, a snuff coloured coat and jacket, half-worn, with mohair buttons, blue country made cloth breeches, lined with linen. The other named Thomas M'Neely, came in last May from Ireland, about 20 years of age, by trade a cooper ; had on, a light-coloured country made coat, with blue and white drugget lining, and white metal buttons, a double breasted scarlet jacket, and snuff coloured cloth breeches, stockings uncertain, as he had several pair with him, old and new shoes, with Pinchbeck buckles. Both about 5 feet 5 inches high, and wore their own short brown hair; they are both good scholars, and it is like may forge a pass. Whoever takes up and secures said servants, so that the subscriber may have them again, shall have three Pounds reward, or thirty Shillings for either, and reasonable charges paid by
AMOS ALEXANDER.

N. B. Said M'Neely has followed the soap boiling business.

The Pennsylvania Gazette, May 14, 1767; May 21, 1767; May 28, 1767; June 4, 1767; June 11, 1767; June 25, 1767; July 2, 1767.

April 29, 1767.

RUN away last night from the subscriber's plantation, in the Fork of Gunpowder, in Baltimore county, Maryland, CHARLES CAMPBELL, born in the west of England, and speaks in that dialect, about 5 feet 8 inches high, has sandy hair, grey eyes, and is very pale, has a very simple look, and stutters; had on, when he went away, a light fulled country cloth jacket, blue lappelled under ditto, without sleeves, old white cotton breeches much patched, ozenbrigs shirt, new felt hat, grey yarn stockings, and old shoes.

PATRICK FACHY, an indented Irish Lad, about 5 feet 8 inches high, and very spare; has long brown hair, and grey eyes, fair complexion, and speaks very pert; had on, when he went away, a white country fulled jacket, a snuff coloured under ditto, old white cotton breeches, much patched, ozenbrigs shirt, felt hat, white yarn stockings, and old shoes, with large broad headed nails in the heels. They had iron collars on, and have taken with them, an old grey cloth coat, faced or lined with shalloon, a striped jacket, patched, two check, and one ozenbrigs shirt. Whoever takes up the said servants, and secures them, so that their master gets them again, shall have Twenty Shillings reward for each, or if taken out of the county Forty Shillings for each, and if out of the province, Three Pounds, and reasonable charges if brought home, paid by   CHARLES RIDGELY, junior.

N. B. They have been in the country about six months, it is probable they will steal other clothes.

The Pennsylvania Gazette, May 14, 1767; May 28, 1767; June 11, 1767; June 25, 1767; July 23, 1767. See *The Maryland Gazette*, March 5, 1767, for Fachy, and *The Maryland Gazette*, April 30, 1767, for both men.

COMMITTED to *Prince-George's* County Jail, the following Runaways, viz. A Convict Lad by the name of *Robert Nelson*, as belonging to Mr. *Nicholas Maccubbin*, but now says his name is *John*, and belongs to Mr. *John Worthington*; also a Molatto Man named *Joe*, and a white Woman named *Mary*, who say they belong to Mr. *George Lee*. Their Masters are desired to take them away and pay Charges.
WILLIAM T. WOOTTON, Sheriff.
The Maryland Gazette, May 21, 1767.

May 18, 1767.
RAN away, on Thursday last, from the Subscriber, living on *Little-Pipe-Creek*, in *Frederick* County, *Maryland*, the Three following Convicts, viz.

MICHAEL MURRAY, an *Irishman*, about 21 Years of Age, a well-set Fellow, about 5 Feet 8 or 9 Inches high, has black Hair, thin beard, down Look, fair Complexion, and grey Eyes: Had on and took with him when he went away, an old Felt Hat, old Cotton Jacket, a Shirt made of this Country Linen, Tow Trowsers, a Pair of old Yarn Leggins, and an old Pair of Shoes with the Heels nailed.

    THOMAS WALTON, a *Yorkshireman*, speaks bad *English*, about 28 Years of Age, about 5 Feet 8 or 9 Inches high, a well-set Fellow, has a down Look, grey Eyes, black Hair, and brown Complexion: Had on and took with him when he went away, an old Felt Hat, a Kersey Coat of a Lead Colour, half worn, an old blue Jacket, one Ditto with the fore Part Plush, a Pair of Leather Breeches about half worn, one Shirt made out of this Country Linen, new Tow Trowsers, and a Pair of Shoes with the Heels nailed.

    JOHN WILCOCKS, an *Englishman*, 6 Feet high, 21 Years of Age, a slim straight well made Fellow, black Hair, thin Beard, fair Complexion, has a sickly Look, and is attended with a Cough. Had on and took with him when he went away, an old light coloured Kersey Coat, an old blue Jacket, an half worn Shirt made out of this Country Linen, new Tow Trowsers, white Yarn Stockings, almost new, and old Shoes with the Heels nailed.

    It is supposed that Two of them will cut off their Hair, as they took with them two Linen Caps, and an old Silk Handkerchief, one Ditto new, the Middle is of a black Colour and the Edges red.

    Whoever takes up and secures the said Servants in any Jail, if out of the County, shall receive the above reward; if taken 20 Miles from home Nine Pounds, if taken any Distance under 20 Miles from home, shall receive 3 Pounds Reward, or in Proportion for either, paid by
EDWARD STEVENSON.

    All Masters of Vessels are forewarned carrying off any of the above Servants at their Peril.

    The Maryland Gazette, May 21, 1767; May 28, 1767; June 4, 1767; June 11, 1767; June 25, 1767. See *The Pennsylvania Gazette,* May 28, 1767.

May 3, 1767.

RAN away from *Bush-River* Furnace, a Convict Servant Man, named *Patrick Hirley,* born in *Ireland,* is a little pitted with the Small-Pox, thin visaged, very narrow a-cross the Eyes, his right Thigh has been broke, and causes him to walk very lame, his right Foot stands out by the said Hurt, and has short brown Hair: Had on when he went away, a Cotton Jacket, Petticoat Trowsers, Felt Hat, and old Shoes and Stockings.

    Whoever takes up said Servant, and secures him in any Jail, shall have Forty Shillings Reward, besides what the Law allows, and reasonable

Charges if brought home, paid by his Master living at the Head of *South-River*.   BENJAMIN WELSH.

The *Maryland Gazette*, May 21, 1767; May 28, 1767; June 11, 1767; June 18, 1767; June 25, 1767; July 2, 1767; July 9, 1767; July 16, 1767; July 23, 1767; August 27, 1767; September 3, 1767; September 10, 1767; September 24, 1767; October 1, 1767; October 8, 1767.

Charles County, *May* 16, 1767.

RAN away, the 27th of last Month, from the Subscribers, the Three following *Irish* Convict Servants, viz.

KANE OHARRA, (belonging to *Samuel Hanson,*) aged about 22 Years, about 5 Feet 7 or 8 Inches high, has a fresh Complexion, wears his own Hair, which curls, and is of a light Colour: Had on and took with him, a fine blue Broadcloth Coat, a new Fustian Ditto and Breeches, Broadcloth Jacket, Osnabrig Breeches and Trowsers, 2 or 3 Check Shirts, and 2 Osnabrigs Ditto.

LAURANCE NOWLAND, (belonging to *Dennis M'Lemar,*) aged about 21 Years, about 5 Feet high, and of a fair Complexion: Had on a blue Duffle Surtout Coat, trimm'd with yellow Buttons, a Pair of brown Thickset Breeches, and a striped Linsey lappel'd Jacket.

PATRICK LARKIN, (belonging to *Thomas Melchizedech Green,*) aged about 23 Years, about 5 Feet high, and wears his own Hair: Had on, a Snuff colour'd Cloth Coat, blue Broadcloth lappel'd Jacket, and black Leather Breeches.

As each of them has Wig, it is probable they may cut off their Hair.

Whoever takes up the abovementioned Servants, if taken within 20 Miles and brought home, shall receive THREE POUNDS, or Twenty Shillings for each; if any farther Distance, SIX POUNDS, or Forty Shillings for each, if brought home; and, if out of the Province, FOUR POUNDS for each Servant.

SAMUEL HANSON,   DENNIS M'LEMAR,
THOMAS MELCHIZEDECH GREEN.

The *Maryland Gazette*, May 21, 1767; May 28, 1767; June 4, 1767; June 11, 1767; June 18, 1767; June 25, 1767. See *The Pennsylvania Gazette*, January 19, 1769, for Oharra.

RUN away, on the 28th Day of April last, from the Subscriber, living in Cecil County, Maryland, near the Head of Elk, a Native Irish Servant Man, named Michael M'Guyer, about 5 Feet high, with short black Hair, round Face, has a Mark of a Cut on the right side of his Chin; had on, when he went away, a short light coloured Cloth Jacket, and red one under it,

Ozenbrigs Shirt, half worn green Cloth Breeches, brown ribbed Worsted Stockings, and half worn Shoes. Whoever takes up and secures said Servant in any of his Majesty's Goals, so as his Mistress may have him again, shall have Forty Shillings Reward, and reasonable Charges, paid by SUSANNAH M'LAUGHLIN.

N. B. As said Servant has been seen in Philadelphia, and will perhaps want to pass for a Sailor, all Masters of Vessels, and others, are hereby forwarned not to harbour or carry off said Servant, as they shall answer for the same.

The Pennsylvania Gazette, May 21, 1767; May 28, 1767; June 4, 1767.

FIVE POUNDS REWARD.

May 20, 1767.

RAN away from *Dorsey's* Forge, a Convict Servant-Man, named THOMAS JAMES, about 5 Feet 8 Inches high, has yellow Hair and Beard, and whitish Eye-Brows, grey Eyes, with an unusual Degree of White in them; down-look; had on his Working Clothes, but may probably change them.

Whoever takes up the said Fellow, shall have, if taken above Ten Miles, Thirty Shillings; if above Thirty Miles, Forty Shillings; and, if out of the Province, the above Reward, and reasonable Charges, if brought home, paid by   CALEB DORSEY.

The Maryland Gazette, May 28, 1767; June 11, 1767; June 18, 1767; June 25, 1767. See *The Maryland Gazette*, June 8, 1769, and *The Maryland Gazette*, July 27, 1769.

RUN away, on the 12th of May instant, from the subscriber, living near the head of North-East, in Caecil County, Maryland, an Irish servant man, named Michael Hagerty, about 5 feet 10 inches high, has a down look, and long black hair; had on, when he went away, a half worn fine hat, a lead coloured coat (which he stole, and is too short and tight for him) with moulded metal buttons, a cape and long cuffs, a camblet jacket, without buttons, except one or two at the top, a fine shirt, with new wristbands, much finer than the shirt, a new black silk handkerchief, lightish coloured cloth breeches, with small metal buttons, deep blue yarn stockings, and new shoes, with odd buckles, tho' he may purchase new ones, as it is thought he has plenty of money; his breeches much whitened with meal, as he has tended a mill these two years He is a very good scholar, and may probably forge a pass. Whoever takes up and secures said servant in any goal, so as his master may have him again, shall have Three Pounds reward, and reasonable charges, paid by   HENRY MILLER.

N. B. All masters of vessels are forbid to carry him off at their peril.

The Pennsylvania Gazette, May 21, 1767; May 28, 1767; June 4, 1767.

May 18, 1767.

RAN away Yesterday from the Subscriber, living on *Elk-Ridge*, in *Anne-Arundel* County, a Convict Servant Man, named WILLIAM KNELLER, near 6 Feet high, of a white Complexion, wears his own brown Hair, tied behind, is a pert saucy Fellow, and speaks pretty much in the West-Country Dialect, and has a remarkable large Knot on the Joint of one of his great Toes: He had on a blue broad Cloth Coat, and a Jacket, the Front of which is Callico, and the Hind Parts of white Linen; Russia Drab Breeches, a white Linen Shirt, ruffled at the Bosom and Slits; grey Worsted Stockings, a Pair of Turn'd Pumps, which are rather too large, and yellow Metal Buckles. He took with him a kind of dapple, or blue dun Horse, about 13½ Hands high, branded on the near Side thus, **G. R.**

Whoever brings home the Servant and Horse, shall have a Reward of THREE POUNDS Current Money, paid by

GREENBURY RIDGELY.

The Maryland Gazette, May 28, 1767.

TEN POUNDS REWARD.

May 26, 1767.

RAN away from the Subscribers, living on *Kent-Island*, on Sunday last, the Four following Convicts, viz.

ALEXANDER MASON, a Shoemaker by Trade, about 26 Years of Age, of a pale Complexion, black Hair, and about 5 Feet 6 Inches high; had on when he went away a stripp'd Country Cloth Vest and Breeches, an old Felt Hat, and an Osnabrig Shirt.

MICHAEL CALVERT, a Labourer, about 20 Years of Age, of a fresh Complexion, with short brown Hair, and about 5 Feet 7 Inches high; had on a stripp'd Country Cloth Jacket and Breeches, an Osnabrig Shirt, Felt Hat, bound round the Edge with Plaiding, white ribb'd Yarn Stockings, and a Pair of coarse Negro Shoes.

JOHN BOULD, a Weaver by Trade, about 44 Years old, and 6 Feet high, of a fair Complexion, is very lusty, and wears his own black Hair; had on, and took with him, an old Castor Hat, a blue Coat and Vest with black Horn buttons (one of which excepted, which was of Brass, fixed to the Top of the Breast of his Coat) an Osnabrig Shirt, white Thread Stockings, and a Pair of Calf-Skin Pumps.

DUNCAN M'FEE, a Labourer, of a brown Complexion, with grey Hair, tied behind, and is about 5 Feet 9 Inches high, and about 40 Years of Age; had on, and took with him, a Kersey Jacket, a Pair of brown Cloth Breeches, white Stockings, and coarse Shoes, a Felt Hat, and an Under-red Jacket, [sic] without Sleeves. They all went off in a Canoe, about 26 Feet long, pay'd over with Tar and red Paint, and is suppos'd to have gone down the Bay. If any Person or Persons will secure the said Servants, they shall be entituled to the above Reward, or in Proportion for either, and reasonable Charges if brought home, paid by
DANIEL WEEDON,   JAMES BRYAN,   THOMAS YEWELL.
N. B. It is suppos'd they will make themselves Trowsers, as they took a Quantity of Osnabrig with them. All masters of Vessels are forbid harbouring or carrying them off.

The Maryland Gazette, May 28, 1767; June 4, 1767. See *The Maryland Gazette*, June 11, 1767.

FIFTEEN POUNDS Reward.

RUN away from the Subscriber, living in Frederick County, Maryland, on Thursday Night, the 14th of May inst. three Convict Servant Men, viz. Michael Murray, an Irishman, a well set Fellow, about 5 Feet 8 Inches high, black Hair, down Look, fair Complexion, grey Eyes, and pitted with the Small-pox; had on, when he went away, an old Felt Hat, old brown Cotton Jacket, new Tow Trowsers, Country Linen Shirt, old Country made Shoes, with the Heels nailed, an Iron Collar round his Neck, but supposed he may have taken it off.

Thomas Walton, a Yorkshire Man, a well set Fellow, about 5 Feet 8 Inches high, black Hair, down Look, grey Eyes, speaks bad English; had on, and took with him, an old Felt Hat, Kersey Coat, of a Lead Colour, about half worn, old blue Jacket, one black Ditto, the fore Skirts Plush, Leather Breeches, about half-worn, new Tow Trowsers, Country Linen Shirt, old blue Worsted Stockings, old Country made Shoes, with the Heels nailed.

John Wilcocks, an Englishman, a spare slim Fellow, about 6 Feet high, black Hair, dark Eyes, speaks good English; had on, when he went away, an old Felt Hat, old light coloured Kersey Coat, old blue Jacket, new Tow Linen Trowsers, Country Linen Shirt, new Yarn Stockings, and old Country made Shoes, with the Heels nailed. Whoever takes up said Servants, and brings them home, shall receive the above Reward, if out of the County; and if taken within 20 Miles from home Nine Pounds; and if taken any Distance under 20 Miles Three Pounds, and so in Proportion for each; or if secured in any Goal, so as their Master may have them again, shall receive the above Reward, paid by
EDWARD STEVENSON.

N. B. It is supposed that two of the three will cut off their Hair, as they stole two Linen Caps.
The Pennsylvania Gazette, May 28, 1767; June 4, 1767; June 11, 1767. See *The Maryland Gazette*, May 21, 1767.

Maryland, Kent County, May 17, 1767.
RUN away from the Subscriber, a Convict Servant Man, named Henry Paiton, 22 Years of Age, 5 Feet 6 Inches high, well set, bluff faced, round shouldered, has a down Look, his Hair cut off, an Englishman, brought up to the Sea, is a good Scholar, and very remarkable for drawing Drafts, and boasts much of his Travels, and no doubt will forge a Pass; had on, when he went away, a Home-spun Shirt and Trowsers, old Shoes, with Buckles, old Hat, bound round with Ferret, a Sailor's Cap, a grey half worn Fearnought Vest; he will either pass for a Painter or a Sailor, as he understands both. Whoever takes up and secures said Servant, so that his Master may have him again, shall have Three Pounds Reward,
paid by JACOB COMEGYS.
N. B. All Masters of Vessels are forbid to carry him off at their Peril.
The Pennsylvania Gazette, May 28, 1767; June 11, 1767; June 25, 1767.

Joppa, Baltimore County, May 28, 1767.
RAN away from the Subscriber, living in *Joppa, Baltimore* County, *Maryland*, on the 10th of *May*, the three following Servant Men, *viz.*

John Chappel, aged about 43 Years, but appears to be much older, as he has a very grey Head, he is an *Englishman* born, tall slim Man, except his having broad Shoulders, has a Sore on one of his Legs which causes him to walk a little lame; his Dress when he came away, was an Osnbrig Frock, one ditto Waistcoat, one old blue Kersey ditto, one Pair of brown Kersey Breeches, Osnabrig Trowsers, one Check Shirt, one Osnbrig ditto, Yarn Stockings, and Country made Shoes, had a Felt Hat bound round the Edge with black Worsted, and wears a brown Bob Wig. The said *Chappel*, has been much used to the Seas, understands Navigation perfectly well, and has been a Captain of a Man of War, has a Register from the Admiralty at home, which makes him appear to have acted in that Capacity; he is under Indentures for Five Years.

John Barret, an *English* Convict Lad, about 20 Years of Age, well grown, of a fair Complexion, has a down Look, and stammers when he talks, wears his own Hair, which is straight, and on the blackish Order, his Cloathing, when he went away, was but mean, being coarse Country Cloth, had several Osnabrig Shirts, and Trowsers, an old Hat, and Country made Shoes.

Timothy Linch, an *Irish* Convict, is a short well set Fellow, much pitted with the Small-Pox; had on when he went away, a good snuff-coloured Cloth Coat, full long for him, a red Waistcoat, a brown Kersey ditto, a Pair of Breeches of the same, one white Sheeting Shirt, Two Osnabrigs ditto, Country Yarn Stockings, and a Pair of Shoes; wears a brown Wig, a Felt Hat, bound round the Edge with black Worsted; he is a pert artful Fellow. Whoever takes up the said Servants, and secures them in any Jail in this Province, the Province of *Pennsylvania*, or the Colony of *Virginia*, so that their Master gets them again, shall have a Reward of NINE POUNDS, *Maryland* or *Pennsylvania* Currency, or THREE POUNDS, like Money, for each, and reasonable Charges, if brought home, paid by
HENRY GASSAWAY.

N. B. The above Servants went away in a large Pettiaugre, with a Suit of Sails belonging to their Master.

The Maryland Gazette, June 4, 1767; June 11, 1767; June 18, 1767; June 25, 1767; July 2, 1767; July 9, 1767; July 16, 1767; July 23, 1767; July 30, 1767; August 6, 1767.

Virginia, April 28, 1767.

RAN away from the Subscriber, of *Fairfax* County, on the 23d Instant, an *Irish* Convict Servant Man, named PATRICK BYRN, upwards of 26 Years of Age, about 5 Feet 7 Inches high; has remarkable Scar on his Forehead, which he is very careful to conceal, by not pulling off his Hat to any Person.—He is of a pale Complexion, red Hair, cut short, and the Fore Part of his Head shaved. Had on, when he went away, a short dyed Cotton Coat, an old fine Cloth Jacket, an old Fine Hat, and a short brown Wig. Whoever apprehends the said Servant, and conveys him to me, shall receive, if taken in this Colony, Forty Shillings; if in any other Province, Four Pistoles Reward, besides what the Law allows; or Forty Shillings, if secured in any Goal.

'Tis suppos'd he has forged a Pass, changed his Cloaths, and gone towards *Philadelphia*, in Company with several *Irish* Servants, who went off at the above time.   PETER WAGENER.

The Maryland Gazette, June 4, 1767; June 11, 1767; June 18, 1767.

June 3, 1767.

RAN away Yesterday from the Subscriber, living in *Queen-Anne's* County, an Indented *Irishman*, named MICHAEL CRAIG, about 5 Feet 6 or 8 Inches high, of a down-look, wears his own black Hair, which he sometimes ties behind: Had on, and took with him, Two Osnabrig Shirts, and a Pair of Trowsers; a half worn brown Cloth coloured Coat, with Buttons of the same Colour; old Shoes, much patched in the Heels and Quarters. 'Tis suppos'd he will try, by some Excuse, to get over the Bay, as I have a Brother living there.

Whoever takes up, or secures him, so as I may have him again, shall have THREE POUNDS Reward, if taken out of the County, paid by
JOHN IRELAND.

The Maryland Gazette, June 4, 1767; June 11, 1767; June 25, 1767; July 2, 1767; July 16, 1767. See *The Pennsylvania Gazette*, June 18, 1767.

June 1, 1767.

BROKE *Anne-Arundel* County Gaol, last Night, the Two following Prisoners, *viz.*

Alexander M'Quillin, an *Irishman*, committed as a Runaway, but has since acknowledged that he is a Deserter from the Royal Train of Artillery; he is about 5 Feet 8 Inches high, wears his own Hair, which is black, is of a ruddy Complexion: Had on when he made his Escape, a blue Cloth Coat, and Breeches of the same, both much worn, white Cotton Jacket, Yarn Stockings, Country made Shoes, and Brass Buckles.

Henry Harrison, committed on Suspicion of Felony, a tall thin Fellow, of a swarthy Complexion: Had on when he made his Escape, a white Country made Cloth Jacket, Oznabrig Shirt, and Trowsers, and a Worsted Cap.

Whoever apprehends and secures the aforesaid *M'Quillin*, and *Henry Harrison*, so as they may be had again, shall receive SEVEN POUNDS Reward, or FIVE POUNDS for *Alexander M'Quillin*, and FORTY SHILLINGS for *Harrison*.   WILLIAM STEUART, Sheriff.

The Maryland Gazette, June 4, 1767; June 11, 1767; June 18, 1767; July 9, 1767; July 16, 1767; July 12, 1766.

RUN away from the snow Fitzherbert, lying in Nanticoke river, Maryland, a sailor, named John Berry, an Irishman, and supposed to have stole four pieces bag holland, containing 84 yards. Whoever secures the fellow in any goal in Maryland or Pennsylvania, with the goods, or any part thereof, shall receive Three Pounds reward, by applying to Alexander Laing at Vienna, or the subscriber,   SAMUEL EDMONDSON.

The Pennsylvania Gazette, June 4, 1767; June 11, 1767.

Lancaster, May 27, 1767.

WAS committed to my custody, the 21st of last April, on suspicion of being runaway servants, Richard Merryman, a low set fellow, about 5 feet 4 inches high, red hair, much freckled, and speaks much with the Irish accent; says he served his time in George Town, on Potowmack, Maryland, with one James Divin, and has the counter part of his indenture with him. And Thomas M'Venny, about 5 feet 6 inches high, well built, dark brown hair, of a dark complexion, and says he came in here from Ireland last fall with Captain Davis, and that he paid him for his passage, but can produce no receipt for the same. Their masters, if any they have, are desired, in four weeks after the date hereof, to come, pay their charges, and take them away, or they will be sold out for their fees by
MATTHIAS BUGH, Goaler.
The Pennsylvania Gazette, June 4, 1767.

Bladensburg, June 10, 1767.
RAN away from the Subscribers, on Tuesday the 9th Instant, Two Convict Servant Men, *viz.*

William Daniel Angess, a Shoemaker by Trade, about 5 Feet 2 or 3 Inches high, of a fair Complexion, about 22 Years of Age, very full Faced, dark Eyes; had on a light Cloth Coat with a Velvet Cape, white Swanskin, or Flannel Waistcoat, with Sleeves, Buckskin Breeches, black Stockings, a white Shirt much worn, a Pair of *English* Shoes, an old Hat, and wears a large Cut Wig; is very foreward in his Speech, and talks good English.

William Sterling, an *Irishman*, and speaks very much in that Dialect; about 5 Feet 7 Inches high, of a dark Complexion, about 28 Years of Age, wears his black Hair, mark'd with the Small-Pox; had on a blue Cloth Coat and Jacket, Osnabrig Shirt and Trowsers, a Pair of Sheepskin Breeches, a Beaver Hat much worn, and cut round the Brim.

Whoever takes up and secures said Servants, so that their Masters may get them again, shall receive THREE POUNDS Reward, or in Proportion for either, besides what the Law allows, and reasonable Charges, paid by
JOHN FRANCIS,   CLEMENT TRIGG.
The Maryland Gazette, June 11, 1767; June 18, 1767; June 25, 1767; July 2, 1767; July 9, 1767.

TEN POUNDS REWARD.
May 26, 1767.
RAN away from the Subscribers, living on *Kent-Island*, on Sunday last, the Four following Convicts, *viz.*

ALEXANDER MASON, an *Englishman*, a Shoemaker by Trade, about 26 Years of Age, of a pale Complexion, black Hair, and about 5 Feet 6 Inches high; had on when he went away a stripp'd Country Cloth Vest and Breeches, a black Cloth under Jacket without Sleeves, an old Felt Hat, and an Osnabrig Shirt. He also took his Tools with him.

MICHAEL CALVERT, an *Englishman*, a Labourer, about 20 Years of Age, of a fresh Complexion, with short brown Hair, and about 5 Feet 7 Inches high; had on a stripped Country Cloth Jacket and Breeches, a stripped Gingham Jacket without Sleeves, an Osnabrig Shirt, Felt Hat, bound round the Edge with Plaiding, white ribb'd Yarn Stockings, and a Pair of coarse Negro Shoes.

JOHN BOULD, an *Englishman*, a Weaver by Trade, about 44 Years old, and 6 Feet high, of a fair Complexion, is very lusty, has a black Beard, and wears his own black Hair; had on, and took with him, an old Castor Hat, a blue Coat and Vest with black Horn buttons (one of which excepted, which was of Brass, fixed to the Top of the Breast of his Coat) an Osnabrig Shirt, white Thread Stockings, and a Pair of Calf-Skin Pumps.

DUNCAN M'FEE, a *Scotchman*, Labourer, of a brown Complexion, with grey Hair, tied behind, and is about 5 Feet 9 Inches high, and about 40 Years of Age; had on, and took with him, a Kersey Jacket, a Pair of brown Cloth Breeches, white Stockings, and coarse Shoes, a Felt Hat, and an Under-red Jacket, [*sic*] without Sleeves. They all went off in a Canoe, about 26 Feet long, pay'd over with Tar and red Paint, and is suppos'd to have gone down the Bay. If any Person or Persons will secure the said Servants, they shall be entituled to the above Reward, or in Proportion for either, and reasonable Charges if brought home, paid by
DANIEL WEEDON,   JAMES BRYAN,   THOMAS YEWELL.

N. B. It is suppos'd they will make themselves Trowsers, as they took a Quantity of Osnabrig with them. All masters of Vessels are forbid harbouring or carrying them off.

The Maryland Gazette, June 11, 1767; June 18, 1767; June 25, 1767.
See *The Maryland Gazette*, May 28, 1767

June 11, 1767.
RAN away on Sunday Night last, from the Subscriber, living in *Pr. George's* County, a Convict Servant Man, named *John Cooper*, about 5 Feet 8 or 9 Inches high, of a swarthy Complexion, dark Eyes and short black Hair: Had on and took with him, two blue Pea Jackets, one without Sleeves; the one with Sleeves is much worn and patch'd, and white Metal Buttons to each, a small Castor Hat, one Osnabrig Shirt, and one white Linen ditto, a Pair of red Cloth Breeches, blue ribb'd Worsted Stockings, one Pair ditto not ribb'd, and a Pair of old Shoes, with broad Nails in the

Heels. He likewise Stole a small bay Horse, about 12½ Hands high, branded on the off Buttock and Shoulder, thus 7, a small half worn Saddle, and blue fring'd Housing much worn.

Whoever takes up the said Servant, and secures him in any Jail, so as he may be had again, shall have, if taken in the County, Eight Dollars Reward, and if out, Ten Dollars, and reasonable Charges if brought home, paid by   ABRAHAM CLARK.
The Maryland Gazette, June 11, 1767.

June 11, 1767.

RAN away, on the 9th Instant, from the Subscriber, living at *London-Town*, an *Irish* Convict Lad, named *Michael Connoway*, wears his own Hair, which is short, has a little Out-breaking on one of his Lips, occasioned by the Fever and Ague: Had on, and took with him, when he went away, an old Bearskin Upper Jacket, with a stripp'd Flannel Under one, a Pair of old Bearskin Breeches, and brown Thread Stockings, a new Pair of *English* made Pumps, one Check, and one Osnabrig Shirt, and an Osnabrig Wallet.

Whoever takes up or secures the said Servant, so as his Master may have him again, shall have TWENTY SHILLINGS Reward, besides what the Law allows, paid by   WILLIAM BROWN.
The Maryland Gazette, June 11, 1767; June 25, 1767. See *The Maryland Gazette*, June 23, 1768, for Conaway/Connaway.

TWENTY POUNDS REWARD.

Annapolis, June 8, 1767.
RAN away last Night from *Annapolis*, Two Servant Men, One a Convict, about 5 Feet 9 Inches high, a well-set square-made Fellow, about 36 Years old, dark Complexion, thick black Beard and bushy black Hair, a House-Carpenter and Joiner by Trade; has on or with him a white Kersey Coat with white Metal Buttons, Buckskin Breeches, an old blue Cloth Waistcoat, Thread Stockings, a Pair of old Silver Buckles; his Name is *William Dunn*, and belongs to *Joshua Frazier*.

The other an *Irish* Lad, about 20 Years of Age, much about the same heighth as the other; fair Complexion, with light Hair commonly tied behind, rather spare in his make; has been used to wait in a House, nor knows any Thing of a Trade; he has on most probably a mix'd coarse Cloth Coat, he had another light colour'd Duffil Coat, which perhaps he may have taken with him, the rest of his Cloaths uncertain; he may too have a Pair of Boots which are missing, and a Portmanteau; his Name is *Edward Butler*, and belongs to *Thomas Johnson*, Junr. of *Annapolis*, which whom he hath been used to ride occasionally.

There are two Saddles and Bridles missing out of Mr. *Johnson's* Stable, both half Kirbs, one of them a solid Bit and Ban across, they have probably furnished themselves with Horses, and made through *Baltimore.*

TEN POUNDS *Pennsylvania* Money Reward for *William Dunn,* and FIVE POUNDS like Money for *Edward Butler,* if taken in the Province, or TEN POUNDS for Edward Butler, if taken out of the Province, on Delivery to   JOSHUA FRAZIER,   THOMAS JOHNSON, Junr.

The Maryland Gazette, June 11, 1767; June 18, 1767; June 25, 1767; July 9, 1767; July 16, 1767.

RUN away from the Subscriber, living in Baltimore County, on the 12th of May, a Convict Servant Woman, named Susannah Cowden, a thick well set Woman, of low Stature, about 20 Years of Age, her Hair is dark brown, which she wears tied behind, has got a large Scar on one of her Legs, and is a round faced pert saucy Wench; had on, and took with her, when she went away, a white Country-made Lincey Jacket, and Petticoat, very dirty, an old Cotton Ditto, Ozenbrigs Shift, old Callimanco Shoes, a Callico Jacket and Bed-gown, an old Pair of red Stockings, a white Bonnet, and white Apron. Whoever takes up and secures the said Servant Woman, so as her Master may have her again, shall receive, if taken up in the County, Twenty Shillings, if out of the County, Forty Shillings and if out of the Province Three Pounds, Reward, and reasonable Charges, if brought home, paid by me   WILLIAM RANDALL.

N. B. She was seen at the Head of Elk, and enquired for Philadelphia.

The Pennsylvania Gazette, June 11, 1767.

June 9, 1767.

RAN away, on Monday the 8th Inst. from the Subscribers, living in *Kent* County, two Convict Servant Men, *viz.*

Francis Hayward, an *Englishman,* Aged about 45 Years, about 5 Feet 7 or 8 Inches high, and wears his own black Hair: Had on when he went away, an old blue surtout Coat, with hair Buttons, stripped Linsey Jacket and Breeches, and Osnabrig Trowsers, One white Shirt, One Country Linen ditto, and an old Castor Hat.

Daniel Peters, about 24 Years of Age, 5 Feet 4 Inches high: Had on when he went away, an old white Frize Coat, old Buckskin Breeches, One Pair of Osnabrig Trowsers, One good white Shirt, and an old Felt Hat.

Whoever takes up the said Servants, and secures them in any Jail in this Province, shall receive a Reward of 5 *l.* or 50 *s.* for each, if brought home, paid by   SAMUEL WICKES,   HANS HANSON.

The Maryland Gazette, June 18, 1767; June 25, 1767; July 2, 1767; July 9, 1767.

May 29, 1767.

RAN away, on the 27th Instant, from the Subscriber, living at *Falmouth*, on *Rappahannock* River, *Virginia*, Three *Scots* Convict Servant Men, *viz.*

WILLIAM NEILSON, suppos'd to be the Ringleader: He is a likely young Fellow, about 28 Years of Age, 5 Feet 10 Inches high, wears his own Hair, of a light sandy Colour, hanging generally loose, has had the Small-Pox, his Nose somewhat flatter than common, especially towards the Point, where it declines to his Mouth. Had on, and took with him, when he went away, a Hat, with a black Band, and a Metal Buckle, which he wears generally cock'd behind, a short light coloured Coat and Jacket, a Pair of Linen tweel'd Breeches, with Shoes and Stockings. He speaks pretty good *English*, having been many Years with Mr. *Holmes*, near *Newcastle upon Tyne*, where he learn'd Jockeyship, which he professes.

HUGH BOYD, a slender Lad, about 19 Years of Age, 5 Feet 8 Inches high, and much freckled; wears his own Hair; had on a Hat, with a black Tape Band and Buckle; a light coloured Cloth Coat, rather too long, a stripp'd Cotton Jacket, blue Breeches, and a Pair of Stockings and Shoes.

GABRIEL STEWART, a thick well-set Fellow above the Knees, of a ruddy Complexion, and smooth Face, wears his own dark coloured Hair, loose. He is about 24 Years of Age, and about 5 Feet 7 or 8 Inches high; he had on a ragged brown coloured Coat and Jacket, with Breeches of the same, all tattered; a Pair of Shoes and Stockings, and a Hat, generally slouch'd. He cuts on the whole but a mean Appearance.

Neilson writes a tolerable good Hand, and, by his superior Knowledge of the *English* Tongue, 'tis imagin'd he will write Passes, and act as Speaker for the rest. He and *Boyd* have both blue Surtout Coats, which, 'tis probable they will wear.

Whoever takes up the said Servants, and conveys them to me, shall receive a Reward of TWENTY SHILLINGS for each, and reasonable Charges, paid by ALEXANDER CUNNINGHAM.

The Maryland Gazette, June 18, 1767; June 25, 1767; July 2, 1767.

Baltimore-Town, *June* 10, 1767.

RAN away last Night, from the *Northampton* Iron-Works, *Baltimore* County, *Maryland*, the following Servant Men, *viz.*

Edmond Grimshaw, an *Englishman*, a well set Fellow, aged about 21 Years, 5 Feet 9 Inches high, red Hair, fair Complexion, much pitted with the Small-Pox, and has a large Pit, or small Scar, about an Inch from his Mouth, his right Eye Tooth doubles over his other Teeth, is a Weaver and

Taylor by Trade: Had on when he went away, a dark coloured Fearnothing Pea Jacket, white Cotton ditto, Osnabrig Shirt, Hempen Roll Trowsers, half worn Shoes with Hob Nails in the Heels, a Felt Hat, and has taken with him a narrow Ax.

John Hardy, an *Englishman*, a well set Fellow, about 38 Years of Age, 5 Feet 9 Inches high, much pitted with the Small Pox, the Bridge of his Nose is broke, and talks very hoarse: Had on when he went away, an Osnabrig Shirt, Hempen Roll Trowsers, new Shoes, and Felt Hat, and has taken with him a narrow Ax.

Whoever takes up the said Servants, and secures them in any Jail, shall have 40 *s*. for each, if taken above 20 Miles from home, 3 *l*. if out of the County, and 5 *l*. if out of the Province, and reasonable Charges if brought home.   CHARLES RIDGELY, senior, & Co.

The Maryland Gazette, June 18, 1767; June 25, 1767; July 2, 1767; July 9, 1767. See *The Maryland Gazette*, April 30, 1767, and *The Pennsylvania Gazette*, August 13, 1767, for Grimshaw and Hardy.

RAN away from the Subscribers, living in *Alexandria*, Two Convict *Irish* Servants.

Edward Bryan, by Trade a Weaver, about 5 Feet 6 Inches high, and 30 Years of Age, has an old blue Coat, red Waistcoat, brown Breeches, a Pair of Check Linen Trowsers, Shoes and Stockings, a dark brown cut Bob-Wig, and a tolerable good Hat: He may vary this Dress by pilferring others. He is much pitted with the Small-Pox, his Nose turning up, has thick Lips and nigh Sighted, in short a very unpromising Countenance, though a plausible Tongue, much upon the Brogue, and addicted to Liquor.

Will Canely, about 16 or 17 Years of Age, 4 Feet 10 Inches high, or thereabouts, pert looking, and smooth Faced, has a remarkable Scar on his Chin, by the Kick of a Horse, also a large Scar on one of his Hands: Had on when he went away, an old Fearnought Jacket, a stripped blue Under ditto, and when closely examined, will stutter. It is expected they will make towards *Baltimore*, or probably towards some Ships down *Patowmack*.

Whoever takes up and secures the said Servants, so as they may be had again, shall have 40 *s*. for each, and reasonable Charges, if brought home, paid by   JOHN DALTON,   ROBERT ADAM.

The Maryland Gazette, June 18, 1767; June 25, 1767; July 2, 1767; July 9, 1767.

TEN POUNDS Reward.

RUN away last Night, from the Patapsco Furnace, near Elkridge Landing, in Anne Arundel, Maryland, two English Convict Servant Men, viz. Levy Barnett, about 23 Years of Age, about 5 Feet 8 Inches high, spare made, swarthy Complexion, smooth Face, light brown Hair, dark Eyes, and down look; took with him the following clothes, viz. one brown Fearnought Jacket, one Pair light blue Duroy Breeches, one Pair brown Rolls Trowsers, one Pair Sailors Ditto, two Ozenbrigs Shirts, one Pair blue Yarn Stockings, one Pair Country Shoes, with Copper Buckles, and one Felt Hat. William Roberts, a Welchman, about 26 Years of Age, 5 Feet 9 Inches high, a well made Fellow, of a dark Complexion, full Face, dark brown Hair, dark Eyes, and down Look; speaks much on the Welch Dialect, and is much addicted to strong Drink; had on, when he went away, one white Fearnought Jacket, one Pair brown Roll Trowsers, two Ozenbrigs Shirts, one Felt Hat, and a pair of old Shoes. Whoever takes up and secures said Servants, so that they may be had again, shall receive for each, if taken 15 Miles from home, Thirty Shillings if 20 Miles, Forty Shillings, if 40 Miles, Three Pounds, and if out of the Province, the above Reward, and reasonable Charges, if brought home to said Furnace, of Messieurs, THOMAS HARRISON, and Company, per   JAMES WALKER.

N. B. As they are meanly clad, it is likely they may steal more Clothes, and endeavour to go off by Water; therefore all Masters of Vessels are forbid to harbour or carry them off at their Peril.

The Pennsylvania Gazette, June 18, 1767; June 25, 1767; July 23, 1767; August 27, 1767; November 11, 1767.

New-Castle, June 8, 1767.
NOW in the Goal of this County, the following Persons, committed as Runaway Servants, viz. JOHN CARROLL....

MICHAEL CRAIG, about 25 Years of Age, 5 Feet 10 Inches high, black Hair, fair Complexion; had on, when committed, a white Flannel Waistcoat, without Sleeves, a Tow Shirt, long Trowsers, and Shoes, without Stockings; says he belongs to John Ireland, near Queen's Town, Maryland.

And JOHN DAVIS, about 30 Years of Age, about 5 Feet 8 Inches high, a well set Fellow; says he belongs to Thomas Harrison in Baltimore Town, Maryland. The Owners of the above Servants, if any they have, are desired to come, pay Charges, and take them away in 6 Weeks from this Date, or they will be sold out for the same, by
THOMAS PUSEY, Goaler.

The Pennsylvania Gazette, June 18, 1767; June 25, 1767; July 2, 1767; July 9, 1767; July 16, 1767; July 23, 1767. See *The Maryland Gazette,* June 4, 1767, for Craig.

TEN POUNDS REWARD.
Prince-George's County, *Piscataway,* June 16.

RAN away from the Subscribers, on the 8th Instant, a Country-born Indented Servant Man, named BASIL PILES, a Blacksmith by Trade, about Six Feet and an Inch high, or thereabouts; had on and took with him, when he went away, a light brown coarse Broad Cloth Coat and Breeches, half worn; a blue Camblet Coat, half worn, a new Pair of *English* made Shoes, a Pair of Worsted Stockings, a Pair of Sailor's Trowsers, Osnabrigs Shirts, White ditto, and a half-worn Hat; 'tis likely he may have other Apparel, tho' unknown. He wears his own Hair, of a light brownish Colour, has a fair pale Complexion, and grey Eyes. He is very fond of Strong Liquor, and will get drunk if it is to be had. 'Tis probable, if he is taken, he will produce an Indenture signed by us, in which he is to serve, at the rate of 25 *l. per Annum*, until his Debts are all paid off. If he has a Discharge to said Indenture, we declare it to be forged. It is imagin'd he will make up towards *Leesburg*, near *Goose-Creek*, where he has a Brother, named *Francis Piles*, and some other Relations.

Whoever takes up and secures said Servant, so as he may be had again, shall have, if taken in the County, SIX DOLLARS; if out of the County, EIGHT DOLLARS; if in *Virginia*, FIVE POUNDS; and, if in *Carolina*, TEN POUNDS Reward, and reasonable Charges, if brought home, paid by   GEO. HARDEY, Jun.   HENRY HARDEY, Jun.

The Maryland Gazette, June 25, 1767; July 2, 1767; July 9, 1767; July 16, 1767; July 23, 1767; July 30, 1767; August 6, 1767.

FIVE POUNDS REWARD.

RAN away from the Subscriber, living in *Gilford* Township, *Cumberland* County, on the 29th of *June* last, a Servant Man, named JOHN PORTER, of a fair Complexion, pitted with the Small-Pox, has short light colour'd Hair, and is about 5 Feet 4 Inches high: One of his Ankle Bones differs from the other in Thickness. He is about 19 Years of Age, was born in SCOTLAND, and has for some Time past been used to Sea, but is a Weaver by Trade: He had on, and took with him, when he went away, a brown Jacket, with short Sleeves, lined with Linsey, a coarse Shirt and Trowsers, an old Hat, old Shoes, and Brass Buckles, has a black Silk Handkerchief, and a Sickle, so 'tis thought he will endeavour to pass for a Reaper.

Whoever takes up said Servant, and secures him, so that his Master may have him again, shall receive the above Reward from
EDWARD COOK.

N. B. All Masters of Vessels are forbid harbouring or carrying him off at their Peril.

The Maryland Gazette, July 2, 1767; July 9, 1767; July 16, 1767; July 23, 1767.

June 22, 1767.

RAN away, on the 2d Instant, from the Subscriber, living in SALEM County, in WEST-JERSEY, an IRISH Servant Man, named PATRICK HUSSEY, about 22 Years of Age, and about 5 Feet 10 Inches high, has dark brown Hair, black Eyes, and pitted with the Small-Pox: Had on, and took with him, when he went away, a new Felt Hat, a new homespun Sheep-grey fulled Cloth Vest and Breeches, with Metal Buttons, and Cuffs to the Sleeves, a blue grey Cloth Vest, with Metal Buttons, one Pair of homespun Trowsers, one coarse Shirt ditto, Yarn Stockings, old patched Pumps, with Brass Buckles. He has a large Scar on the Great-Toe of the right Foot, occasioned by the Cut of an Axe.

Whoever secures the said Servant so as he may be had again, shall receive FOUR POUNDS Reward, and reasonable Charges, if brought home, paid by   RICHARD HACKET.

The Maryland Gazette, July 2, 1767; July 9, 1767. See *The Pennsylvania Gazette*, August 13, 1767.

Alexandria, June 17, 1767.

RAN away last Night from the Subscriber, living in *Alexandria*, Three Convict Servants, viz.

Charles Killeen, an *Irishman*, about 28 Years old, 5 Feet 7 Inches high, of a fair Complexion, white Eye-brows, has a remarkable Scar on one of his Hands, resembling a W, occasioned by the Cut of a Knife, and is pitted with the Small-Pox: Had on when he went away, a white woollen Jacket, double breasted, with black Horn Buttons, a Check Shirt, Osnabrig Trowsers, and an old yellowish Wig; he was brought up a Buckle-maker, but since he has been in the Country has followed the Water, and is pretty expert in that Way, and may probably get on board some Vessel.

Charles Dally, an *Irishman*, is a slender lively Fellow, with dark Hair, about 21 Years of Age, has much of the Brogue in his Speech: Had on when he went away, an old Hat, Osnabrig Shirt and Trowsers.

Mary, the Wife of *Charles*, is about 20 Years of Age, blind of the right Eye, and one of her Legs much swelled; she had on an old with Bed-Gown, and a white woollen Pitticoat. [sic] They are all much given to Liquor: The Woman had Two Guineas, and while they last, they will not want Drink.

Whoever takes up, and secures said Servants, shall have FIFTEEN DOLLARS Reward, and if brought, reasonable Charges, paid by MICHAEL GRETTER.

The Maryland Gazette, July 2, 1767.

June 22, 1767.

RAN away last Night from the Subscriber, living in *Annapolis*, a Convict Servant Woman, named MARY OWENS, born at *Shrewsbury*, in *England*, and speaks in that Dialect: She is a short well-set Woman, about 36 Years of Age, has light brown Hair, fresh Complexion, and lost some of her Fore-Teeth, has a large Dimple in her left Cheek when she laughs, and takes Snuff: She had on and took with her, Two Country white Linen Shifts, and Two Country stripped Linen Wolsey Petticoats, and one stripped Flannel ditto; likewise an old black quilted Coat, lined with green, and an old Pair of Stays; a blue Shalloon Gown, one of dark Calico, and an old Purple-Ground Cotton ditto; three white Aprons, one of Check, and two of coarse Country Linen ditto; a white *Leghorn* Hat, with wash'd Ribbon round its Crown; a Pair of Shoes, and an old Pair of Leather Pumps, and walks much with her Toes inward. 'Tis probable she will change her Name and Dress, as she is a sly artful Hussy.

Whoever takes up the said Servant, and secures her, so as she may be had again, shall receive FORTY SHILLINGS, and reasonable Charges if brought home, paid by   WILLIAM SIMPSON.

The Maryland Gazette, July 2, 1767.

June 29, 1767.

RAN away Yesterday, from the Subscribers, living near *George-Town*, in *Frederick* County, Two *Irish* Convict Servants.

John Broughton, a short well-made Fellow, of a dark Complexion, and black Hair, which is very thin on the Crown: Had on and took with him, a light coloured Fustian Coat, brown Holland Waistcoat, one Pair of short Osnabrig Breeches; also one old black Coat, one stripped Shirt, one check ditto, and two Osnabrig ditto, two Pair of Osnabrig Trowsers, blue worsted Stockings, one Pair of Shoes or Pumps lined and bound, and a Cut Wig, has been bound, but now taken off, and has on one of his Arms a Crucifix mark'd with Gunpowder.

Thomas Tynan, a short well-set Fellow, of a brown Complexion, and has a large Scar under the right Corner of his Mouth, long bushy Hair, on his Forehead and Temples, but has been shaved, and he is very fond of Liquor: Had on a Bearskin Surtout Coat, with Buttons near the colour of the Cloth, a Bearskin Jacket with Sleeves, and Checked with red worsted, and only one Lapel on it, a white Shirt, with two Letters on one of the Wristbands, work'd with Silk, a Pair of Osnabrig Trowsers much patched, and Country made Shoes with Straps, but tied with Strings.

Whoever takes up and secures said Servants, so that they may be had again, shall receive 30 *s. Pennsylvania* Money Reward, for *Broughton*, and

20 s. for *Tynan*; if taken Twenty Miles from home, 40 s. for *Broughton*, if Thirty Miles, and if Fifty Miles, 3 *l.* and 40 s. for Tynan, paid by
RICHARD BOWS, ANTHONY HOLMEAD.
　The Maryland Gazette, July 2, 1767; July 9, 1767; July 16, 1767; July 23, 1767.

June 29, 1767.
COMMITTED to *Prince George's* County Jail, the following Runaways, viz. *Daniel Churchwell*, an *Irishman*, says he belongs to *Michael Gretter*, of *Virginia*; *Edward Kelly*, *Mary Kelly*, *John Barnett*, and *James Burk*, who will not own that they are Servants, but say they came from *Virginia*, and intended to *Baltimore* Town; *Mary Kelly* hath but one Eye. Their Masters are desired to take them away, and pay Charges.
WILLIAM T. WOOTTON, Sheriff.
　The Maryland Gazette, July 2, 1767; July 9, 1767; July 16, 1767; July 23, 1767.

TWENTY PISTOLES Reward.
RUN away on Saturday, the 20th of June last, from the Nottingham Forges, on the Great Falls of Gunpowder, in Baltimore County, Maryland, an indented Scotch Servant Man, named George Simpson, upwards of 5 feet high, of a yellow Complexion, with long black Hair; had on, and took with him, Ozenbrigs Shirts and Trowsers, black Breeches, light grey ribbed Stockings, a blue Broadcloth Coat, about half worn, a striped Jacket, a pretty good white Shirt, a new Castor Hat, a brown Silk Handkerchief, and yellow Pinchbeck Buckles. He stole and rode away a dark bay Mare, seven years old, about 14 hands high, branded on her near Shoulder **I**, and on her near Buttock **SP**, paces pretty fast, was shod before, and has a small Star in her Forehead, with a large Foretop and Mane, and is a Mare of pretty good Spirit. Besides the Clothes above-mentioned, he took with him a pretty good Wig, and probably designed to cut off his Hair. Whoever takes up said Servant, and secures him in any Goal, or brings him to the Subscriber, at the aforesaid Forges, or to Mr. SAMUEL PURVIANCE, junior, Merchant, in Philadelphia, shall have the above Reward.
CORBIN LEE.
　The Pennsylvania Gazette, July 9, 1767; July 16, 1767; August 20, 1767; August 27, 1767.

ANNAPOLIS, *May* 19, 1767.
RAN away from the Subscriber, a Servant Woman, named ANNE GRIFFITH, born in *Wales*, but speaks pretty good *English*; she is a stout

well grown Woman, but not of the largest Size, about 25 or 30 Years of Age, dark brown Hair, grey Eyes, and tolerable fresh Complexion: Had on and took with her, an old light coloured Camblet Gown, and a Country Woollen ditto, with the Warp white, and Filling in blue, with other wearing Apparel, not known; she had a young Child, a Boy, near 12 Months old, who had a red stripped Linen Frock, and a Purple Calico ditto, &c. She was seen on the Road towards *Baltimore*, and said she was going to *Philadelphia*, to her Husband, but she has none; and shewed a counterfeit Letter, as if from him, requesting her to come to him. It is very likely she may have a false Pass, as I have since understood she applied for one.

    Likewise Ran away, the last of *April*, or beginning of *May*, a Servant Man, named THOMAS SHORES, who lately lived with *Sele Tucker*, in the *Swamp*, near West-River.

    Whoever takes up and secures said Servants, so that they may be had again, shall receive 20*s.* if in the County, and if out of the County 40*s.* if out of the Province, 3*l.* Reward for *Anne Griffith*, and 20*s.* Reward for *Thomas Shores*.   JOHN SHAW.

    The Maryland Gazette, July 16, 1767; July 23, 1767; August 6, 1767; August 13, 1767; August 20, 1767. See *The Maryland Gazette*, April 18, 1765.

THREE PISTOLES Reward.

RUN away, from the subscriber, in the night of the 27th of June last, living in Queen Ann's county, in Maryland, a convict servant man, named Thomas Lamprey, about 28 years of age, and about 5 feet 10 inches high, has a fair complexion, wears his own hair, if not taken off since he went away, which is of a fair colour, and took great pride in it; is a little pockmarked, has a small scar under his left or right eye; had on, and took with him, a light coloured broadcloth coat, with a small velvet collar, a brown or snuff coloured jacket, which has been flowered in the fulling-mill, dark striped linen trowsers, a new felt hat, old pumps, one of which is patched at the toe, but as he had money, he may perhaps buy him new ones. He likewise took with him, a dark brown horse, about 13 hands high, was in good order when he went away, with a snip on this nose, one of his forehoofs split almost up to the hair, a saddle and bridle, marks unknown; he says he is a wool-comber and stocking weaver, and has often time importuned his master to sell him in Germantown, or thereabouts, so as he might be at his trade; he has been in the foot guards in England, and says he was convicted for attempting a rape upon a woman. Whoever takes up and secures said servant, so that his master may have him again, shall have the above reward of Three Pistoles, paid by me NATHAN FARROW.

N. B. All persons are forbid from buying said horse, and harbouring said servant, and masters of vessels from carrying him off, at their peril.

The Pennsylvania Gazette, July 16, 1767; August 27, 1767. See *The Maryland Gazette*, October 1, 1767.

July 6, 1767.

RAN away from the Subscriber, living in *Charles* County, on Thursday Evening last, an *Irish* Convict Servant Man, whose Name is JOHN KELLY, of a fair Complexion, about 5 Feet 8 or 9 Inches high, wears his own Hair, which is brown, speaks much in his own Country Dialect, and has a Blemish in one of his Eyes. He had on, and took with him, a blue Broad Cloth Coat, a brown Holland lapelled Jacket, and Breeches of the same, all much worn; a Pair of clouded Country-made Stockings, a Dowlas Shirt, an *Irish* Linen ditto, and an old Felt Hat. As he can both read and write, 'tis probable he may forge a Pass.

Whoever takes up said Servant, and brings him to me, near Mr. *Samuel Hanson's*, in the County aforesaid, if within 20 Miles, shall have TWENTY SHILLINGS Reward; and if at a greater Distance, or out of the Province, THREE POUNDS, and reasonable travelling Charges allowed.

CHARLES GATES.

N. B. The above Servant is about 26 or 27 Years of Age.

The Maryland Gazette, July 23, 1767; July 30, 1767; August 6, 1767.

Carlisle Goal, in Cumberland county, July 13, 1767.

WAS committed to said goal, the 6th instant, a young man, by the name of Andrew Berrett....Also William Riglay, a runaway, servant to Richard Thompson, snuff maker in George-town, Maryland, who hath been notified both by writing and otherwise of the fellow's being here; and William Sherlock, a runaway, servant to John Enser, of Baltimore Town, Maryland. Their masters are therefore desired to come forthwith, and take them away; and any person having any demand against said Brookes, [sic] is desired to come with speed, and lay in the same, otherwise (as the Goal is almost full) they will be all sold or discharged shortly, for their prison fees, by HENRY CUNNINGHAM, Goaler.

The Pennsylvania Gazette, July 30, 1767; August 6, 1767; August 27, 1767.

Chester, July 4, 1767.

NOW in my custody, committed as run-aways, the three following persons, viz. Patrick Mullan....Nicholas Hart, a lad, about 14 years of age, and says he belongs to Michael Stites, at the head of North East. Also a Negroe man, named Charles....Their masters are desired to come and pay charges, and take them away, by JOSEPH THOMAS, Goaler.

N.B. Now in my custody, supposed to be stolen by one Joseph Williams, who is committed for felony, a mouse coloured horse, about 14 or 15 hands high, his two hind feet white, and branded on the near buttock with a horse shoe. Any Person having lost the said horse is desired to come and prove his property.

The Pennsylvania Gazette, July 30, 1767; August 6, 1767; August 27, 1767.

Baltimore County, August 3, 1767.

RUN away last Night, from the Northampton Furnace, in Baltimore County, Maryland, the two following Convicts, viz. EDMUND GRIMSHAW, a well set Fellow, about 5 Feet 9 Inches high, has red Hair, fair Complexion, much pitted with the Small-Pox, and has a large Pit or small Scar about an Inch from the left Corner of his Mouth, his right Eye-Tooth doubles over his other Teeth, about 21 Years of Age, born in Lancashire, in England, and is a Weaver and Taylor by Trade; had on, when he went away, a coarse blue Cloth Coat, half worn, Ozenbrigs Shirt, Hempen Roll Trowsers, half worn Shoes, old Felt Hat, and an Iron Collar. JOHN HARDY, a well set Fellow, about 5 Feet 9 Inches high, much pitted with the Small-Pox, the Bridge of his Nose broken, about 38 Years of Age, born in Lancashire, in England, and talks very hoarse; had on, when he went away, an old coarse grey Coat, Ozenbrigs Shirt and Trowsers, one old Shoe, and one Pump, a Felt Hat, and an Iron Collar. 'Tis supposed they will change their Names and Clothes. Whoever takes up and secures the said Servants, so as their Masters get them again, shall have Forty Shillings for each, if taken above 20 Miles from home; Three Pounds if out of the County; FIVE POUNDS Reward, if out of the Province, and reasonable Charges, if brought home, paid by
CHARLES RIDGLEY senr. and Comp.

The Pennsylvania Gazette, August 13, 1767; August 20, 1765; September 3, 1767. See *The Maryland Gazette*, April 30, 1767, and *The Maryland Gazette*, June 18, 1767.

Maryland, July 31, 1767.

TAKEN up by the Subscriber, and committed to the Custody of the Sheriff of Talbot County, an Irish Servant Man, supposed to be the Person advertised in the Maryland Gazette last Week, by Richard Hackett, Salem County, West Jersey, he answering every Description there given of him,

only he denies his Name, and says it is Patrick Kerney, he has a large Scar on his great Toe as said Hackett mentions.
ALLENBY MILLINGTON.
The Pennsylvania Gazette, August 13, 1767; September 3, 1767; October 1, 1767. See *The Maryland Gazette*, July 2, 1767.

August 17, 1767.
RAN away last Night from the *Patuxent* Iron-Works, the Three following Convict Servant Men, *viz*.

JOHN CARROLL, an *Irishman*, 30 Years of Age, a stout well-made Fellow, and has had his Hair lately cut off: Had on and took with him when he went away, an Osnabrig Shirt, Crocus Trowsers, and an old light colour'd Cloth Coat, pretty much worn, an old Felt Hat, and a Pair of Shoes with Steel Buckles.

JOHN HILL, an *Englishman*, 30 Years of Age, about 5 Feet 7 or 8 Inches high, and has a dark Complexion: Had on and took with him when he went away, an Osnabrig Shirt, Crocus Trowsers, new Felt Hat, Country-made Shoes, with Strings, an old grey Wig, and a Matchcoat Blanket.

PATRICK CONNER, 22 Years of Age, about 5 Feet 5 or 6 Inches high, much pitted with the Small-Pox, and wears his own short brown Hair: Had on and took with him when he went away, an Osnabrig Shirt, Crocus Trowsers, new Felt Hat, and a Pair of Negro Shoes.

Whoever takes up and secures the said Servants so that they may be had again, shall receive Forty Shilings eward for each, if Twenty Miles from home, or Three Pounds if out of the Province, paid by
THOs. SAMl. & JOHN SNOWDEN.
The Maryland Gazette, August 20, 1767; August 27, 1767; September 3, 1767; September 10, 1767; September 17, 1767; September 24, 1767. See *The Maryland Gazette*, June 30, 1768, and *The Maryland Gazette*, August 3, 1769, for Hill.

Prince-George's County.
COMMITTED to my Custody, the following Runaways, *viz*.

RICHARD ADDOWELL, a well made young Fellow, about 5 Feet 10 Inches high, very talkative, says he is a Free Man, and known to be such, by Capt. *Charles Ridgely*, of *Baltimore-Town*, with whom he lived Twelve Months as a hired Servant; by Mr. *Thomas Smith*, of *Charles* County; by Mr. *Thomas Welsh*, Collier, near Mess. *Snowden's* Iron-Works, and requests the Favour of one of them, to make his Assertion appear to some Justice of the Peace for the County aforesaid, which will procure his Releasement.

A New Negro Wench, named PHENEY....
A New Negro Fellow....his Name is BARRACK....
Their Masters are desired to take them away, and pay Charges.
Wm. TURNER WOOTTON, Sheriff.
The Maryland Gazette, August 27, 1767.

THERE is now in the goal of Caecil county, an Irish servant man, that was taken up on suspicion of being a runaway, he says his name is JAMES BRADEY, about 6 feet high, and supposed to belong to one Nathan Farrow, in Queen Ann's county, Maryland. His master is desired to come and take him out, and pay his fees, otherwise he will be sold out for the same, by DANIEL TURNER, Goaler.
The Pennsylvania Gazette, August 27, 1767; September 10, 1767.

RUN away from the subscriber, living near Sasquehanna Lower Ferry, on Sunday, the second instant, a servant lad, named Roger Hagon, lately come from Ireland, aged about 16 years, about 5 feet high; had on when he went away, an old felt hat, a flax and tow shirt, a pair of old leather breeches, no shoes or stockings, neither coat or jacket, his hair of a black colour, and lately cut off, pretty fair complexion. He speaks with something of the brogue, and is very talkative. It is thought he went in company with a certain James Barns, a young man, about 18 years old, 5 feet 10 inches high, and well set; he had on and took with him, when he went away, a castor hat, check shirt, black calimanco jacket, blue breeches, thread stockings, a pair of shoes or pumps, having both kinds with him he had also two coats, one of blue cloth, bound with ferreting, the other of country cloth, of a lightish colour, two fine shirts, and a black silk handkerchief; it is very probable they will keep together as much as possible. Whoever takes up the above Roger Hagon and secures him, so that his master may have him again, shall have FOUR DOLLARS, reward and reasonable charges, paid by JAMES PORTER.
The Pennsylvania Gazette, August 27, 1767.

September 1, 1767.
RAN away from, and robbed the Ship MELORA, lying off the Mouth of *Chester-River*, on the 28th of *August* last, the Two following Men, viz.
HENRY PRATT, aged 26; middle sized, a well-looking dark complexioned Fellow, and wears his own black Hair, which is curled.
JOHN HENRY, aged about 22, a very swarthy short Fellow, round faced, wears a Wig, and they both chew Tobacco. They went away in a new

Yawl, belonging to the Ship, 18 Feet long, with four red painted Square-loom'd Oars. a Sprit-sail bent to an Oar, for a Mast, and a Southerly Wind. Whoever secures the said Men, and brings them to *Queen's-Town*, or to the Ship in *Wye-River*, shall receive FOUR PISTOLES Reward, and ONE PISTOLE for the Boat, and all reasonable Charges, paid by JOHN MONTGOMERIE.

The Maryland Gazette, September 3, 1767; September 10, 1767; September 17, 1767. See *The Pennsylvania Gazette*, September 10, 1767.

Baltimore town, August 4, 1767.

RUN away, on the 30th of July last, from the subscriber, an Irish servant man, named William Burk, about 18 years of age, he is a tall slim fellow, of a pale complexion, short strait light coloured hair, pock-marked, his right leg is crooked, by reason it has been broke, he has worked some time at the cooper's trade: Had on when he went away, a half worn hat, a tow shirt and trowsers, very dirty, a short linsey striped jacket, without sleeves, patched, an old pair of shoes, he has been about a year in the country. Whoever takes up the said servant, and brings him to William Davis in Baltimore town, shall receive THIRTY SHILLINGS reward, and reasonable charges, paid by   WILLIAM DAVIS.

The Pennsylvania Gazette, September 3, 1767; October 1, 1767; October 15, 1767.

ROBBED, *and run away from the ship Meliora, about 2 o'clock in the morning, August 28, then lying at anchor off the mouth of Chester river, two sailors; one named Henry Pratt, aged about 26 years is a well looking fellow, dark complexion, black curled hair, and of a middle size; the other named John Henry, aged about 22 years, is a short fellow, round face, swarthy complexion, and wears a wig. They carried off the ship's yaul, 18 feet long, four oars, a sprit sail, bent on an oar instead of a mast. Whoever secures both sailors and yaul, and brings them to Queen's town, or to the ship in Wye river, shall receive Four Pistoles, or for the yaul only, One Pistole, and all reasonable charges, paid by* JOHN MONTGOMERIE.

The Pennsylvania Gazette, September 10, 1767. See *The Maryland Gazette*, September 3, 1767.

Baltimore County, *September* 1, 1767.

RAN away from the Subscriber, living near the *Soldier's Delight*, *Baltimore County*, the 16th of *August* last, a Convict Servant Man, named

JOHN PRICHET, a Skinner by Trade, about 5 Feet 6 Inches high, 25 Years of Age, born in the West of England, and talks very broad; has one of his fore Teeth out, in the left Side of the upper Jaw, and stoops in his Walk: Had on and took with him, an old Castor Hat, an old grey Wig, a light coloured Broad Cloth Jacket, burnt with the Sparks of a Smith's Fire, a white Flannel ditto, without Sleeves, tweel'd, and made lappell'd Fashion, with Yellow Metal Buttons, Two Osnabrig Shirts, Two Pair of Country Linen Trowsers, and a Pair of old half Boots: He is a very great Rogue, and it is very probable he will change his Name and Cloaths.

Whoever takes up and secures said Servant in any Jail, so that the Subscriber may have him again, shall receive THIRTY SHILLINGS Reward, and if 20 Miles from home, THREE POUNDS, and if 40 Miles, SEVEN POUNDS TEN SHILLINGS, and reasonable Charges, if brought home, paid by   ALEXANDER WELLS.
N. B. All Masters of Vessels are forewarned to harbour said Servant on board at their Peril.

The Maryland Gazette, September 17, 1767; *The Maryland Gazette*, September 24, 1767; October 1, 1767; October 8, 1767; October 15, 1767; October 22, 1767; October 29, 1767; November 5, 1767; November 12, 1767. The last three ads give the runaway's first name as JACOB. See *The Maryland Gazette*, March 10, 1768, for Prichet/Pritchard.

SIX POUNDS REWARD.

RAN away on Sunday Evening, the 30th of *August* last, from the *Patuxent* Iron-Works, the Three following Convict Servant Men, (lately brought in by the *Thornton*, Capt. *Reed*) viz.

JOSEPH SMITH, an old Man, a Gypsie, very much resembling a swarthy Mulatto in Colour: Had on and took with him, an Osnabrig Shirt, Crocus Trowsers, a light coloured Cloath Great-Coat, a Kersey Waistcoat of the same Colour, a stript Linsey Ditto, an old Felt Hat, and a Pair of old Shoes.

WILLIAM SMITH, a Gypsie, aged Forty Years, or thereabout, Brother to the said *Joseph*, and nearly of the same Colour: Had on, and took with him, a Check Shirt, one Osnabrig ditto, a blue Cloath Coat, trimmed with Twist Buttons, a blue double-breasted Waistcoat, a Pair of red Cloath Breeches, a Pair of Crocus Trowsers, a Pair of old blue Worsted Stockings, old Hat, and old Shoes.

JOHN SMITH, Son of the said *Joseph*, a strong hearty young Fellow, nearly of the same Complexion with that of his Father and Uncle: Had on, and took with him, when he went away, a tarnished Thickset Coat, a new Cotton Jacket, with grey Mohair Buttons, one Osnabrig Shirt, one Cotton or stript Holland ditto, a Pair of Crocus Trowsers, Sail-duck Breeches, trimmed with Leather Buttons, old Hat, old blue Worsted Stockings, and old Shoes.

Whoever takes up said Servants, or secures them, so that they may be had again, shall have the above Reward, or FORTY SHILLINGS for each, paid by   THOs. SAMl. & JOHN SNOWDEN.

The Maryland Gazette, September 17, 1767; September 24, 1767; October 1, 1767; October 8, 1767. See *The Maryland Gazette*, June 30, 1768, and *The Maryland Gazette*, August 3, 1769, for John Smith.

RUN away from the subscriber, living near Magotty-mill, on the head of the river, in Ann Arundell county, and province of Maryland, the 16th of August last, a convict servant man, named George Williams, thin visage, short black hair, which curls, is about 5 feet 7 inches high, and has an impediment in his speech; had on, when he went away, a brown coat, flannel waistcoat, brown linen shirt, and trowsers, with old shoes. As this is the second time of his transportation to America, he may be artful enough to deceive any person who examines him, and make them believe he is no runaway. Whoever secures him in any goal, so that he may be had again, shall receive Three Pounds reward, if taken in Pennsylvania.
WILLIAM MACCUBBIN, son of John.

The Pennsylvania Gazette, September 17, 1767; September 24, 1767; November 19, 1767.

PORT-TOBACCO, *Sept.* 2, 1767,
BROKE Jail, and made their Escape, on Tuesday, the 1st Instant, the following Persons, Sailors, *viz.*

HUGH BURNEY, an *Irishman*, about Five Feet Eight Inches high; had on a blue Jacket, and Sailor's Trowsers.

CHARLES SWANN, a *Dane*, about Five Feet Four Inches high; had on a blue Jacket, and Sailor's Trowsers.

CORNELIUS SULLIVAN, an *Irishman*, a thick clumsy Fellow, about Five Feet high; had on a brown linen Shirt, Negro Cloth Breeches, and a red Calf-Skin Cap.

THOMAS LOFTIS, Country born, a slim tall Man, a Ship Carpenter, had on a blue Broad-Cloth Coat and Jacket, and Buckskin Breeches.

Whoever apprehends the said Persons, and secures them in any Jail, or delivers them to the Subscriber, shall receive TWO PISTOLES for each.
CHARLES S. SMITH, Sheriff.

The Maryland Gazette, September 24, 1767; October 1, 1767; October 8, 1767.

Prince-George's County, Sept. 12, 1767.
SEVEN POUNDS Reward.
BROKE Jail, last Night, the Two following Fellows, *viz.*

JOHN STABLER, for House-breaking, about 5 Feet 5 or 6 Inches high, of a pale Complexion, and down Look: Had on a light coloured Coat, an old Hat, Osnabrig Shirt and Trowsers, no Shoes nor Stockings.

RICHARD ADWELL, a suspected Runaway, about 5 Feet 10 Inches high, of a sandy Complexion, a pert Fellow, but a great Coward: Had on a yellowish Waistcoat, without Sleeves, old white Shirt, and Osnabrig Trowsers, and old Hat, a yellow Wig, no Shoes nor Stockings.

Whoever takes up the said Fellows, or either of them, and delivers them to the Subscriber, shall receive for *John Stabler*, FIVE POUNDS Currency, and for *Richard Adwell*, FORTY SHILLINGS.
Wm. T. WOOTTON, Sheriff.

The Maryland Gazette, September 24, 1767. See *The Maryland Gazette*, December 3, 1767, for Adwell/Cross.

SIX POUNDS Reward.
RUN away from the Subscriber, living on Elkridge, two Convict Servant Men, viz. Thomas Stafford, an Irishman, about 21 Years of Age, a tall slim Fellow; had on, when he went away, a short brown Kersey Coat, an Ozenbrigs Shirt and Trowsers, old Shoes, a brown Wig, and a pretty good Felt Hat. Christopher White, a native Irishman, has much of the Brogue upon his Tongue, pitted with the Small-Pox, is about 30 Years of Age, full 6 Feet high, and is a stout able bodied Fellow; had on, when he went away, a Snuff coloured Broadcloth Coat, a brown Wig, and a Felt Hat, fine Linen Shirt, Thread Stockings, and black Leather Shoes; it is supposed they have changed their Apparel, or will endeavour to change them. Whoever takes up and secures said Runaways, so as their masters may have them again, shall have if taken in Ann-Arundel County, Twenty Shillings Reward, besides what the Law allows for each, and if out of the County, Three Pounds for each, including what the Law allows, and if brought home, reasonable Charges, paid by   HENRY OWINGS, and THOMAS BEACH.

The Pennsylvania Gazette, September 24, 1767; November 19, 1767; December 10, 1767.

RUN away from the Subscriber, in Cecil County, Sasquehannah Hundred, Maryland, a likely Irish Servant Woman, named Mary Delany, about 24 Years of Age, can sew well, and likes to be employed in that Way, has sandy coloured Hair, about 5 Feet 6 Inches high, speaks with the Brogue, is a good Scholar, and perhaps will change her Name. She took with her two

Gowns; the one a white twilled Cotton, pretty much worn; the other a Calicoe, of a purple Stamp, Check Apron, old quilted black Petticoat, a Pair of old Stay Boddice, and black Calimancoe Shoes; an old Pewter Tea Pot, and midling large Prayer Book. Whoever secures said Servant in any Goal, or otherwise, so that her master may have her again, shall have TWENTY SHILLINGS Reward, and reasonable Charges, paid by
JOHN COOPER.

The Pennsylvania Gazette, September 24, 1767; November 19, 1767.

TWENTY DOLLARS REWARD.

MADE his Escape from BALTIMORE County Jail, on Thursday the 10th of *September* last.

THOMAS KING, (committed for Felony,) born in *Pennsylvania*, and bred to the Sea, about 35 Years of Age, 5 Feet 3 or 4 Inches high, sharp Nose, pitted with the Small-Pox, bow-legg'd, and wears dark curl'd Hair. As he has sundry Cloathing with him, his Dress cannot be describ'd. Whoever apprehends the said KING, and secures him in any Jail in this Province, shall receive the above Reward, paid by
ROBERT ADAIR, Sheriff.

The Maryland Gazette, October 1, 1767; October 8, 1767; October 15, 1767; October 22, 1767; October 29, 1767.

TEN POUNDS REWARD.

September 22, 1767.

RAN away from the *Kingsbury* Furnace Mine-Bank, near BALTIMORE, the Three following Servants, *viz.*

WILLIAM HATTON, (*i. e.* JACKSON,) by Trade a Stocking-Weaver, about 28 or 30 Years of Age, and about 5 Feet 6 or 7 Inches high; has a down Look, and a remarkable Way of staring any Person in the Face that speaks to him, stout made, fresh Complexion, and light brown Hair: Had on, and took with him, One Felt or Castor Hat, with a Metal Button to it; One Osnabrig, and One Dowlas Shirt, an old red Jacket, an old green short Hunter's Coat, with Pockets under the Arms, and yellow Metal Buttons, One Pair of Osnabrig Drawers, and One Pair Buckskin Breeches, black ribb'd Worsted Stockings, *English* Falls, and a Pair of square plated Buckles. This is the second Time he has ran away these Three Years.

THOMAS CHAPMAN, a pale looking Fellow, about 25 Years of Age, 5 Feet 3 or 4 Inches high; has a Scar under his Chin, and a remarkable Cast with his Eyes; wears a brown Wig, or a Cap, a new Felt Hat, a white Dowlas, or Osnabrig Shirt; has on, or with him, One Cotton, and One Fearnought Jacket, a Pair of Buckskin Breeches, a Pair of Osnabrig

Drawers, a Pair of Thread, and a Pair of Yarn Stockings, Country-made Shoes, with Nails in the Heels, and several other Things unknown.

SAMUEL SMITH, *(i. e.* SIMMONDS,) by Trade a Barber, about 22 or 23 Years of Age, 5 Feet 3 or 4 Inches high: Had on, and took with him, an old black Coat, a Thickset ditto, an old red double-breasted Jacket, with Metal Buttons, black Breeches, strip'd Trowsers, an old Dowlas Shirt, black Stockings, an old Felt or Castor Hat, One Pump, and One Shoe.

Whoever apprehends the said Servants, so as they may be had again, shall receive FORTY SHILLINGS Reward for each, if taken in this Province; and, if taken out of the Province, the above Reward, and reasonable Charges, if brought to the Subscriber, at the above Furnace, paid by   FRANCIS PHILIPS.

N. B. HATTON and CHAPMAN went off together, the other about the Middle of *August* last.

The *Maryland Gazette*, October 1, 1767; October 8, 1767; October 15, 1767; October 22, 1767; October 29, 1767. See *The Maryland Gazette*, September 27, 1764, for Hatton, *The Pennsylvania Gazette*, October 1, 1767, for all three, *The Maryland Gazette*, March 10, 1768, for Hatton and Chapman, *The Maryland Gazette*, September 8, 1768, *The Pennsylvania Gazette*, September 15, 1768, and *The Pennsylvana Gazette*, July 6, 1769, for Hatton.

TEN POUNDS Reward.

RUN away from the Kingsbury furnace mine bank, near Baltimore town, the three following servants, viz. WILLIAM HATTON, or JACKSON, by trade a stocking weaver, about 28 or 30 years of age, and about 5 feet 6 or 7 inches high, has a down look, and a remarkable way of staring any person in the face that speaks to him, stout made, fresh complexion, and light brown hair; had on, and took with him, the following things, viz. one felt or castor hat, with a metal button to it, one ozenbrigs and one dowlas shirt, old red jacket, old green short hunter's coat, with pockets under the arms, and yellow metal buttons to it, one pair of ozenbrigs drawers, one pair buckskin breeches, black ribbed worsted stockings, English falls, one pair of figured square plated buckles. This is the second time the said Hatton has been convicted within three years.

THOMAS CHAPMAN, a pale looking fellow, about 25 years of age, and about 5 feet 3 or 4 inches high, has a scar under his chin, a remarkable cast with his eyes, and wears a brown wig or cap; had on, and took with him, one new felt hat, white dowlas or ozenbrigs shirt, one cotton, and one fearnought jacket, buckskin breeches, one pair of ozenbrigs drawers, one pair of thread, and one pair of yarn stockings, country made shoes, with nails in the heels, brass buckles, with tongues and anchors of the same, and several other things unknown.

SAMUEL SMITH, or SIMMINS, by trade a barber, about 22 or 23 years of age, and about 5 feet 3 or 4 inches high; had on, and took with him, one old black coat, and one thickset ditto, old red double breasted jacket, with metal buttons, black breeches, striped trowsers, old dowlas shirt, black stockings, old felt or castor hat, and one pump, and one shoe. It is supposed they will forge passes, and change their names. Whoever apprehends the said servants, so that they may be had again, if in the province, Forty Shillings for each, if out of the province, the above reward, and reasonable charges, if brought to the subscriber, at the furnace aforesaid, to be paid by Kingsbury furnace, Sept. 22, 1767.   F. PHILLIPS.

N. B. Hatton and Chapman went off this day together, and Smith about the middle of August last.

The Pennsylvania Gazette, October 1, 1767. See *The Maryland Gazette*, September 27, 1764, for Hatton, *The Maryland Gazette*, October 1, 1767, for all three, *The Maryland Gazette*, March 10, 1768, for Hatton and Chapman, *The Maryland Gazette*, September 8, 1768, *The Pennsylvania Gazette*, September 15, 1768, and *The Pennsylvania Gazette*, July 6, 1769, for Hatton.

THREE PISTOLES REWARD.

September 21, 1767.

RAN away, from the Subscriber, living in *Queen-Anne's* County, *Maryland*, in the Night of the 27th of *June* last, a Convict Servant, named THOMAS LAMPREY, about 28 Years of Age, about 5 Feet 10 Inches high; fair Complexion, wears his own Hair, if not cut off since he went away, of a fair Colour, and which he takes great Pride in; he is a little marked with the Small-Pox, and has a small Scar under one of his Eyes. Had on, and took with him, a light coloured Broad-Cloth Coat, with a small Velvet Collar, brown or snuff-coloured Jacket, dark strip'd Linen Trowsers, a new Felt Hat, old Pumps, one of which was patch'd at the Toe; but, as he has Money with him, he may perhaps buy new ones. He likewise stole, and took with him, a dark brown Horse, about 13 Hands high, in good Order when he went away; has a Snip on his Nose; one of his fore Hoofs is split almost up to the Hair, with a Saddle and Bridle, but his Marks are unknown. He says he is a Wool-Comber and Stocking-Weaver; and has often importun'd his Master to sell him to his Trade, at, or near *German-Town*. He has been a Soldier in the Foot Guards at Home, and says he was convicted for attempting to commit a Rape upon a Woman there.

Whoever takes up and secures said Man, so as he may be had again, shall receive the above Reward, and reasonable Charges, paid by

NATHAN FARROW.

All Persons are forbid to buy said Horse; and all Masters of Vessels, or others, are forbid harbouring or carrying off said Servant.

The Maryland Gazette, October 1, 1767. See *The Pennsylvania Gazette*, July 16, 1767.

TWENTY POUNDS Reward.

RUN away the 16th ult. from NATHAN DORSEY, on Elk Ridge, the following servant men, viz. Thomas Owens, an Irishman, about twenty five years of age, a stout well set fellow, about 5 feet 8 or 9 inches high, hath short dark coloured hair, is pitted with the small pox, and speaks good English; had on and took with him, when he went away, a blue broadcloth coat, a blue cloth jacket, without sleeves, a brown holland jacket lapelled, black knit breeches, old thread stockings, and a pair of old yarn ditto, ribbed, a pair of old shoes, a felt hat, about half worn, one brown linen shirt, and one check linen ditto, and one pair of oznabrigs trowsers.

James Ridgely, a tall slim fellow, pale look, short brown hair, has a large nose and roguish look, can write a good hand, and will probably forge a pass, had on a blue cloth coat, a white shirt, a brown country linen jacket, with pearl buttons, oznabrigs trowsers, a pair of pumps, and white thread stockings, they went in company with a tall slim fellow, who had red hair, and a grey wig; took with him a nankeen jacket, and white shirt, and oznabrigs trowsers; he is advertised to have lately broke Queen Ann's Goal. Whoever takes up the said servants, and secures them, so as their masters may have them again, shall have a reward, if taken within 20 miles, of Forty Shillings, if in Arundel or Baltimore county, Three Pounds, if out of those counties, and in the province, Five Pounds, and if out of the province, Ten Pounds for each, and reasonable charges, if brought home, paid by

JOHN DEAVER, of Baltimore Town, or NATHAN DORSEY, on Elk Ridge.

N. B. It is supposed the said servants will make to Philadelphia, as the said Owens has a brother living there.

The Pennsylvania Gazette, October 1, 1767; December 3, 1767. See *The Pennsylvania Gazette*, November 26, 1767, for Owens/Owings.

OCTOBER 15, 1767.

FIFTEEN DOLLARS Reward.

BROKE Jail, on Friday last, the 9th of this Instant,

WILLIAM SPEAKS, a Ship-Carpenter, was late Master Builder at Mr. *Phillip's* Yard, on *Bush-River*, born in *Virginia*, about 30 Years of Age, of middle Stature, square, and well made, dark Complexion, wears dark brown straight Hair, and commonly wears blue Cloaths, which Dress he went away in; he is an active young Fellow, and brags much of his Manhood: He went down the Bay in a Pettiaguer, and is supposed to made for the Eastern-Shore. He carried with him a Negro Boy, about 18 Years of Age.

    Whoever apprehends the said *William Speaks*, and brings him to *Baltimore* County Jail, shall receive the above Reward.
ROBERT ADAIR.
The Maryland Gazette, October 15, 1767; October 22, 1767.

Port-Tobacco, October 10, 1767.

RAN away from the Subscriber, a Convict Servant Man, named MICHAEL MAHONEY, an *Irishman*, by Trade a Tailor, about 5 Feet 6 Inches high, well made, and about 28 Years of Age, of a dark Complexion, much pitted with the Small-Pox, dark Hair, cut very short, and shaved before: Had on when he went away, a dark coloured Wig, a Pompadour coloured Broad Cloth Coat, a Jacket, with the Fore-Parts of cut Velvet, with the Flowers of a dark Crimson, and white Colour, the Back-Parts of red Stuff, and gilt Twist Buttons, light coloured Cloth Breeches, the Buttons, Holes, and Knee-bands of which, are all much wore. It is probable he has a forged Pass, and assumes another Name.—Whoever takes up the said Servant, and brings him to the Subscriber, or secures him, so as he may be had again, shall receive a Reward of THREE POUNDS, if taken in the County; and if out of the County, FIVE POUNDS, paid by
GEORGE BRICHAN.
The Maryland Gazette, October 15, 1767; October 22, 1767; October 29, 1767; November 5, 1767; November 12, 1767.

FIVE POUNDS Reward.

RUN away, the second of October inst. from the subscribers, living in Maryland, and in Frederick county, near Hawling's river, an Irish servant man, named Johnston M'Annelly, has high education, and was just set up to teach school, he talks much, seems to be about 25 years of age, is about 5 feet 8 or 10 inches high, fair complexion, his hand spotted with freckles, and wears his own short hair, which is of a redish colour; his apparel, a coat of a blue grey colour, a striped flannel jacket, breeches of very coarse cloth, an old coarse shirt, yarn stockings, and common shoes. Whoever takes up the said man, and brings him home to either of subscribers, shall have the above reward, paid by
JOHN MUSGROVE, EDWARD GAITHER, or HENRY GAITHER.

N. B. He has some relations living at Philadelphia, calls himself Daniel Johnston M'Annelly, and has forged a pass.

The Pennsylvania Gazette, October 22, 1767; November 5, 1767; November 12, 1767.

RAN away from the Subscriber, living at *Swan-Creek, Baltimore* County, on Saturday the 3d Instant, in the Evening, a Convict Servant Man, named ABRAHAM WILD, born near *Manchester*, in *England*, and speaks very much in that Dialect, by Trade a Weaver, a short well-set Fellow, about 5 Feet 4 inches high, swarthy Complexion, wears his own Hair, which is brown: Had on, and took with him, a white coloured Cloth Coat, half trimmed, and a white coloured Jacket, the Sides of both are pieced with Cloth of another Colour, Buckskin Breeches, half wore, and is very short for him, an Osnabrig Shirt, whitish coloured Yarn Stockings, old Shoes Brass Buckles, and an old Felt Hat; but may alter his Dress, as he took other Things with him. It is supposed he has a Pass.

Whoever takes up said Servant, and brings him to the Subscriber, shall receive FIVE POUNDS Reward, and reasonable Charges, paid by
AMOS GARRETT.

The Maryland Gazette, October 29, 1767; November 5, 1767; November 12, 1767; November 19, 1767. The last three ads show he ran away "on Saturday the 3d of *October* last, in the Evening". See *The Pennsylvania Chronicle, and Universal Advertiser*, November 11, 1767. Wild and White are assumed to be the same person.

Caecil County, November 3, 1767.
RUN away from the SUBSCRIBER, a native Irish servant man, named *Edward Coalman,* by trade a skinner and leather breeches-maker, makes great profession of that business; is very talkative, and much addicted to swearing; is about 5 feet 8 inches high, pretty lusty, of a black complexion, and his beard much so; very positive in his answers, and very seldom answers yes or no, but I will, or I did, or I will not, or I did not, &c. is about 30 years of age, came from Ireland last March with one Captain White: Had on, and took with him, a good felt hat, bound with a black ribbon, an old brown wig, an old white shirt, and a check ditto, short brown jacket, with sleeves, and back of a different sort, and two white ditto, one flowered with needle work, oznabrigs trowsers, old leather breeches, old camblet ditto, and perhaps he may make himself another pair of breeches, as he took some skins with him, two pair of worsted stockings, one pale blue, the other blue and white, old black grained leather shoes, and brass buckles. Whoever takes up and secures said servant, so that his master may have him again,

shall have SIX DOLLARS reward, and, if brought home, reasonable charges paid, by HENRY BAKER.

The Pennsylvania Chronicle, and Universal Advertiser, From Monday, November 2, to Monday, November 9, 1767; November 11, 1767; From Monday, November 16, to Monday, November 23, 1767.

RUN away from the subscriber, living at Swan-Creek, in Baltimore county, on Saturday the 3d instant at night:—A convict servant man named Abraham White,—born near Manchester in England, and speaks much with that dialect, by trade a linen weaver, a short well-set fellow, swarthy complexion, wears his own brown hair. Had on and took with him, a whitish coloured cloth coat, half trimmed, and let out in the sides with cloth of another colour, a jacket of the same kind of cloth, and the same let out in the sides, having been for a person of a smaller stature, half-worn buckskin breeches, very short for him, oznabrigs shirt, black ribbed stockings, old shoes, brass buckles, and an old felt hat; but may alter his dress, as he took other things with him:—He has been seen since he went away in company with a woman, who it is expected may pass for his wife, she is of low stature, she is either a Scotch or Irish woman, of a fair Complexion, the widow of one Mullen, and by her own account, has often travelled in Pennsylvania and Maryland, and it is probable they may make for Philadelphia or the eastern-shore of Maryland, and it is expected they have stole some vessel to cross Susquehanna in.

Whoever takes up and secures said servant, that he may be had again, shall receive FIVE POUNDS reward, and if brought home, reasonable charges, of AMOS GARRETT.
Octob. 27, 1767.

The Pennsylvania Chronicle, and Universal Advertiser, From Monday, November 2, to Monday, November 9, 1767; November 11, 1767; From Monday, November 16, to Monday, November 23, 1767. See *The Maryland Gazette*, October 29, 1767. Wild and White are assumed to be the same person.

FIVE POUNDS Reward.

RAN away from the Subscriber, living at *Ante-Eatam*, *Frederick* County, a Servant Man, named WILLIAM BRIGGS, born in *Charles* County, about 26 Years of Age, fair Complexion, Five Feet Two Inches high, a very talkative Fellow, fond of Company, Gambling, and Liquor: Had on, when he went away, a blue Cloth Coat, black Jacket, and Breeches, with Sundry Changes of other Jackets, and Breeches; also a Blanket Coat. It is supposed he went to the lower Parts of this Province, or into *Virginia*.—Whoever

takes up, and secures said Servant, in any Jail, so that his Master may have him again, shall receive the above Reward, and reasonable Charges, paid by JAMES KENNEDY.
The Maryland Gazette, November 12, 1767.

Baltimore County, *Nov.* 12. 1767.
EIGHT DOLLARS Reward.

RAN away from the Subscriber, an *English* Convict Servant Man, named WILLIAM THOMSON GILLIARD, about 30 Years of Age, a tall slender Fellow, with a full Mouth, lively dark Eyes, pale round Face, and short dark Hair: Had on, and took with him, an old Racoon Hat, a Coarse light grey Cloth Coat, light coloured Broad Cloth Jacket, has been turn'd, and the Button Holes closed on the wrong Side, a Pair of old red Stockings, wove Breeches, a Pair of Tow Linen Trowsers, wears an old Penny tied about his Neck, under his Shirt, with a Silk Cord: He has been Cook to the Duke of NORTHUMBERLAND, and travelled thro' England, Ireland, and France; can speak French, and has been employed as a Schoolmaster. He took away with him a young bright Sorrel Horse, with a white Tail and Mane, has a Blaze in his Face, paces, no Brand, with a good Saddle and Housing. It is likely he will change his Name, and forge a Pass.

Whoever takes up, and brings said Servant to his Master, shall receive THREE POUNDS Reward.
ABRAHAM JARRETT.
The Maryland Gazette, November 12, 1767; November 17, 1767; November 26, 1767; December 3, 1767. See *The Pennsylvania Gazette*, November 12, 1767.

RAN away from the Subscriber, an *Irish* Convict Servant Man, named HUGH CLARK, a Tanner by Trade, about 25 Years of age, 5 Feet 9 inches high, wears a small long Lock of Hair behind: Had on, when he went away, a coarse brown Coat and Breeches, much stained with Leather, a Check Shirt, coarse Stockings, middling good Shoes, and a pretty good Felt Hat; he had an Iron Collar on, though it is possible he has got it off. Whoever takes up said Servant, and brings him to his Master, shall receive a Reward of FORTY SHILLINGS, if taken in the Province; and, if out of the Province, THREE POUNDS, paid by   VACHEL WARFIELD.
The Maryland Gazette, November 12, 1767.

FOUR DOLLARS Reward.
RUN away from the subscriber, an English convict servant man, about 30 years of age, named William Thomson, alias Thomson Gilliard, imported in

the ship Thornton, Captain Reid, last July; he is a tall slim man, with a full mouth, lively dark eyes, pale round face, short black hair, wears an old small racoon hat, coarse grey cloth or frize coat, light coloured, broad cloth jacket, which has been turned, and the button holes closed on the wrong side, a pair of old red stocking wove breeches, and a pair of tow linen trowsers; he is a cook and confectioner by trade, and has been in the service of several great men in England, Ireland and France, speaks French, writes a good hand, and will probably change his name, and forge a pass. He stole away a young bright sorrel horse, with a blaze in his face, and white tail and mane, paces a travel, [sic] and has no brand, with a good saddle and housings. Whoever takes up and secures the said servant, that his master may have him again, shall receive the above reward, and reasonable charges, if brought home, paid by
ABRAHAM JARRETT, in Baltimore county.
The Pennsylvania Gazette, November 12, 1767; December 3, 1767.
See *The Maryland Gazette*, November 12, 1767.

Carlisle goal, Cumberland county, October 24, 1767.
WAS committed some time ago, to said goal, on suspicion of being runaways, the two following persons, viz. JACOB KESLER, a young Dutch lad, has since confessed that he belongs to John Roop, Shoemaker, living in Second street, between Arch and Race streets; the other was committed by the name of ANDREW KEAZ, but has since confessed his name to JOE DIXON, is a slender, thin faced, little fellow, a collier by trade, speaks the Spanish and Portugueze tongues well, says he was born in Fyall, and is well acquainted about Baltimore Town. Their masters, if any there be, are hereby notified to come, forthwith, and take them away, otherwise they will be sold, in a short time, for their expences,
by HENRY CUNNINGHAM, Goaler.
The Pennsylvania Gazette, November 12, 1767. See *The Pennsylvania Gazette*, November 26, 1767.

Kent-Island, November 19, 1767.
RAN away from the Subscriber, a Convict Servant Man, named JOSEPH HAINES, about 30 Years of Age, and about 5 Feet 5 Inches high, swarthy Complexion, short black Hair, and his Beard grey, his Body is much scarified, if well look'd into, his Cloaths are uncertain; it is thought he is a good Scholar, writes a pretty good Hand, and drolls in his Speech.
Whoever takes up and secures said Servant, so as his Master may have him again, shall receive Four Dollars Reward, paid by
JOHN LEGG.

The Maryland Gazette, November 19, 1767; December 3, 1767; December 31, 1767; January 21, 1768; January 28, 1768; February 4, 1768; February 11, 1768.

November 16, 1767.
RAN away last Sunday Evening, from the Subscriber, living at the Head of SEVERN, a Convict Servant Man, named JOHN TREND, by Trade a Weaver, about 28 Years of Age, 5 Feet 6 Inches high, much pitted with the Small-Pox, and wears his own Hair, which is short, and of a light Colour: Had on, when he went away, a green Cloth Upper-Jacket, patch'd on the Sleeves with Cloth of a different Colour; a double-breasted Under-Jacket, of a leaden Colour, with Leather Buttons; an old Pair of white drill Breeches, with a blue Patch on the left Thigh; a Pair of old white Stockings, and old Shoes and Hat.

Whoever takes up or secures said Fellow, so as I may get him again, shall receive a reward of TWENTY SHILLINGS, besides what the Law allows, and reasonable Charges, if brought home, paid by
EDWARD OSMOND.

The Maryland Gazette, November 19, 1767; November 26, 1767; December 3, 1767; Devember 10, 1767; December 17, 1767.

Anne-Arundel County, *November* 24, 1767.
RAN away last Night, from the Subscriber, living near *Patapsco* Ferry, an *English* Convict Servant Man, named BARTHOLOMEW CROSS, about 30 Years of Age, a tall slender Fellow, sandy Complexion, and has a scald Head: Had on when he went away, a brown *Devonshire* Jacket, a Nankeen ditto under it, old white Shirt, a new Pair of brown Half-thick Breeches, with one Pocket, a Pair of black and white Stockings, footed with white Yarn, an old Pair of *English* Shoes, two old Felt Hats sewed together round the Edge with blue Yarn, and a new worsted Cap. Whoever takes up said Servant and brings him to the Subscriber, or secures him so as he may be had again, shall have a Reward of TWENTY SHILLINGS if taken in the County, and FORTY SHILLINGS if out of the County, besides what the Law allows, paid by   CHRISTOPHER GARDENER.

He broke *Queen-Anne* Jail sometime in *September* last, and went by the Name of *Richard Adwell*.

The Maryland Gazette, November 26, 1767; December 3, 1767; December 10, 1767; December 17, 1767; December 24, 1767; December 31, 1767; January 7, 1768; January 21, 1768; January 28, 1768. See *The Maryland Gazette*, September 24, 1767, for Adwell.

TEN POUNDS Reward.
RUN away, the 16th inst. from the Subscriber, living in Baltimore Town, an indented Irish Servant, named Thomas Owings, a stout well set Fellow, about 25 Years of Age, has a large Mouth, and speaks good English, wears short brown Hair; had on, and took with him, a blue Cloth Coat, half worn, an old Snuff coloured Coat, a white Flannel Jacket, lappelled, without Sleeves, a Pair of blue coarse Cloth Breeches, lined with Ozenbrigs, quite new, a Pair of coarse yarn Stockings, ribbed, Country made Shoes, an old Felt Hat, and Ozenbrigs Shirt; he is a Plaisterer by Trade, and his Cloaths are stained with Lime. He stole and took away with him, a large black Gelding, a Man's Hunting Saddle, with Buckskin Seat, and an old Bridle; the Horse is lame in his Shoulder, has constantly been used in a Waggon, paces heavy, and is shod all round; it is supposed he has stole some other Cloaths, may have a Pass, and change his Name; he has been in the Country about four Months. Whoever takes up and brings him said Servant, shall have Five Pounds Reward, and for the Servant and Horse, the above Reward, paid by   JOHN DEAVER.
The Pennsylvania Gazette, November 26, 1767; December 24, 1767; January 7, 1768; January 28, 1768; March 10, 1768; April 14, 1768.
See *The Pennsylvania Gazette*, October 1, 1767, for Owens/Owings.

Carlisle goal, Cumberland county, October 24, 1767.
WAS committed some time ago, to said goal, on suspicion of being a runaway, a person who called himself ANDREW KEAZ, but has since confessed his name to JOE DIXON, is a slender, thin faced, little fellow, a collier by trade, speaks the Spanish and Portugueze tongues well, says he was born in Fyall, and is well acquainted about Baltimore-Town. His master, if any he has, is hereby notified to come forthwith, and take him away, otherwise he will be sold, in a short time, for his expences, by HENRY CUNNINGHAM, Goaler.
The Pennsylvania Gazette, November 26, 1767; December 3, 1767.
See *The Pennsylvania Gazette*, November 12, 1767.

December 9, 1767.
RAN away from the Subscriber, living in *London-Town*, on *South-River*, an Indented Servant Man, named WILLIAM COOKE, born in *Staffordshire*, in *England*, and has been in most parts of *Ireland*, is about 5 Feet 6 Inches high, has a small Lump in his Forehead, a Mole on his left Cheek, thin Visag'd, and dark Eyes: Had on, when he went away, a Coarse Hat, bound round with Worsted Binding, thin black Hair, tied behind, and curled, a short grey Half-thick Coat, and Breeches, with black Horn Buttons on the

Breeches, old Scarlet Cloth Waistcoat, turn'd, white Yarn Stockings, turn'd Pumps, white Shirt, and Muslin Stock, with a Brass Buckle: He may have other Cloaths with him, and probably will change his Name. He has been in the *East-Indies*, on board a Man of War, and boasts much of it, when drunk, in which he will not fail, if he can get Liquor. He was seen in *Annapolis*, on Monday Night, drunk. It is supposed he will go over the Bay, if he can.

Whoever takes up said Servant, and brings him home to his Master, shall receive THIRTY SHILLINGS, if taken within Ten Miles from *Annapolis*, and, if farther, THREE POUNDS Reward, and reasonable Charges, paid by ALEXANDER FERGUSON.

He is a Taylor by Trade, and may pass for a Stay-maker, as he has work'd at that Business some Time.

The Maryland Gazette, December 10, 1767; December 17, 1767; December 31, 1767; January 7, 1768; January 21, 1768; January 28, 1768. See *The Maryland Gazette*, January 5, 1769.

December 16, 1768.

RAN away last Night from the Subscriber, living at *Elk-Ridge* Landing, an indented *Irish* Servant Man, named EDWARD EAGAN, a Taylor by Trade, about 20 Years of Age, 5 Feet 6 or 7 Inches high, has much of the Brogue, a full-fac'd Fellow, well-set, pitted with the Small-Pox, has strait black Hair, and 'tis likely he has forged a Pass, as he can write a pretty good Hand. Had on and took with him, a mixed coloured Cloth Coat with long Skirts, Nankeen Jacket, spotted Flannel ditto, mixed coloured Cloth Breeches, Two Check Shirts, blue Country made Stockings, Felt Hat, Country made Shoes, and several other Cloaths. Whoever takes up the said Servant, and secures him so as his Master may have him again, shall receive a Reward of Twenty Shillings, besides what the Law allows, paid by
RICHARD HARDESTY.

The Maryland Gazette, December 17, 1767; December 31, 1767; January 7, 1768.

New Castle county, December 16, 1767.

NOW in the goal of said county the following persons, viz. Bartholomew Johnson, aged about 35 years, of a fair complexion, had on, when committed, a suit of blue clothes, much abused, as if he wore them on his passage to this country; he says he came in with Captain Jeremiah Bennet, to Maryland.

Also William Sheppard, about 20 years of age, by trade a taylor, about 5 feet and a half high, and very slender made; had on, when committed, a white broadcloth coat, with black knit breeches; he confesses that he left Captain Langly at Philadelphia.

Likewise Curtis Cat, aged about 35 years, of a middle size; had on, when committed, a sailor's jacket, of a red colour, with black breeches; he also confesses he left Captain Stewart, of the province of Maryland. The masters of said servants are desired to come in 4 weeks from this date, and pay their fees, and take them away, or they will be sold for the same by THOMAS PUSEY, Goaler.

The Pennsylvania Gazette, December 17, 1767; December 24, 1767; December 31, 1767; January 7, 1768.

SIXTEEN DOLLARS Reward.

BROKE out of *Dorchester* County Jail, on Sunday the 13th of *December* Instant, one EDWARD HUSSEY, (alias *James Rush*) being committed on Suspicion of Horse-Stealing. He is about Five Feet Eight Inches high, of a dark Complexion, wears his own Hair, and has a very dull heavy Countenance: Had on, when he broke out, a brownish colour'd coarse Cloth Coat, Waistcoat, and Breeches; his last Place of Residence was near *William Stewart's* Tavern, in *Kent* County, and 'tis very probable he may endeavour to secret himself about that Neighbourhood.

Whoever apprehends the said Fellow, and brings him to the Subscriber, shall be paid the above Reward, and all reasonable Charges, by ROBERT HARRISON, Sheriff.

The Maryland Gazette, December 24, 1767; December 31, 1767; January 14, 1768. See *The Maryland Gazette*, March 31, 1768.

December 21, 1767.
FIVE POUNDS Reward.

RUN away from the subscriber, living in Chester-Town, Maryland, the 14th of December instant, a Servant Man, named LOCHLAN RIAN, about 5 Feet 8 Inches high, of a fair pale Complexion, and wears his own black Hair: He had on, and took with him, a dark Frize Coat, white Cotton and lappelled Fearnought Vests, a Pair of half worn black Plush Breeches, a Pair of half worn English shoe Boots, good Country Shoes and Stockings, and a good Hat. He rode a small white Horse, and an English Saddle, half worn; he is supposed to be now in Philadelphia, as he was seen there about 4 or 5 Days ago. Whoever takes up the said Servant, and secures him, so as he may be had again, shall have the above Reward, and reasonable Charges if brought home, paid by EMORY SUDLER.

The Pennsylvania Gazette, December 24, 1767; December 31, 1767; January 7, 1768; January 14, 1768. Only the first two ads have the date at the top.

Prince-George's County, *Dec.* 17, 1767.
FIVE POUNDS REWARD.

RAN away, last Night, from the Subscribers, a Convict Servant Man, named JOHN EVANS, a Tailor by Trade, about Five Feet Eight Inches high, has short black Hair, and a smooth Face and Look, and stammers much when surprized: Had on, and carried with him, an old blue Surtout Coat, with Metal Buttons, a brown Sagathy Suit, lined with white, the Waistcoat has Metal Buttons; a brown lapell'd Frize Waistcoat; a white Flannel ditto; a new Castor Hat, Yarn Stockings, white and check Shirts; a blue Ratteen Pair of Breeches, and several other Things unknown. He also took with him a likely bay Horse, about 14 Hands high, has a small white Spot on the End of his Nose, branded on the near Shoulder and Buttock, O S; a good Saddle, with large Swivel Stirrups, a blue fringed Cloth Housing, stripp'd Swanskin Saddle Cloth, and Snaffle Bridle.

Whoever secures the said Servant and Horse, so that they may be had again, shall have Three Pounds for the Horse and Saddle, and Forty Shillings for the Servant, and reasonable Charges, if brought home, paid by BASIL WARING, JOHN WARING.

The Maryland Gazette, December 31, 1767; January 7, 1768; January 21, 1768; January 28, 1768. See *The Maryland Gazette,* September 18, 1766.

1768

COMMITTED to *Queen-Anne's* County Jail, on Suspicion of being a Runaway, a certain JOHN M'GUMRY, an *Irishman,* aged about 23 Years, has with him, an Osnabrig Shirt, an old white Vest, and an old brown ditto, a Pair of old stripped [*sic*] Trowsers, one Pair of old Shoes.—Any Person claiming the aforesaid *John M'Gumry,* is desired to take him away, pay Charges, and the Expence of this Advertisement.
Jas. BUTLER, Jailer
The Maryland Gazette, January 7, 1768.

RAN away from the Subscriber, living in *Frederick* County, near *George-Town, Maryland,* a Convict Servant Man, named JAMES JOHNSON, alias *Ingram,* about 18 Years of Age, 5 Feet 3 Inches high, has short black Hair, is much pitted with the Small-Pox, and has been employed as a Schoolmaster. Had on, and took with him, a new Forrest Cloth Coat, with Mohair Buttons, a white Broad Cloth Jacket, which was a little too large for him, a Pair of white Serge Breeches, a white Shirt, and a Pair of Shoe Boots that has been lately Soled, a Castor Hat, and brown great Coat, about half worn, He likewise took with him, a bright bay Horse, about 14 Hands high, with a Star in his Forehead, paces, very fast, trots and gallops; had a Man's new Saddle, Saddle-Cloth, and a blue Housing.

Whoever takes up said Servant, and delivers him to his Master, shall receive Three Pounds Reward, and Thirty Shillings for the Horse.
JOHN CLAGETT.

The Maryland Gazette, January 14, 1768; January 21, 1768; January 28, 1768; February 4, 1768; February 11, 1768.

January 1, 1768.

RAN away from the Subscriber, in *November* last, an *Irish* Convict Woman, named MARY FLOYD. She was imported in *October* 1766, in the *Randolph*, Capt. Price. She is of a middle Stature, thin visag'd, has light brown Hair, a fresh Complexion, and is very bold and talkative. Her Dress is uncertain, as she has been harboured and entertained a considerable Time in the City of *Annapolis*.

Whoever takes up the said Convict Servant Woman, and commits her to any Jail, shall receive a Reward of FOUR DOLLARS, on applying to EDMUND JENNINGS.

The Maryland Gazette, January 21, 1768; January 28, 1768; February 4, 1768; February 11, 1768.

Prince-George's County, *Jan.* 10, 1768.

RAN away from the Subscriber, living within Four Miles of *Bladensburg*, an Apprentice Lad, named DAVID HENNIS, by Trade a Cordwainer and Tanner, near 18 Years of Age, about 5 Feet 10 Inches high, of a ruddy Complexion, with dark brown Hair, tied behind: Had on, when he went away, a spotted Swanskin Jacket, a black Broad Cloth ditto, pretty much worn, an Osnabrig Shirt, a Pair of old Buckskin Breeches, and Osnabrig Trowsers, a Pair of white Yarn Stockings, a Pair of Fall Shoes, with Buckle-Straps, and an old Felt Hat, very much worn.

Whoever takes up said Apprentice, and brings him to the Subscriber, or secures him in any Jail, shall receive a Reward of Thirty Shillings, if taken in the County, if out of the County, Forty Shillings, paid by Jail, shall receive a Reward of Thirty Shillings, if taken in the County, if out of the County, Forty Shillings, paid by   RICHARD BEALL.

The Maryland Gazette, January 21, 1768; January 28, 1768; February 4, 1768; February 11, 1768.

Baltimore-Town, January 11, 1768.
COMMITTED to my Custody, on Suspicion of being Runaways, and are now lying in *Joppa* Jail, the following Persons, *viz.*
    A Negro Fellow, who calls himself JACK....
    ELISABETH BRYAN, a thin visag'd Woman, of small Stature, has a high Nose, and is very handy at her Needle. She says she served her Time in Philadelphia, to one of the Name of *Tolly.*
    MICHAEL OBILDER, about 5 Feet 2 or 3 Inches high, he is full faced, and about 20 Years of Age; and says he bound himself to a certain *William Greenfield,* in *Patapsco* Neck, in *Baltimore* County.
Now lying in the Jail in BALTIMORE-TOWN,
    JOHN HINES, an *Irishman,* says he is a Servant to *William Hide,* near *Bladensburg,* is about 35 Years of Age, 5 Feet 8 Inches high, and has been lately shot in the left Thigh, near his Ham, which he says was done in *Virginia,* when he formerly ran away: He wears a grey Wig, has a new white Cotton Jacket and Breeches, and Country Stockings and Shoes.
    A Negro Fellow....
    WILLIAM JOHNSTON, *alias* MALONE, a Painter by Trade, and appears to be the same as is advertis'd in the *Philadelphia* Papers, by *John Gratton,* of *Brox's Gap,* in *Augusta* County, *Virginia.*
    Whoever owns any of the above Servants or Slaves, are desired to come, and fetch them away, within the Time limited by Law, and to pay Fees and Charges, otherwise they will be sold for the same, as the Law directs.   DANIEL CHAMIER.
    Sheriff of *Baltimore* County.

The Maryland Gazette, January 28, 1768; February 4, 1768; February 11, 1768; February 18, 1768; February 25, 1767; March 10, 1768; March 17, 1768; March 24, 1768.

RUN away from the subscriber, living in *King's-Town, Queen Ann's* county, *Maryland,* an *Irish* servant woman, about 24 years of age, of a fresh complexion, is supposed to have had on when she went away, a red stuff gown and petticoat, but her dress is uncertain, as she carried other clothes with her. She is thought to have gone off with a couple of sailors, deserted from the ship *Randolph,* Captain *Price,* lying at *Chester* town, *Kent* county. Whoever takes up said woman, and confines her in any gaol, so that her master may have her again, shall have *Twenty Shillings* reward, and all reasonable charges, paid by   JOHN BIRSTALL.

Queen Ann's, Jan. 24, 1768.
The Pennsylvania Chronicle, and Universal Advertiser, From Monday, January 25, to Monday, February 1, 1768. See *The Pennsylvania Chronicle, and Universal Advertiser*, From Monday, February 8, to Monday, February 15, 1768.

COMMITTED to *Kent* County Jail, on Suspicion of being Runaways, a certain *William Hudson,* and *James Smith,* who say they are Servants to *William Groves* of *Baltimore* County.
 Their Master is desired to take them out of Jail, or they will be sold for their Fees.   J. NICHOLSON, Sheriff of Kent County.
The Maryland Gazette, February 4, 1768; February 11, 1768; February 18, 1767; February 25, 1767; March 3, 1768; March 17, 1768; March 24, 1768.

Philadelphia, February 1, 1768.
WHEREAS JACOB DECAMP, servant to John Beale Boardley, Esq; of Baltimore town, Maryland; GEORGE JACK, servant to Henry King, of Chestnut Ridge, Baltimore county, Maryland; THOMAS WILKINSON... JOHN FREDERICK HARBURN...JOHN M'DERMOTT...JOHN CARROLL...ISAAC BEATE...and ANDREW PEELE, servant to Dr. Boyd, of Baltimore; being confined in the public goal of this county, as runaway servants, public notice is hereby given to the masters of the said servants, that I intend to apply to the court of quarter sessions, to be held in the city of Philadelphia, for the county of Philadelphia, on Monday, the 7th day of March next, for an order to sell the said servants for their fees, unless their masters redeem them before that time.
JEHU JONES, goaler.
The Pennsylvania Gazette, February 4, 1768; Febuary 11, 1768.

RUN away from JOHN BENNETT, hatter, at Talbot Court house, Maryland, an apprentice lad, named Oliver Bush; had on when he went away, a blue jacket, made sailor fashion, bearskin breeches, a wool hat, new shoes. Whoever takes up and brings home the said apprentice, shall have FORTY SHILLINGS reward. All persons are forewarned not to harbour him at their peril.   JOHN BENNETT.
The Pennsylvania Gazette, February 11, 1768

RUN away from the subscriber, living in *King's-Town*, *Queen Ann's* county, *Maryland*, an *Irish* servant woman, named *Martha Carr*, about 24 years of age, of a fresh complexion, is supposed to have had on when she went away, a red stuff gown and petticoat, but her dress is uncertain, as she carried other clothes with her. She is thought to have gone off with a couple of sailors, deserted from the ship *Randolph*, Captain *Price*, lying at *Chester* town, *Kent* county. Whoever takes up said woman, and confines her in any gaol, so that her master may have her again, shall have *Twenty Shillings* reward, and all reasonable charges, paid by
JOHN BIRSTALL. *Queen Ann's, Jan.* 24, 1768.
 N. B. Said Servant was in *New-Castle* gaeol along [sic] time, and left it about nineteen months ago.
 The Pennsylvania Chronicle, and Universal Advertiser, From Monday, February 8, to Monday, February 15, 1768. See *The Pennsylvania Chronicle, and Universal Advertiser*, From Monday, January 25, to Monday, February 1, 1768, for the unidentifed woman runaway.

RAN away from the Subscriber, living on the great Road, near *Abbot's* Town, *York* County, *Pennsylvania*, a Servant Man, named JOHN LAMB, about 5 Feet 7 Inches high, and about 25 Years of Age, of a ruddy Complexion, long visaged, brown Hair, pretty long, speaks thick, and has a stern Look, is apt to swear, and much given to drinking, and is by Trade a Taylor: Had on, when he went away, a pretty good Suit of blue Cloaths, with *Bath* Metal Buttons, and his Cloaths is much greased.
 Whoever takes up said Servant, and secures him in any Jail, so as the Subscriber may have him again, shall receive Five Pounds Reward, and reasonable Charges, paid by Mr. *George Stricker*, in *Frederick-Town*, *Maryland*, Mr. *Bryan Bruen*, Merchant in *Winchester*, or the Subscriber, living at *Brook's* Gap, *Augusta* County, *Virginia*.
JOHN GRATTAN.
 The Maryland Gazette, February 18, 1768; March 3, 1768; March 17, 1768.

RAN away on the 24th of *January* last, an indented Servant Man, named THOMAS THROP, a thick well-set Fellow, about 5 Feet 8 or 10 Inches high, much pitted with the Small-Pox, has light brown Hair, and a remarkable large Foot: Had on when he went away, an old Snuff coloured Broad Cloth Coat, and Waistcoat, the Coat has a Velvet Cape, with the Button-holes, and the Pocket-flaps bound round with Ferret, near the Colour of the Coat, a Pair of old Leather Breeches, an Osnabrig Shirt, a Pair

of Country made Shoes, and a Felt Hat, bound round with Linen. Whoever takes up the said Servant, and delivers him to the Subscriber, shall have a Reward of THREE POUNDS, and reasonable Charges, paid by
THOMAS HOPKINS.
The Maryland Gazette, February 18, 1768; February 25, 1768; March 10, 1768. The third ad has "*Talbot* County, *February* 1, 1768." at the top.

RUN away from the subscriber, at the head of Bush River, in Baltimore county, Maryland, on the 26th day of December last, a Dutch servant man, named GASPER BREEMER, a stout able fellow, about 6 feet high; he had on when he went away, a claret coloured broad cloth coat, the rest of his dress now known, he came into America, in Captain Thompson, in the year 1764, to Baltimore town, and brought in with him three children; one he put out in Baltimore town, and the other two in York county, Pennsylvania, where it is believed he has gone amongst his countrymen. Any person that will secure the said servant, so that he may be had again, shall receive FIVE POUNDS reward, and if brought back, reasonable charges, paid by
AQUILA HALL.
The Pennsylvania Gazette, February 25, 1768; March 3, 1768; March 10, 1768.

Carlisle goal, Cumberland county, Feb, 4, 1768.
NOW in said goal, on suspicion of being runaways, the following persons, viz. William Hartsworth, who says he belongs to William Coal, senior, of Baltimore county, at Western Run, Maryland; also John M'Kissock, or M'Castlen, supposed to belong to Mr. Chase, an attorney in Annapolis, he is a bluff faced young fellow, about 5 feet 7 or 8 inches high, black hair, and pretty thick built. William Pettison...their masters, if they have any, are desired to come forthwith, and take them away, otherwise they will be sold for their fees and expences, in 5 weeks after the date hereof, by
HENRY CUNNINGHAM, Goaler.
The Pennsylvania Gazette, February 25, 1768; March 3, 1767; March 17, 1768.

March 8, 1768.
RAN away from the Subscribers, living near the Mouth of *Great Choptank* River, on Sunday the 6th of this Instant, an *Irish* Servant Man, named THOMAS BYRNE, is about 5 Feet 3 or 4 Inches high, and is a little round shouldered, fair Complexion, and wears his Hair tied behind, and is much

addicted to the Principles of Free Masonry: Had on, when he went away, a new Snuff coloured Coat, with a small Cape, and an old white Broad Cloth Vest, Leather Breeches, and a Black Handkerchief round his Neck, a Country Linen Shirt, and an old Hat.—Whoever takes up said Servant, and secures him in any Jail, shall be well satisfied for their Trouble, beside what the Law allows, paid by ANTHONY & WILLIAM LECOMPE.

The Maryland Gazette, March 10, 1768; March 17, 1768.

March 8, 1768.
TEN POUNDS REWARD.

RAN away last Night from *Kingsbury* Furnace, in *Baltimore* County, the Three following Servants, *viz.*

THOMAS HAWKES, aged about 30 Years, 5 Feet 9 or 10 Inches high, thin Visage, brown Hair, slow of Speech, thick of Hearing, and has a Mole between his Eyes: Had on, when he went away, a Fearnought and Cotton Jacket, a Calico ditto, a white Linen Shirt, and an Osnabrig ditto, Cotton Breeches, or light coloured Cloth ditto, Worsted Hose, and ribb'd Thread ditto, Felt Hat, Country made Shoes, and some other Things unknown.

WILLIAM HATTON, *(i. e.)* JACKSON, by Trade a Stocking-Weaver, aged about 28 or 30 Years, 5 Feet 6 or 7 Inches high, light brown Hair, has a down Look, and a remarkable Way of staring any Person in the Face that speaks to him, has a Scar from the Side of his Mouth to his Chin, is stout made, and a fresh Complexion: Had on, and took with him, when he went away, a Fearnought Jacket, a blue Duffle, a Cotton, and a blue lappelled ditto, Cotton Breeches, Check Shirt, Osnabrig ditto, ribb'd Yarn Stockings, Country made Shoes, Metal Buckles, and Felt Hat.

THOMAS CHAPMAN, a pale looking Fellow, 25 Years of Age, 5 Feet 3 or 4 Inches high, has a Scar under his Chin, a remarkable Cast with his Eyes, and short black Hair: Had on, and took with him, when he went away, a Fearnought Jacket, Cotton ditto, and Breeches, a pretty good Felt Hat, Osnabrig Shirt, ribb'd Yarn Hose, Country made Shoes, and Metal Buckles.

Whoever apprehends the said Servants, so that they may be had again, shall receive FORTY SHILLINGS for each, if taken in this Province, and if out of the Province, the above Reward, and reasonable Charges, if brought to the Subscriber. FRANCIS PHILLIPS.

The Maryland Gazette, March 10, 1768; March 17, 1768; March 24, 1768; March 31, 1768; April 7, 1768; April 14, 1768. See *The Maryland Gazette*, March 31, 1763, for Hawkes, *The Maryland Gazette*, September 27, 1764, for Hatton, *The Maryland Gazette*,

October 1, 1767; for Hatton and Chapman, *The Maryland Gazette*, September 8, 1768, *The Pennsylvania Gazette*, September 15, 1768, and *The Pennsylvania Gazette*, July 6, 1769, for Hatton.

February 21, 1768.
FIFTEEN POUNDS Reward.

RAN away, last Night, from the Subscriber, living near the *Soldier's Delight*, in *Baltimore* County, *Maryland*, the Two following Convict Servant Men, *viz.*

JOHN KINGHAM, an *Englishman*, a good Scholar, and is about 27 Years of Age, 5 Feet 10 Inches high, he has a long Visage, a full Mouth, but a pleasant Countenance, speaks hoarse, has a small Scar over his left Eye, has lost one of his Fore-Teeth in the Upper-Jaw on the right Side, and he stoops in his Walk: He had on and took with him, a new Felt Hat, a dark grey coloured Surtout Coat, Cloth Cape, and Velvet Neck, with some spots of Tar on the Coat; a grey Country Cloth Jacket, with Sleeves, a black Broad Cloth Jacket, much worn, Buckskin Breeches, grey Yarn Stockings, and Country made Shoes, and One Holland, and Two Osnabrig Shirts, and sundry other Things unknown.

JACOB PRITCHARD, a Skinner by Trade, about 5 Feet 6 Inches high, 26 Years of Age, born in the West of *England*, and talks broad, has lost some of his Fore-Teeth in the Upper Jaw, he is knock-knee'd, stoops in his Walk, and has short brown Hair: Had on, and took with him, a Castor Hat, a blue grey Cloth Coat, burnt with Smith's Fire, Two Pair of Buckskin Breeches, white Yarn Stockings, double soled Shoes, one Holland Shirt, and Two coarse ditto; with sundry other Things unknown.—They took with them Two Horses and Saddles, one of them is a dark Bay, and has a crooked Blaze down his Face, light Flanks, and some White on his Feet, 4 Years old, and about 13 Hands 3 Inches high, and is branded on the near Buttock with the letters **A W**, (joined together) and had on a small Hunting Saddle.—The other is a light Bay, with a large Star in his Forehead, if any Brand, unknown, and had on a Saddle with a blue fringed Plush Housing. Both Horses pace, trot, and gallop.—They also took with them a small Gun, with a curl'd Mapel Stock, Five Deer Skins, half drest, and one Match-Coat Blanket.—It is supposed they will forge Passes, and perhaps may change their Names and Cloaths.

Whoever takes up or secures said Servants, so as their Master may have them again, shall receive a reward of THREE POUNDS for each Man, and THIRTY SHILLINGS for each Horse and Saddle, if Twenty Miles from home; and if Forty Miles from home, FIVE POUNDS for each Man, and FIFTY SHILLINGS for each Horse and Saddle, and reasonable Charges, if brought home, paid by   ALEXANDER WELLS.

The above *Jacob Pritchard* ran away last Fall, and got over the *Allegheny* Mountains, and was, on his Travels, at the South Branch of *Patowmack*.

The Maryland Gazette, March 10, 1768; March 17, 1768; March 24, 1768; March 31, 1768; April 7, 1768. See *The Maryland Gazette*, September 17, 1767, for for Prichet/Pritchard.

New-Castle, March 1, 1768.

WAS committed to the jail of this county, the 2d day of February last, a certain EDWARD WARRAN, on suspicion of breaking out of the jail of Frederick county, in Maryland, having been committed there (as is supposed) for felony. He is about 28 years of age, about 5 feet 6 inches high, well set, of a ruddy complexion, and has short black hair; had on, when committed, a brown country cloth coat, white cloth waistcoat, and buckskin breeches. The keeper of the said jail, if he has any demands against the said WARRAN, and all others, are desired to take notice, that unless they appear in four weeks from this date, and take the said WARRAN out of this jail, and pay his fees, he will be discharged.
By order of the court at New-Castle, this 29th of February, 1768
THOMAS PUSEY, Jailer.

The Pennsylvania Gazette, March 10, 1768, March 17, 1768.

February 27, 1768.
TEN POUNDS REWARD.

STOLEN out of the Subscriber's STABLE, in *York-Town*, last Night, a large dark brown GELDING, about 15 Hands high, a natural Pacer, with a large Star in his Forehead, long Neck, and holds his Head very high. Also a black GELDING with a bald Face, Four white Legs, paces, trots, and hand gallops, very sprightly, and of a good Carriage, the property of Mr. *John Ord*. The Thief's Name is JAMES BIGGAR; he was Twice whipt in *Carlisle*, for Horse-stealing, was in Prison in *Maryland*, and *North-Carolina*; he is about 5 Feet 8 Inches high, fair Complexion, wears his Hair, has an old Blanket-Coat, an old blue Coat, old striped Jacket, red Plush Breeches, and Leggings.—Whoever takes up the Thief and Horses, and brings them to the Subscriber, or to Mr. *Swearingham's* in *Frederick-Town*, shall have the above Reward, or Four Pounds for each Horse.
JAMES SMITH.

The Thief and Horses were seen, on Saturday Night, at *Tawny-Town*, and on Sunday crossed *Monokasy*.

The Maryland Gazette, March 17, 1768; March 24, 1768; April 14, 1768; April 21, 1768; April 28, 1768; May 5, 1768. The first two ads do not have a date at the top.. See *The Pennsylvania Gazette*, October 9, 1766, and *The Maryland Gazette*, December 1, 1768.

York Goal, in York Town.

WAS committed to my Custody, the 22d of November last, a certain MICHAEL M'DOWELL, as he calls himself, on Suspicion of murdering one Gibson, in Maryland, and of being a Runaway Servant; he is a short well-set Fellow, about 5 Feet 8 or 9 Inches high, about 25 Years of Age, wears his own Hair, and is a Shoemaker by Trade. As there has no Proof appeared against him, his Master is desired to come, if any he has, and pay Charges, and take him away, otherwise he will be sold out, in 30 Days after this Advertisement appears, for the Charges, by me
ALEXANDER RAMSAY, Goaler.
The Pennsylvania Gazette, March 24, 1768.

March 29, 1768.

BROKE out of *Queen-Anne's* County Jail, on the 26th of this Instant, the following Prisoners, *viz.*

JOSEPH NEVILL, about 25 Years of Age, Country-born, 5 Feet 8 Inches high, remarkable black Hair and Eyes, thin Visage, and brown Complexion: Had on a light coloured Country-made Coat, a blue lappell'd Cloth Vest, Leather Breeches, and good Shoes and Stockings.

EDWARD HUSSEY, Country-born, was committed for stealing a Negro and Mare; is about 23 Years of Age, 5 Feet 6 Inches high, a well-set Fellow, brown Complexion, and a remarkable Down-look: Had on a Snuff coloured Cloth Coat, and Vest, Leather Breeches, and good Shoes and Stockings.

JAMES FOWLER, about 22 Years of Age, Country-born, 5 Feet 10 Inches high, of a pale Complexion, thin Visag'd, a pert impudent looking Fellow, and wears his own Hair, which is of a brown Colour: Had on a blue lappell'd Vest, Leather Breeches, good Shoes, and white Worsted Stockings.

Whoever takes up said Prisoners, and secures them, or brings them to *Queen-Anne's* County Jail, shall receive, for *Nevill*, TEN POUNDS, for *Hussey*, FIVE POUNDS, and for *Fowler*, THIRTY SHILLINGS Reward, paid by   WILLIAM HINDMAN, Sheriff.
The Maryland Gazette, March 31, 1768; April 7, 1768; April 14, 1768; April 21, 1768; April 28, 1768; May 5, 1768. See *The Pennsylvania Gazette*, April 7, 1768. See *The Maryland Gazette*, December 24, 1767, for Hussey.

RAN away from the Subscriber, on the 28th of *October* last, living at the Head of *Hungre-River*, in *Dorchester* County, a Negro Fellow, named Tom....It is supposed he was carried away by one *John Shinton*, that went away for Debt, and it is imagined he will make for the Lower Part of *Virginia*, or *Carolina*, he went away in a small Shallop. The said *John Shinton* is a thick well-set Fellow, about 30 or 35 Years of Age, and about 5 Feet high, of a light Complexion, light coloured Hair, has large blue Eyes, a full Beard, and a heavy Look; his Apparel is uncertain.

Whoever takes up and secures said *Shinton*, and finds the Negro in his Possession, or where he has sold or hired him, shall receive TEN POUNDS, if taken out of the County, and if in the County, FIVE POUND Reward, paid by   ELLINER M'GRAW.

The Maryland Gazette, March 31, 1768; April 7, 1768; April 14, 1768; April 21, 1768.

RUN away, the Fifth of March inst. from CORNELIUS GAESON, Breeches-maker, in the City of Annapolis, an English Servant Man, named ROBERT DOWNING, a Breeches-maker by Trade (he is the Property of William Carlin, at Alexandria, in Fairfax County, Virginia) about 5 Feet 5 or 6 Inches high, of a dark Complexion, short black curled Hair, stoop shouldered, has a remarkable uncommon Way of walking; had on, when he went away, a Claret coloured Coat, black Waistcoat, and Leather Breeches. It is supposed he is gone to Philadelphia, as he has been seen in Baltimore-Town, and Nottingham, and he said he would go to Newport, Rhode-Island.

Whoever secures said Servant in any Goal on the Continent, so that his Master, or his Assigns, may have him again, shall receive EIGHT DOLLARS Reward, and reasonable Charges, paid by me
WILLIAM CARLIN.

The Pennsylvania Gazette, March 31, 1768; April 7, 1768; April 28, 1768; May 5, 1768.

BROKE out of Queen Ann's county goal, in the province of Maryland, on the 26th of March last, the three following prisoners, viz. JOSEPH NEVILL, about 25 years of age, country born, 5 feet 8 inches high, remarkable black hair and eyes, thin visage, and brown complexion; had on, a light coloured country made coat, blue lapelled cloth jacket, leather breeches, and good shoes and stockings. EDWARD HUSSEY, about 23 years of age, country born, 5 feet 7 inches high, a well set fellow, of a brown complexion, a remarkable down look; had on, a snuff coloured cloth

coat and jacket, leather breeches, good shoes and stockings; was committed for stealing a Negroe boy, and a Mare. And JAMES FOWLER, about 22 years of age, country born, 5 feet 10 inches high, of a pale complexion, and thin visage, a pert impudent looking fellow, wears brown coloured hair; had on, a blue lapelled vest, leather breeches, good shoes, and white worsted stockings. Whoever takes up said prisoners, and brings them to Queen Ann's county goal, or secures them, so as they may be had again, shall have Ten Pounds reward for Joseph Nevill; Five Pounds for Edward Hussey; and Thirty Shillings for James Fowler, paid by
WILLIAM HINDMAN, Sheriff.

The Pennsylvania Gazette, April 7, 1768; April 14, 1768; April 21, 1768; May 5, 1768. See *The Maryland Gazette*, March 31, 1768, and *The Maryland Gazette*, December 24, 1767, for Hussey.

RUN away, on the 29th of March last, from the Subscriber, living at the Head of Chester River, in Kent County, Maryland, a Convict Servant Man, named THOMAS RICHARDS, about 5 Feet 8 Inches high, well set, wears his Hair, is much pitted with the Small-Pox, and has lost his left Thumb, he is a Welchman, and speaks bad English: Had on, when he went away, a blue Fearnought Vest, Kersey under Ditto, and Breeches, old Shoes and Stockings, and Hat. Whoever takes up and secures the said Servant, so that his Master have him again, shall have Forty Shillings Reward, and reasonable Charges, paid by   JACOB COMEGYS.

The Pennsylvania Gazette, April 7, 1768; April 14, 1768; May 12, 1768. See *The Pennsylvania Gazette*, June 30, 1768.

FIVE POUNDS Reward.

RUN away, on the 29th of March last, from the Subscriber, living near Anti-Etam, in Frederick County, two convict Servants, one named FRANCIS WARD, an Englishman, by Trade a Stocking Weaver, a thick set Fellow, about 5 Feet 6 Inches high, has short red Hair, and lost one of his upper fore Teeth: Had on, a light coloured Jacket, with large flat Buttons, and two black Jackets, one of Broadcloth, half worn, with black Glass Buttons, the other flowered Stuff, with white Metal Buttons, half worn Leather Breeches, two Pair of light blue Worsted Stockings, new Shoes, two coarse white Shirts, and a Castor Hat. The other, a Welchman, named WILLIAM JONES, a slim Fellow, 5 Feet 8 or 9 Inches high, has short light Hair, tied behind, and is bald on the top of his Head: Had on, a dark brown Coat, with Catgut Buttons, a light coloured Summer Coat, half worn, with Mohair Buttons, an old red Flannel under Jacket, a brown Jacket with Sleeves, half worn Leather Breeches, with Strings at the Knees, two Pair of blue Worsted Stockings, old Shoes, two coarse white Shirts, and stole a Holland Shirt, and two Stocks. They formerly lived with William Reynolds, Tavern-keeper, at Annapolis. All Masters of Vessels are forbid to carry them off. Whoever takes up said Servants, and secures them in any Goal, so that their Master may have them again, shall have the above Reward, paid by WILLIAM REYNOLDS , Hatter, in ANNAPOLIS, or, the Subscriber, in Frederick County.   JOSEPH REYNOLDS.

The Pennsylvania Gazette, April 14, 1768; April 21, 1768; April 28, 1768; May 5, 1768.

FIVE POUNDS Reward.

MADE his escape from Caecil county goal, on Wednesday the 6th of this inst. April, Edward Johnson (committed for felony) born in Ireland, about 27 years of age, 5 feet 3 or 4 inches high, wears his own dark brown hair, tied behind, a long sharp nose, a little pitted with the small-pox, fresh complexion; it has been reported, that he went formerly by the name of Edward Carney; had on, when he went away, a short brown cloth coat, with large metal buttons, old buckskin breeches, grey yarn stockings, but no shoes. Whoever apprehends the said Johnson, and brings him to the goal in Charles-Town, in the aforesaid county, shall receive the above reward, and reasonable charges, paid by
W. MITCHELL, Sheriff of said county.

The Pennsylvania Gazette, April 28, 1768; May 5, 1768.

FOUR POUNDS Reward.

RAN away from the subscribers, living in Queen Ann's county, Maryland, the following servant men, viz. one named William Fetherson, a schoolmaster, a stout well set fellow, about thirty-six years of age, about five feet ten inches high, and has two moles on the side of his face, in a direct line between the corner of his mouth and his ear; had on and took with him, a blue broadcloth coat and vest, with yellow buttons; a white ditto, with black hair buttons, a pair of leather breeches half worn, with several small patches about the knees; a white sheeting linen shirt, an old black silk handkerchief, a good pair of shoes, a pair of pumps, and two pair of yarn stockings; a castor hat about half worn, an old great coat, scorched on the left side, and a slit on the right fore skirt, which it is thought, he let the other have, whose name is Stephen Rogers; he is about five feet six inches high, a thick well set fellow, and is about thirty years of age; he speaks in the west country dialect; he had on when he went away, a felt hat, about half worn, with a small hole burnt through the crown, an old jacket, an old shirt, and short wide trowsers of country tow linen; old grey ribb'd

stockings, a pair of old shoes (but it is thought the other will help him to better clothes) he has short brown hair; he has been a collier in his own country.—Whoever takes up and secures the said servants, so that their masters may get them again, shall have the above reward, or Forty Shillings for each, and reasonable charges if brought home, paid by
WILLIAM BENNETT, or THOMAS DEROACHBROOM.
N. B. As the said Fetherson is a good scholar, it is thought he will forge passes.

The Pennsylvania Chronicle, and Universal Advertiser, From Monday, April 18, to Monday, April 25, 1768; *The Pennsylvania Gazette*, April 28, 1768; May 26, 1768; June 9, 1768. Minor differences between the papers.

Loudoun County, *Virginia, April* 29, 1768.
FIFTEEN DOLLARS Reward.

RAN away from the Subscriber, living in *Loudoun* County, near *Rocky-Run* Chapel, Two *English* Convict Servant Men, both Blacksmiths, *viz.*

JOHN BENHAM, about 28 Years of Age, a slender made Fellow, stoops in his Shoulders, and has a very hoarse Voice, wears his own short Hair, is about 5 Feet 5 or 6 Inches high: Had on, when he went away, an Osnabrig Shirt, a short Cotton Jacket, Cotton Breeches, coarse Stockings, and Country Shoes or Pumps.

JOHN MILLER, a short well-set Fellow, wears his own short Hair, has a large Scar in his Forehead, is about 5 Feet 2 or 3 Inches high, and about 28 Years of Age, he talks very much, and is very deceitful: Had on, when he went away, a grey Bearskin Jacket and Breeches, an Osnabrig Shirt, no Stockings, and Country Shoes. They may both perhaps change their Dress, as they took with them Osnabrig Trowsers, and other Cloaths. They also took with them, a Negro Lad, named *Jack*....They stole out of my Stable, Two Horses, one a bay about 14 Hands high, shod before, has a Star in his Forehead, hanging Mane and Switch Tail, Brand not known; the other a large sorrel Horse, shod all round, has a Star in his Forehead, and goes well: The Negro Boy took with him, a small grey Horse, about 12 Hands high, with a Bob Tail.

Whoever takes up said Servants, and Negro, and brings them to my House, in *Loudoun* County, near *Rocky-Run* Chapel, shall receive the above Reward, and if taken apart, Five Pounds Reward for each.
WILLIAM CARR LANE,

t is supposed they have black'd themselves, as there was some Coal and Tallow found in a Kettle of theirs.

The Pennsylvania Gazette, May 5, 1768; May 12, 1768; May 26, 1768. See *The Maryland Gazette*, September 15, 1768.

EIGHT POUNDS REWARD.

May 2, 1768.

RAN away last Night from the Subscriber, living in *Frederick* County, about Seven Miles from *Bladensburg*, one WILLIAM SCOTT, an Overseer, a Country-born fellow, full-faced well made Man, about Twenty-two Years of Age, Five Feet Eight or Nine Inches high: Had on, and took with him, the following Cloaths, viz. a *German* Serge Coat, of a red and white Colour, a Nankeen Jacket, a Pair of Breeches on the same of his Coat, a Pair of black Worsted Stockings, a Pair of Thread ditto, a red spotted Silk Handkerchief, a Linen ditto, a good Castor Hat, and sundry other Things. It is supposed he took away with him a Convict Fellow, a likely well made Man, named WILLIAM ABBUTT, an Englishman, about Twenty-six Years of Age, Five Feet Eight Inches high, wears his own Hair, of a brownish Colour, tied behind: Had on, and took with him when he went away, a *German* Serge Coat, of a Leaden Colour, white Fustian Jacket, a Pair of Osnabrig Trowsers, Two *Holland* Shirts, and Two Pair of Yarn Stockings. They also took a dark bay Horse, about Fourteen and an Half Hands high, in very good Order, and well made, branded on the near Shoulder, **G. P**, and on the Buttock, **O**, also on the near Shoulder, **I**, and on the Buttock, **A**, has a Star in his Forehead, Bob Tail, fretted with Traces on the Sides, and is about Seven Years old; also a bay Mare, about Thirteen Hands Three Inches high, branded on the near Shoulder **I**, and on the Buttock, **A**, about Five Years old, an old Saddle, with a good blue fringed Housing, a Pair of Leather Bags, and a Broad-Sword. Whoever takes up the said Fellows, and brings them to the Subscriber, shall have Three Pounds Currency for each, and Twenty Shillings for each of the Creatures, paid by
JOHN ADAMSON.

N. B. It is supposed they will both change their Names, and Cloaths.

The Maryland Gazette, May 12, 1768; May 19, 1768; May 26, 1768.
See *The Maryland Gazette,* July 3, 1766, for Abbutt.

May 17, 1768.

RAN away from the Subscriber, in *St. Mary's* County, on the 2d of this Instant, an Indented Lad, named JAMES JOHNSTON, about 20 Years of Age, has been brought up as a Gentleman's Servant; he is about 5 Feet 5 Inches high, is very fond of Liquor. He carried with him a new Duroy Coat, and Shag lapell'd Jacket, and different Changes of Linen. He also carried with him a bay Horse, about 14 Hands high, with a bob Tail; paces, trots, gallops, and has a remarkable handsome Carriage, when in the Bridle.

Whoever secures said Fellow, so that I can get him again, shall have THREE POUNDS Reward, and the like for the Horse.
THOMAS KEY.

The Maryland Gazette, May 19, 1768; June 2, 1768; June 9, 1768; June 16, 1768; June 23, 1768; June 30, 1768; July 7, 1768; July 14, 1768.

TEN POUNDS Reward.

RUN away, the 26th of March last, from Frederick forge, in Frederick county, Maryland, at the mouth of Anti-Eatam creek, on Potowmack river, the two following servants, indented in London about July last; DAVID MEEK, a Scotchman, fond of strong drink, writes well, and is capable of any writing business, or being a schoolmaster, who was wholly employed as an assistant clerk at the said forges, and is about 24 years of age, 5 feet 8 or 9 inches high, pretty broad in his shoulders, with long black hair, which he sometimes ties behind, and sleeps in a kind of thin knit cap; he had on, and took with him, a coat and jacket of light coloured cloth, and a black jacket with sleeves, buckskin breeches, pieced in the seat, a little sullied, a good hat, and several white shirts, some of them ruffled and marked on the hip D. M. with red silk. THOMAS WILKINS, supposed to be an English man, and is about 26 years of age, about 5 feet 3 or 4 inches high, stoops in his shoulder, and has a short neck, with brown hair, a joiner and house-carpenter by trade; had on, and took with him, a coat, jacket and breeches, of grey coarse bearskin cloth, and a blue jacket, a small hat, old and rusty, and his other apparel but ordinary; I am informed they have a pass, or rather a discharge, signed Christopher Lowndes, perhaps on searching their baggage, which they carried in a wide short coarse linen bag, and a wallet, or a pair of trowsers, paper may be found that Meek has had some correspondence with Peter Brown, particularly in Edinburgh, his native place, and some kind of power to draw bills on his uncle, as he calls him. Whoever takes up the said servants, so as their master (Dr. David Ross, living in Bladensburg, Maryland) may have them again, shall be paid the above reward, or Five Pounds for either, and reasonable charges, if brought home (or to their master) by him, or by SAMUEL BEALL, junior, manager of the forges aforesaid.

The Pennsylvania Gazette, May 19, 1768; June 23, 1768; June 30, 1768; July 21, 1768; September 1, 1768.

Carlisle Goal, Cumberland County, May 12, 1768.
NOW in said Goal the following Persons, committed on Suspicion of being Runaway Servants, viz. MATTHEW TAYLOR, a little old grey haired

Man, wears a Leather Cap, says he belongs to Mr. John Gill, at Chestnut Ridge, in Baltimore County. ANGUS CAMPBELL, a well set young Fellow, with very black Hair, tied behind, smooth Face, and very swarthy, wears an old red Coat. And JAMES BARNETT, a tall slender Fellow, has short brown Hair, thin faced, out mouthed, peeked Chin, thin Beard, and very ragged Cloathing; the two last were taken up together, and had two Mares with them, which are supposed to be stolen; one is grey, with a very long Mane, the other black. The Masters of said Fellows, if any they have, are desired to come and take them away, otherwise they will be sold out for their Fees in four Weeks after the Date hereof, by
HENRY CUNNINGHAM, Goaler.

The Pennsylvania Gazette, May 19, 1768; June 9, 1768.

COMMITTED to *Prince-George's* County Jail. as Runaways. Negro SAM....

WILLIAM CLARK, an *Englishman*, about 5 Feet 6 Inches high, a well looking Fellow, about 30 Years of Age, has on his own dark coloured Hair, and a Sailor's Apparel: He says he is a Sailor, and well known to be a Free Man by Mr. *Edward Harriss*, of *Baltimore Town*. Their Masters are desired to take them away, and pay Charges, else they will be sold, as the Law directs.   WILLIAM T. WOOTTON, Sheriff.

The Maryland Gazette, May 26, 1768.

RUN away, on Sunday, the 15th of May inst. from the Subscriber, living in Baltimore County, Maryland, a Servant Man, named Richard Wickly, but has changed it to John White, in a Discharge, or Pass, he carries with him, he says he got from Captain Manley, of the Nottingham Man of War, or Merchantman; the said Servant wears a dark coloured Fearnought Jacket, a light coloured Ditto, lined with black, without Sleeves, a Tow Shirt, old Leather Breeches, old dark coloured ribbed Stockings, half worn Shoes, and old Metal Buckles in them; he also carried with him, a half worn fine Hat, a fine white shirt, and a Pair of ribbed Thread Stockings; he is about 5 Feet 9 or 10 Inches high, of a dark Complexion, down Look, and an Englishman born. Whoever takes up and secures the said Servant, so as the Subscriber, his Master, may have him again, or brings him to the Lower Ferry, on Sasquehannah, shall have Three Pounds Reward, if taken within ten Miles of Baltimore County, paid by   WILLIAM BONAR.
N.B. All Masters of Vessels are forbid to carry him off at their Peril.

The Pennsylvania Gazette, May 26, 1768; June 16, 1768; July 14, 1768.

FIVE POUNDS Reward.
RUN away, the 10th of May inst. from the subscriber, living in Frederick county, Maryland, the two following convicts, viz. JAMES DOBY, about 40 years of age, 5 feet 8 or 9 inches high, he has black hair, tied, a very large beard, somewhat grey, and is pitted with the small-pox; had on, and took with him, two cotton, and one white broadcloth waistcoats, a pair of old cotton breeches, black yarn stockings, ozenbrigs shirt, country made shoes, and a new felt hat; he is a sly artful fellow, very talkative when spoke to, and is a piece of a sailor. THOMAS GOOD, by trade a miller, a lusty well looking fellow, about 35 years of age, of a dark complexion, and about 5 feet 7 or 8 inches high, born in the north of England, and speaks broad; had on, and took with him, a Russia drab frock and breeches, an old cotton jacket, white broadcloth ditto, white yarn and grey worsted stockings, country made shoes, with strings, two ozenbrigs and two white shirts, and a grey cut wig: It is supposed they have wrote themselves a pass, as they were seen writing. Whoever will apprehend and secure the said servants, so that their master gets them again, shall have the above reward, of
CHARLES GREENBURY GRIFFITH.

The Pennsylvania Gazette, May 26, 1768; June 9, 1768; June 23, 1768; July 7, 1768; September 1, 1768; September 15, 1768.

Benedict, May 13, 1768.
RAN away on Tuesday Morning last, from the Subscriber, living in *Benedict-Town*, an Indented Servant Man, named JAMES CLARK, a Tailor by Trade, he is about Thirty-five Years of Age, Five Feet Six Inches high, of a pale Complexion, slow of Speech, and pretty much addicted to strong Drink: Had on, when he went away, a light coloured Broad Cloth Coat, Nankeen Jacket, and Sagathy Breeches; the Coat and Breeches about half worn, and the Jacket almost new; he carried with him only Two Shirts, one of them of very fine Holland, the other of little Value. Whoever takes up the said Servant Man, and secures him in any Jail in the Province, shall be entitled to a Reward of Fifty Shillings Current Money, and Five Pounds, if brought home.   ROBERT YOUNG.

The Maryland Gazette, June 2, 1768; June 9, 1768.

May 25, 1768.
RAN away, last Night, from on board the Snow *Sally*, now lying in *South-River*, a Servant Man, named *Thomas Jones*, a Groom by Profession; is of a brown Complexion, and wears a Cue Wig, or short brown Hair: He had on, when he went off, a Pair of Trowsers, and a white spotted Jacket, and had

other Cloaths with him, tied up in a Bundle. He made his Escape from the Vessel by Means of a Canoe.

It is not unlikely that he may pass for a Sailor; but, as he is an entire Stranger in the Country, its presumed he will be easily found. Whoever takes up said Servant, and delivers him to me, on board said Snow, shall have Twenty Shillings Reward, besides what the Law allows. And, it is hoped, that none of my Brother Captains will harbour, or carry off said Servant.   THOMAS SMITH.

The Maryland Gazette, June 2, 1768; June 9, 1768.

Wye-River, May 31, 1768.
THREE POUNDS REWARD.

RAN away last Night, from the Ship *Betsey*, Capt. *Love*, now lying in *Wye-River*, the following Seaman, *viz.*

WILLIAM COOK, of a middle Stature, ruddy Complexion, pretty lusty and full faced; the Top of his Head shaved.

JAMES THOMPSON, thin faced, pitted with the Small-Pox, and wears his own short Hair. They went away in a Canoe, and took with them all their Cloaths, and Bedding. 'Tis supposed they would make towards *Baltimore-Town*.

Whoever takes up the above Seamen, and secures them in any Jail, within this Province, shall be paid a Reward of THREE POUNDS, or THIRTY SHILLINGS for either of them.   ROBERT LOVE.

The Maryland Gazette, June 2, 1768; June 9, 1768; June 16, 1768.

Elk-Ridge Furnace, *May* 30, 1768.

RAN away, last Night, from the Subscriber, Two Convict Servant Men, *viz.*

JAMES RAIN, a Mason by Trade, about 35 Years of Age, 5 Feet 9 Inches high, of a brown Complexion, has short black Hair, large Eye-Brows, a frowning Down-look, large Legs, and talks in the West-Country Dialect: He took with him a Cotton Jacket and Breeches, a Pair of black and white Yarn Stockings, and a new Felt Hat.

THOMAS HUGHS, a Carpenter by Trade, about 25 Years of Age, 5 Feet 6 Inches high, has Brown Hair, and a pretty agreeable Way of Address, but often looks down, and has a large Nose, rising at the End; he has lately had a sore Leg, which is yet of a dark red Colour about the Small: [sic] Had on, when he went away, a blue Surtout Coat, with Brass Buttons, and a Belt to buckle round him. a red Plush Jacket, stained with black, on one Side of the Breast, with red Mohair Buttons, one Check Shirt, one white ditto, and a Pair of old black knit Breeches, a Castor Hat, bound round the Brim, with black Silk Ferrit, and a blue and white spotted Handkerchief. It is also supposed that they have taken with them, a black Cloth Coat, and one dark brown ditto, with green Lining, a Pair of *German* Serge Breeches, a red Plush Jacket, Two white Shirts, a Pair of striped Holland Trowsers, a black *Barcelona* Silk Handkerchief, a turned broad Cloth Coat, with white Lining, and Brass Buttons, with sundry other Things.

Whoever takes up the said Runaways, and brings them home, shall have, if taken 10 Miles from said Furnace, Thirty Shillings; if 20 Miles, Forty Shillings; if 40 Miles, Three Pounds; and if out of the Province, Six Pounds Reward, for each, (including what the Law allows) paid by
CALEB DORSEY.

N. B. Whoever takes up said Runaways, are desired to take great Care of them, for they are great Villains, and will try, if possible, to escape.

The Maryland Gazette, June 2, 1768; June 9, 1768; June 16, 1768; June 23, 1768; July 7, 1768; July 14, 1768; July 21, 1768; July 28, 1768; August 4, 1768; August 11, 1768; August 18, 1768; August 25, 1768; September 1, 1768; September 8, 1768. See *The Maryland Gazette,* January 12, 1769, and *The Pennsylvania Chronicle, and Universal Advertiser,* From Monday, January 9, to Monday, January 16, 1769, for Hughs.

May 30, 1768.

RAN away from the Subscriber, living in *Baltimore* County, on Sunday Evening the 29th Instant, the Two following Servants, viz. THOMAS STEVENS, a Convict, about 25 or 26 Years of Age, about 5 Feet 9 or 10 Inches high, has large round Shoulders, dark Hair, grey Eyes, his Nose stands forward in his Face, and has been in the Country about Ten Months: Had on, and took with him, a short black and white Country Cloth Coat, a white Country Cloth Waistcoat, a Pair ditto Breeches, a Pair of old Shoes, with Hob Nails in both Soles and Heels, Osnabrig Shirt, and old Castor Hat. It is supposed he has purchased new Cloaths, and has Cash with him. SARAH CONWAY, an indented *Irish* Servant, has been in the Country about Two Years, about 24 Years of Age, about 5 Feet high, pale Complexion, black Hair, grey Eyes, and is a good Spinner: Had on, and took with her, a blue and white Linsey Petticoat, a yellow and white ditto, a yellow and white Bed Gown, a Pair of Leather Shoes, a Pair of Stockings, a Dowlas Shift, a purple and white Calico Gown, and sundry Caps and Handkerchiefs. Whoever apprehends said Servants, and secures them, so that their Master gets them again, shall have, if taken in the County, Thirty Shillings each, if out of the County, Forty Shillings, and if out of the Province, Fifty Shillings, and reasonable Charges if brought home, paid by
THOMAS SOLLERS.

It is supposed they are gone by Water, and that the Man has a Discharge from a Man of War, or a Regiment, and it's likely they may pass for Man and Wife. T. S.

The Maryland Gazette, June 2, 1768; June 9, 1768; June 16, 1768; June 23, 1768; June 30, 1768; July 7, 1768; July 14, 1768.

RUN away from the subscriber, living in Talbot county, Maryland, a servant man, named JOHN DICK, a taylor by trade, but pretends to be a sailor, he has a forged discharge from Captain Hadding, commander of the ship Good Intent, and as it is supposed, has also a forged pass. He had on when he went away, a grey coloured serge coat, bound with black, a jacket the back part the same as the coat, the fore part of light coloured cloth, a pair of old trowsers, and black breeches under them, an ozenbrigs shirt, a half worn Carolina felt hat, a pair of country made shoes, a pair of yarn stockings, and a pair of thread ones; he is middling well set, about 5 feet 8 inches high, has a whitely look, and was born in Scotland. Whoever takes up the said servant, and brings him home, or secures him, so that his master gets him again, shall have Four Pounds reward, paid by
ROBERT HALL.

N. B. The said John Dick has run away ever since the 7th of May last. It is said he is gone towards Philadelphia.

The Pennsylvania Gazette, June 16, 1768; June 23, 1768; June 30, 1768.

London-Town, June 22, 1768.

RAN away last Night, from the Subscriber, a Convict Servant Man named MICHAEL CONAWAY, an *Irishman*, and speaks much in that Dialect: He is a little short Fellow, about 5 Feet high, has black curled Hair, and had on, when he went away, a white Fearnought Jacket, with broad white Metal Buttons, a Cotton Under-Jacket, a Pair of Cotton Breeches, much wore and tattered, tho' mended in several Places, an old slouch'd Felt Hat, Osnabrig Shirt, and a Pair of tolerable good Negro Shoes.

Whoever takes up and secures said Servant, shall receive a Reward of TWENTY SHILLINGS; and, if brought home, reasonable Charges, paid by WILLIAM BROWN.

***He has with him an old rusty Bayonet, which he pulled out of his Bosom, when a Negro Fellow attempted to bring him home.

The Maryland Gazette, June 23, 1768; June 30, 1768; July 7, 1768; July 14, 1768; July 21, 1768; July 28, 1768; August 4, 1768; August 11, 1768; August 18, 1768; August 25, 1768; September 1, 1768; September 8, 1768; September 15, 1768; September 22, 1768;

September 29, 1768. See *The Maryland Gazette*, June 11, 1767, for Conaway/Connaway.

Bladensburgh, May 31, 1768.

RAN away, last Night, from the Ship *Keith*, an indented Servant Man, belonging to the Subscriber, named WILLIAM STEWART, just imported in the said Ship. He is an *Irishman*, about 38 Years of Age, 5 Feet 8 or 9 Inches high: Had on, when he went away, a brown cloth Coat, with white Lining, a brown or blue Jacket, Buckskin Breeches, white Thread Stockings, and a ruffled Shirt. He is of a dark Complexion, has black Hair, tied behind, a little mixed with grey; he has little or no Beard, is bow-legged, and has One or Two small Moles on his right Cheek. Whoever brings said Servant to the Subscriber, at *Bladensburgh*, shall receive a Reward of THREE POUNDS, paid by   ROBERT DICK.

The Maryland Gazette, June 23, 1768; June 30, 1768; July 7, 1768; July 14, 1768.

May 30, 1768.

RAN away last Night from the Subscriber, living in *Frederick* County, near Mr. *James Brookes*, a Convict Servant Man, named WILLIAM BAKER, about 5 Feet 7 Inches high, has black Hair about 5 Inches long, thin Beard, slim made, dark Complexion, and a remarkable black Mole on his left Cheek: Had on and took with him when he went away, an old Felt Hat, with a Hole in the Crown of it, Osnabrig Shirt, Check ditto, dark Kersey Jacket, with large Horn Buttons, strip'd Flannel ditto, without Sleeves, Country Linen Trowsers, Crocus ditto, white Yarn Stockings, and old Shoes.

Whoever apprehends the said Servant, and brings him home, shall receive FORTY SHILLINGS Reward, paid by
RICHARD MORGAN.

The Maryland Gazette, June 23, 1768; June 30, 1768; July 7, 1768.

June 21, 1768.

RAN away from the Subscriber, living near the Mouth of *Magothy* River, in *Anne-Arundel* County, the 13th Instant, a Convict Servant Man, named JAMES GROVES, about 30 Years of Age, thin Visage, dark Complexion, black Hair, tied behind, and one of his Legs crooked: Had on, when he went away, a Fearnothing Jacket, an Osnabrig Shirt, a Pair of Crocus Trowsers, and Negro Shoes.

Whoever takes up said Servant, and brings him home, shall have FORTY SHILLINGS Reward, paid by

ANNE PETTIBONE.
The Maryland Gazette, June 23, 1768; June 30, 1768; July 7, 1768; July 14, 1768; July 21, 1768; July 28, 1768; August 4, 1768; August 11, 1768; August 18, 1768; August 25, 1768; September 1, 1768; September 8, 1768; September 15, 1768; September 22, 1768; September 29, 1768. No date on top for on Sept 15, 22, 29.

TEN POUNDS Reward.
RUN away, the 8th of November last, from the subscriber, living at the head of Bohemia, Cecil county, Maryland, the following persons, viz. JAMES BROADY, a native Irishman, aged 30 years, about 6 feet 2 inches high, sandy complexion; had on, when he went away, an old felt hat, pissburnt [sic] wig, white linen coat, long trowsers, and new shoes, but perhaps may change his clothes; he talks low, and has much of the brogue on his tongue. The other named ROBERT LOWRY, about 6 feet high, yellow complexion, large eyes, long visage, down look, his under lip hangs down, talks thick, forward in company, and much given to gaming; had on, when he went away, a small felt hat, bound round with black ferriting, an old brown wig, brown coat, with yellow buttons, striped jacket, long trowsers, and new shoes, but perhaps may change his clothes, as he took others with him. Whoever secures the above persons, so as the subscriber may have them again, shall receive the above reward, or FIVE POUNDS for Lowry and SIX for Broady, paid by
DANIEL TURNER.
The Pennsylvania Gazette, June 23, 1768; June 30, 1768; July 7, 1768.

June 12, 1768.
FIVE POUNDS Reward.
RUN away, from James Wroth, John Curbuc, and Oliver Hastings, living in Kent County, near Chester-Town, three Convict Servant Men; one a large brown complexioned Man, who has lost one of his Thumbs; another a small brown complexioned Man, with black Hair: The other, a slim Man, about 40 Years of Age, about 5 Feet 10 Inches high; had on, when he went away, a half-worn, Broadcloth Coat, and Vest, with white buttons, old Castor Hat, and took with him more Clothes, that cannot be described. Whoever secures the said Servants, so as their Masters may have them again, shall have the above Reward, and reasonable Charges, paid by
JAMES WROTH, OLIVER HASTINGS, and JOHN CURBUC.
The Pennsylvania Gazette, June 23, 1768; June 30, 1768.

June 23, 1768.

RAN away from the Subscriber, living at the Head of *Severn*, a Convict Servant Man, named WILLIAM CARTER, about 20 Years of Age, 5 Feet 6 Inches high, and has black curled Hair: He had on a blue Fearnought Jacket, a green double-breasted ditto, Osnabrig Shirt and Trowsers, old Shoes, and a new coarse Hat. Whoever takes up said Man, if Ten Miles from home, shall receive TEN SHILLINGS, besides what the Law allows, paid by
      EDWARD OSMOND.
He has a Razor with him, and 'tis thought he has a Pass.
The Maryland Gazette, June 30, 1768.

June 15, 1768.

RAN away from the Ship *Faquier*, lying at *Lyon's* Creek, in *Patuxent*, the Two following Sailors, *viz.* JAMES CONNELY, a short well-set Fellow, 24 Years of Age, fresh Complexion, and wears his own Hair. JAMES QUINDLAND, a short Man, aged 22 Years, of a pale Complexion, and wears his own Hair.

Whoever takes up the said Runaways, and secures them in any County Jail, shall receive one Pistole for each of them, besides what the Law allows, paid by   WILLIAM MAYNARD.
The Maryland Gazette, June 30, 1768; July 7, 1768; July 14, 1768; July 21, 1768.

June 27, 1768.

RAN away, last Night, from the *Patuxent* Iron-Works, the Two following Convict Servant Men, viz.

JOHN HILL, an *Englishman*, about 30 Years of Age, 5 Feet 7 or 8 Inches high, has a swarthy Complexion, and wears his own short black Hair: Had on, and with him, Two Osnabrig Shirts, and a Pair of Osnabrig Trowsers, old Felt Hat, old Cotton Jacket, and old Shoes.

JOHN SMITH, (a Gipsy, 5 Feet 7 or 8 Inches high, has a very dark Complexion, and wears his own short black Hair, and is dressed in the same Manner as *Hill*.

Whoever takes up said Servants, and secures them in any Jail, so that they may be had again, shall receive, if taken 10 Miles from home, Twenty Shillings; if 30 Miles, Thirty Shillings; and if 50 Miles, Fifty Shillings for each; and if brought home, reasonable Travelling Charges, paid by
THOs. SAMl. & JOHN SNOWDEN.
The Maryland Gazette, June 30, 1768; July 7, 1768; July 14, 1768; July 21, 1768; July 28, 1768; August 4, 1768; August 11, 1768. See *The Maryland Gazette*, August 20, 1767, for Hill, *The Maryland Gazette*, September 17, 1767, for Smith, and *The Maryland Gazette*, August 3, 1769, for both men.

June 18, 1768.

RUN away from the subscriber, living in Queen-Anne's County, near the head of Chester river, a Welch convict servant man, named Thomas Richards, about 30 years of age, well set, much pitted with the small-pox, wears his hair, of a brown colour, speaks bad English, has a down look, and has lost his left thumb, off at the upper joint, by his hand, and is about 5 feet 8 inches high; had on, and took with him, one fine shirt, one coarse ditto and trowsers, a half worn blue fearnought over jacket, home made kersey under ditto, old stockings and shoes, and an old castor hat. Whoever takes up and secures the said servant, so that the owner may have him again, shall have, if taken within 15 miles of home, Twenty Shillings, if further Forty Shillings, and reasonable charges, paid by
JACOB COMEGYS.

The Pennsylvania Gazette, June 30, 1768. See *The Pennsylvania Gazette*, April 7, 1768.

Baltimore Town, June 20, 1768.

TAKEN up, and committed to Baltimore Town Goal, on suspicion of being runaways, viz.

Timothy Mahony, an Irishman, about 5 feet 10 inches high, dark brown hair, tied behind, his nose somewhat bent more towards one side than the other, he writes a very good hand, and is well acquainted with the inhabitants at North-River, quite up to Albany, and from whence, he says, he came last March; he had on, when taken up, a ruffled shirt, with the mark cut out from the side gushet, and he is remarkably fond of liquor; a letter has been found, wrote by him, which he dates from Quebec, and therein mentions, that he left Sugar Loaf in March last, this letter was directed to Edmund Keho, on Cow-foot Hill, near the tanyard, New-York.

Richard Whitaker, or Whitacre, a shoemaker by trade, about 22 or 23 years of age, short black hair, has a mole under his right eye, near the ear, and another on the left side of his neck; he had, when taken, a leathern budget, with the words New-Jersey, in yellow or gold letters, in which are his tools; he produces a pass, signed John Jarman, one of his Majesty's justices of the peace for the county of Salem, which pass is supposed to be forged, it being very badly wrote, and much worse spelt; there was also found on him a bond, signed by John Buck, of Deerfield township, in the county of Cumberland, and province of West-Jersey, for 46 l. lawful money of West-Jersey, payable to Richard Whitaker, and witnessed by William M'Gill.

If not claimed, and fetched away, in one month from the date hereof, they will be sold out for their fees, by   DANIEL CHAMIER, Sheriff.

The Pennsylvania Gazette, June 30, 1768; July 14, 1768.

FIVE POUNDS Reward.

RUN away from the subscriber, living in the Fork of Gunpowder, Baltimore county, Maryland, on Monday, the 26th day of June last, an English convict servant man, named William Blake, about 5 feet 9 inches high, between 30 and 40 years of age, of a fair complexion, full faced, large nose, and large full eyes, pitted with the small-pox, a shoemaker by trade, and very much addicted to liquor; had on, when he went away, a colt-skin jacket, with hair on, of a black colour, the back parts made of coarse napt cloth, of a lightish colour, old leather breeches, coloured with the sole leather, turned pumps, and brass buckles, a black wig, a small new felt hat, a white shirt, half-worn coarse kersey fly coat, without lining, the buttons on the breast not fellows. He took with him a black mare, about 13 hands high, 6 years old this spring, a star in her forehead, and a small snip down her nose, paces and trots, her off fore foot white, a half-worn saddle, and a new-saddle cloth, cross-barred. Whoever secures the said servant, and mare, so that the owner may have them again, shall receive the above reward, or Fifty Shillings for either, paid by   PETER HUNTER.

N. B. It is supposed he will change his name to John Barker, as it is thought he has an old indenture with that name.

The Pennsylvania Gazette, July 7, 1768; July 14, 1768; August 18, 1768.

RAN away, on the 3d inst. from the subscriber, living in Queen Anne's county, Maryland, near the Chapel, two convict servants, both Englishmen. One named Henry Roberts, about 25 years old, about five feet nine or ten inches high, has short black hair, and some cuts on his head. He had on, when he went away, a white fly coat, a dowlas shirt, oznabrigs trowsers, blue stockings, a pair of shoes half worn, an old hat bound round with black ferriting, and a band of the same.

The other, named Samuel Pope, about twenty-one or two years of age, about 5 feet eight inches high, stoops a little in his shoulders, he has light coloured hair, which curls very neat, his face is tanned, and he talks very much in the West Country tongue. He had on, when he went away, a red plush jacket, with some tar on the back, with slits in the sleeves, and black horn buttons on them, and a dark coloured jacket, with black cloth in the back, and black horn buttons, a pair of light coloured breeches, with a fall before, a fine shirt, a very good hat, a pair of blue stockings, and a pair of shoes with the soles full on small nails.

Whoever secures the said servants so that their masters may have them again, shall have THREE POUNDS REWARD paid by
JOHN LAMBDIN,   and   GEORGE STEPHENS.

The Pennsylvania Chronicle, and Universal Advertiser, From Monday, July 11, to Monday, July 18, 1768; From Monday, July 18, to Monday, July 25, 1768.

July 15, 1768.
FOUR POUNDS REWARD.
RAN away last Night, from the Subscriber, living in *Prince-George's* County, the following Convict Servants, *viz.*

JAMES COORT, *(alias* COURT), born in the County of *Kent*, in *England*, about 5 Feet 7 Inches high, of a dark Complexion, and about 28 Years of Age, has an oval Face, and short Hair, which is dark, his Nose has a Cast to one Side, and his right Foot turns in more than his left, speaks the *Kentish* Dialect: Had on, and took with him, a blue Fearnought Jacket, Two Osnabrig Shirts, Osnabrig Trowsers, an old Cloth Coat, and Breeches of a *Spanish* brown Colour, and the Coat has been mended in the Lining, with Pompadour coloured Shalloon, a flowered cut Velvet Jacket, Yarn Stockings, half worn Shoes, and a new *Carolina* Felt Hat.

ISABELLA WATSON, of a fair Complexion, sandy coloured Hair, has a round Face, pitted with the Small-Pox, of a middle Stature, but thick, and about 24 Years of Age: Had on, and took with her, an Osnabrig Shift, and a white Linen ditto, a striped Country Cloth Petticoat, a new blue Shalloon ditto, and a new Osnabrig ditto, a new Purple Sprig Stamp'd Cotton Gown, a blue and white short Gown, old Stays, and a black Silk Bonnet, a Silk Handkerchief, Two red stamp'd Linen ditto, white Yarn Stockings, and a Pair of Country-made Pumps, and a small Looking-Glass, with sundry other Things.—The above Servants came into the Country in the Years 1764, in the *Neptune*, Capt. *Somerville*.—Whoever takes up said Servants, and brings them to their Master, or secures them in any Jail, and gives Notice thereof, so as he may hear of them soon after their Committment, shall have Forty Shillings Reward for each, and if taken and brought home, reasonable Charges, paid by
JOHN F. A. PRIGGS.

The Maryland Gazette, July 21, 1768; July 28, 1768; August 11, 1768; August 18, 1768. See *The Maryland Gazette*, March 29, 1764, for Corrt/Coort, *The Maryland Gazette*, June 21, 1764, and *The Maryland Gazette*, October 27, 1768.

Maryland, July 12, 1768.
RAN away from the Subscriber, living at *Elk-Ridge* Landing, on Monday last, Three Convict Servants, *viz.*

DAVID JOHNSON, about 5 Feet 8 Inches high, and 28 Years of Age: Had on, when he went away, a green Frieze Jacket, Check Shirt, old white Cloth Breeches, old Shoes and Stockings, and a Castor Hat half worn; he is very remarkable, his left Hand being off at the Wrist.

WILLIAM SIMMONS, a Barber by Trade, fair Complexion wears his own Hair, is about 5 Feet 9 Inches high: Had on, when he went away, a new Check Shirt, a brown Bearskin Surtout Coat, bound all round, old Leather Breeches, old Shoes and Stockings, a Pair of Plate Silver Buckles, old Castor Hat.

JAMES CROSBY, an *Irish* Lad, about 21 Years of Age, 5 Feet 8 Inches high, very fair Complexion, and a little Cross-eyed: Had on, and took with him, a blue Surtout Coat, Check Shirt, long Trowsers, very black, and much tar'd, old Shoes, no Buckles, and a new Castor Hat.—It is supposed they will pass for Sailors, and make for *Chester*, in *Pennsylvania*: They were seen near *Baltimore-Town*, on Tuesday last.

Whoever takes up and secures the above Servants, so that their Master have them again, shall be entitled to the above Reward, or in Proportion for either of them, with reasonable Charges, if brought home, paid by
WILLIAM DUVALL.

The Maryland Gazette, July 21, 1768; July 28, 1768; August 11, 1768; August 18, 1768; August 25, 1768; September 1, 1768; September 8, 1768. See *The Maryland Gazette*, November 10, 1768, for Simmons.

Frederick County, *July 4*, 1768.
RAN away last Night, from the Subscriber, a white Servant, named *Mary Murray*, a *Scots* Woman, who formerly served her Time with the Widow *Crawford*, near *Chicamuxent*, in *Charles* County, she is a short thick Woman, about Forty Years of Age, and of a brown Complexion: Had on, when she went away, a white Shift, a brown Linen ditto, a coarse Cap, with a Lawn Border, a Silk spotted Handkerchief, a Linen Check ditto, a brownish Linsey short Gown, which has been fulled, a striped Linsey Petticoat, a Pair of Woman's Wooden Heel'd Shoes, a Pair of black Yarn Mirrings, cut off by the Wrist.—Whoever secures said Servant, and brings her to the Subscriber, living near Mr. *James Brookes's*, shall have Three Pounds Reward, paid by   JOHN VILLIERS.

The Maryland Gazette, July 21, 1768.

July 22, 1768.
RAN away last Night, from the Subscriber, living in *Baltimore-Town*, an indented *French* Servant lad, named LERAY THEODORE, about 19 Years of Age, 5 Feet 5 or 6 Inches high, he is well set, has light coloured Hair,

tied behind, grey Eyes, and walks very wide; he is by Trade a Barber, and was lately imported in the *William* and *Thomas*, Capt. *Cock*: Had on, and took with him, a dark mix'd Cloth Coat, and Waistcoat, black Cloth Breeches, a Pair of old Shoes, dirty strip'd Linen Trowsers, strip'd Linen Shirt, white Thread Stockings, and coarse Country-made Shoes, White-Metal Buckles, an old Castor Hat, much greased and flour'd.—It is probable he may change his Dress, as he has other Cloaths in Town; he has stole Two dark coloured Wigs, the one tail'd, and the other a Two curled Bob, with Two Cases of Razors, one contains Four, and the other Two.

Whoever takes up the said Servant, and secures him, so that his Master may have him again, shall have, if taken in Town, Twenty Shillings, if Twenty Miles from Town, Forty Shillings, and if out of the Province, Three Pounds Reward, and reasonable Charges, if brought home, paid by WILLIAM ADAMS.

N. B. All Masters of Vessels are desired not to harbour said Lad on board, or carry him off at their Peril.

The Maryland Gazette, July 28, 1768; August 4, 1768; August 11, 1768; *The Pennsylvania Gazette,* August 4, 1768; August 18, 1768; September 1, 1768; September 15, 1768; September 22, 1768. Minor differences between the papers. *The Pennsylvania Gazette* does not have the date at the top.

Baltimore County, *July* 23, 1768.

RAN away last Night, from the Subscriber, living at *My Lady's Manor*, near the Chapel, a Convict Servant Man, named WILLIAM OAK, of a middle Stature, and wears his own short brown Hair, which curls; he is a pretty good Scholar, a cunning artful Fellow, and will endeavour to forge a Pass, has lately had a Hurt over his left Eye, which is now sore, and has an old Scar on his left Ancle: Had on, when he went away, a large Iron Collar, with Two Rivets in each End, an old Felt Hat, a lappelled chequer'd Saddle-Cloth Jacket, a Country Linen Shirt, a Pair of Hempen-Roll Trowsers, a Pair of old Stockings, but no shoes.—It is supposed he will endeavour to get his Collar off, before he travels, also furnish himself with other Cloaths, and then either steal a Horse to go off, or get a Reaping-hook, and pass for a Reaper, as he is a very good one.—Whoever takes up, and secures said Servant, so as his Master may have him again, shall receive, if taken within 20 Miles, Three Pounds, and if 40 Miles, Five Pounds, with reasonable Charges, paid by   THOMAS TALBOTT.

The Maryland Gazette, July 28, 1768; August 4, 1768. See *The Pennsylvania Gazette,* August 7, 1766.

RAN away from the Subscriber, living in *Chester-Town*, *Kent* County, *Maryland*, on the 16th of June last, a Convict Servant Woman, named *Elisabeth Lloyd*, about 4 Feet 8 Inches high, short brown Hair, stoops very much in her Walking, and is round shouldered: Had on, when she went away, a Linsey Woolsey Gown, Two Osnabrig Shifts, with false Sleeves to them, made out of old Shirts. It is supposed that she went with one *Thomas Moore*, and will probably pass for his Wife; the said *Moore* has a thin Visage, straight black Hair, mean Apparel, and is by Trade a Barber.— Whoever secures the said Servant, so that her Master may have her again, shall be well rewarded, besides what the Law allows.
THOMAS JOHNSON.
The Maryland Gazette, July 28, 1768.

MADE his escape, in going from Lancaster to Maryland, a certain JOHN BARKER, about 25 years of age, and about 5 feet 7 inches high, has strait hair, and a good wool hat, cocked all round, a good coarse country made shirt, and brown jacket, with good stockings and shoes and square steel buckles in them. The said John Barker ran away from Samuel Dorsey, in Maryland, some time ago, and was taken up, and committed to Lancaster goal; he is a cunning artful fellow, and probably will change his name, and produce a forged pass on the road. Whoever takes up the said John Barker, and secures him in any of his Majesty's goals in this province, or bring him to the subscriber, in the Borough of Lancaster, shall have FOUR DOLLARS reward, and reasonable charges, paid by GEORGE HOFFNAKLE.
The Pennsylania Gazette, July 28, 1768; August 18, 1768.

Maryland, June 20, 1768.
RAN away last Night, from *Hockley* Forge, on the Head of *Patapsco*, Two Convict Servant Men, *viz.*

SAMUEL DAVENANT, a Gardener by Trade, about 30 Years of Age, 5 Feet 6 or 7 Inches high, speaks short, is well-set, of a good Complexion, mark'd with the Small-Pox, has black Eyes, and very dark Hair, tolerable long, which he wears tied: Had on, and took with him, a brown Cloth Jacket, and Breeches, Felt Hat, Two Osnabrig Shirts, One old Check ditto, Holland ditto, a Pair of old blue and white Yarn Stockings, Crocus Trowsers, and Country-made Shoes.

SAMUEL FLOOD, a Labourer, about 25 Years of Age, and near the same Height as the other, of a brown Complexion, has a smooth Face, dark Eyes, and short dark straight Hair, a down Look, speaks low, and very plain: Had on, when went away, an old Felt Hat, old brown Kersey Jacket, Osnabrig Shirt, Crocus Trowsers, and a Pair of *English* Shoes, almost new.

Whoever brings home said Servants, shall receive a Reward of Ten Pounds for both, or Five Pounds for either.
R. CROXALL.
N. B. They had Collars and Leg-Irons on, when they went away. The Gardener sometimes went by the Name of *Samuel Dryton*, and may probably pass by that Name.

The Maryland Gazette, August 4, 1768; August 11, 1768; August 18, 1768; August 25, 1768; September 8, 1768; September 15, 1768.

Nottingham Forges, Baltimore county, August 3, 1768.
RUN away from the Subscriber, living on the Great Fall of Gunpowder, an Irish servant man, named MARTIN DOWLAND, about 6 feet high, of a fair complexion, much pitted with the small-pox, stoops much, has a down look, and generally complains of sore eyes, he wore short black curled hair. A middle sized bay horse was missing with him, which he is supposed to have stole, the horse was used to the geers, has a very black mane and tail, and was shod all round. He had on, and took with him, a brown thickset coat, a pair of lead coloured breeches and jacket, two old white shirts, ozenbrigs shirts and trowsers, two pair of old blue worsted stockings, a new felt hat, a pair of old turned pumps, and two striped silk handkerchiefs. Whoever apprehends said servant, and brings him home, or secures him in any goal, shall have FIFTY DOLLARS reward, paid by me
CORBIN LEE.

The Pennsylvania Gazette, August 18, 1768; September 8, 1768.

Baltimore county, Maryland, July 27, 1768.
RUN away, last night, from the subscriber, living near Baltimore-Town, an Irish servant man, named William Fields, a linen weaver by trade, a well set fellow, about 24 years of age, 5 feet 7 or 8 inches high, of a dark complexion, pretty much pitted with the-small pox, one eye brow-shaved, but a little grown out again, a natural mark on one of his wrists, a claret colour; had on, when he went away, a felt hat, half-worn lincey coat and jacket, old country linen shirt and trowsers, dogskin pumps, and one large brass buckle.

Whoever takes up and secures said servant, so that his master may get him again, shall have a reward of Three Pounds, current money, and if taken out of the province Five Pounds currency, paid by
JOSHUA OWINGS, junior.

The Pennsylvania Gazette, August 18, 1768.

August 18, 1768.

BROKE out of *Anne-Arundel* County Jail, *John Hosley*, a Lad about Eighteen or Nineteen Years of Age, of a fair Complexion, Five Feet Four Inches high: Had on, when he made his Escape, a light coloured Cloth Coat, with Silver Twist Buttons. Also a Negro Man, named *Jem*....Whoever secures the aforesaid *John Hosley*, and Negro *Jem*, so that they may be had again, shall receive Twenty Shillings Reward for each, besides what the Law allows. They have been seen a few Days ago, about the Head of *South-River*.

Committed to the Jail aforesaid, as Runaways, *William Jackson*, and *William Russell*, who deny they are Servants; and say, they run away from a Vessel at New-York. Also *Sarah Butler*, an *Irish* Woman, committed as a Runaway; and likewise denies she is a Servant. She was in Company with the aforesaid *Jackson* and *Russell*, when taken up.

WILLIAM STEWART, Sheriff.

The Maryland Gazette, August 25, 1768; September 1, 1768; September 8, 1768. See *The Maryland Gazette*, December 15, 1768, for Russell.

August 13, 1768.
To all SHERIFFS and CONSTABLES, &c.

MARYLAND, *ss*. WHEREAS Complaint has been made to me, the Subscriber, one of his Lordship, the Right Honourable the Lord Proprietor of the Province of *Maryland*, his Justices of the Provincial Court; and am informed, by the Oaths of several credible Persons, that *Thomas Lewis*, by Trade a Shoemaker, did, on or about the Thirteenth Day of *June* Last, cruelly murder a certain *John Free*, of *Prince-George's* County, Saddler.

Thomas Lewis, is 5 Feet 7 Inches and an Half high, or thereabouts, of a pale Complexion, with a long Visage, well made, his Limbs rather large than otherwise, hazel Eyes, round Shoulders, one of his Toe Nails has been hurt, which occasions it to grow crooked: His Wearing-Apparel, was a green Camblet Coat, Nankeen Breeches, a light coloured napp'd Frize Coat, a Pair of Thread Stockings, and a Pair of white Cotton ditto; but, as he has Plenty of Money, (which he is said to have robb'd *John Free* of) he may change his Apparel: And, as he has absconded from Justice, and is not yet apprehended;

THESE ARE THEREFORE, in the Name of the Right Honourable, the Lord Proprietor of this Province, to command you, forthwith, to make diligent Search within your Counties, and Hundreds, for the said *Thomas Lewis*, and to make HUE and CRY after him, from County to County, and from Hundred to Hundred, and that, as well by Horsemen, as by Footmen, according to Law, and if that you should find him, that then you bring him before me, or some other Justice of the Provincial Court, that he may be

dealt with according to Law. And hereof fail not at your Peril. Given under my Hand at *Annapolis*, this 22d Day of *August* 1768.
GEORGE STEWART.

AND, *in order to encourage Persons to be active, in apprehending and securing the aforesaid* Thomas Lewis, *so that he be brought to Justice, the Subscribers offer a Reward of Thirty Pounds Current Money.*
NELLY FREE, NICHOLAS FREE.
The Maryland Gazette, August 25, 1768; September 1, 1768.

August 18, 1768.
THREE POUNDS REWARD.
RAN away from the Subscriber, in *Kent* County, *Maryland*, on the 16th Ult. a Convict Servant Man, named THOMAS HARGROVE, an *Englishman*, about 20 Years of Age, a lusty portly Man, about 6 Feet high, a hearty well looking Fellow, or a ruddy Complexion, red or sandy coloured Hair, short, inclined to curl, no Beard: Had on when he went away, a Check Shirt, and long wide Tow Linen Trowsers, but is supposed to have stole some Cloaths from Two of the Neighbours that lived near; amongst which was one red Plush Jacket, without Sleeves. He came over from *England*, in the Year 1765, in the Ship *Albion*, *Thomas Spencer* Commander. It appears from Intelligence received, that he crossed the Bay, from *Talbot* County, near *Poplar-Island*, with an Intent to go over to the Western Shore.

Whoever takes up, and secures the said Servant, so that his Master may have him again, shall have the above Reward, and reasonable Charges, paid by SAMUEL MANSFIELD.
The Maryland Gazette, August 25, 1768; September 1, 1768; September 8, 1768; September 15, 1768; September 22, 1768.

Frederick County, *August* 18, 1768.
RAN away from the Subscriber, living within Three Miles of the Mouth of *Concocheague*, on the first on *June* last, a Convict Servant Man, named *Edward Tricked*, who pretends to be a Watchmaker: He is about 5 Feet 6 Inches high, is much marked with the Small-Pox, and has a pale Complexion. Had on him, when he went away, a blue Camblet Coat, made after the *Dutch* Fashion, a blue Linsey Jacket, old Trowsers, and old Shoes, patched on one Side.—Whoever takes up, and secures said Servant, so that his Master may get him again, shall receive a Reward of Three Pounds, and reasonable Charges, if brought home, paid by
CHRISTOPHER PRUNCK.
The Maryland Gazette, August 25, 1768.

Virginia, Richmond County, *August* 15, 1768.
RAN away from the Subscribers, on the 13th Instant, Two Servant Men, and a Negro Fellow, viz. GEORGE PITT, convicted into *Virginia*, in the *Justitia*, Capt. *Somerville*, in the Fall 1766, has served in the 112th Regiment of Foot, under Major *Markham*, as appears by a printed Certificate: He is about 5 Feet 5 Inches high, of a brown Complexion, somewhat pitted with the Small-Pox, wears his own Hair, which is black, short, and curls, has been shot through the right Foot with a Bullet; is a good Shoemaker, much given to Liquor, and has a very smooth Tongue: He carried away with him a Goat-skin Knapsack, a blue Fear-nothing Jacket, one old red Cloth do. Two Cotton Shirts, a Pair of Oznabrig Trowsers, one Osnabrig Frock, a Felt Hat, good Shoes, One Pair of Copper Plain Buckles, One Pair of Thread Hose, One Pair of Yarn do.

HENRY VALENTINE, born in *Leicestershire*, about 18 Years of Age, has been in the Country about 3 Years, Speaks very plain, is about 5 Feet 3 Inches high, and very well made, has a fair Countenance, and, tho' a very great Villain, has a very harmless inoffensive Look. He carried off with him two Osnabrig Shirts and Trowsers, a white Russia Drill Coat, with flat Metal Buttons, a striped Holland Jacket, one old white Shirt, one Pair of Cloth Breeches, (dark colour'd) with Twist Basket Buttons, a Felt Hat, half worn; wears his own short brown Hair, has Two Pair of new Shoes with him. He is the Property of Mr. *Samuel Hipkins*, at *Totuskey-Bridge*, and by attending about the House, is well known to many Gentlemen in the Colony.

Negro JACK....It is supposed they have all Passes, as *George Pitt* writes a good Hand, and was seen to have Pen Ink and Paper, the Night they went off. Whoever secures the above Servants, and Negro, so that they may be recovered again, shall receive SIX POUNDS Reward, or in Proportion for either of them, with reasonable Charges.
SAMUEL HIPKINS.   GRIFFIN GARLAND.
The Maryland Gazette, September 1, 1768; September 8, 1768; September 15, 1768; September 29, 1768; October 6, 1768.

ANNE-ARUNDEL County, *August* 25, 1768.
RAN away from Subscriber, on Wednesday, the Twenty-fourth Instant, a white Servant Lad, named RICHARD WELCH, imported in the Brig *Hannah* and *Nancy*, Capt. CIRCAUD, last Fall was Twelve-Months, is about Fifteen Years of Age, full faced, and of a red Complexion; had on, when he went away, an Osnabrig Shirt and Trowsers, and a Pair of Crocus ditto, and a Felt Hat; as also, a Negro Man, named SAM....Whoever will take up, and bring them home, shall have THREE PISTOLES Reward; or for either of them, One Pistole and a Half, paid by

WILLIAM CRANDELL.
The Maryland Gazette, September 1, 1768; September 8, 1768; September 15, 1768; September 22, 1768; September 29, 1768; October 6, 1768; October 13, 1768; October 27, 1768; November 3, 1768.

August 31, 1768.
EIGHT POUNDS REWARD.

RAN away last Night, from *Kingsbury* Furnace Mine-Bank, near *Baltimore-Town*,
    WILLIAM HATTON, (otherwise JACKSON) a Convict, by Trade a Stocking-Weaver, about 28 or 30 Years of Age, 5 Feet 6 or 7 Inches high; has a Down-Look, and a remarkable Way of staring in any Person's Face, that speaks to him; he has a Scar from the Corner of his Mouth, to his Chin, stout made, fresh Complexion, light brown Hair: Had on, and took with him, a new Osnabrig Shirt, that never was washed, a Cotton Country-made, and a Fearnought Jacket, Osnabrig Trowsers, a Pair of *English* Falls, Metal Buckles, and Felt Hat, bound with black Binding.
    Negro Cyrus....
    THOMAS STRINGER, about 25 Years of Age, 5 Feet 6 Inches high, short brown Hair, has Two Moles on his Face, and speaks pretty fast: Had on, when he went away, a white *Russia* Drab Coat, Double-breasted Cotton Jacket, fine Linen Shirt, Osnabrig Breeches, Thread Stockings, and Country-made Pumps, striped Silk Handkerchief, a pretty good Felt Hat, and sundry other Things, unknown.
    Whoever apprehends the said Runaways, so that they may be had again, shall receive FIFTY SHILLINGS for each of the Convicts, and THIRTY SHILLINGS for the Negro, if taken in the Province; and, if out of the Province, THREE POUNDS each, for *Hatton* and *Stringer*, and TWO POUNDS for Negro *Cyrus*, paid by
FRANCIS PHILLIPS.
***The said *Stringer* went off, by himself, the first of the Month.
    The Maryland Gazette, September 8, 1768; September 15, 1768; September 22, 1768; October 6, 1768; October 13, 1768. See The Maryland Gazette, March 31, 1763, and The Pennsylvania Gazette, September 15, 1768; for Stringer. The Maryland Gazette, September 27, 1764; The Maryland Gazette, October 1, 1767, The Maryland Gazette, March 10, 1768, The Pennsylvania Gazette, September 15, 1768, and The Pennsylvania Gazette, July 6, 1769, for Hatton.

September 1, 1768.
TEN POUNDS REWARD.

RAN away from the Subscriber, in *Loudoun* County, on the Night of the 30th of *August* last, Two Convict Servant Men, both Blacksmiths by Trade.

JOHN BENHAM, 28 Years of Age, 5 Feet 5 Inches high, stoops in his Shoulders, has a very hoarse Voice, is slender made, and his Hair cut off, has a Scar or two in his Neck, which he says was by Shot; and was clothed in Osnabrig.

JOHN MILLER, 28 Years of Age, 5 Feet 2 Inches high, a thick-set Fellow, and wears his own Hair; has a large Scar in his Forehead, has been in the Country before, talks much, and very impudent, and is the most deceitful Fellow I ever knew, is very capable of deceiving by his Polaver: He was drest in Osnabrig, and had on a Felt Hat. 'Tis likely they will change their Dress, as they were endeavouring to steal Cloaths, the Night they went away. They are the Two Servants that run away last *May*, from me, and advertised in the several Gazettes of the several adjoining Colonies. They were then taken up in *Maryland*; and, I am satisfied, they will endeavour to get on board some Vessel, so as to get a Passage home, or to the West-Indies; so Masters of Vessels are cautioned not to entertain them. They had each of them large Steel Collars about their Necks, but possibly will get them off. Whoever takes them up, and delivers, or causes them to be delivered, at my House, in the said County, shall receive the above Reward, or FIVE POUNDS for either, if taken seperate, paid by
WILLIAM CARR LANE.

The Maryland Gazette, September 15, 1768; September 22, 1768. See *The Pennsylvania Gazette*, May 12, 1768.

Maryland, Elk-Ridge, September 7, 1768.
TEN POUNDS REWARD.
RAN away from *Dorsey's* Forge, Two Convict Servant Men, *viz.* On the 16th Ult. one named THOMAS PHILIPS, about 35 Years of Age, full 5 Feet 8 Inches high, has dark Eyes, short brown Hair, which curls, a pretty pleasant Countenance, but looks down, and is very mannerly in his Address, but somewhat slow in his Speech, and is crippled in the little Finger, of his left Hand: He took with him, besides his working Cloaths, an old blue Broad-Cloth Coat, and a short red Jacket, with a double Breast: It is supposed he has also taken with him, a dark ground Chintz Gown, a green Damask Petticoat, Four Holland Shifts, and sundry other Things, which he will, no doubt, try to dispose of, or change for Mens Cloaths.— And, on the 30th Ult. one named JAMES CALLIS, about 30 Years of Age, near 5 Feet 5 Inches high, has short light Brown Hair, which also curls a

little, and is very thin on the Top of his Head, so as to appear almost bald; he has a pale whitish look, a fair Complexion, and is very pert in Conversation: Had on, and took with him, a Bearskin Jacket, with short close Cuffs, lapelled, or double breasted, with large Metal Buttons, a spotted Swanskin Jacket, a Castor Hat, Check Shirt, and one white ditto: It is supposed they have got forged Passes, and have changed their Names and Cloaths. Whoever apprehends the said Runaways, or either of them, and brings him, or them, home, shall have, for each, if taken Ten Miles from said Forge, Thirty Shillings; if Twenty Miles, Forty Shillings; if Forty Miles, Three Pounds; and, if out of the Province, Five Pounds Reward, including what the Law allows, paid by   CALEB DORSEY.

The Maryland Gazette, September 15, 1768; September 22, 1768; September 29, 1768; October 6, 1768.

EIGHT POUNDS REWARD.

RUN away, last night, from Kingsbury Furnace, Mine Bank, near Baltimore town, viz.

WILLIAM HATTON, (otherwise Jackson) a convict servant, by trade a stocking weaver, about 28 or 30 years of age, 5 feet 6 or 7 inches high, has a down look, and a very remarkable way of staring any body in the face that speaks to him; he has a scar from the corner of his mouth to his chin, stout made, fresh complexion, and light brown hair; had on, and took with him, a new ozenbrigs shirt, that had never been washed, cotton country made, and one fearnought jacket, ozenbrigs trowsers, a pair English falls, with metal buckles, and felt hat, bound round with black binding.

Negroe CYRUS....

THOMAS STRINGER, aged about 25 years, 5 feet 6 inches high, short brown hair, has two moles on his face, speaks pretty fast; had on a white Russia drab coat, fine linen shirt, white double breasted cotton Jacket, ozenbrigs breeches, thread stockings, country made pumps, striped silk handkerchief, a pretty good felt hat, and sundry other things, unknown. The said Stringer went off by himself the first of the month.

Whoever apprehends the said Runaways, so that they may be had again, shall receive Fifty Shillings for each of the two convicts, and Thirty Shillings for the Negro, if taken in the province; and, if out of the province, Three Pounds each, for William Hatton and Thomas Stringer, and Two Pounds for Negroe Cyrus, paid by
FRANCIS PHILLIPS.
Kingsbury Furnace, *August* 31, 1768.

The Pennsylvania Gazette, September 15, 1768; September 22, 1768; October 13, 1768; October 20, 1768. See *The Maryland Gazette*, March 31, 1763, and *The Maryland Gazette*, September 8, 1768 for

Stringer. *The Maryland Gazette*, September 27, 1764; *The Maryland Gazette*, October 1, 1767, *The Maryland Gazette*, March 10, 1768, *The Maryland Gazette*, September 8, 1768, and *The Pennsylvania Gazette*, July 6, 1769, for Hatton.

SIX POUNDS Reward.

RUN away from his bail, living in Kent county, Maryland, about six years ago, a certain JOHN BOYER, but has changed his name to JOHN SEILER, born in Maryland, between 30 and 40 years of age, about 5 feet 10 inches high, stoops in his shoulders, a dark complexion, black hair, tied behind, an agreeable countenance, very much given to strong liquor, but very quiet in the same; he is a very good farmer, and it is supposed he is now at Eggharbour, or Morris's river. Whoever takes up the said John Boyer, alias Seiler, and secures him in any of his Majesty's goals, and gives notice to the subscriber, shall have the above reward, and reasonable charges, paid by DANIEL SIMMONS.

The Pennsylvania Gazette, September 22, 1768; October 13, 1768; October 20, 1768.

Lancashire furnace, Baltimore county, Maryland, Sept. 10, 1768.
FIFTEEN DOLLARS Reward.

RUN away from the above furnace, an Irish convict servant named HUGH JONES, by trade a miller, he wears his own dark coloured hair, some times tied, he is about 30 years of age, 5 feet 5 inches high; had on, and took with him, a fearnought jacket, a pair of ozenbrigs petticoat [sic] trowsers, a hat, bound with ferrit or ribbon, also a light coloured fustian or kersey coat, and a yellow or straw-coloured jacket. Mary Dugan, a tall lusty woman, is a companion in his flight, and pretends to be his wife, altho' she has a husband living; she hath a child with her, about 3 years old: The woman is an artful hussey, and a great thief. Whoever takes up and secures the said Hugh Jones, shall receive, if taken 10 miles from home, Ten Shillings; if 30 miles Fifty Shillings; and if out of the province the above reward; over and above the allowance granted by act of assembly, with reasonable charges, if brought either to Mr. John Smith, at North-east forge, in Caecil county, or to the subscriber, at the Lancashire furnace,
GEORGE RANDELL.

The Pennsylvania Gazette, September 22, 1768; October 20, 1768. See *The Pennsylvania Chronicle, and Universal Advertiser*, From Monday, September 19, to Monday, September 26, 1768, and *The Pennsylvania Gazette*, October 20, 1768, for Jones.

SIX POUNDS Reward.

RUN away, the 12th of September inst. from the subscriber's fulling-mill, near Frederick-Town, in Frederick county, Maryland, an indented servant man, named Francis Blackburn, a Scotchman, and talks broad, a fuller by trade, a short well-set fellow, with short brown hair, full faced, very talkative, about 22 years old; had on, and took with him, a new London brown cloth coat, with yellow flowered gilt buttons, a blue lappelled camblet waistcoat, with gilt buttons, a pair of black calimancoe breeches, two pair of grey worsted stockings, a pair of pumps, a fine white shirt, a new felt hat, and a silk handkerchief. Whoever takes up said servant, and secures him, so that his master may have him again, shall have the above reward, paid by me CHARLES BEATTY.

N. B. The said servant, about three years ago, worked with one Dunnem, a fuller in the Jerseys, as a freeman.

The Pennsylvania Gazette, September 22, 1768. See *The Pennsylvania Gazette*, October 13, 1768.

Baltimore County, Maryland, Sept. 10, 1768.
Lancashire Furnace,
Four Dollars Reward.

RUN away from this furnace, an Irish convict, named Hugh Jones, by trade a miller; he wears his own dark coloured hair, sometimes tied; is about 30 years of age, 5 feet 5 inches high: Had on, and took with him, a fearnought jacket, petticoat oznabrig trowsers, [sic] and a hat, either ferrit or ribbon bound. He has also with him a light coloured fustian or kersey coat, and a yellow or straw coloured jacket.

Mary Dungan, a fat lusty woman, is a companion in his flight; she has a child with her about 3 years old. The woman is an artful hussey, and a great thief. Whoever takes up and secures the said runaway, shall receive, if taken 10 miles from home, Ten Shillings, if 30 miles Twenty Shillings, and if out of the province the above reward of Thirty Shillings, over and above the allowance granted by act of assembly, and reasonable charges paid, if brought either to Mr. John Smith, at North-East forge, or to the subscriber, at Lancashire furnace. GEORGE RANDELL.

The Pennsylvania Chronicle, and Universal Advertiser, From Monday, September 19, to Monday, September 26, 1768; October 10, 1768. See *The Pennsylvania Gazette*, September 22, 1768, and *The Pennsylvania Gazette*, October 20, 1768, for Jones.

September 27, 1768.

RAN away from the Subscriber, living in *Fairfax* County, in *Virginia* on the 25th Instant, a Convict Man, named THOMAS FOSSIT, a Weaver by

Trade, born in the County of *Cumberland*, in *England*; he is a likely Fellow, about Five Feet Eight or Nine Inches high, has black Eyes, long brown Hair, but it is probable he has cut it off, and steps very high in his Walk: Had on, and took with him, when he went away, a Check shirt, coarse white ditto, dark coloured Cloth Coat, red Waistcoat, coarse grey Breeches, grey Worsted Stockings, Castor Hat, English Shoes, and a Pair of Buckles, not Fellows.

Whoever takes up and secures said Servant, so that his Master gets him again, shall have FORTY SHILLINGS Reward, if taken in Maryland, and TWENTY SHILLINGS, in taken in Virginia, paid by
SAMPSON DARRELL.
The Maryland Gazette, September 29, 1768.

RUN away, on Wednesday, the 7th of September inst. from the subscriber, in Baltimore county, Maryland, an English servant woman, named SARAH HEAMES, about 22 years of age, about 5 feet 4 inches high, has a scar on her cheek, is pock-marked, fair complexion, and has flaxen hair; had on, when she ran away, a white silk hat, green quilted petticoat, shoes, and silver buckles in them; she stole and carried off cash, to the amount of Fifty Shillings, a silver watch, and womens apparel, to the value of Twenty Pounds. As she has gowns, &c. of different colours, her dress cannot be described; she went, as is supposed, with two sailors, towards Philadelphia. Whoever takes up and secures said woman, so that her master may have her again, shall have THREE POUNDS reward, including what the law allows.
WILLIAM BANNISTER.
The Pennsylvania Gazette, September 29, 1768; October 20, 1768.

Alexandria, Fairfax County, *Sept.* 19, 1768.
COMMITTED to Jail, on Suspicion of being a Runaway Servant, a Man, who says his Name is *John Hoget*, and belongs to Capt. *John Mathews*, in *Baltimore*; had on a Fearnought Coat, a Pair of Crocus Trowsers, and an Osnabrig Shirt, has a down Look, light brown bushy Hair, a large Scar on his left Hand, and one over his Nose, not very perceivable. He bears the Marks of a late Whipping.

Whoever owns said Servant, may have him, on paying Charges, to
MICHAEL GRETTER, Jailer.
The Maryland Gazette, October 6, 1768.

Baltimore Town, September 27, 1768.
TEN POUNDS Reward.

RUN away, last night, THOMAS BENNET, about 33 or 34 years of age, and about 5 feet 6 or 7 inches high, has a pale look, wears short brown hair; had on, and took with him, a white country cloth coat, with hair buttons at the sleeves, and pockets of the same colour, check and white linen shirts, blue stockings, English falls, metal buckles, and sundry other things unknown. He is gone off in company with an Irish woman, that he calls his wife; she is a short pale looking person, black eyes, brown hair, is very apt to get drunk, and commonly wears a blue and white calicoe gown. SAMUEL FORSTER, about 5 feet 10 inches high, about 30 years of age, very much marked with the small pox, and wears brown hair; had on, and took with him, an old brown cloth coat, cotton jacket, ozenbrigs shirt and trowsers, and sundry other things unknown. They have likewise taken with them a pretty good feather bed, with Russia drilling tick, and three or four pretty good match coat blankets; probably they may sell the last articles, to help them on their journey. Whoever apprehends the said runaways, so that they may be had again, shall receive, if taken in this province, Forty Shillings, and if out of the province, the above reward, and reasonable charges, if brought to Mr. Henry James, in Baltimore Town, or to the subscriber, at Bond's mine bank, near said town, JOHN MURRAY.

The Pennsylvania Gazette, October 6, 1768.

Woodbridge, October 8, 1768.
NOTICE is hereby given to Charles Beatty, of Frederic Town and County, Maryland, that Dennis Combes, of Woodbridge, hath taken up and committed, Francis Blackburn, to Jail, in Perth-Amboy, East New-Jersey, who on examination owned that he, the said Francis Blackburn, was an indented servant to Charles Beatty; and unless said Beatty come and take his said servant, and pay the Charges, within five weeks from this date, he will be sold for the same. DENNIS COMBES.

The Pennsylvania Gazette, October 13, 1768. See *The Pennsylvania Gazette*, September 22, 1768.

October 10, 1768.
RAN away Yesterday Morning from the Subscriber, living in *Prince-George's* County, near *Nottingham*, an indented Servant Man, named GEORGE DILLADD, a Bricklayer by Trade, about Five Feet Nine Inches high, he is about Forty Years of Age, an *Englishman*, born in or near *Liverpool*, of a dark Complexion, and pitted with the Small-Pox; is afflicted with a remarkable Lameness, occasioned by being shot through the left Leg, when in the Service, as a Soldier, in One of the Regiments in the late Wars in *America*, which makes him halt and tread on his left Toes; the Calf of which Leg is much withered, and is much smaller than the other: Had on,

when he went away, a blue Coat with Horn Buttons, a brown Jacket, Osnabrig Shirt, Breeches and Trowsers, Yarn Stockings, old Shoes, a Bob-Wig, and an old Hat: has also with him sundry Papers, among which is a Discharge from the Regiment he served in, and a Discharge from the Hospital where the Cure of his Leg was effected, (which is now broke out again) he may probably make Use of the said Discharges to pass him off as a Freeman.—Whoever takes up the said Servant, and brings him to the Subscriber, shall have Forty Shillings Reward, and reasonable Charges, paid by   JOHN F. A. PRIGGS.

The Maryland Gazette, October 20, 1768; October 27, 1768; November 10, 1768; November 17, 1768; November 24, 1768; December 1, 1768; December 8, 1768; December 15, 1768.

Milford Hundred, Caecil County, Maryland, October 18, 1767.
SEVEN DOLLARS Reward.

RUN away, on Sunday night last, from the subscriber, an English servant man, named JOHN ROBINSON, about 22 years of age, of a swarthy complexion, with dark hair, sometimes tied behind; had on, when he went away, a felt hat, check shirt, striped handkerchief, and a spotted flannel jacket, made sailor fashion, and a blue under jacket, and breeches of the same, with coarse long trowsers over them, blue worsted stockings, and old shoes; he is pretty full faced, his upper lip pretty thick, cannot be very particular as to his features or dress, as I have had him but about 2 days and nights; he is, by appearance, a lively fellow, and a great rogue. Whoever takes up said runaway, and secures him in any of his Majesty's goals, so that his master may have him again, shall have the above reward, and all reasonable charges, paid by me   JOHN STRAWBRIDGE.

N. B. The above servant came to Philadelphia, two or three weeks ago, with Captain Caton, from Cork. All masters of vessels are forbid to carry him off.

The Pennsylvania Gazette, October 20, 1768; November 17, 1768; January 26, 1769. See *The Pennsylvania Gazette,* December 15, 1768, for Robison. *The Pennsylvania Gazette,* February 9, 1769.

Northampton county, Pennsylvania, Oct. 7, 1768.

WAS committed to the common goal of this county, a certain HUGH JONES, by trade a miller, and servant to George Randell, at the Lancashire Furnace, Baltimore county, Maryland, according to his own acknowledgement; and an advertisement, in Hall and Seller's paper, No. 2074, dated September 10, 1768; these are to acquaint his master to come

and pay the reward and charges, according to his advertisement, and take him away. JACOB BACKMAN, Goaler.
The Pennsylvania Gazette, October 20, 1768; November 3, 1768; November 10, 1768. See *The Pennsylvania Chronicle, and Universal Advertiser*, From Monday, September 19, to Monday, September 26, 1768, and *The Pennsylvania Gazette*, October 20, 1768.

RAN away, the 16th of this instant, from the subscriber, living in Baltimore county, near Deer-creek, a servant man, named PATRICK SMITH, a native Irishman, has a good deal of the brogue on his tongue, about 5 feet 4 or 5 inches high: Had on when he went away, a blue and white linsey jacket, and an old dark coloured one over it, tow and linen shirt, and trowsers of the same, a pair of half worn shoes, and a felt hat: He has a lump between his shoulders, easily discerned, and it is likely he will change his name. Whoever takes up said servant, and secures him, so as the subscriber may have him again, shall have Thirty Shillings reward, and reasonable charges, paid by THOMAS BRYARLY.
The Pennsylvania Gazette, October 20, 1768; November 17, 1768.

October 23, 1768.
RAN away from the Subscriber, living in *Chester-Town*, *Kent* County, *Maryland*, the 2d of this last, an *English* Servant Man, named CHARLES WILLIAMS, about 5 Feet 8 or 9 Inches high, slender made, pretty good Complexion, wears his own Hair, which is brown, and curls; it is supposed he has a Watch, and Money, which must have been stolen: Had on, when he went away, a Castor Hat, blue Cloth Coat, white Shirt, a Calico Jacket, with Lappels, white Ticking Breeches, white ribb'd Stockings, a good Pair of Pumps, stitched round the Quarters, and it is possible he may have other Cloaths. Whoever takes up, and secures said Servant, so that his Master may have him again, shall receive Forty Shillings Reward, paid by
GEORGE LEYBOURN.
The Maryland Gazette, October 27, 1768.

October 27, 1768.
EIGHT POUNDS REWARD.
RAN away on the Night of the 14th of *July* last, from the Subscriber, living in *Prince-George's* County, the following Convict Servants, *viz.*
JAMES COORT, *(alias* COURT), born in the County of *Kent*, in *England*, about 5 Feet 7 Inches high, of a dark Complexion, and about 28 Years of Age, has an oval Face, and short Hair, which is dark; his Nose has

a Cast to one Side, and his right Foot turns in more than his left, speaks the *Kentish* Dialect: Had on, and took with him, a blue Fearnought Jacket, Two Osnabrig Shirts, Osnabrig Trowsers, an old Cloth Coat, and Breeches of a *Spanish* brown Colour, and the Coat has been mended in the Lining, with Pompadour coloured Shalloon, a flowered cut Velvet Jacket, Yarn Stockings, half worn Shoes, and a new *Carolina* Felt Hat.

ISABELLA WATSON, of a fair Complexion, sandy coloured Hair, has a round Face, pitted with the Small-Pox, of a middle Stature, but thick, and about 24 Years of Age: Had on, and took with her, an Osnabrig Shift, and a white Linen ditto, a striped Country Cloth Petticoat, a new blue Shalloon ditto, and a new Osnabrig ditto, a new Purple Sprig Stamp'd Cotton Gown, a blue and white short Gown, old Stays, and a black Silk Bonnet, a Silk Handkerchief, Two red stamped Linen ditto, white Yarn Stockings, and a Pair of Country-made Pumps, and a small Looking-Glass, with sundry other Things.—The above Servants came into the Country in the Years 1764, in the *Neptune*, Capt. *Somerville*.—Whoever takes up said Servants, and brings them to their Master, or secures them in any Jail, and gives Notice thereof, so as he may hear of them soon after their Committment, shall have FOUR POUNDS Reward for each, and if taken and brought home, reasonable Charges, paid by
JOHN F. A. PRIGGS.

The Maryland Gazette, October 27, 1768; November 3, 1768; November 10, 1768; November 17, 1768; November 24, 1768; December 1, 1768. See *The Maryland* Gazette, March 29, 1764, for Corrt/Coort, *The Maryland Gazette*, June 21, 1764, and *The Maryland Gazette*, July 21, 1768.

Talbot County, *October* 31, 1768.
RAN away from the Subscriber, the 30th Instant, a Servant Man, named JOHN CYAS, a Shoemaker by Trade, about 5 Feet 4 Inches high, fair Complexion, about 28 Years of Age, born in *Chester*, but liv'd 10 or 12 Years in *London*, and speaks very good *English*: Had on, and took with him, a Dowlais Shirt, One Osnabrig ditto, One Pair of dark striped Holland Trowsers, and One Pair of Osnabrig ditto, a Snuff coloured Broad Cloth Coat and Waistcoat, the Coat lined with Green, pretty much worn, One Pair of new grey Stockings, Country-made, and One Pair of new Pumps, with a good Hat, and an old Wig. It is supposed that one *William Blanch* is gone with him, who belong to Mr. *Francis Baker*. Said *Cyas*, when he works, holds his Fore-Finger on his right Hand strait out, occasioned by a Cut.— Whoever takes up said Servant, and secures him in any Jail, so as the Owner may get him again, shall have Forty Shillings Reward, besides what the Law allows, paid by   WILLIAM BLAKE.

Said *Cyas* came in the Ship *Good-Intent*, Captain *George Haddon*, Commander, consigned to Mr. *Anthony Banning*, of *Miles-River*, the 24th Day of January last. All Masters of Ships are forewarn'd from carrying him off, at their Peril.   *W. B.*

The Maryland Gazette, November 3, 1768; November 17, 1768; November 24, 1768.

Kent county, Maryland, near the head of Chester-river.

RUN away from the subscriber, an Irish servant man, named JOHN HUGHES, by trade a smith, about 20 years of age, supposed to be 5 feet high; had on, when he went away, a surtout or sheep black, blue jacket, plush breeches, of a winestone colour, black or blue stockings, old shoes, and old felt hat; he is very crooked in the hams. Whoever takes up the said servant, and secures him, so as his master may have him again, shall receive FORTY SHILLINGS reward, paid by   WILLIAM GRANT.

The Pennsylvania Gazette, November 3, 1768; November 10, 1768; November 17, 1768; December 22, 1768.

TEN POUNDS REWARD.

Maryland, Sept. 1, 1768.

RAN away from the Subscriber, living on *Bush-Creek*, near *Frederick-Town*, in *Frederick* County, the Two following Convict Servants, *viz.*

WILLIAM SIMMONS, an *Englishman*, by Trade a Barber, is fond of expressing his Calling; he is about 5 Feet 6 Inches high, of a fair Complexion, wears his own Hair, of a sandy Colour, has large white Eyes, and very high Cheek Bones: Had on a Check Shirt, blue Cloth double-breasted Jacket, a Pair of Country Linen Trowsers, old Shoes, and a Castor Hat, half worn.

WILLIAM BURNS, an *Englishman*, a lusty well made Fellow, 5 Feet 8 Inches high, of a fair Complexion, wears his own Hair, of a yellow Colour, has a very brazen Look, and is much given to Swearing, he also has a large Scar on his right Arm, which he often shows when in Company: Had on a Crocus Shirt, brown Kersey Jacket, a Pair of full'd Country Cloth Breeches, old Hat and Shoes; they also took with them, a strip'd Match-Coat Blanket. Whoever takes up the said Servants, and secures them, so as their Master may get them again, shall have the above Reward, and reasonable Charges, if brought home, paid by
WILLIAM DUVALL.

I have been informed of Two Men, answering the above Description, being seen passing from *Lower-Marlborough*, down *Patuxent* River; and, as Freemen, offering themselves to man any Vessel going to Sea. If any

Captains of Vessels, or others, should remember employing them, on giving me Notice thereof, the Favour shall be gratefully acknowledged; and, if they are taken up. 'tis requested particular Care may be taken of them, as they are both grand Villains, and will endeavour, if possible, to make their Escape. *W. D.*

The Maryland Gazette, November 10, 1768; November 17, 1768; November 24, 1768; December 1, 1768; December 8, 1768; December 22, 1768; January 5, 1768. See *The Maryland Gazette*, July 21, 1768, for Simmons.

WENT off this day, a certain JAMES ROWE, and stole a sorrel HORSE, with a blazed face, and a bridle, from Abraham Curseiur, of Cecil county, Maryland, near Elk ferry. He also stole and took with him, from Thomas Price, of the place aforesaid, a hunting saddle, about half wore, remarkably large, a bearskin surtout coat, a claret coloured broad cloth coat, and a pair of black knit breeches, a good castor hat, almost new, one new saggathy jacket, and one ditto of thickset, with the lining much wore. Whoever apprehends and secures the said fellow and effects, so that the may be brought to justice, shall have Five Pounds reward, paid by
ABRAHAM CURSEIUR, or THOMAS PRICE.

N. B. He is a short thick fellow, about 5 feet 5 inches high, of a dark complexion, and has a scattering beard; about 28 years of age, his common clothes. a blue coat, gray jacket, and white ticken breeches.
November 5, 1768.

The Pennsylvania Gazette, November 10, 1768; November 17, 1768; December 1, 1768.

RUN away, on the 30th of October last, from the subscriber, living in Gunpowder Forrest, a convict servant woman, who formerly belonged to Edward Breston, of Baltimore-Town, named NELLY ENGLISH, about 40 years of age; had on, when she went away, a black calimancoe gown, and a black silk bonnet with lace, and a blue cloak, she is a lusty fat woman, with a scar down her cheek. Whoever takes up the said woman, and brings her to Mr. William Barney's, in Baltimore-Town, or secures her, so as her master may have her again, shall have, if taken in the county, Twenty Shillings, and if out of the county, Forty Shillings reward and reasonable charges, paid by   NICHOLAS BRITTIAN.

The Pennsylvania Gazette, November 10, 1768; December 1, 1768.

TEN POUNDS REWARD.

Annapolis, November 14, 1768.

RAN away last Night from the Subscribers, the Two following indented Servants, *viz.*

WILLIAM SMITH, born in the West of *England*, by Trade a Joiner and Carpenter, about Five Feet Eight Inches high, of a fair Complexion, and about Twenty-three Years of Age, has short brown Hair, and had on, and took with him, when he went away, a light-coloured Cloth Coat, a spotted Flannel Jacket, a white Shirt, one Check ditto, black Stocking Breeches, black Worsted Stockings, a new Pair of Country-made Shoes, and a Pair of plain Brass Buckles.

JOHN BERRAGE, by Trade a Clock and Watchmaker, born in the West of *England*, about Five Feet Eleven Inches high, of a very dark Complexion, marked much with the Small-Pox, and has short black Hair: Had on, and took with him, a short Bearskin Coat, a strip'd Flannel Under-Jacket, Two strip'd Check Shirts, new Leather Breeches, Yarn Stockings, new Country-made Shoes, and a new Hat.

Whoever takes up the said Servants, or secures them, so as they may be had again, shall receive FIVE POUNDS for each, or the above Reward for both, and reasonable Charges, if brought home, paid by
PHILIP MERONEY,   WILLIAM KNAPP.

The Maryland Gazette, November 17, 1768.

Somerset County, Maryland, November 7, 1768.
FOUR POUNDS Reward.

RUN away from the subscriber, an Irish servant man, named JOHN SULLIVANE, lately imported from Cork by Mr. Littleton Dennis; the said John Sullivane hath been run away about two weeks; he had on when he absconded, an upper blue jacket, and an under spotted ditto, a check shirt, black plush breeches, shoes and stockings, and a new coarse hat; he is about 5 feet 9 inches high, well built, of a fair complexion, and has straight short white hair: A person answering this description was seen near Duck-creek, under the name of John Neel or Oneel, enquiring for Philadelphia; but as there is a person of the name of Sullivane at the head of Bohemia, to whom I suppose him related, it is not improbable he may have steered that way. Whoever takes up the said servant, and secures him, so that his master may have him again, shall (if taken in Maryland) receive a reward of Forty Shillings, if in Pennsylvania, the above reward of Four Pounds, paid by
ISAAC HANDY.

The Pennsylvania Gazette, November 24, 1768; December 1, 1768; December 29, 1768.

STOLEN from the Subscriber, living near *Hugh's* Forge, on the 10th of *October* last, a black Mare, Seven Years old, about 14 Hands high, has a white Spot in her Forehead, shoed all round, trots, and is branded on the

near Buttock, **B R**.—Whoever takes up, and secures said Mare, and Thief, shall have Five Pounds Reward, and for the Mare alone, Forty Shillings. I have strong Suspicion of one *James Biggar*, a noted Rogue, who has, within these Three Years, broke several Jails: He was seen near my House the Night before, and had on a new Pair of Leather Breeches, with blue Leggings over them, and had on a Hunting-Shirt over his other Cloaths; he is about Five Feet Nine inches high, of a red Complexion.
JOHN ROHRER.
The Maryland Gazette, December 1, 1768. See *The Pennsylvania Gazette*, October 9, 1766, and *The Maryland Gazette*, March 17, 1768.

December 14, 1768.
BROKE out of *Anne-Arundel* County Jail, on the Night of the 13th Instant, the Two following Men, *viz*.
    WILLIAM RUSSELL, a Sailor, low Stature, black Hair, was committed as a Runaway last *July*. His Dress is uncertain.
    THOMAS LEWIS, a Middle-sized Man, pale Complexion, fair Hair: Had on, when he went away, an old Bearskin Coat, red Everlasting Jacket, with Metal Buttons, and a Pair of Leather Breeches, and is by Trade a Shoemaker.—He was tried at last *April* Assize Court, on Suspicion of murdering *John Free*, and was committed by said Court, for Want of Security, for his good Behaviour.
    Whoever secures the above Men, shall have what Reward the Law allows, paid by   WILLIAM STEUART.
The Maryland Gazette, December 15, 1768; January 12, 1769. See *The Maryland Gazette*, August 25, 1768, for Russell.

Cecil County, Maryland, Dec. 8, 1768.
RUN away, this day, from the subscriber, an English servant man, named JOHN ROBISON, about 21 years of age, of a swarthy complexion, is about 5 feet 9 or 10 inches high, with dark brown hair, sometimes tied behind; had on, when he went away, a spotted flannel jacket, made sailor fashion, a blue under ditto, and breeches of the same, light blue worsted stockings, good shoes, an old felt hat, white shirt, and check handkerchief round his neck, but I need not be very particular to his dress, as he may change it. He is to appearance a lively fellow, pretty full faced, a thick upper lip; he can pass very well for a sailor. Whoever secures said servant, so as his master may have him again, shall have Seven Dollars reward, paid by me
JOHN STRAWBRIDGE.
    N. B. He has on one of his arms a mark with the first letters of his name.

The Pennsylvania Gazette, December 15, 1768; January 5, 1769. See *The Pennsylvania Gazette*, October 20, 1768, for Robison/Robinson.

December 12, 1768.
RAN away from the Subscriber, living near *Piscataway*, an indented Servant Man, named THOMAS CORESHIL, by Trade a Stone-Mason, about 5 Feet 8 Inches high, is well set, and turns his Toes in when he walks. He had on, when he went away, an Osnabrig Shirt, and a new light-coloured Kersey Coat and Breeches, with flat Metal Buttons. Whoever secures the said CORESHIL, so that he may be had again, shall receive a Reward of TWENTY SHILLINGS, besides what the Law allows, paid by WILLIAM DIGGES.
The Maryland Gazette, December 22, 1768. See *The Pennsylvania Gazette*, January 19, 1769.

1769

January 5, 1769.
RAN away from the Subscriber, in *London-Town*, on the First Instant, an Indented Servant Man, named WILLIAM COOKE, a Tailor by Trade, an *Englishman*, born in *Staffordshire*, and has been in most Parts of *Ireland*, is about 5 Feet 6 Inches high, has a small Lump in his Forehead, a Mole on his Face, which he has shaved off, thin Visage, and dark Eyes: Had on when he went away, a coarse Hat, bound round with Worsted Binding, thin black Hair, tied behind, and curled, a dark Bearskin Coat, a light coloured nap'd Duffil Waistcoat, and Everlasting Breeches, with Metal Buttons; the Coat and Waistcoat and the Edges of the Coat and Waistcoat bound, white Yarn Stockings, a Pair of Country-made Shoes, pretty good, a Pair of carved yellow Buckles, a brown Sheeting Shirt, and sundry other Cloaths unknown.—It is supposed he is gone with his Wife, an *Irishwoman*, who served her Time with Mr. *Charles Stewart*, on *South-River*, who has got Mr. *Stewart's* Discharge on the back of her Indenture, about Nine Months ago, and has likewise got another Discharge on the 31st of *December* last, from Mr. *Stewart*, on her pretending she has lost her Indenture; she has also got a Certificate from the Reverend Mr. *David Love*, of their Marriage, which, I make no Doubt, but they will be very apt to show both the Discharge and the Certificate.—He has been in the *East-Indies*, on board a Man of War, and boasts much of it when drunk, in which he will not fail, if he can get Liquor.—He has been Two Years in the Country.—It is supposed they will enquire for *Hugh Miriarlie's**, in *Frederick* County, a

Weaver by Trade, (which, I believe, is not a settled Person in *Frederick County*) or more probably intends to *Philadelphia*.—Whoever takes up the said Servant Man, and brings him home to his Master, shall receive Three Pounds Reward, and reasonable Charges, paid by
ALEXANDER FERGUSON.
*This *Miriarlie* is Brother to the Woman.
The Maryland Gazette, January 5, 1769. See *The Maryland Gazette*, December 17, 1767.

TEN POUNDS REWARD.
Elk-Ridge Furnace, *Jan.* 7, 1769.

RUN away from the Subscriber, a Convict Servant Man, named *Thomas Hughs*, about 36 [sic] Years of Age, near 5 Feet 5 Inches high, has short brown Hair, Hazel Eyes, and his Nose rises up at the End: He has a mild Way of Address, and often looks down when spoken to. It is pretty certain that he lately broke into the store of Mr. *French*, at *Elk-Ridge* landing, and took from thence about Sixty Pounds Cash, consisting of Gold and Silver, chiefly Half-Johannes's and Pieces of Eight: He has also taken with him a light-coloured broad Cloth Coat, a new Pair of Buckskin Breeches, and other Cloaths, not certainly known. He ran away last Spring, and was taken up in *Pennsylvania*, and confined for some time in *Chester* Jail, where he called himself *Thomas Steelman:* he is a good Carpenter and Joiner, and a very handy Fellow. Whoever apprehends the said Runaway, and brings him home, shall have, if taken in the Province, Five Pounds; and, if out of the Province Ten Pounds Reward, paid by   CALEB DORSEY.

The Maryland Gazette, January 12, 1769; January 19, 1769; January 26, 1769; February 2, 1769; February 9, 1769; *The Pennsylvania Gazette*, January 19, 1769. Minor differences between the papers. *The Pennsylvania Gazette* shows his age as 30. See *The Maryland Gazette*, June 2, 1768; and *The Pennsylvania Chronicle, and Universal Advertiser*, From Monday, January 9, to Monday, January 16, 1769.

Maryland, Elk-Ridge Furnace, Jan. 7, 1769.
TEN POUNDS Reward.

RUN away from the subscriber, a convict servant man, named Thomas Hughs, about 30 years of age, near 5 feet 5 inches high, has short brown hair, hazel eyes, his nose rises at the end, and he has a mild way of address, and often looks down when spoken to. It is pretty certain that he lately broke into the store of Mr. French, at Elk-Ridge landing, and took from thence about Sixty Pounds cash, consisting of gold and silver, chiefly half Johannas and pieces of eight. He has also taken with him a light coloured broadcloth coat, a pair of new buckskin breeches, and other clothes not certainly known. He ran away last spring, and was taken up in Pennsylvania, and confined some time in Chester Gaol, and there called himself Thomas Steelman; he is a good carpenter and joiner, and a very handy fellow. Whoever apprehends the said runaway, and brings him home, shall have, if taken in the province, Five Pounds, and if out of the province Ten Pounds reward, paid by   CALEB DORSEY.

The Pennsylvania Chronicle, and Universal Advertiser, From Monday, January 9, to Monday, January 16, 1769. See *The Maryland Gazette*, June 2, 1768.

December 30, 1768.

RAN away from the Subscriber, living near *Airs's* Ford, on the Falls of *Patapsco*, on *Elk-Ridge*, an *Irish* indented Servant Man, named PETER DENNY, about 20 Years of Age, about Five Feet Two Inches high, of a fair Complexion, thin visaged, grey eyed, and a little pitted with the Small-Pox, short brown Hair, and carries his Head crooked, is very much addicted to Liquor, and when drunk, is very quarrelsome: Had on, when he went away, a new Check Shirt, a new Bearskin Coat, bound round with black Binding, a blue Sagathy Jacket, with the Shirts lin'd with the same, and yellow Buttons, a Pair of new Broad Cloth Breeches, a Pair of plain Yarn Stockings, a Pair of new Shoes, and Steel Buckles, a Felt Hat, bound with black Ferreting, a new red Duffil great Coat, and took with him, a black Stallion, about 13 Hands high, and near Nine Years old, with a half worn *English* Saddle, and Snaffle Bridle: He also took with him Three Bills, One of Twenty Shillings, One of Fifteen, and One of Five; and, as he is well acquainted in *Baltimore-Town*, he may probably change his Dress.

Whoever takes up the said Servant, and brings him to the Subscriber, shall receive Three Pounds for the Man, and Thirty Shillings for the Horse, beside what the Law allows, paid by
VALENTINE BROWN, Junior.

The Maryland Gazette, January 19, 1769; January 26, 1769; February 2, 1769; February 9, 1767; February 16, 1769; February 23, 1769; March 2, 1769; March 9, 1769; March 16, 1769; March 23, 1769.

Maryland, Piscataway, December 14, 1769.

RUN away from the subscriber, an indented servant man, named THOMAS CORESHILL, by trade a Stone-mason, is well set, turns his toes in when he walks, and is about 5 feet 8 inches high; had on, when he went away, an ozenbrigs shirt, a new light coloured kersey coat and breeches, with flat metal buttons, and an old beaver hat. Whoever secures said Coreshill, so that he may be had again, shall receive the reward of three Pounds, if taken

out of the province, and Twenty Shillings, if taken within, besides the allowance by law. WILLIAM DIGGES.
N. B. It is supposed that this servant will make for York or Lancaster.
The Pennsylvania Gazette, January 19, 1769. See *The Maryland Gazette*, December 22, 1768.

WHEREAS on Wednesday, the 14th of December last, I the subscriber, living in Baltimore county, Maryland, gave my bond to a certain William Wilson, of New-Castle county, near Christiana bridge, for Twenty-seven Pounds, Pennsylvania currency, to be paid to said William Wilson, or his certain attorney, heirs or assigns, payable on the 13th or 14th of December next, for a convict servant man, named Kane O Hara, and his wife Mary, for 4 years;—as it appears from good authority, and from Kane O Hara's own confession, that he was convicted into this country, and sold to one Samuel Hanson, Esq; of Charles county, Maryland, from whom he ran way about two years ago, having served but a small part of his time, and returned to Europe, from whence he was again convicted to this county, and sold by said Wilson to the subscriber;—therefore, until the matter be determined, these are to forewarn all persons from taking an assignment of said bond, as the subscriber will not pay it.
THOMAS ARCHER.
N. B. I tendered the indentures to said Wilson, that he might settle the matter with Samuel Hanson, Esq; but he refused accepting of it.
The Pennsylvania Gazette, January 19, 1769. See *The Maryland Gazette*, May 21, 1767.

January 19, 1769.
RAN away from the Subscriber, living in *Frederick-Town, Maryland*, on the 9th of *October* 1767, an indented Servant Man, named JOHN QUIN, an *Irishman*, and says he was born in *Dublin*. He is about 5 Feet 5 Inches high, has some Scars in his Face, is a Shoemaker by Trade, and very much given to Liquor and Company. He has been several Years in this Country, and has resided both in *Pennsylvania* and the *Jersies*. I bought him from one *William Blair*, Shoemaker, living at *Carlyle*, in *Cumberland* County, *Pennsylvania*.
Whoever takes up, or secures said Servant, so as the Subscriber may have him again, shall receive a Reward of THIRTY SHILLINGS, from
JOSEPH BURNESTON.
N. B. I am informed he was at Work with Mr. *Hyde*, in *Annapolis*, about Two or Three Weeks ago.
The Maryland Gazette, February 2, 1769; February 9, 1769; February 16, 1769. The second and third ads do not have the date at the top.

THERE is in *Frederick* County Jail...a Negro Man named PETER. Likewise taken up and committed the 19th Day of *January*, a Servant Man, named RICHARD FLOOD, who says he belongs to Richard Murphy, in *Baltimore* County.
The Owners are desired to take them away, and pay Charges.
NORMAND BRUCE, Sheriff.
The Maryland Gazette, February 2, 1769; February 16, 1769; February 23, 1769; March 2, 1769.

January 29, 1769.
RAN away from the Subscriber, and from his Bail, a certain ROBERT SWAN, who serv'd his Time with *Thomas Rutland*, near the City of *Annapolis*, and is a stout well-set Fellow: Had on any took with him, a light coloured Kersey Jacket, Osnabrig Shirt, and a Pair of Half-Boots, almost new: His other Clothes uncertain. Whoever takes up the said ROBERT SWAN, and brings him to the Sheriff of *Baltimore* County, or to the Subscriber, living in *Baltimore-Town*, shall receive FORTY SHILLNGS Reward, and reasonable Charges, paid by JOHN DEAVER.
The Maryland Gazette, February 2, 1769.

Chester Goal, January 24, 1769.
THIS day was committed to my custody, as a runaway servant, an Englishman, who calls himself JOSEPH PENNOCK, and confesses that he is a servant to Mr. Thomas Rutland, of Anne Arundel county, near Annapolis, in Maryland; his master is desired to come, pay charges, and take him away, or he will be discharged in four weeks, according to law, by JOSEPH THOMAS, Goaler.
The Pennsylvania Gazette, February 2, 1769. See *The Pennsylvania Gazette*, June 1, 1769' for Penick/Pennock.

February 2, 1769.
RAN away from the Subscriber, living at Mr. *Thomas Addison's* Ferry, an *Irish* Servant Lad, named JOHN ALLEN, about 19 Years of Age, and supposed to be 5 Feet high, he has a round fresh coloured Face, with a Scar between his Eyes, wears short light brown curled Hair, cut on the fore Part of his Head: He had on, and took with him, when he went away, an old dark great Coat, very much tore before, one old Cotton Jacket, with one of the fore Skirts tore off, and another of Narrow-Broads, lined with Scotch Plaid, of a lightish Colour, a new Osnabrig Shirt, with Ilet [*sic*] Holes in the Collar and Wrists, a Pair of Buckskin Breeches, very much tore, a Pair of black

and white ribb'd Stockings, much the worse for Wear, a Pair of Shoes, with Steel Buckles in them, and an old Felt Hat, cock'd Two Ways.—Whoever takes up, and brings home said Servant, shall receive THIRTY SHILLINGS Reward, beside what the Law allows, paid by
SUSANNAH PATTERSON.
The Maryland Gazette, February 9, 1769; February 16, 1769.

FOUR DOLLARS Reward.

RUN away on the 31st of January last, from the subscriber, living at Peach Bottom Ferry, on Sasquehanna, Cecil County, Maryland, an Irish convict servant man, named Patrick Horan, alias M'Guire, about 25 years of age, 5 feet 5 or 6 inches high, well set, has short black hair, inclining to curl, and of a ruddy complexion: Had on, when he went away, a brown forrest cloth jacket, ill made; without lining, a brown jacket, much worn, striped ditto, with the stripes across, and an old kersey ditto, with sleeves, ozenbrigs shirt, buckskin breeches, much too long for him, old light blue stockings, and sheeps grey, footed with white, and appears above his shoes, which are good, and a coarse half worn wool hat. Whoever secures the said servant in any goal, so that his master may have him again, shall have the above reward, paid by WILLIAM CARSON, at the sign of the Harp and Crown, in Philadelphia, or GEORGE EWING.
The Pennsylvania Gazette, February 9, 1769; April 13, 1769.

Gloucester County, February 7, 1769.
WAS committed to the Goal of this County, a certain Englishman (who calls himself Walter Maloney) on Suspicion of being a Runaway, says he is a free Man, but he is thought to be the Man advertised in the Pennsylvania Gazette of October 18 last, by John Strawbridge, of Maryland, by the name of John Robinson, as he answers the Description of said Person; therefore his Master, if any he has, is desired to come, pay Charges, and take him away in three Weeks from this Date, or he will be sold out for his Charges, by JOSIAH CHATTIN, Goaler.
The Pennsylvania Gazette, February 9, 1769. See *The Pennsylvania Gazette*, October 20, 1768.

RUN away, on the 22d of January, from the subscriber, living near Rock Run, in Cecil county, Maryland, an Irish servant man, named George Peters Newcomb, but is apt to change his name to Johnson, and Dougherty, a short thick fellow, about 5 feet 4 inches high, has black hair tied behind, and a down look, by trade a shoemaker, loves strong drink, given to picking

pockets, and was bought out of Philadelphia goal last June: Had on, when he went away, a brown great coat, an old grey ditto, with black binding, blue serge jacket, lined with red buckskin breeches, Germantown stockings, black grain shoes, with silver buckles, and a fur hat; supposed to have a watch; and two Five Pounds notes of hand, and it is thought he is gone to Philadelphia. Whoever takes up and secures said servant, so as his master may have him again, shall have Three Pounds reward, and reasonable charges, paid by   WILLIAM GRIFFIE.
The Pennsylvania Gazette, February 9, 1769.

February 7, 1769.
TWENTY ONE POUNDS Reward.
RUN away, last night, from the subscribers, in Baltimore county, near Baltimore-Town, Maryland, the three following convict servants, viz. William Smith, an Englishman, about 30 years of age, 6 feet high, a fresh coloured, well looking fellow, of a brown complexion, short black hair, and black eyes, broad shouldered, with slim legs, big hands and arms; had on, and took with him, a grey fearnought jacket, a white cotton under ditto, an old cloth coloured great coat, old black buckskin breeches, old felt hat, two ozenbrigs shirts, one Pair white yarn stockings, one pair grey ribbed worsted ditto, one pair plain ditto, and country made shoes, nailed, with iron on the heels. Robert Williams, an Englishman, between 40 and 50 years of age, about 5 feet 6 inches high, thin visage, grey eyes, small flat nose, a large scar under his left ear; had on, and took with him, an old felt hat, old brown wig, old worsted cap, two halfworn coats, one of a dirty snuff colour, the other dark grey, faced with red shaloon, new white kersey under jacket, with sleeves, one blue ditto, a pair of half worn buckskin breeches, one pair of black and white yarn stockings, a pair of ribbed ditto, and a pair of country made shoes, nailed. Richard Mulanie, an Irishman, about 40 or 50 years of age, 5 feet 7 or 8 inches high, thin visage, pitted with the small-pox, high nose; had on, an iron collar, old castor hat, two wigs, one yellow, the other white, old blue coat, the sleeves patched with cloth of a yellow colour, old cloth coloured waistcoat, old black leather breeches, much worn, two pair of ribbed stockings, country made shoes, nailed, with iron on the heels. Whoever takes up and secures the said servants, or either of them, in any goal, so that their masters may get them again, shall have, if 10 miles from home, Forty Shillings reward, and if 20 miles, Five Pounds, and if out of the province, Seven Pounds for each of them, including what the law allows, and reasonable charges, if brought home, paid by
JOSHUA OWINGS, and JOHN COCKEY OWINGS.
The Pennsylvania Gazette, February 16, 1769; April 13, 1769.

February 28, 1769.
FORTY-SIX DOLLARS REWARD.

RAN away, on Sunday Night the 19th Instant, from *Bush-Creek*, near *Frederick-Town*, in *Frederick* County, Two Convicts, one of them named JOHN THOMAS, a likely young Man, about 25 Years of Age, 5 Feet 7 or 8 Inches high, ruddy Complexion, dark brown, or black Hair, and curls in his Neck, has large Wrists, is stout made, he was imported last Spring from *Bristol*, is a good Farmer, and is rather slow in his Speech: He took with him a light coloured Broad Cloth Coat and Breeches, the Breeches finer than his Coat, and his Coat mended at the Elbows, *Welsh* Cotton Jacket and Breeches, a black Cravet, a half worn Felt Hat, one Check'd, and Two Osnabrig Shirts, a Pair of Country made Shoes, one of them has been split, and mended on the Top, Country-made Yarn Stockings, black, or white and black Threads twisted, and probably some other Cloaths; he belongs to *Thomas Johnson*, Jun.—The other about 5 Feet 6 Inches high, fair Complexion, black curled Hair, about 25 Years of Age: He took with him a Country Cloth, and another *Welsh* Cotton Jacket, Two Osnabrig Shirts, a Pair of Country Cloth Breeches, all old, a Pair of old Shoes and Stockings, and an old Hat patched with Cloth; he is remarkably talkative, and belongs to *Benjamin Sapp*.—They are supposed to have taken with them a grey Horse, branded, I believe, **T I**, and a grey Mare, and I believe, a natural Pacer, and broken rumped, both used to the Draft. *John Thomas* will probably change his Name, and rig his Companion, as well as he can, with his spare Cloathing. The respective Master [sic] will give Twenty Dollars for either of the Servants apprehended and returned, or secured in any Jail, and Notice given, so that they may be had again; and Three Dollars for each of the Beasts returned. THOMAS JOHNSON, Jun.

N. B. If the Fellows should be apprehended, they will escape, unless well secured.

The Maryland Gazette, March 2, 1769; March 9, 1769; March 16, 1769; March 23, 1769; March 30, 1769; April 6, 1769; April 13, 1769; April 27, 1769; May 11, 1769. See *The Pennsylvania Chronicle, and Universal Advertiser*, From Monday, March 13, to Monday, March 20, 1769.

RUN from the subscriber, living near Joppa Town, in Baltimore county, Maryland, on Friday night, the 17th of February last, an indented Irish servant lad, about 18 years of age, dark complexion, pitted with the small pox, about 5 feet 5 inches high, had on, stole, and took with him, when he went away, a red halfthick jacket, with sleeves, and breeches of the same, not lined, a white saggathy coat, tore on the top of the left shoulder, blue stockings, and half-worn shoes; he also stole at the same time his master's

watch, the inside works cased, maker's name James Warne, London. Whoever takes up said servant, and brings him to his master, shall receive for himself, Three Pounds, and for the watch and servant, five Pounds current money, paid by PHILIP CALVIN.
The Pennsylvania Gazette, March 2, 1769.

March 13, 1769.

MADE his Escape from the Sheriff of *Prince-George's* County, a certain *Joseph Zachariah Thomson*, born in *St. Mary's* County, a young Man, about Five Feet Seven Inches high, of a thin Visage, a fair Complexion: Had on him, when he went away, an old short Sagothy Coat, a strip'd Linsey Woolsey Waistcoat, old brown Cloth Breeches, old Shoes and Stockings, and a slouch'd Hat.—Whoever will bring said Person to the Subscriber, or secure him, so as I may get him again, shall receive a Reward of FIVE POUNDS, from   JOHN ADDISON, Sheriff.
The Maryland Gazette, March 16, 1769; March 23, 1769; March 30, 1769.

Port-Tobacco, Feb. 28, 1769.

RAN away, on the First of *January* last, from the Subscriber, an indented Servant Woman, named *Hannah Carr*:—Had on, when she went away, a blue and white stript *Manchester* Cotton Gown, a black and white Silk and Cotton Handkerchief, Check Apron, and a black silk Bonnet. She is a strong middle-siz'd Woman, of a fair ruddy Complexion, large visaged, brown Hair, pitted much with the Small-Pox, and her Eyes inclinable to be sore.

Whoever takes up the said Servant, and brings her to the Subscriber, shall receive THIRTY SHILLINGS, besides what the Law allows, paid by me,   JOSEPH ADERTON.
The Maryland Gazette, March 16, 1769; March 23, 1769; April 6, 1769; April 13, 1769.

TEN POUNDS Reward.

RUN away on Sunday night, the 19*th of February last, from Bush Creek, near Frederick Town, in Frederick County, Maryland, the two following convicts, viz.*

John Thomas, *a likely young man, about 25 years of age, 5 feet 7 or 8 inches high, of a ruddy complexion, dark brown or black hair, curls in his neck, has large wrists, is stout made and rather slow of speech. He is a good farmer. Had on and took with him, a light coloured broadcloth coat and breeches, the coat has been mended at the elbows, Welch cotton jacket and breeches, black cravat, half-worn felt hat, one check shirt, and two* ozenbrigs ditto, country made shoes, one of them split open on the top, and mended again; it is probable he may have some other clothes. He belongs to Thomas Johnson, jun. in Annapolis.

William Warner, *an Englishman, about 5 feet 6 or 7 inches high, fair complexion, black curled hair, 25 years of age. He took with him a country cloth jacket, and a Welch cotton ditto, two ozenbrigs shirts, old shoes and stockings, and an old hat patched with cloth. He is remarkably talkative, and belongs to Benjamin Sapp, whose place they went from.* John Thomas will probably change his name, and rig his companion, as well as he can, with his spare cloathing. Their respective masters will give Five Pounds for either of them apprehended and returned, or secured in any gaol, and notice given, so that they may be had again, and reasonable charges if brought home, paid by

THOMAS JOHNSON, junior.   BENJAMIN SAPP.

N. B. *If the fellows should be apprehended, they will escape unless well secured.*

The Pennsylvania Chronicle, and Universal Advertiser, From Monday, March 13, to Monday, March 20, 1769. See *The Maryland Gazette*, March 2, 1769.

TEN POUNDS REWARD.

Virginia, March 4, 1769.

RAN away from the Subscriber, in *New-Kent* County, on Monday last, an *English* Convict Servant Man, named THOMAS BELCHER, about 28 Years olf, 5 Feet 7 or 8 Inches high, well made, fair Complexion, light Hair, which he wears, red thin Beard, and speaks effeminately: His Occupation is Farming, which he understands, but pretends to Knowledge in many other Kinds of Businesses: Had on, and took with him, a Felt Hat, almost new, an old brown Cut Wig, a light Duffil Coat, half worn, with round white Metal Buttons, mix'd Country Cloth Jacket and Breeches of white Cotton, filled with yellow Wool, one Pair of Sagothy Breeches, one Osnabrig Shirt, Country-made mix'd Yarn Hose, one Pair of white Cotton ditto, one Pair of Country-Made Shoes, nailed all round with Hob-Nails, one Pair of old Pumps, with carved Brass Buckles. He was seen, it is supposed, passing *Todd's* Bridge, going to the Northward, the Morning following, in Company with some Man who wore a blue Coat. He has very likely forged a Pass, or Discharge; and he may probably attempt to make his Escape by Water.—All Masters of Vessels are forbid employing, or harbouring him.— Whoever takes up and secures said Servant, and gives Intelligence thereof, so as he may be had again, shall be paid at the Rate of Sixpence *per* Mile for any Number he may be from home, under Forty; and then for any greater Number, at the Rate of Ninepence *per* Mile; if out of the Colony,

Five Pounds, more than the Law allows; and, if brought home, reasonable Charges, paid by JOSEPH WATKINS.
The Maryland Gazette, March 23, 1769.

Virginia, March 5, 1769.

RAN away from the Subscriber, on Friday the 27th of *January* last, near the Falls of *Rappahannock*, in the County of *Spotsylvania*, EDWARD DANIEL, alias JAMES M'DONALD, he is a Blacksmith by Trade, and by Birth an *Irishman*, is about 50 Years of Age, between 5 Feet 6 and 9 Inches high, and has lost several of his fore Teeth: Had on, and took with him, a blue Frock, green Jacket, Leather Breeches, sundry white, Check, and brown Linen Shirts, a new Felt Hat, brown Wig, and a thick Woollen Cap.—He was convicted for robbing on the High-Way, and was imported in the *Justitia*, Capt. *Somerville*.—Whoever delivers said Servant to Mr. *Stapleton Crutchfield*, at *Elk-Ridge*, near the Falls of *Patapsco*, shall receive Five Pounds *Maryland* Currency, besides reasonable Expences, if brought any considerable Distance; or Forty Shillings, if committed to any Jail, (of which public Notice is requested) so that I may get him again, which shall be paid to the Jailer, when he is taken out of Jail. As he was convicted some Years ago, and made his Escape, it is probable he will endeavour to get on board some Ship, or travel to the Northward, in order to follow his Occupation.—All Masters of Ships are requested to have him secured, if he should be found on board of any Vessel under their Command; and all Smiths, if he should offer himself to them for Employment.
BENJAMIN GRYMES, jun.

The Maryland Gazette, March 23, 1768; March 30, 1769; April 6, 1769.

Kent County, Maryland, February 24, 1769.
TWENTY DOLLARS Reward.

RUN away from the subscriber, living in Kent county, Maryland, about the 12th of this instant, a convict servant man, named *Michael Kern* or *Hern*, a Taylor by trade, about 5 feet 7 inches high, slim made, thin visaged, dark complexion, black hair, a German born, and is so much like a French Neutral, that he many very well pass for one; had on, when he went away, a dark coloured jacket, or half coat, of beaver coating, much worn, a double breasted jacket, of white cotton, green half thick breeches, a neat pair of pumps, good stockings, and several good shirts; he is an artful cunning fellow, can write, and has money; he many change his name and dress, likewise forge a pass. Whoever takes up the said servant, and brings him home, if taken within the county, shall receive Eight dollars reward, if out of the province, and brought home, Twenty Dollars reward, and if taken out of the county, and secured in any goal, so that his master may have him again, shall receive Ten dollars reward, provided immediate notice be given, paid by RICHARD GRESHAM.

The Pennsylvania Gazette, March 23, 1769; April 13, 1769. See *The Maryland Gazette*, July 6, 1769, *The Pennsylvania Gazette*, August 17, 1769, and *The Pennsylvania Gazette*, December 14, 1769, as Hern/Kern is probably Hewne/Keirn/Hayne.

March 29, 1769.

RAN away last Night from the Subscribers, living on *Kent-Island*, Two Convict Servant Men, *viz.*

EDWARD PONTING, born in *Bristol*, about 25 Years of Age, 5 Feet 6 or 7 Inches high, has a pert impudent Look, thin Visage, with brown curled Hair, is by Trade a Shoemaker, and has some blue Marks on the Upper Part of his Hands, near the Thumbs, which are unknown: Had on, when he went away, an old brown coloured *Wilton* Coat, spotted Flannel Jacket, a Pair of half worn Leather Breeches, old blue ribb'd Stockings, old Shoes, with plated Buckles, half worn Castor Hat, and a Check Shirt.

EVAN DAVIS, born in *Wales*, or on the Borders thereof, about 30 Years of Age, 5 Feet 9 or 10 Inches high, a well set Fellow, round Visage, a short Nose, which turns up at the End, sandy Complexion, and has short curled or frizled Hair; he speaks pretty good *English*, but a little in the *Welsh* Dialect, and has been bred to the Plantation Business: Had on, and took with him, when he went away, Two short Jackets, the uppermost double breasted, of blue coarse Cloth, with white Metal Buttons, the other yellowish striped Flannel, or Swanskin, a Pair of blue Plush Breeches, much worn, and mended on the Knees with blue Cloth, Two Pair of Stockings, the one blue Yarn, the other white Yarn, or Cotton, a good Pair of Shoes, with broad Brass Buckles, an Osnabrig Shirt, and a Felt Hat almost new.—Whoever takes up and secures said Convicts, so that their Masters may get them again, shall receive for each, Thirty Shillings, besides what the Law allows, and reasonable Charges, if brought home, paid by SAMUEL BLUNT, JONATHAN ROBERTS.

The Maryland Gazette, March 30, 1769; April 6, 1769; April 20, 1769; May 4, 1769; May 11, 1769; May 18, 1769. See *The Pennsylvania Gazette*, April 27, 1769, and *The Pennsylvania Gazette*, June 29, 1769.

RAN away, on the 2d Inst. from the Ship *Polly*, at *Annapolis*, a Sailor, named *John Fipps*, about 25 Years of Age, Five Feet Eight Inches high, wears his own brown Hair, is pitted with the Small-pox, carbuncled Face, and looks pleasant: Had on, when he went away, an old green Jacket, and *Dutch* Cap.

Whoever apprehends the above *John Fipps*, and secures him, so that the Subscriber may have him, shall have Two Pistoles Reward, paid by
JOHN KILTY.

The Maryland Gazette, April 6, 1769; April 20, 1769.

Baltimore-Town, March 29, 1769.

RAN away from the Subscribers, the Two following Servant Men, *viz.*
JOHN OWINGS, about 25 Years of Age, 5 Feet high, by Trade a Coach-Harness Maker, and has short brown curl'd Hair: Had on and took with him when he went away, One double-breasted Swanskin Jacket, spotted with red, a coarse Drab ditto, with Brass Buttons, a Broad-Cloth under ditto, of a light Colour, a Pair of blue Breeches, Two Pair of Stockings, One of a yellowish Colour, and the other of a coarse grey, a Pair of Country made Pumps, with Brass Buckles. He may have several other Things, is much given to Liquor, and when drunk is very quarrelsome.

WILLIAM SHEPHERD, about Five Feet Five Inches high, Nineteen Years of Age, by Trade a Watch-Maker, of a dark Complexion, black Eyes, short dark curl'd Hair, stoops a little in his Walk, and turns in his Toes: Had on and took with him, when he went away, a brown Bearskin Surtout Coat, bound round with narrow Binding, a coarse brown close-bodied ditto, patch'd under the Arms with light grey, a scarlet napp'd Waistcoat, a Pair of black Stocking Breeches, a Pair of light blue Stockings, Country-made Shoes, and a coarse Felt Hat, with a Slit in the Crown; he likewise took an *English* Crown Piece of Queen *Anne's* Coin.

Whoever takes up said Servants, and gives Intelligence to *Jacob Myers*, in said Town, so as their Masters may have them again, shall receive a Reward of Forty Shillings, if in, or near Town, and Five Pounds if Twelve Miles from home, and if out of the Province, Five Pounds for each, paid by
JACOB MYERS & BASIS FRANCIS.

The said *John Owings* can write a good Hand, and may probably forge a Pass.

The Maryland Gazette, April 6, 1769; April 13, 1769; April 20, 1769.

April 6, 1769.

RAN away from the Subscriber, on Tuesday the 3d Inst. a Servant Man, named WILLIAM WHATELEY, has been in the Country about 13 Months, is of a dark Complexion, about 6 Feet High, stout limb'd, and one of his Knees seems as if it was double jointed, and he has been, as he says, a Soldier in the late War: Had on, when he went away, an old Bearskin

Jacket, and a white Kersey double-breasted Jacket under it, has short black Hair, and was brought up a Ribbon-Weaver, but can turn his Hand to any Thing that is done upon a Plantation, and understands something of the Sailors Business.

Whoever takes up, and secures said Servant Man, shall have Three Pounds Reward, and reasonable Charges, paid by
ASAEL GITTINGS.

The Maryland Gazette, April 13, 1769; April 27, 1769; May 4, 1769; May 18, 1769.

April 10, 1769.
TWENTY POUNDS REWARD.
RAN away on Sunday Night, the 2d Instant, from the Subscriber, living on *Fell's* Point, *Baltimore* County, the Four following Indented Servant Men, viz.

JOHN EVANS, an *Englishman*, about 5 Feet 8 or 9 Inches high, 28 or 30 Years of Age, of a fair Complexion, pretty much pitted with the Small-Pox, and wears a light coloured Wig: Had on and took with him, an old light blue Cloth Surtout, a strip'd Linsey Under-Jacket, old Leather Breeches, Yarn Stockings, old Shoes, and Brass Buckles.

JOHN BARBER, an *Englishman*, about 5 Feet 9 or 10 Inches high, 26 or 28 Years of Age, stout made, of a dark Complexion, wears his own strait black Hair, and has a very down Look: Had on and took with him, a good Broad-Cloth Coat, Waistcoat, and Breeches, of a Claret, or rather Pompadour Colour, an old blue out-side Jacket, a white Flannel Under ditto, old Leather Breeches, Yarn Stockings, and old Shoes.—He, and *Evans*, are both Sawyers by Trade, and took with them a Whip-Saw.

HENRY WILLIAMS, an *Englishman*, by Trade a Ship-Carpenter, about 5 Feet 9 Inches high, 36 Years of Age, a slim made Fellow, and wears his own short brown Hair: Had on and took with him, a mix'd grey Bearskin Surtout, an old blue Jacket, a strip'd Linsey Under ditto, Claret colour'd Cloth Breeches, Yarn Stockings, and old Shoes.

WILLIAM ADAIR, a *Scotchman*, about 5 Feet 8 or 9 Inches high, a stout lusty well made Fellow, a little mark'd with the Small-Pox, wears his own short brown curl'd Hair, of an easy and pleasant Address, and speaks much in the *Scotch* Dialect: Had on and took with him, a long light colour'd Outside Jacket, lined with red Flannel, a strip'd Linsey Under ditto, short white Cotton Trowsers, brown Cloth Breeches, Yarn Stockings, old Shoes, and Brass Buckles.

They took with them a Boat about 17 Feet Keel, with a Turpentine Coat on her Bottom, and Upper Streaks painted red, her Stem broke off short, and marked with Marking Irons on the Inside of her Stern, with the Letters **B D**: 'Tis likely they may change their Apparel, and forge a Pass.

All Masters of Vessels are forbid harbouring or carrying them off, at their Peril.

Whoever takes up and secures said Runaways, so that their Master may get them again, shall have, if taken in the County, Twenty Shillings for each, if out of the County, Thirty Shillings, and if out of the Province, the above Reward, for all, or in Proportion for either, with reasonable Charges, including what the Law allows, paid by
GEORGE WELLS.

The Maryland Gazette, April 13, 1769; April 20, 1769; April 27, 1769; May 4, 1769; May 11, 1769; May 18, 1769. See *The Pennsylvania Chronicle, and Universal Advertiser*, From Monday, October 30, to Monday, November 6, 1769, for Adair and Barber.

Anne-Arundel County, *April* 12, 1769.
TEN POUNDS REWARD.

RAN away from the Subscriber, on Sunday Night the 9th Instant, living near *Elk-Ridge* Church, a Servant Man, named JOHN WINTER, he is about Forty Years of Age, Five Feet Eight Inches high, mark'd with the Small-Pox, and wears his own black Hair: Had on, and with him, a Fearnought Upper Jacket, a blue and brown Under Cloth ditto, an Osnabrig and Check Shirt, a Pair of Black Breeches, an also a Pair of Osnabrig Trousers, coarse Yarn Stockings, common Negro Shoes, and a Castor Hat, half worn: He is a very complaisant dissembling Fellow, it will be necessary to be aware of his fair Promises. Whoever takes up the said Fellow, and secures him in Jail, so that his Master gets him again, shall receive Forty Shillings Reward; tho' if brought home, and taken out of the Province, Five Pounds; if within the Province, Fifty Shillings, paid by   EPHRAIM HOWARD.

The Maryland Gazette, April 20, 1769.

RUN away the 28th of March last, from the Subscribers, living on Kent-Island, Queen-Anne's County, Maryland, two Convict Servant Men, viz.

EDWARD PONTING, born in Bristol, about 25 Years of Age, 5 Feet 6 or 7 Inches high, has a pert impudent Look, thin Visage, with brown curled Hair, is by Trade a Shoemaker, and has some blue Marks on the Upper Part of his Hands, near the Thumbs, which are unknown: Had on, when he went away, an old Bloom coloured Wilton Coat, spotted Flannel Jacket, a Pair of half-worn Leather Breeches, old blue ribbed Stockings, old Shoes, with plated Buckles, half-worn Castor Hat, and a Check Shirt.

EVAN DAVIS, born in Wales, or on the Borders thereof, about 30 Years of Age, 5 Feet 9 or 10 Inches high, a well set Fellow, round Visage, a short Nose, which turns up at the End, sandy Complexion, and has short curled or frizzled Hair; he speaks pretty good English, but a little in the Welsh Dialect; and has been bred to the Plantation Business: Had on, and took with him, when he went away, two short Jackets, the uppermost double breasted, of blue coarse Cloth, with white Metal Buttons, the other yellowish striped Flannel, or Swanskin, a Pair of blue Plush Breeches, much worn, and mended on the Knees with blue Cloth, Two Pair of Stockings, the one blue Yarn, the other white Yarn, or Cotton, a good Pair of Shoes, with broad Brass Buckles, an Osnabrig Shirt, and a Felt Hat almost new.

Both the above Servants were imported into the Province of Maryland, last November, in the Ship Randolph, Captain Price.

Whoever takes up and secures the said Convicts, so that their Masters may get them again, shall receive, for each, FIFTY SHILLINGS, and reasonable Charges besides, if brought home, paid by
JONATHAN ROBERTS,   SAMUEL BLUNT.

N. B. It is likely they may have forged Passes, or Discharges, as PONTING can write, though very indifferently.

The Pennsylvania Gazette, April 27, 1769. See *The Maryland Gazette,* March 30, 1769, and *The Pennsylvania Gazette,* June 29, 1769.

April 23, 1769.

RAN away last Night from the Subscriber, living in the Forrest of *Baltimore* County, a Convict Servant Man, named SAMUEL WATTS: He is a short well set Fellow, about 30 Years of Age, 5 Feet 6 Inches high, wears his own Hair, which is very red, his Beard the same Colour, and of a ruddy Complexion. Had on and took with him, a new Felt Hat, blue gray Fearnothing Jacket, Cotton ditto and Breeches, One Osnabrig Shirt, and One Check ditto, Yarn Stockings, and Negro Shoes—He also stole, and took with him, a good Broad Cloth Coat and Breeches, of a brown Colour, too large for him, red Frieze Jacket, new Castor Hat, with a yellow gilt Button and Loop, a good Holland Shirt, with Ruffles at the Bosom, a Stock, with Silver Clasps, old Leather Breeches, black Worsted Stockings, and Yarn ditto, good *English* Shoes, much too large for him, odd Buckles, and a Pair of Buckskin Gloves, and several other Things. Whoever takes up said Servant, and secures him, so as his Master may have him again, shall have, if taken Twenty Miles from home, Twenty Shillings; if Forty Miles, Forty Shillings; and if out of the Province, Three Pounds, paid by
JOSEPH JACOBS.

It is likely he my [*sic*] change his Name, and forge a Pass.

The Maryland Gazette, May 4, 1769; May 11, 1769.

RUN away from the subscriber, living in Cecil county, Maryland, an Irish servant man, named PHILIP MURPHEY, about 5 feet 7 or 8 inches high; had on when he went away, a half worn hat, 2 jackets, the one spotted flannel, with sleeves, the other a brown, without sleeves, lately turned, and lined with white shaloon, a tow shirt patched, a pair of coarse linen trowsers, made breeches fashion, old claret coloured cloth breeches, a pair of stockings fitted with lincey, and half worn pumps. He says he is a Coppersmith, and has been some time at sea; he has been 2 or 3 years in the army, and was at the taking of the Havanna; he says he received a wound in his stomach, and carries the mark; he is a good Cobler, and a handy ingenious fellow at almost any thing. Whoever takes up and secures said servant in any goal, so that his master may have him again, shall have Three Pounds reward, paid by me   JONAS CHAMBERS.

N. B. The said Philip Murphey has short brown curled hair, and may change his name and clothes. All masters of vessels are forewarned not to carry him off at their peril.

The Pennsylvania Gazette, May 4, 1769.

FIVE POUNDS Reward.

RUN-away from the subscribers, living in Frederick-Town, Maryland, the two following servants, viz. Thomas Homes, an Englishman, by trade a gardener, about 25 or 26 years of age, about 5 feet 6 inches high, of a sandy complexion, and wears his hair tied some times; he has been branded on both his arms, but 'tis very remarkable to be seen that he is branded or marked with gunpowder on his left hand with a resemblance of the seven stars: He took with him when he went away, two wool hats, a blanket coat with yellow binding, and a pair of old leather breeches, with four pair of stockings; he has a sore leg, and it is seemingly thicker than the well one.

The other named Henry Weply, by trade a brick-layer, an Englishman, about 5 feet 3 or 4 inches, very stooping, and has a remarkable lump on, or above his right eye: He took with him when he went away, a brown jacket with sleeves, and a double breasted white jacket, with a good strong pair of leather breeches, and a good pair of woollen blue stockings. They both went off together, and as Homes can write a good hand, its probable he may forge passes for both. Whoever takes up the said servants, and secures them in any of his Majesty's dominions, or in any goal, so that their masters may have them again, shall have a reward of Five Pounds, or Fifty Shillings for each, paid by us,

JACOB BRANGLE, CHRISTIAN SCHOOL.

The New-York Gazette; and the Weekly Mercury, May 8, 1769; May 15, 1769; May 29, 1769; June 12, 1769.

April 7, 1769.

RAN away from the *Elk-Ridge* Furnace, a Convict Servant Man, named WILLIAM SNOW, about Forty Years of Age, near Five Feet Four Inches high, has long brown Hair, a down look, a long Hawk-Bill Nose, is whining or plaintive, and slow in his Speech: Had on and took with him, an old Felt Hat, old Cotton Jacket, one new under ditto, without Sleeves: Four Osnabrig Shirts, a Pair of Cotton Breeches, a Pair of white Yarn Stockings, and old coarse Shoes.—Whoever apprehends said Runaway, and brings him home, shall have, if taken Ten Miles from said Furnace, Twenty-five Shillings; if Twenty Miles, Forty Shillings; if Forty Miles, Three Pounds; and, if out of the Province of Maryland, Five Pounds Reward, paid by
CALEB DORSEY.

The Maryland Gazette, May 11, 1769; May 18, 1769; May 25, 1769; June 8, 1769. See *The Maryland Gazette*, March 19, 1767.

Baltimore-Town, May 8, 1769.

RAN away last night, from the subscriber, living in Baltimore-Town, an English servant man, named HENRY CARTWRIGHT, about 5 feet 8 inches high, 24 years of age, fresh complexion, has short light brown hair, wears it loose about his shoulders, wants several of his teeth, broad shouldered, greatly bow-legged, had on when he went away, a new felt hat, a good green jacket, made sailor fashion, with buttons on the sleeves, a striped under ditto, a pair of black shag breeches, a light pair of worsted stockings, and a pair of yarn ribbed ditto in his pocket, a pair of soled shoes, and plain yellow buckles, a check shirt, and check handkerchief about his neck. Whoever takes up said servant, and secures him in any goal, so that his master may have him again, shall have, if 20 miles from home, Twenty Shillings, if 40 miles, Forty Shillings, and if out of the province, Three Pounds reward, and reasonable charges, paid by
GEORGE PRESSTMAN.

The Pennsylvania Gazette, May 18, 1769; June 1, 1769. See *The Pennsylvania Chronicle, and Universal Advertiser*, From Monday, July 3, to Monday, July 10, 1769, and *The Pennsylvania Gazette*, July 13, 1769.

RUN away from his bail, living in Queen-Anne's county, Maryland, a certain AARON YOE, he is about 5 feet 6 inches high, of a dark complexion, wears his own hair; had on, and took with him, when he went away, an old felt hat, an old claret coloured coat, a country made shirt, and a pair of old black breeches; his other apparel unknown. Whoever takes up said person, and secures him, so that the Subscribers (who are his bail in

several actions) may get him again, shall receive Forty Shillings Pennsylvania currency reward, paid by
April 26, 1769.   THOMAS WRIGHT, WILLIAM YOE.
The Pennsylvania Gazette, May 25, 1769.

TEN POUNDS Reward.

RUN away from the Subscriber, living on Kent-Island, Queen-Anne's county, Maryland, the 9th of May instant, at night, two servant men, viz. John Jennings, a convict, by trade a shoemaker; and Benjamin Webber, an indented servant, a weaver by trade; said Jennings is about 5 feet 9 or 10 inches high, of a thin visage, has a scar across his left cheek, has thin brown hair, fresh cut on the crown, but may have it cut off, is fond of strong liquor, and when drunk is very bold; both of them are Englishmen, born in or near Coventry; Jennings took a pair of leather breeches, patched, and sewed with white thread, a bearskin jacket, made in a plain manner, a bearskin great coat, almost new, of a light cloth colour, old hat, a pair of new shoes that do not fit him, and other things unknown; it is probable they may change their dress and names, and I do expect they have a forged pass or discharge, on some assignment or indenture. Benjamin Webber has a bearskin jacket, made in a plain manner, a bearskin surtout, mended on the elbows with another sort of cloth, white hose, his shoes have been lately soaled, with other things unknown. Whoever takes up said servants, and secures them in any goal in this province, shall have Three Pounds reward, current money, for Jennings, and Forty Shillings for Webber, and if out of the province Six Pounds for Jennings, and Four Pounds for Webber, and reasonable charges, if brought to Queen's-Town goal, paid by
BENJAMIN KIRBY.

N. B. Jennings took with him a good sett of shoe-maker's tools, and some leather; I forewarn all masters of vessels taking them on board.

The Pennsylvania Gazette, May 25, 1769; June 1, 1769.

RAN away from the Subscriber, living near the Head of *Chester* River, in *Queen-Anne's* County, on the 14th of *May*, a Convict Servant Man, named WILLIAM PREES, about 50 Years of Age, 5 Feet 6 or 7 Inches high, is broad set, his Hair almost white, the Top of his Head bald, and has a particular Wink, or Leer with his Eyes, when Talking. Also a Negro Fellow, named BEN....They took with them Four Pair of Leather Breeches, Three white Shirts, one of which is new, and Two Brown ditto, much worn, Two white Country Kersey Jackets, not mill'd, a dark colour'd Fearnought Jacket, a white *Welch* Cotton ditto, a Claret coloured and brown ditto, both Cloth, a brown Camblet Coat, Three Felt Hats, and Four Pair of Shoes.

Whoever takes up, and secures the said Convict, and Negro, or either of them, so that the Subscriber may have them again, shall receive 20 s. each, if taken in this Province, or 40 s. each, if taken out of this Province, and reasonable Charges.   JOHN SEALE.

The Maryland Gazette, June 1, 1769; June 8, 1769; June 22, 1769; June 29, 1769; *The Pennsylvania Gazette*, June 1, 1769; June 29, 1769. Minor differences between the papers. The first *Pennsylvania Gazette* has May 22, 1769, at the bottom, the second has June 22, 1769, at the bottom.

Elk-Ridge, May 15, 1769.

RAN away from the Subscriber, a Convict Servant Man, named THOMAS DANELY, about 36 Years of Age, 5 Feet 9 Inches high, has black Hair, is of a dark Complexion, has a flat Nose, and snuffles in his Speech: Had on, when he went away, a half worn Castor Hat, a Cotton Jacket, an Osnabrig Shirt and Trowsers, gray Yarn Stockings, a Pair of old Shoes, and plain Buckles: He went off in Company with a free Man, named *Patrick Maguire*, who came some Time ago from *Pennsylvania*, and is well acquainted in *Baltimore, Prince-George's, St. Mary's*, &c. *Maryland*, is remarkable for a Trembling in his Hands, has short black Hair, bald headed, speaks low, slow, and is very hoarse: He likewise took with him a Snuff-colour'd superfine Cloth Coat and Jacket, two Jackets gray Cloth, lined with white Flannel, an old light coloured Great Coat, white Linen Shirt, Osnabrig ditto, and Trowsers; he had also Razors, Hone, and a Roman Prayer-Book, with other Things unknown—He will no Doubt give *Danely* Part of the Cloaths.

Whoever takes up said Runaway, or *Danely*, shall have, if taken in *Anne-Arundel County*, 30 s. and, if out of the County, 3 l. Reward, paid by WILLIAM LEVINS.

The Maryland Gazette, June 1, 1769.

RUN away, on the 4th of May last, from the Subscriber, living near Annapolis, in Maryland, two convict servant men, viz. JOSEPH PENICK, about 5 feet 8 inches high, of a brown complexion, black hair, and black eyes; had on, when he went away, a light coloured fearnought jacket; his other apparel uncertain: It is supposed one of them, has a pair of leather breeches, with a gore down each thigh, he speaks quick, and pretends to many things, and is a young man, about 23 or 24 years of age. THOMAS ELTON, about 25 or 26 years of age, a short well made man, of a brown complexion, black hair, cut close on the top of his head; had on, when he went away, a blue fearnought upper jacket, a dyed cotton ditto under it; he pretends to understand farming, and butchering: As to their apparel, it is very likely they may have changed them; it is supposed they will make towards Philadelphia, as one of them had run away some time ago, and was taken up and committed to Chester goal. Whoever takes up the said servants, and secures them, so that their master may get them again, shall have a reward of Four Dollars, including what the law allows, paid by THOMAS RUTLAND.

The Pennsylvania Gazette, June 1, 1769. See *The Pennsylvania Gazette*, February 2, 1769, for Penick/Pennock. See *The Pennsylvania Chronicle, and Universal Advertiser*, From Monday, September 25, to Monday, October 2, 1769, *The Pennsylvania Gazette*, October 12, 1769, and *The Maryland Gazette*, October 19, 1769, for Elton.

RAN away from the *Elk-Ridge* Furnace, a Convict Servant Man, named THOMAS JAMES, about 35 Years of Age, near 5 Feet 8 Inches high, has yellow Hair, light coloured Eyebrows, and shows much of the White of his Eyes; he has a down Look, but is pert and hasty in his Address: Had on, when he went away, a new Felt Hat, a blue Broad Cloth Jacket lined with white Flannel, a fine Linen Shirt, a striped Silk Handkerchief, Osnabrig Trowsers, and a Pair of Dogskin Pumps, with plain Copper Buckles.— Whoever apprehends the said Runaway, and brings him home, shall have, if taken Ten Miles from said Furnace, Thirty Shillings; if Twenty Miles, Forty Shillings; if Thirty Miles, Three Pounds; and, if out of the Province, Five Pounds Reward (including what the Law allows) and reasonable Charges, paid by CALEB DORSEY.

The Maryland Gazette, June 8, 1769; June 15, 1769; June 22, 1769; June 29, 1769. See *The Maryland Gazette*, May 28, 1767, and *The Maryland Gazette*, August 3, 1769.

Four Dollars Reward.

RUN away last night from the subscriber, in Frederick town, Cecil County, Maryland, a servant man, named Thomas Lovott, born in Cheshire, in England, of a yellow complexion, and remarkable black eyes and hair: he is about 24 years of age, and about six feet high; had on and took with him a narrow brimmed hat, bound with black binding, an old snuff coloured coat, a striped linsey vest, a white shirt, and an old check ditto, a pair of old buckskin breeches, (lately washed) a pair of new oznabrigs trowsers, and an old pair ditto, a pair of half worn pumps, with a pair of pinchbeck buckles. He formerly lived with Mr. Anthony Banning, of Talbot county; writes a good hand, and probably may forge a pass. Whoever secures said servant, so that his master may have him again, or delivers him to Mr. Benjamin

Kendall, in Philadelphia, shall receive the above reward, and reasonable charges paid by   PHILIP WEATHRALL.

The Pennsylvania Chronicle, and Universal Advertiser, From Monday, June 5, to Monday, June 12, 1769; From Monday, June 12, to Monday, June 19, 1769; From Monday, June 19, to Monday, June 26, 1769.

RUN away from the Subscriber, living in Baltimore County, Maryland, near the head of Bush River, the 16th of April 1769, an Irish convict servant man, named Patrick Dermon, a stone mason by trade, a well set fellow, about five feet nine inches high, red complexion, marked with the small pox, his nose droops, black eyes, black hair, some grey hairs on the top of his head, wears his hair short, about thirty-five years of age, walks wide in the knees: Had on, when he went away, a castor hat, blue surtout coat, brown kersey jacket, a black ditto, a pair of cloth breeches, a pair of grey worsted stockings, a pair of yarn ditto, one Holland shirt, an oznabrig ditto, half worn, a pair of shoes, and odd steel buckles; he also took with him a yellow cut wig, and a striped cap. Whoever takes up the said servant, and secures him so that his master may have him again, shall have FIVE POUNDS Reward, and reasonable charges paid by me
          THOMAS SANDERS.
N. B. He speaks bad English.

The Pennsylvania Chronicle, and Universal Advertiser, From Monday, June 5, to Monday, June 12, 1769; From Monday, June 12, to Monday, June 19, 1769; From Monday, June 19, to Monday, June 26, 1769.

SIX POUNDS REWARD.

RAN away from the subscribers, living in Baltimore county, Maryland, near the lower ferry, on Susquehannah, two convict servant men, viz. John and Daniel Stepelton, brothers, both born in Coneck, in Ireland: John is about thirty years old, and speaks with the brogue; he is about five feet four or five inches high, a well set fellow, of a very dark complexion, with his hair turning grey. Had on when he went away an old castor hat, a dark brown jacket, and striped ticken breeches, patched on the knees with striped linsey, one country made check shirt, and a pair of homespun stockings, and a pair of single channel pumps, with old buckles: He writes a good hand, and it is likely he will forge a pass.—Daniel is about twenty-seven years old, and about five feet eight or nine inches high, of a middling fair complexion, pitted with the small pox, and a large scar from his ears down to his throat: had on when he went away, a brown half-thick jacket, with slash sleeves, a striped ditto, a check shirt, a felt hat, a brown wig, a pair of

sheep-skin breeches, striped ditto, a pair of coarse stockings, and a pair of single channel pumps, tied with strings. It is probable that they will both change their names and cloathing, as they went off the fifteenth of January last. Whoever takes up said servants, so that their masters may have them again, shall receive the above reward, paid by us,
ANDREW WILSON, and HENRY RUTTER.
June 10, 1769.
> *The Pennsylvania Chronicle, and Universal Advertiser*, From Monday, June 12, to Monday, June 19, 1769; From Monday, June 19, to Monday, June 26, 1769. See *The New-York Journal; or, the General Advertiser*, June 29, 1769.

TEN POUNDS REWARD.

RAN away and absconded, from his servitude and bail, in the night between the 20th and 21st of May last, a certain James Moobrey, late of Baltimore county, Maryland, being about 35 years of age, about 5 feet, 7 or 8 inches high, black hair, bushy and curled, which he will probably cut off, a very large beard; had on and took with him a black coat, double breasted jacket, plush breeches, half worn beaver hat, check trowsers, and sundry other things. Went away at the same time, a certain Mary Carty, the wife of a certain Robert Carty, and a young child, and the said Mary Carty's sister. It is supposed they are together, as the said Moobrey, unlawfully cohabitated with the said Robert Carty's wife. Whoever takes up the said run-away, and brings him to his master or bail, or secures him in any gaol, in this, or any of the neighbouring provinces, shall be paid the above reward and reasonable charges, by
JACOB GILES, his master, or THOMAS DURBIN, Bail.
> *The Pennsylvania Chronicle, and Universal Advertiser*, From Monday, June 12, to Monday, June 19, 1769; From Monday, June 19, to Monday, June 26, 1769.

June 10, 1769.

RAN away from the Subscriber, living in *Nod Forest*, *Baltimore* County, near the Rocks of *Deer-Creek*, on the 5th Instant, an *English* Convict Servant Man, named ROBERT JOHNSON, about 5 Feet 7 Inches high, between 20 and 30 Years of Age, of a swarthy Complexion, has straight black Hair, and is very bold and talkative: Had on, when he went away, an old fine Hat, torn, and sewed with white Thread, an old black Broad Cloth Coat, green Waistcoat, an old coarse Shirt, old Trowsers, patch'd with Ticken, old Shoes, Steel Buckles, plated with Silver, and is troubled with the Rupture.—Whoever takes up said Servant, and brings him home, or

secures him in any Jail in the Province, shall have Forty Shillings Reward; if out of the Province, Five Pounds, and reasonable Charges, paid by WILLIAM HOW.
As he is a good Scholar, it is probable he will forge a Pass.
The Maryland Gazette, June 15, 1769.

RAN away, on the Sixth of *June*, from the Subscriber, living in *Annapolis*, a *Welsh* Servant Man, nam'd DANIEL THOMAS, about 27 Years of Age, 5 Feet 8 Inches high, has short brown Hair, thin Visage, swarthy Complexion, and by Trade a Sawyer: Had on, and took with him, One Shirt, One blue Cloth Jacket, One red and yellow strip'd Flannel ditto, with Brass Buttons, One Pair of half worn Buckskin Breeches, One pair of blue Yarn Stockings, a Pair of Pumps newly soled, and old Castor Hat, and One Whip-Saw.—Whoever takes up the said Servant, and secures him in any Jail, so that his Master may have him again, shall receive, if taken within this Province, Forty Shillings; and, if out of the Province, Five Pounds and reasonable Charges, paid by   JOHN BROWN.
The Maryland Gazette, June 22, 1769.

May 18, 1769.
RAN away last Night, from the Subscriber, living on *Mattawoman* Creek, *Charles* County, a Convict Servant Man, named GEORGE GAULL, born in *Scotland*, but speaks plain, is about 35 Years of Age, has a ruddy full Face, black Beard, full Eyebrows, dark Eyes, and a Scar over one of them, is about 5 Feet 8 Inches high, pretty well Limb'd and Body'd: Had on when he went away, a Broad Cloth Coat, of a Snuff Colour, lined with red, and a light coloured Cloth Jacket, a Pair of Velvet Breeches, a Pair of brown Thread Hose, a Pair of *English* made Shoes, a Pair of yellow Metal Buckles, with narrow Rims, a Check'd Shirt, a red Silk spotted Handkerchief, a small Felt Hat, bound with black Worsted Ferrit, he has several Pair of different coloured Stockings, which he took with him. He served in the Capacity of a Schoolmaster, and perhaps may forge a Pass. He has a Discharge from the Service of a Man of War, which may serve for a Pass. Whoever takes up, and delivers the said Runaway to us, shall have Three Pounds Currency, if taken in the County; if taken out of the County, Four Pounds; and if out of the Province, Five Pounds, and reasonable Charges, if brought home, paid by
JOHN M'ATEE,   HENRY M'PHERSON.
The Maryland Gazette, June 22, 1769; June 29, 1769; July 13, 1769.

June 22, 1769.
RAN away from on board the *Patuxent*, Captain *David Lewis*, lying at *Selby's* Landing in *Patuxent* River, on the Night between the 15th and 16th Instant, Two Indented Servant Men, *viz.* JAMES CHILD, about 5 feet 1 Inches high, dark Complexion, short brown Hair, about 26 Years of Age, and is by Trade, a Carpenter and Joiner.—HENRY THOMPSON, about 5 Feet 5 Inches high, short black Hair, dark Complexion, about 25 Years of Age, and is a Painter and Glazier by Trade: Had on, when they went away, Check Shirts, strip'd Flannel Jackets, and blue Pea Jackets over them. It is probable they will change their Dress, and pass for Sailors. Whoever takes up said Men, and will bring them on board the Patuxent, or to *Frank Leeke*, in *Upper-Marlborough*, shall receive Twenty Shillings Reward for each, paid by   DAVID LEWIS.

The Maryland Gazette, June 22, 1769; July 6, 1769; July 13, 1769. First ad does not have the date at the top.

TEN POUNDS REWARD.

RAN away on the 22d day of *May* last from the Subscriber, living in *Conococheague*, an *Irish* Servant, named MATHEW KEAN, about 22 Years of Age, 5 Feet and an Half high, thick and well built, short frizled Hair, tied behind, of a red Colour, round Visag'd, and has a smiling Countenance; he is a great Snuffer, which makes him speak through his Nose; he is a little dull of Hearing, and is left handed; says he was born in *Dublin*, and pretends to be an Upholster by Trade; his Cloaths are very uncertain, as he robbed a House, and killed a Man about 20 Miles off, and took with him a great many Things, but it is probable he will wear a whitish coloured Broad Cloth Coat with yellow gilt Buttons, a Scarlet lappelled Jacket, with Hair Buttons, a Pair of Leather Breeches, with Seams across the Seat, a Pair of half worn Shoes, with Brass Buckles; he has some Letters mark'd with Powder on one of his Legs. It is hoped that he every honest Man will endeavour to secure him, that he may be brought to Justice, for which they may receive the above Reward, and reasonable Charges, paid by DAVID SCOTT.

N. B. He has been used to the Sea, and will endeavour to go on board some Vessel. All Masters of Vessels are forewarned to carry him off at their Peril.

The Maryland Gazette, June 29, 1769.

SIX POUNDS REWARD.

RUN away from the Subscribers, living in Baltimore County, Maryland, near the lower Ferry, on Susquahanna, two Convict Servant Men, viz. John and Daniel Stepleton, Brothers, both born in Conaugh in Ireland; John is about thirty Years old, and speaks with the Brogue, he is about 5 Feet four or 5 Inches high, a well set Fellow, of a very dark Complection, with his Hair turning grey; had on when he went away, an old Castor Hat, a dark brown Jacket, with Green Sleeves, a striped under Jacket, and striped Ticken Breeches, patched on the Knees with striped Lincey, one Country made Shirt, and one check'd, Country made Stockings, single Channel Pumps, with odd Buckles, he writes a good Hand, and may forge a Pass. Daniel is about twenty-seven Years old, and about five Feet 8 or 9 Inches high, of middling fair Complection, pitted with the Small Pox, and a large Scar from his Ear to Ear, down to his Throat; had on when he went away, a brown half Thick Jacket, with slash Sleeves, a striped ditto, a Check Shirt, a Felt Hat, a brown Wig, a Pair of Sheepskin Breeches, a Pair striped Ticken Do. a Pair of coarse Stockings, a Pair of single Channel Pumps tied with Strings; it is probable that they both may change their Names and Clothing, as they went off on the 15th of January last. Whoever takes up said Servants, so that their Masters may have them again, shall receive the above Reward, paid by us,

ANDREW WILLSON,   HENRY RUTTER.
June 10, 1769.

The New-York Journal; or, the General Advertiser, June 29, 1769; July 6, 1769. See *The Pennsylvania Chronicle, and Universal Advertiser*, From Monday, June 12, to Monday, June 19, 1769.

Easton, June 23, 1769.
WAS committed to the goal of this county, a man, who calls himself JAMES CLARK, *he was sent here on suspicion of being a run-away servant; his right name is supposed to be* EVAN DAVIS, *who was advertised lately in Maryland, by Jonathan Roberts, and Samuel Blunt; he is about 5 feet 7 or 8 inches high, sandy complexion, his dress very indifferent. Whoever has any right to this man, is desired to come and take him away, in 6 weeks time, or else he will be discharged.*

ALSO a man, who calls himself JAMES M'KINSEY, *is about 5 feet 9 or 10 inches high, full faced, of a blackish complexion; he says he is a servant belonging to John Abbot, on the east side of the North River, in New-York government. His master is desired to come and take him away, in 6 weeks time, or else he will be discharged, by* JACOB BACHMAN, Goaler.

The Pennsylvania Gazette, June 29, 1769. See *The Maryland Gazette*, March 30, 1769, and *The Pennsylvania Gazette*, April 27, 1769.

Carlisle Goal, June 13, 1769.

WAS committed here, five men; one who calls himself *James Bell*, says he is a servant to John Champ, near Duck-creek in Virginia, about 10 or 11 miles from Leesburgh; another who calls himself *John Wilson*, says he is a servant to John Ogden, waterman, in the West-Jerseys, about 12 or 14 miles from Brunswick, and about 10 miles from the sign of the Red Lion; he has on a large iron collar. Likewise two others, who call themselves *William Kittoe*, and *Richard May*, say they belong to Philip Hall, in Prince George's county, Maryland, one of them has a large scar on his cheek, and is blind of an eye. The fifth calls himself *Lawrence Kearney*, says he is a servant to Richard Longin, in the said county, in Maryland, near Duck Creek, about 10 miles from Bladensburg. Their masters (if any they have) are desired to come, within six weeks, pay their charges, and take them away, otherwise they will be sold for the same, by
ROBERT SEMPLE, *Goaler.*
The Pennsylvania Gazette, June 29, 1769.

RAN away, on the 31st of *May*, from the Subscriber's Plantation, in *Synapuxon* Neck, in *Worcester* County, a Servant Man named CON ROURKE, born in the West of *Ireland*, he is a thick well set Fellow, about 5 Feet 8 or 10 Inches high, pitted with the Small-Pox, wears his own short thin straight sandy coloured Hair, about 30 Years of Age and has very little of the Brogue: Had on, and took with him, when he went away, an old blue fly Coat, and Jacket, the back Parts of the Jacket are of a different Colour, a Pair of half worn Leather Breeches, Two coarse Country-made Shirts, One of which is striped, the other Check. One Pair of ditto Trousers, a brown Cut Wig, which he sometimes wore over his Hair, and a new Felt Hat; he also took with him a large Shovel and Spade in a Wallet, and probably may pass for a Banker and Ditcher. As he has often talked about *St. Mary's* County, perhaps he may have gone that Way.

Whoever secures the said Servant, so that he may have him again, shall receive Fifty Shillings; and, if brought home, reasonable Charges, paid by   JAMES ROWND.
The above *Con Rourke* has since changed his Name to *James Campbell.*
The Maryland Gazette, July 6, 1769; July 13, 1769; July 20, 1769.

June 22, 1769.

RAN away last Monday Night, from the Subscriber, living in *Kent* County, *Maryland*, Two Convict Servant Men, viz. MICHAEL HEWNE, or KEIRN, born in *Germany*, and is by Trade a Tailor; he is slim made, has a thin Visage, dark Complexion, black Hair, and an old Sore on his Head, a little above his Temple: He so much represents a *French* Neutral, that he may very well pass for one: Had on, and took with him, when he went away, a blue Cloth Surtout Coat, with Mohair Buttons, a striped red and white lapelled Jacket, of single Grogram, a Pair of ribbed Worsted Stockings, a black Silk Handkerchief, a new Castor Hat, with Silk Loopings, and a good Pair of Shoes, with the Grain out.

NATHANIEL POWELL, about 30 Years of Age, a slim made Fellow, thin Visaged, dark Complexion, thick black curled Hair, which grows very low down his Back, is an *Englishman* born, talks much in the West Country Dialect, and has a very down Look; he understands Plowing, Reaping, and Mowing, and is a nimble brisk Fellow: Had on, and took with him, when he went away, a blue Broad Cloth Coat, with a small Cape, and Mohair Buttons, a Pair of Snuff coloured fine Cloth Breeches, half worn. As they have other Clothes, they may perhaps change their Dress. They have Money with them, and it is probable, they will change their Names, and forge Passes.

Whoever takes up said Servants, and brings them home, if taken out of the Province, shall have a Reward of Ten Dollars; and if in the Province, Six Dollars, for either, and for both, the above Reward, paid by
R. GRESHAM.

It is supposed they went off in a Canoe, and made down the Bay, from *Chester* River.

The Maryland Gazette, July 6, 1769; July 13, 1769; July 20, 1769; August 3, 1769; August 17, 1769; August 24, 1769; September 7, 1769; September 14, 1769. See *The Pennsylvania Gazette*, March 23, 1769, *The Pennsylvania Gazette*, July 6, 1769, and *The Pennsylvania Gazette*, December 14, 1769, as Hewne/Keirn is probably Hern/Kern/Hayne. See *The Pennsylvania Gazette*, July 6, 1769, *The Pennsylvania Gazette*, August 17, 1769, and *The Maryland Gazette*, September 21, 1769, for Powell.

June 28, 1769.
THREE POUNDS REWARD.
RAN away from the Subscribers, living near *Pig-Point*, on Sunday the 18th Instant, Two Indented *Irish* Servants, viz.—DANIEL MURPHY, aged about 17 or 18 Years, about 5 Feet high, a thick well set Fellow: Had on, and took with him, when he went away, Two Osnabrig Shirts a little worn, a Pair of Crocus Trousers, and an old Felt Hat; he hath a remarkable large Scar on one of his Legs, and as soon as spoke to will put his Hand to his Head.—TIMOTHY CARTHY, by Trade a Weaver, is about 5 Feet 10 Inches high, is full faced, has black Hair and Eyes, and a Kind of Hollow on his right Cheek. His Apparel is unknown.—Whoever will secure them in

any Jail, so that their Masters may get them again, shall be entitled to the above Reward, or Thirty Shillings for either of them, paid by
BENJAMIN ALLEIN,   HENRY JONES.
The Maryland Gazette, July 6, 1769.

COMMITTED *to St. Mary's* County Jail, as Runaways, the Two following Servants, *viz.*

DANIEL MURPHEY, an *Irish* Lad about 17 or 18 Years of Age, and says he belongs to Mr. *Benjamin Allein* of *Anne-Arundel* County.

TIMOTHY M'CARTY, an *Irishman*, about 25 Years of Age, and says he belongs to Mr. *Henry Jones*, of Said County.—Their Masters are desired to take them away and pay Charges, to
ROBERT WATTS, Sheriff.
The Maryland Gazette, July 6, 1769; July 13, 1769. See *The Maryland Gazette*, July 6, 1769, for both men.

TWENTY DOLLARS Reward.
RAN away from the subscriber, living in Kent county, Maryland, the 26th ult. two convict servant men; the one named Michael Hayne, a taylor by trade, and a German born, about 32 years of age, slim made, thin visage, dark complexion, black hair, has an old sore on his head, a little above his temple; he is about 5 feet 7 inches high, and so much like a French Neutral, that he may well pass for one; had on, and took with him, a blue broadcloth surtout coat, with mohair buttons, lapelled jacket, striped red and white, half grogram, a pair of dark coloured broadcloth breeches, a good pair of shoes, grain outward, and many other things, such as trowsers, shirts, handkerchiefs, and a good castor hat, with silk loops; the other named Nathaniel Powell, born in England, talks much on the west country dialect, about 30 years of age, slim made, thin visage, dark complexion, black bushy curled hair, and grows more than common down his face; he carried with him a blue broadcloth coat, with a small cape, and mohair buttons, a pair of snuff coloured breeches, half worn, but they have many other things with them; and as both are cunning crafty fellows and the taylor can write, they may forge a pass, and change their names and dress. Whoever secures the said servants, if out of the province, and brought home, shall receive the above reward, and reasonable charges paid, or Ten Dollars for both; if taken within the province, and brought home, Ten Dollars for each or either or them; if secured in prison, and speedy notice given, Five Dollars for either or each of them, paid by   R. GRESHAM.
The Pennsylvania Gazette, July 6, 1769; August 10, 1769. See *The Pennsylvania Gazette*, March 23, 1769, *The Maryland Gazette*, July 6,

1769, and *The Pennsylvania Gazette*, December 14, 1769, as Hewne/Keirn is probably Hern/Kern/Hayne. See *The Maryland Gazette*, July 6, 1769, *The Pennsylvania Gazette*, August 17, 1769, and *The Maryland Gazette*, September 21, 1769, for Powell.

THREE POUNDS Reward.

RUN away from Kingsbury Furnace Mine-Bank, near Baltimore-Town, on the 16th of May last, a convict servant, named William Hatton, otherwise Jackson, by trade a stocking weaver, about 28 or 30 years of age, and about 5 feet 6 or 7 inches high, has a down look, and a remarkable way of staring any person in the face that speaks to him, stout made, fresh complexion, and light brown hair; had on, and took with him, ozenbrigs shirt, cotton and new fearnought jackets, with broad white metal buttons, ozenbrigs trowsers, English falls, or pumps, metal buckles, and felt hat; he has a remarkable scar from the side of his mouth to his chin; he went off in company with one who is since taken on the Frederick Town road; he is a noted rogue, and had on a collar. Whoever secures the said runaway in any goal, so that he may be had again, shall have the above reward, paid by F. PHILLIPS.

The Pennsylvania Gazette, July 6, 1769; August 10, 1769. See *The Maryland Gazette*, September 13, 1764, *The Maryland Gazette*, October 1, 1767, *The Pennsylvania Gazette*, October 1, 1767, *The Maryland Gazette*, March 10, 1768, *The Maryland Gazette*, September 8, 1768, and *The Pennsylvania Gazette*, September 15, 1768.

RAN away from the subscriber, living near Pipe Creek Furnace, in Frederick County, Maryland, on Tuesday the 16th of May last, a convict servant man, named Henry Manning, born in the West of England, and talks much in that dialect, is about 5 feet 10 Inches high, of a dark complexion, and his left jaw has been broke, also the ridge of his nose, which renders him very remarkable: Had on when he went away, an old dark coloured broadcloth coat, and an old red cloth jacket, and light coloured plush breeches, a pair of blue grey worsted ribbed stockings, an oznabrig shirt, and an old felt hat, a pair of strong country shoes, with plates of iron in the heels, and hob nails in the soles, wears his own dark brown hair, by trade a butcher. Any person securing the said servant in any gaol so that his master may have him again, shall have Five Pounds currency reward, if taken out of this Province, but if taken in this Province, Four Pounds, and reasonable charges, if brought home, paid by JOHN GAINER.

The Pennsylvania Chronicle, and Universal Advertiser, From Monday, July 3, to Monday, July 10, 1769; From Monday, July 10, to Monday, July 17, 1769.

June 26, 1769.

RAN away last night from the subscriber, living in Baltimore town, an English servant man, named Henry Cartwright, perhaps he has changed his name, is about 5 feet 7 inches high, 24 years of age, fresh complexion, short brown hair, wants some of his teeth. Had on when he went away a green jacket, with buttons on the sleeves, a striped linsey one under it, a check shirt, oznabrigs trowsers, half worn shoes, and carved steel buckles. He stole and carried with him, a silver watch, made by William Mercer, Liverpool, and 2 silver table spoons, marked M
P R.
and a good beaver hat. He is greatly bow-legged, broad shouldered, with a stoop. Whoever takes up said servant, and secures him in any goal, so that his master may get him again, shall have a reward of Forty Shillings, if taken in the province, and Three Pounds, if out of it, with reasonable charges, paid by   GEORGE PRESTMAN.

N. B. There is reason to believe he has forged a pass, and discharge from the ship.

The Pennsylvania Chronicle, and Universal Advertiser, From Monday, July 3, to Monday, July 10, 1769; From Monday, July 10, to Monday, July 17, 1769. See *The Pennsylvania Gazette*, May 18, 1769, and *The Pennsylvania Gazette*, July 13, 1769.

July 8, 1769.

RAN away from the Subscriber, living on *Sandy-Point, Anne-Arundel* County, on the 6th Instant, the Three following Convict Servant Men, *viz.*

JOHN HUMPHRIES, about 20 Years of Age, 5 Feet 8 Inches high, of a fair Complexion, brown Hair, red Beard, and is lame in his left Arm: Had on when he went away, an Osnabrig Shirt, and brown Roll Trousers.

JOHN BROWNSNOW, 20 Years of Age, 5 Feet 6 Inches high, of a fair Complexion, brown Hair, much curled, and is a very sly fellow.

JAMES STEEL, a Lad about 18 Years of Age, 5 Feet 6 Inches high, of a fair Complexion, light coloured Hair, and speaks in a whining Manner.—They went off in a small Boat, and is supposed to have gone down the Bay.

Whoever takes up said Servants, and secures them in any Jail, so that their Master may have them again, shall have Nine Pounds Reward, (including what the Law allows) and reasonable Charges, if brought home, paid by   RICHARD WEEDON,

All Masters of Vessels are forewarned from carrying off said Servants, or harbouring them at their Peril.

The Maryland Gazette, July 13, 1769.

RUN away the 25th of June last, at night, from the Subscriber, living in Baltimore-Town, Maryland, an English servant man, named Henry Cartwright, about 5 feet 7 inches high, 24 years of age, fresh complexion, short brown hair, and wants some of his teeth; had on, when he went away, a green jacket, with buttons to the sleeves, a striped lincey one under it, a check shirt, ozenbrigs trowsers, half worn shoes, and carved steel buckles.—He stole and carried with him, a silver watch, made by William Mercer, Liverpool, two silver table spoons, marked M

P R, and a good beaver hat. He is much bow-legged, and broad-shouldered, with a stoop; perhaps he has changed his name, and there is reason to believe he has forged a pass, and a discharge from the ship. Whoever takes up said servant, and secures him in any goal, so that his master may get him again, shall have Forty Shillings reward, if taken in the province, and Three Pounds, if out of the province, and reasonable charges, paid by   GEORGE PRESSTMAN.

The Pennsylvania Gazette, July 13, 1769; August 10, 1769. See *The Pennsylvania Gazette,* May 18, 1769, and *The Pennsylvania Chronicle, and Universal Advertiser,* From Monday, July 3, to Monday, July 10, 1769.

Chester-Town, July 17, 1769.

RAN away from on board the Snow *Isabella,* the 6th Instant, a Convict Servant Man, named RALPH GAMBALL, about 40 Years of Age, Five Feet Eight Inches high, fresh coloured, and pitted with the Small-Pox, and has lost all his Teeth: Had on, when he went away, a dark coloured Cloth Coat and Jacket, Yarn Stockings, old Shoes, and wears his own Hair.

Also, ran away, on the 8th Instant, from the said Snow, Three other Convict Men, *viz.*

SOLOMON LEGG, about 45 Years of Age, and of dark Complexion: Had on a blue Cloth Coat, wears a Wig, and a Flap'd Hat.

ROBERT HUNT, about 40 Years of Age, Five Feet Five Inches high, pitted with the Small-Pox, has a Sore on each of his Ancles, and wears a Wig.

WILLIAM TURNER, about Five Feet Six Inches high: Had on when he went away, a blue Cloth Coat, and wears his own short Hair.—Whoever secures the said Convicts, or either of them, in any Jail, shall have Thirty Shillings Reward for each, and reasonable Charges if brought to Chester-Town, paid by   SMYTH & SUDLER.
The Maryland Gazette, July 20, 1769; July 27, 1769; August 3, 1769.

July 4, 1769.
RAN away last Night from the Subscriber, living near *George-Town, Frederick* County, Two Convict Servant Men, *viz.* JAMES BAILEY. a Blacksmith by Trade, about Twenty-One Years of Age, Five Feet Five or Six Inches high, well set, of a swarthy Complexion, has a down Look, wears his own short black Hair: Had on, and took with him, One Check Shirt, One Osnabrig ditto, Two Pair of Osnabrig Trousers, One Pair of Shoes, One spotted Swanskin Waistcoat, One old black Cloth Coat and Breeches, and One Felt Hat.
     JOHN ROBERTS, an *Englishman*, about Twenty-one Years of Age, Five Feet Six Inches high, thin Visage, pale Complexion: Had on, and took with him, a white Linen Shirt, a Pair of new Check Trousers, a Pair of old Pumps, with Two odd Buckles, a new Felt Hat, and a white Flannel Waistcoat. Whoever takes up said Fellows, and brings them home, shall receive Five Pounds for each, paid by
SAMUEL WADE MAGRUDER,   BENEDICT CRAIGER.
     The Maryland Gazette, July 20, 1769.

July 11, 1769.
RAN away from the Subscribers, living in *Baltimore-Town*, on the 9th Instant, an *English* Servant Lad, named CHARLES ALAN, by Trade a Biscuit-Maker, 17 Years of Age, about 5 Feet 3 or 4 Inches high, slender made, of a middling fair Complexion, his Knees inclines in, is lame in both his Feet, by a Swelling on his Toes, and has a sore Place on one of his Ancles, light brown Hair, which he may have cut off, his Eyes are weak, and appear to be sore, has a sharp Visage, talks much, and pretty loud: Took with him, when he went away, a light coloured Broad Cloth Coat, and Breeches, with white gilt Buttons, a fine double breasted red knapt duffil Jacket, with a Coat Button at the Top, and another at the Bottom, a Pair of redish coloured mottled Stockings, Shoes, and large Block-Tin Buckles, with Brass Tongs and Anchors, a blue Fearnought Sailors Jacket, too large for him, a Castor Hat, trimmed round the Brim, a yellow striped Cotton double breasted Jacket, Silver Knee Buckles, and sundry other Cloaths.

JOSEPH ALAN, a Blacksmith by Trade, Nineteen Years of Age, about Five Feet Six Inches high, has short straight black Hair: Had on, and took with him, a brown Cloth Coat and Jacket, with Mohair Buttons, a Pair of Leather, and a Pair of Hair Shag Breeches, a Check Shirt, an Osnabrig ditto and Trousers, old Hat, and good strong Shoes, with Brass Buckles. They are Brothers, and, as they can both write, it is probable they may forge Passes.

Whoever apprehends said Servants, and secures them, so that their Masters may have them again, shall have Two Pistoles for each, if taken in the Province; and, if out of the Province, Four Pistoles Reward, (including what the Law allows) and reasonable Charges, if brought home, paid by
RICHARD MOALE,   CHARLES RIDGELEY, Junior.

The Maryland Gazette, July 20, 1769. See *The Pennsylvania Chronicle, and Universal Advertiser*, From Monday, July 17, to Monday, July 24, 1769.

EIGHT DOLLARS Reward.

RUN away, the 10th of July instant, from the Subscriber, living in the Fork of Gunpowder, in Baltimore county, Maryland, near the Manor Chapel, a convict servant man, born in Yorkshire (and consequently speaks broad) named JOHN READ, about 24 or 25 years of age, about 5 feet 8 inches high, of a swarthy complexion, has short brown hair, and a little scar on the top of his nose; had on, when he went away, a new felt hat, a brownish thickset coat, with some whitish spots on the back of it, and waistcoat of the same stuff, both with brass carved buttons, linsey breeches of a pale mixed colour, with white metal buttons, blue worsted stockings, good shoes, with plain steel buckles, a white shirt, and black silk handkerchief. He came in on the first of this month; he has been seen on the Lancaster road; and it is supposed intends to go to New York. Whoever takes up the said servant, and secures him, so that his master may have him again, shall have the above reward of Eight Dollars and reasonable charges, paid by me,
EDWARD BOSMAN.

The Pennsylvania Gazette, July 20, 1769; July 27, 1769; August 10, 1769.

On Thursday the 7th instant, was committed to the gaol of this city, by John Dennis, Esq; William Tomlin (a servant to Thomas Gent) and a negro fellow named Berkshire, a slave to Mr. Christopher Cannon, both of the county of Baltimore, in the Province of Maryland; fifteen miles from Baltimore town, near Mr. Benjamin Badger's mills, the Great Falls of Gunpowder, and Garrison church, on the great road to Connawawgo; the

servant and slave stole from each of their masters, a mare; the one from Thomas Gent, is a likely black mare, with saddle and bridle, the other stolen by the negro, the property of Mr. Christopher Cannon, is a fine bay mare, both of which are secured. Messrs. Cannon and Gent are desired to send for their servant, slave, mares, &c. as soon as possible, and they will much oblige their humble servant.   JACOB WISER.
City of New Brunswick, in the province of
East New-Jersey, July 18, 1769.

> The Pennsylvania Chronicle, and Universal Advertiser, From Monday, July 17, to Monday, July 24, 1769; From Monday, July 24, to Monday, July 31, 1769; From Monday, July 31, to Monday, August 7, 1769.

RAN away, the 9th inst, from the subscribers, living in Baltimore town, Charles Alan, an English servant lad, 17 years of age, about 5 feet 3 or 4 inches high, slender made, and of a middling fair complexion, his knees inclines in, is lame in both his feet, by a swelling on his toes, and on one of his ancles he has a sore place, has light brown hair, which he may have cut off, his eyes are weak, and appear red and sore, of a sharp visage, talks much, and pretty loud. Took with him when he went away, a light coloured broadcloth coat and breeches, with white gilt buttons, a fine double-breasted red knapped duffil jacket, with one coat button at the top, and one at the bottom, a pair of reddish coloured mottled stockings, shoes, and large white block-tin shoe buckles, with brass tongues and anchors, a blue fearnought sailor jacket, two [sic] large for him, castor hat, trimmed round the brim, a yellow striped cotton double-breasted jacket, silver knee buckles, and sundry other clothes.

Joseph Alan, a Blacksmith by Trade, 19 Years of age, about 5 feet 6 inches high, has short straight black hair, had on and took with him a brown cloth jacket, a pair of leather and a pair of hair shag breeches, a check shirt, oznabrig ditto and trowsers, old hat, and good strong shoes, with brass buckles; they are brothers, and as they can both write, it's probable they may forge passes and discharges.

Whoever apprehends said servants, and secures them so as their masters may get them again shall have two Pistoles for each, if taken in the province, and four Pistoles for each if out of the province (including what the law allows) and reasonable charges if brought home, paid by
RICHARD MOALE, and   CHARLES RIDGELEY, Junior.

N. B. The said CHARLES ALAN is a bisket-baker by trade. Joseph has black eye-brows and grey eyes and a brown coat with mohair buttons.

> The Pennsylvania Chronicle, and Universal Advertiser, From Monday, July 17, to Monday, July 24, 1769; From Monday, July 24,

to Monday, July 31, 1769 From Monday, August 7, to Monday, August 14, 1769. See *The Maryland Gazette*, July 20, 1769.

July 20, 1769.

RAN away from the Subscriber, living in *Kent* County, *Maryland*, a Convict Servant Man, named JOHN TURNER, about thirty-five Years old, Five Feet Eight or Nine Inches high, very thick made, pale Visage, and dark Hair, has a large Sore on his right Leg, speak West Country Dialect: Had on, and took with him, Two Osnabrig Shirts, Two Pair of Osnabrig Trousers, an old spotted Flannel Jacket, good Shoes, and an old Hat, it is possible he may have, or get other Cloaths: He has worked some Time in a Smith's-Shop.

Whoever takes up said Runaway, and secures him in any Jail, so that his Master may have him again, shall receive Fifteen Shillings Reward, besides what the Law allows, paid by
JOHN BERRYMAN.

The Maryland Gazette, July 27, 1769; August 3, 1769.

RAN away from the Subscriber, living in *Annapolis*, an indented Servant, named JOHN BURRAGE, by Trade a Clock and Watchmaker, born in the West of *England*, about Five Feet Eleven Inches high, of a dark Complexion, mark'd much with the Small-Pox, and has short black Hair: Had on, and took with him, a Drab Colour Surtout Coat, cut short, Check Shirt, striped Linen Trousers, Castor Hat, and Country made Shoes.— Whoever secures the said Servant, and delivers him to the Subscriber, shall have Five Pounds Reward, and reasonable Charges, paid by
FRANCES KNAPP.

The Maryland Gazette, July 27, 1769; August 3, 1769; August 17, 1769; August 24, 1769; August 31, 1769; September 14, 1769; September 21, 1769; September 28, 1769; October 5, 1769; October 12, 1769; October 19, 1769; October 26, 1769; November 9, 1769; November 16, 1769; November 23, 1769; November 30, 1769; December 7, 1769; December 14, 1769.

RAN away from the Subscriber, on the 21st of *June* last, a Servant Lad, named SAMUEL KENNING, about 18 or 19 Years of Age, by Trade a Shoemaker, and of a Sandy Complexion: Had on, when he went away, a Pair of Shoes and yellow Buckles, a Pair of Osnabrig Trousers, a Country Linen Shirt, an old brown Jacket, and a new Felt Hat. Part of the Crown of which was eat by the Rats. Whoever takes up said Servant, and brings him

to his Master, living in *Queen-Anne's* County, or secures him so that he may be had again, shall have Fifty Shillings Reward, paid by
EZEKIEL HUNTER.

The Maryland Gazette, July 27, 1769; August 3, 1769. See *The Pennsylvania Gazette*, August 3, 1769.

Alexandria, July 22, 1769.
RAN away from the Subscriber, on Sunday last, a Convict Servant Man, named JAMES LOWE, by Trade a Barber, about Twenty-five Years of Age, Five Feet Six Inches high, has been much pitted with the Small-Pox, but now wore pretty smooth, thin Visage, and black Hair: Had on, when he went away, a Wilton mixt Cloth Coat, white Jacket, Nankeen Breeches, and Check long Breeches over them, and a new Castor Hat. He carried also with him, a brown Cloth Coat, a black Cloth ditto, and a green Jacket, so it is supposed he will change his Cloaths, he is a smooth tongu'd Fellow, speaks fast, and writes a good Hand, and I suppose will forge a Pass, as he had Liberty to go to *Upper-Marlborough*, in *Maryland*, to purchase some Hair: He went in Company with a certain *Luke Kenney* a Freeman, by Trade a Saddler, they were seen on a bye Road to Annapolis, who hired for him a grey Mare: The said *Kenney* went to do some Business at *Annapolis*, in *Maryland*, and was to have returned with the said Mare in a few Days, but as he has not, they are supposed to have run away together, either to *Baltimore* or *Philadelphia*, and I expect *Lowe* will attempt to get on board some Ship for *England*.—All Captains are forewarned against taking him out of the Country, and any Person that will take up, and commit the said *Lowe* to any Jail in *Maryland*, shall receive Three Pounds Reward, if to any jail in *Pennsylvania*, Five Pounds, and if brought home, the said Reward, with all reasonable Charges, paid by
ROBERT ADAM.

The Maryland Gazette, July 27, 1769.

COMMITTED to *Calvert* County Jail, a few Days ago, a Fellow who calls himself *William Cowens*, and says he belongs to Mr. *George Carter*, of *Baltimore* County. Also a Fellow who calls himself *Thomas James*, and says he belongs to Mr. *Caleb Dorsey*, of *Elk-Ridge*. Their Masters are requested to take them away and pay Charges to
JOHN WEEMS, jun. Sheriff.

The Maryland Gazette, July 27, 1769; August 3, 1769. See *The Maryland Gazette*, June 8, 1769; June 26, 1769, and *The Maryland Gazette*, May 28, 1767, for James.

TWENTY DOLLARS Reward.

RUN away, the 10th of July ult. from the Subscriber, living in Kent county, Maryland, two servant men, viz. EDWARD BOSDEN, an Englishman, of a darkish complexion, pock-marked, about 5 feet 6 or 7 inches high, a drooping nose, highest in the middle, and has been used to the sea; had on, a felt hat, striped lincey waistcoat, check shirt, blue worsted plush breeches, blue and grey ribbed hose, half-worn shoes, and broad rimmed buckles. The other, named THOMAS MEGRAW, an Irishman, speaks broken, and strains in his speech; and 3 blue dots on his right hand, and on his right arm, the letters T. M. dotted in blue; about 5 feet 10 inches high, has short black hair, very small feet for his size, round faced, and somewhat pock-marked; he is cloathed like Bosden, and was a marine during the last war. Whoever takes up said servants and secures them, so as they may be had again, shall have the above reward, or Ten Dollars, for either, paid by me
JOHN VANSANT.

The Pennsylvania Gazette, July 27, 1769; August 10, 1769.

RUN away, the 20th of June last, from the Subscriber, living near Watkins's Ferry, on Patowmack river, an English convict servant woman, named Susanna Yates, middle sized, 37 or 38 years of age, short black hair; had on, when she went away, a coarse striped country-linen petticoat and bed gown, and a coarse linen bonnet without any paper; she was seen near Carlisle, and is supposed to make for Philadelphia. Whoever takes up the said servant and secures her in any goal, so that she may be had again, shall have Forty Shillings, beside what the law allows, paid by me
JOHN PEARCE DUVALL.

The Pennsylvania Gazette, July 27, 1769; August 10, 1769.

FIFTEEN POUNDS Reward.

July 17, 1769.

RUN away last night from the Patapsco Furnace, near Elk Ridge Landing, in Anne-Arundel county, Maryland, three convict servant men, viz. WILLIAM WILLIAMS, about 30 years of age, about 5 feet 6 inches high, a thick well set fellow, short brown hair, pitted with the small-pox; had on and took with him, a striped country jacket, a snuff coloured fustian under ditto, two ozenbrigs shirts, one blue and white linen handkerchief, one pair roll trowsers, one pair blue ribbed worsted hose, a pair of old country made shoes, a pair of large white metal buckles, and an old felt hat. WILLIAM TOWNSING, about 20 years of age, about 5 feet 6 inches high, a thick well set fellow, short brown hair, smooth face; had on, and took with him, one

striped country cloth jacket, one pair of old leather breeches, two ozenbrigs shirts, one pair roll trowsers, country made shoes, and an old felt hat. JOHN SOULSBY, he was born in Scotland, and was imported the last of June, in Captain Morrison, [sic] a short thick well made fellow, swarthy complexion, short black hair; had on, and took with him, a brown cloth coat, a black jacket, with horn buttons, an old red silk handkerchief, a pair of strong shoes, with odd buckles, an ozenbrigs shirt, a pair of roll trowsers, a pair of grey ribbed stockings, a pair old leather breeches, and a new felt hat. Whoever will take up and secure the said servants, so that they may be had again, shall receive for each, if taken 15 miles from home, Twenty Shillings; if 20 miles from home, Forty Shillings, if 40 miles, Three Pounds; and if out of the province, Five Pounds reward, and reasonable charges, if brought home to said Furnace, paid by
THOMAS HARRISON, and JAMES WALKER.
The Pennsylvania Gazette, July 27, 1769; August 10, 1769.

Forty Shillings Reward.
RUN away from the subscriber, on the 10th inst. an Irish servant lad named Patrick Nerney, about 16 or 17 years old, 5 Feet 5 or 6 inches high, much mark'd with the small-pox; had on when he went away, an oznabrigs shirt and trowsers, an old light-coloured outside jacket, an old blue under jacket, a pair of half-worn shoes, and a felt hat about half worn.—Whoever takes up and secures said lad, so that the owner may have him again, shall have the above reward, and all reasonable charges paid by
Tobias Rudulph.   Head of Elk, July 14, 1769.
The Pennsylvania Chronicle, and Universal Advertiser, From Monday, July 24, to Monday, July 31, 1769; From Monday, August 7, to Monday, August 14, 1769.

July, 8, 1769.
RAN away this morning from the subscriber, living in Baltimore county, Maryland, near Joseph Sutton's, an English convict servant man, named Benjamin Parkinson, a likely well set young fellow, about 30 years of age, fresh complexion, has had the small-pox, though not much marked, has a scar a-cross his left cheek, about an inch long, seems as if it had been cut with a knife or sword: He was born in Yorkshire, he speaks pretty broad, is about five feet six or eight inches high, wears his own brown coloured hair, pretty short, but curls, wore a fine hat, good brown coat full trimmed, and bound round the edges with brass buttons, a dirty fine shirt, a pair of good buckskin breeches with buckles at the knees, 1 pair of light coloured worsted stockings, and another pair of mixed yarn, a pair of new shoes and

buckles, a black silk handkerchief, two spotted cotton or linen ditto. He took a bridle with him, has one pistareen in money, and no more to my knowledge. Whoever takes up the said servant, and brings him home, or secures him in any gaol, so that his master may have him again, shall receive Fifty Shillings reward if taken in the county, if out of it Three Pounds, besides what the law allows, from
EDWARD NORRIS, son of Joseph.

The Pennsylvania Chronicle, and Universal Advertiser, From Monday, July 24, to Monday, July 31, 1769; From Monday, July 31, to Monday, August 7, 1769; *The Pennsylvania Gazette*, August 17, 1769. Minor differences between the papers.

July 24, 1769.
RAN away last Night, from the *Patuxent* Iron-Works, the Two following Convict Servant Men, viz. JOHN HILL an *Englishman*, about Thirty, or Thirty-five Years of Age, dark Complexion, and wears his own short black Hair; he is about Five Feet Nine or Ten Inches high: Had on, when he went away, an Osnabrig Shirt, Crocus Trousers, old Cotton Jacket, old Felt Hat, and old Shoes.

JOHN SMITH, a *Gypsy*, about Twenty-five Years of Age, Five Feet Nine or Ten Inches high, of a very dark Complexion, and is cloath'd in the same Manner as *Hill*.—Whoever takes up the said Servants, shall receive on delivering them, if taken Twenty Miles from home, Thirty Shillings, and if Fifty Miles or out of the Province, Fifty Shillings for each (including what the Law allows) paid by
THOs. SAMl. & JOHN SNOWDEN.

The Maryland Gazette, August 3, 1769; August 10, 1769; August 17, 1769; August 24, 1769; August 31, 1769; September 7, 1769; September 21, 1769; September 28, 1769; October 5, 1769; October 12, 1769; October 19, 1769; October 26, 1769; November 9, 1769; November 16, 1769; November 23, 1769; November 23, 1769; December 7, 1769; December 14, 1769. See *The Maryland Gazette*, August 20, 1767, for Hill, *The Maryland Gazette*, September 17, 1767, for Smith, and *The Maryland Gazette*, June 30, 1768, for both men.

RUN away, the 18th of July last, from the Subscriber, near the Head of Elk, two servant men, one named William Evans, an Englishman, about 20 years of age, 5 feet 9 inches high, of a dark complexion, slim made, wears his own short black hair; had on, when he went away, a narrow brimed wool hat, bound round with yellow binding, a double breasted striped jacket, the

stripes across, coarse shirt and trowsers, half worn shoes, with buckles. The other named Thomas Mecan, an Irish man, about 17 years of age, 5 feet high, wears his own short dark brown hair; had on, when he went away, an old wool hat, coarse shirt and trowsers, middling good shoes, tied with strings. Whoever takes up said servants, and secures them so as their master may get them again, shall have Three Pounds reward, or Thirty Shillings for either, paid by ROBERT EVANS.
The Pennsylvania Gazette, August 3, 1769; August 10, 1769.

RUN away from the Subscriber, the 21st day of June last, a servant lad, named SAMUEL KENNING, about 18 or 19 years of age, of a sandy fair complexion, a shoemaker by trade; had on, when he went away, a pair of shoes, with yellow buckles, ozenbrigs trowsers, a country linen shirt, and a new felt hat, the edge of the crown rat-eaten; he carried away with him, an old brown jacket. Whoever takes up said servant lad, and brings him home to his master, living between Tuckahoe and Choptank bridges, in Queen-Anne's county, Maryland, or secures him, so as his master may get him again, shall have Fifty Shillings reward, paid by
EZEKIEL HUNTER.
The Pennsylvania Gazette, August 3, 1769; August 10, 1769. See *The Maryland Gazette*, July 27, 1769.

RUN away from the Subscriber, living in Kent county, Maryland, on the 16th of July, 1769, an Irish servant woman, named MARY BRYAN (but may change her name to Howard, as she has done before, or to any other sirname) she is a middle-sized woman, but slender, brown hair, her eyes look redish and tender; had on, when she went away, a country lincey petticoat, striped black, blue and white, a lincey jacket, striped blue and white, a country linen shift, and has another with her of the same linen, a white linen bonnet, but no shoes, or stockings, that I know of. Whoever secures the said servant in any of his Majesty's goals so as her master may have her again, or brings her to him, shall have Twenty Shillings reward, if taken up out of province and all reasonable charges, paid by
GEORGE LITTELL.
The Pennsylvania Gazette, August 3, 1769; August 10, 1769.

Baltimore, July 26th, 1769.
SIX PISTOLES Reward.
RAN-AWAY from on board the ship Britannia, the morning of the 17th instant, three Irish convict servant men, viz. JAMES COBOURN, a stout

well made fellow, about six feet high, has short brown hair, had on a blue cloth coat, has a cut above his forehead, by trade a butcher, JAMES OHAIR, a well set fellow, about five feet six inches high, bald head: Had on a black cut wig, a brown cloth coat with mohair buttons, by trade a white smith. HENRY GRIFFIN, a stout made fellow about five feet eight or nine inches high, fair hair: had on a grey cloth coat, with mohair buttons. They were seen attempting to cross Susquehanna ferry, the night of the 20th instant, where they were taken up, but afterwards made their escape; it's thought they are gone to Philadelphia. Whoever will bring them back to the subscribers in Baltimore town, shall have the above reward, (including what the law allows) and reasonable charges paid by
EWING and BROWN.

The Pennsylvania Chronicle, and Universal Advertiser, From Monday, July 31, to Monday, August 7, 1769.

July 10, 1769.

RAN away from the Subscriber, a well set *Irish* Lad, named ANDREW LARKIN, about Five Feet high, round Face, fresh Colour, short black Hair, and speaks much in the *Irish* Dialect: Had on, and took with him, a black Bearskin Coat, and a Pair of Breeches of the same, Check Shirt, Felt Hat, light colour'd Yarn Stockings, a Pair of Half worn Shoes, and Crocus Trousers.—Whoever takes up the said Servant, and brings him home to the Subscriber, living on the Upper Part of *Elk-Ridge*, or secures him in any Jail, so that the Owner may get him again, shall have Three Pistoles Reward, paid by   JOSHUA GRIMES.

The Maryland Gazette, August 10, 1769.

Baltimore-Town, August 4, 1769.

RAN away last Night from the Subscriber, living in *Baltimore* County, a Convict Servant Man, named GEORGE ADAMS, about 35 Years of Age, 6 Feet high: Had on, when he went away, a brown Coat, blue Waistcoat, with wash'd Buttons, Two brown Linen Shirts, and One coarse Holland ditto, a Pair of new Boots, and One Pair of new Shoes with Copper Buckles, Felt Hat bound round, old Wig, Three Pair of Worsted Stockings, Leather Breeches, coarse Trousers, and One spotted Silk Handkerchief.—Whoever takes up the said Servant, and secures him in any Jail, so that his Master may get him again, shall have, if taken Ten Miles from home, Twenty Shillings; if Twenty Miles, Forty Shillings; and, if out of the County, Three Pounds; and, if out of the Province, Four Pounds Reward, and reasonable Charges if brought home, paid by   JOHN MURRAY.

The Maryland Gazette, August 10, 1769.

FOUR POUNDS REWARD.

RAN away from the Subscriber, living near *Patapsco Ferry*, in *Anne-Arundel* County, on the 31st of *July* last, a Convict Servant Man, named WILLIAM GAFFORD, about 30 Years of Age, 5 Feet 6 or 7 Inches high, he is a square well made Fellow, has a smiling Countenance, a way of shutting one of his Eyes when spoke to, has a remarkable Scar on the left Side of his Neck, is mark'd with the Small-Pox, and on both Arms with blue Letters, has short light brown Hair, sandy Beard, and light blue Eyes: Had on, and took with him, an old brown Broad Cloth Coat, with a small Cape, old red Cloth Jacket, with Sleeves, Cotton Breeches, One Osnabrig and One striped Shirt, old Shoes nailed in the Soles, Pewter Buckles, and old Felt Hat; he has some Cash, and will probably pass for a Sailor: He went off in a Pettiauger, and took with him, a Broad-Axe, Hand-Saw, and Taper-Bit.—Whoever takes up, and secures said Servant, so that his Master may get him again, shall receive, if taken in the County, Twenty Shillings; if out of the County, Forty Shillings; and, if out of the Province, Four Pounds Reward, paid by   THOMAS HAWKINS.

The Maryland Gazette, August 10, 1769.

RAN away from the Subscriber, living in *Baltimore* County, a Convict Servant Man, named JONATHAN EATING, about 26 Years of Age, 5 Feet 8 Inches high, slim made, thin visag'd, has a fair Complexion, and light coloured Hair: Had on a coarse Tow Linen Shirt and Trousers, Cloth Jacket, without Sleeves, half worn, Felt Hat, and a Pair of Pumps, lately soled with half Soles.—Whoever takes up Said Servant, and brings him home, or secures him so that his Master may get him again, shall have Forty Shillings, and if out of the Province Three Pounds Reward, paid by STEPHEN GILL, jun.

The Maryland Gazette, August 10, 1769.

August 1, 1769.

RAN away from the Subscriber, living at *Port-Tobacco* in *Charles* County, an indented Servant Man, named ALEXANDER SCOTT, born in *Scotland*, he is remarkable little, a well made Fellow, about 30 Years of Age, has a round Face, fair Complexion, grey Eyes, light brown Hair, cut short and curls, and he is pitted with the Small-Pox: Had on, when he went away, a redish mixture Superfine Broad-Cloth Coat, the Button-Holes and Edges on each Side are bound with Worsted Binding much faded, a striped flower'd Cotton Waistcoat, has a Straw colour'd Ground, with purple, red and black small running Flowers, white Shirt, yellow and white Silk Handkerchief round his Neck, brown Linen Breeches, white Thread Stockings, and

English Shoes tied with Strings. It is imagined that the said Servant has made for *Baltimore* or *Pennsylvania*, he served his Time some Years ago, as an indented Servant with Mr. *Grub*, a Farmer, who keeps a Merchant-Mill in *Pennsylvania*, which he says lives near the Lines of *Maryland*, and not far from *Baltimore*.

Whoever takes up said Servant, and brings him home, shall receive Five Pounds (including what the Law allows) paid by
JOSEPH ADERTON.

N. B. The said Servant is a good Farmer.

The Maryland Gazette, August 17, 1769; August 24, 1769; August 31, 1769; September 7, 1769; September 28, 1769; October 12, 1769.

August 7, 1769.

RAN away from the Subscribers, living in *Baltimore* County, in *Maryland*, on Monday the 31st of *July* last, a Servant Man, named THOMAS MOORE, a Tailor by Trade, about 27 Years of Age, a young Look, born in *Coventry* in *Great-Britain*, speaks plain *English*, but something louder than common in his ordinary Discourse; he is slim made, about 5 feet 9 or 10 Inches high—belonged to some Regiment of Soldiers in 1766, and came into this Country from *Dublin*, in the Year 1767, for some Misdemeanor whilst in the Army—He has been severely whipt, which appears on his Back now in Scars, is a good Workman by his Trade, and is very fond of Dress, has good Cloaths with him, and don't appear any way like a Servant; he wears a Snuff colour'd Cloth Coat, lined with white Tammy or Shalloon, with Pinchbeck Buttons, Linen or Nankeen Jackets, and white Russia Drab or Nankeen Breeches, with Osnabrig and strip'd Trousers, white and Check Shirts, Castor Hat, and may have many other Cloaths, whereby he may Change his Dress, being much given to show in that Way, wears his Hair, and generally ties it behind with a Ribbon; he walks straight and well, and is much given to strong Drink. It's thought he will direct his Course to the Northward, as he pretended since in this Country, when free, he would go to a Brother in *New-York* Government.

Whoever takes up said Servant, and delivers him to the Subscribers, or confines him in any Jail, that he may be had again, shall receive Ten Pounds Reward, and if brought home, reasonable Charges, paid by
AQUILA HALL, and AMOS GARRETT.

N. B. The said Servant took several Cloaths with him, which he had not finished, in particular, one Piece of Nankeen. He had Money with him, and probably may sell the unfinished Cloaths to raise more.

The Maryland Gazette, August 17, 1769; August 31, 1769; September 14, 1769; September 21, 1769.

RUN away, the 4th of July last, from the Subscriber, living in Baltimore county, near Joseph Sutton's, on the York road, a convict servant man, named Thomas Lockhart, about 6 feet high, much marked with the small-pox, has long brown hair, which he ties behind, and he is blind of one of his eyes, though it is not sunk; had on, when he went away, a good felt hat, tow linen shirt and trowsers, both pretty much worn, good shoes and small steel buckles; he is suspected to have stolen a coat and jacket, the coat of a light coloured saggathy, full trimmed, with mohair buttons, of a darker colour, a red jacket, without sleeves, has been patched on the fore part, with red shaloon. Whoever takes up the said servant, and confines him in any jail, shall have Five Pounds reward, and if brought home, reasonable charges, paid by me   JOHN ALMORE.

The Pennsylvania Gazette, August 17, 1769, September 21, 1769.

Lancaster Goal, August 17, 1769.
WAS committed to said goal, on suspicion of being runaways, the following persons, viz. A certain John Middleton (as he called himself) but has confessed that his name is William Grant, and that he is a servant to John Wright, of Frederick county, Virginia, committed 13th of June.—William Barker, as he calls himself, confesses he came to Baltimore from England, in the Friendship, Captain Morrison, and that he ran away from said Morrison; he is 5 feet 10 inches high, rough faced, with short black hair; had on, old leather breeches, black stockings, good shoes, and a good shirt and hat; was committed the first instant.—And Nathaniel Brown, as he calls himself, but supposed to be the person advertised in the public papers by the name of Nathaniel Powell, from Kent county, Maryland, as he answers all the descriptions of that advertisement, and was committed the 2d instant. The masters of said servants, if any they have, are desired to come, pay the charges, and take them away, otherwise they will be sold out for their fees in three weeks from the date hereof, by GEORGE EBERLY, Goaler.

The Pennsylvania Gazette, August 17, 1769. See *The Maryland Gazette*, July 6, 1769, *The Pennsylvania Gazette*, July 6, 1769, and *The Maryland Gazette*, September 21, 1769, for Powell.

RAN away from the Subscriber, on the 23d of *July* last, living in *Queen-Anne's* County, the Two following Servant Men, *viz.* JOHN ADAMS, about 24 Years of Age, 5 Feet 8 or 9 Inches high, well set, ruddy Complexion, much pitted with the Small-Pox, has a bold impudent Look, a Blemish in One of his Eyes, short light Hair, and is mark'd on One Arm with the Letters I A, and something else, but can't be certain what: Had on, a half worn Hat, green Broad Cloth-Coat, with Gold Twist or Basket Buttons, striped Linen lappelled Jacket, old Sheepskin Breeches, white rib'd worsted Stockings, and old Shoes, the Soles and Heels filled with Stub Nails, Steel Buckles, and a white Shirt.

JOSEPH BISHOP, about 23 Years of Age, 5 Feet 7 or 8 Inches high, broad Shoulders, and very well set, short black Hair, just cut of before, black Eyes, swarthy Complexion, and a down Look, several of his Upper Teeth are gone from before, but not altogether, One being between each Vacancy: Had on, an old Felt Hat, Osnabrig Shirt and Trousers, a light colour'd Cloth Coat, Linsey Woolsey Jacket, with a Cloth Back, old blew [sic] Stockings, old Shoes, the Soles and Heels fill'd with Stub Nails.

Whoever takes up, and secures the said Servants, in any Jail in *Maryland*, shall have Forty Shillings Reward for each, or if secured in any Jail in any other Province, shall have Three Pounds for each, besides what the Law allows, and reasonable Charges paid if brought home, by
DAVID LINDSEY,   TURBUTT BETTON.

The Maryland Gazette, August 24, 1769; September 7, 1769; September 14, 1769. See *The Pennsylvania Gazette*, September 7, 1769, and *The Pennsylvania Gazette*, September 21, 1769.

August 23, 1769.
RAN away from the Plantation of WALTER DULANY, Esq; in the Fork of *Gunpowder*, on the 21st of this Instant, Two *Welsh* Convict Servant Men, viz.

WILLIAM VOICE, a Plasterer by Trade, about 45 Years of Age, 5 Feet 10 Inches high, of a swarthy Complexion, has a Mole on his right Cheek, black Eyes, some Scars on his Face, on his right Arm the Representation of a Crucifix, with the Figures 1760, and the Two first Letters of his Name, put on with *Indian* Ink: Had on, and took with him, a *Dutch* Cap, a Buff coloured Cloth Upper Jacket, with round top'd yellow Metal Buttons, a light coloured brown Under ditto, a fine Linen Shirt, much patched, a coarse Linen one, much wore, a Pair of Osnabrig Trousers, a Pair of worn white Yarn Stockings, a Pair of turn'd Pumps, almost new, and carved yellow Buckles; he took with him Two plastering Trowels, and One Mason's ditto, with a Lathing Hammer; he is an insinuting [sic] fair spoken Fellow, when sober, but when drunk, (which he will be if he can get Liquor) is impudent, noisy, and turbulent.

HENRY GREEFES, about 40 Years of Age, 5 Feet 6 or 7 Inches high, of a redish Complexion, is a slow spoken Fellow, and sometimes stammers in his Speech: Had on, and took with him, a Castor Hat, a dark coloured gray Coat, almost black, a Thickset Jacket, a new Osnabrig Shirt, a Linen ditto which has been wore, a Pair of Hempen Roll Trousers, old Buckskin Breeches, ribb'd gray Yarn Stockings, and new Shoes.

N. B. They stole a Pair of plain Silver Sleeve Buttons, a Pair of carved plate Buckles, an *Indian* Blanket, Two Bridles, and will probably steal Two Horses. *William Voice* has a forged Pass, by which he will endeavour to pass for a free Man, by the Name of *William Brown*. Whoever takes up the said Runaways, and delivers them to the Subscriber, or secures them in any Jail, shall receive FORTY SHILLINGS Reward for each.

THOMAS CHISHOLM.

The Maryland Gazette, August 24, 1769; August 31, 1769; September 7, 1769; September 21, 1769; September 28, 1769; *The Pennsylvania Gazette*, August 31, 1769. Minor differences between the papers.

FIVE POUNDS REWARD.

RAN away from the subscriber, on Wednesday the 16th of August, a white servant man, about 19 years old, called Richard Holder, is a slim fellow about five feet eight inches high, marked much with the small pox, and is thin visaged and white complexion, with blackish hair; had on when he went away, an oznabrig shirt and trowsers and a felt hat; it is supposed he will change his name and steal other clothes. Whoever apprehends said fellow, and secures him in gaol and sends me word thereof, to Snow-hill Town, in Worcester County, Maryland, shall be intitled to the above mentioned reward, from   WILLIAM WHITTINGTON.

The Pennsylvania Chronicle, and Universal Advertiser, From Monday, August 21, to Monday, August 28, 1769; From Monday, September 11, to Monday, September 18, 1769.

RAN away from the subscriber, living in Joppa, in Baltimore County on the 13th of this instant, at night, two convict servant men, and one indented servant, viz. WILLIAM VAIL, a convict servant man, about five feet high, a thick well set fellow, red hair and beard, some of his teeth out before; had on, and took with him, a small new felt hat, country linen or brown role shirt and trowsers, country made shoes, and an old cotton jacket, also a match coat or English blankets. CHARLES HILL, a convict, near about the stature of William Vail, and in or near the same dress, a Bricklayer by trade, and has worked in a Smith's shop some time. JOHN RICKMAN, an indented servant man, of a swarthy complexion, about five feet 8 or 9 inches high, a Sawyer, and has worked in a Smith's shop, in or near the same dress as the other two servants, William Vail and Charles Hill. They may possibly has forged passes or discharges with them. Whoever takes up the said servants, and brings them home, if taken in this county, shall have

Forty Shillings, if out of the county, Three Pounds, and if out of the province, Five Pounds Currency, for each of them, paid by
WILLIAM ANDREW.   Joppa, August 16th, 1769.
    N. B. All Masters of vessels and others are forbid, at their peril, harbouring or carrying away any of the above servants.
    The Pennsylvania Chronicle, and Universal Advertiser, From Monday, August 21, to Monday, August 28, 1769.

RAN away from the Subscriber, a Convict Servant Man, named ANTHONY CAYTON, or KURTON, a Taylor by Trade, about 6 Feet high, pretty lusty, a very fair Skin, his Face and Hands much freckled, short Hair of a deep red or Carrot colour, drawling Voice, a very remarkable wide Mouth, thick red Lips, and has a small Cut over his Left Eye, and it is bruised and black under it: His Appare when he went away, was a light colour'd Cloth Coat and Breeches, red Jacket, good Shoes and Stockings, and Hat.   RICHARD LEE.
    N. B. 'Tis supposed he has other Cloaths with him, and therefore may change his Apparel; likewise supposed there went away with him, a Convict Servant Woman, named *Margaret Flannakin*, belonging to Mr. *George Smoot* of *Charles* County.
    The Maryland Gazette, August 31, 1769; September 14, 1769; September 21, 1769; October 5, 1769; October 12, 1769; October 19, 1769.

                                            August 29, 1769.
RAN away from the Subscriber on the Ninth Instant, at *Allen's* Fresh in *Charles* County, a Convict Servant Man, named CHARLES M'DONALD, a Plasterer by Trade, about 30 Years of Age, 5 Feet 7 or 8 Inches high, slim made, swarthy Complexion, and blind in the left Eye, he is talkative, but smooth spoken, he has several painted Marks on his Arms and above his Knees: Those on his right Arm have the Representation of a Crucifix, with a Crown at the Top, and within the Crown are the Letters I. N. R. I on the Outside of the Arm are a Heart and Four Darts; below them,
          S P.
are the Letters, F M On the Inside of his left Arm, are the Letters, S. LEE, and below those, Two Hearts; above his right Knee, are the Letters M^d. M^c. D. above the left Knee a Heart, and below it, the Figure of Six. Had on, when he went away, an Osnabrig Shirt, Petticoat Trousers, a Pair of Shoes and Stockings, blue striped Country Cloth Jacket, and a round *Dutch* Cap.—Whoever takes up the said Runaway, and delivers him to the Subscriber, shall have Forty Shillings Reward if taken in the County, if out of the County Eight Dollars and reasonable Charges.—I have lately heard

he told a Companion of his, he intended to go off with *George Liddell* a Showman, I suppose he did so, as *Liddell* went out of the Creek in his Boat the same Day as the Runaway absconded: I therefore promise to give any Person that will convict the said *Liddell* of carrying off the said Servant, Five Pounds besides the above Reward.
JAMES CAMPBELL.
N. B. He has been on board a Man of War, and may pass for a Sailor.
   The Maryland Gazette, September 7, 1769; September 14, 1769; September 28, 1769; October 5, 1769.

Queen-Anne's County, Maryland, July 23, 1769.
RUN away from the Subscribers, two convict servant men, one named JOHN ADAMS, about 24 years of age, about 5 feet 8 or 9 inches high, well set, of a fair complexion, pitted with the small-pox, bold impudent look, has a blemish on one of his eyes, short hair, and the two first letters of his name marked on one of his arms thus, I. A. with the date of the year; had on, when he went away, a half-worn hat, green broadcloth coat, with gold basket buttons, red and white striped double-breasted jacket, old sheepskin breeches, white ribbed worsted stockings, and old shoes, the soles and heels full of stub nails. The other named JOSEPH BISHOP, about 23 years of age, 5 feet 7 or 8 inches high, of a dark complexion, down look, broad shouldered, and well set, has short black hair, black eyes, and lost some of his teeth from before; had on, when he went away, a light coloured cloth coat, linsey woolsey jacket, the back of which is old stuff-coloured broadcloth, old blue stockings, and old shoes, the soles and heels filled with stub nails. Whoever secures the said servants in any jail in Maryland, shall have Forty Shillings reward for each, or if out of the province THREE POUNDS for each, besides what the law allows, and reasonable charges, paid if brought home.
DAVID LINDSAY,   TURBUTT BETTON, senior.
   The Pennsylvania Gazette, September 7, 1769; September 21, 1769; October 12, 1769. See *The Maryland Gazette,* August 24, 1769, and *The Pennsylvania Gazette,* September 21, 1769.

Elk Ridge, Maryland, August 28, 1769.
RUN away from the Subscriber, a convict servant man, named JOHN LANDON, born in England, about 22 or 23 years of age, between 5 feet 8 and 10 inches high, has short black hair, marked a little with the small-pox, and of a brown complexion; had on, and took with him a black broadcloth coat, and a new vest and breeches of the same colour, a black Barcelona handkerchief, 2 or 3 white shirts, and 1 check ditto, a pair of striped

trowsers, 1 or 2 pair of light blue worsted stockings, a pair of pumps, and a pair of shoes, a castor hat, half worn; he has procured an old indenture, and a forged pass, and has plenty of cash with him. Whoever takes up the said servant, and confines him in any goal, so that his master may have him again, shall have Twenty shillings reward, besides what the law allows, if within 20 miles from home; if out of the province FIVE POUNDS reward, and reasonable charges, paid by WILLIAM INMAN.
The Pennsylvania Gazette, September 7, 1769; September 21, 1769.

RAN away from the Subscriber, living in *Annapolis*, a Convict Servant Woman, named MARY PRICE, of a middle Stature, has a sour down Look, and bloated under her Eyes: She had on, and took with her, a black quilted Petticoat, striped Linen Bed-gown, blue and white spotted Handkerchief, Womans old Felt Hat, brown Sheeting Shifts and Aprons, and an old Pair of Shoes and Stockings.—Whoever takes up the said Servant, and brings here to Annapolis, shall have Twenty Shillings Reward, paid by
ROBERT REITH.
The Maryland Gazette, September 14, 1769; September 21, 1769.

COMMITTED to *Queen-Anne's* County Jail supposed to be Runaways, the Three following Men, *viz*.
JOHN TOOL, about 5 Feet 10 Inches high, black Hair: Had on, a blue Jacket with a double Set of small Buttons, a small Check Shirt, and wide Petticoat Trousers.
EDWARD DREW, wears a brown Wig, a white Surtout Coat, black Velvet Breeches, broad striped Cotton blue and white Shirt, a Pair of large carved Silver Buckles.
ROBERT STEVENSON, has a red Cloth Jacket, striped Shirt, One Pair of large white Linen Petticoat Trousers, a thin Pair of Pumps, white Metal carved Buckles.—The above Men say they belonged to the *Tatees*, Captain *Gregory* lying at *Baltimore*, which Vessel they say they were discharged from, the 9th or 10th of *August*, and were going to *Chester-Town* on *Chester* River, *Kent* County, but did not receive their Discharge from the said Vessel. They came over from *Baltimore* in a Vessel's Boat. If the said Persons do belong to Captain *Gregory*, or to any other Captain, they are desired to take them out of Prison and pay Charges, or otherwise they will be Sold out to pay Charges, by
JAMES BUTLER, Jailer.
P. S. If the said Persons belonged to Captain *Gregory*, and was discharged from the said Vessel, it is desired that Captain *Gregory* will send them a proper Discharge.

The Maryland Gazette, September 14, 1769.

FIVE POUNDS REWARD.
Baltimore-Town, August 30, 1769.

RAN away Yesterday Evening from the Subscriber, an English Convict Servant Man, named JONATHAN STICKWOOD, born in *Cambridgeshire*, he is about 21 Years of Age, 5 Feet 8 or 9 Inches high, grey Eyes, short dark colour'd Hair which curls a little, he has been sick sometime, looks very yellow and poor: Had on, and took with him, an old Hat, Osnabrig Shirt and Trousers, light blue Cloth Jacket with Sleeves and Metal Buttons, the Under Part of the Sleeves are let out with deep blue Cloth; blue Yarn Stockings, good strong Shoes, odd Buckles, *Irish* Linen Shirt, red and white Calico Jacket with Horn Buttons covered with the Calico, a Pair of *Russia* Drab Breeches with white Metal Buttons, a good striped Silk, a spotted Linen, and an old black *Barcelona* Handkerchief, a Pair of blue ribb'd Worsted Stockings, and One Pair of scarlet Garters.

Whoever takes up the said Servant, and secures him so that the Subscriber gets him again, shall have Thirty Shillings if taken Twenty Miles from home, if Forty Miles Three Pounds, if out of the Province the above Reward (including what the Law allows) and reasonable Charges if brought home, paid by   WILLIAM GOODWIN.

The Maryland Gazette, September 14, 1769; September 21, 1769; September 28, 1769; October 19, 1769; October 26, 1769; November 2, 1769; *The Pennsylvania Gazette*, September 14, 1769; October 21, 1769; November 23, 1769; December 7, 1769; December 21, 1769; December 28, 1769. Minor differences between the papers. See *The Pennsylvania Chronicle, and Universal Advertiser*, From Monday, September 11, to Monday, September 18, 1769.

Maryland, BaltimoreTown, August 30, 1769.
Five Pounds Reward.

RAN away yesterday evening, from the subscriber, an English convict servant man, named Jonathan Stickwood, born in Cambridgeshire, is about 21 years of age, 5 feet 8 or 9 inches high, has grey eyes, and short dark coloured hair, which curls a little, has been sick some time, and looks very yellow and poor; had on an old hat, oznabrigs shirt and trowsers, a light blue cloth jacket with sleeves and metal buttons, the under part of the sleeves are let out with deep blue cloth, blue yarn stockings, good strong shoes and old buckles, took with him a fine Irish linen shirt, a red and white callico jacket, with horn moulds thereto, covered with the callico, a pair of white Russia drab breeches, with white metal buttons, a good striped silk, a

spotted linen, and an old black Barcelona handkerchief, a pair of blue ribbed worsted stockings, and a pair of scarlet garters.—Whoever takes up said servant, and secures him so that his master may get him again, shall have Thirty Shillings if taken twenty miles from home, Three Pounds if forty miles, and the above reward if out of the province (including what the law allows) and reasonable charges if brought home, paid by
WILLIAM GOODWIN.
    N. B. He was imported this summer, in the Friendship, Capt. Morrison. All masters of vessels are forewarned to harbour or carry him off at their peril.
    The Pennsylvania Chronicle, and Universal Advertiser, From Monday, September 11, to Monday, September 18, 1769; *The Pennsylvania Gazette*, October 12, 1769. Minor differences between the papers. See *The Maryland Gazette*, September 14, 1769.

THREE POUNDS Reward.
RUN away, the 20th of August last, from Birch Grove Blumery, Maryland, two servants, viz. One named JOHN SPENCER, about 25 years of age, has a remarkable stoop in his shoulders, fair hair, and was born and raised on Chicknecomoco river in Dorchester county; had on, and took with him, a claret coloured cloth coat, blue cloth breeches, 2 old ozenbrigs shirts, an old beaver hat, lined with white linen, and half worn shoes. The other a lad, named GIBBONS CHRISTOPHERS, about 18 years of age, and about 5 feet 6 inches high, well set, very full faced, his hair short, he was born and raised in Worcester county; it is not known that he has any other clothes with him, than an ozenbrigs shirt and trowsers, new shoes, and a felt hat. It is supposed they intend for the Jerseys. Whoever takes up said servants, and secures them in any goal, shall receive the above reward, or thirty Shillings for each, paid by
JOHN *and* WILLIAM DOUGLASS, *and* COMPANY.
    The Pennsylvania Gazette, September 14, 1769.

FIVE POUNDS Reward.
RUN away, the 3d of this instant September, from the Subscriber, living in Upper Deer-creek Hundred, Baltimore county, Maryland, a convict servant man, named MICHAEL KELLY, of a fair complexion, about 5 feet 8 inches high, 24 years of age, born in Dublin, a little pock marked, has a scar on his neck under one of his ears, speaks mannerly, and not been much more than a month in the country, and intends for Philadelphia; had on, and took with him, a grey lappelled coat, red vest, without sleeves, blue ditto, with sleeves, brown breeches, blue and white yarn stockings, without a

back seam, good shoes, with buckles not fellows, new felt hat; he had no money, but told his fellow servant he would plunder, and change his apparel the first opportunity. Whoever takes up said servant, and secures him, so that his master may have him again, shall have Forty Shillings reward, if taken in said province; if out of it Three Pounds; and, if 40 miles from home, the above mentioned reward, and reasonable charges, paid by JAMES HUTCHISON.
N. B. All masters of vessels are forbid to carry him off at their peril.
The Pennsylvania Gazette, September 14, 1769.

August 31, 1769.
RAN away on Sunday last from the Subscriber, in *Queen-Anne's* County, near the *Red-Lion* Branch, an *English* Convict Servant Man, named NATHANIEL POWELL, about 30 Years of Age, a slim made Fellow, thin Visage, of a dark Complexion, wears his thick black Hair, which grows very low down his Forehead, speaks in the West Country Dialect, he is a very brisk Fellow, and has a Down-Look, he understands Ploughing, Reaping and Mowing: Had on, when he went away, a light colour'd Jacket, with long Skirts, Check Shirt, a Pair of Snuff colour'd Breeches, speckled Worsted Stockings, with Holes in the Heels, a Pair of Shoes, with a Hole in One of the Upper Leathers.—Whoever takes up said Runaway, and secures him in any Jail, so that his Master may have him again, shall have Three Pounds Ten Shillings Reward, and reasonable Charges, if brought home, paid by   ROGER COLMAN.
N. B. The said Person was taken and committed to *Lancaster* Prison, by the Name of *Nathaniel Brown*.
The Maryland Gazette, September 21, 1769; September 28, 1769; October 12, 1769; October 19, 1769; October 26, 1769; November 9, 1769; November 16, 1769. See *The Maryland Gazette*, July 6, 1769, *The Pennsylvania Gazette*, July 6, 1769, and *The Pennsylvania Gazette*, August 17, 1769.

WAS committed to the goal of the county of Gloucester, in the province of West New-Jersey, one JOSEPH BISHOP, who says he is a servant to one Taulbert Battin, of Queen's-Town, in Queen-Anne's county, Maryland, and also one JOHN ADAMS, from the same place, who says he belongs to one David Linsey, a planter. Their masters are requested to come, or send for them, within one month of the date hereof, or they will be sold for their charges, by RICHARD JOHNSON, Goaler.
September 18, 1769.

The Pennsylvania Gazette, September 21, 1769. See *The Maryland Gazette*, August 24, 1769, and *The Pennsylvania Gazette*, September 7, 1769.

FORTY POUNDS REWARD.
Baltimore Town, 16th Sept, 1769.
Broke gaol last night about Eleven o'clock the following prisoners, viz.

JOHN NAILING, a tall thin faced square set young fellow, about 20 years of age, born in Ireland and imported from Dublin, speaks much of the brogue, is remarkably talkative, addicted to drinking and swearing, brags much of his manhood, and is a great bruiser; this was the fourth time of his being committed to goal in one year that he has been in the country.

WILLIAM STARLING, a well set man, about five feet eight inches high, by trade a leather breeches maker, born in Ireland, about 30 years of age, both his eyes have been lately bruized in fighting, and one of them appears very blood-shotten, he has a very ill look, and at present appears very sickly.

JOHN STINSON, who says he was born in Pennsylvania, near Schuylkill, about five feet ten inches high, a portly well set man, wears his own black hair, tied behind, has a down look, gogle eyes, thick lips and a mole on one cheek, he has also a wound on the back of his left hand, by which he has lost the use of one finger, he is a notorious horse thief and house breaker, has twice been tried for his life in Virginia, under the name of Shepherd, but constantly broke gaol. He has with him a light coloured Wilton coat without lining, also a green sagathy coat and leather breeches.

JOHN DOUGLASS, an Irishman born, about six feet high, stoops much in the shoulders, has sore eyes, he was detected conveying servants from this town to Virginia; he speaks a little on the brogue and is very drunken and talkative; he chiefly goes by water, and says he lived in Norfolk.

ROBERT COALE, a Negro....

RICHARD WHEELER, was born in this county, about 25 years of age, a tall, thin young man, he has a very dark down cast look, and has been in gaol near fourteen months, much pitted with the small pox which he has had not long since.

WILLIAM WOODMAN, about five feet ten or eleven inches high, he is a down looking fellow, and had on an old oznabrig shirt and trousers.

THOMAS ELTON, a servant of Mr. Rutland's near Annapolis, a short square set man, he is a very sober orderly fellow; had on a blue ragged coat, old shirt and leather breeches, which are very old and too short for him, without shoes or stockings, one of his eyes appears much bruised by fighting, by trade a farmer, and has a very pale thick faced countenance.

As many of them have been long confined, they appear pale and their skin tender, though they are tolerable well in flesh, their cloathing is uncertain, as many of them had scarce any, and most of them barefooted. Whoever secures and brings back said prisoners, shall have Forty Pounds reward for the whole, or Five Pounds for each, paid by
DANIEL CHEMIER, Sheriff of Baltimore County.

The Pennsylvania Chronicle, and Universal Advertiser, From Monday, September 25, to Monday, October 2, 1769; From Monday, October 2, to Monday, October 9, 1769; From Monday, October 16, to Monday, October 23, 1769; *The Pennsylvania Gazette*, October 5, 1769. Minor differences between the papers. See *The Pennsylvania Gazette*, June 1, 1769, and *The Pennsylvania Gazette*, October 12, 1769, for Elton. See *The Maryland Gazette*, October 19, 1769. See *The Maryland Gazette*, October 26, 1769, for Woodman.

Bladensburgh, September 27, 1769.
RAN away from the Subscriber, living in *Philadelphia*, an *English* Servant Man, named THOMAS TAYLOR, by Trade a Shoemaker, he is of a low Stature, slim made, mark'd with the Small-Pox, and has dark Hair: Had on, a brown Jacket without Sleeves, black Buckskin Breeches, Check Shirt, an old Hat. He has changed his Name, and calls himself JOHN SMITH, and has been confined in *Baltimore* Jail, but through his false Name was discharged: He has been seen on the Road between this Town and *Annapolis*, and it is supposed he is gone towards *Virginia*.—Whoever delivers the said Servant, to *Thomas Hyde*, in *Annapolis*, or to the Subscriber, shall receive Three Pounds Reward, if Lieu of what the Law allows. JOSEPH GAVIN.

The Maryland Gazette, October 5, 1769; October 19, 1769; November 2, 1769.

RAN away from the Subscriber living in *Frederick*, an Apprentice Boy, named RICHARD KEEN, by Trade a Breeches-maker, about 19 Years of Age, 5 Feet 10 Inches high: Had on, when he went away, a green napped Coat, with yellow Buttons, and bound with green Binding, a red lappelled Waistcoat, a Pair of Leather Breeches, good Shoes and Stockings. Whoever takes up said Apprentice, and brings him to his Master, in *Frederick Town*, shall have Thirty Shillings Reward, paid by
LUDWICK WELTNER.

The Maryland Gazette, October 12, 1769.

October 1, 1769.
COMMITTED to *Calvert* County Jail, a few Days ago, as Runaways, the following Men, *viz*. JONATHAN MARTIN, who says he is a Freeman, and a Bricklayer by Trade, and has for some Time past work'd for Mr. *John Hyde*, in *Annapolis*. JOSEPH WARD, who says he is of the same Trade, and belongs to *Samuel Chase*, Esq; Attorney at Law. Also Negro TOM....— The Owners of said Runaways, are requested to take them away and pay Charges, by JOHN WEEMS, junr. Sheriff.
The Maryland Gazette, October 12, 1769.

Chester Goal, October 9, 1769.
THIS day was committed to my custody, an Irishman, who calls himself Joseph Bennet, he is a thick faced man, pock marked, and of a pale countenance, and very mild spoken, about 5 feet 6 or 7 inches high, and well set, had on when committed, a spotted swanskin jacket, an old broadcloth ditto, without sleeves, and blue shaloon lining, an old pair of cloth breeches, old shirt, an old pair of shoes, and no stockings, an old felt hat; he very much answers the description of Thomas Elton, a servant of Mr. Rutland, near Annapolis, who broke out of Baltimore Goal with several others, the 18th of September last, and advertised by the Sheriff of Baltimore in the Pennsylvania Gazette, No. 2128. His master, if any, or any person that has any claim, are desired to come in five weeks, and pay cost, or he will be discharged. JOSEPH THOMAS, Goaler.
The Pennsylvania Gazette, October 12, 1769. See *The Pennsylvania Gazette*, June 1, 1769, *The Pennsylvania Chronicle, and Universal Advertiser*, From Monday, September 25, to Monday, October 2, 1769, and *The Maryland Gazette*, October 19, 1769, for Elton.

Ran away from the subscriber, living in Tully's Neck, Queen Ann's County, Maryland, two convict English servant men, one named George Kidwell, a blacksmith by trade, about 35 years of age, 5 feet, 5 inches high, has short black hair, small black eyes, a crook in one of his fingers on his left hand; had on and took with him two oznabrigs shirts, one old white one, a pair of long trowsers, a pair of blue knit breeches, an old light German serge coat, a coarse felt hat, almost new, and old shoes with plated buckles, the plating almost worn off. The other is named Charles Clarke, about 45 years of age, 5 feet 8 inches high, of a dark complexion, stoops in his shoulders, had on and took with him two old sheeting linen shirts, oznabrigs trowsers, mended on the knees with brown role, a coarse broad-cloth coat, and a pair of old pumps much too large for him, he has short black hair, a little grey. Whoever takes up the said servants, and secures them in any

gaol, so that the owner may get them again, shall receive a reward of Four Pistoles, and reasonable charges paid, (if brought home) by
JOHN PRICE.   *Tully's Neck, Sept.* 30, 1769.

> *The Pennsylvania Chronicle, and Universal Advertiser*, From Monday, October 9, to Monday, October 16, 1769; From Monday, October 16, to Monday, October 23, 1769; From Monday, October 23, to Monday, October 30, 1769.

WHEREAS John Richman, William Vale, and Charles Hill, are now confined in the public gaol, at Dover, in Kent County, on Delaware, who say they are servants to a certain William Andris, tavern keeper in Joppa, Baltimore County, in the province of Maryland.—These are therefore to give notice to the said William Andris, to come and take the said John, William, and Charles out of the gaol, and pay charges; otherwise, in six weeks, from the date hereof, the said servants will be sold, at the public vendue, for their prison fees, by
JAMES WELLS, Sheriff.   October 5, 1769.

> *The Pennsylvania Chronicle, and Universal Advertiser*, From Monday, October 9, to Monday, October 16, 1769.

THIRTY FIVE-POUNDS REWARD.
Baltimore-Town, September 16, 1769.
BROKE Jail last night about Eleven o'Clock, the following Prisoners, *viz.*

JOHN NAILING, a tall thin faced square set young Fellow, about 20 Years of Age, born in *Ireland* and imported from *Dublin*, speaks much of the brogue, is remarkably talkative, addicted to drinking and swearing, brags much of his Manhood, and is a great Bruiser; this was the Fourth Time of his being committed to Jail in one Year that he has been in the Country.

WILLIAM STARLING, a well set Man, about 5 Feet 8 Inches high, by Trade a Leather Breeches-maker, born in *Ireland*, about 30 years of Age, both his Eyes have been lately bruised in fighting, and one of them very Bloodshotten, he has a very ill look, and at present appears very sickly.

JOHN DOUGLAS, an Irishman born, about six feet high, stoops much in the shoulders, has sore eyes, he was detected conveying servants from this town to Virginia; he speaks a little on the brogue and is very drunken and talkative; he chiefly goes by water, and says he lived in Norfolk.

ROBERT COALE, a Negro....

JACOB, a Negro....

WILLIAM WOODMAN, about 5 Feet 10 or 11 Inches high, he is a down looking Fellow, and had on an old Osnabrig Shirt and Trousers.

THOMAS ELTON, a Servant of Mr. *Rutland's* near *Annapolis*, a short square set Man, and is a very sober orderly Fellow: Had on a blue ragged Coat, old Shirt, and Leather Breeches, which are very old and too short for him, without Shoes or Stockings, one of his Eyes appears much bruised by fighting, by Trade a Farmer, and has a very thick Face and pale Countenance.

As many of them have been long confined, they appear pale and their Skin tender, though they are tolerable well in Flesh. Their Cloathing is uncertain, as many of them had scarce any, and most of them bare footed.

Whoever secures and brings back said Prisoners, shall have Thirty-five Pounds for the whole, or Five Pounds for each, paid by
DANIEL CHEMIER, Sheriff of *Baltimore* County.

The Maryland Gazette, October 19, 1769. See *The Pennsylvania Gazette*, June 1, 1769, and *The Pennsylvania Gazette*, October 12, 1769, for Elton. See *The Pennsylvania Chronicle, and Universal Advertiser*, From Monday, September 25, to Monday, October 2, 1769. See *The Maryland Gazette*, October 26, 1769, for Woodman.

TEN POUNDS REWARD.
Baltimore-Town, September 16, 1769.
BROKE Jail last Night, about Eleven o'Clock, the following Prisoners, *viz.*
JACOB, a Negro....
WILLIAM WOODMAN, about 5 Feet 10 or 11 Inches high, he is a down looking Fellow, and had on an old Osnabrig Shirt and Trousers.

Whoever secures and brings back said Prisoners, shall have Ten Pounds for both, or Five Pounds for each, paid by
DANIEL CHAMIER,   Sheriff of *Baltimore* County.

The Maryland Gazette, October 26, 1769; November 2, 1769; November 16, 1769; November 23, 1769; November 30, 1769; December 7, 1769; December 14, 1769. See *The Pennsylvania Chronicle, and Universal Advertiser*, From Monday, September 25, to Monday, October 2, 1769, and *The Maryland Gazette*, October 19, 1769, for Woodman.

FIVE POUNDS REWARD.
October 30, 1769.
RAN away from the Subscriber, last Sunday Night, an *English* Convict Servant Man, named JESSE JORDAN, about 25 Years of Age, 5 Feet 11 Inches high, has a pale Complexion, gray Eyes, light fair short Hair, and is by Trade a Shoemaker: Had on, an Osnabrig Shirt, red Breeches, with Trousers over them, Two Jackets, the Under one a knit scarlet, the other a

blue flower'd Serge; he also took with him his Shoemakers Tools, and a sorrel Horse, about 14 Hands high, with a white Blaze down his Face, an old Saddle and Bridle; it is supposed he had a Companion with him, as the Subscriber has also missed a Horse, branded on the near Buttock H. Whoever takes up the said Servant and Horses, and brings them to the Subscriber, living near Annapolis, if taken within the County, Forty Shillings for the Fellow, and Twenty for the Creatures; or if out of the County and brought home, Five Pounds Reward, paid by
JOHN HESSELIUS.

The Maryland Gazette, November 2, 1769; November 9, 1769; November 30, 1769; December 7, 1769; December 14, 1769.

TWENTY-FIVE POUNDS Reward

October 30, 1769.

RAN away last night from Baltimore Town, the five following servants, viz. WILLIAM ADAIR, a Scotch man, 5 feet, 8 or 9 inches high, a lusty well set fellow, wears his own short brown curled hair, a little marked with the small pox, speaks pretty much on his own country dialect, had on when he went away a short blue outside jacket, and red flannel under ditto, new leather breeches, brown thread hose and new shoes; he may pass for a blacksmith or sailor. JOHN BARBER, an Englishman, 5 feet, 9 or 10 inches high, a lusty well set fellow, wears his own short black hair, of a dark complexion, and has a surly down look when spoke to, by trade a sawyer; had on when he went away a short blue cloth outside jacket, white flannel under ditto, new leather breeches, yarn stockings, and new shoes; oznabrig shirt, and an old hat. EDWARD MURPHEY, an Irishman, about 5 feet 5 inches high, slim made, wears his own short brown curled hair, and pretty much marked with the small pox, by trade a blacksmith; had on when he went away a blue cloth outside jacket, and a callico under ditto, plush breeches, worsted hose, new shoes, oznabrig shirt, and an old hat. WILLIAM BAKER, an Irishman, about 5 feet 7 inches high, a well set fellow, speaks good English, wears an old brown wigg, a dark coloured coarse cloth jacket, much stained with lime, two pair of oznabrig trowsers, an oznabrig shirt, felt hat, and old shoes. DAVID WELCH, an Irishman, about 26 years of age, 5 feet 10 inches high, a lusty well set fellow, has lost some of his teeth, has short black hair, is a cooper by trade; had on and took with him a lead coloured coarse kersey outside jacket and breeches, striped under jacket, blue worsted hose, half worn shoes, a white frock and white shirt. Whoever takes up said runaways, if taken in the county, and brought home, shall have Forty Shillings for each, if out of the county, and if brought home Fifty Shillings, and if out of the province, and secured in any county gaol, giving intelligence thereof, shall have Three Pounds for each,

and if brought home Five Pounds reward for each, paid by us, *George Wills, Brittingham Dickenson, John Deaver,* and *Edward Hanson.*
N. B. It is supposed they have taken horses with them, and will push back into the country, and very likely change their names and apparel; whether they are all gone together or no, is not known.

The Pennsylvania Chronicle, and Universal Advertiser, From Monday, October 30, to Monday, November 6, 1769; From Monday, November 6, to Monday, November 13, 1769; *The Pennsylvania Gazette,* November 9, 1769. Minor differences between the papers. The *Gazette* does not have the date at the top. See *The Maryland Gazette,* April 13, 1769, for Adair and Barber.

RAN away from the Subscriber, living in *Kent* County, *Maryland,* on the 25th of *October* last, a Convict Servant Man, named ROBERT HAINES, an *Englishman,* about 22 Years of Age, and 5 Feet 7 or 8 Inches high: Had on and took with him, a dark colour'd Half-worn Cloth Coat, with flower'd Block-Tin Buttons, and dark colour'd Lining, a purple nap'd Halfthick Jacket, with red Flannel Lining, without Buttons, and the Nap almost worn off, a short Under ditto, the Fore Parts made of striped Flannel, and the Hind Parts of blue Fearnought, Two Osnabrig Shirts, One white Sheeting ditto, Two Pair of old long Trousers, Half-worn Shoes, with Buckles, old Stocking Legs, Half-worn Hat, an Osnabrig Wallet, and a Glass Bottle. Whoever takes up and secures said Servant, so that his Master may have him again, shall have Forty Shillings Reward, besides reasonable Charges, paid by MICHAEL BYRNE.

The Maryland Gazette, November 9, 1769; November 16, 1769; November 23, 1769; November 30, 1769; *The Pennsylvania Gazette,* November 9, 1769. Minor differences between the papers.

TEN POUNDS REWARD.

Elk-Ridge Furnace, *October* 24, 1769.

RAN away from the Subscriber, the Two following Convict Servant Men, viz.

THOMAS DAVIS, an Irishman, 27 Years of Age, 5 Feet 11 Inches high, a straight well made Fellow, of a fair Complexion, speaks good English, has long black Hair, and wears it club'd, black Beard, and large hazel Eyes: Had on, a Cotton Jacket, Osnabrig Shirt, Crocus Trousers, new English Shoes, yellow Metal Buckles, and a new Castor Hat.

SIMON SALE, about 21 Years of Age, 5 Feet 9 Inches high, a straight well made Fellow, of a light Complexion, short brown Hair, and wears it tied, has hazel Eyes, and a Scar on his left Elbow: Had on, a Cotton Jacket, Osnabrig Shirt and Trousers, a Pair of old Country made Shoes, and a new Castor Hat. They broke open a House, and Stole the following Goods, *viz.* A Blue Country Cloth Coat, lin'd with Shalloon, and trim'd with large white Metal Buttons, Nankeen Jacket, a Pair of Leather Breeches patch'd, One Pair of brown Cloth ditto, Two Pair of blue Worsted Stockings, Two white Shirts, mark'd W H, Two cross-bar'd Silk Handkerchiefs, One Bird-eyed ditto, and a Gun.

Whoever apprehends the said Runaways, and brings them home, shall have, if taken within 20 Miles of said Furnace, 30 Shillings; if 30 Miles, 40 Shillings; and if out of the Province, 5 Pounds Reward for each, (including what the Law allows) paid by   CALEB DORSEY.

The Maryland Gazette, November 9, 1769; November 16, 1769; November 30, 1769.

COMMITTED to *Prince-George's* County Jail, the Two following Persons, viz. *Sarah Webb*, about 5 Feet high, fair Complexion, pretty much mark'd with the Small-Pox, she says she belongs to Mr. *John Wiseman*, near *Cedar Point*.—William Foursith, about Six Feet high, dark Complexion: Has on, a red short Jacket, and a Pair of long Cotton Trousers.

The Owners are desired to take them away and pay Charges.
JOHN ADDISON, Sheriff.

The Maryland Gazette, November 9, 1769.

Annapolis, November 3, 1769.
RAN away from the Subscribers, on the 29th of *October* last, Two *Irish* indented Servant Men, *viz.*

DANIEL M'CRITCH, alias *M'Grath*, a Carpenter by Trade, about 5 Feet 5 Inches high, pale Complexion, short and bow legged, has a down Look: Had on, an old brown Wig, but his Hair is growing, and is very black, brown Jacket, double breasted, short black ditto, also double breasted, Leather Breeches, Yarn Stockings, and black Shoes.

GEORGE CAVENDISH, also a Carpenter by Trade, about 6 Feet high, round shoulder'd, and his Toes lap'd one over the other: Had on, and took with him, a Bearskin Jacket, with a Cape, blue Cloth ditto, *Norway* Buck Breeches, *Russia* Drab ditto, a Pair of white Thread Hose, a Pair of mix'd Yarn ditto, One Check Shirt, and One Dowlas ditto, and black Shoes.

Whoever takes up said Servants, and brings them to the Subscribers, shall have Five Pounds Currency for *Daniel M'Critch*, and Three Pounds for *Cavendish*, paid by
JAMES BRICE,   JUBB FOWLER.
The Maryland Gazette, November 16, 1769; November 23, 1769; November 30, 1769; December 7, 1769.

Anne-Arundel County, *October* 13, 1769.
RAN away, last Night, from the Subscriber, living on *Elk-Ridge*, a Convict Servant Man, named, SAMUEL ALLSWORTH, by Trade a Gunstocker, about 20 Years of Age, 5 Feet 7 Inches high, has short brown curl'd Hair, short Face, and brown Complexion: Had on when went away, an old Castor Hat, a light colour'd Broadcloth Coat and Jacket, the coller of his Coat is lined with red Velvet, Osnabrig Shirt and Trousers, patch'd with coarse Linen, and a Pair of Country made Shoes, nailed. Whoever takes up the said Servant, and brings him home, shall have Twenty Dollars Reward, and reasonable Charges, paid by   SAMUEL POOLE.
The Maryland Gazette, November 23, 1769; November 30, 1769.

Bladensburg, November 19, 1769.
RAN away from the Subscriber, a Convict Servant Man, named WILLIAM WILLIAMSON, alias WAINWRIGHT, a thick well made Fellow, about 5 Feet high, has no Beard, a round full Face, fresh Colour, short light brown Hair, has a Cut on his under Lip, and an effeminate Voice. Had on and took with him, a white Linen Shirt, a Pair of white Drilling Breeches, strip'd red and white Jacket, a short brown ditto, a Pair of light blue gray Stockings, white Thread ditto, a Stock and Stock-Buckle, white Neckcloth, with a red and white Border at each End, a white Handkerchief, with a red and white Border, good Shoes, Pumps, Brass Buckles, and a Half-worn Hat. Whoever takes up the said Servant, and brings him home, if taken 20 Miles from home, Twenty Shillings, if 30 Miles, Thirty Shillings, if 40 Miles, Forty Shillings, and so in Proportion for a shorter or longer Distance, and if out of the Province, Five Pounds Reward, and reasonable Charges if brought home, paid by   WAIT STILL SINGELLTON CHURCH.
The Maryland Gazette, November 23, 1769; November 30, 1769; December 7, 1769; December 14, 1769; December 21, 1769.

November 1, 1769.
FIVE POUNDS Reward.
RUN away from the subscriber, last night, three convict servant men, viz. Daniel Whitefield, John Passanham, and James Brahen; the latter of which

has lost his left hand, which is a good mark. Whitefield is a very small fellow, of a very sandy complexion, wears his own red hair; had on, when he went away, a blue linen jacket, a tow linen shirt, cotton breeches, good shoes and stockings, and a new felt hat. Passanham about 5 feet 8 or 9 inches high, about 40 years of age, of a fair complexion, has a large scar on his throat; took with him a light coloured cloth surtout coat, a fine shirt, a black pair of greasy buckskin breeches, black worsted stockings, good shoes, and silver plated buckles, an old hat; was lately transported into this country. Whoever takes up said servants, and secures them, so that the owner may have them, again, shall have Three Pounds, if taken in the county; but if out of the county, the reward, paid by WILLIAM EDWARDS, on Lady's Manor, near the Chapel, in Baltimore county.

The Pennsylvania Gazette, November 23, 1769.

Lancaster Goal, November 14, 1769.
WAS committed to my custody, on the 25th of October, on suspicion of being a run away servant, a certain John Davis, as he calls himself, is a Welshman, and says he served his time out with Jacob Roara, of Conegocheague, in Maryland; he is 5 feet 7 or 8 inches high, black complexion, near 35 years of age; had on, when committed, a blanket coat, a red spotted flannel jacket, tow trowsers, good hat, shoes and stockings. Also was committed to my custody, on the 6th inst. on suspicion of being a run away servant, a certain John Gorman, as he calls himself, about 5 feet 9 or 10 inches high, short black hair; had on, when committed, a old short brown jacket, an old blue one, breeches the colour of the jacket, old shoes and stockings, an old shirt, and hat; on his own confession, says he did belong to the Niger Frigate, of New York, Captain Wilkinson, commander. Their masters, if any they have, are desired to come and pay their said servants charges, and take them away, otherwise they will be sold out for their fees, in three weeks from the date hereof, by
GEORGE EBERLY, Goaler.

The Pennsylvania Gazette, November 23, 1769.

FIVE POUNDS REWARD.
Dumfries, October 14, 1769.
RAN away last Night, a Convict Servant Man, named WILLIAM POWELL, about 40 Years of Age, or upwards, born in some of the inland Counties in *England*, and speaks very plain English, he is 5 Feet 9 Inches high, has short dark gray Hair, writes a pretty good Hand, and has probably wrote some Letters, or made out a Pass, as he is an artful Fellow: Had on, when he went away, a strong Kersey Jacket, or short Coat, pretty much

wore, a Pair of Buckskin Breeches, too large for him, a Pair of *Aberdeen* ribbed Hose, and a Pair of good Country Shoes almost new. He has also taken with him, an old Suit of black Cloaths, some Stockings and Shirts, he left Word in the Kitchen that he was going to kill Ducks, so that he was not directly missed. It is very likely he is either gone down *Patowmack* River, or got over to *Maryland*. Whoever takes up said Servant, and brings him to me, shall be paid Five Pounds, if taken Twenty Miles, from thence, or upwards, and if nearer, Three Pounds.
RICHARD GRAHAM.
The Maryland Gazette, November 30, 1769; December 7, 1769; December 14, 1769.

Frederick-Town, November 14, 1769.
RUN away from the Subscriber, yesterday morning, an indented servant, named Adrian Haplitzel, by trade a hatter, a well set fellow, about 21 or 22 years of age, about 5 feet high, born in Switzerland; had on, when he went away, a new felt hat, a silk handkerchief, brown on one side, and red on the other, a fine blue cloth coat and waistcoat, both with brass and steel buttons, a scarlet jacket, black leather breeches, blue light grey wove stockings, new shoes, with steel buckles, and a new check shirt. Whoever secures the said fellow, so as his master may get him again, or brings him home to his master, shall have FOUR POUNDS reward, paid by NICHOLAS HOWER.
The Pennsylvania Gazette, November 30, 1769.

RUN away from the subscriber hereof, living near the Blue Rocks, on the great road leading to Baltimore-town, Maryland, an Irish servant man, named John Gormon, of about 24 years of age, of a dark complexion, black hair, pitted with the small-pox, of a middle stature, wants one joint of the fore finger of his right hand; had on, when he went away, an old felt hat, newly-trimmed, a light coloured jacket, a green and blue damask under jacket, with red back parts, old grey kersey breeches, with founders buttons, blue yarn stockings, good shoes, and copper buckles; he has an iron yoke about his neck. Whoever takes up said servant in said county, shall have FIVE POUNDS reward, and all reasonable charges, paid by me
JOHN QUERNS.
The Pennsylvania Gazette, November 30, 1769.

Frederick-Town, Cecil County, Maryland, Nov. 27, 1769.
RUN away yesterday, from the subscriber, an Irish servant man, named Robert Bencroft, by trade a Stone Mason, he is about 22 years of age, and about 5 feet 10 inches high; had on, and took with him, a drab kersey coat,

and jacket, a pair of leather breeches, worsted stockings, castor hat, black wig, one white shirt, one check ditto, half worn shoes, odd steel buckles. He came over from London, in the ship Charming Isabella, Captain Johnson, in September last. Whoever secures said servant, so as his master may have him again, shall receive six Dollars reward, paid by
PHILIP WEATHERALL.
The Pennsylvania Gazette, December 7, 1769; December 14, 1769.

November 19, 1769.
RUN away from the subscriber, living on Elkridge, in Ann Arundel county, Maryland, an Irish convict servant man, named John Fowler; he is a tanner by trade, about 30 years of age, 5 feet 10 inches high, a lusty down looking fellow, and much pitted with the small-pox, has long black hair, not tied; he had on and took with him, a Carolina felt hat, newly dressed, a blue surtout coat, a black broadcloth coat, a pair of brown cloth breeches, a pair coarse country knit stockings, coarse shoes, and check shirt. Whoever takes up said servant, and brings him to the subscriber, shall have, if taken 10 miles from home, TWENTY SHILLINGS, and if out of the province, FIVE POUNDS reward, paid by   GEORGE SCOTT.
N. B. It is supposed that said servant has papers of Jacob Hoolbrooke.
The Pennsylvania Gazette, December 7, 1769.

Baltimore Town, November 30, 1769.
COMMITTED to my Custody, as Runaways, the following Persons, *viz.* MATHEW YOUNG, a tall down-looking young Fellow, born in *Ireland*, who with MICHAEL KELLEY, a short square set Fellow, say they ran away from a certain James Stinson, at *Bull's Shin*, near *Winchester*, in *Virginia*. HUMPHRY HILL, a Mulatto....JEM or SAM, a new Negro....
The respective Owners of the above Persons, are desired to come, pay charges, and take them away, or else they will sold out for their Fees, by DANIEL CHAMIER, Sheriff.
The Maryland Gazette, December 21, 1769.

TWENTY DOLLARS Reward.
RUN away from the subscriber, living in Kent county, Maryland, the 26th ult. two convict servant men; the one named Michael Hayne, a taylor by trade, and a German born, about 32 years of age, slim made, thin visage, dark complexion, black hair, has an old sore on his head, a little above his temple; he is about 5 feet 7 inches high, and so much like a French Neutral, that he may well pass for one; had on, and took with him a blue broadcloth

surtout coat, with mohair buttons, lapelled jacket, striped red and white, half grogram, a pair of dark coloured broadcloth breeches, a good pair of shoes, grain outward, and many other things, such as trowsers, shirts, handkerchiefs, and a good castor hat, with silk loops; the other named Nathaniel Powell, born in England, talks much on the west country dialect, abut 30 years of age, slim made, thin visage, dark complexion, black bushy curled hair, and grows more than common down his face; he carried with him a blue broadcloth coat, with a small cape, and mohair buttons, a pair of snuff coloured breeches, half worn, but they have many other things with them; and as both are cunning crafty fellows, and the taylor can write, they may forge a pass, and change their names and dress. Whoever secures the said servants, if out of the province, and brought home, shall receive the above reward, and reasonable charges paid, or Ten Dollars for each or either of them; if secured in goal, and speedy notice given, Six Dollars for each, or Twelve Dollars for both; if taken within the province, and brought home, Ten Dollars for each or either of them; if secured in prison, and speedy notice given, Five Dollars for either of each of them, paid by R. GERSHAM.

N. B. They had a Musket with them, marked J. Jenkins on the Lock; and were seen the 27th of June, near Wilmington.

The Pennsylvania Gazette, December 14, 1769. See *The Pennsylvania Gazette*, March 23, 1769, *The Maryland Gazette*, July 6, 1769, and *The Pennsylvania Gazette*, July 6, 1769, Hayne is probably Hewne/Keirn/Hern/Kern. See *The Maryland Gazette*, July 6, 1769, *The Pennsylvania Gazette*, July 6, 1769, *The Pennsylvania Gazette*, August 17, 1769 and *The Maryland Gazette*, September 21, 1769, for Powell.

RAN away from the Subscriber, living at *Patapsco* Ferry, a Convict Servant Man, named JOHN PRAT, about 6 feet high, with red Hair, and a very down Look: Had on, when he went away, a blue long Jacket, with Leather Buttons, a white Flannel under ditto, bound round with black [   ]ing, a Pair of long Osnabrig Trousers, with Flannel Drawers under them, an Osnabrig Shirt, a Pair of blue ribbed Stockings, Country-made Shoes, with Buckles, a Sailors Cap; and it is probable he [will] change his Name and Dress, and pass for a Sailor. He complains of a Weakness in his Back, to remedy which, he wears a broad Belt next his Shirt.

Whoever takes up said Servant, and secures him, shall have Two Pounds reward, if taken in the Province; if out of the Province, THREE POUNDS, and reasonable Charges, if brought home, paid by
FLORA DORSEY.

The Maryland Gazette, December 21, 1769. See *The Pennsylvania Gazette,* December 28, 1769.

Lancashire Furnace, Baltimore County, Dec. 4.

RAN away last Night, from the Subscriber, a Convict Servant, named EDWARD HOOPER, about Twenty-four Years of Age, fair Complexion, about 5 Feet 3 or 4 Inches high, wears his own dark brown Hair: Had on, and took with him, an Osnabrig Shirt and Trousers, an old Fearnought Jacket, and Cotton Breeches. This fellow has on an Iron Collar when he went away, being under a Prosecution for Housebreaking.

Ran away from his Bail, at the same Time, JOHN BISHOP, by Trade a Collier, about Thirty Years of Age, 5 Feet 6 or 7 Inches high, wears his own lank dark brown Hair, is a thin Fellow, speaks in the *Shropshire* Dialect, and has a remarkable Scar on his left Hand: Had on, and took with him, a Copper coloured Suit of Cloaths, a drab lappelled Waistcoat, new blue Cloth Breeches, old blue Coat, and a close bodied Great Coat. It is supposed he is a great Villain, and has inveigled away the said Servant, who, it's supposed, he will be in company with, and possibly will spare him some of his Cloaths; as likewise a Woman, who passeth for his Wife, and a Child, about Two Years old; the Woman is about Twenty-one, or Twenty two Years of Age, about 5 Feet 1 or 2 Inches high, fair Complexion, and brown Hair; she had on a dark coloured Shalloon Gown, red Petticoat, and black Silk Hat; she strolled some Time ago from *Queen-Anne's* County, on the Eastern Shore. Her maiden name was *Ann Hand.* Whoever apprehends said Runaways, so that they may be had again, and gives Notice to the Subscriber, shall have Forty Shillings Reward for *Edward Hooper,* and Three Pounds for *John Bishop,* with reasonable Charges, if brought home. GEORGE RANDELL.

The Maryland Gazette, December 21, 1769; January 4, 1770; January 11, 1770; January 18, 1770.

Maryland, October 24, 1769.

WHEREAS Complaint has been made to me, One of his Lordship's the Right Honourable the Lord Proprietary's Justices for *Baltimore* County, by MARY CHAPMAN, that on the 19th Day of *September* last past, Two Men, one named THOMAS PLANT, the other JAMES GORDON, took of her Property, an Apparatus of a PUPPET SHOW, *Punch's* Head remarkably large: GORDON is a Taylor by Trade, and had many Clothes with him, he is about 25 Years of Age. THOMAS PLANT is an uncommon short Man, and looks strangely with his Eyes, pretty much deformed in his

Limbs, beats the Drum and plays Legerdemain. Whoever takes up said Men abovementioned, and secures them in any Jail in this Province, shall have Four Pounds Reward, paid by the above MARY CHAPMAN, on their sending Intelligence to Capt. JAMES MAXWELL, in *Gunpowder* Neck, *Baltimore* County, where said MARY CHAPMAN now resides.

THESE are therefore to require and command all his Lordship's good People of this Province, to make diligent Enquiry after the said *Thomas Plant*, and *James Gordon*, by Way of HUE and CRY, and apprehend the said *Thomas Plant*, and *James Gordon, or* either of them, and to carry them, or him, to some Justice where taken, to be dealt with according Law; and for their so doing this shall be their Warrant, Given under my Hand and Seal, the Day and Year first abovewritten.
WILLIAM YOUNG.
To all Sheriffs, Constables, and others, His Lordship's good People in this Province.
The Maryland Gazette, December 21, 1769.

RUN away from the subscriber, living at Patapsco Ferry, Maryland, on the 14th of this instant December, a convict servant man, named JOHN PRAT, about 6 feet high, with red hair, and a down look, he appears of be about 25 years of age; had on, when he went away, a long blue jacket, with leather buttons, a white flannel under jacket, bound round with black, an ozenbrigs shirt, long ozenbrigs trowsers, with white flannel drawers under them, blue ribbed stockings, and country made shoes, with buckles; had on a sailor's cap; he complains of a weakness in his back, and wears a broad duck belt next to his shirt, he passes for a sailor, and possibly may change his name and clothes, and I imagine he has a forged pass. Whoever takes up said servant, and secures him, so that the owner may have him again, shall have Two Pounds reward, if taken in the province, if out of the province, THREE POUNDS, paid by   FLORA DORSEY.
The Pennsylvania Gazette, December 28, 1769; January 18, 1770.

INDEX

Abbot, John, 315
Abbutt, William, 154, 256
Abdell, John, 55
Adair, Robert, 111, 229, 233
Adair, William, 303, 348
Adam, Robert, 152, 214, 326
Adams, George, 331
Adams, John, 334, 338, 342
Adams, Nathaniel, 195
Adams, William, 270
Adamson, John, 155, 256
Addison, John, 298, 350
Addison, Thomas, 294
Addowell, Richard, 223
Aderton, Joseph, 298, 333
Adwell, Richard, 228, 238
Ager, James, 49, 50
Aires, Charles, 125, 131
Alan, Charles, 322, 324
Alan, Joseph, 323, 324
Alexander, Amos, 199
Alexander, James, 111
Aliscram, James Henry, 128
Allein, Benjamin, 318
Allen, Captain, 31
Allen, Charles, 102
Allen, James, 17, 19
Allen, John, 294
Allsworth, Samuel, 351
Almore, John, 334
Ancell, John, 166
Anderson, James, 13, 15, 30
Anderson, John, 39
Anderson, William, 145
Andrew, Nicholas, 33, 116
Andrew, William, 337
Andrews, John, 22
Andrews, Joseph, 94
Andris, William, 346
Angess, William Daniel, 209

Archer, Benjamin, 47
Archer, Thomas, 293
Arens, John, 169
Armstrong, John, 167
Arthur, Hannah, 29
Bachman, Jacob, 315
Backman, Jacob, 284
Bacon, Joseph Neale, 74
Badger, Benjamin, 323
Bailer, Mr., 180
Bailey, James, 322
Baker, Francis, 285
Baker, Henry, 235
Baker, William, 263, 348
Bambridge, John, 129
Banks, William, 37
Banning, Anthony, 286, 310
Banning, Jeremiah, 144
Bannister, William, 281
Barber, John, 62, 303, 348
Barham, Joseph, 111
Barker, John, 271
Barker, William, 334
Barnett, James, 35, 258
Barnett, John, 219
Barnett, Levy, 181, 214
Barney, William, 287
Barns, James, 224
Barret, John, 206
Barron, Bartholomew, 39
Bartley, William, 183
Bath, John, 176
Battin, Taulbert, 342
Baxter, James, 5
Baxter, William, 74
Beach, Samuel, 102
Beach, Thomas, 228
Beal, Samuel, 168
Beall, Joshua, 23
Beall, Richard, 243

Beall, Samuel, Jr., 62, 144, 157, 257
Beall, Walter, 183, 194
Beate, Isaac, 245
Beatty, Charles, 280, 282
Beck, Samuel Duvall, 3
Beech, Thomas, 184
Belcher, Thomas, 299
Bell, Benjamin, 97
Bell, James, 316
Bence, Michael, 20
Bencroft, Robert, 353
Bener, Charles, 194
Benham, John, 255, 277
Bennet, Jeremiah, 240
Bennet, John, 143
Bennet, Joseph, 345
Bennet, Thomas, 282
Bennett, James, 3, 4
Bennett, John, 146, 245
Bennett, William, 121, 255
Benson, Fleetwood, 93
Berrage, John, 288
Berrett, Andrew, 221
Berry, John, 208
Berryman, Richard, 325
Best, Thomas, 98
Betton, Turbutt, 335, 338
Bevan, John, 189
Bewmire, Gerrard, 17
Biddle, Noah, 195
Biggar, James, 176, 250, 289
Billington, William, 145
Birstall, John, 53, 244, 246
Bishen, Edward, 79
Bishop, John, 356
Bishop, Joseph, 335, 338, 342
Blackburn, Francis, 280, 282
Blair, John, 177
Blair, William, 293
Blake, William, 267, 285
Blanch, William, 285
Blunt, Samuel, 301, 305, 315

Boardley, John Beale, 245
Bolton, John, 143, 146
Bonar, William, 258
Boon, William, 51
Boot, Daniel, 48
Bosden, Edward, 327
Bosley, Joseph, Jr., 167
Bosman, Edward, 323
Bostock, William, 116
Bould, John, 204, 210
Bowen, Josias, 166
Bowes, Richard, 10, 26
Bowman, Thomas, 191
Bows, Richard, 219
Box, Jesse, 132
Boyd, Dr., 245
Boyd, Hugh, 213
Boyer, John, 279
Boyer, Thomas, 125
Bozman, John, 43, 49, 172
Bradey, James, 224
Bradford, Henry, 56
Brady, Mary, 82
Brahen, James, 351
Brangle, Jacob, 306
Breemer, Gasper, 247
Brenon, Patrick, 167
Brent, William, 57, 77
Breston, Edward, 287
Brice, James, 351
Brice, John, 29
Brichan, George, 233
Briggs, John, 88
Briggs, William, 235
Brisko, Mary, 11
Britt, Patrick, 15
Brittian, Nicholas, 287
Broadbent, John, 24
Broadwater, Mordecai, 29
Broady, James, 264
Brook, Richard, 175
Brooke, Thomas, 20
Brookes, Henry, 89

Brookes, James, 263, 269
Brookes, Richard, 94
Brookes, Thomas, 65, 176
Brooks, William, 10
Broughton, John, 218
Brown, Aquila, 42
Brown, George, 168, 180
Brown, John, 313
Brown, Mr., 331
Brown, Nathaniel, 334, 342
Brown, Peter, 257
Brown, Robert, 78
Brown, Samuel, 188
Brown, Valentine, Jr., 128, 292
Brown, William, 8, 76, 211, 262, 336
Brown, William Chew, 128
Brownsnow, John, 320
Bruce, Normand, 294
Bruen, Bryan, 246
Bryan, Edward, 214
Bryan, Elisabeth, 244
Bryan, Elizabeth, 50
Bryan, James, 205, 210
Bryan, John, 23
Bryan, Mary, 330
Bryan, Stephen, 13
Bryarly, Thomas, 284
Buchanan, James, 79
Buck, John, 266
Buckingham, John, 77
Bugh, Matthias, 209
Burch, Thomas, 46
Burgess, Caleb, 46
Burgess, John, 172
Burgoine, John, 130
Burgon, Joshua, 177
Burk, James, 219
Burk, John, 131
Burk, William, 225
Burkitt, Michael, 107
Burn, Sweatnam, 172, 178
Burneston, Joseph, 293

Burns, James, 130
Burns, William, 286
Burrage, John, 325
Burrell, Alexander, 195
Burritt, Isaac, 76
Burrough, George, 120, 122
Burt, Andrew, 170
Bush, Oliver, 245
Butler, Edward, 211
Butler, James, 339
Butler, Jas., 242
Butler, Sarah, 273
Byrn, Patrick, 207
Byrne, Michael, 349
Byrne, Thomas, 247
Cain, John, 99
Callahan, William, 115, 169
Calle, William, 58
Callis, James, 277
Calvert, John, 59, 67
Calvert, Michael, 204, 210
Calvin, Philip, 298
Campbell, Angus, 258
Campbell, Charles, 198, 200
Campbell, James, 316, 338
Cane, Margaret, 81, 84
Canely, Will, 214
Cannon, Christopher, 323
Cannon, John, 134
Carlin, William, 252
Carnes, Arundale, 170
Carney, Edward, 254
Carpenter, Mary, 44
Carr, Hannah, 298
Carr, Henry, 28
Carr, Martha, 246
Carr, Michael, 112
Carravan, Partrick, 193
Carroll, Charles, 29, 97, 129, 141, 172
Carroll, John, 215, 223, 245
Carroll, Patrick, 85
Carroll, William, 8

Carson, William, 295
Carter, George, 326
Carter, William, 265
Carthy, Timothy, 317
Cartwright, Henry, 307, 320, 321
Cartwrite, Joseph, 5
Carty, Mary, 312
Carty, Robert, 312
Cary, John, 24
Casey, James, 65
Casey, William, 56
Cat, Curtis, 241
Caton, Captain, 283
Cavendish, George, 350
Cayton, Anthony, 337
Chaires, Joseph, 136
Chambers, John, 116
Chambers, Jonas, 306
Chamier, Daniel, 244, 266, 347
Champ, John, 316
Chandler, William, 59
Chant, Robert, 27
Chapell, Lucy, 103
Chapman, James, 118, 181
Chapman, Mary, 356
Chapman, Thomas, 229, 230, 248
Chappel, John, 206
Chase, Mr., 247
Chase, Samuel, 190, 345
Chattin, Josiah, 295
Chavies, Joseph, 101
Chemier, Daniel, 344, 347
Chew, John, 142
Chew, Samuel, 80
Chews, Samuel, 116
Child, James, 314
Child, John, 37, 38, 54, 67
Chisholm, Thomas, 336
Christie, James, Jr., 190
Christie, Robert, Jr., 188
Christopher, Thomas, 171
Christophers, Gibbons, 341

Church, Wait Still Singellton, 351
Churchwell, Daniel, 219
Circaud, Captain, 275
Clagett, John, 243
Clapham, Josias, 176
Clark, Abraham, 211
Clark, George, 146
Clark, Hugh, 236
Clark, James, 34, 259, 315
Clark, John, 82, 166
Clark, Joseph, 99
Clark, Mary, 34
Clark, Neal, Jr., 93
Clark, Richard, 5
Clark, William, 104, 106, 258
Clarke, Charles, 345
Clarke, Joseph, 76
Clarke, Robin, 137
Clement, Richard, 118
Clenn, Christopher, 110, 112
Clinton, Thomas, 25
Cloauss, John Christopher, 135
Coal, John, 69, 85
Coal, Willam, 247
Coale, William, 46
Coalman, Edward, 234
Cobourn, James, 330
Cock, Captain, 270
Cockran, Joseph, 20
Cole, Captain, 29
Cole, Cuthbert, 178
Cole, George, 98
Cole, James, 46
Cole, John, 60
Colegate, Thomas, 166
Colens, Patrick, 114
Collings, Patrick, 122
Collins, Edmund, 114
Collins, John, 6, 12, 16
Colman, Roger, 342
Colwell, William, 42, 49
Combes, Dennis, 282

Comegys, Jacob, 206, 253, 266
Commins, John, 112
Conawa, John, 114
Conaway, Michael, 262
Connally, Philip, 176
Connant, William, 82
Connel, Michael, 79
Connell, Alexander, 123
Connely, James, 265
Conner, Patrick, 223
Conner, Thomas, 14
Connerly, Patrick, 194
Connoway, John, 122
Connoway, Michael, 211
Conway, Sarah, 261
Conyngham, Mr., 39
Cook, Edward, 216
Cook, Miles, 13, 15, 30
Cook, Mrs., 51
Cook, Thomas, 84
Cook, William, 260
Cooke, John, 26
Cooke, Philip, 118, 120
Cooke, Richard, 31
Cooke, William, 239, 290
Cooper, John, 210, 229
Cooper, Joseph, 110
Cooper, Joshua, 87
Coort/Court, James, 268, 284
Coppage, John, 41, 42
Corbet, James, 100
Coreshil/Coreshill Thomas, 290, 292
Corkrill, William, 27
Corrt, James, 41
Corrt/Court, James, 57
Corsa, William, 30
Cosgrove, Charles, 195
Cosh, Samuel, 39
Costolow, Edward, 92
Couley, James, 154
Cowden, Susannah, 212
Cowens, William, 326

Cox, John, 163
Cox, Richard, 99
Cox, William, 149, 165
Craig, Michael, 207, 215
Craiger, Benedict, 322
Crandell, William, 276
Crawford, John, 171
Crawford, Mrs., 269
Crawley, Jacob, 135
Craymer, Captain, 15
Craymer, Mathew/Matthew, 13, 30
Craytan, James, 166
Crop, Mr., 88
Crosby, James, 269
Cross, Bartholomew, 238
Cross, Robert, 175
Cross, Thomas, 175
Crosswell, James, 65, 70
Crouch, William, 150
Croxall, R., 17, 37, 97, 272
Crutchfield, Stapleton, 300
Cullamore, William, 105
Cullimoor, William, 132
Cullom, Henry, 29
Cunningham, Alexander, 213
Cunningham, Andrew, 184
Cunningham, Henry, 171, 176, 221, 237, 239, 247, 258
Curbuc, John, 264
Curling, John, 152
Curry, Michael, 112
Curseiur, Abraham, 287
Cyas, John, 285
Dabs, John, 97
Dailey, Cornelius, 148
Daily, Barney, 21
Daily, Cornelius, 137, 168
Dally, Charles, 217
Dally, Mary, 217
Dalton, John, 214
Dance, Thomas, 172, 178
Dane, William, 45, 65

Danely, Thomas, 309
Daniel, Edward, 300
Darbyshire, Jonathan, 78, 79, 130
Darding, William, 27
Darrach, Thomas, 122
Darrel, George, 75
Darrell, Sampson, 281
Davenant, Samuel, 271
Davis, Alice, 82
Davis, Edward, 59, 67, 133
Davis, Evan, 301, 304, 315
Davis, John, 23, 122, 215, 352
Davis, John Lewis, 107
Davis, Michael, 112
Davis, Mr., 89
Davis, Richard, 23
Davis, Thomas, 349
Davis, William, 225
Davy, Thomas, 195
Dawson, Benjamin, 56, 123
Day, Edward, 36, 37
Dealy, William, 38
Deaver, John, 232, 239, 294, 349
DeCamp, Jacob, 245
Delany, Daniel, 173
Delany, Mary, 228
Dennis, John, 323
Dennis, Littleton, 288
Dennit, William, 174
Denny, Peter, 292
Denny, William, 186
Dent, John, 35, 36
Dent, Joseph, 108, 153, 159
Dent, Mary, 195
Dermon, Patrick, 311
Deroachbroom, Thomas, 255
Derrick, Thomas, 120
Devorse, Stephen, 151
Dial, Francis, 163, 178
Dick, John, 262
Dick, Robert, 263
Dickason, Joseph, 9

Dickenson, Brittingham, 349
Dickinson, John, 109
Dicks, James, 24
Diggan, Patrick, 68
Digges, William, 290, 293
Dilladd, George, 282
Divin, James, 209
Dixon, Francis, 63
Dixon, James, 113
Dixon, Joe, 237
Dixon, John, 59, 239
Dixon, Simon, 93
Dobson, Thomas, 135
Doby, James, 259
Dockery, Thomas, 133
Dodson, John, 192
Doloson, James, 15
Dome, William, 48
Donaldson, James, 14, 30
Donelly, Felix, 54
Donerly, Patrick, 62
Doran, Brian, 28
Doran, Bryan, 30
Dorney, Thomas, 126
Dorsey, Benjamin, 128
Dorsey, Caleb, 12, 76, 163, 193, 203, 261, 278, 291, 307, 310, 326, 350
Dorsey, Flora, 83, 93, 96, 100, 355, 357
Dorsey, Henry, 1, 7, 32
Dorsey, John, 74, 98, 141
Dorsey, Nathan, 59, 71, 232
Dorsey, Samuel, 271
Dorsey, Thomas, 292
Dougherty, George Peters, 295
Douglas, John, 346
Douglass, John, 341, 343
Douglass, William, 55, 341
Dowland, Martin, 272
Downing, Robert, 252
Downing, Samuel, 104
Downing, William, 72, 73

Downy, Samuel, 2
Dowsman, John, 180
Drew, Edward, 339
Driver, John, 17
Driver, William, 76
Dryton, Samuel, 272
Ducker, John, 1, 50
Dudley, William, 31
Duely, Cornelius, 132
Dugan, Mary, 279
Dulany, Samuel, 75
Dulany, Walter, 335
Dungan, Mary, 280
Dunkin, James, 48
Dunn, Catherine, 195
Dunn, Robert, 88, 89
Dunn, William, 194, 211
Dunnavon, Dennis, 24
Dunnem, Mr., 280
Durbin, Thomas, 312
Duvall, Aquila, 94
Duvall, John Pearce, 327
Duvall, William, 269, 286
Eagan, Edward, 240
Eagle, Edward, 31
Ealgor, Joseph, 54
Earle, Daniel, 189
Earle, Joseph, 133
Earle, Michael, 140
Earley, John, 127
Eating, Jonathan, 332
Eberly, George, 334, 352
Edmondson, Samuel, 208
Edwards, William, 114, 352
Edwin, Francis, 121, 179
Elder, James, 175
Elliott, Thomas, 107, 130
Elton, Thomas, 309, 343, 345, 347
Elwood, John, 199
Engle, John, 142
English, Nelly, 287
English, William, 31

Ennalls, Bartholomew, 13
Ennalls, William, 138, 145
Enser, John, 221
Ensor, John, Jr., 95
Errington, Captain, 100
Erskine, Robert, 63
Eunuch, John, 154
Eustis, Augustus, 63
Evans, George, 96
Evans, John, 168, 179, 242, 303
Evans, Robert, 330
Evans, Thomas, 22, 179
Evans, William, 329
Everhatt, Abraham, 87
Ewing, George, 295
Ewing, Mr., 331
Ewing, Thomas, 142
Fachy, Patrick, 191, 198, 200
Fagin/Fagon, Garret, 120, 122
Faris, William, 112
Farran, Charles, 103, 138, 164
Farrell, John, 99
Farrow, James, 45
Farrow, Nathan, 220, 224, 232
Fea, Thomas, 53
Ferguson, Alexander, 240
Ferguson, Colin, 137
Ferguson, William, 85
Ferran, Charles, 150
Ferroll, Dennis, 86, 104
Ferroll, John, 29, 86
Ferroll, Martin, 29
Fetherson, William, 254
Fields, William, 272
Finn, John, 124
Fipps, John, 301
Firth, William, 152, 158, 161
Fisher, Ebenezer, 68
Fisher, George, 97
Fishwick, James, 25
Fishwick, Mr., 102
Fitch, Joseph, 180
Fitzhugh, Colonel, 109

Fitzhugh, William, 109, 153, 160, 161
Flannakin, Margaret, 337
Flewharty, Michael, 19
Flood, Nicholas, 196
Flood, Richard, 294
Flood, Samuel, 271
Floyd, Mary, 243
Footman, Peter, 129
Footman, Richard, 129
Forsey, Thomas, 180
Forster, Samuel, 282
Forsythe, Matthew, 71
Fossit, Thomas, 280
Foster, Thomas, 61, 70, 85
Foursith, William, 350
Fowler, James, 251, 253
Fowler, John, 29, 354
Fowler, Jubb, 351
Fowler, Richard, 113
Francis, Basis, 302
Francis, John, 209
Franklin, James, 38, 54, 67
Franklin, Thomas, 49, 80
Frazier, Joshua, 211
Free, John, 273, 289
Free, Nelly, 274
Free, Nicholas, 274
Freeman, Daniel, 129
French, Mr., 291
Fricker, John, 57, 77
Fry, Joseph, 128
Fry, William, 54
Fryer, John, 185, 187
Fullerallcary, Edward, 113
Fussell, Captain, 30
Gabrel, Solomon, 61
Gabriel, Solomon, 62
Gaeson, Cornelius, 252
Gafford, William, 332
Gainer, John, 319
Gaither, Benjamin, 158
Gaither, Edward, 158, 233

Gaither, Henry, 233
Gale, Joseph, 195
Gallion, James, 34
Galloway, David, 92
Galloway, Joseph, 50, 65, 87, 96, 102, 104, 155
Galloway, Samuel, 184
Gamball, Ralph, 321
Gambrill, William, 36, 55
Gantt, Thomas, 118, 121
Gardener, Christopher, 238
Gardiner, John, 12
Gardner, John, 62, 123
Gardner, Samuel, 63
Garland, Griffin, 275
Garraughty, John, 162, 173
Garret, William, 124
Garrett, Amos, 234, 235, 333
Gartrell, William, 51
Gassaway, Henry, 207
Gassaway, Nicholas, 109
Gassaway, Tho., 109
Gates, Charles, 221
Gaull, George, 313
Gavin, Joseph, 344
Gent, Thomas, 323
George, William, 174
Gibbins, George, 91
Gibson, Mr., 251
Gibson, W., 8
Giles, Jacob, 12, 312
Giles, Nathaniel, 194
Giles, Nathaniel John, 87
Gill, John, 258
Gill, Stephen, Jr., 332
Gillhespy, Joseph, 53
Gilliard, Thomson, 236
Gilliard, William Thomson, 236
Gittings, Asael, 303
Glanding, John, 188
Glasford, Hugh, 84
Glassell, John, 63
Glover, Henry, 136

Gold, Elizabeth, 129
Goldsmith, Charles, 3, 4
Good, Thomas, 259
Goodan, John, 127
Goodwin, William, 162, 340, 341
Gordon, James, 356
Gordon, John, 165, 167, 171
Gorman/Gorman, John, 127, 352, 353
Gorsuch, David, 95
Gouge, Richard, 66
Graham, Reginald, 113
Graham, Richard, 100, 353
Graham, William, 188, 190
Grahame, Charles, 95
Graigg, John, 23
Grant, Thomas, 17
Grant, William, 286, 334
Grattan, John, 246
Gratton, John, 244
Graves, Richard, 133
Gray, Thomas, 114
Graybell/Graybill, Jacob, 165, 173
Greefes, Henry, 335
Green, Joseph, 195
Green, Richard, 172
Green, Thomas Melchizedech, 202
Greenfield, William, 244
Gregory, Captain, 339
Gresham, R., 117, 126, 317, 318, 355
Gresham, Richard, 161, 301
Gresham, Thomas, 117
Gretter, Michael, 217, 219, 281
Griffie, William, 296
Griffin, Anne, 86
Griffin, Henry, 331
Griffith, Anne, 94, 219
Griffith, Charles Greenbury, 259
Griffith, Henry, 110

Griffith, Joshua, 110
Griffith, Orlando, 110
Griffits, John, 13
Grimes, Joshua, 331
Grimshaw, Edmund, 197, 222
Grimshaw, Edward, 213
Grimshaw, Job, 40
Groves, James, 60, 69, 85, 263
Groves, William, 245
Grub, Mr., 333
Grussely, Peter, 77
Grymes, Benjamin, Jr., 300
Guiddine, William, 176
Gumry, John, 242
Hacket, Richard, 217, 222
Hadding, Captain, 262
Haddon, George, 286
Hagerty, Michael, 203
Hagon, Roger, 224
Haile, George, 24
Hails, George, 164
Haines, Joseph, 237
Haines, Robert, 349
Haley, John, 156
Hall, Aquila, 64, 247, 333
Hall, Felix, 27
Hall, George, 107
Hall, Henry, 33
Hall, John, 69
Hall, Philip, 316
Hall, Robert, 262
Hall, William, 72
Hamilton, James, 51
Hamilton, William, 114, 122, 170, 171
Hammond, Mordecai, 124
Hammond, Philip, 190
Hand, Ann, 356
Hands, John, 151
Handy, Isaac, 288
Haney, Henry, 180
Haney, Charles, 180
Hannah, William, 84

Hanson, Edward, 349
Hanson, Hans, 212
Hanson, Samuel, 202, 221, 293
Haplitzel, Adrian, 353
Harbett, Richard, 162
Harburn, John Frederick, 245
Hardesty, Richard, 240
Hardey, Geo., Jr., 216
Hardey, Henry, 123
Hardey, Henry, Jr., 216
Harding, William, 2
Hardwick, James, 51
Hardy, Henry, Jr., 127
Hardy, John, 197, 214, 222
Hargrove, Thomas, 274
Harris, Isaac, 9, 69, 82
Harris, John, 147, 168
Harrison, Henry, 208
Harrison, John, 109
Harrison, Mr., 131, 176
Harrison, Robert, 241
Harrison, Thomas, 34, 116, 166, 215, 328
Harriss, Edward, 258
Harriss, George, 27
Harriss, John, 142
Harriss, William, 148
Hart, Nicholas, 221
Hart, Robert, 31
Hartsworth, William, 247
Harvey, Alexander, 12, 30, 129, 168
Harvey, William, 106
Haslup, William, 180
Hastings, Oliver, 264
Hatton, William, 74, 229, 230, 248, 276, 278, 319
Hawkerday, John, 140
Hawkes, Thomas, 5, 248
Hawkins, James, 91
Hawkins, Thomas, 332
Hay, Captain, 87
Hayes, George, 48

Hayne, Michael, 318, 354
Haynes, Absalom, 18, 21
Hays, Thomas, 12
Hayton, Richard, 102, 104, 108
Hayward, Francis, 212
Hayward, William, 94
Heames, Sarah, 281
Hearly, Timothy, 108
Hebb, Vernon, 150
Heires, Jane, 44
Henley, Michael, 75
Hennis, David, 243
Henry, James, 26
Henry, John, 224, 225
Henry, Jonathan, 3
Henward, Robert, 84, 85
Heran, John, 150
Hern, Michael, 300
Hernly, Darby, 64
Heron, John, 134
Hesselius, John, 348
Hewne, Michael, 316
Hicks, Elias, 40
Hicks, Joseph, 175
Hide, William, 244
Hill, Charles, 336, 346
Hill, John, 174, 223, 265, 329
Hindman, William, 251, 253
Hines, Absalom, 18, 21
Hines, John, 244
Hipkins, Samuel, 275
Hirley, Patrick, 201
Hix, Elias, 39
Hobbs, Benjamin, 87
Hobbs, Joseph, 145
Hockaday, John, 139
Hoffman, William, 193
Hoffnakle, George, 271
Hoget, John, 281
Holder, Richard, 336
Holliday, John, 162
Hollingsworth, Henry, 103, 139, 150, 164, 167

Hollingsworth, Jesse, 134
Holmead, Anthony, 219
Holmes, John, 176
Holmes, Mr., 213
Holmes, Samuel, 142, 147
Holmes, Thomas, 174
Holton, Solomon, 6
Homes, Samuel, 160
Homes, Thomas, 306
Hood, James, 84
Hood, John, 60
Hoolbrooke, Jacob, 354
Hooper, Edward, 356
Hooper, Robert, 64
Hopkins, Gerard, 33
Hopkins, Thomas, 247
Hopper, Col., 117
Horan, Patrick, 295
Horn, Richard, 53
Horn, William, 179
Hoskins, John, 134
Hosley, John, 273
Hoult, Mary, 11
How, William, 313
Howard, Ephraim, 41, 67, 304
Howard, John Greniff/John Grenis, 61, 114
Howard, William, 91
Howe, Estes, 180
Hower, Nicholas, 353
Hubbard, John, 83
Hubberd, John, 78
Hudson, William, 245
Hughes, Elisha, 100
Hughes, James, 111
Hughes, John, 155, 165, 286
Hughs, Thomas, 260, 291
Hulet, William, 91
Humphreys, Matthew, 43
Humphries, John, 320
Hunt, John, 149
Hunt, Robert, 321
Hunter, Ezekiel, 326, 330

Hunter, John, 26
Hunter, Peter, 267
Hurd, James, 35
Hussey, Edward, 241, 251, 252
Hussey, Patrick, 217
Huston, William, 66
Hutchings, James, 2, 147
Hutchings, Thomas Elliott, 106
Hutchison, James, 342
Hyde, John, 345
Hyde, Mr., 293
Hyde, Thomas, 344
Hyley, William, 57
Hyligar, John, 180
Hysley, Charles, 133
Igo, Dennis, 192
Ingram, Benjamin, 114
Inman, William, 339
Ireland, John, 208
Irwing, James, 92
Isgreg/Isgrig William, 40
Jack, George, 245
Jackson, William, 109, 229, 230, 248, 273, 276, 278, 319
Jacobs, Joseph, 37, 162, 305
Jacobs, Samuel, 107
Jacques, Lancelot, 12, 18
James, Henry, 282
James, Peter, 53
James, Thomas, 101, 203, 310, 326
Janney, Isaac, 28
Janvier, Isaac, 151
Jarrett, Abraham, 236, 237
Jarvis, Mr., 4
Jeffcock, Joseph, 119
Jenkins, Edward, 161
Jenkins, J., 355
Jennings, Edmund, 243
Jennings, John, 308
Jennings, William, 111
Johns, Jeremiah, 32
Johnson, Bartholomew, 240

Johnson, Captain, 354
Johnson, David, 269
Johnson, Edward, 254
Johnson, George Peters, 295
Johnson, James, 149, 242
Johnson, Randle, 46
Johnson, Richard, 342
Johnson, Riely, 177
Johnson, Robert, 312
Johnson, Thomas, 33, 271
Johnson, Thomas, Jr., 211, 297, 299
Johnston, James, 256
Johnston, Mr., 137
Johnston, Thomas, 75
Johnston, William, 244
Jones, Henry, 318
Jones, Hugh, 279, 280, 283
Jones, Jehu, 245
Jones, John, 40
Jones, Richard, 2
Jones, Thomas, 61, 63, 259
Jones, William, 253
Jordan, Jeremiah, 86
Jordan, Jesse, 347
Jordan, John, 72
Jordan, William, 44, 114
Kanare, William, 52
Kean, Mathew, 314
Kean, William, 146
Kearney, Lawrence, 316
Keaz, Andrew, 237, 239
Keen, Richard, 344
Keho, Edmund, 266
Keirn, Michael, 316
Kelkelly, Patrick, 101
Kelley, Matthew, 60
Kelley, Michael, 354
Kelley, Mordecai, 33
Kelley, William, 51
Kellock, Mary, 4
Kelly, Edward, 171, 219
Kelly, John, 221

Kelly, Martin, 25
Kelly, Mary, 219
Kelly, Matthew, 70, 86
Kelly, Michael, 341
Kelly, Nicholas, 193
Kelsey, John, 152
Kendall, Benjamin, 310
Kendall, John, 63
Kennall, James, 63
Kennedy, Edward, 46
Kennedy, James, 236
Kenney, Luke, 326
Kenning, Samuel, 325, 330
Kent, John, 155
Kern, Michael, 300
Kerney, Patrick, 223
Kesler, Jacob, 237
Key, Richard Ward, 31
Key, Thomas, 116, 257
Kidwell, George, 345
Killeen, Charles, 217
Kilty, John, 154, 302
King, Francis, 123, 127
King, Henry, 245
King, Robert, 110, 112
King, Thomas, 190, 229
Kingham, John, 249
Kirby, Benjamin, 76, 308
Kittle, John, 25
Kittoe, William, 316
Knapp, Frances, 325
Knapp, William, 288
Kneller, William, 204
Knight, John, 53
Kurton, Anthony, 337
Lacey, Catherine, 195
Laha, Priscilla, 45
Laing, Alexander, 208
Lamb, Francis, 19
Lamb, John, 246
Lambdin, John, 267
Lamprey, Thomas, 220, 231
Landon, John, 338

Landray, Jos., 150
Lane, Nathan, 3
Lane, William, 58, 70
Lane, William Carr, 255, 277
Lansdale, John, 32
Larkin, Andrew, 331
Larkin, Patrick, 202
Lasher, Henry, 63
Laurie, James, 80
Lawrence, Benjamin, 102
Lawson, Thomas, 68, 170
Leary, John, 153, 159
Lecompe, Anthony, 248
Lecompe, William, 248
Lee, Charles, 131
Lee, Corbin, 219, 272
Lee, George, 200
Lee, Philip, 84
Lee, Richard, 337
Leech, Mary, 99
Leeke, Frank, 314
Lefavour, John, 176
Legate, Benjamin, 99
Legg, John, 237
Legg, Solomon, 321
Leith, Frederick, 118, 181
Lemon, John, 111
Leonard, Clement, 5
Levins, William, 309
Lewes, John, 146
Lewis, David, 174, 314
Lewis, John, 143
Lewis, Philip, 180
Lewis, Thomas, 114, 122, 273, 289
Lewis, William, 114, 165
Leybourn, George, 284
Liddell, George, 338
Linch, Timothy, 207
Lindenberger/Linderberger, George, 73
Lindsey, David, 335, 338
Linsey, David, 342

Linsey, John, 180
Littell, George, 330
Little, Walter, 108
Livers, Arnold, 56
Liverton, Mr., 168
Lloyd, Elisabeth, 271
Lloyd, William, 26
Locker, Thomas, 16
Lockhart, Thomas, 334
Lockier, Thomas, 6
Loftis, Thomas, 227
Logan, Alexander, 6
Longin, Richard, 316
Lotan, Richard, 7
Love, Captain, 260
Love, David, 290
Loveday, Thomas, 27
Lovewell, Richard, 110
Lovott, Thomas, 310
Low, David, 27
Lowe, David, 128
Lowe, James, 326
Lowman, Joseph, 111
Lowndes, Christopher, 136
Lowry, Robert, 264
Lux, Mr., 14, 30
Lux, William, 47
Macclesish, Mr., 96
Maccubbin, John, 227
Maccubbin, Nicholas, 200
Maccubbin, William, 227
Maccubin, Nicholas, 7
MacDonall, John, 192
Mackall, Benjamin, 45
Mackey, John, 156, 172
Macky, John, 57
Magruder, Enoch, 78, 79
Magruder, Samuel Wade, 322
Maguire, Patrick, 309
Mahoney, Michael, 233
Mahoney, Thomas, 197
Mahony, William, 266
Makall, Mr., 101

Mallett, Joseph, 152
Maln, John, 71
Malone, John, 126
Malone, William, 244
Maloney, Walter, 295
Malvill, Thomas, 155
Manley, Captain, 258
Manning, Henry, 319
Mansell, Samuel, 190
Mansfield, Samuel, 274
Marcer, Robert, 28
Markham, Major, 275
Marlow, Samuel, 182
Marren, Archibald, 19
Marren, John, 19
Martin, Jonathan, 345
Mason, Alexander, 204, 210
Mason, Thomson, 138
Mathews, Jacob, 104
Mathews, John, 281
Mattex, Samuel, 149
Matthews, Jacob, 108
Matthews, John, 29
Matthews, Thomas, 71
Matthewson, William, 169
Maund, James, 101
Maxwell, James, 357
May, Richard, 316
Maynard, William, 53, 265
McAnnelly, Johnston, 233
McAtee, John, 313
McCarty, Timothy, 318
McCastlen, John, 247
McCay, Mary, 11, 12
McClane, Daniel, 186
McClellan, William, 106
McCollins, Andrew, 184
McCormick, Bridget, 187
McCowan, Michael, 189
McCritch, Daniel, 350
McCulloch, Anthony, 63, 147
McDaniel, James, 190
McDavett, William, 100

McDonald, Charles, 337
McDonald, Hugh, 105
McDonald, James, 300
McDonald, Mr., 109
McDonnell, John, 21
McDougall, Captain, 67
McDowell, Michael, 251
McDowell, Nathaniel, 6
McDuff, John, 51
McEnerry, Patrick, 98
McFee, Duncan, 205, 210
McGachin, Captain, 92
McGee, Jane, 31
McGill, William, 266
McGlochlan, Mr., 15
McGrath, Daniel, 350
McGraw, Elliner, 252
McGuier, Matthias, 106
McGuire, Patrick, 295
McGuyer, Michael, 202
McIntosh, Alexander, 15, 60, 185
McIntyre, Henry, 147
McKeen, Roger, 44
McKenny, Michael, 184
McKinsey, James, 315
McKissock, John, 247
McKogh, Patrick, 199
McLacklen, James, 11
McLaughlin, Susannah, 203
McLemar, Dennis, 202
McMullan, Patrick, 176
McNeely, Thomas, 199
McPherson, Daniel, 21, 65, 176
McPherson, Henry, 313
McPherson, Robert, 71
McQuillin, Patrick, 208
McVenny, Thomas, 209
Mecan, Thomas, 330
Mecklenburg, William, 127
Meclene, Thomas, 144, 157, 168
Meek, David, 257
Megraw, Thomas, 327

373

Mercer, William, 320, 321
Merchant, Sarah, 192
Meroney, Philip, 288
Merrett, William, 120
Merritt, William, 122
Merryman, Richard, 209
Merryweather, Roger, 122
Middleton, John, 334
Millar, James, 102
Miller, Henry, 204
Miller, John, 255, 277
Milliner, Thomas, 61
Millington, Allenby, 223
Milme, Robert, 95
Milne, Edmund, 3, 4
Milton, John, 75
Miriarlie, Hugh, 290
Mitchell, John, 51
Mitchell, W., 254
Moale, Richard, 323, 324
Modesley, William, 99
Molison, James, 26
Mollison, James Henry, 128
Monk, Renoldo, 106
Montgomerie, John, 225
Moobrey, James, 312
Mooney, Michael, 184
Moore, George, 121
Moore, Thomas, 271, 333
Moore, William, 180
Moran, Mary, 15
More, George, 118
Morgan, John, 44, 154
Morgan, Richard, 263
Morgan, Thomas Spry, 117, 129
Morris, Evan, 157
Morris, James, 187
Morris, John, 90, 117
Morrison, Captain, 24, 328, 334, 341
Morrison, James, 102
Morriss, George, 158
Morrow, John, 51

Motherby, Charles, 16
Moulton, James, 93
Mudd, Mr., 150
Muheaw, William, 184
Muir, Robert, 22, 52
Mulanie, Richard, 296
Mullan, Patrick, 221
Mullan, Thomas, 107
Mullen, Mrs., 235
Murdo, William, 5
Murdock, George, 107
Murphey, Daniel, 318
Murphey, Edward, 348
Murphey, Philip, 306
Murphy, Daniel, 317
Murphy, Mr., 150
Murphy, Richard, 294
Murray, John, 282, 331
Murray, Mary, 269
Murray, Michael, 200, 205
Murray, Mr., 148
Murray, William, 129
Musgrove, John, 98, 233
Myers, Jacob, 302
Nail, Charles, 98
Nailing, John, 343, 346
Neel, John, 288
Negroes, Amey, 116; Barrack, 224; Ben, 37, 38, 308; Berkshire, 323; Bewdly, 115; Bob, 18; Cato, 171, 184; Charles, 71, 222; Coale, Robert, 343, 346; Collins, George, 111; Cyrus, 276, 278; Frank, 188; Harry, 58; Hen[nobie], Will, 155; Hill, Humphry, 354; Jack, 30, 97, 182, 244, 255, 275; Jacob, 346, 347; James, 58; Jeffery, 75; Jem, 273; Joe, 200; Peter, 294; Pheney, 224; Philip, 171; Philips, Hannah, 47; Pompey, 58; Sam, 115, 186, 258, 275;

Negroes, Sam/Jem, 354; Sancho, 105; Tom, 252, 345; William, 71
Neile, Jane, 4
Neilson, William, 213
Nelson, John, 200
Nelson, Robert, 200
Nelson, Sarah, 163, 178
Nerney, Patrick, 328
Nesbet, Robert, 114
Nesbitt, Mr., 39
Nevill, Joseph, 251, 252
Newcomb, George Peters, 295
Newcomb, Samuel, 192
Newcomb, William, 192
Newman, William, 172
Nicholson, J., 156, 245
Nicholson, Joseph, Jr., 185
Nickles, John, 102
Nicols, Nathaniel, 156
Nisbet, Robert, 122
Niven, William, 156
Norman, John, 190
Norris, Edward, 329
Norris, John, 169
Norris, Joseph, 329
Norris, Patrick, 169
North, Thomas, 186, 187
Norton, Patrick, 128
Nowland, Laurance, 202
Nursler, Adam, 47
Oak, William, 164, 270
Obilder, Michael, 244
Obrian, James, 125
O'Brien, George, 183
O'Driskill, Rhomas, 177
Ogden, John, 316
Ogesen, John, 102
Ohair, James, 331
O'Hara, Kane, 293
O'Hara, Mary, 293
O'Harra, Kane, 202
Onan, Thomas, 144, 157

Oneel, John, 288
Ord, John, 250
Ormsby, John, 65
Orrick, Caroline, 26
Osborn, Joseph, 131
Osburn, Henry, 171
Osburn, Mary, 32
Osmond, Edward, 86, 94, 238, 265
Owen, Edward, Jr., 175
Owens, Mary, 218
Owens, Thomas, 232
Owings, Henry, 228
Owings, John, 302
Owings, John Cockey, 296
Owings, Joshua, 296
Owings, Joshua, Jr., 272
Owings, Thomas, 35, 239
Paca, William, 154
Page, George, 123
Paiton, Henry, 206
Pamer, Thomas, 75
Pane, Stephen, 173
Parker, John, 83
Parkinson, Benjamin, 328
Partinton, Nancy, 31
Passanham, John, 351
Paterson, Basil, 44
Patterson, Susannah, 295
Payne, John, 10, 25
Payne, William, 138, 144
Peale, Charles Wilson, 14
Pearce, Andrew, 115, 169
Pearce, Henry W., 115, 140
Pearce, Henry Ward, 139, 140
Pearce, Richard, 56
Pecker, Thomas, 14
Peele, Andrew, 245
Pence, Michael, 182
Penemore, John, 38
Penick, Joseph, 309
Pennock, Joseph, 294
Pennybacker, Derrick, 169

Perepoint, George, 39
Perkin, George, 19
Perry, Edward, 193
Peters, Daniel, 212
Pettibone, Anne, 264
Pharley, Owen, 80
Philips, Francis, 187, 230
Philips, John, 180
Philips, Thomas, 277
Philips, William, 71
Phillips, Ephraim, 171
Phillips, F., 231, 319
Phillips, Francis, 186, 248, 276, 278
Phillips, Mr., 232
Philpot, Brian, 55
Philpott, Benjamin, 81, 84
Philpott, James, 101
Pickron, John, 10
Pigman, John, 54
Piles, Basil, 216
Piles, Francis, 216
Pinamore, John, 37
Pinemore, John, 16
Pinkney, Jonathan, 9, 59, 69, 82
Pinshen, George, 168
Pitcher, Thomas, 22
Pitt, George, 275
Place, John, 2
Plant, Thomas, 356
Plato, James, 90
Plevy, Thomas, 97
Plint, Sarah, 192
Polk, Hugh, 137, 148
Ponting, Edward, 301, 304
Poole, Richard, 11
Poole, Samuel, 351
Pope, Nathaniel, 85
Pope, Samuel, 267
Porter, James, 224
Porter, John, 216
Potter, Francis, 70
Poulk, Hugh, 132

Powell, Howell, 26
Powell, Nathaniel, 317, 318, 334, 342, 355
Powell, Sarah, 192
Powell, William, 352
Powny, Thomas, 52
Prat, John, 355, 357
Prather, Thomas, 47, 70
Pratt, Henry, 224, 225
Prees, William, 308
Presstman/Prestman, George, 307, 320, 321
Price, Captain, 243, 244, 246, 305
Price, John, 346
Price, Mary, 339
Price, Mordecai, 63
Price, Rice, 45, 48
Price, Thomas, 287
Priest, Richard, 6
Priggs, John F. A., 268, 283, 285
Priggs, John Frederick, 58
Priggs, John Frederick Augustus, 42
Pritchard, Jacob, 249
Pritchard, John, 13
Pritchet, John/Jacob, 226
Prue, William, 127, 150
Prunck, Christopher, 274
Pugh, Simon, 13, 15, 30
Purchase, Richard, 116
Pursley, William, 163, 176
Purviance, David, 180
Purviance, Samuel, Jr., 219
Pusey, Thomas, 184, 215, 241, 250
Querns, John, 353
Quick, Robert, 125
Quin, John, 293
Quindland, James, 265
Ragon, Cornelius, 60, 70, 86
Rain, James, 260
Ramsay, Alexander, 184, 251

Randall, William, 212
Randell, George, 279, 280, 283, 356
Raven, Thomas, 183
Rawlings, John, 159
Rawson, Daniel, 75
Read, John, 105, 323
Red, James, 134
Redkin, Edward, 64
Reed, Captain, 226
Reed, James, 87, 183
Reid, Captain, 113, 237
Reid, John, 132, 137, 148
Reith, James, 63
Reith, Robert, 339
Reynolds, Joseph, 254
Reynolds, William, 3, 254
Rhoads, Richard, 63
Rian, Lochlan, 241
Rice, John, 79
Richard, Francis, 11, 12
Richards, Captain, 165
Richards, Richard, 73, 75
Richards, Thomas, 253, 266
Richards, William, 42
Richardson, Francis, 110
Richardson, Joseph, 112
Richardson, William, 120
Richman, John, 346
Rickman, John, 336
Ridgely, Charles, 81, 86, 112, 157, 162, 197, 214, 222, 223
Ridgely, Charles, Jr., 43, 191, 198, 200, 323, 324
Ridgely, Greenbury, 204
Ridgely, H., 145
Ridgely, James, 232
Ridgely, Charles, 173
Riggs, Elias, 46
Riggs, James, 48, 97
Riglay, William, 221
Rigton, Zachariah, 21, 25
Ringgold, Thomas, 48, 145

Ringgold, William, 48
Risteau, George, 198
Riston, Zachariah, 18
Ritchie, Archibald, 90
Roads, Robert, 88
Roara, Jacob, 352
Roberson, William, 71
Roberts, Evan, 101, 135
Roberts, Henry, 267
Roberts, John, 322
Roberts, Jonathan, 301, 305, 315
Roberts, Robert, 28, 45, 48, 56
Roberts, William, 148, 215
Robertson, William, 59
Robeson, John, 75
Robeson, Peter, 28
Robinson, John, 283, 295
Robinson, Owen, 12
Robison, John, 289
Robson, Mr., 180
Roden, Joseph, 110
Rodgers, Sarah, 137
Roe, James, 137
Rogers, Benjamin, 95
Rogers, Sarah, 132, 148
Rogers, Stephen, 254
Rohrer, John, 289
Rolings, John, 153
Roop, John, 237
Rorck, Patrick, 165
Rose, Alexander, 52
Rose, Peter, 56
Ross, David, 257
Rourke, Con, 316
Rowe, James, 287
Rowin, John, 119
Rownd, James, 316
Royle, Joseph, 98
Rudisely, Tobias, 164
Rudulph, Tobias, 328
Rush, James, 241
Russel, Alexander, 111
Russell, James, 153, 159

Russell, William, 273, 289
Rutland, Mr., 343, 345, 347
Rutland, Thomas, 9, 68, 124, 168, 294, 310
Rutter, Henry, 312, 315
Ryan, Richard, 127
Sale, Simon, 350
Sales, Mortimore, 16
Sandals, John, 139
Sandels, John, 140
Sanders, John, 157
Sanders, Thomas, 311
Sapp, Benjamin, 297, 299
Saunders, William, 11
Scham, John, 84
School, Christian, 306
Scot, Thomas, 177
Scott, Alexander, 332
Scott, David, 314
Scott, Geo., 147
Scott, George, 130, 167, 354
Scott, James, 100
Scott, Lieutenant Governor, 180
Scott, Michael, 64
Scott, Upton, 142
Scott, William, 256
Scrivener, George, 52
Seale, John, 309
Searson, Samuel, 186, 187
Segrmes, Thomas, 53
Seiler, John, 279
Semple, John, 144
Semple, Robert, 316
Sertain, James, 141
Severan, John, 55
Sewell, John, 126
Sharp, Samuel, 165, 167, 171
Shaw, John, 220
Sheffield, John, 130
Shepard, John, 129
Shepherd, John, 107, 343
Shepherd, William, 302
Sheppard, William, 176, 240

Sheredine, Jeremiah, 11, 103, 119, 182
Sherlock, William, 221
Sherridin, Jeremiah, 194
Shinton, John, 252
Shores, Thomas, 220
Shovel, John, 98
Simmins, Samuel, 231
Simmonds, Samuel, 230
Simmons, Daniel, 279
Simmons, Thomas, 94
Simmons, William, 269, 286
Simpson, Gaither, 72
Simpson, George, 219
Simpson, John, 180
Simpson, Thomas, 49, 50
Simpson, William, 218
Skinner, Sarah, 33
Skinner, Trueman, 62, 73, 75, 110, 112
Slade, Josiah, 12
Slade, Josias, 7, 16
Slade, William, 2
Slyder, Christopher, 105
Smith, Charles S., 172, 227
Smith, Conrad, 18, 21, 25, 134, 151
Smith, George, 49, 50, 81
Smith, Henry, 24
Smith, James, 125, 132, 141, 245, 250
Smith, John, 20, 58, 163, 226, 265, 279, 280, 329, 344
Smith, Joseph, 143, 226
Smith, Joseph Addison, 5
Smith, Mr., 180
Smith, Nicholas, 66
Smith, Patrick, 284
Smith, Richard, 41, 66, 96
Smith, Samuel, 230, 231
Smith, Thomas, 3, 22, 223, 260
Smith, William, 226, 288, 296
Smoot, George, 337

Smyth, Mr., 322
Smyth, Thomas, 60
Snell, Thomas, 170
Snow, William, 192, 307
Snowden, John, 136, 223, 227, 265, 329
Snowden, Mr., 17, 20, 29
Snowden, Saml./Samuel, 92, 104, 108, 136223, 227, 265, 329
Snowden, Thomas/Thos., 136, 223, 227, 265, 329
Snowdon, Mr., 19
Socket, Andrew, 96
Sollers, Thomas, 261
Somervill/Somerville Captain, 41, 268, 275, 285, 300
Somerwell, Colin, 196
Somerwell, John, 110
Soulsby, John, 328
Speaks, William, 232
Spencer, John, 341
Spencer, Thomas, 8, 75, 116, 274
Sprout, Joseph, 185
St. Laurance, Ambrose, 8
Stabler, John, 228
Stafford, Nathaniel, 109
Stafford, Thomas, 228
Stansely, William, 8
Stanton, William, 106
Starland, John, 171
Starling, William, 343, 346
Steel, James, 320
Steelman, Thomas, 291, 292
Stepelton, Daniel, 311
Stepelton, John, 311
Stephen, Levi, 172
Stephens, Abraham, 88
Stephens, George, 267
Stephens, James, 33
Stephens, Levi, 156
Stepleton, John, 314, 315
Sterling, William, 209

Steuart, Geo., 10
Steuart, George, 109
Steuart, William, 189, 289
Stevens, Richard, 1
Stevens, Thomas, 261
Stevenson, Edward, 201, 205
Stevenson, Henry, 135
Stevenson, John, 39, 82
Stevenson, Robert, 339
Stewart, Captain, 241
Stewart, Charles, 290
Stewart, Gabriel, 213
Stewart, George, 274
Stewart, Hugh, 110
Stewart, Mr., 14, 30
Stewart, William, 241, 263, 273
Stickwood, Jonathan, 340
Stilling, John, 168
Stinsicomb, Thomas, 14
Stinson, James, 354
Stinson, John, 343
Stites, Michael, 221
Stocksdale, Solomon, 105
Stone, Godfrey, 112
Stone, John, 96
Strawbridge, John, 6, 283, 289, 295
Stricker, George, 246
Strictfoot, Matthias, 182
Stringer, Thomas, 5, 276, 278
Stringfellow, Mr., 52
Sudler, Emory, 241
Sudler, Mr., 322
Sullivan, Cornelius, 227
Sullivan, John, 18, 55
Sullivane, John, 288
Summers, John, 63
Sutton, Joseph, 328, 334
Swan, Robert, 294
Swann, Charles, 227
Swearingham, Mr., 250
Swope, Benjamin, 91
Sydenham, Mr., 102

Taite, William, 143, 148, 160
Talbot, Henry, 9, 24, 69
Talbott, Edmund, 99
Talbott, Thomas, 164, 270
Tasker, Margaret, 33
Tayloe, John, 67, 170
Taylor, Alexander, 170
Taylor, Benjamin, 169
Taylor, Bray, 126
Taylor, Captain, 132, 137, 180
Taylor, John, 17, 75, 117, 126
Taylor, Matthew, 257
Taylor, Mr., 148
Taylor, Thomas, 344
Tennent, John, 189
Teves, Robert, 179
Tevis, Robert, 121
Thackfeild, William, 89
Theodore, Leray, 269
Thomas, Daniel, 313
Thomas, James, 182
Thomas, John, 100, 110, 112, 124, 297, 298
Thomas, Joseph, 170, 222, 294, 345
Thomas, Richard, 70
Thompson, Captain, 247
Thompson, Edward, 115, 139, 140
Thompson, Henry, 314
Thompson, James, 260
Thompson, John, Jr., 51
Thompson, Richard, 221
Thompson, William, 34, 154, 193
Thomson, Joseph Zachariah, 298
Thomson, William, 236
Throp, Thomas, 246
Todd, Alexander, 141
Todd, John, 74
Tolly, Mr., 244
Tomlin, William, 323
Tongue, James, 42

Tongue, John, 41
Tool, John, 339
Townsing, William, 327
Trayner, Simon, 184
Trend, John, 238
Tricked, Edward, 274
Trigg, Clement, 209
Trimble, Cornelius, 81
Tripplett, William, 155
Trump, James, 151
Trundle, John, 194
Tucker, George, 123
Tucker, Samuel, 25
Tucker, Sele, 220
Tuite, Tobias, 158
Tummer, John, 47
Turner, Daniel, 186, 224, 264
Turner, John, 325
Turner, William, 322
Tutes, Tobias, 149
Tylor, Edward, 198
Tynan, Thomas, 218
Vail, William, 336
Vale, William, 346
Valentine, Henry, 275
Vallaly, Charles, 169
Van Bebbe, Abraham, 183
Van de Huville, Jan Jonas, 80
Vanhorn, Mr., 159
Vansant, Benjamin, 177, 178
Vansant, John, 327
Vanstavoren, Cornelius, 181
Vanswaringgen, Joseph, 171
Vaughan, Jonathan, 25, 55
Veach, Jeremiah, 107
Veasy, Captain, 169
Verdiman, Jacob, 75
Villiers, John, 269
Voice, William, 335
Wagener, Peter, 207
Wainwright, William, 351
Wales, Thomas, 8

Walker, James, 117, 166, 215, 328
Walker, John, 60
Walker, Robert, 14, 15, 30
Walker, Samuel, 156
Wallace, John, 125
Walton, Thomas, 201, 205
Warburton, William, 161
Ward, Francis, 253
Ward, John, 68, 115
Ward, Joseph, 345
Warfield, Vachel, 236
Waring, Basil, 118, 121, 169, 242
Waring, John, 169, 242
Waring, William, 124
Warne, James, 298
Warner, Isaac, 119
Warner, William, 299
Warran, Edward, 250
Washington, Baily, 77
Waters, Roger Mere, 114
Waters, Thomas, 18, 19
Watkins, John, 92
Watkins, Joseph, 34, 300
Watkins, Thomas, 87
Watson, Isabella, 58, 268, 285
Watson, James, 48
Watson, Thomas, 112
Watts, Robert, 318
Watts, Samuel, 305
Watts, Thomas, 9
Wayman, John, 113
Weatherall/Weathrall, Philip, 311, 354
Webb, Samuel, 2
Webb, Sarah, 350
Webber, Benjamin, 308
Webster, James, 130, 158
Webster, John Lee, 141, 150, 191
Weedon, Daniel, 205, 210
Weedon, Richard, 321

Weems, John, Jr., 199, 326, 345
Welch, David, 348
Welch, Richard, 275
Wells, Alexander, 1, 8, 32, 226, 249
Wells, George, 304
Wells, James, 346
Wells, John, 52
Welsh, John, 135
Welsh, Patrick, 202
Welsh, Richard, 128
Welsh, Thomas, 9, 223
Weltner, Ludwick, 344
Weply, Henry, 306
West, James, 101
West, Stephen, 181
West, Thomas, 111
Whateley, William, 302
Wheeler, Richard, 343
Whitacre/Whitaker, Richard, 266
White, Abraham, 235
White, Captain, 234
White, Christopher, 228
White, George, 61, 63
White, John, 71, 258
White, Mr., 168
White, Thomas, 22
White, William, 175, 182
Whitefield, Daniel, 351
Whiton, Henry/John, 43
Whittington, William, 336
Whitton, John, 191
Wickenden, David, 1, 7, 32
Wickersaam, Isaac, 150
Wickes, S., 56
Wickes, Samuel, 212
Wickes, Simon, 45, 66
Wickly, Richard, 258
Widon, George, 66
Wilcocks, John, 201, 205
Wild, Abraham, 234
Wilkes, S., 48
Wilkins, James, 181

Wilkins, John, 83, 93, 95
Wilkins, Thomas, 257
Wilkinson, Bettey, 83
Wilkinson, Captain, 352
Wilkinson, George, 20
Wilkinson, John, 34, 52
Wilkinson, Thomas, 245
Willcoxen, Thomas, 80
Williams, Benjamin, 5
Williams, Charles, 284
Williams, George, 227
Williams, Henry, 303
Williams, James, 36, 55
Williams, John, 27, 51, 119, 143, 146
Williams, Joseph, 173, 222
Williams, Robert, 296
Williams, Thomas, 163, 176
Williams, William, 132, 199, 327
Williamson, George, 150
Williamson, William, 351
Willis, James, 165
Willis, Lewis, 66
Wills, George, 349
Willson, Andrew, 315
Wilmot, John, 115
Wilson, Andrew, 312
Wilson, Dennis, 64, 70
Wilson, John, 194, 316
Wilson, William, 293
Wingle, Francis, 151
Winter, John, 304
Winterton, John, 132
Winwood, Thomas, 155
Wise, Peter, 152
Wiseman, John, 350
Wiser, Jacob, 324
Witmore, Joseph, 173
Wood, Benedict, 182
Wood, James, 78, 166
Wood, John, 90
Woodman, William, 343, 346, 347
Woods, George, 49, 50
Woods, Thomas, 155
Woolford, John, 127
Wootton, Thomas Sprigg, 58
Wootton, William T., 189, 200, 219, 258
Wootton, Wm. T., 158, 163, 176, 182, 228
Wootton, Wm. Turner, 224
Worberton, William, 160
Worthington, John, 200
Worthington, Vachel, 72
Wrench, Henry, 188
Wrench, William, 44
Wright, John, 165, 175, 334
Wright, Nathan Samuel Turbutt, 147
Wright, Thomas, 308
Wroth, James, 264
Wyle, Walter, 174
Yates, Susanna, 327
Yeates, Joseph, 102
Yewell, Thomas, 205, 210
Yoe, Aaron, 307
Yoe, William, 308
Young, Margaret, 147
Young, Mathew, 354
Young, Robert, 259
Young, William, 34, 72, 73, 357
Young, Wm., 177